Benedict Arnold

REVOLUTIONARY HERO

An etching of Benedict Arnold (1741–1801) drawn in the 1890s, from an original portrait by John Trumbull. *Courtesy, Library of Congress.*

Benedict Arnold
REVOLUTIONARY HERO

An American Warrior Reconsidered

James Kirby Martin

New York University Press

NEW YORK AND LONDON

NEW YORK UNIVERSITY PRESS
New York and London

Copyright © 1997 by New York University

The scripture in the epigraph is reprinted from the Holy Bible, New International Version ®. NIV ®. Coyright © 1973, 1978, 1984 by International Bible Society. Used by permission of Zonderran Publishing House. All rights reserved.

Library of Congress Cataloging-in-Publication Data
Martin, James Kirby, 1943–
Benedict Arnold, revolutionary hero : an American warrior
reconsidered / James Kirby Martin.
p.   cm.
Includes bibliographical references and index.
ISBN 0-8147-5560-7 (alk. paper)
1. Arnold, Benedict, 1741–1801.   2. American
loyalists—Biography.
3. Generals—United States—Biography.   4. United States.
Continental Army—Biography.   5. United
States—History—Revolution,
1775–1783.   I. Title.
E278.A7M37   1997
973.3'82'092—dc21
[B]   97-4631
                    CIP

New York University Press books are printed on acid-free paper,
and their binding materials are chosen for strength and durability.

Manufactured in the United States of America

10 9 8 7 6 5 4 3 2 1

For my daughters

DARCY ELIZABETH,

SARAH-MARIE,

and

JOELLE KATHRYN GARRETT

with unbounded love,
and pride in your accomplishments

Contents

Maps

Illustrations appear as a group following p. 186.

Preface

The historical impressions we first encounter as school-children have a way of staying fixed in our memories. In my case, earnest teachers wanted me to appreciate certain ideals, among them worthy and dedicated citizenship. To demonstrate these qualities, they taught me about George Washington, the youngster who could not tell a lie and went on to greatness as commander in chief of the Continental army and the first president of the United States. They also characterized the populace of Revolutionary America as extraordinarily virtuous. This unique generation, they claimed, placed no bounds on its patriotic fervor and persistence in overcoming the far more powerful redcoated forces of George III, thereby guaranteeing liberty and freedom for posterity.

To complete the scenario, these teachers also mentioned the shadowy, tainted figure of Benedict Arnold. Not since Judas, I recall one of them saying, had a human being left so wicked a mark on the pages of history. Greedy, vain, self-serving Arnold, the man who tried to sell out his selfless Revolutionary brethren, was truly the personification of human deviance and devilry.

I credit these grade school teachers with nurturing my fascination with history. The stories they told, reinforced in primary school texts, caused me to read more widely, especially biographies. Being a young person, I did not realize that I was imbibing a "whiggish" interpretation of history, which defines the human experience in terms of a centuries-long contest between the forces of tyranny and liberty. In this framework, notable figures abound who devote themselves to improving the lot of humanity, and liberty triumphant represents the loftiest essence of progress.

Over the years I have learned that the past is far more complex than this interpretive framework would allow. George Washington, a figure who certainly deserves to be held in the highest respect, manipulated the truth when he saw good reason to do so. As for an accurate characterization of the Revolutionary populace, unwavering commitment and perseverance were anything but pervasive qualities. Benedict Arnold, by comparison, manifested far more fervency of purpose in serving the cause of liberty than did the typical American patriot during the early years of the War for Independence.

In studying the American Revolution for more than a quarter century, I have come to realize how much this formative era, unlike any other in the history of the United States, remains enshrouded in popular myth of a whiggish kind—featuring a tyrannical imperial government, a mad king, a resolute band of provincial Americans unstintingly sacrificing their all until they secured their liberties, and an extremely rare patriot renegade, such as Arnold, whose villainous behavior only served to underscore the Revolutionary generation's irrefutable virtue.

Many years ago, when I began doing research for this book, I did not fully appreciate how much this popular mythology had influenced biographical treatments of Arnold. Nor was I aware of the distorting nature of a series of Arnold folktales. What I did understand was that Arnold biographers invariably wrote about his life by envisioning him retrospectively through the prism of treason. Looking for signs of his allegedly greedy, malicious, obnoxious, vain, self-serving temperament, they seemed to find plenty of proof, even if derived in many instances from the Arnold tales. In their research they took little, if any, notice of evidence that might cast doubt on the popular image of his depraved character. Rather, they focused on attempting to decipher why Arnold, despite some begrudgingly admitted contributions to the American cause, was such a reprehensible human being. Slaying him in every way was invariably the result, perhaps out of concern for being labeled an Arnold apologist or, worse yet, a disloyal American.

Arnold's act of treason was what these writers wanted to explain, even if by caricature, and with the effect of downgrading his contributions to the Revolution. This deflation of Arnold actually began in the days immediately after the exposure of his dealings with the British. The common refrain then was that a person so obviously evil could not possibly have been, at one time, so valuable. That was part of Arnold's deceptive nature. His biographers have generally followed along in reducing Arnold to a Revolutionary era curiosity, perhaps a dangerous one at that, who deserved only some updated rendering of his flawed character and deviant behavior.

If Arnold was so inconsequential, nothing more than a patriot leader and warrior of the second rank, then why all the fuss, beginning with his contemporaries, about his decision to return his allegiance to the British? After all, thousands, indeed hundreds of thousands of colonial Americans remained loyal to the British Crown, were neutral toward both sides, or even changed their allegiance (toward either the British or the Americans) during the Revolutionary War. What Arnold's contemporaries knew was that he was no bit actor but a marquee performer in establishing the conditions that ultimately brought victory to the American cause. His treason was shocking because of the magnitude of his contributions to the Revolutionary effort. That was what made his actions so potentially devastating, especially in light of the critique he was offering about the cause of liberty, and that was why, at least initially, his part in the great drama of revolution had to be minimized.

In reconstructing the past we have many obligations. We must engage in extensive research and present our evidence fair-mindedly, even when that evidence does not fit our preconceptions. In Arnold's case, I had expected to find an avaricious, egocentric, ever manipulating person. Extant records show, however, that Arnold, unlike many of his peers, was willing to risk a portion of his personal financial assets in supporting the Revolutionary cause. Arnold, like most people, had his temperamental moments, but for the most part he was considerate in his dealings with others, unless he thought his reputation as a meritorious gentleman-patriot was under attack. Although he was an ambitious person with clear goals, he was not a smooth-talking self-promoter. In short, my research—I have sought to look at every available source—did not confirm what so many others have said Arnold was or what the folktales made him out to be.

We have other obligations as well, not the least of which is to treat chronology with respect—to move forward through time from beginnings, as lives are actually lived, without allowing outcomes to skew the plotline. The beginning for Arnold was not 1780, the year of his treason, but 1741, the year of his birth. No real evidence suggests that he was predestined to commit treason, even though many commentators have assumed that he was somehow foreordained to perpetrate evil acts. Arnold, despite this deterministic approach, was like all other human beings. He made choices for himself based on his experiences in life, and his experiences in trying to measure up to the ideal of the selfless patriot warrior congealed in such a way as to convince him that the cause of liberty was actually hollow—and even fraudulent—at its core.

To comprehend Arnold more completely, we must also reckon properly with his times. His world was very different from our own. He grew up in a culture that dictated deference toward one's superiors; he realized that advancement, whether in commerce or in making war, depended on gaining the favor of patrons; and he held fervently to the gentleman's code of honor, which required that he defend his reputation against those who willfully desecrated his good name. For him, the greatest achievement would have been to win the Revolutionary community's respect and everlasting favor.

That he so intently tried but failed is the essence of his ultimately tragic story.

In this portrait of Arnold's rise from obscurity through his career as Washington's remarkable fighting general, I have not made whiggish assumptions about the Revolutionary generation. Self-serving, venal behavior was just as common in the days of the nation's founding as in our own era. As such, I have placed Arnold in a context of historical realism as part of my overall objective of reconsidering all the evidence and seeking to understand while avoiding facile judgments. That Arnold, from my point of view, made the wrong decision in abandoning the American cause is irrelevant to narrating his story as he lived it. Nor are my personal feelings about his temperament and character pertinent to the presentation. What is relevant is that by the end of the Saratoga campaign of 1777, which for Arnold was the defining moment of his existence, the reasons that he would turn against the American cause were becoming obvious. As such, I have not chosen to dwell on the actual process of his descent into villainy—a dramatic story in itself, perhaps worthy of a good retelling someday. Rather, this is an account of a Revolutionary warrior and hero in which the answer to the question—why treason?—also resides.

Acknowledgments

No author stands alone. My debts are legion, and I am very grateful to both persons and institutions for critical support over the years. For valuable suggestions that helped me better reckon with Arnold, I am greatly indebted to George A. Billias, Wayne Bodle, James C. Bradford, J. M. Bumsted, David Burner, Larry E. Cable, E. Wayne Carp, Theodore J. Crackel, George M. Curtis III, Joseph G. Dawson III, John Ettling, Roy K. Flint, David J. Fowler, Don R. Gerlach, Joseph T. Glatthaar, Ira D. Gruber, Karen Guenther, John Mason Hart, Don Higginbotham, Wilson J. Hoffman, Frank Holt, James H. Jones, Richard H. Kohn, Maurice D. Lee Jr., Mark E. Lender, Jan Lewis, Marc Mappen, Lloyd J. Matthews, Amos C. Miller, John Murrin, Charles Patrick Neimeyer, Paul David Nelson, Thomas F. O'Brien, David M. Oshinsky, Randy Roberts, Charles Royster, Robert S. Rutter, Constance B. Schulz, Hal T. Shelton, Sheila Skemp, Roger J. Spiller, Mark E. Steiner, Karen R. Stubaus, Jack Sweetman, Loyd Swenson, David Szatmary, and Ursula Weigold. I also owe special thanks to graduate students who not only assisted with research but showed a keen interest in getting to know Arnold better. They include Robert J. Babbitz, Catherine Felsmann, Barry Q. Kienholz, J. Kent McGaughy, Rodney Miles, Robert Miller, Cynthia Thomas Mizelle, Jill Schumann, and Diane Vandenburg.

Richard Fyffe performed yeoman service in helping me obtain essential research materials from the American Antiquarian Society. John L. Hawkes of Dorset, Vermont, was kind enough to share from his personal collections a copy of a valuable Arnold letter. Elizabeth B. Knox, curator of the New London County Historical Society in Connecticut, was most thoughtful in responding to my inquiry about diseases and epidemics that swept through eastern Connecticut in the mid-eighteenth century.

The University of Houston provided a pivotal semester's leave that allowed me to get back to working on the manuscript. During that time I was able to affiliate with the David Library of the American Revolution, located in Washington Crossing, Pennsylvania, and the Philadelphia Center for Early American Studies, based at the University of Pennsylvania. Richard R. Beeman of the University of Pennsylvania history department was a most gracious host. The late Ezra Stone, then president of the David Library, became a special friend, and Dave Fowler, the library's research director, gave lavishly of his time in sharing his immense knowledge of source materials on Revolutionary America. The David Library represents an inestimable national asset in the encouragement of research and writing in Revolutionary era history.

Various institutions and groups afforded me the opportunity to share my findings about Arnold. These include the University of Akron; the Columbia University Faculty Seminar in Early American History; the David Library of the American Revolution; Hiram College; the United States Military Academy at West Point, New York; the United States Army Military History Institute at Carlisle Barracks, Pennsylvania; and Villanova University (through the Philadelphia Center for Early American Studies). I especially benefited from audience commentary, some of which caused me to rethink portions of my conclusions.

Historians would be lost without archival assistance. Many individuals at numerous repositories went far beyond the call of duty in answering my queries and making me feel at home when I was able to visit their collections. My unbounded thanks go out to the following institutions and their staffs: Maine Historical Society, Portland; Vermont Historical Society, Montpelier; Mugar Memorial Library at Boston University, Boston Public Library, and Massachusetts Historical Society, Boston; Houghton Library at Harvard University, Cambridge, Massachusetts; American Antiquarian Society, Worcester, Massachusetts; Smith College Library, Northampton, Massachusetts; Berkshire Athenaeum, Pittsfield, Massachusetts; Rhode Island Historical Society, Providence; Connecticut Historical Society and Connecticut State Library, Hartford; Beinecke Rare Book and Manuscript Library and Sterling Memorial Library at Yale University and New Haven Colony Historical Society, New Haven, Connecticut; New York State Archives, Albany; United States Military Academy Library, West Point, New York; New-York Historical Society, New York Public Library, and Pierpont Morgan Library, New York City; New Jersey Historical Society, Newark; Morristown National Historical Park, Morristown, New Jersey; Alexander Library at Rutgers University, New Brunswick, New Jersey; Firestone Library at Princeton University, Princeton, New Jersey; American Philosophical Society and Pennsylvania Historical Society, Philadelphia; Maryland Historical Society, Baltimore; Maryland Hall of Records, Annapolis; Library of Congress and National Archives, Washington, D.C.; Alderman Library at the University of Virginia, Charlottesville; Western Reserve Historical Society, Cleveland, Ohio; American Jewish Archives, Cincinnati, Ohio; William L. Clements Library at the University of Michigan, Ann Arbor; Joseph Regenstein Library at the University of Chicago, Illinois; M. D. Anderson Library at the University of Houston, Texas; Stanford University Library, Stanford, California; and Huntington Library, San Marino, California.

At New York University Press, former director Colin Jones and current director Niko Pfund have exemplified the very highest standards of professionalism in the world of publishing. Years ago, Colin and I worked together on another project that came to successful fruition, for which I remain grateful. Niko Pfund, quite simply, has few peers in book publishing. Not only is his enthusiasm infectious and encouraging, but his keen editorial insight and sensible judgment has made this a much stronger book. I am likewise indebted to Gerard F. McCauley, my agent, who through the years has remained a valued adviser and good friend. Austin Allen deserves special recognition for his care and workmanship in developing the maps; so does Vic Pennell, for his timely and talented assistance with illustrations and photography.

My family remains ever supportive. My brother, Frederick W. Martin, has repeatedly provided a writer's refuge at his Cheney's Point home on Chautauqua Lake. My late mother, Dorothy Marie Garrett Martin, and my father, Paul E. Martin, will always be an inspiration to me for so many reasons, including their love of history and joy in reading. My mother, a history major in college, cared deeply about life and knew no bounds as a giving person. My wife, Karen, as always has generously provided editorial advice and shrewd commentary. Our daughters, to whom this volume is lovingly dedicated, have been a very special inspiration to their father. To them and to each person and institution named above, my sense of gratitude is truly profound.

James Kirby Martin
Cheney's Point
Chautauqua Lake, New York

You were the model of perfection,
full of wisdom and perfect in
beauty.
You were in Eden,
the garden of God;
every precious stone adorned you: . . .
Your settings and mountings were
made of gold;
on the day you were created they
were prepared.
You were anointed as a guardian
cherub,
for so I ordained you.
You were on the holy mount of God;
you walked among the fiery stones.
You were blameless in your ways
from the day you were created
till wickedness was found in you. . . .
So I drove you in disgrace from the
mount of God,
and I expelled you, O guardian
cherub,
from among the fiery stones.
Your heart became proud
on account of your beauty,
and you corrupted your wisdom
because of your splendor.
So I threw you to the earth;
I made a spectacle of you before
kings.
By your many sins and dishonest
trade
you have desecrated your
sanctuaries.

So I made a fire come out from you,
and it consumed you,
and I reduced you to ashes on the
ground
in the sight of all who were
watching.
All the nations who knew you
are appalled at you;
you have come to a horrible end
and will be no more.

—Selections from Ezekiel 28:12–19,
New International Version

Benedict Arnold

REVOLUTIONARY HERO

Prologue

Treason! Treason! Treason! Black as Hell

No one will ever know whether Benedict Arnold looked back. The day was Monday, September 25, 1780, a resplendent time of the year when the colorful hues of early autumn were just taking hold of the foliage in the Hudson Highlands region of New York. The place was Robinson's Landing on the east bank of the Hudson River, a mile south of the Continental army's strategically vital West Point defensive base on the opposite shore. The hour was mid-morning, a few minutes past ten o'clock. For the past several months, Major General Arnold had engaged in secret negotiations with British military leaders, most notably Major John André, adjutant general of the main British army based some fifty miles to the south in New York City. Arnold had just learned about the unraveling of his scheme to deliver a mortal blow to the cause of American liberty by allowing the enemy to seize the West Point defenses. He was about to flee down the Hudson River, toward both the safety of British lines and the most dishonorable of places in American history.

Arnold's haste reflected a person nearly caught off guard by unexpected circumstances. The general had begun his day tranquilly at the elegant residence of Beverley Robinson, a prominent loyalist who had abandoned his property in going over to the British. Robinson's House had served as Arnold's headquarters since early August, when he first took command of patriot defenses in the Highlands region.

While Arnold was eating breakfast, two officers, Major James McHenry and Captain Samuel Shaw, rode up with anticipated news. Commander in Chief George Washington, along with the dashing young Marquis de Lafayette, Artillery Chief Henry Knox, and various staff aides, would soon reach Robinson's House, where they had scheduled a meeting with Arnold. They also were looking forward to breakfast. Greeting the two officers warmly, Arnold invited them to join him at his table. Within minutes, another officer, Lieutenant Solomon Allen, also appeared. He had ridden hard up the east side of the Hudson to bring Arnold important dispatches. Before looking at them, the West Point commander asked Allen to sit down and enjoy some company and breakfast with the group.

It was not unusual for Arnold to show hospitality toward military subordinates. These men, in turn, admired and respected him. They knew about his legendary martial feats, as well as the two serious wounds to his left leg that had left him all but crippled. They viewed him as their "fighting general, and a bloody fellow he was," who "was as brave a man as ever lived." He was likewise a gallant officer, they believed, who cared deeply about the welfare of his comrades in arms.[1]

As the three officers conversed with the heroic West Point commander, they were regarding a man who had begun to show his age. At one time, not many years before, Arnold's light but penetrating eyes, hawklike nose, bronzed complexion, dark hair, and athletic physique had conveyed a ruggedly handsome appearance, despite a tendency toward stoutness. Since the general was no more than five feet four or five inches tall, his contemporaries referred to him as both short and middling in stature, in an era when many men, among them John Adams and James Madison, were hardly five feet tall and anyone over six feet, such as George Washington, seemed like a giant. Now, at thirty-nine years of age, Arnold's hair was graying, and his face, if one looked closely enough, revealed deepening lines, as if the ordeal of fighting so long a war had made a permanent imprint on his countenance. Yet, even with his conspicuous limp, Arnold remained an imposing figure, a man who evoked command presence. The three officers particularly noted how relaxed he seemed as he sat with them that morning, almost as if he were demonstrating the composure for which he was legendary when he engaged in combat with the British enemy.[2]

As his guests talked and ate, Arnold perused the dispatches. Much to his astonishment, one letter contained personally disastrous news. Major André, traveling south through the Highlands in civilian clothing under the assumed name of John Anderson, had been captured outside British lines near Tarrytown. On André's person was a pass signed by Arnold, as well as detailed sketches of the network of redoubts and fortresses making up the West Point defensive network. Worse yet, a courier had taken these incriminating documents to Washington. He would certainly comprehend their meaning, and he could appear at any moment, not in friendship for leisurely conversation and breakfast but in wrath with armed soldiers, ready to arrest his West Point commander.[3]

Arnold evidenced little sign of discomfort, nothing more than what McHenry recalled as a fleeting moment of "embarrassment." He stopped reading, stood up, and motioned Allen aside, then whispered to him to keep silent about the capture of André. Still unruffled, he excused himself and limped clumsily upstairs in search of his beautiful, vivacious, twenty-year-old wife, Margaret "Peggy" Shippen. Exactly what Arnold said to her remains a mystery. Historians have not resolved the extent of her involvement in her husband's perfidy, although Peggy certainly knew about his contacts with André. Arnold likely told Peggy of his urgent need to escape downriver to the British. He also promised to provide for her, if he could somehow find the means, as well as for their six-month-old son, Edward, who was in the bedroom with Peggy.[4]

Major David Franks, one of Arnold's staff aides, suddenly knocked at the bedroom door, interrupting the furtive conversation. He announced that Washington's personal servant had just ridden up. The commander in chief could not be far behind. Arnold darted out of the room, descended the stairway, and brushed past the three officers at the breakfast table while ordering Franks to get him a horse. Urgent business had come up at West Point, the general claimed, and he promised to return within an hour to welcome Washington and his party.

Hobbling out the front door of Robinson's House, Arnold waited anxiously, not sure whether he could get away before Washington appeared. Finally, a groomsman brought up a saddled horse. An expert rider, Arnold soon had his mount galloping northward along the main road. Then he wheeled the horse to the left onto a narrow path that descended through a deepening ravine leading to Robinson's Landing. Much to his relief, he found his eight-man boat crew alert and on duty, ready to serve him whenever he needed water transportation. Bolting onto the barge (sometimes described as a whaleboat), Arnold ordered the crew to put muscle to their oars and row as they never had before—first into the center of the Hudson and then downriver, away from West Point. Unbeknownst to them, their destination point was the British sloop of war *Vulture,* anchored some twenty miles to the south off Tellers Point at the lower end of Haverstraw Bay.

Arnold's flight down the Hudson took somewhere between one and a half and two hours. As he made his infamous passage to the enemy, he worried about the safety of his family. Surely, too, he considered the tortured course of his life after he had so enthusiastically committed himself to serving the

American rebellion back in early 1775. He thought of his ambition to gain enduring fame for himself and his desire to restore an eminence, if not magnificence, to his once-venerated New England family bloodline. Arnold, a name dating back to twelfth-century England, meant "honor." Upholding his personal honor—his reputation as a gentleman worthy of the community's highest respect—still represented a preeminent concern in his life, as did his desire to refurbish the Arnold family name.[5]

Unfortunately, too many false patriots, as he comprehended his own experiences, had unfairly maligned him—and his good name—at almost every turn during the War for American Independence. Small-minded patriots such as these, among them prominent civilian leaders, had made a mockery of the Revolution and its high ideals, or so he had long since come to perceive reality. The only sensible course, he had concluded, was to return his political loyalty to its original source, the British parent nation, before everything dear to him was forever lost.

Even though his scheming with André had gone awry, Arnold still hoped that his defection would help destroy what he now believed was an errant, misguided attempt to establish a new republican polity in America. He even fancied himself a pied piper of reconciliation whose willingness to act decisively, which had invariably denoted his mercantile and military careers, would encourage other worthy patriots, most particularly disgruntled soldiers in the Continental army, to come to their senses, renounce the Revolution, and revert to their natural British allegiance. In his imagination he envisioned thousands of disillusioned Americans following his own bold example.

As Arnold reflected on all of these possibilities, he kept wondering whether he would make good his escape. No craft was following his barge, so he was able to relax somewhat, perhaps to the point of noticing the vibrant colors along the mountainous terrain on both sides of the river. Finally, the British sloop of war came into view. Arnold speedily hoisted a white cloth, and he ordered his oarsmen to pull alongside the *Vulture.* Soon he was meeting belowdecks with the ship's captain, Andrew Sutherland. Then he reappeared topside and invited his barge crew to return to "the standard of his Britannic Majesty," as he was now doing. Arnold promised them advancement in rank, but his coxswain, Corporal James Lurvey, responded scornfully that "he would be damned if he fought on both sides." Lurvey's comment revealed just how futile Arnold's vision of reunification with the British parent nation really was, especially after five and a half years of warfare.[6]

Aboard the *Vulture* that evening, Arnold labored over a communication to his once-valued patron, George Washington. He implored the commander in chief to protect Peggy, whom he described "as good, and as innocent as an angel, and [who] is incapable of doing wrong." He also offered a rationalization for his own behavior. Arnold's "heart" was "conscious of its own rectitude." Even if he had taken "a step, which the world may censure as wrong," he had "ever acted from a principle of love to my country," and "the same principle of love to my country actuates my present conduct, however it may appear inconsistent to the world, who very seldom judge right of any man's actions." Arnold would now have to wait for the reactions of American patriots. At this juncture at least, he certainly did not doubt his perception of a cause hopelessly lost and erstwhile colonists who were standing ready to follow his lead in renewing their allegiance to Great Britain.[7]

Seasons of mounting bitterness lay behind Arnold's transformation from an intensely enthusiastic patriot to a dangerous enemy of the Revolution. Deeply bruised by so many personal confrontations and disappointments, he had come to regard the cause of liberty in the same battered terms. "The mass of the people are heartily tired of the war," he had written secretly to John André in July 1780, and he compared the "present struggles" convulsing the patriot war effort to "the pangs of a dying man, violent but of a short duration."[8]

Arnold was not wholly inaccurate in his diagnosis. The Revolution had reached its nadir during the summer of 1780, and future prospects looked remarkably bleak. The patriot war effort had repeatedly suffered from lackluster, if not at various times incompetent, civilian leadership. In recent months, Continental officers and soldiers alike had emitted loud grumblings about another basic problem: languishing popular support. In August 1780, angry members of Washington's officer corps went so far as to threaten Congress with mass resignations unless they received guaranteed recognition for their services in the form of postwar pensions. But among the army's ranking generals, only Benedict Arnold had so trenchantly expressed his disenchantment by plotting with the British in what proved to be both an isolated and a tragic attempt to snuff all remaining life out of the ailing cause of liberty.[9]

Arnold's vision of a general reconciliation represented one solution to the many ills that had long since cast a pallor over the Revolution. It was a palliative from which he and his family would benefit financially, and one that would likewise elevate his name to revered status as the great reconciler of the British empire. His comrades in rebellion, after all, had pronounced him America's Hannibal for his dauntless efforts to seize Quebec in late 1775. Because patriot dreams of a better world had metamorphosed into nightmares since those heady early days of civil war, most rebels were now anxious "to be on their former footing," or so Arnold had assured André back in July. The hero had thus convinced himself that patriots would again applaud his boldness in forging the pathway to revived imperial allegiance. On this point, his discernment of reality was completely aslant.[10]

What Arnold had failed to calculate properly was the possibility of overwhelmingly negative responses to his actions. Intending to eradicate lingering vestiges of patriot resolve, his audacious course had the ironic effect, at least for him, of reigniting faltering sensations of popular support for the rebel cause. Also unexpected was the fundamental public recasting of his heroic image. As Arnold made his water passage down the Hudson, he could not imagine how his fate would resemble that awaiting the autumn foliage all around him. His once radiant colors were about to dry up, fall to the ground, and become a crumbled, decaying memory. In his case the descent was straight into the netherworld, the spiritual source of all human mayhem—Satan's hellish abode.

After September 25, 1780, Benedict Arnold's name was to be forever associated with the absence of light, which Revolutionary patriots linked to the darkness of British tyranny and the devil's infernal wickedness. Almost immediately the popular cry rang out: "Treason! Treason! Treason! Black as Hell." So striking an inversion of imagery destroyed Arnold's reputation and the credibility of his concept of a reconciled empire. What he had offered, patriot citizens concluded, was nothing more than a grand delusion inspired by Satan.[11]

On the morning of Tuesday, September 26, Captain Samuel Frost, stationed downriver from West Point at Tappan, New York, entered a statement in the Orderly Book of the 6th Massachusetts regiment. "Treason of the blackest dye was yesterday discovered," Frost scribbled. "Such an event would have given the American cause a deadly wound, if not a fatal stab," but "happily the treason has been timely discovered to prevent the fatal misfortune." Something far more profound than mere happenstance or good fortune had rescued the patriots at so perilous an hour. Wrote Frost, "the providential train of circumstances . . . affords the most convincing proof that the liberties of America are the object of . . . divine protection."[12]

Good had overcome evil because Almighty God, a benevolent and just deity, cared deeply about the fate of the American Revolution. Wrote Major Sebastian Bauman from West Point, "there is a guardian angel who watches over this country and his Excellency [Washington] and that imperceptible two million who dwell in it." "Providence," echoed William Beaumont at Tappan, had "disconnected this deep laid, dark, and treasonable plot in a way that plainly shows the hand of Him in the discovery. The providential train of circumstances ... are enough to convince the most stupid rustic of an overruling Providence that has to this time preserved the liberties of America and brought to light this daring conspiracy." [13]

Arnold's scheme had failed, according to any number of commentators, because the turncoat general had lost sight of the cosmic struggle that overlay the temporal martial contest with Britain. He had not appreciated the spiritual dimension of the human battle to preserve—and even expand—liberties in what patriots invariably described as a dark and corrupt world, personified in the tyrannical political regime of Great Britain.

Explanations of Arnold's thwarted treachery thus came to involve the intervention of Divine Providence in the affairs of nations—and on behalf of a noble cause seeking to secure fundamental human liberties. American patriots found such reasoning particularly reassuring; as long as the Almighty was on their side and they had the stamina to continue the fight, the British tyrants were ultimately doomed to failure. In this sense, the providential explanation represented a statement of abiding hope—and faith—that the Revolutionary cause would regain its earlier momentum and ultimately prevail in its special purpose of uplifting the lot of an oppressed people. [14]

Arnold had abandoned that faith, and commentators sought to comprehend his motives. As with Colonel Alexander Scammell, stationed south of West Point, they wanted to know why "an officer so high on the list of fame ... would, or could be lost to every sense of honor, patriotism, and his own true interest." For Scammell, the puzzle was not complex. Arnold's "bravery at Saratoga has in the eyes of his country and army, covered a multitude of his villainous actions." A few courageous deeds had blinded far too many patriots to the inherently flawed character of America's Hannibal. Scammell was among those who now recalled how Arnold had "practiced for a long time the most dirty, infamous measures to acquire gain." [15]

According to such interpretations, Arnold was a seasoned master of deception. He had never really served the cause of liberty as a selfless patriot. He had only feigned a posture of public virtue—of sacrificing his own interests for the good of his fellow citizens—to obtain what he most craved: fame and fortune, exclusively for himself. It all should have been so obvious, but somehow truly virtuous patriots, striving so diligently to win their War for Independence, had mistakenly assumed that they needed Arnold's martial talents to defeat the enemy. So they had ignored the obvious signs of his perfidious nature and unwittingly jeopardized the Revolution.

The common belief held Satan, the spiritual master of deception, responsible for having temporarily blinded the eyes of so many. At the same time, only the devil himself could have so debauched Arnold's appreciation of his own best interests. The tyrannical British, themselves representatives of a corrupt, oppressive political order, had only done Satan's dirty work by tempting the wanton Arnold with a handsome monetary stipend for betraying so glorious and righteous a cause.

On Saturday, September 30, patriotic citizens in Philadelphia gave visual expression to the satanic explanation. They paraded a float that centered on "an effigy of General Arnold sitting" through the streets of their city. The effigy portrayed America's Hannibal as having "two faces, emblematical of his traitorous conduct, a mask in his left hand, and a letter in his right from Beelzebub, telling him that he had done all the mischief he could do." The devil was "shaking a purse of money at the general's left ear, and in his right hand [was] a pitchfork, ready to drive him into hell as the reward due for the many crimes which the thief of gold had made him commit." Only Satan could have come so close to destroying the vitals of a Revolution so worthy in its purpose as to be an object of divine protection.[16]

Elsewhere "the horrid account of Arnold's perfidy," reported an army officer in Connecticut, quickly became "the almost universal topic of conversation." Despite the reassurance of the protecting hand of Providence, many patriots worried lest "maybe there are more Arnolds among the Americans." To help allay such fears, civilian leaders in New York proclaimed "a day of public thanksgiving to Almighty God, for His remarkable deliverance, in the discovery of the horrid conspiracy for delivering up the fortress at West Point." Various New England communities, among them Boston and Providence, Rhode Island, discouraged other potential Arnolds by holding public demonstrations similar to the Philadelphia spectacle. To assure the complete isolation of Arnold, some patriots even advocated turning "the ever memorable 25th of September (the day when the blackest of crimes was unfolded)" into an annual holiday, so that Arnold's horrifying duplicity could be "handed down to the latest posterity, to the eternal disgrace of the traitor."[17]

What everything came down to was that Satan, as the adversary of an enlightened world, had seriously threatened the Revolution by taking advantage of Arnold's defective character, or what General Nathanael Greene, once an admiring friend, now called "the villainy and meanness of that man." The turncoat general was nothing more than "a reproach to human nature," continued Greene, "and a disgrace to America, especially to New England." A newspaper commentator was more specific. He beheld in Arnold a "poor sordid wretch" whose many "demerits" included "the base born passion, love of gold." Explained a satirist, writing as if he were Arnold, "It was my misfortune not to be born in affluent circumstances. My ruling passion is, and ever has been vanity and love of money." The Marquis de Lafayette encapsulated these impressions by categorically stating that Arnold suffered from an uncontrollable "rascality" of temperament.[18]

As if corrupted by the wily old serpent from the moment of his birth, Arnold came to personify the depraved, darkened side of human nature. Within weeks of his flight, American patriots had fully recast him as a thoroughgoing scoundrel, nothing more than "a mean toadeater" suited only for "robbery," "peculation," "mean deception," "falsehood," "barbarity," "ingratitude," "hypocrisy," "avarice," and, worst of all, "treason."[19]

Hence came into being the depiction of a truly wicked human being who deserved "a fixed detestation and abhorrence ... which can receive no addition," as Colonel Scammell summarized contemporary reappraisals. Scammell would have heartily agreed with the writer of "An Acrostic—On Arnold," a poetical denunciation that first appeared in October 1780:

> Born for a curse to virtue and Mankind,
> Earth's broadest realms can't show so black a mind.
> Night's sable veil your crimes can never hide,
> Each one's so great—they glut the historic tide.
> Defunct—your memory will live
> In all the glare that infamy can give.
> Curses of ages will attend your name,
> Traitors alone will glory in your shame.
>
> Almighty justice sternly waits to roll
> Rivers of sulphur on your traitorous soul.
> Nature looks back, with conscious error sad,
> On such a tainted blot that she has made,
> Let Hell receive you rivetted in chains,
> Damn'd to the hottest of its flames.

Much more succinctly, a Philadelphian summarized the feelings of thousands of patriots:

> *Mothers shall still their children, and say—Arnold!—*
> *Arnold shall be the bugbear of their years.*
> *Arnold!—vile, treacherous, and leagued with Satan.*

Nathanael Greene was the most direct of all in expressing popular attitudes when he wrote, "Never since the fall of Lucifer has a fall equaled his."[20]

On October 4, 1780, the Continental Congress ordered its Board of War to "erase" Benedict Arnold's name from the sacred rolls of the army. No one among the Revolutionary leaders wanted to admit to ever having had any association with so abhorrent a person. In the years ahead, those who would confess to having known Arnold took full advantage of such selective hindsight; they chose to recall only the very worst. Aging Revolutionaries even began to spin tall tales about Arnold's squandered youth and dissipated adulthood. In time these stories took on a life of their own, further adding to the reams of negative commentary about the Revolution's greatest temporal enemy.[21]

Yet the vividly contrasting, even haunting images of the luminescent hero and the serpentine villain remain. In reckoning with so imposing a contradiction, Nathanael Greene spoke of a parallel between Arnold's life and the cosmic journey of Satan, who first, as the angel Lucifer, the "guardian cherub" of the Garden of Eden, had been "full of wisdom and perfect in beauty," before he corrupted paradise. Then God "threw" Lucifer, once "adorned" by "every precious stone," down "to the earth," at which point the disgraced Lucifer took on the garb of Satan and retaliated by making perpetual war on God and his people. Greene's analogy served as an inadvertent admission that triumph and magnificence had denoted the life of Benedict Arnold before his tragic downfall. Were it otherwise, his plunge from grace as the Revolution's most renowned fighting general would have been much less ignominious. What follows is the actual story of Benedict Arnold, stripped of its heavily encrusted myths, and his rise from obscurity to heroic stature, so much of which explains his tragic descent to perpetual ignominy.[22]

One

A Childhood of Legends

I

In the years following the American Revolution, civilians and battlefield veterans alike delighted in retelling the heroic accomplishments of their illustrious generation. Many of these aging Revolutionaries naturally embellished their own deeds while avoiding any mention of personal fainthearted-ness. Using their memories selectively as they spun their glorified tales, they also glossed over the knotty spots of the Revolution and ignored the debili-tating internal conflicts that had nearly destroyed their cause from the inside. In so doing, they helped form a national mythology about a deeply committed citizenry rising up as one on behalf of political liberty and shattering forever the shackles of British tyranny. During eight long years of war, the old-timers insisted, zealous patriots such as themselves had suffered horribly but endured, thereby creating an independent, freedom-loving, republican polity; and because of their sacrifices, future generations would not have to face the wrenching prospect of political tyranny, as long as they stood faithfully by the ideals of the Revolution.[1]

Looking back over their achievements, the aging Revolutionaries dwelled on the themes of unity, commitment, and endurance. When they spoke of differences among the colonists, they focused on tories, casting aspersions on those thousands of loyalists whose allegiance to the British empire made them appear as traitors to the noble cause of American liberty. For some old-timers, the word "traitor" conjured up images of turncoat Benedict Arnold, allegedly the greatest villain of them all. Denouncing the devious, self-serving Arnold was yet another way of certifying their own credentials as virtuous, selfless patriots.

As the aging Revolutionaries gathered around warm fires on winter eve-nings or sat rocking on country-store porches on sunny summer days, they begot many a cracker-barrel tale about the reasons for Arnold's traitorous conduct. In their explanations they often drew on immediate posttreason assessments of the turncoat general. Some New England locals even reached into the recesses of Arnold's childhood in Norwich, Connecticut. Little Benedict, the old-timers liked to relate, was an uncontrollable boy, "hell bent" for destruction. From the moment of his birth he was a devilish lad, corrupted by some mysterious implantation of Satan's poisonous seed.[2]

Each story functioned as a parable and implicitly warned of the dangers associated with destructive personal character traits. Just as the cherry-tree tale, an apocryphal fabrication of Washington's early biographer Parson Mason L. Weems, established young George's unflinching rectitude, the Arnold tales helped delineate little Benedict's defects. Thus one of the traitor's "earliest amusements" was allegedly "the robbing of birds' nests." A thoroughly depraved youngster, he loved "to maim and mangle young birds in sight of the old ones, that he might be diverted by their cries." Only a child so wantonly cruel could revel, when later an apprentice, in spreading sharp pieces of broken glass, "by which the children would cut their feet," along the main dirt path "in coming from the school." The stripling Benedict, then, was compulsively mean-spirited from infancy, which finally became obvious when he plotted with the British to crush the Revolution.[3]

Still, someone had to explain Arnold's effectiveness as a military leader, since so despicable a person had gained a hero's reputation as America's Hannibal early in the Revolutionary War. Pausing to think, the old-timers quickly explained away the inconsistency by mentioning Arnold's leadership qualities in his youth—the type that caused other children to go astray. They framed Benedict's actions as those of a "dauntless ringleader" in molding youthful delinquents. Always stirring up "mischief," he was also a bullying lad, "as despotic among the boys as an absolute monarch," and therefore an archenemy of responsible behavior among his playmates.[4]

To prove their case, the aging Revolutionaries told the story of fourteen-year-old Benedict persuading "a gang of boys" to steal tar barrels from a local shipyard. Arnold's intent, it appears, was to fuel a great bonfire on a holiday; however, the local constable caught them. Not surprisingly, the boys' obstreperous ringleader "was so enraged that he stripped off his coat upon the spot, and *dared* the constable, a stout and grave man, *to fight*." So flagrant a disregard for those in authority showed how this young ruffian would bully his way through life, even to the point of assaulting the ideals of American liberty because of his unquenchable thirst for mindless mayhem.[5]

Just as horrifying to listeners were tales of Arnold's coldly vengeful and violent nature. During his late youth or early adulthood, he supposedly threatened the life of a foreign gentleman, often described as a French dancing master, who was courting his sister Hannah. As the story goes, Arnold took an intense disliking to the suitor, thinking him a rake. One evening he returned home to find the Frenchman again visiting Hannah. Standing in front of the house with a loaded pistol, he ordered the suitor outside. Hannah's frightened admirer fled through a side window and escaped, but apparently not before Arnold fired at least one shot. Demanding a showdown, the merciless future traitor insisted on a duel, and the Frenchman got the worst of it, nearly succumbing to his wounds. Alas, this victim of Arnold's wrath was never heard from again, one consequence of which, pronounced some storytellers, was that Hannah suffered the lamentable fate of spinsterhood.[6]

To maintain credibility and to avoid making the flawless likes of George Washington appear injudicious for having promoted Arnold's military career, the old-timers had to admit to some meritorious characteristics. "When a boy," they pointed out, Arnold "was bold, enterprising, ambitious, active as lightning, and with a ready wit always at command." Of course, he would invariably twist these positive qualities, such as when he found some gunpowder and tried to fire a cannon—Arnold was always causing trouble, it seems, on holidays, with this particular occasion being a day of thanksgiving for a military victory over the French. For some reason, perhaps to make the tale more exciting, young Benedict supposedly pointed the barrel of the fieldpiece in a sharp upward angle to facilitate dropping home the powder and, *"from his hand,* a blazing firebrand." Only his agility—he was quite athletic before war wounds mangled his left leg—saved the bumptious lad from more severe burns as he jumped back from the cannon's mouth just as it belched forth its flames. This time his compatriots cheered his foolish bravery, as they would in the early years of the Revolutionary War; but listeners also appreciated that only show-offs and potential troublemakers would take such foolhardy risks.[7]

Stories seemed to abound about young Arnold's physical agility. The old-timers remembered feats of athletic prowess, such as performances at a Norwich gristmill when the fearless lad would "astonish his playmates and alarm the lookers-on" by riding "the great waterwheel, and holding on as it made its revolutions." What such tales emphasized was Arnold's inborn recklessness in pursuit of fame, the kind of egotistical bidding for the applause of the crowd that initially fooled citizens into viewing him as a true military hero. In reality, the old-timers concluded, Arnold was a self-centered, aggrandizing person who invariably employed his natural physical and mental talents in distorted ways.[8]

Young Benedict the consummate "daredevil" was only a short step away from the malevolent adult controlled by Satan. To solidify the connection, the aging Revolutionaries spoke of the time when teenager Benedict hollered madly and shouted obscenities at the height of a severe thunderstorm. A demon-ridden deviant virtually from the moment of his birth, Arnold was a lad, according to his first serious biographer, who, "to an innate love of mischief, . . . added an obduracy of conscience, a cruelty of disposition, an irritability of temper, and a reckless indifference to the good or ill of others," all of which "left but a slender foundation upon which to erect a system of correct principles or habits." [9]

Arnold's perverse childhood, the aging Revolutionaries sadly observed, broke the heart of his mother Hannah—they remembered her as "a pattern of piety, patience, and virtue"—and drove her to an early grave—she "was a saint on earth, and is now a saint in heaven." Benedict had received "wholesome instruction" from his persevering mother, who constantly struggled to subdue his obstinate, self-centered will. The "lamentable" product, however, was "a proud, obstinate, and unprincipled man," in glaring contrast to the old-timers of the Revolution, who had respected their parents' nurturing and consequently had become praiseworthy exemplars of selfless republican citizenship in adulthood. [10]

As a virtuous mother, Hannah Arnold had sacrificed her health and life, but she never quit trying to instill correct habits of behavior in her little hellion. Republican mothers committed to the proper nurturing of worthy children, according to a widely read nineteenth-century author of childrearing literature, were likewise never to give up, no matter how obstinate the child. They were to model their actions on Mary Ball Washington, George's mother, who appreciated "that the first lesson to every incipient ruler should be, '*how to obey.*'" In addition, they were to instruct each "infant pupil" in "kindness to all around," which they could best demonstrate "by the treatment of animals." The cruel lad Arnold, this author stressed, had "loved to destroy insects, to mutilate toads, to steal the eggs of the mourning bird, and torture quiet, domestic animals." Accordingly, mothers who stifled any instincts in their children toward viciousness were helping to protect the republic from future Benedict Arnolds, the kind of fiendish adult who "would have drained the life-blood of his endangered country." [11]

Thus an additional purpose of the Arnold tales was to advise parents, particularly mothers, on the critical importance of nurturing children in values that resulted in responsible republican citizenship. The stories also served to warn children about what not to do—and how not to turn out. They represented guideposts about the dangers of misspent youth and the terrible penalties waiting in adulthood for youngsters who habitually behaved in a self-centered, boisterous, and defiant fashion. Children who aspired to revered status as adults were those who gained an appreciation of the value of giving to others and serving the greater good of the whole community—the core ideal of virtuous citizenship. Youngsters who behaved otherwise were potential Benedict Arnolds, despicable creatures with the potential to destroy the American republican experiment.[12]

II

The Arnold tales seriously distort the realities of Benedict's childhood days and the ways in which various formative experiences affected his adult behavior. Although surviving records are scant, enough materials exist to reconstruct Arnold's early years and place him in the context of his youth in eastern Connecticut. Family and community networks and problems certainly influenced his development. So did compelling issues that shaped the contours of life in colonial British North America during the two decades surrounding the midpoint of the eighteenth century.

Arnold's New England bloodline reached back to 1635, when William Arnold (1587–1675) sailed with other Puritans to Massachusetts to escape what they were sure was the oppressive religious atmosphere of Stuart England under autocratic King Charles I. William brought along his family, including his eldest son, Benedict (1615–1678). These Arnolds soon decided the Bay Colony was too stifling in its religious conformity. In 1636 they followed dissenter Roger Williams to Rhode Island, where William and his sons purchased vast tracts of land, nearly ten thousand acres, in the Pawtuxet River region. By the 1640s they were among the wealthiest settlers in Rhode Island.

Benedict I soon gained the community's political favor. During the late 1650s, Rhode Islanders deemed him the logical successor to Roger Williams as the colony's governor. Benedict I held Rhode Island's highest office on and off for several terms until his death in 1678. His property holdings were so extensive and his social and political stature so revered that nearly one thousand mourners attended his funeral.[13]

Of middling status in England, the Arnolds had quickly emerged as a front-rank family of elevated reputation in the more fluid social and economic milieu of mid-seventeenth-century English America. Governor Arnold's eldest son, Benedict II (1642–1727), served in the Rhode Island General Court and even became the speaker of the House of Deputies. Since his father, who designated eight heirs, practiced partible inheritance, he received only a small portion of the family estate, something over five hundred acres. Consequently, Benedict II had much less land to distribute among his own heirs. His five surviving children received rather modest inheritances. To his son Benedict III (1683–1719) he bequeathed 140 acres in the vicinity of Newport.[14]

Despite impressive family credentials, Benedict III did not own enough property or live long enough to make a reputation for himself. He married Patience Cogswell in 1705, and they had several children, one of whom was Benedict IV (?–1761). Born in Providence and apprenticed to a cooper, this fourth Benedict Arnold grew to adulthood with the scant prospect, as a younger son of an ordinary farmer, of receiving any landed inheritance. If he wanted to distinguish himself, he would have to use his own ingenuity in stretching beyond the calling of a barrel maker.[15]

The Arnolds, after just three generations of subdividing their land through the practice of partible inheritance, had begun to crowd themselves off the land. They were among thousands of third- and fourth-generation families in colonial New England who faced the dilemma of overcrowding as they multiplied rapidly and attempted to squeeze their numerous progeny onto relatively fixed amounts of farm acreage. Ultimately, further divisions of land would have resulted in freehold farming units too circumscribed in size to support families at even subsistence levels. As such, splitting the 140 acres of Benedict III among his six surviving children made no practical economic sense. One, most likely the eldest son, Caleb, received the whole of his father's freehold estate. The younger brothers and sisters had to accept alternate forms of inheritance. In the case of Benedict IV, his bequest was an apprenticeship, which endowed him with the capacity to earn a modest living, unless he possessed the energy and ambition to extend his range of economic opportunities.[16]

To gain his livelihood as a cooper held scant appeal for Benedict IV, given his heritage. He intended to accomplish more with his life, even if that meant relocating away from family and friends. Around 1730 he traveled westward with his younger brother Oliver to the inland port town of Norwich in eastern Connecticut. The two brothers were looking for opportunities to tap into trade and commerce exchange. Through his own labors Benedict IV hoped to realize the day when the downwardly mobile Arnold family trajectory would again be on an ascending course.

Before long Benedict IV was flourishing in Norwich, a town originally settled in the mid-seventeenth century. The principal port village sat at a geographic point where the navigable Thames River, cutting its way some twelve miles inland from the Atlantic Ocean, split into two smaller rivers that penetrated yet farther into the hilly countryside. Over the years, Norwich village had thrived as a shipbuilding and regional trading center. It easily competed with its coastal rival, New London, located at the mouth of the Thames, because of the geographic advantage of closer proximity to freehold farmers in more remote settlements. Some Norwich merchants, like those of New Haven to the west, enjoyed substantial personal prosperity by aggressively trading in ports along the American coast and in the West Indies and British Isles. Back home, their customers were mainly interior farmers who kept demanding a steady supply of luxury goods—pewter, fine linens, glassware, and books—in return for their surplus agricultural products.[17]

Dismissing any thought of someday remolding himself as a freehold farmer in the image of his Puritan forebears, Benedict IV fully embraced the rising commercial ethos of the acquisitive, hard-driving New England Yankee trader. He first found work as a cooper but kept looking for the opportunity to become involved in Norwich's mercantile trade. Circumstances turned out to be his greatest ally. He met and won the hand of Hannah Waterman King (1706–1759), a recent widow whose first husband, Absalom King, was a respected Norwich merchant. In September 1732, while returning from a trading voyage to Ireland, King had disappeared at sea. Benedict IV may have been in King's employ at this time. After a suitable period of mourning, Hannah married Benedict in November 1733, which by law placed him in charge of her substantial estate. He likewise gained access to King's trading connections, as well as valuable bloodline ties with two influential Norwich families, the Watermans and the Lathrops. Hannah's paternal grandfather, Thomas Waterman, had been one of Norwich's original town proprietors, and her mother, Elizabeth, was from the locally prominent Lathrop clan.[18]

Benedict IV quickly settled into his new life of mercantile respectability. He became heavily involved in trading goods along the coast of New England and back and forth to the West Indies. He purchased a handsome two-story home on five acres just outside the village, and in 1739 he took the oath as a freeman of the town. In the years ahead he accepted various town offices, including those of surveyor, constable, and selectman. From every point of view, Benedict IV was now a respected, upwardly mobile citizen of Norwich. Friends and neighbors no longer thought of him as an outsider from Rhode Island or a mere cooper. They took to calling him "Captain" Arnold, not only because he often sailed to the West Indies as master of his own trading vessels but also because he could claim association, through his marriage to Hannah, with the local elite families of Norwich.[19]

A harmonious union, the marriage of Benedict and Hannah Arnold produced six children. In August 1738, Hannah gave birth to their first child, whom the parents proudly named Benedict; but this infant died less than a year later. Parents in mid-eighteenth-century New England, especially in heavily populated areas where contagious killer diseases spread more easily, could consider themselves among the fortunate if more than 75 to 80 percent of their progeny survived to adulthood. The Arnolds were not so lucky. They lost four of their six children during outbreaks of epidemic disease.[20]

On January 14, 1741 (new style), Hannah, while lying-in at home, gave birth to another son. This infant, too, would bear the name Benedict. Choosing to repeat the family forename, the parents followed accepted custom dating back to the earliest Puritan settlements. In keeping alive a family forename that reached back through four generations to an ancestor of revered community standing in early Rhode Island, the Captain was also paying homage to himself. He had, after all, reversed the downward spiral in family fortunes. With proper nurturing, this new son could build on his father's achievements. With Waterman, Lathrop, and Arnold blood flowing in his veins, he might even someday attain a reputation of grand proportions, returning a once-proud New England family line to the most visible heights of community recognition. If childhood death could only be avoided, this second Benedict V had the potential to add many increments of glory to his father's noteworthy accomplishments. The baby Benedict thus represented hope for the fulfillment of the Captain's worldly ambitions—and perhaps even immortality. With a strikingly ironic twist, the Captain's hopes were to be realized.[21]

The Arnolds presented their babe for baptism before the First Congregational Church of Norwich just eight days after his birth. The Reverend Benjamin Lord performed the ceremony. Like other Congregationalists, Arnold's parents did not believe that baptism per se would protect their son from the wrath of God and eternal damnation. Still, in dedicating him to God and His work, the parents reached out for an established blessing in the mysterious process of divine judgment—of spending eternity with God in heaven rather than with Satan in the bowels of hell. Prospects of their son someday possibly securing God's eternal grace offered them special comfort even as the Reverend Lord baptized Benedict V and as the congregants prayed together for the preservation of the baby's soul.[22]

Born into the nest of a prospering family, Benedict V entered the world surrounded by the unconditional affection of parents, relatives, and friends. Surviving correspondence from Hannah suggests that his parents were as indulgent of his needs as they were restrictive of his behavior. The Captain and Hannah manifested a deep and abiding sense of love toward all their children, for which they paid dearly when killer diseases devastated their household in the early 1750s.

Captain Arnold functioned as the patriarchal head of his family unit, but he was no tyrant. He immersed himself in family and community activities when not attending to his local mercantile affairs or sailing back and forth to the West Indies. Hannah focused her energies on managing the family household. As the Captain's surrogate when he was away from home, she served as the primary source of daily instruction in implanting rules of acceptable behavior in her children. She nurtured them with gentle but firm instructions, such as when she counseled young Benedict to "keep a steady watch over your thoughts, words, and actions." She likewise advised him, "Be dutiful to superiors, obliging to equals, and affable to inferiors, if any such there be. Always choose that your companions be your betters, that by their good example you may learn." These admonitions reflected the deferential values of mid-eighteenth-century colonial society. His parents expected him to know his place, but they also encouraged him to aim high in seeking the favor of patrons who might recognize his merits and assist him in advancing to truly honorable stations.[23]

III

As a youngster, Benedict Arnold learned about the realities of life from many different sources. Three sets of childhood experiences helped shape his views of the world around him: the incessant warfare of the eighteenth century; the religious turmoil of the first Great Awakening; and the killer epidemics that besieged portions of New England. The overall effect was to introduce Benedict to the contentious, brutal, and tragic aspects of human existence. He learned that pain and suffering were as much a part of life as the happiness and personal contentment of growing to adulthood in a mutually supportive family environment.

Arnold was born in a year when warfare was convulsing the British empire. The British parent nation, in a frenzy of anti-Spanish hysteria, had raised the battle standard in 1739—the War of Jenkins's Ear—over differences about the extent of British trading rights in the Spanish Caribbean empire. Then a royal succession crisis developed in Europe in the wake of the death of the Hapsburg emperor Charles VI of Austria. The crown passed to his daughter, Maria Theresa, but young Frederick of Prussia, later known as Frederick the Great, joined with some dissident Hapsburg males in objecting to Maria. France and Spain aligned themselves with Frederick while Britain and Holland sided with Maria Theresa in what turned into the War of the Austrian Succession (1744–1748). As was the case with European conflicts dating back to 1689, warfare spilled onto the North American continent.

The British North American colonists called the current contest King George's War, and New Englanders became heavily involved. In 1745 they mounted a major expedition against the mighty French fortress of Louisbourg that guarded the entrance to the St. Lawrence River, the major artery leading into France's Canadian empire. A virtually impregnable edifice, Louisbourg fell to forty-two hundred besieging New Englanders, including many young soldiers from Connecticut. New Englanders took great pride in this victory, but in the peace settlement the king's negotiators returned the fortress to France in exchange for territory lost in India. The message was clear. The purpose of Anglo-American contributions was to secure and advance Britain's worldwide mercantile pretensions. As for the colonists, they existed to serve the empire but not to question the elevated wisdom of the parent nation.[24]

Only seven years old when the conflict ended, Arnold overheard many family and community discussions about King George's War. He learned to think of the French and Spanish as the traditional—and much hated—enemies of British subjects everywhere. The Spanish were malicious butchers, as epitomized in the mutilation of Robert Jenkins—he had his ear chopped off—when he was allegedly trading legally in the Caribbean. Little Benedict absorbed equally gruesome stories about French and Indian raiding parties massacring settlers along New England's frontier, and he internalized the long-felt British desire to eradicate French authority in Canada. Young Arnold also formulated impressions about the central role of warfare in deciding national differences, especially when leaders in Norwich like his father spoke of the imminence of yet more hostilities to reduce, if not destroy, the power of Britain's French and Spanish antagonists in America.

Besides identifying national enemies, King George's War helped Benedict conceptualize an embryonic sense of his own Englishness. Home government officials and British regular officers in America, he gleaned from the conversations around him, viewed the colonists as outlanders or country cousins, hardly worthy of their full respect. He listened as Norwichites denounced the return of Louisbourg to France. Still, as he heard so many times, to be a British subject, even though of secondary rank, was to have the advantage of belonging to the most powerful, enlightened, and liberty-loving empire in the world.

King George's War did not touch the Arnold family directly, except in making trade with the West Indies a more dangerous undertaking for the Captain. The contest likely forced Arnold's father to decrease or suspend his voyages to the West Indies, causing a downturn in the scale of family income. A lad as young as Benedict would not have noticed the difference. For him, the war functioned as a riveting—and frightening—kind of abstraction that likely produced childlike daydreams of martial glory and heroic achievement.[25]

At the same time, young Benedict harbored doubts about testing his own valor in combat. Years later, during the Revolutionary War, he described himself as "a coward until he was fifteen years of age." He characterized his vaunted "courage" as an "acquired" trait. Arnold did not explain why he underwent this transformation, but the causal factor lay with a series of devastating crises that beset his family during the 1750s.[26]

Meanwhile, reticent young Benedict would obtain a firsthand introduction to the turbulent and spiteful side of human relations. His education took root in the caustic bickering among Norwichites over matters of religious conscience and experience. At the time of Arnold's birth, the first Great Awakening was stirring up folk all over New England. Events in Norwich typified the widespread outpouring of concern over securing God's eternal grace. In the two decades before 1740, a declining number of Norwichites had petitioned for full church membership, the criterion for which included publicly testifying to evidence of having secured God's saving grace. Unsure or unconcerned about their spiritual state, most local citizens, including Benedict's parents, were only halfway church members. They could have their children baptized, but they could not participate in the sacred rite of communion.[27]

Ministers such as Benjamin Lord, whose pastorate with the First Congregational Church dated back to 1717, wanted to reverse the pattern but could not find the means. Then itinerant preachers, among them the charismatic evangelist George Whitefield, began to proclaim the vitality of the new-birth message in communities throughout New England, prompting a sudden rush of conversions. Whereas in 1740 no Norwichite presented himself or herself for full membership, during the year of Arnold's birth, eighteen women and fourteen men sought full membership, matching in one year the total number of full church admissions in Norwich during the previous decade. In 1742, forty-five persons became full members, including Arnold's parents. The Captain and Hannah had searched their hearts and found the comforting presence of Christ. The numbers of new full members dropped off again after 1742, but in towns such as Norwich, as well in the Arnold home, a new sense of religious enthusiasm had replaced the perfunctory ceremonialism of earlier years.[28]

Now more secure in the prospect of eternal salvation, the Captain and Hannah focused on preparing their children for God's saving grace. Each of the surviving letters by Hannah, five of which she addressed to young Benedict, stressed the need to "let your first concern be to make your peace with God, as it is of all concerns of the greatest importance." Hannah worried continuously about her son's spiritual state and repeatedly reminded him, "My dear, . . . make the Lord your dwelling place and try and trust His care. We have a very uncertain stay in this world, and it stands us all in hand to see that we have an interest in Christ, without which we must be eternally miserable."[29]

Arnold's parents also insisted on their son's instruction in vital faith as part of his formal education. When they first sent him away to school, Hannah asked the teacher "to instill the first rudiments of religion and enforce virtue and explode all manner of vice" in her son. "If you should find him backward and unteachable," she wrote, "pray don't be soon discouraged." The boy was "uncultivated" in his understanding of God's saving grace and required instruction. If necessary, corporal discipline was permissible: "Pray don't spare the rod and spoil the child," Hannah declared, since nothing was more important than checking the inborn will of human beings toward sin, which too often kept them from seeking conversion and eternal salvation.[30]

Despite his mother's exhortations, Benedict ultimately could not bring himself to accept the Calvinist-rooted beliefs of his parents. Certainly affecting his outlook was all the turmoil that developed among Norwichites in the immediate aftermath of the Awakening. Friends and neighbors were both contentious and vile with one another, which no doubt left Benedict wondering about the benefits of holding religious beliefs that seemed to spark endless bickering rather than a sense of spiritual and communal harmony.

Congregational ministers throughout New England were genuinely grateful when their churches came back to life. Soon, however, they had second thoughts. Enthusiastic itinerant preachers had done much more than help awaken the populace. Some residents now felt called to preach and serve as witnesses of God's Word without clerical authorization. Still others demanded church facilities closer to their homes and insisted on employing only ministers who could convincingly relate their own conversion experiences and would preach the "new light" gospel.

Established Congregational clergymen found themselves under attack from their own parishioners. In Norwich, some inhabitants decried the First Church and the Reverend Lord for being too lenient in the scrutiny of parishioners who offered public testimonies of conversion. These purists, also known as Separates, balked at having just anyone partake in the hallowed privilege of full church membership, the communion service. When the Reverend Lord objected, they accused him of lacking commitment to the new-light gospel. Norwich's Separates also threatened to form their own congregation, headed by someone fully committed to correct church practices.

In 1745 a full-scale separatist revolt took place in Norwich. Refusing to attend services conducted by the Reverend Lord, one group of dissenters petitioned the Connecticut Assembly for their own society. The First Church responded by suspending these folk from communion until such time as they repented. A bitter struggle over fundamental beliefs, which included bludgeoning assaults on Lord's personal character and spiritual state, had split Norwich wide open, as was the case in so many other ostensibly well ordered New England towns.[31]

The Captain and Hannah stood with their church pastor, but some distant relatives, including three Lathrops and three Watermans, aligned with the Separates. Benedict was four years old at the time. The young lad watched as the Separates' challenge—and resulting neighborly vindictiveness—reached full crescendo, and relatives and friends turned to snubbing and ridiculing one another. All the acrimony surely frightened him, making him wonder why adults, particularly the most significant persons in his life, had become so dreadfully contentious.

Indeed, if Benedict Arnold was the kind of troublesome youth portrayed by the Revolutionary old-timers, he received excellent instruction in the art of willful, self-righteous belligerence from the inhabitants of Norwich. At the same time, his memories of hateful squabbling over matters of religious faith, when linked with the tragedy of losing three of four younger siblings to killer diseases in the early 1750s, helped convince Arnold to reject the austere Calvinism of his parents.[32]

Throughout the 1740s, the Captain and Hannah made the First Church a root institution in their family's life. With the Reverend Lord serving as their spiritual mentor, the family prayed and worshiped together; but piety did not spare the Arnold household from the terrible epidemics that devastated so many eighteenth-century New England families. Uncontrollable, virulent diseases swept down with unremitting regularity. Medical knowledge, fixated as it was on the science of bleeding, or phlebotomy, was a useless ally in warding off such scurrilous enemies as scarlet fever, the measles, whooping cough, the mumps, influenza, and smallpox, among a host of potent killers.

During 1739, a serious diphtheria epidemic swept through much of Connecticut. This virulent disease most likely claimed the life of the Arnolds' first Benedict. Family members watched helplessly as loved ones struggled to maintain their ability to breathe. The "throat distemper," as diphtheria was then commonly called, slowly choked its victims to death, just as surely as fevers from smallpox raised body temperatures beyond the point of human endurance.[33]

The Arnolds' second Benedict was fortunate by comparison. He avoided the worst of these killer diseases, but three of his four younger siblings were not so favored. Arnold's siblings included Hannah, who was born in December 1742; Mary, born in June 1745; Absalom King, born in April 1747; and Elizabeth, born in November 1749. Only Hannah survived into adulthood. Absalom King succumbed to some mysterious ailment in December 1750. Mary and Elizabeth died within nineteen days of each other in the autumn of 1753. Before Benedict reached thirteen years of age, only his sister Hannah remained—along with his distraught parents.[34]

Young Arnold was away at boarding school when his sisters Mary and Elizabeth perished during a virulent diphtheria epidemic. His mother sent him two letters during this awful period. On August 13, 1753, she reported that "deaths are multiplied all around us and more [are] daily expected." She admonished her son not to "neglect your precious soul which, once lost, can never be regained." On August 30, she gladly let Benedict know "that your poor sisters are yet in the land of the living." Mary, who had been "just stepping on the banks of time," was now "something revived," but Hannah, who did survive, was "waxing weaker and weaker." The Captain was also "very poor," and "I myself have had a touch of the distemper but through divine goodness it is past of light with me."[35]

For Arnold's mother, firmly fixed as she was in Calvinist doctrine, the explanation for this deadly assault was self-evident: "God seems to be saying to all, children be you also ready." Hannah described the epidemic as "His servant," and she again urged her sole surviving son to "pray improve your time and beg of God to grant his spirit, or death may overtake you unprepared, for his commission seems sealed for a great many, and for ought you know you may be one of them."[36]

As a dutiful Calvinist, Hannah defined God with an Old Testament emphasis. Her supreme being was not only omniscient but arbitrary, the kind of deity that inflicted communities with dreadful maladies to warn everyone, especially those not seeking salvation, of the eternal damnation awaiting the unsaved. Trapped between her conception of a highly judgmental, even wrathful deity and deep emotional anguish for her family, she wanted Benedict, above all else, to keep soliciting God's grace. At the same time, she could not help being an indulgent parent, sending him a pound of chocolate with the second letter. A month and a half later, both Mary and Elizabeth were dead, along with dozens of others in the Norwich region. Hannah's only solace was the survival of her husband and remaining daughter and son.

No surviving record indicates how young Arnold reacted to the deaths of his siblings. Part of a close-knit family unit, he most likely experienced deep and lasting grief, having learned at a tender age how short and tragic human existence could be. He had likewise discovered how easily contention and strife, whether over matters of religious belief or over the affairs of nations, could despoil human relationships. Even though his mother offered him solace through her Calvinist mentality, she spoke not of a God of love and hope but of a being that arbitrarily struck down innocents as a warning to others about the sinful nature of humankind. This same deity, his bereaved mother reiterated, had taken his two brothers and two sisters to warn him and everyone else about the penalties for ungodly human behavior. ·

In the days ahead, Hannah continued to urge her son to seek this same God's grace, but he did not. As Benedict grew to adulthood, with brothers and sisters forever left behind, he eschewed the Calvinist expression of a judgmental, angry, vengeful deity in favor of a more humane and enlightened God. Unlike his grieving mother, he would not blame himself for tragedies in life beyond his control. Even more important, he would show little tolerance for those who, like his mother's wrathful Calvinist God, expected complete obedience to their will but demonstrated little or no beneficence toward others. He would challenge arbitrary power wherever it lurked, especially when directed against his person, character, and reputation—and those whom he loved. Well before adulthood, then, Arnold would abandon a certain passivity toward life by adopting a set of personal values intolerant of anyone he deemed threatening, unjust, or repressive in any way.

IV

Young Benedict still had more painful lessons to endure. In 1753 the Arnold family, devastated by disease, held the community's sympathy. Over the next few years, unfortunately, the Captain developed a serious drinking problem, and commiseration metamorphosed into contempt for a once-respected community figure. Historians have speculated that Benedict IV's troubles with alcohol stemmed from his failure as a merchant. He either overextended his trading activities during the 1740s or failed to weather interruptions in the West Indies trade caused by King George's War.[37]

This causal sequence is out of kilter. Like most Anglo-Americans of his day, Captain Arnold drank regularly and heavily, but his consumption of alcohol did not begin to threaten his personal productivity or his family's financial well-being until 1754 or 1755. No evidence exists to show that his drinking got out of control until after the diphtheria epidemic of 1753 claimed the lives of Mary and Elizabeth. A loving father, the Captain found the deaths of these two daughters and the lingering threat of losing Benedict and Hannah too difficult to bear. Great quantities of alcohol dulled his senses and temporarily eased the emotional pain associated with the ongoing devastation of his family.

In 1754 there was still enough money for Benedict's schooling. On April 12, Hannah sent her son fifty shillings, and the Captain added another twenty shillings, not for tuition but for personal expenses. He was to spend the money "prudently, as you are accountable to God and your father." Four months later, Hannah reported to Benedict that "your father is in a poor state of health," so much so that the Captain was not yet sure whether he could make a trip to Newport, Rhode Island. Hannah offered no description of the ailment. Six months later the parents reluctantly withdrew Benedict from school. With the Captain unable to work on a regular basis, the Arnolds could no longer pay for their son's formal education. Soon they would be short of money for much of anything else.[38]

Ambitious for their son, the Captain and Hannah wanted Benedict to have the benefits of a formal education. They had first enrolled him in Dr. Jewett's school in Montville, a few miles south of Norwich. Then they sent him to Canterbury, Connecticut, in 1752 to attend a school kept by the Reverend James Cogswell. Cogswell was well known as a dedicated minister, gifted logician, and demanding taskmaster who prepared his students well for further education. In Canterbury, Benedict lived with other young scholars under the tutelage of Cogswell, who drilled them in the rudiments of Greek and Latin, mathematics, and public speaking. For nearly three years he learned from such Latin texts as *Cornelius Nepos*. He owned the 1748 edition of this volume in which he inscribed, "Benedict Arnold, Ejus Liber [his book]."[39]

Arnold's parents were clearly preparing their son for a college education, most likely hoping for matriculation at Yale College. Some of Cogswell's students did attend Yale; one, Naphtali Daggett, eventually became president of that institution. Then, in 1755, all of Benedict's formal schooling came to an abrupt halt. He would have to make his way in life without the immense advantage of a gentleman's education.

The Captain's ill health likewise severely restricted his capacity to offer his namesake son supervised training in the mercantile business. Fortunately for Benedict, his mother had many prominent relatives in Norwich. She approached her cousins, Daniel and Joshua Lathrop, who, besides being graduates of Yale, had prospered as partners in the apothecary and general merchandise trade. They ranked among the wealthiest citizens of Norwich. Fully aware of the Arnold family's plight, the brothers agreed to assume responsibility for Benedict's vocational education. They accepted him as an apprentice and soon came to admire his high aptitude for business.[40]

V

The Captain's attempt to reverse the socioeconomic decline of his family had thus ultimately failed. His efforts had amounted only to a brief interlude of recaptured respectability. By 1756, he could offer his namesake son little more than Benedict III had given him, an apprenticeship—and this only because of the intervention of Hannah. Instead of Yale College and certification as a young Connecticut gentleman of local family rank and distinction, Benedict had to accept his apprenticeship to the apothecary's trade as his primary familial inheritance. Like the Captain, he was quick to seize the initiative and make the most of the opportunity before him.

If Benedict harbored resentment toward a father who had stirred his ambition but failed to equip him with the tools for rapid advancement or with connections to powerful patrons, he never indicated as much. As a dutiful son, young Arnold kept his feelings under disciplined control. Nor did he purge any anger or disappointment by running away from home to participate in the military campaigning in New York and French Canada associated with the worldwide Seven Years' War (1756–1763), also known in America as the French and Indian War.

One of the most persistent—and misleading—of the Arnold tales dwelled on the teenaged Benedict's alleged passion for warfare and the opportunity to profit personally from military service. The aging Revolutionaries relished in explaining how Benedict, with his pugnacious temperament and insatiable greed, became involved in a war that again pitted denizens of the British empire against the French—and eventually, the Spanish—in a decisive test of imperial strength. Arnold allegedly kept running off to New York, where the bounty moneys for enlisting were supposedly greater than in Connecticut. In 1756, according to one version, the Reverend Lord acted on the pleas of Benedict's desperate mother, intervened with officials in New York, and got her son back to Norwich, presumably with lots of bounty money lining his avaricious pockets.

Despite his indenture agreement with the Lathrops, the unreliable apprentice could not be restrained, or so claimed the old-timers. Benedict again bolted from Norwich in the spring of 1758, this time with the prospect of grabbing bounty money then being offered by the Westchester, New York, militia company of Captain Jonathan Holmes. In March 1759 he reenlisted for a second year of service, receiving yet more bonus money. On this occasion, however, young Arnold deserted, having supposedly become bored with camp life. By so doing, according to this lore, he revealed his cunning nature in what was an obvious rehearsal for his treason.[41]

A more charitable version stated that Benedict, shortly after reenlisting, had received disturbing news from Norwich that his mother was desperately ill. He rushed home to be at her side. The understanding Lathrops, who did not seem to mind their apprentice running off for months at a time, generously allowed Benedict to return to New York for yet another enlistment term in 1760. Apparently, the military authorities in New York, also being charitable folk, overlooked the previous year's desertion and welcomed back the peripatetic youth, with nary a stripe laid on as punishment.[42]

These stories come apart under closer inspection. The circumstances of Arnold's life after 1755 contradict the possibility that he first joined and then deserted the New York militia. There was a "Benedick" (also rendered "Bowdick" and "Benidick") Arnold who enlisted with the Westchester militia in 1758, 1759, and 1760. This young man gave his residence as Norwalk in western Connecticut, just a few miles east of Westchester County. Why young Benedict would have traveled so far—across most of Connecticut— to enlist when many companies closer to home also were short of troops has no satisfactory explanation; and the greed motive carries little weight without proof that enlistment bounties were significantly higher in New York.

The records twice describe the Benedict in question as a "weaver" and once as a "laborer," which should lead one to ask why Arnold would have lied about his place of residence and occupation while giving his real name, if he intended to hide his true identity. That this person did not change his name does not support the argument that Arnold's objective, in going so far from home, was to make sure his mother and the Lathrops could not find him. Surely he would have taken the obvious precaution of altering his name, since he was clever enough to describe himself as a laborer and a weaver from Norwalk, Connecticut.[43]

The stories, in the end, represent a case of mistaken identity. Although the desertion description of 1759—"18 years of age, dark complexion, light eyes, and black hair"—generally fits the Norwich Arnold, the height listed for "Benidick" in 1760 was five feet nine inches, certainly above average in physical stature for a male during the late colonial era. No contemporary ever described Arnold as more than middling in height. Still, if there were some physical similarities, these could be accounted for by ties of blood. Members of the extended Arnold clan were living in Norwalk during the mid-eighteenth century, and they were distant relatives of the Norwich family. The most logical conclusion is that the Benedict who deserted in 1759 was from this Norwalk branch of the family.[44]

Young Arnold, furthermore, was under an apprenticeship contract. The Lathrop brothers, although tolerant benefactors, were not fools who allowed their apprentices to neglect their training and whimsically wander off to war. Between 1756 and 1760, Benedict spent his days in Norwich with the Lathrops, who considered him a model apprentice. They, in turn, demonstrated their full confidence after 1760 by initially financing him as their junior business associate in New Haven. As shrewd merchants and eminent local leaders, they would not have wasted their time, energy, and working capital on Arnold, no matter how fervent his mother's pleas, had he repeatedly violated his apprenticeship by running off to war.[45]

On one occasion, Benedict apparently mustered arms with the Norwich militia, but only briefly, during the Seven Years' War. In early August 1757, French and Indian raiders under the command of the French Canadian governor, Louis Joseph, Marquis de Montcalm, besieged and captured British-held Fort William Henry on the southern shore of Lake George. Much of western New England suddenly lay exposed to attack. Even before the fort's defenders capitulated and fell victim to a bloody massacre, Connecticut militiamen, including those of Norwich, were rallying to counter the enemy's advance. Arnold, now sixteen and just old enough for militia service, may have joined the Norwich column as it marched for Albany. However, Montcalm's force, concerned about overreaching its supply lines, quickly retreated northward, and the Connecticut units returned home before the end of August. Most likely, Arnold's short stint of service with the Norwich militia, representing his only martial experience before the Revolutionary War, along with the confusion of names, somehow combined to produce the desertion tales.[46]

Rather than sulking over disappointments or irresponsibly rushing off to snatch up enlistment bounties, young Arnold reckoned carefully with his prospects and future. A modestly well educated person with more formal schooling than most of his New England contemporaries, he had the energy to transpose personal adversity into a wide pathway of opportunity. The key, he understood, lay with his mercantile mentors and patrons, the Lathrop brothers, and he did everything possible to impress them with his abilities.

Before Arnold's apprenticeship was over, the Lathrops were treating him like a son of their own. What they beheld in him was an intelligent, earnest, intense young man, full of ambition, willing to work hard, and determined to master every aspect of their complex trading network. Since the Lathrops had well-established mercantile connections in the Caribbean and Britain, they even sent their protégé on trading voyages, first to the West Indies and then to London, where Benedict gained valuable experience in negotiating the purchase of commodities with merchants who regularly supplied the Lathrops.[47]

Still, Arnold's apprenticeship years were anything but untroubled. Before the decade was out, his mother was dead. Mother and son surely had become more dependent on each other as they suffered through the loss of family members, as they dealt with the Captain's intensifying alcohol problem, and as they endured the shame of their collapsing financial circumstances. Arnold dearly loved his mother, but he could not ease her distress. Hannah's shattered dreams, certainly as much as some mysterious ailment, caused her death in August 1759, while she was still in her early fifties.[48]

His mother gone, Benedict, though living away from home, had to look after his father as well as his remaining sibling, Hannah. The Captain's bouts of drinking, which grew worse after the loss of his wife, became a source of lasting embarrassment for his two children. In May 1760 a Norwich justice of the peace issued a warrant for Captain Arnold's arrest. Citizens had complained that he "was drunk" in public, "so that he was disabled in the use of his understanding and reason," based on his "speech, gesture[s], and behavior." Excessive drinking was simply unacceptable in well-ordered New England towns, most certainly in public, and the local court fined the Captain, besides warning him about further abuses of the bottle.[49]

Members of the First Church were not so lenient. They could not abide a full church member stumbling around their community in a drunken stupor. In late June 1760, Deacon Ebenezer Huntington demanded the Captain's appearance before the congregation, to be admonished for "drunkenness in diverse instances." The elder Arnold scoffed at the invitation, thereby rejecting established church authority. Church leaders responded by sending a committee to meet with the Captain but conceded that "they had not recovered him to his duty—that he was still impertinent and refused to make a public confession" regarding his socially disruptive behavior. The full church members then "voted a public admonition which renders him incapable of communion in special circumstances." Wholly defiant, the Captain again refused to appear at the meetinghouse, to ask forgiveness, and to submit to standard church discipline.

By early 1761, some church members were whispering about the ultimate penalty: excommunication. At this juncture, the Reverend Lord intervened. He promised to write "this poor man . . . a pungent letter," although that gesture failed to help. Because of "his great incapacity," the elder Arnold continued "in great disorder" of mind. Lord suspected correctly that sustained alcohol abuse had done its damage, that the Captain's health was completely broken. He asked his parishioners to show charity toward a once-respected church member, one who had stood steadfastly by him during the turbulent Separate years of the mid-1740s.

Before the end of 1761, Benedict Arnold IV was dead. For the First Church and its minister and members, there was "no more to be done." The problem of having a chronically drunk parishioner in their midst had found its own resolution.[50]

VI

Their father's tragic demise took a bruising toll on Benedict V and his sister Hannah. In addition to the sense of shame they experienced in daily contacts with relatives and friends, Benedict harbored feelings of indignation toward those Norwichites who looked at him sanctimoniously rather than sympathetically, as if they were measuring his worth by the failures of his namesake father. Another burden was Benedict IV's financial legacy, which amounted to nothing; to satisfy pressing creditors, the family homestead had to be sold, seemingly desecrating the memories of a once contented and loving family unit. Had the Lathrops not offered moral encouragement and financial support, the two surviving Arnolds might have entered adulthood destitute.

Thus Benedict, almost twenty-one years old in late 1761, had to reckon with his shattered sense of family honor. He would never forget his father's wretched downfall and death, nor would he forgive those Norwichites who were asking themselves, or so he suspected, whether the surviving son of Benedict IV would end his days as disreputably as had his father. He resolved to demonstrate to the folk of Norwich, at the first opportunity, that the Arnold name was as worthy of respect as any other in eastern Connecticut. He likewise made a commitment to devote his adult years to returning the Arnold name to its once lustrous heights. In doing so, he would be respectful toward his superiors and courteous toward his inferiors, as his mother had advised him; but he vowed never again to think of himself as a cowardly person but to confront anyone, however high or low in birth, who questioned his honor, reputation, or family name. Those with the temerity to do so would find him unrelenting in challenging their slurs—again and again and again.

Benedict also had to sort through his religious feelings. He would finally choose to accept a God of love, a supreme being that served as a source of light and comfort, not human misery and death. As he later wrote to his first wife after a particularly dangerous sailing voyage, "pray put up a petition of thanks that my life has been spared and pray for recovery and health." Arnold's deity would support rather than subvert his personal quest for greatness; and his God would encourage him to depend on his own intelligence, wit, and energy as he clambered up the socioeconomic ladder of secular achievement.[51]

Looking back to late 1761, Benedict Arnold emerged from his childhood days as a person of wounded pride but determined ambition. Born to comfort, that comfort had been taken from him. Raised to magnify the family name that he bore, he had seen that name lose its community respectability. Expecting a handsome monetary inheritance on which to carry forward his father's dream, he now had none. What he did have was his sister Hannah and a treasury of once-happy childhood days—the times of contentment before everything had gone so terribly wrong.

Benedict likewise had the patronage of the Lathrop brothers. With their support he would make his initial mark as an apothecary-merchant, knowing that gaining wealth from dealings in the marketplace would bring him status and prestige. Perhaps someday, as he projected an image of his own future, he would even enter politics and become a widely admired political patriarch, in the mold of his great-great-grandfather. Such tantalizing prospects, he appreciated, lay in the far distant future for a young adult of no family influence or respectability. First and foremost, he had to succeed in commerce, and the Lathrops stood ready to finance his new beginnings. Young Benedict Arnold thus took the obvious pathway open to him, and it led directly to New Haven.

CHAPTER Two

A Person to Be Reckoned
With in New Haven

I

Mid-eighteenth century New Haven was booming. Between 1750 and 1775 the town's population quadrupled, from two thousand to eight thousand. About one-fourth of its citizenry lived in the port village. More than a century had passed since early Puritan settlers had laid out this trading hub in a gridlike design on flat, marshy land where the Quinnipiac, Mill, and West rivers emptied into a deep, natural harbor. Beyond the harbor lay Long Island Sound, providing water access to markets in New York, Boston, the West Indies, and the British Isles. Immediately behind the village were hills, farmland, and a well-developed road network to interior towns over which agricultural goods could be transported to New Haven.[1]

By the early 1760s, the port village surged with dynamism and even conveyed cosmopolitan sensations. Yale College stood regally on the west side of the village green. The town could boast the colony's first newspaper, the *Connecticut Gazette,* founded in 1753. Citizens took special pride that their community served as one of two seats of provincial government— Hartford was the other. New Haven had also emerged as a center of religious diversity, at least by Connecticut standards. Besides two Congregational churches (the second was a product of a Separate movement similar to Norwich's), inhabitants could choose among Anglican and Roman Catholic services. Perhaps most visible of all, the marketplace fairly buzzed with activity as dozens of merchant vessels stood watch in the harbor while shipmasters waited to have cargoes loaded or unloaded.[2]

An explosive, fortyfold increase in commercial tonnage handled by the port in the third quarter of the century belied the demise of traditional

Puritan values, especially the maintenance of a communal sense of piety, harmony, and good order. Old-line families now longed for the days when residents knew their stations in life, deferred to their betters in political and social matters, and thought it more important to seek God's grace than to clamor obsessively after worldly riches. The old guard resented the spreading diversity of values, rampant competitiveness, and conspicuous consumption that Yankee traders seemed to personify; yet they could only carp, complain, and, whenever possible, snub those new persons on the make who kept arriving in their boomtown.[3]

In migrating to New Haven, Benedict Arnold cast his lot with the forces of competitive, acquisitive commercialism. He, too, would become the quintessential Yankee merchant-trader, joining many other aspiring migrants, including such notables as Roger Sherman, who signed both the Declaration of Independence and the Constitution of 1787, and David Wooster, who served as a general (much less successfully so than Arnold) in the Continental army. New Haven radiated unbounded opportunity for such ambitious and energetic persons. In Arnold's case, the New Haven marketplace became the arena in which he launched his personal quest to reestablish the respectability that once had denoted his family line.[4]

New Haven had other advantages for Arnold. The town was far enough from Norwich, a distance of about fifty miles, to free him of association with his father's sullied reputation. Potential customers would, he hoped, regard and accept him for his own deeds and strength of character. In Norwich he would have likewise faced constant reminders of his mother's heartfelt desire to see him earn God's saving grace, and worshiping at the First Church would have constantly reminded him of his father's failures. In contrast, Arnold could pursue his own form of faith in New Haven's more pluralistic religious atmosphere. The notion of finally becoming his own person greatly appealed to him. Even if the old-guard families treated him as an upstart outsider, he could still chart his own course in seeking what success the world had to offer—and he could do so unfettered by the past.

In moving to New Haven, Arnold also benefited from the largesse of his merchant patrons, Daniel and Joshua Lathrop. The two brothers were not just locally minded apothecaries; they were decidedly expansive in the range of their business contacts and interests. They worked to have mercantile associates with a sense of obligation toward them in the principal economic centers in Connecticut. As such, the Lathrops had recently set up a talented apprentice as an apothecary-merchant in Hartford. In 1761 they did the same with their young nephew and protégé Arnold. They encouraged him to tap into the commercial opportunities in New Haven, where he would initially operate as another key link in their trading network.[5]

The Lathrop brothers provided Arnold with an initial inventory of merchandise on their credit—the standard estimate is £500 sterling. Directly ordering these goods was likely one purpose for sending him to the British Isles. Not only could he purchase an array of medicines, books, and other trade items for his mercantile shop, but he could establish vital connections with suppliers. Arnold thus began his trading career as the Lathrops' junior partner, certainly a desirable status for a young adult lacking in working capital of his own.[6]

Before moving, Arnold and his sister Hannah decided that she should stay behind, at least until he was comfortably resettled. Once in New Haven, he resided temporarily with his uncle Oliver, the same person who so many years before had traveled with his father from Rhode Island and who now made his living in New Haven. Oliver gladly offered his nephew food and lodging—and much useful information about the community—during the weeks when Arnold set up and opened his shop.

II

The Lathrops were not mistaken about Arnold's capacities. Their protégé had a keen aptitude for commercial dealings. The first marks of success were soon evident, despite another posttreason tale that had Arnold failing miserably and ending up in debtors' prison before the end of 1763. He worked diligently and judiciously to establish his business and then expand his interests. At the outset, he rented space for a small shop on Chapel Street. As the volume and scope of his trading activities increased, he moved to more accommodating quarters—first to Church Street and then to Water Street, adjacent to New Haven's harbor.[7]

Early on, Arnold wanted to let New Havenites know that his purpose was to serve their needs with ample supplies of medicines, books, and related merchandise. He did so by hanging a black-and-gold lettered sign above the entrance of his shop, which read:

> *B. Arnold*
> *Druggist, Bookseller, &c.*
> *From London.*
> *Sibi Totique*

"For himself and for all," that was to be his motto in trade. Commentators have since claimed that Arnold much preferred the *sibi* to the *totique,* a backward-looking judgment at best. The young adult Arnold knew better than that. At the outset of a mercantile career in a community where he was a virtual stranger, he carefully cultivated a positive reputation. He wanted his customers to view him as a person who was astute enough to appreciate that serving himself depended on his being of service to them. He likewise hoped they would understand that working for their welfare should produce rewards for him as their servant. Choosing Latin to convey these thoughts represented a way to show his training, however incomplete, in the classics, certainly an important message in a community that contained college students as potential customers.[8]

As a neophyte apothecary-merchant, Arnold sold medicine products meant to improve health and to heal, such as "Bateman's Pectoral Drops," "Turlington's Balsam Life," "Tincture of Valerian," "Spirits of Scurvy Grass," and "James's Fever Powder." He offered a lengthy listing of books, ranging from "Hebrew Bibles," "Paradise Lost and Regained," and "Watts's Poems, Sermons, Psalms, and Hymns" to "Dryden's Poems," "Locke on Human Understanding," "Ben Johnson's Works," "Every Man his own Lawyer," and "a large collection of plays and novels, with many other books and pamphlets too numerous to mention." Indicating future directions, he also advertised the availability of "rum, sugar, . . . [and] many other articles . . . for cash or short credit." His customers found him to be both knowledgeable and helpful. As his trade flourished, New Havenites even began referring to him as "Dr. Arnold," the same title of respect used by Norwichites when they addressed the Lathrop brothers.[9]

Some New Havenites, particularly among the old-guard elite, did come to fear and despise Arnold before 1775, but their loathing had mostly to do with the ambitious newcomer's unwavering stand against Britain's new flurry of constraining imperial policies. Whatever their recollections, New Havenites favored Arnold generously with their business. They came to respect him as a merchant who wanted good relations with his clientele—and who proved it through generous extensions of credit to customers hard pressed for cash.[10]

By the summer of 1762, Arnold was looking toward the sea and the West Indies trade for additional commercial opportunities. By 1764 he had formed a loose partnership with Adam Babcock, another prospering New Haven merchant; together they operated a brigantine named *Fortune* (forty tons). By 1765 they had acquired two more vessels, *Charming Sally* (thirty tons) and *Three Brothers* (twenty-eight tons). Arnold still maintained his ties with the Lathrops and kept operating his apothecary shop. However, the sea and large profits to be derived from trade in horses, rum, molasses, pork, grain crops, and timber products became the primary focus of his attention. Like his father before him, he took to the sea and gained the appellation "Captain" Arnold as he sailed, depending on the season of the year, as far north as Canada and as far south as the West Indies.[11]

Business concerns absorbed most of Arnold's energies, but he occasionally returned to Norwich to visit the Lathrops and his sister Hannah. Such a trip occurred in the early autumn of 1763, during which Arnold made final arrangements to buy back his family homestead. Daniel Lathrop served as his agent in working out the purchase agreement with creditors who had earlier assumed control of the property in settlement of his father's estate.[12]

Then, in March 1764, Arnold abruptly turned around and sold his homestead for a handsome profit. He had two major reasons for doing so. First, as a young adult passionately devoted to commerce, he had little practical use for a piece of property that included just five acres—far too small a plot of land to serve as a base for a viable farming unit. Acquiring additional acreage was out of the question, since rapid population growth in eastern Connecticut had land prices soaring. Controlling large tracts had helped make the first Arnolds in Rhode Island prominent settlers. Perhaps, in time, he might want to emulate their landed lifestyle by having his own country estate, the true mark of an eighteenth-century gentleman; but not yet. To reach that goal, he had to amass substantial personal wealth, which depended on plunging into and maneuvering amid the competitive challenges and impersonal risks of the mercantile economy. To take full advantage of marketplace opportunities, he most of all needed working capital—over and above what the Lathrops had offered him. Thus, when Arnold received a lucrative offer, he showed no sentimentality. He would use the £400 profit from the sale of his homestead to help underwrite future business ventures.[13]

The other reason was intensely personal. The painful memories of his father's downfall, disgrace, and death, as well as his own sense of humiliation, were still very fresh in his mind. Arnold regarded the Norwichites, with the Lathrops as notable exceptions, as harshly judgmental, mean-spirited folk. In buying back the family homestead, Arnold had conveyed a message to them about how unjustly they had appraised his qualities, the testament of which was his rapid rush toward material achievement. At the same time, he was reclaiming a portion of his father's defamed reputation by paying the property's owners—and onetime unsatisfied creditors—a fair market price. Then, in so quickly reselling the property, Arnold projected how little he desired further associations with so small-minded a community. He thus exhibited his defiance toward those whom he felt had wronged him; and he did so, as would so often be the case, with the objective of vindicating his personal and family honor.

At this juncture, Arnold asked Hannah to move to New Haven, which she willingly did. An intelligent and capable person in her own right, Hannah devoted her life to her brother's welfare. After relocating in New Haven, she became his primary assistant in his commercial dealings. She also provided him a more comfortable home life, and she continued playing both roles even after Arnold married. For the rest of her life (she outlived her brother by two years), Hannah remained Benedict's valued confidante and partner in both business and family matters. She lent him solace and stability because she understood his past.[14]

Arnold's initial success in business buoyed his confidence. He spent considerable time seeking to prove his talents and personal worth. He did so in a variety of ways. On frigid winter evenings in New Haven he often went ice-skating, which gave him the opportunity to display his considerable athletic abilities. A neighbor described him "as the most accomplished and graceful skater . . . that he had ever seen." Arnold intended to make a favorable impression. He often spoke of his namesake ancestor who "was the first governor of Rhode Island," and he claimed "that an estate in England belonging to his family would probably fall to him," according to one less-than-dazzled informant. This person did not understand that Arnold was trying to fill the void caused by his father's—and, by association, his own—loss of community respect in Norwich. Above all else, he desired, at a minimum, to become a highly respected member of the New Haven community.[15]

What Arnold had to accept was that some New Havenites, particularly members of the more staid, old-guard families, were not going to be impressed—no matter what he accomplished. From their point of view, he was nothing more than a parvenu in their midst who dressed in the latest fashions, talked far too often about distinguished ancestors, and threatened their sense of proper hierarchy in human relations. Not wanting to share their place at the top of the local socioeconomic pyramid with the likes of him, they were quick to notice that he almost never spoke of his parents. Gossipmongers furnished them with what they needed to know, and there was plenty of whispering behind Arnold's back about his nearly excommunicated, drunkard father. On that count alone, they kept dismissing him as an upstart nobody; but no matter how hard they tried, they could not ignore him.

What old-guard New Havenites were learning was that Benedict Arnold, first and foremost, was a man of energy, purpose, and direct action. Although he craved respect, he would not pander himself or grovel for favors. Nor would he exercise tolerance toward those who, like the Norwichites, in some way seemed bent on discrediting his reputation and good name. Like many other future Revolutionary leaders, his profile was that of an individual ambitious for achievement, with low levels of tolerance toward those who threatened the full realization of his personal aspirations. Because of his sensitivities, temperament, and ambitions, old-line leaders should not have been surprised when Arnold emerged as a persistent—and for them, often annoying—advocate of American rights in resistance to perceived British tyranny.[16]

III

The Peace of Paris of 1763 ratified a stunningly successful series of British martial conquests in bringing an end to the Seven Years' War. The French reluctantly surrendered their far-flung Canadian holdings, and the Spanish gave up East and West Florida to regain Cuba. As a consequence, the first British empire had reached an all-new muscular apex among the major powers of Europe. The little island kingdom and its many colonial append-ages thus stood triumphantly in 1763 as the mightiest political force among the nations of the world.

Britons celebrated everywhere, but lingering imperial problems would mar the festivities. The youthful, energetic King George III and his chief ministers had come to view the American colonists as shirkers in their responsibilities to the empire's welfare. During the late war, for example, some wily colonial merchants had traded covertly with the French and Spanish enemy, so the Privy Council adopted new Orders in Council in October 1763 to assign Royal naval vessels to American waters, with the power to run down suspected smugglers. That same month, to preclude expenses of frontier Indian wars, the council announced the Proclamation of 1763. The idea was to draw a geographic boundary, running north to south at the edge of the Appalachian Mountains, beyond which the ever land-hungry provincials could not settle.

Home government leaders had good reason for deep concern about government expenditures. The Seven Years' War had almost doubled En-gland's national debt—from roughly £75 to £137 million sterling. Colonial governments, by comparison, were all but debt free, so another idea was for the Americans to pay for the eight thousand to ten thousand redcoated regulars the king's ministers had decided to station in North America—during peacetime, no less—to enforce the imperial ruling against continued westward expansion. Of course, these troops could also be deployed, if the need arose, to quell disturbances by fractious colonists living in eastern settlements.[17]

Once in motion, Britain's home leaders hastened forward on their crackdown course. In April 1764, King and Parliament legislated both the Currency Act and the Sugar Act. The first outlawed the use of unbacked—and on rare occasion, wildly inflationary—colonial currencies as legal tender in private debt payments. Among the many provisions of the second was a trade-duty reduction from six to three pence per gallon on foreign molasses shipped to the provinces (with the intention of actually collecting the levy) and a delineation of new procedures to strengthen the ability of local customs officials in ferreting out colonial smugglers.

In 1765 King and Parliament struck again, twice. The purpose of the Quartering Act was to shift to the colonists the financial burden of billeting the king's regulars in America. Most disturbing of all, the Stamp Act placed unprecedented direct taxes on the colonists by means of stamps attached to some fifty items, ranging from newspapers, almanacs, and pamphlets to wills, land deeds, college diplomas, and port clearance papers for trading vessels.[18]

This flurry of imperial legislation, after decades of "salutary neglect," reflected an attitude that the colonists had forgotten their fundamental responsibility of steadfastly serving, above all other consideration, the paramount needs of the empire. In the aftermath of the Seven Years' War, leaders in England were asking in shrill voices whether the Americans truly appreciated how "the colonies . . . have been of late the darling object of their mother country's care." The war effort, best epitomized in General James Wolfe's glorious victory over the forces of the Marquis de Montcalm at Quebec in September 1759, had removed the French imperial enemy from North American soil and rolled back the geographic range of Spanish hegemony. George Grenville, head of the king's cabinet between 1763 and 1765, questioned whether the colonists comprehended—or even cared—how the solicitous parent "nation has run itself into an immense debt to give them protection." His position was uncompromising: "Great Britain protects America: America is bound to yield obedience."[19]

In the metaphor of the times, the king's ministers perceived Britain's children in North America as spoiled and misbehaving, the product of parental overindulgence. The time was at hand to reprove them after too many years of gratifying their every whim. King and Parliament thus mandated a series of disciplinary strokes, ranging in content from Royal naval vessels ready to pounce on suspected smugglers and redcoats standing by to inhibit frontier expansion to Parliament, a body in which the Americans had no elected voice, demanding tax moneys in support of more constraining imperial policies. This tightened regimen would compel greater obedience among the colonial children toward their generous parent. If not, they might well face far more inhibiting restraints in the days ahead.

The American perspective was very different. Colonists everywhere, Benedict Arnold among them, regarded themselves as dutiful subjects who were maturing toward political adulthood. As one widely read pamphleteer stated, Americans had "facilitated . . . those operations by which so many glorious conquests were achieved" during the late war. Nor was the parent nation totally selfless in rolling back imperial enemies. The empire's conquests were "necessary for the defense of . . . herself" because tiny Britain "could not long subsist as an independent kingdom after the loss of her colonies" to those enemies. From the American perspective, the parent was now demeaning the contributions of its Anglo-American progeny to the empire's long-term welfare. This gaping dissimilarity in perceptions foreshadowed major difficulties in the making.[20]

Although the colonists lodged official complaints about the violation of such fundamental rights as taxation only by duly elected representatives, they behaved with relative equanimity until the summer of 1765. By that time some American agitators, more commonly referred to as "radical" or "popular" leaders, thought they had evidence of a deep-laid plot among home government leaders and royal officeholders in America to deprive the children of their fundamental liberties and to ensnare them in the tyrannical chains of political slavery. The lust for power had corrupted the king's ministers, insisted the popular leaders, and, with the passage of the Stamp Act, liberty itself seemed now at stake. These agitators—Boston's Samuel Adams was the most prominent among them—organized colonial resistance. Using confrontational tactics, including intimidation through controlled crowd violence, the colonists rendered the Stamp Act impotent before it went into effect.

In Connecticut's case, the home government named a much-respected New Haven attorney, Jared Ingersoll, as its stamp distributor. Ingersoll, who knew Arnold well and served on occasion as his lawyer, was surrounded by the local Sons of Liberty while riding to Hartford in mid-September 1765. Before the Sons finished with him, he had signed a sworn statement renouncing any intention to administer the Stamp Act. Just to make sure, the Sons made him verbally reject Parliament's tax plan in favor of "liberty and property, with three cheers" at two separate locations. Each time the deeply shaken Ingersoll followed orders to throw his hat in the air, causing onlookers to guffaw and merrily shout huzzahs. Not surprisingly, no one else was foolhardy enough to step forward and claim Connecticut's stamp distributorship.[21]

IV

Arnold did not participate in these crowd actions. He was most likely at sea trying to get a shipload of goods back to New Haven before November 1, the date when the Stamp Act was to become law (and the first day that stamped papers would be necessary for bringing commodities in and out of port). When that fateful date arrived, commercial activity came to a screeching halt in American port towns. Not only were stamps unavailable, but merchants, sometimes with a bit of coercion, were pronouncing themselves in favor of boycotting the importation of British goods until Parliament rescinded the Stamp Act. Even though coastal trading was possible, if carrying merchants were willing to risk doing business without stamps, few initially had the temerity to do so. Then, as November gave way to December and the new year of 1766 arrived, more and more colonists returned to conducting their business affairs, as if the Stamp Act did not exist. Arnold was among their number.

In late January 1766 one of Arnold's brigantines, the *Fortune,* docked in New Haven. The vessel's crew managed to sneak some of the cargo, probably molasses from the West Indies, past local customs officers without paying the three-pence-per-gallon trade duty. Peter Boles was a mariner who assisted in this operation, and he indicated to Arnold that an increase in his wages would help to keep his mouth shut. The apothecary-merchant curtly refused the bribe. An angry Boles marched off to the New Haven customs office and asked for the port collector, who was not available. Boles then queried the assistant collector about how much money he would earn for informing on a cargo of smuggled trade goods. The assistant was not sure, so Boles left the office but not before indicating that he would soon return to speak directly with the collector.[22]

Arnold was one among hundreds of New England merchants—John Hancock of Boston was perhaps the most notorious among them—who evaded the payment of trade duties whenever they could. The postwar imperial shift toward more vigorous customs collections served as a challenge to these merchants to become more creative in their smuggling activities. Their essential argument was that the duties were unfair and only made goods too expensive, thereby stifling local economic activity. Customs collectors, in turn, depended on informers to help them identify and seize illicit cargoes for condemnation in vice-admiralty courts. Mariners and dockworkers rarely cooperated with customs officials, since sudden financial setbacks for their employers could leave them bereft of work opportunities and wages. As a result, those who did inform quickly became pariahs in their respective communities.[23]

When Arnold learned about Boles's visit to the customs house, he sought him out and "gave him a little chastisement." Feigning intimidation, the mariner promised to leave town. Two days later Arnold learned that Boles was still in New Haven, hanging about Beecher's Tavern, where he was downing great quantities of alcohol. Now incensed, Arnold gathered together some of his workers and led them to the tavern. The force of their numbers quickly convinced Boles to sign a prepared confession regarding his alleged misdeeds. He admitted that, "not having the fear of God before my eyes, but being instigated by the Devil," he had attempted to inform on Arnold "for importing contraband goods." Boles agreed that "I justly deserve a halter for my malicious and cruel intentions." He swore never to make such accusations again, against Arnold or any other merchant, and he also promised to leave New Haven immediately and "never enter the same [town] again."[24]

Four hours later, at 11 p.m., a very foolish, stubborn, or drunk Boles was still loitering about Beecher's Tavern. Arnold and his crew, having gained additional numbers, went inside, grabbed the mariner, dragged him outside, and "took him to the whipping post where he received near forty lashes with a small cord, and was conducted out of town." No one saw Boles again in New Haven.[25]

Had these events occurred in Samuel Adams's Boston, the site of serious anti–Stamp Act rioting in August 1765, no one would have thought much of the incident. Inhabitants there viewed informers like Boles as threats to the community's welfare and their right to earn a decent livelihood. In New Haven, however, old-guard leaders still maintained firm political control, and residents had not engaged in anti–Stamp Act violence. The community had remained placid, almost as if unwanted imperial policies and taxes would go away if everyone did nothing. For the sake of established order in their town, New Haven's old guard was not going to let an upstart outsider like Benedict Arnold destroy the harmony they so wanted to preserve.

On January 31, two grand jurors, Tilley Blakeslee and John Wise, issued an indictment against Arnold and nine others. The local constable, Jonathan Mix, reluctantly did his duty and arrested the band of troublemakers three days later. Ironically, Jared Ingersoll, so recently defrocked as Connecticut's stamp distributor, defended Arnold in a hearing before Justice of the Peace Roger Sherman, but Ingersoll's arguments did not prevent his client from being fined fifty shillings for having disturbed the peace.[26]

If old-guard leaders had not learned it from the Peter Boles incident, they were about to find out that Arnold, when aggrieved, could be assertively confrontational. On the evening of January 31, the date of the indictment, a sizable crowd assembled near the village green. In a demonstration no doubt spearheaded by Arnold, they listened to rousing speeches about defending America's liberties. Then they paraded effigies of Blakeslee and Wise in a torch-lit procession through the streets of New Haven. The effigies had ropes about their necks, tied to a pretend gallows. After marching to and fro with the symbols of these alleged despoilers of American liberties held high for all to see, the crowd roared its approval as the organizers heaved the effigies into a huge bonfire.[27]

Good street theater, the demonstration was also a testament to festering discontent among New Haven's working people. They were enduring a postwar depression, which the virtual stoppage in trade associated with the Stamp Act had only aggravated. For them, a person such as Benedict Arnold, who drove off customs informers and defied British authority, was a courageous defender of liberty. Having just celebrated his twenty-fifth birthday, the future Revolutionary general had exhibited his skills in inspiring, mobilizing, and leading groups of people. In the process and by accident, he had become a popular leader of sorts in New Haven.

The old guard called a special town meeting for February 3. In doing so, they in essence admitted that the flames incinerating the effigies had intimidated them. The gathering discussed the specter of seeming anarchy in their midst. Since they could do little else, they voted to "mutually assist one another and particularly the civil authority" in putting a stop to "the growing disorder and violence and breaches of law" that so recently had become so "very threatening to the public peace and even dangerous to civil society" in New Haven.[28]

Arnold scoffed at such statements. Considering such pious words insulting to those with the resolve to stand up for American rights, he, too, now had a constituency to which he could appeal. He addressed the concerns of his partisans by arguing that informers were agents of impending tyranny, just as the Stamp Act was. His rationale appeared in the *Connecticut Gazette* as follows:

> *Query.* Is it good policy, or would so great a number of people, in any trading town on the Continent (New Haven excepted), vindicate, protect, and caress an informer—a character particularly at this alarming time so justly odious to

the public? Every such information tends to suppress our trade, so advantageous to the colony, and to almost every individual both here and in Great Britain, and which is nearly ruined by the late detestable Stamp and other oppressive acts—acts which we have so severely felt, and so loudly complained of, and so earnestly remonstrated against, that one would imagine every sensible man would strive to encourage trade and discountenance such useless, such infamous informers.

New Haven's old-guard leaders had called for law and order; Arnold challenged their appeal by insisting that complacency would result in the loss of liberties, including so fundamental a right as earning a livelihood.[29]

Arnold paid his fifty-shilling fine but was not contrite and refused to admit his culpability with regard to charges of smuggling. His public posture was that of an aggrieved subject who would stand up to any person who lacked the foresight to see how imperial willfulness, even when symbolized by nothing more than an inconspicuous customs informer, held portentous consequences for all Americans. He had come to view the old guard as pusillanimous folk who would quickly compromise everyone's liberties for the pitiful privilege of maintaining their trifling status and comforts. Because Arnold had acted, he was no longer just another inconspicuous New England merchant. He was now a man to be taken seriously in New Haven.[30]

The contest in early 1766 between Arnold and the old-guard leaders ended in a stalemate, but the problem of toughened imperial administration did not go away. Bowing to American pressures, King and Parliament repealed the Stamp Act in March 1766. To save face, they also adopted the Declaratory Act, thereby proclaiming their "full power and authority to make laws and statutes of sufficient force to bind the colonies and people in America, subjects of the Crown of Great Britain, in all cases whatsoever."[31]

The parent nation thus insisted on its sovereign right to tax the provincials—indeed, to do whatever it pleased. In time, such determination resulted in such ill-conceived legislation as the Townshend Duties of 1767 and the Tea Act of 1773. These acts kept royal officials in British North America and local old-guard leaders like those in New Haven on the defensive. In their collective mind-set, imperial ties were essential to societal stability and the maintenance of their favored status as persons of rank and fortune. Ambitious upstarts like Arnold, more concerned about possible constraints on their range of opportunities and about their right to maximize their standing in Anglo-American society, could not so easily countenance imperial policies. Events after 1765 favored Arnold; he had positioned himself well for future triumphs.

V

In defending his actions during the Peter Boles affair, Arnold spoke of the negative effects of recent British policies on the local economy. His observation was not just hyperbole, but he did oversimplify matters. A great number of colonial merchants found themselves overextended after the Seven Years' War. They had feasted on wartime contracts to provision land and naval forces. When the war ended, they were stuck with large inventories they had purchased on credit. Caught short, they had to stave off creditors, including many prominent British mercantile firms, clamoring loudly for payments.

Arnold was typical of local merchants who blamed economic stagnation on the home government's toughened imperial policies; and the brief hiatus in trade caused by the Stamp Act seemed to prove their argument. Merchants everywhere were facing insolvency. Connecticut's Revolutionary period war governor, Jonathan Trumbull, for example, had made substantial profits from a trading partnership during the Seven Years' War but was in debt by as much as £15,000 in 1766. Hundreds of other merchants were facing bankruptcy, and New England's newspapers regularly listed insolvencies. During the summer of 1767, Arnold almost joined the ranks of those merchants whose contracted debts were crushing their capacity to stay in business.[32]

In Arnold's case, he was caught short of cash to pay for various goods long since purchased on credit from six London merchants. Their American agent, a merchant-lawyer named Bernard Lintot, a resident of New York, confronted Arnold in May 1767 about his outstanding obligations. The London merchants wanted both security against the debt and a repayment schedule for the £1,700 due to them.[33]

Arnold had to make another appearance before Justice of the Peace Roger Sherman, this time to present a sworn statement regarding his "debts and effects." His assets, including debts due him by various parties, amounted to slightly over £2,000; and his obligations, including his sister's share in the sale of the family property (£240), added up to £1,408, in addition to the claim of the London merchants. By any ledger assessment, Arnold's debts were some £1,000 greater than his assets.[34]

Caught in a financial vise, Arnold maneuvered adroitly and managed to extricate himself. His attorney, Jared Ingersoll, drew up an indenture agreement between Lintot and Arnold. The New Haven merchant was to turn over his sloop *Sally* and its cargo "for the security and payment of one half of the demands" against him. The trade goods would "be disposed of in the West Indies," there to be redeemed in commodities that would be transported back to Connecticut and "converted into cash." The indenture assumed that this process would bring in something over £850 in hard money. If that figure could be met, then Arnold would be released from "the whole of said creditors' demands against him."[35]

Lintot was willing to write off one-half of the obligation because of the languid economic climate. Arnold gladly accepted these terms. With the West Indies voyage completed by August, he went about the task of converting the goods shipped back into cash. Lintot then spoke of a new "difficulty," regarding currency exchange rates. Arnold was paying off his obligation in inflated provincial currencies rather than in rates properly adjusted to their actual sterling value. An irritated Lintot wrote to Ingersoll, "But as bills rise and fall and are generally higher [worth less] than the rate he calculates at, I think it but just that it should be calculated at a price I actually can buy bills at; otherwise I am not paid the proposed sum."[36]

Arnold was struggling to obtain financial liquidity. Like other merchants caught short, he took advantage of fluctuating currency rates to decrease his payout—on top of what was already a heavily discounted financial obligation. He calculated that Lintot would likely complain but not press him too forcefully. If the agent did, he might get little or nothing for his London clients should Arnold declare himself insolvent and dare Lintot into further costly legal actions, including the prospect of trying to seize his assets or remand him to debtors' prison. Additional information about the case has not survived. One of the most pervasive Arnold tales notwithstanding, the ambitious young merchant spent no time in debtors' prison, and it must be assumed that Lintot eventually declared the indenture agreement settled—on Arnold's terms rather than his own.[37]

Arnold had narrowly averted a personal disaster that typified the risks faced by merchants on both sides of the Atlantic. His London-based suppliers had to absorb a significant loss; but from his perspective the problem related to the constraining web of imperial policies, which he and others blamed for the postwar depression. As such, he was willing to defy laws and rules that might inhibit his right to trade and prosper as a free English subject in provincial America. Arnold had also learned his lesson about the perils of overextending himself. Determined not to fail as his father had before him, he would still take calculated risks, but he also vowed to guard more carefully against getting caught short—no matter what the circumstances.

Like all merchants, Arnold perpetually maneuvered to balance his ledger books between credits and debits. When creditors demanded payments, he, in turn, had to press those who owed him for goods. Arnold usually maintained a gracious but firm posture when calling in debts. He had no desire to offend his network of good customers, who might take their business elsewhere, or other merchants, who might retaliate by suddenly pulling him up short when he was slightly overextended. In late 1763, for example, Arnold tactfully wrote to Dr. William Jepson, an apothecary in Hartford, and explained how he was having "trouble collecting a little hard money, which I very much want [lack], so that necessity obliges me to ask you for the money." In 1765 the Lathrop brothers assisted their protégé in collecting on a promissory note drawn against Thomas Mumford, a merchant based in Groton. In almost genteel terms, they noted that Arnold had advised them how "you were to take your leisure about the payment." However, since "Mr. Arnold is in a straight for money," the brothers asked Mumford to settle his obligation as quickly as he could.[38]

In most samplings from Arnold's business records, the transactions—both credits and debits—were for relatively small sums. On occasion, however, usually when the amounts were substantial and debts long overdue, Arnold could become downright obstreperous in demanding payments. In 1768, for example, New York merchant John Remsen apparently had no intention of settling with his New Haven counterpart, at least short of a lawsuit. Arnold insisted on knowing "what pleasure it is for you to keep the balance due me in your hands; . . . it has been due three years, and I want it very much." When Remsen replied with personal invectives, Arnold displayed his own talent for venomous prose. He dismissed with "indifference . . . your threats in regard [to] the contract." Such "impertinency" deserved every gentleman's contempt. In a telling phrase invariably used by Arnold when feeling that his personal honor was at stake, he expressed "a consciousness of my uprightness and fairness in regard to our concerns"; and he made it absolutely clear to Remsen that he would "never suffer the opinion of you or any other blockhead to give me any uneasiness."[39]

In the end, nothing of consequence resulted from this heated exchange. Arnold was on the mend financially in 1768, as was the provincial economy. By the early 1770s he was one of New Haven's most prosperous merchants, even as he kept expanding his trading network. Bits and scraps of information place him at various times in the port communities of Boston, Quebec, and Montreal, as well as the Richelieu River region southeast of Montreal, besides on his regular trading voyages back and forth to the West Indies. As a person of keen business acumen and immense personal energy, his name became more widely known with each mercantile triumph.

Arnold was rarely frivolous with his time. Even in his social life he preferred activities with the potential to expand or solidify his range of business connections. Such being the case, he welcomed induction into Freemasonry in April 1765 when he became an initiate of New Haven's Hiram Lodge no. 1. He enjoyed his fraternal association with other Masons in New Haven, some of whom were also aggrandizing outsiders with few ties to New Haven's old-guard elite families. His lodge affiliation also accorded him a kindred bond with Masons beyond New Haven, on which he could construct useful social and business relationships.[40]

Spreading out of London, eighteenth-century Freemasonry placed a high value on religious toleration while rejecting the kind of unforgiving, interventionist deity worshiped by Arnold's mother. Prominent Masons, George Washington and Benjamin Franklin among them, generally eschewed the doctrine of the Trinity and believed in one creator, most often described as Divine Providence, which had put the universe in motion but rarely intervened in worldly affairs, unless for positive purposes. As befitting rationalist thinking during the era of the Enlightenment, Masonry subscribed to the ideal that human beings should channel their collective intelligence to improve the quality of life for all persons. Masonic tenets thus fit well with Arnold's rejection of his Calvinist training and his determination to become a person of great secular consequence through the performance of exemplary deeds.[41]

Arnold was neither a lodge activist nor a holder of Masonic offices. Meetings at the Hiram Lodge served as a social outlet for him when he was not at sea. They also brought him into contact with his future father-in-law, Samuel Mansfield, a modestly successful local merchant who also served as the sheriff of New Haven County. Mansfield introduced Arnold to his family, and the eligible young merchant soon fell in love with a daughter named Margaret (born on April 24, 1745). Courting her became a new obsession for Arnold, and they were married on February 27, 1767.[42]

Very little is known about this first "Peggy" in Arnold's life. Apparently she was quite sickly as a child. As a young adult, she could offer any future husband ties with a venerable and respected local family. Arnold, on his part, had long since decided to marry. In 1764 he had made separate wagers with two bachelor acquaintances regarding who would wed first. He bet Abraham Beach a silver tankard and salver and Andrew Thomson a silver teapot, each worth £15 local currency. Three years passed, however, before he married Peggy, and he may have lost one or both wagers. As had his father before him, Arnold had found a partner whom he dearly loved. Further, he had married into an old family of solid local reputation and respectable financial means. Arnold also developed a close friendship with "Papa" Mansfield, as he affectionately referred to his father-in-law. Even before the marriage, these two merchants had launched what was to become a profitable collaboration in trading ventures to the West Indies.[43]

Benedict and Peggy enjoyed a harmonious relationship, at least during their first three or four years of marriage. Before her untimely death from some mysterious illness in June 1775, she gave birth to three sons: Benedict VI, on February 14, 1768; Richard, on August 22, 1769; and Henry, on September 19, 1772. In addition, Peggy involved herself in her husband's mercantile pursuits, working closely with his sister Hannah when Arnold was at sea. Initially she accepted her husband's peripatetic lifestyle, but she did not write to him as often as he would have liked. Over and over again in letters sent home from distant ports, Arnold mentioned his disappointment about not having received any written messages from her. At one point, when in Quebec, he expressed genuine hurt: "I am now under the greatest anxiety and suspense, not knowing whether I write to the dead or the living, not having heard the least syllable from you this four months."[44]

Arnold composed these words in late 1773. Peggy's silence for so long a period likely meant something more than a poor penchant for correspondence. She may have been too ill to write, or she may not have been writing on purpose, knowing that her silence would aggravate her husband. Problems had developed that may have seriously undermined any sense of abiding love or mutual friendship in their marriage.

VI

A number of Arnold's letters to Peggy and to his business contacts, particularly in the West Indies, have survived, making it possible to patch together some of his trading ventures. During the summer of 1768, for example, Arnold sailed to the West Indies with a cargo of cattle, horses, and lumber. He wrote Peggy repeatedly regarding his concern about so long a period of separation. It had taken him thirty-four days, "a very fatiguing and horrendous passage" with "extreme bad weather," to get from New Haven to Martinique in the Windward Islands. He declared on June 25, "My dear girl, you and you only can imagine how long the time seems since we parted and how impatient I am to see you and the dear little pledge [Benedict VI] of our mutual love. God bless you both and send us a happy meeting soon."

Then Arnold was off to St. Christopher (St. Kitts) in the Leeward Islands, hoping to get a better price for his lumber. On July 14 he reported success and spoke of having "engaged a freight" for St. Croix in the Virgin Islands. He also announced, "I have bought you a Negro girl—very cheap." Two days later, while still at St. Christopher, he expressed excitement over "receiving your very agreeable favor" and "was very glad to hear you, little Ben, and all our family are well." Relieved to have had a letter from Peggy after two months of separation, he "never was so heartily tired of the West Indies as at present" and was "impatient for home." With unabashed sentimentality he confessed, "The most pleasing scenes are not agreeable when absent from you."[45]

Although impatient to sail for New Haven, Arnold had committed himself to go to St. Croix, so he decided to stop at St. Eustatius for further trading along the way. On August 8 he was not in a buoyant mood. He had failed to collect on debts owed him by two St. Croix merchants, and he had endured "a few days illness with a fever (but thank God am very well at present)." Likewise, he seemed perturbed about not receiving a second letter from Peggy, "though there have been several vessels from New Haven." Turning to other matters, he asked her to obtain insurance for the return cargo at a value of £600, mentioned "a violent shake of as earthquakes" that "did no damage" to the island, and talked about a serious shortage of rainfall making it impossible to obtain fruit.

Five days later he drafted yet another letter. He would soon be sailing for home, expecting to make only one stop in the Bahamas to sell sixty hogsheads of rum. He was pleased that the captain of another New Haven vessel, which had just arrived at St. Croix, had reported "that you and all our family were well the 9th of July." Despite this welcome news, he expressed irritation that "you have written me only once when there have been so many opportunities." He closed what may have been his last letter of this voyage by telling Peggy "how anxious I am to see you, and be once more among my friends. May the best of Heaven's blessings attend you, and may we both be under the care of a kind Providence, and soon, very soon, have a happy meeting is the sincere prayer of your ever affectionate husband."[46]

Arnold continued these lengthy trading voyages on a regular basis, sailing throughout the Caribbean among British, French, Dutch, and Danish islands in search of cargoes and profits. Wherever he sailed, he sent letter after letter to his "dear Peggy," explaining what was happening, asking for letters, and proclaiming how much he missed her. Typical was a missive from Barbados of April 1769. Arnold remarked how "each day seems an age" without her, before exclaiming, "Oh, when shall we be so happy to meet and part no more." It was "with the greatest impatience I long to see you, dear little Ben, and all the family." Yet Arnold could not afford to give up these trading expeditions. He was prospering as never before and rapidly becoming one of New Haven's wealthiest merchants.[47]

So much separation, however, was almost bound to cause marital difficulties. Peggy may have suspected that her husband's trading ventures meant more to him than she did, despite his written protestations. She may have come to dread and resent the long periods of loneliness whenever he went to sea. Then, just before the end of 1770, an odious rumor began circulating through New Haven. According to Arnold, slanderers were telling everyone that he "had [contracted] the venereal disease" while trading in the Caribbean the previous year. In a masterful understatement, Arnold noted how such gossip "has hurt my character here very much and given my family and friends much uneasiness." To vindicate his good name, he sought depositions from Caribbean business associates "in regard to my being in perfect health all the time I was in the Bay [of Honduras]." He also asked for their comments "in regard to my living, eating, and drinking wine and punch, and any spiritous liquors as freely as any person," as well as "in regard to the company I kept . . . in the Bay." Such depositions were crucial to ending the scandalous talk "that has been spread here by some of my enemies." At the same time, he met with Jared Ingersoll and filed a lawsuit against a local ship's captain, perhaps once in his employ and now disaffected, to recover damages for willful defamation of his character.[48]

Certainly, Arnold had not contracted syphilis; he never manifested any symptoms of that disease. However, on occasion he may well have engaged in sexual liaisons with prostitutes in Caribbean and Canadian ports. To have had furtive sexual relationships with women for hire in rough-hewn, unseemly dockyard brothels or taverns when he was away from home for months at a time was not beyond the realm of possibility, and his repeated pleas for letters from Peggy may have helped him rationalize any feelings of guilt.

Arnold's letters regarding the venereal disease scandal also pertained to hearsay regarding his involvement in duels while trading in the Caribbean. As part of his request for depositions, Arnold asked for statements "in regard to the duel fought with Mr. Brookman." He explained why: "It is reported here to have been occasioned by a dispute about a whore I wanted to take from him." Whether this contest of personal honor was over a prostitute or something else, he at least admitted to the incident. This duel took place in the Bay of Honduras, where Arnold also apparently settled differences with a Captain Croskie over a brace of pistols. These dueling incidents may have been one and the same, yet the names of Arnold's adversaries do not resemble each other, thus suggesting two separate confrontations. The once-cowardly lad from Norwich had long since made the determination to call his adversaries to account whenever his reputation was at stake. He certainly demonstrated his unyielding disposition, regardless of his personal safety, when standing up to the likes of Brookman and Croskie.[49]

The story of Arnold's encounter with Croskie, as handed down by Arnold's descendants, had the New Haven merchant getting ready to sail for Connecticut from the Bay. Caught up in the final flurry of preparations, Arnold received an invitation from a British merchantman, Captain Croskie, who wanted him to attend a social gathering that evening. Neglecting to reply, but not wanting to be considered impolite, Arnold visited Croskie the next morning to explain his circumstances. The Britisher disdained his apology and called him "a damned Yankee, destitute of good manners or those of a gentleman." A shocked Arnold demanded satisfaction, and the two adversaries, complete with surgeons and seconds, soon met on the field of honor.

Since Croskie had accepted the challenge, he had the right to the first pistol shot. He missed. Arnold then leveled his weapon and fired, but he only wounded his adversary slightly. Once the surgeons had dressed Croskie's wound, Arnold enjoined the Britisher to stand forth again, indignantly stating, "I give you notice, if you miss this time, I shall kill you." Thoroughly chastised, feeling the effects of being shot, and now fearing for his life, Croskie apologized for his rudeness. The incident came to an end with a firm handshake. According to the *code duello,* Arnold had thereby fully regained his personal honor.[50]

In many ways, the competitive existence of eighteenth-century merchant-traders, especially those who commanded their own vessels, demanded the cultivation of a certain truculence of manner. An assertive disposition was often a necessity while trying to make the most profitable transaction amid the din of the marketplace. Ambitious men like Arnold also had to be constantly alert in searching out the best markets, bargaining for the most favorable prices, and manipulating to their advantage the dozens of paper notes and currencies as they traded. The acquisition of commercially based wealth likewise required the ability to address and resolve unexpected problems and the capacity to confront willful adversaries at any time.

In November 1770, for instance, Arnold took a large gamble when he underwrote an expensive load of mahogany that needed shipment from the West Indies to Philadelphia. He hired a captain whom he considered trustworthy, but that mariner reported foul weather on the voyage north; put into the harbor at Charleston, South Carolina; quickly sold most of the cargo; and then absconded with the profits. Arnold's correspondence on this case breathed fire. For at least a year, he worked feverishly to run down the culprit. No record confirms whether he ever succeeded, but entrusting so valuable a cargo to a potential thief represented the kind of risk he had to take in his never-ending search for profits and personal wealth.[51]

There were other hazards as well. Arnold often battled dangerous weather while at sea. "We had the misfortune to blow away our jib . . . and struck on the rocks, but very luckily received no damage, but the loss of our jib," he reported after reaching New York in September 1768. At the same time, he invariably expressed his thanks to a benevolent deity—"Thank God [I] am well"—for having been spared his life. Sometimes he would state that better, more comfortable moments lay ahead, such as in a letter from Boston in which he asked Peggy for the "time and patience which overcome all things" and "will I hope produce fairer prospects and happier days to us both."[52]

Arnold's continual absences were clearly debilitating to his marriage, especially when his voyages produced stories of venereal disease, whoring, and dueling—at least some of which were true. Arnold was trying to ameliorate his strained marital relations by promising Peggy "fairer prospects and happier days." Yet commercial exchange dominated his life; he could not become a great and respected citizen without these endless trips to far-flung ports. As for sickly, uncommunicative Peggy, she remained outwardly dedicated to Arnold, and she may have found solace—and some pride—in knowing that her husband had become a person to be reckoned with in New Haven. In turn, Arnold expected Peggy to support his aspirations and enjoy the material comforts he was providing her and his family. In the end, however, their marriage was something less than wholly satisfying.

VII

On the brink of financial ruin in 1767, Arnold had recovered by the early 1770s—so much so that he set about the task of building a stately new residence on Water Street. Some forty-eight feet wide and thirty-eight feet deep overall and an additional ten feet deep on the first floor, the exterior would be covered with white clapboard siding in a plan that called for the placement of two majestic pillars to frame the main entrance. On the inside were two luxurious floors of living space, as well as an attic topped by a widow's walk on the roof. A white picket fence separated the front of the property, which consisted of three prime acres, from Water Street. To the rear of the home were elaborate formal gardens, as well as stables and a coach house.

In expending considerable time on the details of design and construction, Arnold desired to create a truly impressive edifice. Certainly he could afford to do so, providing opulent living quarters for Peggy, his three sons, his sister

Hannah, and various household servants. As a New Haven correspondent observed late in 1774, "as to his ability to pay [for trade goods] there are few or no men here that are thought more sufficient at present, as he has had great luck at sea of late."[53]

As Arnold regarded his handiwork, he thought of the new home as the setting for those happier times he had pledged to Peggy. In addition, he meant the residence to stand as a statement about his own worldly achievements—and the name that he bore. The traditional clapboard siding was like a testament to his deep family roots in Puritan New England. The grandly placed front pillars were symbolic of his personal aspirations. He wanted guests who passed through the main entrance to feel as if they were entering the home of not just a successful merchant but a gentleman of merit, whose attainments were worthy of their abiding respect.

In little more than ten years, Arnold had surmounted many obstacles. He had recovered from the failures of his father and become one of the wealthiest citizens of New Haven, if not all of Connecticut. Repeatedly showing his talent and energy in the world of commerce, he now hoped that friends and neighbors would see in him a potential patriarch of Connecticut politics and society. With his multiplying wealth he would have the leisure time of a gentleman to devote to disinterested public service in the spirit of his ancestor, Governor Benedict Arnold I of Rhode Island. What he could not yet envision were the ways in which the looming imperial crisis would deny him the pleasure of ever obtaining patriarchal status, or even much of an opportunity to enjoy his magnificent new home.

CHAPTER *Three*

Irrepressible Acts of Martial Resistance

I

Even as Benedict Arnold prospered and became a noteworthy resident of New Haven, the British imperial world of his early adulthood was crumbling. Home government officials just could not stop meddling with the Americans. In June 1767, fifteen months after repealing the Stamp Act, King and Parliament legislated the Townshend Duties Act, which placed import taxes on British-manufactured glass, lead, painters' colors, paper, and tea. A tax was a tax, the colonists responded, whether direct, as with stamps, or indirect, in the form of hidden trade duties mandated for the sole purpose of raising imperial revenue. Resistance followed, most notably in the form of a trade boycott that dramatically reduced the importation of goods from the British Isles.[1]

Cuffed once more by their provincial children, Crown officials had to back down again. In March 1770, Lord Frederick North, the king's new chief minister, asked Parliament to repeal the Townshend duties, except for the three-pence-a-pound tax on tea. That duty was to remain as a symbol of Parliament's "declared" sovereignty in all matters of imperial legislation, including taxation. The colonists soon abandoned their trade boycott, although they did not return to buying tea from England. Wily American traders kept smuggling in foreign tea, supplied primarily by the Dutch, thereby continuing to evade payment of the Townshend duty.

Not wanting to irritate further their irascible American subjects, King George and Lord North ignored this issue until problems from another center of the empire beset them. By early 1773, the powerful East India Company was near financial collapse, and a source of company ailments was its lost revenues from tea sales in America. King and Parliament adopted a comprehensive bailout plan in May 1773. One bill, the Tea Act, legislated new procedures for the shipment of tea to America. Company tea would henceforth be sent to designated merchants, not traders of Arnold's localist ilk but well-known royal favorites. The price would be lowered by virtue of direct shipments from India to America, thus eliminating a whole series of costs related to merchandising the tea through England. Company tea, even with the Townshend duty, would now be as cheap as, if not cheaper than, smuggled Dutch blends.[2]

Colonial popular leaders reacted swiftly. They disliked the favoritism shown merchants with close ties to parent England, but they most of all decried the Townshend duty on tea as a key element in the devious conspiracy of power-hungry imperial officials to deprive Americans of fundamental liberties. In December 1773 the ever-feisty Bostonians, rallying around the radical clique of Samuel Adams, showed their vigilance in resisting every form of suspected tyranny by dumping into the harbor the first consignments of company tea to reach their port city.

The Boston "Tea Party" infuriated home government leaders. Lord North went before Parliament in March 1774 and called for legislation to discipline the citizens of Massachusetts. "We are considered as two independent states" in Boston, he proclaimed on behalf of George III, and he gained overwhelming approval for a series of bills—the so-called "Coercive Acts." Among other actions, this flurry of legislation closed the port of Boston until its denizens paid for the destroyed tea and altered the charter basis of Massachusetts government by giving the royal governor something akin to a tyrant's political authority. To drive home the confrontational message, the ministry named General Thomas Gage, commander of His Majesty's military forces in North America, as the Bay Colony governor.[3]

Gage soon arrived in Boston, as did some thirty-five hundred redcoats, which represented the second placement of king's regulars in that port city during the period of deteriorating British-American relations. Redcoats had first appeared in the autumn of 1768 to quell anti-imperial violence, at which point troop-baiting became a common sport among Bostonians. Then, on March 5, 1770, an ugly incident occurred when a small detachment of soldiers fired into a menacing crowd after being harassed and pressed up against the front of the customs house. Five civilians died in the "Boston Massacre," and appalled colonists took to memorializing them as righteous martyrs in the defense of American liberties.[4]

Arnold was trading in the West Indies when he first learned of the massacre. He described himself as "very much shocked" by "the accounts of the most cruel, wanton, and inhuman murders, committed in Boston by the soldiers." "Good God," he wrote in a seeming frenzy, "are the Americans all asleep and tamely giving up their liberties, or are they all turned philosophers, that they don't take immediate vengeance on such miscreants." Characteristically, Arnold demanded a bold response, fearing that if his fellow colonists did not stand up for their rights, "we shall as soon see ourselves as poor and as much oppressed as ever [a] heathen philosopher was." Animating his concern was his sense of personal grievance over what he viewed as the inhibiting constraints of British commercial policies, which fed his willingness to challenge the power of imperial officials through acts of rebellion later in the decade.[5]

When news of the Coercive Acts swept through the colonies during the spring and summer of 1774, popular leaders likewise cried oppression and called for intercolonial resistance. In early September, the First Continental Congress began meeting in Philadelphia. More radical delegates soon controlled the agenda. Among various decrees, Congress called on militia companies throughout the provinces to commence vigorous training, should patriots have to defend hearth and home against menacing British regulars. The delegates also approved a comprehensive boycott plan—the Continental Association—of British goods. Every community was to establish a committee of observation and inspection charged with monitoring the behavior of friends and neighbors. Persons who imported, sold, or purchased British merchandise were to be identified as "foes to the rights of British America" in local newspapers. They were to be isolated, shunned, and "universally condemned as the enemies of American liberty."[6]

Having chosen the path of defiance, the First Continental Congress disbanded in late October, but not before mandating a second intercolonial congress to assemble in May 1775, should the home government not renounce the Coercive Acts and redress American grievances. While the colonists waited for British reactions, local patriots began "purifying" the landscape. Even before the First Congress met, they had started to harass those in their midst who had expressed doubts about continually challenging the mighty imperial parent. Patriots smeared such persons with the epithet "tory," although they preferred to think of themselves as "loyal" to the British Crown.[7]

One such outspoken subject was the Reverend Samuel Peters, an Anglican clergyman of old New England stock who resided in Hebron, Connecticut. Peters was utterly self-assured, if not overly supercilious. Putting modesty aside, he described himself as so full "of such truth and integrity as to command great weight in all that concerned the benefits of the colony."

However, in the summer of 1774 many Connecticut folk had come to doubt his unabashed rectitude, especially after he convinced a Hebron town meeting not to contribute "charitable help" to the suffering Bostonians. Soon many were saying that Peters "was a dangerous enemy to America." Angry crowds began harassing the clergyman, and in September he fled to New Haven, where friends offered him sanctuary.[8]

According to Peters, one New Haven resident had promised him the protection of his home. This gentleman, however, changed his mind because he was leery of "the mobs of Colonel [David] Wooster and Dr. Benedict Arnold, who are mobbing the Sandemanians [a small Scottish religious sect in New Haven] for having spoken against the outrageous conduct of the destroyers of the tea in Boston harbor." Peters finally found sanctuary at the home of the Reverend Bela Hubbard, the leader of New Haven's Anglican congregation. Word soon spread "that Arnold and Wooster . . . had said they would visit Peters and Hubbard as soon as they had finished with the Sandemanians." Hubbard fled with his family to a neighbor's house, even as the belligerent Peters claimed to have obtained twenty muskets and, with servants and a friend, made ready for battle.[9]

The confrontation occurred around ten o'clock at night. Peters described the incident in self-congratulatory fashion as follows:

> Dr. Arnold and his mob came to the gate, and found it shut and barred. He called out to open the gate, and Dr. Peters answered: "The gate shall not be opened this night but on pain of death!"—holding a musket in his hand.
>
> The mob cried: "Dr. Arnold, break down the gate, and we will follow you, and punish that tory Peters!"
>
> Arnold replied: "Bring an axe, and split down the gate!"
>
> Dr. Peters said: "Arnold, so sure as you split the gate, I will blow your brains out, and all that enter this yard tonight!"
>
> Arnold retired from the gate, and told one of his fellows to go forward and split the gate. The mob then cried out: "Dr. Arnold is a coward!"
>
> Arnold replied: "I am no coward; but I know Dr. Peters's disposition and temper, and he will fulfill every promise he makes; and I have no wish for death at present."
>
> The mob then cried: "Let us depart from this tory house!"

The beleaguered Anglican divine also asserted that he used the same boisterous tactics later that evening to scare off a mob headed by Wooster.[10]

Peters's courage in the face of adversity seemed to know no bounds. His version of the attempted mobbing, which is the only one that survives, is certainly suspect. Had Arnold's purpose been to capture Peters, he would have found the means, since he was anything but a bumbling, cowardly bully. Most likely the crowd's sole objective was to frighten and intimidate Peters so that he would leave town. To dramatize the seriousness of their purpose, the bands of Arnold and Wooster even hoisted up a liberty pole on Hubbard's property. Peters got the message. Despite his putative boldness, he fled New Haven the next morning—in hastily assembled disguise, no less.[11]

Having made himself *persona non grata* in Connecticut, Peters soon made a precipitous flight to Boston and the safety of General Gage's army. Like others with the temerity to speak out on behalf of the Crown or unwilling to sign the Continental Association, Peters had failed the key litmus test of patriotism. Before the year was out he sailed for England, where he became a prominent early exile from his native land. Not turning the other cheek, Peters never forgot his brief encounter with Arnold. In the early 1780s he paid back his adversary by circulating a number of derogatory stories at the time of Arnold's arrival in England. In the process, Peters became yet another source of Arnold folktales.[12]

The Peters incident also demonstrates that Arnold still had a committed following among New Haven's working persons. They viewed him as a determined advocate of American liberties whose aggressive leadership was serving the needs of their community. They also admired him because he stood ready, unlike more cautious members of New Haven's old-guard elite, to act decisively in resisting the ever-spreading tentacles of British tyranny. By the time of the First Continental Congress, Arnold was ready to dedicate himself wholly to the defense of American rights, even if that meant immense personal sacrifice, including the neglect of his young family and thriving mercantile business. The alternative, he believed, was to accept the looming prospect of political slavery. So Arnold counted himself among the most fervent of Connecticut's patriots. Had he had any idea what lay ahead for him, he might well have tempered his enthusiasm for selfless service— the hallmark of the truly virtuous patriot.

II

During the winter of 1774–1775, relations between Britain and America became as cold and bleak as New England's frozen landscape. Convinced that the imperial government had compromised with the Americans too many times, George III stated to Lord North in September 1774, "We must not retreat." By November, the king was even more intransigent. "The New England governments are in a state of rebellion," he asserted angrily, and then stated that "blows must decide whether they are to be subject to this country or independent."[13]

By and large, the king's ministers agreed. Most now favored a military showdown with what the Earl of Sandwich, speaking before the House of Lords, condescendingly called "raw, undisciplined, cowardly" colonists. "The very sound of a cannon would carry them off," Sandwich assured his fellow peers, just "as fast their feet could carry them." The commonly held, official opinion thus rated the provincials as a faint-hearted lot of bumpkins who lacked the mettle to wage prolonged war against the king's regulars.[14]

Convinced of the necessity for a strong dose of martial repression, King and Parliament appropriated funds to garrison additional troops in Boston. The ministry named three high-ranking officers—Major Generals William Howe, Henry Clinton, and John Burgoyne—to join Gage and his soon-to-be-augmented cadre of regulars. In February 1775, King George declared the Bay Colony to be in a state of rebellion. Martial law would now allow the king's troops to act without due-process niceties in incarcerating or, if need be, maiming and killing troublesome colonists. To assure a showdown, the ministry sent orders to Gage demanding greater activity in halting the "violences committed by those who have taken up arms in Massachusetts Bay." The sense was that Gage was too fearful of "a rude rabble without plan, without concert, and without conduct" who were totally "unprepared to encounter with a regular force." He was "to arrest and imprison the principal actors and abettors" of sedition or carry out a serious demonstration of force. A little spilling of blood and destruction of property would frighten the colonists into submission, believed King and Parliament. They could not have been more wrong.[15]

General Gage received his orders on Friday, April 14, 1775. Four evenings later he sent a select column of redcoats into the field. When the disastrous day of Lexington and Concord had ended, Gage's troops had suffered 273 casualties in comparison to only 95 for the colonists. The hundreds of citizen-soldiers who were ready to engage in combat on April 19 proved how seriously patriot activists in New England had heeded the entreaty of the First Continental Congress for a renewed emphasis on militia training.[16]

That was also the case in New Haven, where in late 1774 sixty-five persons, among them Benedict Arnold, organized themselves into a militia company. They agreed to furnish their own arms and equipment and to hire an expert in "the military exercise" to direct their training. In March 1775, Connecticut officials rewarded their diligence by formally establishing them as the Governor's 2d Company of Guards. Also authorized to elect their own

aroused in defense of home, family, and property, could prevail over red-coated hirelings.

Doubting neither their own rectitude nor their courage, these patriots thought they were ready to deflect every tyrannical thrust until their liberties were forever secure. Because patronizing imperial leaders viewed them as both errant children and a rude rabble lacking the fortitude to endure the punishment of concentrated firepower and deadly bayonet charges, their defiance under arms was as much an invitation to full-scale civil war as was the ministry's decision to have a martial reckoning. Neither the imperial protagonists nor the colonial antagonists expected a drawn-out conflict, but they were both wrong; and while the former paid dearly for their condescending posture, the latter barely succeeded because of their lack of sustained commitment to their glorious cause.[23]

III

Along the road to Massachusetts, Arnold had a brief but fateful meeting with Colonel Samuel Holden Parsons, a Connecticut patriot who was returning from Cambridge to begin recruiting troops in Hartford. Parsons mentioned the shortage of cannons and other ordnance pieces in the rebel camp that might assure the continued entrapment of Gage and his redcoats. According to Parsons, Arnold responded with "an account of the state of [Fort] Ticonderoga, and [pointed out] that a great number of brass cannons were there." This exchange of information soon resulted in nasty problems for the American cause after Arnold and Parsons, going their separate ways, each decided that the once-mighty fortress on Lake Champlain should be seized—specifically to appropriate the artillery pieces that it contained.[24]

Colonel Parsons rushed on to Hartford. He met with a handful of provincial leaders, among them merchant Silas Deane, who had attended the First Continental Congress. These gentlemen saw merit in taking Ticonderoga—as soon as possible. On no one's authority but their own, they drew £300 from the provincial treasury and named Captain Edward Mott to head the expedition. They also got in touch with Heman Allen and sent him scurrying off to the New Hampshire Grants (Vermont). He was to enlist the services of his older brother Ethan and the Green Mountain Boys. Mott and his small raiding party started north on Saturday, April 29, the very day Captain Arnold and the Footguards marched into Cambridge.[25]

Stimulated by his discussion with Parsons, Arnold kept thinking about an expedition against Fort Ticonderoga. By the time he reached Cambridge, he had decided to seek support for so bold an undertaking. Before doing so he provided for his company, getting his troops comfortable billets in the mansion of Andrew Oliver, the recently deceased royalist lieutenant governor of Massachusetts. The next day Arnold sought out the noted Boston patriot Dr. Joseph Warren, a fellow Mason, and other members of the Massachusetts Committee of Safety. This administrative body of the Provincial Congress watched over day-to-day operations against Gage's troops, but Arnold spoke of matters elsewhere. Besides small arms and abundant military stores, he estimated that as many as 130 pieces of artillery could be seized at Fort Ticonderoga, which was in "ruinous condition" and only lightly garrisoned. "The place could not hold out an hour against a vigorous onset," Arnold declared. This information, procured from mercantile contacts while trading in the vicinity of Montreal, was fundamentally accurate.[26]

Arnold's commentary corroborated an earlier report from John Brown of Pittsfield, Massachusetts. At the behest of the Boston Committee of Correspondence, Brown had endured horrible winter weather in traveling covertly to Montreal not only to gain intelligence but also to encourage Canadians to join the American cause. Once back in Massachusetts, Brown urged the seizure of Ticonderoga "as soon as possible, should hostilities be committed by the king's troops." In a meaningful phrase, he had also advised, "The people on New Hampshire Grants have engaged to do this business, and in my opinion they are the most proper persons for this job."[27]

Warren and the Committee of Safety voted on Tuesday, May 2, to place its confidence in Arnold's "judgment, fidelity, and valor." They named him a colonel in the Massachusetts service "and commander in chief over a body of men not exceeding four hundred," for the "secret" purpose of capturing British-held Ticonderoga. Arnold's regiment was to take "possession of the cannons, mortars, stores, etc., upon the lake" and then return with all "serviceable" weaponry to Cambridge. The committee members handed Arnold £100 in cash as well as two hundred pounds each of gunpowder and lead balls, one thousand flints, and ten horses. Because these supplies were so paltry, they also authorized him to draw on their financial credit in obtaining "suitable provisions and stores for the army."[28]

With orders in hand, Colonel Arnold said goodbye to the Footguards and rode westward with a handful of hastily designated captains who were to recruit companies for the regiment. Among them was his close friend from the Footguards, the youthful New Haven distiller Eleazer Oswald. Personal glory and widespread fame awaited those who dared to conquer Ticonderoga, but dreams of popular acclaim were not uppermost in Arnold's mind. Rather, his primary concern was getting his regiment enlisted in time to seize Ticonderoga before British reinforcements appeared, since reports were commonplace that various Crown officials had called for the strengthening of the Lake Champlain forts. On the day of Lexington and Concord, for instance, General Gage had written to Governor Guy Carleton in Canada and counseled him to rush regulars from the 7th Regiment of Foot, then located in Quebec City, along with Canadian auxiliaries and Indians, to Ticonderoga and Crown Point. Captain William Delaplace, who commanded the handful of redcoats of the 26th Regiment of Foot then garrisoning these two sites, had received warnings to keep alert to the prospect of a rebel foray. Delaplace should have listened because the Green Mountain Boys, led by the muscular, pugnacious, hard-drinking Ethan Allen, lived within easy striking distance.[29]

Riding relentlessly day and night, Arnold laid plans with his captains for a quick recruiting campaign in western Massachusetts. He also gave thought to getting Allen and the Green Mountain Boys under his command. Their numbers were large enough to assure the necessary strength for a successful assault. Unfortunately, Arnold was unaware of the linkup between Allen's free-spirited rowdies and the Connecticut-sponsored band of Edward Mott.[30]

As the Mott party traveled north, they did not dally in search of recruits. They were confident Heman Allen would obtain his big brother's support. Heman caught up with Ethan at Catamount Tavern, the unofficial capitol of the New Hampshire Grants in Bennington—and the base of operations for the Green Mountain Boys in their ongoing personal clash with New York. Allen and the Boys held patents to their Vermont lands from New Hampshire, but New York also claimed title to this territory. New York's leaders regarded Allen and his following as nothing more than ill-kempt, squatting frontier banditti, yet they had failed in their attempts to dislodge them. In 1774 the New York officials even posted a £100 reward for the capture of Allen; however, he still roamed free as the master of the New Hampshire Grants region.

By involving the Boys in a strike against Ticonderoga, Allen could attack the king's property in New York while acting the part of disinterested patriot. A successful assault might also solidify the Boys' control of the Grants region by casting them as indispensable defenders of American rights. In time, such role-playing could even result in fully certified land patents as a reward for extraordinary services to the cause of liberty. If nothing else, seizing Ticonderoga would represent another, perhaps telling blow against hated royal authority in New York, which could only work to the Boys' advantage.

Even as Allen prepared to call out the Green Mountain Boys, Mott's party was passing through the town of Pittsfield in far-western Massachusetts.

Mott welcomed the support of about fifty volunteers from the immediate area who also wanted a crack at capturing Ticonderoga. These patriots had rallied under the banner of two locally prominent gentlemen: Colonel James Easton, who commanded Pittsfield's militia, and John Brown, the very same person who had visited Montreal at the behest of the Provincial Congress. Easton was both a tavern keeper and a local merchant, but he had overextended himself and was heavily in debt. As for Brown, he likely had become casually acquainted with Arnold while attending Yale College. Graduating in 1771, he had already trained for the law under Oliver Arnold, a prominent Rhode Island attorney and cousin of Benedict's; and he had also married Oliver's sister. These connections should have pointed toward harmonious relations between Benedict and Brown. For whatever reason, the obverse would be the case. In the days ahead, nasty disagreements abounded that had damaging effects on Arnold's personal reputation and the course of his military career.[31]

On May 3, the same date that Arnold began his journey across Massachusetts, the enlarged Mott force made contact with Ethan Allen in Bennington. At once, everyone went to work to secure a full complement of supplies. The growing legion then headed north some fifty miles to Castleton. Early on Monday morning, May 8, the self-proclaimed patriot force gathered at Zadock Remington's tavern to discuss matters of military organization. Edward Mott agreed to chair a "committee of war," which in turn placed "Colonel" Ethan Allen in charge of the invasion column. No one seemed surprised, since the Boys had categorically declared their unwillingness to serve under anyone else. The committee then named Easton as second in command and the Green Mountain stalwart, giant-sized Seth Warner, as third. Later that morning Allen began moving his detachment to Shoreham, three miles west of the designated launching point—Hand's Cove on the Vermont side of Lake Champlain—for the assault on Ticonderoga.[32]

Early that evening Arnold, having picked up rumors of the impending foray, rode at breakneck speed into Castleton. Charging into Remington's tavern, he found only a few rear-guard troops. Dramatically pointing to his commission, Arnold did not mince words. He expected to be placed in charge of the operation. Although startled, those present retorted with equal conviction that Ethan Allen was their chosen leader. Arnold scoffed; he alone held a legitimate commission to command. In response, the party asked Arnold whether he had any troops to back up his claims. His captains were actively recruiting in western Massachusetts, the Massachusetts colonel replied, and would soon be available for duty. The party wondered how he expected to command without those troops at hand. He intended to discuss

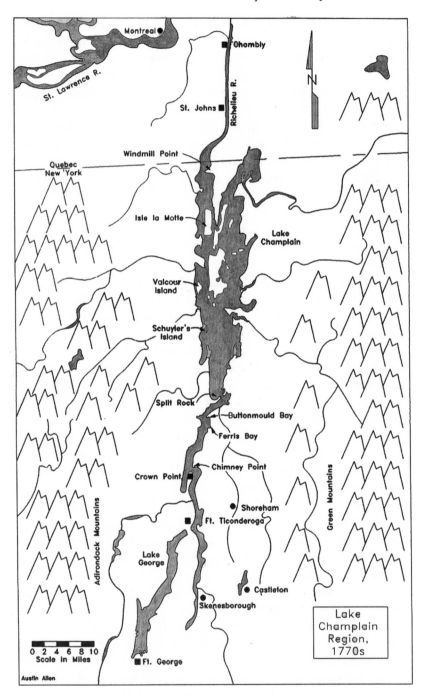

Montreal

Chambly

St. Lawrence R.

Richelieu R.

St. Johns

N

Windmill Point

Quebec
New York

Isle la Motte

Lake
Champlain

Valcour
Island

Schuyler's
Island

Split Rock

Buttonmould Bay

Ferris Bay

Chimney Point

Crown Point

Shoreham

Ft. Ticonderoga

Adirondack Mountains

Green Mountains

Lake
George

Castleton

Skenesborough

0 2 4 6 8 10
Scale in Miles

Ft. George

Austin Allen

Lake
Champlain
Region,
1770s

that issue with Allen, Arnold responded. Meanwhile, he needed some food and rest. Before daybreak the next morning, Tuesday, May 9, Arnold started north for Shoreham, determined to clarify command relations with Allen and the Committee of War. The rear-guard party tagged along at some distance. Not liking Arnold's brash manner, according to Edward Mott, they feared that he "should prevail on Colonel Allen to resign the command."[33]

Even if he was being more brash than realistic, Arnold did have a trump card—his Massachusetts commission. By comparison, the Allen-Mott force was little more than a misbegotten gathering acting on nothing more than the authority of a few prominent Connecticut civilians. Arnold, however, was now in Ethan Allen's country, and the Green Mountain Boys, some two hundred of whom were converging on Shoreham, gave Allen all the legitimacy he needed to remain in command. Still, when Arnold reached Allen at about noontime, the frontiersman did not dismiss the commission. Reports vary with regard to what happened, but Allen most likely suggested a joint command. The Boys disliked that idea and threatened to march home at once. Attempting to placate the fuming and duly commissioned Arnold, Allen apparently invited him to take a place at the head of the column as a volunteer officer. Having come so far and determined to participate, Arnold reluctantly acceded. He would join the attackers, he said, but only to see to the execution of his primary mission to secure the ordnance pieces and related war goods for the patriot army back east.[34]

IV

The French had begun the construction of the Ticonderoga fortress in 1755. They had called it Carillon, "a chime of bells," because of the distant sound of the falls over which waters from Lake George to the southeast spilled into Lake Champlain. Guarding the southern reaches of Lake Champlain as well as the northern entrance to Lake George, Fort Carillon served briefly as a major defensive barrier in obstructing any attempted British invasion of Canada through the Hudson River–Lake Champlain–Richelieu River corridor.

Fort Carillon proved to be a mighty obstacle. At the height of the Seven Years' War in July 1758, the British sent an army of fifteen thousand regular and provincial troops against a much smaller French force of four thousand defending the fortress under the Marquis de Montcalm. The French repulsed the British, who suffered very heavy casualties at outer works to the west of the main stone fortress. In August 1759 the French retreated into Canada in the face of renewed British pressure. As the last of Montcalm's units pulled out, they seriously damaged the main Carillon structure by setting fires and igniting the powder magazine.

The British captors expended little effort in rebuilding the edifice, which they renamed Ticonderoga. They instead constructed a new fortress some twelve miles to the north at Crown Point, where a peninsula juts into Lake Champlain to create one of the narrowest passage points on the lake. Fully operational by 1762, the Crown Point stronghold was the largest British military installation in North America up to that time. Eleven years later an accidental fire all but destroyed the inner barracks and blew up the powder magazine. By 1775 Crown Point, like Ticonderoga, was a very lightly garrisoned frontier depot used primarily for the storage of military weaponry and supplies.[35]

Ethan Allen knew how weak these garrisons were. He had received detailed intelligence from venturesome Noah Phelps, one of Mott's followers who entered Ticonderoga playing the part of a local farmer looking for a shave. The British fell for the ruse, and Phelps verified that Ticonderoga's soldiers were not conducting themselves as if they were on alert, despite orders to that effect. Since the pickings would likely be easy, Allen hardly needed Arnold's assistance, but the frontiersman was nobody's fool. The presence of his commissioned rival would lend legitimacy to the Ticonderoga assault. If anything went wrong, Allen could blame Arnold. Should glory ensue, Allen could grab it; but if disgrace, that would be Arnold's, whose presence as a volunteer could not possibly hurt Allen in any way.[36]

Early on Wednesday, May 10, 1775, the rebel band launched its assault from Hand's Cove. Short on watercraft, the first challenge was to get across a milewide expanse of lake amid turbulent gusts of thrashing rain. After only 83 of the available pool of some 250 men had reached the New York side, Allen and Arnold decided to press ahead. They did not want to lose the element of surprise or the advantage of maneuvering under cover of darkness. Allen ordered Seth Warner to keep bringing over troops. Then he moved the column out with Arnold and himself in the lead. For a half mile they followed a narrow path near the water that brought them around the fort to its south side. There the strike force furtively took position, preparing to burst through the main wicket gate leading to the interior parade ground and barracks.[37]

By Arnold's reckoning, the attack commenced at about 4 a.m. According to Allen, a lone redcoated sentry was on duty at the gate. He first stood motionless in startled amazement when the Green Mountain leader charged toward him. Then he leveled his musket and "snapped his fusee" at Allen before starting to yell for assistance and retreating hastily through the covered way into the parade ground. Allen, Arnold, and the Boys surged forward, cheering loudly but meeting no resistance as they charged into the parade ground. Another sentry, Allen later claimed, darted out at one of his officers and nicked him with his bayonet. Allen allegedly leveled this soldier with a fearsome blow to the head, then "demanded of him the place where the commanding officer kept." The stunned sentry pointed to the left stairway on the west barrack. The private quarters of Captain William Delaplace were on the second floor. Shoving others aside, Allen "immediately repaired" to the stairway, climbed it, and "ordered the commander . . . to come forth instantly or I would sacrifice the whole garrison." Awakened by all the commotion, Delaplace stumbled groggily to the door "with his breeches in his hand" and, continued Allen, "asked me by what authority I demanded it." At this moment the Green Mountain leader putatively offered his famous reply: "In the name of the great Jehovah, and the Continental Congress."[38]

Ticonderoga fell in fewer than ten minutes. The brief conflict was neither as replete with danger nor as full of memorable moments as Allen's fanciful account allowed. Lieutenant Jocelyn Feltham, second in command of the regulars at Ticonderoga, later offered a more trustworthy version of what actually happened. According to Feltham, all was confusion when the Boys rushed into the parade ground. Feltham, holding pants in hand, appeared at the second-floor doorway and got the attention of Allen and Arnold, who were standing at the bottom of the stairs. Feltham stalled as long as possible by asking a number of questions, "expecting to amuse them until our people fired, which I must certainly own I thought would have been the case." When he queried "by what authority they entered His Majesty's fort," Allen and Arnold shouted that theirs was "a joint command" sponsored by Connecticut and Massachusetts. Then Allen, presuming he was confronting Captain Delaplace, bellowed out "that he must have immediate possession of the fort and all of the effects of George III (those were his words)." In other accounts, Allen's command was "Come out of there, you damned old rat," although it may have been "old skunk" or "old bastard."[39]

Despite Allen's fiery but less than rousing patriotic words, Feltham kept up his questioning, hoping his comrades would rally and counterattack. The Boys, however, had moved in too quickly on the somnolent troops. Most were already prisoners. Having climbed the stairs with Arnold by his side, an exasperated Allen threatened Feltham with "a drawn sword . . . alleging I was commanding officer and to give up the fort, and if it was not complied with, . . . neither man, woman, or child would be left alive." By comparison, "Mr. Arnold begged it in a genteel manner but without success." Finally, Captain Delaplace, now fully dressed, came through the doorway to parley with Allen

and Arnold. He ultimately surrendered the fortress, but not before he made
sure that the forty-four soldiers under his command, as well as twenty-four
women and children in the fort, would be accorded full rights as prisoners
of war.[40]

Whichever account one prefers, the taking of Ticonderoga was a bloodless
affair, primarily because Delaplace had not followed orders and prepared for
an assault. Caught completely off guard, he and his troops had to feel very
foolish as the Boys herded them onto the parade ground long before daylight, after which they locked them up in a large storeroom. The fault,
however, was not completely Delaplace's, since so small a garrison force
could hardly have defended to the last extremity—against five times their
number, no less—an edifice that was in a virtual state of rubble. Responsibility lay with Crown officials who had refused to conceive of "a rude rabble"
possessing the pluck to take advantage of the most obvious of circumstances.

Allen maintained his command presence long enough to make arrangements for moving the prisoners over two different routes—separating officers and common soldiers—to Connecticut. Then he turned the Boys loose
to ransack and plunder the fort and its environs. Someone soon found a
plentiful liquor supply, including ninety gallons of rum belonging to Delaplace. To help celebrate so glorious a victory, the Boys felt called upon to get
roaring drunk. An appalled Arnold, trapped among Allen's cavorting "wild
people," reasserted his claim to full command rights. He expected nothing
less than discipline and good order from patriot troops, but Allen, "taking
umbrage at" anyone "forbidding the people to plunder," sharply rebuked
Arnold and boisterously asserted his right to "the entire command." To
underscore his point, Allen had Mott's Committee of War issue a commission so he would "keep the command" by the authority of Connecticut.
Now, if his rival started to wave around his Massachusetts commission, Allen
could wave back with his own piece of paper.[41]

A thoroughly rebuked Arnold found himself reduced to "a private person
often insulted by him [Allen] and his officers." Some of the besotted Boys
even went so far as to threaten his life, and on two occasions they took shots
at him. They wanted this frowning interloper with ideas of military decorum
out of the fort, but Allen's binging rustics were merely a variant of drunken
mariners to Arnold. He calmly fended off their acts of intimidation. He had
his orders from the Massachusetts Committee of Safety, and he still intended
to assume command whenever the opportunity presented itself.[42]

Most of the Boys, Arnold appreciated, had not joined the expedition in a
frenzy of patriotism but to plunder the fortress and, if lucky, to shoot a
British redcoat or two. Once binged out on rum and loaded down with

whatever booty they could carry, Arnold expected them to drift back across the lake to their farmsteads in the Grants country. That is exactly what happened. The Boys began disappearing in groups of two, three, and four over the next few days, ostensibly, as some stated, to get on with their spring planting. As Allen's following dwindled, Arnold's recruits started to arrive. Once he had the advantage in troop strength, he planned to take charge. Should Allen object, Arnold would remind his rival how the Boys, by right of superior numbers, had insisted on having their own designated commander. Should Allen not like that verdict, he could always leave—and get on with his own spring planting.

Still, the Boys, even if not brimming over with selfless patriotism when they seized Ticonderoga, had made an incontrovertible statement of provincial intransigence, if not open rebellion. They had shown that the colonists, or at least some of them, were willing to wage a shooting war rather than submit to what they perceived as the tyrannical will of King and Parliament.

To add an exclamation point, about fifty Green Mountain Boys under Seth Warner—most of them had missed the Ticonderoga assault—seized Crown Point on Friday, May 12. In their first attempt to maneuver down the lake, strong northerly winds drove them back; but a second sortie succeeded. The tiny garrison force of nine regulars, along with ten women and children, quickly surrendered after Warner, a stoic man of few words in comparison to the gushing Allen, rather prosaically claimed Crown Point "in the name of the country." Warner's party soon located a horde of heavy weaponry, plus ample goods for personal plunder.[43]

Together, Crown Point and Ticonderoga yielded 201 artillery pieces, some 100 of which were in fully usable condition. In time, a patriot column sent from rebel headquarters outside Boston would haul fifty-seven of these weapons, the heaviest of which weighed a ton, back east across the Berkshire Mountains. George Washington then had crews position this "noble train of artillery" on Dorchester Heights, overlooking Boston from the south. The ominous presence of these weapons convinced the British army to evacuate that port city and retreat by sea to Nova Scotia in mid-March 1776.[44]

V

By Sunday, May 14, Arnold was in a position to assume command of the Champlain forts. As he reported to the Massachusetts Committee of Safety, he now had some one hundred recruits at Ticonderoga, with more expected each day. Since Allen and his party were "decreasing," Arnold wrote with genuine relief, "the dispute between us [is] subsiding." He was "extremely sorry" about his problems with Allen and the Boys. In self-congratulatory fashion, he stressed that he had "done everything in my power" despite "many insults to preserve peace and serve the public." [45]

Once secure in his command rights, Arnold unveiled a strategy for further securing Lake Champlain, a plan that required disciplined citizen-soldiers to execute it. Everything gained so far, he reasoned, could be easily lost if Governor Carleton and other royal officials in Quebec Province moved troops up the Richelieu (Sorel) River, ascended the lake, and attacked the Americans. The British had a garrison of unknown size at the fortress town of St. Johns (St.-Jean) on the Richelieu, some twenty-five miles into Canada, as well as a seventy-ton sloop of war. That vessel, routinely used to carry supplies, mail, and fresh troops to Crown Point and Ticonderoga, was essential to mounting a counterassault from Canada. To preclude this possibility, Arnold intended to launch a preemptive strike against St. Johns.

The plan became feasible when a schooner, recently captured at Skenesborough (modern-day Whitehall, New York), appeared at Ticonderoga under the command of Arnold's close friend and captain, Eleazer Oswald. Some Green Mountain Boys had captured this outpost community (and schooner), the personal preserve of Philip Skene, a wealthy landholder and confirmed loyalist who held title to sixty thousand acres along the southern extremities of Lake Champlain. The landlubbing Boys knew nothing about sailing, so they turned the schooner over to Oswald who, along with fifty recruits, had marched into Skenesborough on their way north to Ticonderoga. [46]

As was characteristic, Arnold did more than just consider seizing the initiative; he embraced it. He saw to the arming of Skene's schooner, which he christened the *Liberty*, with four small carriage guns, probably 3- and 6-pounders, and six swivel guns. Before evening on Sunday, May 14, he set sail down the lake to Crown Point with two accompanying bateaux. There he gathered more supplies and fretted impatiently for contrary northerly winds to dissipate. On Tuesday morning, May 16, he and his small expeditionary force finally set off for Canada. By the next evening they were close to the Canadian border, but the schooner could not proceed for lack of wind.

Arnold selected thirty-five men and put them in the two bateaux. They rowed down the Richelieu River all night. At about 6 a.m. on Thursday, May 18, Arnold's raiders swooped down on St. Johns's unsuspecting defenders, a sergeant and twelve regulars of the 26th Regiment guarding old and decaying French military works. These redcoats had heard about events at Ticonderoga and Crown Point but had not tightened their own security. With prisoners in tow, Arnold led his troops in a rush toward the sloop. They easily snatched the vessel from a sleepy crew of seven. Having gained so valuable a prize, they made ready to sail—but not before locating nine bateaux, "four of which being out of repair we destroyed, the others [we] brought away."

Quickly securing all available arms, including two valuable brass 6-pounders, Arnold and his crew embarked at 9 a.m. Their haste reflected intelligence from their prisoners that relief columns were descending on St. Johns from Fort Chambly, twelve miles north on the Richelieu, and Montreal, some twenty miles to the northeast. These troops could arrive at any moment, but with "the wind springing up fair," Arnold's band judiciously retreated and reached the safe waters of Lake Champlain by noon.[47]

American patriots under Arnold had now wantonly attacked a British military post in Canada, the third flagrant act of rebellion within eight days. When fully apprised of these events, British officials in London wrongly concluded that the colonists were irrevocably committed to making war. As a result, they were less willing to take seriously the conciliatory overtures of more cautious provincial civilians, who would keep trying to reconcile differences with the parent nation.

Such consequences did not necessarily occur to Arnold. Having captured the largest naval vessel in the Champlain region, he felt flushed with martial success. Furthermore, he gladly shared the credit. The "mere interposition of Providence," he wrote to the Massachusetts Committee of Safety, had assured "that we arrived at so fortunate an hour" in St. Johns. Since the only way for troops to move in this wilderness theater was by water, "the king's troops, Canadians, or Indians," he further explained, no longer had craft "to cross the lake in, if they have any such intention." Any British counterthrust would require the construction of new vessels. Thus Arnold's raid on St. Johns had the desired outcome of securing, at least temporarily, the patriot hold on Ticonderoga and Crown Point.[48]

Arnold had other reasons to feel ebullient. Once freed from the meddlesome Green Mountain Boys, he had demonstrated the dash, boldness, and enterprise that would make him so dynamic a military leader. His troops had succeeded in the operation, moreover, because they had remained disciplined, something that set them apart from Allen and the Boys. Even though still very much an amateur in the art of war, Arnold hoped that others would recognize his merit and appreciate his worthiness as a virtuous servant of the cause of liberty.

A little after noontime on May 18, just after Arnold's triumphant raiders reached Lake Champlain, an unanticipated specter—four bateaux beating northward against the wind—appeared on the horizon. Upon closer observation, the craft contained Ethan Allen and about one hundred Green Mountain Boys. They had paddled their way north for the past two days, trying to catch up with Arnold's party. Not wanting to miss the action, especially with images of more easy plunder addling their brains, they had neglected to think about certain essentials, such as bringing enough food with them. Arnold, rather than sailing right past those who had so recently treated him so cavalierly, graciously offered some provisions. He also invited Allen aboard the sloop, where they drank a hearty toast to the Second Continental Congress, which had just convened in Philadelphia.

As the two rivals conversed, Allen revealed his determination to have a crack at St. Johns. Arnold attempted to dissuade the Green Mountain leader from this "wild, impracticable scheme," truly a plan "of no consequence, so long as we are masters of the lake." Allen refused to listen, even with warnings about British reinforcements descending on St. Johns. Having no command authority over these "mad fellows," Arnold could not block Allen and the Boys "from so rash a purpose." If they wanted to risk their lives for nothing, except a little booty, they could proceed on their way, no matter how much they might embarrass themselves and the cause of liberty.[49]

Embarrassment was a generous term for what happened. While Arnold maintained his southerly course for Ticonderoga, the Boys rowed down the Richelieu and set up camp on the river's west bank about a mile south of St. Johns. Allen sent out scouts, who returned with bad news. A column of two hundred British regulars, apparently from Montreal, was fast approaching St. Johns. Rather than ordering a retreat, as Allen should have done, he moved the Boys to the Richelieu's east bank. The river would afford ample protection, he reasoned, should the redcoats, whose numbers were twice his own, detect their presence.

Once across the Richelieu, Allen and his party, exhausted and not a little famished, were fast asleep. Near dawn, their dreams of plunder turned into nightmares as cannon fire from the west bank rudely awakened them. With grapeshot raining down on their campsite, the sleepy invaders staggered to their bateaux and, by some miracle, got away—in such haste that they left behind three of their comrades. Allen and the Boys still seemed to be paddling hard when they reappeared at Ticonderoga on Sunday, May 21. More bemused than surprised by the whole fiasco, Arnold wrote in his memorandum book, "It happened as I expected."[50]

Allen's ill-conceived escapade only further legitimized Arnold's claim to command, a role he energetically embraced. Working with Bernard Romans, a trained military engineer, Arnold finished a complete inventory of the captured artillery pieces at Crown Point and Ticonderoga. He traveled to a local mill and ordered "a quantity of plank for carriage boards and bateaux to carry the cannons [south] over Lake George." He launched a search for wheel carriages to assure transportation from the southern end of Lake George to the Hudson River, where the ordnance could be floated downriver to Albany for later transportation to eastern Massachusetts. He employed troops in refurbishing the captured British sloop, which he christened the *Enterprise.* These were not glamorous tasks. They held no appeal for adventurers like Allen, but they were essential to getting the most out of the situation.[51]

No detail was too small for Arnold. An experienced taskmaster as a carrying merchant, he understood the need for order and discipline in camp, just as aboard ship. He obviously had to have combat-ready troops, so he kept his volunteers drilling under arms when they were not performing other essential tasks. His constant message was one of preparation, since he most of all did not want to lose the rebel initiative in the Champlain region.

Even as he barked out orders, Arnold worried about the unexpected, such as a sudden British foray from Canada. As such, he decided to concentrate his main defensive line at Crown Point. He did so after concluding that it would be "next to impossible to repair the old fort at Ticonderoga"; nor did he feel "qualified to direct" work parties "in building a new one." Overall, he estimated that fifteen hundred patriot soldiers would make for an adequate garrison force at the lake forts. This figure did not include the many workers needed to refurbish these sites, which Arnold believed were critical to protecting New England and New York from a massive British assault through Canada, should full-scale warfare eventuate.[52]

On Tuesday, May 23, as Arnold's troops went about their assigned tasks, one of Boys left behind at St. Johns suddenly appeared at Crown Point. Breathlessly he described how four hundred British regulars, Canadians, and Indians were "making all possible preparation for crossing the lake." Concerned that Allen's failed raid had emboldened the British, Arnold sprang into action, promising "to give them a warm reception." He placed his troops, whose strength was then half that of the putative British force, on full alert. Then he rushed messages to Fort George and Skenesborough, asking "for the people to muster and join us." He had already composed a letter that morning to the Connecticut Assembly in which he said it was "highly necessary" for that government "to send here immediately 1,500 men at least, with good arms, ammunition, etc." He now added a postscript, praying "with the smiles of Providence, to keep our ground, if not overpowered by numbers."[53]

The rumored attack proved to be a false alarm. Late on May 23, another of the Boys left behind by Allen made it back to Crown Point. The king's regulars, he reported, had withdrawn from St. Johns after scaring off Allen's party. A relieved Arnold called off the alert but kept everyone on full guard for the next week. He also sped up the training of sailing and artillery crews for the *Enterprise* and the *Liberty*. As one of his lieutenants explained, "Arnold's present design" was to have these vessels "cruise the lake, and defend our frontiers, until men, provisions, and ammunition are furnished to carry on the war." [54]

Genuinely excited when a small party of experienced mariners appeared from Connecticut a few days later, Arnold immediately assigned them to duty on the two vessels. Something else also pleased him. Allen's followers had all but disappeared, so much so that Arnold wrote with obvious pleasure, "Colonel Allen has entirely given up the command." Matters had seemingly come full circle. Arnold had outlasted Allen in their contest for command authority in the Champlain region. Even more important, the cause had benefited from Arnold's vigorous, purposeful leadership. Curiously, however, many civilian patriot leaders had gained the impression that the obverse was the case. [55]

VI

The patriot assaults on Ticonderoga, Crown Point, and St. Johns in May 1775 were nothing less than irrepressible acts of rebellion carried out by semi-organized bands of rebel partisans. Those involved were short on formal military training but long on initiative. They succeeded because the few British regulars at these isolated posts gave scant consideration, even with warnings, to the prospect of colonists possessing enough temerity to attack His Majesty's troops and property. The attitude of the British reflected the disdainful thinking of imperial leaders such as Governor Carleton, who in early June informed his superiors in London that some plebeian "horse-jockey" named Arnold had led the St. Johns raid. Surely so common a person, no gentleman officer of noteworthy lineage but a mere tradesman who dealt in commodities like horses, would break and run in paroxysms of fright when he finally had to reckon with substantial numbers of regulars massed in combat formation. [56]

Imperial leaders should have reexamined their condescending posture. Instead, they admitted only to being momentarily caught off guard by rebel ilk like Arnold. Conveniently, too, they had a scapegoat in General Gage, who had warned them to take the Americans seriously. With his army of four thousand pinned down in Boston by ten thousand to fifteen thousand

patriot enthusiasts, Gage could not release troops to counteract rebel successes in the Champlain region. Furthermore, the tally of British regulars in
Quebec Province—roughly seven hundred—was too small and too scattered in postings to offer immediate assistance. Crown officials were confident, however, that such minor setbacks could be rectified, not by taking
their colonial brethren—and grievances—more seriously but by significantly expanding Britain's martial presence in North America.[57]

Much less sure of themselves, the patriots of 1775 had exhibited a robust
determination to defend their families and property against wanton acts of
political tyranny and military aggression, hoping in the meantime to realize
the full restoration of their liberties. The forays in the Champlain region,
however, stretched beyond credulity the bounds of any definition of defensive war. The attacks were clearly aggressive in intent and an invitation to
expanded warfare, regardless of rationalizations about acquiring heavy artillery or preemptively securing a strong foothold in what could become a
hotly contested theater of war.

Offensive operations so brash disturbed many delegates to the Second
Continental Congress, which commenced deliberations in Philadelphia on
the very same day that Allen, Arnold, and company seized Ticonderoga.
Would this new Congress keep the Champlain forts, since their seizure made
pronouncements about taking up arms only for defensive purposes look
deceitful? Moderates in Congress worried lest this seeming incongruity un-
dermine their attempts to resolve grievances with the parent nation, knowing
full well that ever-escalating warfare would have the same effect.

Because Arnold had taken command in the Champlain theater, his name
became ensnared in congressional wrangling over the forts and the larger
issue of expanding the rebellion to include Canada. In the process his
reputation suffered, mostly provoked by Allen and friends. Arnold had a
general idea of what was happening when he wrote to the Massachusetts
Committee of Safety on Sunday, May 19: "I have had intimations given me,
that some persons had determined to . . . injure me in your esteem, by
misrepresenting matters of fact" regarding his actions in the Champlain
theater. What he did not foresee was the turmoil that was about to erupt
over command rights in the Champlain region, even as mild springtime
temperatures gave way to hotter summer days during the turbulent year of
spreading rebellion in 1775.[58]

Four

The Provincial Politics
of Rebellion

I

"Horse-jockey" Arnold had so focused his energies as a carrying trade merchant that he had not sought local offices or gained experience in the often perplexing undertaking of organized human politics. Thirty-four years old in 1775, he had not yet learned how important images and impressions were in the political arena in comparison to substantive accomplishments. Nor had he acquired a taste for the all-important matter of effective political compromise. As a popular leader in New Haven, Arnold had relied on the tools of confrontation and intimidation, not carefully reasoned public debate and backroom bargaining, to effect his purposes. He was, at best, politically naive, which became abundantly clear when Ethan Allen enrolled him in a crash course on the art of playing politics for private advantage within twenty-four hours of the taking of Ticonderoga. Ably assisted by the likes of Edward Mott, James Easton, and John Brown, Allen exposed Arnold, so naturally quick-witted in commerce and war, as a fumbling student of politics. So politically unschooled was Arnold that before the end of June 1775, and despite inestimable service in the Champlain region, he had nearly destroyed his prospects for continuing his military career.

The Boys' drunkenness and willful plundering aside, Arnold's main problem with Allen related to public recognition for conquering Ticonderoga. Both men had strong personalities, and neither was averse to gaining hero status. Nor did either want to share center stage with the other. Although Arnold was able to outlast Allen in the Champlain corridor, Allen was able to outmaneuver Arnold in creating a far more favorable impression of his own actions at Ticonderoga.

In drafting after-action reports and sending them across the landscape, Allen was not shy about claiming the laurels of victory for himself and those loyal to him. On Thursday, May 11, he prepared two reports, the first of which he directed to the Albany Committee of Correspondence, proclaiming, "I took the fortress of Ticonderoga." He did admit that "Colonel Arnold entered the fortress with me side by side," but only because New Yorkers considered the Green Mountain leader as nothing more than a frontier brigand. Noting Arnold's presence as an agent of Massachusetts was a way to legitimize Allen and the Boys as something more than extralegal, land-grabbing invaders of New York.[1]

In Allen's account to the Massachusetts Provincial Congress, he ignored Arnold. Victory was Allen's alone, along with Boys, of course, who "behaved with . . . resistless fury" in the attack. Allen reserved additional words of praise for his second in command, "Colonel" James Easton, "who behaved with great zeal and fortitude, not only in council, but in the assault," and for John Brown, "who was also an able counselor, and was personally in the attack."[2]

This communication to a body that had not authorized Allen to do anything in the Champlain region was an act of political perspicacity. First accounts with positive news, Allen appreciated, would not only mold favorable opinions about himself but also fix his highly selective version as objective reality in the delegates' minds. By disregarding rather than dunning Arnold, he avoided making himself look like the self-serving rival he was. Allen shrewdly left the matter of denouncing Arnold to Edward Mott, who, as head of the Committee of War, could play the part of an impartial observer, one who surely would not criticize a fellow inhabitant of Connecticut unless completely justified.

The Mott report, also dated May 11, likewise twisted reality. Arnold had appeared only at the last minute, noted Mott, and had arrogantly "presumed to contend for the command of those forces that we had raised." His overbearing manner had almost caused "mutiny among the soldiers which . . . nearly frustrated our whole design." Fortunately, coolheaded Colonels Allen and Easton had dexterously intervened and calmed down their dedicated band of citizen-soldiers, who "were for clubbing their firelocks and marching home." Mott also corroborated Allen by neglecting to mention Arnold's involvement in the assault; the implication was that the Massachusetts colonel had materialized at the fortress only after far braver patriots had carried the day. Having almost ruined everything, Arnold had again waved about his commission and demanded command rights. He was an embarrassment to the colony sponsoring him, was Mott's unstated conclusion, an

unworthy patriot, a troublemaker at best and glory seeker at worst, especially
in comparison to Allen, Easton, and Brown, who had behaved with unusual
valor. Mott then recommended Easton and Brown, both inhabitants of
Massachusetts, for military commissions "equal to their merit," in what
was a veiled intimation to have them replace the annoying outsider from
Connecticut.[3]

To assure an appropriate reception in the Provincial Congress, Allen
selected James Easton to serve as his messenger. This gentleman had already
had a nasty encounter with Arnold. Shortly after the raid, Easton approached
the Massachusetts colonel and asked for a lieutenant colonel's commission in
the latter's regiment. Arnold, still enduring insults from the Boys and also
suspecting Easton of cowardice for not taking a prominent part in the
assault, curtly dismissed him. He shrugged off the Pittsfield tavern keeper,
calling him a rank opportunist; after which, according to Arnold, Easton
"set off for the [Provincial] Congress with an announced intention to injure
me all in his power." Easton was now seeking more than a field-grade
commission in the provincial service—his colonelcy was a militia appointment. He now wanted Arnold's commission for himself. Although Allen and
Mott may not have known about Easton's overtures to Arnold, they were
aware of his deep loathing for their adversary. Thus Easton made an ideal
emissary.[4]

Not yet fully aware of the rivals' machinations, Arnold penned his own
after-action report on May 11. Since he had received his commission from
the Massachusetts Committee of Safety, he followed protocol and directed
his comments to that body. Before the attack, Allen had agreed "to issue
further orders jointly," stated Arnold, who claimed to be "the first person
who entered and took possession of the fort." Shortly thereafter, Mott's
Committee of War had stripped him of command functions because he
forbade the "anarchy" and "plundering and destroying [of] private property"
by the Boys. Although deeply distressed and prepared "to be honorably
acquitted of my commission" so that "a proper person might be appointed
in my room," Arnold intended to keep asserting his right to command until
further orders reached him.[5]

Offering to resign in favor of a more meritorious person became a
common refrain from Arnold over the next month. He would willingly step
aside should the Committee of Safety or its parent body, the Provincial
Congress, select someone with experience more attuned to strengthening the
Champlain forts. The operative phrase for Arnold was "honorably acquitted," code words for any eighteenth-century gentleman expecting to receive
courteous treatment. Should Arnold's stepping aside serve the best interests

of the cause, he expected proper public acknowledgment for his actions—if for no other reason than to protect his good name from the slandering Allen bunch. Anything less could cause him great personal embarrassment, not only because he had rendered truly virtuous service but because of his own intensely held sensitivities about slurs of any kind on his character and reputation.

Because Arnold's commission was from the Committee of Safety, he was at a distinct disadvantage, had he known about Allen's stratagem of dealing directly with the Provincial Congress. Ironically, Allen's group, lacking any base of legitimacy, could communicate with whomever they pleased. They were resourceful enough to choose the highest patriot civil authority in Massachusetts. Not having to work through the Committee of Safety, Easton easily made the first—and most lasting—impression on the Provincial Congress.[6]

On May 17, as Arnold was approaching the northern end of Lake Champlain to strike at St. Johns, Easton was in Watertown, where the Provincial Congress was meeting just a few miles west of patriot lines in eastern Massachusetts. Allen's herald turned over the two reports, and the delegates invited him "to give a narrative" regarding the taking of Ticonderoga. Easton must have been eloquent. Although he did not secure a commission for himself, he got nearly everything the Allen group wanted. The delegates ordered the Green Mountain leader to remain in control of Ticonderoga and any related dependencies until further notice. Then they called on Connecticut to provide additional troops and supplies "until the advice of the Continental Congress can be had in that behalf." They directed Arnold to focus on the core of his original assignment—to take charge of all captured ordnance pieces "and bring them down, with all possible haste." Removing him from Ticonderoga would also represent "a means of settling any disputes which may have arisen between him and some other officers, . . . at a time when our common danger ought to unite us in the strongest bonds of unity and affection."[7]

Arnold thus fared poorly in this initial round of patriot political manipulation. Easton had successfully cast a pall over Arnold's good name. The negative portrait stuck hard with some delegates, who wanted to know why the colonel's commission had not gone to a solid Massachusetts patriot in the first place. Still, in trying to untangle a specious dilemma, the Congress had offered Arnold a face-saving assignment, in essence to get rid of him.

Ironically for Allen, who now possessed an authentic claim to command, he found himself in the same position that was Arnold's before the Ticonderoga assault. He lacked the troop strength to back up his newfound authority.

As such, the only significant outcome of Easton's sojourn to Watertown was the raising of doubts about the worthiness of Arnold's character and judgment. This tainted image would linger and cause Arnold further problems in the days ahead, despite his exemplary public service in the Champlain theater.[8]

II

The Massachusetts Provincial Congress had other concerns about Ticonderoga and Crown Point. With its energies and limited financial resources focused on the British military threat emanating from Boston, that body hoped to avoid sending additional troops and supplies to the Champlain corridor. Hence the delegates appealed to Connecticut for assistance and also asked the Continental Congress for counsel and guidance about defending a region that lay well beyond the borders of Massachusetts.

Many delegates to the Second Congress, so recently assembled in Philadelphia, would have preferred not having to act as an intercolonial coordinating authority in managing the overall patriot military effort. A majority, especially those from the Middle Colonies, wanted to focus squarely on resolving differences with Great Britain. By comparison, most New England delegates had begun to dismiss reconciliation as an illusion, particularly in the wake of Lexington and Concord. Although still very much a minority, some of them had even started to articulate the advantages of declaring independence. Months would pass, however, before these independence-minded leaders had broad enough support to overcome the reconciliationist predilections of Congress.

Meanwhile, more radical delegates had to reckon with cautionary arguments regarding the lack of American preparedness for war, specifically against His Majesty's regulars, considered the best fighting troops in the western world. The reconciliationists also kept warning about the colonies being too disorganized and disunited in purpose to sustain their autonomy among the nations of Europe. Despite the *rage militaire* of the moment, they likewise doubted whether Americans had the depth of commitment to keep fighting when adversity set in, and they fretted about shortages of material resources for waging long-term war. Although more cautious delegates were anxious to preserve American liberties, they still felt the need for the stabilizing influences of British military institutions. As citizens of property, they feared internal anarchy and social upheaval should those ties be completely severed. Thus, when news of the taking of Ticonderoga and Crown Point reached Congress, the reconciliationists reacted negatively. They knew that seizure of the forts would stand as an obstacle in realizing their goal of a reunited empire respectful of American rights.[9]

Ethan Allen could not have imagined an adverse congressional reaction, and he asked John Brown to serve as his personal messenger to Congress. Leaving Ticonderoga on May 11, Brown arrived in Philadelphia six days later, fully prepared to extol the virtues of Allen and company while torching Arnold's reputation. New England delegates welcomed the news, but grave concern characterized the reaction of the reconciliationists. A perceptive Brown thus altered his presentation to Congress to protect the reputation of Allen's party. Masterfully bending reality, he passed himself off as a courier from Arnold, who now became the instigator of the assault, with the effect of making Allen's rival appear as an impetuous troublemaker.[10]

The delegates, having met for only a week and still struggling to get their bearings, were not sure what to do. The reconciliationists grasped the military advantage of controlling the Champlain region, based on "indubitable evidence," apparently from the New England delegates, of a "design ... formed by the British ministry of making a cruel invasion from the province of Quebec, upon these colonies, for the purpose of destroying our lives and liberties." Nevertheless, the reconciliationists wanted to contain spreading acts of rebellion. Their solution was to float all captured military arms and stores to the southern end of Lake George. Patriot troops in the Champlain theater were to reconcentrate at Fort George and stand watch over this war matériel until everything could "be safely returned" to the Champlain forts after "the restoration of the former harmony between Great Britain and these colonies so ardently wished for by the latter shall render it prudent and consistent with the overruling law of self-preservation."[11]

For the reconciliationists, the matter of handing out accolades to Allen or Arnold was tangential nonsense. They did not appreciate the actions of either because both had raised the specter of further martial confrontations with the imperial government. Hence the majority in Congress voted to abandon the Champlain theater as a statement to the Crown of their desire to settle differences short of a full-scale rebellion.

Arnold was at Crown Point on Monday, May 29, when he learned about the pullback ruling of Congress. Much dismayed, he took pen in hand. "The report of Ticonderoga being abandoned" by his force, he wrote to Congress, "has thrown the inhabitants into the greatest confusion." At least five hundred patriot families resided between the forts and Canada, and retreating would expose them to the "mercy" of redcoats and hostile Indians. Ticonderoga, he asserted, was "the key of this extensive country, and if abandoned, leaves a very extensive frontier open to the ravages of the enemy, and to

continual alarms, which will probably cost more than the expense of repairing and garrisoning it." From Arnold's perspective on the front line,
holding Lake Champlain was critical to patriot martial interests. Having
offered his assessment, he hoped Congress would listen — regardless of the
political implications of standing firm.[12]

Arnold's appraisal was not singular. The Massachusetts Provincial Congress held the same opinion. Controlling the Champlain forts assured New
Englanders and New Yorkers "that all movements from Canada, . . . whether
by scalping parties or large bodies, . . . may almost certainly be discovered so
seasonably as that the blow may be generally warded off." Fort George to the
southwest, by comparison, was too far out of the way to afford protection,
and it was "probable that three-fourths of the attempts on the frontiers of
New York and New England, by Champlain, will never be known until
executed." Like Arnold, the Provincial Congress regarded Ticonderoga as a
strategically vital base for launching northern operations, "if it should become necessary and just that the United Colonies should annoy the inhabitants of Canada." The provincial delegates, like their New England brethren
in Congress and like Arnold, thus were adamantly opposed to abandoning
the Champlain forts.[13]

Even before these sentiments reached Philadelphia, Congress had reversed
its earlier decision, based on troublesome tidings contained in a letter from
Arnold (dated Tuesday, May 23) to the Connecticut Assembly. This dispatch
reported the full-alert status at Ticonderoga and Crown Point because of a
rumored British force bearing down on the forts from Canada. Arnold's
courier left Crown Point before the enemy detachment proved a phantom,
but Connecticut's worried governor, Jonathan Trumbull, saw potential "political" clout in Arnold's missive. He quickly forwarded a copy to Philadelphia. The Connecticut delegates, in turn, brandished the news before Congress, a tactic that played on fears, even among reconciliationists, about a
devilish British "design" to attack the colonies from the north.[14]

Late on the afternoon of Wednesday, May 31, Congress voted to retain
control of Ticonderoga and Crown Point. Then, in responding to Massachusetts's pleas of being overburdened, the delegates called on Connecticut to
assemble "a strong reinforcement" of soldiers for duty at the Champlain
forts. They also recommended the retention of some artillery pieces and
military stores "for the immediate defense of those posts," and they asked
the New York Provincial Convention to gather supplies and daily rations for
the enlarged garrison of patriot troops.

In these precedent-setting resolutions, Congress accepted a coordinating
function for rebel military mobilization — on the basis of unintentionally

misleading information. The reconciliationists thus had taken the first step in providing overall direction to a martial contest they wanted, above all else, to avoid. In so doing, they and their colleagues also addressed the issue of local command. Congress called on Governor Trumbull to "appoint a person, in whom he can confide, to command the forces at Crown Point and Ticonderoga."[15]

Trumbull gave scant consideration to Arnold. From what the governor knew about Arnold's differences with Allen and Connecticut men like Mott, he did not seem like a good choice. Arnold also lacked influential political connections and had no patron to sponsor his candidacy. Further, he already held a Massachusetts commission, another liability since that colony was backing away from committing further resources to the Champlain region. If Connecticut was going to assume the burden, Trumbull wanted someone from the government's circle of favorites. Indeed, he was so confident about Congress reversing itself that he had already selected the politically well connected Benjamin Hinman to head the force of one thousand Connecticut troops that would soon be bound for Ticonderoga and Crown Point.[16]

III

At this juncture, the Massachusetts Provincial Congress became an agent of additional commotion. When the Committee of Safety forwarded Arnold's May 11 letter to Watertown, the delegates showed little interest in debating whether Easton had misrepresented Arnold's actions. Their concerns lay elsewhere. Foremost on their agenda was extricating Massachusetts from commitments in the Champlain theater. As a first step, they wanted to see the records relating to the committee's decision to send Arnold on "a secret warlike enterprise to the westward." Not sure "of the relation Colonel Arnold then stood, and now stands in to this colony," including his "authority to raise a regiment to be in the pay of" Massachusetts, the delegates placed him under their direct jurisdiction, at least until they shed themselves of all responsibilities in the Champlain region. This, of course, meant getting rid of Arnold—and possibly even his regiment—as well.[17]

Motivated by the escalating financial burden of keeping Boston under siege, the ·Provincial Congress next angled to have Connecticut and New York take complete charge of the Champlain theater. Therefore, the delegates sent Colonel Joseph Henshaw to Hartford to communicate information about Massachusetts's straitened circumstances to Governor Trumbull and the Assembly. If Henshaw found Connecticut prepared to step into the breach, he was to travel to Ticonderoga and "acquaint Colonel Arnold that it is the order of this Congress that he return, and render accounts of his expenses . . . in order that he may be honorably discharged." Should Connecticut not yet be ready to act, Henshaw was to go to Ticonderoga anyway, "judge" how many troops Massachusetts should support, and tell Arnold to "continue there" in command. Seeking to avoid any misunderstanding, the delegates also dispatched Arnold a copy of Henshaw's instructions.[18]

Henshaw rode into Hartford on Wednesday, May 31. That afternoon he learned from Trumbull that arrangements were well under way to march one thousand troops northward under Hinman—pending the approval of the Continental Congress. Instead of proceeding to Ticonderoga to recall Arnold, he rushed back to Watertown with an important message from Trumbull, but not before hastily jotting an awkwardly phrased note to Arnold. "Respecting the fortress at Ticonderoga," wrote Henshaw, "Hinman was to take the command there." Arnold, however, was not to leave his post. Stated Henshaw, "It is expected you will continue with Colonel Allen, and put the place in the best posture of defense you are able, and guard against any surprise from the enemy until the succors arrive, and you receive further orders from the [Provincial] Congress."[19]

Henshaw never indicated that Hinman was to be senior in command rights, only that he was to assume control of Ticonderoga. For Arnold, who had long since located his headquarters at Crown Point and reported the same to Massachusetts officials, these words meant that he was to remain in overall command of the Champlain theater—Allen was not an active claimant by this time—until he heard differently from the Provincial Congress. Henshaw's decision to call off his scheduled trip to the Champlain forts only reinforced what was a very mistaken interpretation by Arnold.

Anxious to serve the cause and demonstrate his talents, Arnold was structuring reality as he wanted it to be. His foremost desire was to remain in command, but he could not miss the point that Hinman's troop strength was five times his own or that the Provincial Congress had advised him of the imminence of his being "honorably discharged." Before hearing from Henshaw, he had braced himself for the latter possibility. To safeguard his good name, he had earlier asked for treatment as a disinterested patriot who had rendered virtuous service, should he be recalled. Whatever happened, he expected Massachusetts's civilian leaders to behave respectfully toward him. Apparently, that was too much to ask.[20]

Focusing on their own agenda, the provincial delegates kept sending contradictory messages to Arnold. They showed scant regard for his sensibilities. First, thanks to James Easton, Arnold was to return east with a supply of captured ordnance pieces. Next, he was to accept instructions from

Henshaw, most likely meaning an honorable discharge. Then, in a sudden turnabout on Thursday, June 1, the delegates expressed "the greatest confidence in your fidelity, knowledge, courage, and good conduct." In almost obsequious tones, they implored Arnold to "dismiss the thoughts of quitting your important command"; rather, he was to keep building his regiment to its projected strength of four hundred and wait for instructions regarding whether New York or Connecticut "shall take on . . . maintaining and commanding" these troops "agreeable to an order of the Continental Congress."[21]

Arnold fairly glowed when he read these flattering words. At last, he surmised, evidence of his meritorious service had overcome the damaging reports of Allen, Easton, and company. In actuality, he was only displaying his political naivete in drawing such a conclusion.

Putting the best possible light on matters, civilian rebel leaders in Massachusetts were taking advantage of Arnold. The merit of his service was a secondary consideration to them. More immediate was their need to pacify other patriot governing bodies, in this case those of Connecticut and New York. That was the message from Governor Trumbull that Joseph Henshaw had carried back to Watertown. Even though Connecticut would provide one thousand troops, Trumbull expected Massachusetts to continue making proportionate contributions, since the defense of New England from its back side was not just Connecticut's obligation. The goal was to have fifteen hundred soldiers defending Lake Champlain. Leaders in the area of Albany had agreed to enlist a few troops, giving New Yorkers a larger part than just serving as primary suppliers of food and other camp necessities. Even so, a potential shortfall in troop strength still existed. Trumbull, then, had insisted as a price for Connecticut's involvement that Massachusetts not "draw off" its soldiers—more specifically, Arnold's regiment. The Bay Colony was to "leave them to cooperate with theirs for the defense of the post." This was the news that altered Henshaw's assignment and caused the effusive expressions of confidence in Arnold's performance and abilities.[22]

In the name of intercolonial cooperation, patriot leaders in Massachusetts reluctantly agreed to do their part, all of which made the dispensable Arnold now seem indispensable. Because his reputation had also improved with the Provincial Congress in the wake of more positive reports about his recent command activities, it looked as if Arnold might yet emerge from the campaign with some laurels of distinction. The delegates, however, in crafting gratuitous words, still had not confessed the whole truth. The realities of intercolonial politics dictated Arnold's subordination to Benjamin Hinman, since Connecticut was making the largest manpower contribution. Arnold should not have been surprised, since relative troop strength had determined whether he or Allen had enjoyed command rights. An ugly confrontation was now brewing.

All of these political considerations were the natural outcome of individual colonies preparing for war in the absence of central planning and administration. By the middle of June, delegates to the Second Congress would accept that coordinating function by "adopting" the New England armies and proclaiming them to be a Continental military establishment. The decision of May 31 to defend the Champlain region represented a significant step in that direction. But in early June, while Congress continued to debate what role, if any, it would play in the management of patriot military resistance, provincial leaders had to coordinate intercolonial operations as best they could. They had to avoid offending one another; if they fell to squabbling, everything could be lost.[23]

Massachusetts's rebel leaders would have been foolish to challenge their Connecticut brethren, who were also offering them significant financial relief. The matter of who had overall command rights had nothing to do with Arnold's competence, and the Provincial Congress hoped he could appreciate the necessity of balancing off intercolonial interests. Unfortunately, Arnold was not going to understand. In the wake of vacillating orders from Watertown and all the turmoil with the minions of Ethan Allen, he would take the news of Hinman's elevation very personally—and respond as a person whose deepest sense of personal honor was under willful attack.

In early June, Arnold kept attending to the mundane matters of Champlain's defense: the removal of cannons, construction of bateaux, and repair of half-ruined barracks. He also sailed down the lake on a scouting expedition. Through messages from mercantile acquaintances in Montreal, he learned that Governor Guy Carleton had just come up the St. Lawrence River from Quebec. Basing himself in Montreal, Carleton was pressuring the local populace, as well as the Caughnawaga Indians, to disdain rebel pleas for assistance. The governor even threatened to burn Montreal, which contained about seven hundred homes, unless the *habitants*—French subjects of commoner status—and English merchants strengthened local defenses. He also redeployed the few British regulars in the area, sending some three hundred troops to St. Johns. To Arnold's relief, the Canadians and Indians were not embracing Carleton's attempts to put them under arms. Consequently, the regulars remained in a defensive posture and focused on strengthening dilapidated fortifications at such strategic points as Chambly and St. Johns.[24]

Arnold and the scouting party returned to Crown Point early on the evening of Saturday, June 10, only to be confronted by Ethan Allen, James Easton, and a few of the Boys. Based on Easton's out-of-date instructions from the Massachusetts Congress, Allen pronounced himself the legitimate commander. Although very annoyed, Arnold kept his composure and informed the Allen coterie that he was "the only legal commanding officer" in the Champlain region. He "would willingly give up the command when anyone appeared with proper authority to take it." Meanwhile, he would not "suffer" any disagreement with interlopers like them, should they attempt "to raise a mutiny." Since the soldiers at Crown Point were loyal to Arnold, Allen and friends backed down.[25]

When they tried to leave the next morning, personal animosities erupted. Allen's party moved out without "showing their pass." A sentry remanded them to Arnold. Easton became testy and offered gratuitous insults. Arnold, long since aware of the "liberty he [Easton] had taken with his character," exploded in rage. He grabbed his adversary and demanded that he "draw like a gentleman," since Easton had "a hanger [cutlass] by his side, and a case of loaded pistols in his pocket." Pulling back, the startled tavern keeper refused the challenge. Not to be restrained, Arnold "kicked him very heartily" before ordering him, along with the rest of Allen's party, to stay away from Crown Point. A stunned Easton stalked off with the others, angrily vowing to do everything he could to destroy the man who had given him so humiliating a thrashing.[26]

Arnold expressed no regrets about the incident. From his perspective, Easton was a lying, dishonorable coward. As Arnold dealt with the details of command over the next few days, he seemed genuinely pleased with the overall turn of events. New York recruits, he learned, were coming up from Albany with orders to join his regiment, and he reveled in the flattering words of the Massachusetts Provincial Congress. At long last, Arnold thought, he had established his credentials as a virtuous patriot. His dedication and persistence at the Champlain forts were finally producing the respect he so eagerly sought. He could not have been more wrong in his assessment.[27]

IV

Arnold's buoyant frame of mind caused him to think expansively about the Canadian situation. The more he reflected on the intelligence reports available to him, the more enthusiastic he became about a quick-hitting, preemptive invasion designed to bring all of sprawling Quebec Province into the patriot camp. In mid-June, Arnold laid out his reasoning in a long letter to the Continental Congress. He described Governor Carleton's initial failure to rally either the French or the Native American populace. Available British regulars were so few in number and spread so thinly across the landscape that they could not offer concentrated resistance. In this vein, Arnold emphasized how "great numbers of the Canadians have expected a visit from us for sometime, and are very impatient of our delay, as they are determined to join us whenever we appear in the country with any force to support them." For all of these reasons, he encouraged Congress to order a swift invasion by two thousand patriot troops—the projected garrison forces at Ticonderoga and Crown Point but, he stressed, "no Green Mountain Boys."

His "plan of operations" called for half of the soldiers to seize Montreal, "whose gates, on our arrival at that place, will be opened by our friends there, in consequence of a plan for that purpose already entered into by them." The other half would cut off St. Johns and Fort Chambly to secure safe supply lines and easy communications back to the Champlain forts. Once these maneuvers had been effected, patriot forces would recombine and aim straight at Quebec City, the capital of Canada and the most critical target of them all.

Arnold underscored the importance of moving quickly, before Carleton received reinforcements from Britain. He likewise tried to preempt the arguments of reconciliationists, who would surely view such an invasion as a major impediment to resolving differences with the parent nation. "The reduction of those places would discourage the enemies of American liberty," Arnold proclaimed, and "frustrate their cruel and unjust plan of operation, and be the means of restoring that solid peace and harmony between Great Britain and her colonies, so essential to the well being of both."

Part of that "cruel and unjust plan," Arnold stated, related to a rumor about the home government's intention to return Canada to the autocratic French. By comparison, the proposed invasion would guarantee "a free government" for Quebec Province, "agreeable to the English constitution." Further, should King George and his ministers not accede to patriot pleas for liberty, Canada would serve as "an inexhaustible granary in case we are reduced to want" through protracted war. In closing, Arnold reemphasized the importance of proceeding "without loss of time," and he stood ready, if called upon, to "undertake" command of the expedition, hoping, "with the smiles of heaven," to "answer for the success of it." [28]

Arnold's was an audacious campaign design. Yet his thoughts, although detailed and well articulated, were not wholly original. During June, Ethan Allen also appealed to Congress to mount a Canadian invasion—and like

Arnold, he pronounced himself available to lead the expedition. Leaders in Congress, moreover, were vigorously debating the subject. The reconciliationists were adamantly opposed to any such action, but more radical New England delegates kept pressing the issue. On Tuesday, June 27, Congress, after considering further arguments and the operational plan in Arnold's letter in particular, voted to launch such an expedition.[29]

The delegates showed no interest in Arnold as a potential commander. He was too much of a political nobody—and apparently too rash and turbulent in temperament anyway, thanks to the impression created by John Brown. The assignment went to a patriot of far-reaching influence, the wealthy New York landholder and merchant Philip Schuyler, an experienced veteran of the Seven Years' War. In organizing the Continental army, Congress had already named Schuyler one of its major generals, and because his main residence was in Albany, he was the logical person to head operations in the northern theater.[30]

Arnold never had a chance to sulk, since other difficulties had long since ruined his euphoric mood. On Saturday, June 17, Colonel Benjamin Hinman appeared at Crown Point and, as Arnold wrote, "made a demand of the command here, but as he produced no regular order for the same I refused giving it up, on which he embarked for Ticonderoga." Arnold was not just being obstinate. The problem lay with Hinman's written orders, which directed him only to reinforce the Champlain forts and command his regiment. Hinman, an affable, do-nothing sort of a chap, did not seem terribly offended. He retired to Ticonderoga to await clarifying instructions. As for Arnold, he remained confident that his civil superiors in Massachusetts had not sold him out. After all, they had so recently praised his "fidelity, knowledge, courage, and good conduct" at the Champlain forts.[31]

Meanwhile, the Massachusetts Provincial Congress, still worried about the financial burden of maintaining Arnold's regiment, had named a committee of three prominent delegates—Walter Spooner, Jedidiah Foster, and James Sullivan—to travel to Ticonderoga and investigate matters. Spooner and his associates were to decide whether holding the forts was critical to "the general defense of these colonies." Presuming an affirmative answer, they were to correspond with the Continental Congress regarding "further provisions . . . for securing and maintaining" the forts. In addition, they were to examine "in what manner . . . Colonel Arnold has executed his . . . commission and instructions." If convinced of his "spirit, capacity, and conduct," Arnold and his regiment were to be "retained" in the service of Massachusetts, as long as he accepted "the command of such chief officer as is or shall be appointed by ... Connecticut." If not fully satisfied, the Spooner committee was to discharge Arnold and order him to return to the Provincial Congress to settle his accounts.[32]

That Spooner and his associates were to evaluate Arnold was curious indeed, given the fulsome words of praise so recently forwarded to him. Apparently, suspicions about his martial capacities lingered, dating back to the denigrating comments of James Easton. Some delegates were also asking why a Connecticut man should have command of a Massachusetts regiment, especially if permanently established and paid for by the Provincial Congress. Surely, politically influential patriots with enough military experience to command resided in Massachusetts—perhaps someone like local militia colonel James Easton.

Spooner and his committee appeared at Ticonderoga on Friday, June 23. They were less than pleased to hear Hinman's account of his first meeting with Arnold. They immediately went to Crown Point and confronted Arnold. As Spooner later reported, Arnold asked for a copy of their instructions, "upon [the] reading of which he seemed greatly disconcerted." Distressed to learn that he, so recently pronounced so worthy a patriot, was now the object of an investigation, and mortified over not being properly informed about Hinman's elevation over him, Arnold allegedly "declared he would not be second in command to any person whatsoever; and after some time contemplating upon the matter, resigned his post."[33]

Arnold appreciated the need for intercolonial cooperation, and he did not question the desire of Massachusetts to lessen its role. He recognized that Connecticut's commitment to the defense of the Champlain region was now greater than anyone else's, and he certainly knew from firsthand experience that the officer with the most troops had de facto command rights— and Hinman had something else Arnold never had, the agreement of all constituencies that he was to be in charge. Furthermore, Arnold understood that he might possibly retain his commission and regiment if he would only subordinate himself to Hinman and cooperate with the Spooner committee. He still resigned.[34]

What affected Arnold's decision was not just petulant anger. He did not relish the idea of taking orders from "a younger officer [in date of commission] of the same rank" who had not yet contributed anything to the Champlain campaign, which might easily be interpreted as "a most disgraceful reflection on him and the body of troops he commands." Equally if not more bothersome was what Arnold considered the capricious, if not abusive, behavior of the Provincial Congress. Within days of pronouncing him indispensable to the cause, the delegates had instructed the Spooner committee to judge "in what manner I have executed my commission," which he regarded as "a very plain intimation that the Congress is dubious of my rectitude and abilities." Only a buffoon, he concluded, would continue to have confidence in a civil body so whimsical in its actions.[35]

Arnold thought he had acted the part of a truly disinterested patriot by forsaking his booming mercantile business and the comforts of home for martial service in the field. He believed his record at the Champlain forts was above reproach—certainly deserving of respect, and perhaps even advancement, but not arbitrary demotion. Thus he pithily encapsulated his feelings by confiding to his memorandum book, "I have resigned my commission, not being able to hold it longer with honor."[36]

V

At this juncture unexpected turmoil, partially of Arnold's making, beset the Crown Point encampment. After resigning, Arnold spoke with various soldiers in his regiment. They wanted to know what was going to happen to them. He had no inkling whatsoever. Probably they would be released from their terms of service, he replied, since the Massachusetts Provincial Congress seemed so worried about expenses. What about wages due them? He could promise nothing, he said, now that he was no longer their commander.

When these less-than-reassuring words circulated among Arnold's regiment, now numbering nearly three hundred troops, panic set in. A short-lived mutiny erupted on Saturday, June 24, as Arnold was eating lunch aboard the sloop *Enterprise*. A party of soldiers rushed him, and he was "confined in the great cabin" under armed guard. The same agitated group then sent a delegation after the Spooner committee, which had already left Crown Point to meet with Hinman at Ticonderoga. Arnold "complained much of the insult offered," even though the mutineers showed no "personal ill will" toward him. As he later wrote, their objective in making him a hostage was to "stop the committee and oblige them to pay off the regiment or at least some part as will enable them to go home to their families with honor."[37]

The Spooner committee, having related the story of Arnold's resignation to Hinman, next sought out James Easton, who was lurking about Ticonderoga. Without a moment's hesitation, he accepted a colonel's commission as Arnold's replacement. (The committee also named John Brown to the rank of major in this regiment.) Easton and Brown happily agreed to "re-engage" Arnold's troops. At this juncture the emissaries from the mutineers confronted Spooner, Easton, and company, who quickly dispatched representatives to Crown Point. By late evening, Arnold had regained his freedom, and the little tempest was over, largely because the Spooner committee turned over £280 to pay off those troops who wanted to go home and to provide wages for those willing to accept Easton as their regimental commander.

Neither Arnold nor the Spooner committee dwelled on the mutiny. Walter Spooner gave the incident only passing attention in his lengthy summary report to the Provincial Congress. Spooner did say that some of Arnold's soldiers "became dissatisfied and mutinous" because "they had been informed that they were to be defrauded out of the pay for past services." He did not, however, charge Arnold with willfully misleading anyone. Spooner had no evidence to support such an accusation, which Arnold could have countered by indicating how foolish the committee members were to rush away from Crown Point before designating an interim commander or offering the soldiers reassurances.[38]

Others still hovering about Ticonderoga, such Edward Mott, felt compelled to strike with yet another round of slander against the unfrocked Arnold's reputation. With the assistance of Easton and Brown, Mott let his imagination run freely in a letter to Governor Trumbull. When the Spooner committee "discharged" Arnold, he had deliberately inspired and then led the uprising, claimed Mott. Arnold and a few of his soldiers became so frenzied that they cruised up the lake and "fired upon" the retreating committee; and they also "threatened" to sail the *Enterprise* and the *Liberty* to St. Johns and turn these vessels and themselves over to the British—unless they received satisfaction. Mott further stated that he and a few others courageously intervened. They sailed to Crown Point on behalf of the frightened committee and soon contained the uprising, despite the "fixed bayonets" and insults offered by the whole mutinous bunch, who ultimately "declared they had been deceived by Colonel Arnold." Since no other source corroborated Mott's sensationalized yarn, it cannot be taken seriously.[39]

Arnold viewed the mutiny as the product of a regrettable misunderstanding. He neither condemned nor condoned the behavior of his soldiers. What disturbed him most was the Spooner committee's decision to hand his regiment over to Easton and Brown. This action confirmed his suspicions of the serious damage done to his reputation by Easton before the Massachusetts Provincial Congress, as well as his apprehensions about the Spooner committee as little more than a lynching party for the same deceitful patriot Congress.

To purge his indignation, Arnold supervised the preparation of a newspaper essay under the name "Veritas," who posed as a respondent to an earlier published account of the taking of Ticonderoga in which "that very modest gentleman" James Easton almost single-handedly engineered the triumph. This fabricated version of reality, the handiwork of a self-promoting Easton, was "so replete with falsehood" that the public deserved a more "candid detail of the whole matter." As for the truth, declared Veritas, Easton played no part in the attack. No one saw him inside the fortress until around 9 a.m., long after the assault was over. "He was the last man that entered the fort," insisted Veritas, having stayed away "until the [British] soldiers and their arms were secured, he having concealed himself in an old barrack near the redoubt, under the pretense of wiping and drying his gun, which he said had got wet in crossing the lake."

Most of all, Veritas wanted the world to know that James Easton often behaved in a "cowardly manner." He was the kind of person who would abuse "Colonel Arnold behind his back" but always appear "very complaisant before his face." When Arnold finally could take no more and "heartily kicked" this rank opportunist, he did so, Veritas stated, "to the great satisfaction of a number of gentlemen present." So dishonorable a cur deserved no better treatment.[40]

Not surprisingly, the Veritas essay extolled Arnold's role in the Ticonderoga victory, but not to the point of denying Ethan Allen his fair part. The purpose of Veritas was to expound on the truth, as obviously interpreted by Arnold, not to compound mistaken conceptions of reality. In addition, the unfrocked colonel was attempting to act by the code of a gentleman. He hoped the insults offered by Veritas would provoke the pusillanimous Easton into a duel; but this adversary preferred to avoid so risky a proposition. Continuing to smear Arnold's name was certainly much safer. Thus Mott wrote his damning report about Arnold's alleged mutiny at Crown Point in direct response to the Veritas essay. Also, Easton already had the satisfaction of commanding Arnold's regiment.

Having defended his reputation through Veritas, the normally decisive Arnold dawdled in preparing to leave the Champlain forts. Most likely he was waiting to hear from Congress about his proposed invasion plan and the remote prospect of his commanding the expedition. In addition, the Spooner committee had ordered him to settle his accounts, a perplexing matter. Having ridden west with only £100 in cash from the Committee of Safety, Arnold had plowed his personal resources into providing for his regiment and purchased much-needed supplies on his own credit. He suspected the Provincial Congress would attempt to shortchange him, given its penurious mentality and the turmoil surrounding his resignation. Arnold spoke directly to this issue on June 24, when he chastised the Provincial Congress for having "declined sending me money . . . to discharge the small and unavoidable debts I have contracted for necessaries for the use of the army, for which my own credit is at stake." Because the Spooner committee lacked authority to cover these expenses, Arnold found himself "reduced to the necessity of leaving the place with dishonor, or waiting until I can send home and discharge those debts out of my private purse." He apparently chose the latter alternative.[41]

By early July, word had reached Ticonderoga regarding the decision to mount a Canadian invasion with Philip Schuyler in command of the Northern Department. The news disappointed Arnold, but he resolved to travel south to Albany to see if he could meet—and possibly gain favor with—the newly designated commander. Arnold began his journey on July 4, 1775. Before he left the Champlain region behind, local residents buoyed his flagging spirits by gathering at Crown Point to say goodbye and wish him well. They handed him a proclamation of their "gratitude and thankfulness for the uncommon vigilance, vigor, and spirit" he had displayed in providing "for our preservation and safety from the threatened and much dreaded incursions of an inveterate enemy." They praised his "humanity and benevolence," particularly in "supplying them with provisions in their distress." They lauded his "polite manner" and "generosity of soul, which nothing less than real magnaminity and innate virtue could inspire." Finally, they reassured him about ultimately receiving "rewards adequate to your merit."[42]

Arnold took great solace in these words, offering in turn his "sincere thanks for your support, vigilance, and spirited conduct in the public cause." He could not "help regretting the necessity I am under of leaving you so soon," but he was sure that a "kind Providence" would afford them continued protection. He would "at all times," he promised, "be happy in hearing of the welfare of all the inhabitants on Lake Champlain."[43]

Others commented favorably on Arnold's performance at the Champlain forts. A Connecticut civilian leader who visited Crown Point in late May had stated, "Colonel Arnold has been greatly abused and misrepresented by designing persons" of the Allen, Easton, Brown, and Mott variety. He went on to declare that "had it not been for him [Arnold], everything . . . would have been in the utmost confusion and disorder; people would have been plundered of their private property, and no man's person would be safe that was not of the Green Mountain party."[44]

Another patriot leader who had already formed a positive impression of Arnold's capacities was Philip Schuyler. In early July, based on favorable reports, he wrote to Connecticut congressional delegate Silas Deane, who was a business and personal acquaintance of Arnold, and queried, "Could you not get Arnold appointed Deputy Adjutant General in this department? I dare not mention it to Congress, and would not have it known that I had ever hinted it, as it might create jealousy. Be silent, therefore, with respect to me."[45]

Schuyler wanted to avoid any appearance of a ranking military officer trying to dictate to civilian authority. At the same time, he needed a capable adjutant, and he had come to view Arnold as a most useful patriot, based on his gritty performance in the Champlain region. In light of Governor Trumbull's elevation of Benjamin Hinman, Schuyler had discerned that Arnold lacked key political connections to gain military preferment in his home colony. Thus the northern commander drew on his own wide-ranging influence to gain vital backing from Connecticut's congressional delegates, without which there was little prospect of Arnold obtaining this or any other post of even modest consequence in the nascent Continental military establishment.[46]

As Arnold approached Albany, he had no inkling what the politically powerful Schuyler might think of him. His goal was to make a positive impression, presuming the Northern Department commander had a few moments to meet with him. He certainly could not foresee that Schuyler was already his advocate and would become a valuable patron for him in the days ahead. Nor could Arnold have guessed how much their client-patron relationship would affect the turbulent course of his own spectacular but tortured career as a Continental army officer.

VI

Besides their mutual interest in commerce and abhorrence of the Green Mountain Boys, Philip Schuyler and Benedict Arnold had little in common except for their desire to serve the cause of American liberty. More than seven years Arnold's senior, Schuyler, the scion of one of New York's great landed families, grew up in substantial affluence. After laudable service as a logistics officer during the Seven Years' War, he labored tenaciously to expand his inherited domain, which by 1765 had increased to one hundred thousand acres. Schuyler focused his energies on the development of his Saratoga Patent estate, consisting of 1,875 acres some forty miles north of Albany. He also filled various political offices as a respected steward of the more "common sort" of New York folk. In his public dealings, Schuyler maintained the unruffled air of the gentleman-aristocrat. His deep-set eyes and hawklike nose helped cast his appearance in severe terms, and his critics often described him as a condescending patrician. Despite his public bearing, Schuyler was genuinely unassuming, friendly, and even full of good humor when among friends and family. This was the person who pleasantly greeted Arnold at his stylish Albany mansion on the morning of Monday, July 10.[47]

Schuyler had just returned from Philadelphia, where he had been serving in Congress, to commence preparations for the Canadian invasion. He was anxious to obtain a full briefing on conditions at the Champlain forts. Arnold discussed everything from supply shortages to his difficulties over command. Possibly even as they conversed, a courier from Colonel Hinman arrived with a desperate-sounding communiqué for Schuyler. Almost frantically, the Connecticut officer spoke of the absence of "flour and a constant cry for rum and want [of] molasses for beer. . . . The failure of those who provide gives great uneasiness to the men." Even more striking was his admission of an incapacity to deal with these problems. "I wait sir with impatience for your arrival," Hinman confessed, "as I find myself unable to steer in this stormy situation."[48]

Such a letter laid bare how much Hinman, whom one historian labeled "King Log" for his inability to make decisions, was lacking in leadership capacities, especially in comparison to Arnold. As for Schuyler, he could not miss Arnold's deeply injured pride and despoiled sense of personal honor over being cast aside in favor of a virtual incompetent whose best qualification for command was the favor of Governor Trumbull and the Connecticut General Assembly.[49]

To lessen his companion's mortification, Schuyler expressed how highly Congress regarded his performance at the Champlain forts, which gave Arnold a "sensible pleasure." The New Yorker was also "kind enough," Arnold stated, "to offer me his interest to procure me an agreeable post in the army." His only disappointment was Schuyler's report about Congress not adopting "the plan of operation I proposed" for the invasion of Canada. The delegates intended to increase the number of troops before moving forward, which Arnold thought foolish in light of the weak defensive posture of Quebec Province. The "most favorable" moment to strike was at hand, certainly before Governor Carleton received "a sufficient number of king's troops . . . to alter the sentiments of the . . . inhabitants and oblige them to take up arms against us." On this point Arnold was prescient.[50]

As another palliative, Schuyler asked Arnold to prepare a report for Congress on current conditions in the Champlain theater. The unfrocked colonel did so, but without much enthusiasm. He pointed out that "since giving up the command, I have been prevented [from] receiving regular intelligence as heretofore." He did not urge Congress to proceed quickly with an expedition, since the delegates had already rejected that advice. His only heartening comment was about "the disposition of the Canadians and Indians," which by the "latest accounts" remained "very favorable" toward the patriot cause. Everything else seemed bleak, especially with Carleton making "indefatigable" preparations to defend the Richelieu River forts and Montreal. Then, in a curious postscript, Arnold almost apologized for failing "to inform" Congress that "my regiment is disbanded." He was not asking for sympathy; rather, he felt shamed that his regiment had been turned over to Easton and Brown. For Arnold, the regiment had simply ceased to exist.[51]

The melancholy tone of this letter suggests other concerns as well. Although Arnold had "no doubt," as he stated privately, that Schuyler was a "very sensible and active" person with the capacity to "regulate matters" at Ticonderoga and Crown Point, he saw a military disaster in the making "should the present dispute continue longer than this year, which God forbid." His skepticism arose from much more than his humiliating experiences at the Champlain forts or the seemingly cautionary behavior of a reconciliationist-dominated Congress. With the survival, let alone success, of the cause of liberty so dependent on vigorous, enlightened decision making, Arnold was starting to wonder whether patriot civilian leaders had the breadth of vision to withstand the British martial onslaught that was sure to come, particularly when preferment for well-connected patriots, regardless of their competence, and the balancing of competing provincial interests seemed more important than the resolute defense of American rights.[52]

Arnold's initial doubts would receive major reinforcement during the spring of 1776, when he found himself desperately trying to check the British military juggernaut in Canada while Congress, rather ironically, was casting stones of blame in everyone's direction but its own. Again and again Arnold would come back to the theme of short-sighted, self-serving, petty-minded civilian leadership as the Achilles' heel of the Revolution.

VII

Arnold's premonitions of impending disaster also reflected the tragic personal news he had just received from home. Word reached him in Albany that his wife, Peggy, barely thirty years old, had died on June 19. Just three days later, his father-in-law, "Papa" Mansfield, who was regaining his strength after a serious illness, had a sudden relapse, likely triggered by the shock of losing his daughter, and also died. Sharing his personal anguish with Schuyler,

Arnold promptly made preparations to leave behind "a scene of public hurry and confusion" and return home. During the past two and a half months, as he recorded, he had often longed to retreat to his "safe, happy asylum" in New Haven "where mutual love and friendship doubled our joys and bears down our every misfortune." "But, oh, alas," he cried out in sorrow, "how is the scene changed, [and] every recollection of past happiness heightens my present grief, which would be intolerable, were it not buried in the public calamity."[53]

In the light of so much private and public misfortune, a less purposeful person might have given up on serving the cause. But the thought of "an idle life under my present circumstances would be but a lingering death," Arnold wrote. Even though his three "dear innocent prattlers" and his sister Hannah needed his immediate attention and loving comfort, as he needed theirs, he planned to return to the Champlain theater, if patriot "arms are carried into Canada," or "as a volunteer join the army at Cambridge." He was not going to be bullied by the tyrannical imperial government—or by the Ethan Allen crowd, the Massachusetts Provincial Congress, or the Continental Congress, for that matter. Arnold would not forsake his personal mission. He still intended to restore the name that he bore to its former glory by earning the patriot community's lasting respect. And if he had garnered little more than personal dishonor from his Champlain adventures, he had gained the patronage of Philip Schuyler to assist him in his quest.[54]

Within another few days, Arnold rode into New Haven and dismounted before the home where he had promised to enjoy better days with his wife and family. He embraced Hannah and his three sons, and they soon visited the grave sites of "dear" Peggy and Papa Mansfield. Hannah tried to cheer him by relating how much the Footguards had praised him as being "a very humane, tender officer." In turn, he articulated his feelings about rejoining the patriot military effort. He could best submerge his personal sorrow in "consideration of the public" cause, he explained, but only if Hannah would take care of the boys and keep various business ventures going. Since he had to travel to Massachusetts to settle his accounts anyway, he intended to present himself to the new commander in chief, George Washington.[55]

Hannah dearly loved the three boys, and she promised do her best in serving as a surrogate mother. She also agreed to manage his mercantile affairs, as much as the perilous times would permit. Hannah would do whatever she could to support her brother, since she of all people fully appreciated the reasons for his relentless pursuit of respect for himself and the Arnold family name. All he needed was an opportunity to demonstrate his talents, just as he had done so many years ago when the Lathrops had offered him their critical support. Now, with Schuyler's patronage, he was hoping to garner a consequential military assignment. Yet, in this time of personal grief, Arnold gave scant thought to how the provincial politics of rebellion might keep plaguing his efforts to serve the cause of American liberty without jeopardizing his personal honor and reputation as a virtuous patriot.

CHAPTER Five

Into the Howling
Maine Wilderness

I

Like her namesake mother, Hannah Arnold was a prayerful woman. While her brother was still at Crown Point, she sent him a loving letter in which she sympathized with "the fatigue you must unavoidably suffer in the wilderness." Her "hope" for him was to "have health, strength, fortitude, and valor, for whatever you may be called to." Then Hannah pointed to the "broad hand of the Almighty" as she gently reminded Benedict, "It is to Him and Him only, my dear brother, that we can look for safety or success. His power is ever able to shield us from the pestilence that walks in darkness, and the arrows that fly by noonday." [1]

Hannah retained her supplicating attitude in comforting her despondent brother after he returned home in mid-July. Certainly Arnold had reached a low point in his life. Besides the biting grief over the loss of Peggy and Papa Mansfield, he had to reckon with his virtual rejection by the patriot cause. Normally so physically robust, Arnold's health took a sudden turn for the worse. A severe attack of the gout, which periodically struck his lower limbs, kept him bedridden for more than a week.

When he could concentrate, he spoke with Hannah about the care of his sons, the oldest of whom — "Little Ben" — was just seven, and about the dangers of continuing trading activities in the midst of the deepening imperial crisis. He expressed concern about one of his trading vessels, the brigantine *Peggy*, that had recently cleared port for Quebec, literally sailing into a potential war zone. If British officials seized this vessel, he fretted, it could be lost forever as a source of income for his family.[2]

Also disturbing Arnold's equanimity was the matter of settling his accounts with the Massachusetts Provincial Congress, which he doubted would treat him fairly. Since he had to travel to Watertown, he was thinking about visiting Cambridge, just a few miles to the east, with the purpose of meeting the Continental army's new commander in chief, George Washington. He would present himself as a volunteer, he told Hannah, and hope to gain a Continental officer's commission. His still felt strongly about taking part in any patriot invasion of Canada, and he even had some ideas about an appropriate role for himself. Understanding her brother's ambitions as only she could, Hannah did nothing to discourage his dreams of glory. He should keep devoting himself to the cause of the liberty, she advised him, and she would provide for the boys and maintain his business affairs as best she could in these troubled times.

Hannah's deep-felt concern and encouragement seem to have had a salubrious effect on her brother's ailing health. Arnold was soon making arrangements to ship a large cargo of hoops and barrel staves to the West Indies, and he also compiled a detailed listing of his Lake Champlain expenses. Toward the end of July, he embraced his sons and devoted sister, then mounted his horse and began his second journey in just three months to Massachusetts. As before, he intended to find some means to demonstrate his worth as a truly virtuous patriot, even to the point where Hannah's words—"and if called to battle may the God of Armies cover your head in the day of it"—would resonate back to him with extraordinary meaning.[3]

II

Accounts in hand, Arnold presented himself to the Massachusetts Provincial Congress on Tuesday, August 1. The delegates named a committee of five, headed by Dr. Benjamin Church, who not long thereafter would be identified as a British spy, to review his records and recommend a final settlement. On and off during the next two and a half weeks, Church and his colleagues quibbled with Arnold about various entries. They expressed dismay about his claim for wages covering three and a half months of service (£53) when two months (£30) seemed ample. The Spooner committee, they pointed out, had directed him to ride to Watertown immediately to settle his accounts. He had not received authorization to travel by way of New Haven, regardless of his personal circumstances.

Arnold was not particularly pleasant with Church and his committee— nor they with him. Given negative earlier impressions from the likes of James Easton, as well as the Spooner committee report, the committee members poked away at his integrity whenever they could. If Arnold expected reimbursement for oxen, cows, sheep, and horses allegedly purchased at Crown Point, they told him, he would need to obtain more convincing evidence. When he asked how he could do that, they almost playfully advised him to ride to Ticonderoga and secure receipts from Massachusetts's own Colonel James Easton. Arnold scoffed at so ridiculous a suggestion; he knew he would get no help from a man whom he had castigated as a coward and physically humbled. All the haggling and purposeful insults finally ended on Saturday, August 19, when the Church committee dismissed more than half of Arnold's claims in recommending a settlement of £195.13.9, more than £200 short of the reimbursement he had sought.[4]

For all of his reputed greed, Arnold reacted with restraint. He was now focusing his thoughts on the far more consequential matter of invading Canada. In September, he did turn over his financial records to Silas Deane and asked whether he might get satisfaction from the Continental Congress. Deane, who had repeatedly voiced chagrin about his friend's shabby treatment by Massachusetts's patriot leaders, pursued the claim. In late January 1776, Congress awarded Arnold an additional £245.14.1 ($819). The delegates acted favorably at this time because of Arnold's recent surge in stature as a wounded war hero in the rebel quest to conquer Canada.[5]

Arnold did not stay in Watertown idling away nearly three weeks while the Church committee periodically pored over his accounts. Sometime before the middle of August, he rode to Cambridge and had a meeting with General Washington. The new commander, having served in the Second Congress before receiving his appointment, knew about Arnold's creditable but controversial performance in the Champlain region. Anxious to receive as much intelligence as he could, Washington welcomed such a meeting, particularly with plans moving forward in the Champlain region for an invasion of Canada.

Washington beheld in Arnold a man with an animated, loquacious manner as well as penetrating mind. He asked Arnold to summarize his impressions of conditions in Quebec Province, based not only on his observations as a private trader but also on information garnered from various Canadian friends with an affinity for the patriot cause. Arnold likewise described the stores of military ordnance, lead, and powder at Ticonderoga and Crown Point. With his own Continental force having no more than nine rounds of powder and ball per soldier, let alone very few artillery pieces, Washington was grateful for Arnold's report—and soon requested a supply of the lead. The ambitious patriot from Connecticut thus made a favorable first impression.[6]

Arnold may well have brought up his June letter to Congress advocating a Canadian invasion, which Washington likely saw before coming to Cambridge. Arnold wondered about having some part in the invasion, and he broached the subject of a second force entering Canada by way of the Maine wilderness. This column would act in concert with the main attack force then assembling at the Champlain forts under Schuyler's command. Arnold offered to serve as a volunteer but also communicated his desire to secure a Continental officer's commission—at a rank comparable to his vacated Massachusetts colonelcy so as not to compromise his honor.

The idea of dispatching such a force through the Maine wilderness and down the Chaudière River to the capital city of Quebec was very much in the air at the time. No one could claim originality, except perhaps Colonel Jonathan Brewer of Massachusetts. Shortly after the patriot assault on Ticonderoga, Brewer had proposed leading five hundred troops along this route with the purpose of capturing Quebec City. Washington had already contemplated mounting such an expedition. Now Arnold was meeting with him, thinking along the same lines, and no doubt offering himself for command. Brewer was no longer available, having received a serious wound at the Battle of Bunker Hill.[7]

Washington and Arnold appreciated that any such detachment had to march for Quebec as soon as possible before Governor Carleton, who was concentrating his few available regulars some 150 miles to the southwest at Montreal, St. Johns, and Chambly, could organize effective resistance at the fortress-like city. In addition, both men were aware of Lieutenant John Montresor's 1761 journal and map describing this heretofore uncharted wilderness trail. Montresor, a talented British military engineer now resident with Gage's troops in Boston, had moved easily and quickly over the route. So had various French and Indian raiding parties bent on wreaking havoc among New England's frontier settlements during the colonial wars. It was one thing for small groups, which could live off the land, to traverse so unexplored a wilderness. A force large enough to capture even a relatively undefended city would need sustained logistical support or face the prospect of many lives lost. The risks were enormous, Washington and Arnold realized, but success contained the all-important potential of bringing Quebec Province into the rebellion.[8]

The commander told his guest that he wanted a few days to think more about the matter. Arnold readily acceded but also said he would soon have to return to New Haven to attend to his mercantile affairs, should a lengthy delay develop in planning for the expedition. Washington promised a swift decision. On Sunday, August 20, he prepared an "express" letter to Schuyler. The commander wanted "to communicate . . . a plan of an expedition, which has engrossed my thoughts for several days," and for which he could "very well spare a detachment of 1,000 or 1,200 men." The objective would be to "make a diversion that would distract Carleton and facilitate your views." Washington saw an opportunity to squeeze the governor simultaneously from both sides. Should Carleton "break up and follow this party to Quebec," Schuyler's troops could easily seize Montreal. Should he persist in defending Montreal and throw all his resources into challenging Schuyler's force, the capital of Canada would likely "fall into our hands." Either outcome "would have a decisive effect and influence on the public interests."

Washington sought Schuyler's blessing for several reasons. The Northern Department commander was busily assembling troops and supplies at Ticonderoga, but when his expedition would proceed north into the Richelieu River Valley was not yet clear. Both armies had to operate in concert for the two-pronged invasion to succeed. Washington also requested the latest intelligence regarding enemy soldiers and warships present at Quebec City. He did not want the detached column, possibly worn down by a wilderness march, to arrive before Quebec in the face of substantial resistance. Finally, the commander evidenced concern about sending a force through a virtually unknown wilderness so late in the summer season. If operations did not commence quickly, the column could be devastated by frigid autumn weather. Stressing that "not a moment's time is to be lost in the preparation for this enterprise," Washington asked Schuyler to respond immediately.[9]

While Washington waited, he became more convinced of the strategic value of launching the detached column. The lingering question was who should take command. Arnold was the logical choice, despite those who had denigrated his performance on Lake Champlain. Washington admired Arnold's intensity of purpose and indomitable spirit, but other factors abetted his selection. Congress had adjourned for the month of August, and some New England delegates were then visiting the commander in chief in Cambridge. Among them was Silas Deane, who stated how "hardly" Massachusetts had "treated" Arnold and about Schuyler's request to make him his adjutant general. Acting the part of a patron, Deane encouraged Washington to "take . . . advantage of those abilities and activities of which I am sure he is possessed."[10]

Arnold himself further impressed Washington by submitting a written operational plan. Perhaps as important, the commander was unenthusiastic about other New England officers in camp. On the very day he wrote Schuyler, he described them as "the most indifferent kind of people I ever saw." Arnold was anything but indifferent. He had tried to serve the cause well on Lake Champlain; he was very knowledgeable about Quebec Province;

and he was eager for an opportunity to prove his worth. Even before Washington received Schuyler's reply, he informally let Arnold know that he was to lead the diversionary force.[11]

III

The fascination of Washington and Arnold with the Province of Quebec had many dimensions. In each of the colonial wars dating back to 1689, English and colonial leaders had proposed, attempted, or actually mounted expeditions to conquer this bastion of the French empire in North America. When Quebec City and Montreal fell in 1759 and 1760 respectively, all Anglo-American subjects rejoiced. The armies of General James Wolfe and Sir Jeffrey Amherst had scraped what they considered to be a butchering, inveterate enemy off their backs.

The transition to British rule did not mean an end to French cultural influences in Canada. The population was overwhelmingly Roman Catholic, a religious faith that Protestants in the thirteen seaboard provinces perceived as inspired by the devil. French Canadians seemed to care little about representative institutions of government, and their economic and social systems mirrored Europe's highly stratified, class-based relationships. Of the roughly sixty thousand French-speaking Canadian subjects in 1775, the vast majority were *habitants* who worked the soil and paid rents to members of the *seigneural* class. The *seigneurs* controlled vast amounts of acreage along the St. Lawrence, Richelieu, and Chaudière rivers. The urban communities of Quebec, Montreal and Three Rivers (Trois Rivières) contained merchants, skilled artisans, and struggling day laborers. In all locales were Catholic clergy, who strove to keep the French-speaking populace loyal to the Church of Rome.

Making political affairs particularly virulent after 1763 was a vociferous band of English settlers, who began moving to Canada in the 1760s and whose numbers had reached two thousand by 1775. The most visible of these "old subjects," a term used to separate them from the "new" French-speaking subjects, were merchants such as Thomas Walker and James Price in Montreal and John Dyer Mercier in Quebec. Arnold had traded with these gentlemen before 1775. Such old subjects had regularly supplied intelligence regarding Carleton's efforts to defend the province, and they actively supported overtures to have Quebec Province represented in the Continental Congress as the fourteenth province in rebellion.[12]

The old subjects felt betrayed by Carleton and his handiwork, the Quebec Act of June 1774. They had expected to dominate Canadian politics under

British rule. Carleton, by contrast, viewed them as noisome, self-serving colonists no more deserving of a large voice in government than the aristocratic *seigneurs*. King and Parliament sustained the governor. The Quebec Act failed to provide for a popularly elected provincial assembly. Only a royally appointed council would exist to advise the governor. Further, this legislation confirmed Roman Catholicism as a state-sanctioned religion in Quebec Province. Carleton had advocated these provisions to wed the most powerful French Canadians—specifically the *seigneurs* and the priests—to British authority.[13]

For the old subjects, the Quebec Act smacked of tyranny, which was also the perception of colonists south of Canada. As if more than one domino had suddenly fallen, they beheld images of the rampant spread of Roman Catholicism and the potential loss of their elective assemblies. The act also angered ever-expansive colonists by designating the Ohio River as the southwestern boundary of Quebec Province. Through various land companies, provincial gentlemen-speculators had lobbied in England for years to gain patents to the Ohio country, a region set aside after the Seven Years' War as a permanent Indian preserve. Now the expectation of someday acquiring this much-coveted territory seemed to be lost forever.

From a political point of view, winning over Canada as an ally represented an opportunity to build an even more powerful rebel phalanx against the home government. In this light, delegates to the First Continental Congress drafted a lengthy "Letter to the Inhabitants of the Province of Quebec" and sent two thousand copies to old-subject merchant Thomas Walker in Montreal. This document implored Canadians to secure "your interest and happiness" by joining with "your unalterable friends" from below in defeating the manifest despotism of "your inveterate enemies" in Britain.[14]

Walker and other old subjects circulated the letter far and wide, but Carleton shrewdly counterattacked. He obtained a copy of Congress's "Address to the People of Great Britain," written at virtually the same time. This document had incautiously denounced Roman Catholicism as "a religion" that had "dispersed impiety, bigotry, persecution, murder, and rebellion through every part of the world." Carleton had these words posted throughout the province, thereby undercutting congressional claims about common goals by revealing the contempt that patriot American colonists had for the Catholic Church. Except among old subjects, Congress's plea for united resistance gained little support.[15]

Still, one major factor, Carleton's shortage of troops, favored the American rebels. After the fall of the Champlain forts, the *habitants,* when ordered to arms, eschewed the governor's standard. Preferring neutrality, they wanted to plant their crops and provide for their families, not engage in war. To counter such widespread indifference, the Bishop of Quebec, Jean Olivier Briand, issued an ecclesiastical mandate in late May 1775, reminding all Canadian Catholics of their filial obligation to defend their church, king, and country. Failure to do so, by implication, would mean denial of access to the sacraments and to burial sites in sacred church grounds. Hundreds of *habitants,* at least around Montreal, now came forward, but most did so sullenly. By early summer, Carleton realized that the defense of Quebec Province would be borne by the fewer than six hundred "fit for duty" regulars of the 7th and 26th regiments. He could expect only a smattering of additional support from local Indians and those few *seigneurs* who were able to hold, at least for the moment, the allegiance of *habitants* too intimidated to stay away from militia musters.[16]

Winning the allegiance of the mass of French Canadians was certainly an objective of the Second Continental Congress. On Monday, May 29, two days before the delegates voted to keep the Champlain forts, they issued yet another address to Canada's "oppressed inhabitants." Congress now proclaimed "the fate of the Protestant and Catholic colonies to be strongly linked together." The real issue was not religious bigotry, rather "rejecting, with disdain, the fetters of slavery." Once again the delegates implored everyone in Quebec Province to become part of a resistance movement "in the defense of our common liberty" against "a licentious ministry" determined "to riot in the ruins of the rights of mankind."[17]

Patriot leaders had not suddenly forsaken their anti-Catholic prejudices; rather, they had gained a heightened awareness of the strategic importance of Quebec Province in making war against the parent nation. Arnold had emphasized this point in his June letter to Congress calling for an invasion. The most effective position of initial defense, he had argued, was at Quebec City, a natural fortress, rather than at the Champlain forts, which were then in total disrepair. Indeed, gaining an indisputable military advantage as much as a broadened political alliance helped inspire Congress's directive of Tuesday, June 27, to Schuyler. "If . . . practicable, and . . . not . . . disagreeable to the Canadians," he was to "immediately take possession of St. Johns, Montreal, and any other parts of the country, . . . which may have a tendency to promote the peace and security of these colonies."[18]

Congressional reconciliationists winced at this resolution, but they could not deny the logic of commentators like Arnold. Quebec Province represented a vital barrier to invasion, should imperial leaders commit massive resources to put down the rebellion. If that happened, the patriots could expect a large, well-trained force of regulars to sail for Canada and sweep up the St. Lawrence River from Quebec City to the Richelieu River Valley. Then that army could move south across Lake Champlain and down through the Hudson River Valley all the way to New York City. The consequence of British forces gaining control of the Hudson-Champlain water corridor was potential disaster for the rebels because New England, the center of the rebellion, would be cut off from the rest of the provinces—and exposed to being conquered in a series of carefully orchestrated military advances.

Washington, Arnold, and others did not see how massive reinforcements could reach Carleton before winter set in. They wanted to take advantage of these favorable circumstances; and if the expanded league of fourteen colonies failed to settle differences with the imperial government, rebel troops would at least be in position to square off against Britain's redcoats at Quebec City, rather than deep in the interior of New York Province at the much less defensible Champlain forts.

IV

Striking differences separated George Washington and Benedict Arnold. One was quite tall for his times; the other was of average height. One was diffident in personality; the other was highly animated. One was Virginia gentry, appearing to represent deep-rooted social and political standing; the other was of more plebeian origins, somehow connoting the grasping monetary acquisitiveness of the New England Yankee trader.

Such caricatures, however, can be misleading. Washington's ancestry did not run as deep in American soil as did Arnold's; no colonial governor graced his family tree; and he was certainly not a favored eldest surviving son. In comparison to Arnold's support from the Lathrops, Washington had enjoyed access to far more locally influential patrons, particularly his older half brother Lawrence and the land-rich Fairfax clan of Virginia's Northern Neck. Unlike Arnold, he had also married a wealthy woman, Martha Dandridge, the widow of planter Daniel Parke Custis; and by the 1760s Washington had emerged as one of the great planters of Virginia.

Like Arnold, the ambitious Washington had clawed and groveled to make his way up in the world. Unlike Arnold, who was nearly nine years his junior, he had figured prominently in the Seven Years' War. Young Washington performed respectable service while holding a Virginia colonel's commission, but he loathed the condescension of British military officers. When he tried to secure a regular officer's commission, he found that he was not qualified, being a mere provincial. He had known the burning anger of a talented person being held back by lesser individuals whose only real calling was to perpetuate mediocrities like themselves in power.

Thus, when informed by Silas Deane of the high-handed treatment meted out to Arnold by the Massachusetts Provincial Congress, Washington could sympathize. When Deane and others spoke of Arnold's many talents and thwarted attempt at virtuous service, the commander responded favorably. One of Washington's noteworthy traits was his capacity to identify and effectively utilize patriots of extraordinary abilities. In Arnold he had found a resolute person with the capacity to lead the proposed expeditionary force through a rugged wilderness—and perhaps even to a glorious victory at Quebec City.[19]

Expecting a favorable response from General Schuyler, Washington advised Arnold to contact Reuben Colburn, a shipbuilder who had just appeared in Cambridge from Gardinerston (then called Pittston), Maine, on the Kennebec River in company with a few St. Francis Indians. These natives lived in the vicinity of Quebec City and had used the Chaudière-Kennebec trail to reach Colburn's shipyard. Since Arnold was still at Watertown, he penned a note to Colburn on Monday, August 21, inquiring whether two hundred bateaux could "be procured, or built" at his shipyard in the next few weeks. Each bateau needed to be "furnished with four oars, two paddles, and two setting poles" and had to be capable of "carrying six or seven men each with their provisions and baggage (say 100 [pounds] weight to each man)." Arnold likewise asked about provisions, particularly "fresh beef," and requested "particular information" about the wilderness route. With Washington's blessing, Colburn rushed back to Gardinerston to gather up food supplies and put his crews to work in constructing the required quota of bateaux. Logistically, at least, Arnold's expedition was beginning to take shape.[20]

Meanwhile, Arnold's close friend and Champlain associate Eleazer Oswald hurried across Massachusetts with Washington's letter for Schuyler. He found the general in Albany parleying with representatives of the Six Nations—and seeking their neutrality in the spreading "family quarrel" with Britain. Schuyler was also on the verge of sending his growing Champlain force into Canada. News of a diversionary expedition delighted him, and he chided Washington by stating how "happy" he was "to learn your intentions, and only wished that the thought had struck you sooner." Also pleased with the projected choice of Arnold as commander, Schuyler voiced only one concern. He advised Washington "to be particular in your orders to the officer that may command the detachment that there may be no clashing should we join." No matter how highly Schuyler regarded Arnold, he wanted no repetition of the earlier controversy over command rights on Lake Champlain.[21]

Oswald got back to Cambridge late on the afternoon of Saturday, September 2. Washington and Arnold now began working feverishly to get the expedition launched. Before the day was over the commander sent instructions to Nathaniel Tracy, a well-to-do Newburyport, Massachusetts, merchant, asking him to gather enough vessels to transport "a body of troops" on "a secret expedition." Tracy's task was to move Arnold's force from Newburyport to Gardinerston, Maine. The next morning Washington dispatched an express message to Reuben Colburn, formally ordering the construction of two hundred bateaux at the rate of forty shillings per craft; and in addition to gathering food supplies, Colburn was to hire up to twenty men, some to serve as guides and others as carpenters who could repair the bateaux in their transit through the wilderness.[22]

In the midst of attending to logistical needs, Washington offered Arnold a colonel's commission in the Continental army. In so doing, he spoke of Schuyler's concern about accepting the absolute authority of superior officers. Confused, overlapping, and self-serving lines of provincial jurisdiction, Arnold stated in reply, had caused most of the turmoil on Lake Champlain. Besides, circumstances had changed dramatically with the introduction of a clearly defined Continental command structure. Washington accepted this response and informed Schuyler that Arnold would "have no difficulty in adjusting the scale of command," should "a junction of the detachment with your army" take place.[23]

Arnold had learned a valuable lesson about the damaging personal consequences of disputing command rights. At the same time, he greatly appreciated the second chance Washington and Schuyler had given him, and he felt a keen sense of obligation to these two patrons. Indeed, Arnold's dogged determination during the next few months in refusing to break under the weight of so many crushing obstacles reflected something more than his desire to enhance his own name and reputation. He was thanking Washington and Schuyler for the trust they had shown in championing his case. He was also demonstrating to patriot leaders in Massachusetts and Connecticut how wrongheaded they had been in elevating such ineffectual favorites as Benjamin Hinman and James Easton over him.

On Tuesday, September 5, Washington called for "volunteers" from among patriot soldiers in camp "to go upon command with Colonel Arnold of Connecticut." Interested participants were to assemble the next morning "upon the common in Cambridge," where, if chosen, they would receive further instructions, or at least as much information as could be shared with them without conveying the scope of the operation. Secrecy was essential so that General Gage did not concoct some means to disrupt the expedition or, just as bad, forewarn Governor Carleton of the column's existence.

The next morning Arnold found himself inundated with volunteers, most likely because detached duty represented a sure way to escape the boredom, filth, and disease of daily life in camp. Washington's general orders stated only two requirements. Those who came forward were to be "active woodsmen, and well acquainted with bateaux." Arnold had a third requirement: No Green Mountain Boys! He wanted soldiers committed more to fighting for the cause of liberty than for personal plunder.[24]

During the next two days Arnold and Washington's adjutant general, Horatio Gates, selected 786 officers and privates and divided them into two regiments of five musket companies each. Lieutenant Colonel Roger Enos, a veteran of the Seven Years' War from Connecticut, assumed command of the first battalion, to be assisted by Major Return Jonathan Meigs, also from Connecticut. Lieutenant Colonel Christopher Greene, who was from a prominent Rhode Island family (he was also a cousin of General Nathanael Greene), took charge of the second battalion, with Timothy Bigelow of Massachusetts serving as major. Of the ten captains, Henry Dearborn of New Hampshire would become the most prominent. He served as Secretary of War during Thomas Jefferson's presidential administration before suffering through a disastrous tour as a field commander during the War of 1812.[25]

About three hundred others also joined Arnold's detachment. Most were frontiersmen from Virginia and Pennsylvania. Known as excellent marksmen, they carried long rifles, much more accurate weapons at long range than smoothbore muskets but more difficult to reload, thereby reducing any tactical superiority in pitched, set-piece battles. The woodsmen also had tomahawks and scalping knives strapped to their belts; and to set them even further apart from musketmen, their standard dress consisted of fringed hunting shirts, Indian leggings, moccasins, and broad-brimmed hats. Captain Daniel Morgan, a tall, physically imposing man and as talented as any officer who served in the Continental army, had just marched his company from frontier Virginia to Cambridge, a distance of six hundred miles, in three weeks. The two Pennsylvania companies and their captains, handsome William Hendricks and loutish, heavy-drinking Matthew Smith, had trekked some 450 miles in twenty-six days to reach Cambridge.

Representing the kind of experienced woodsmen Arnold needed, these Pennsylvania and Virginia riflemen would have little trouble moving through the Maine wilderness. Unlike Arnold's volunteers, they received orders from

Washington to join the column, not only because of their special skills but because of their obstreperous behavior in camp. They resented military discipline and reveled in provoking brawls with New England soldiers. Washington seemed relieved to have an excuse to get them out of camp. Daniel Morgan, who was sparing of words but fully capable of asserting his authority with the back of his fists, assumed command of the three rifle companies.[26]

Finally, a smattering of volunteers joined the detachment, including four St. Francis Indians to serve as guides. Eleazer Oswald, for whom Arnold could not get an officer's commission, agreed to travel along as his friend's personal secretary. Dr. Isaac Senter of New Hampshire signed on as surgeon, and the Reverend Samuel Spring, a graduate of the College of New Jersey (Princeton), accepted the position of chaplain. Two hardy women, Jemima Warner and a Mrs. Grier, married to Private James Warner and Sergeant Joseph Grier, respectively, of the Pennsylvania rifle companies, refused to stay behind. Two young Jerseyites, Aaron Burr and Matthias Ogden, both in search of military adventure and carrying a glowing letter of introduction from John Hancock, president of the Continental Congress, stepped forth as well. Burr went on to great notoriety as Alexander Hamilton's political rival and Jefferson's vice president before he reputedly spearheaded an elaborate, clumsy plot to establish a grand western empire separate from the United States.[27]

Once supplied with new coats, linen frocks, and blankets, as well as firearms and tents, Arnold's column, numbering something over 1,050 troops, received orders to march some forty miles northeast to Newburyport. Between September 11 and 13, all of the companies began this first leg of what became a legendary journey, but not before a momentary tempest over wages. Some of the troops refused to leave Cambridge until they received a month's advance wages. Washington and Arnold grumbled about insubordinate behavior, but the commander granted the pay, thereby averting any significant delay.[28]

Incredibly, less than a month had lapsed in organizing and launching the expedition. Except for the brief confrontation over wages, virtually everything had proceeded with a minimum of difficulty. Yet on Friday morning, September 15, when Arnold exchanged pleasantries with Washington before leaving for Newburyport, he was conscious of how much could go wrong in the wake of such hurried planning and with warm summer weather rapidly passing. Had he known what travails lay ahead, even the doggedly tenacious Benedict Arnold might well have turned back.[29]

V

Arnold rode hard and fast that day. He stopped at Salem to procure 270 blankets and two hundred pounds of ginger, yet still reached Nathaniel Tracy's lavish brick residence late that evening. Most of his troops had already bivouacked at Newburyport, and they were eager to make sail. Arnold learned from Tracy that eleven sloops and schooners, a collection of "dirty coasters and fish boats," according to one soldier, stood ready for the expedition. Unfortunately, strong head winds were blowing in off the Atlantic Ocean, trapping the assembled flotilla in the harbor. All Arnold could do was wait—and hope this inopportune delay did not cost the expedition some critical advantage in the days ahead.[30]

Tempering his impatience, Arnold carefully scrutinized the detailed orders and instructions provided him by Washington. The commander in chief underscored the pivotal significance of the "present enterprise," which was "of the utmost consequence to the interest and liberties of America." Nothing less than "the safety and welfare of the whole Continent" were at stake, and "success" depended on treating Canadians and Indians as "our friends and brethren," not as "enemies." Any soldier who attempted "to plunder or insult any of the inhabitants of Canada" was to receive "severe and exemplary punishment." Washington issued an admonition "to avoid all disrespect or contempt of the religion of the country and its ceremonies." "While we are contending for our own liberty," he stressed, "we should be very cautious of violating the rights of conscience in others; ever considering that God alone is the judge of the hearts of men and to him only in this case they are answerable." Washington also reminded Arnold of his obligation "to put yourself under" General Schuyler, should the two armies come together for joint operations. He likewise warned against needlessly risking the lives of so many patriot soldiers, "if unforseen difficulties should arise or if the weather should become so severe as to render it hazardous to proceed" deeper into the wilderness. If Arnold, after consulting his senior officers, decided to turn back, the commander asked to receive "as early notice as possible [so] that I may give you such assistance as may be necessary." Finally, Arnold was to circulate copies of a new "Address" that urged the "generous citizens" of Quebec Province to embrace "the standard of general liberty—against which all the force and artifice of tyranny will never be able to prevail."[31]

During the weekend, Arnold rode among his troops and spoke confidently of the military glory that awaited them in Canada. On Sunday morning he led the detachment to the First Presbyterian Church as patriotic townsfolk lined the streets and cheered enthusiastically. The assemblage then

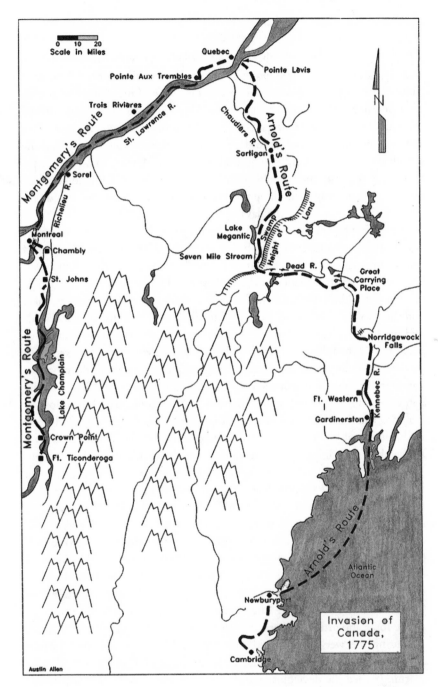

listened to the Reverend Spring sermonize on the topic, "If thy spirit go not with us, carry us not up hence." After the service, Arnold and his officers descended into the crypt below the sanctuary where lay the remains of George Whitefield, the charismatic English evangelist whose travels in the colonies had ignited the Great Awakening. Removing the lid from the coffin, they gazed prayerfully inside before touching "the hallowed corpse . . . with great solemnity." Then they removed a small portion of clothing, which they cut into pieces for each officer to carry as "a precious relic" in seeking the blessings of a benevolent Providence for the expedition.[32]

Arnold believed that his column, called together as it was in the name of human liberty, would be the object of divine favor. Still, he left nothing to chance. While enjoying the hospitality of Nathaniel Tracy, he spoke with his host about having small scouting craft row out beyond the harbor to see if British warships were lurking over the horizon, just waiting to pounce on the fleet. One crew reported back on Monday with assurances that the water route to Maine was free of enemy vessels, which Arnold interpreted as evidence of providential assistance. Had British warships been present, his orders were to lead his troops on a long, slow overland march of some 150 miles to Gardinerston. Water transit guaranteed a much faster trip, and his detachment would enter the wilderness in a freshened rather than exhausted physical state.[33]

Since the soldiers were getting restless, Arnold began loading them on the vessels late Monday afternoon. The next morning, September 19, favorable winds had returned, and the flotilla finally raised anchor. An approving patriot crowd on shore shouted huzzahs as the vessels floated out of the harbor with "drums beating, fifes playing, and colors flying." Arnold was aboard the schooner *Broad Bay*, the fleet's flagship. By noon the fleet was taking on full sail. The ocean water was choppy, and the vessels swayed to and fro as they creaked steadily forward through gusts of rain and a spreading shroud of fog. Many of the soldiers, not used to sailing, became seasick. One wrote, "Had I been thrown into the sea, I should hardly have made an effort to have saved myself." By midnight the vessels were nearing the tangled island entrance to the Kennebec River, having covered about one hundred miles in less than twelve hours. A land march over the same distance would have consumed four or five days.[34]

The weather did not improve overnight, but early the next morning Arnold ordered the vessels to begin picking their way through the offshore islands. A few got lost temporarily when they took the wrong channel, and others ran aground in mud. On the evening of September 20, most dropped anchor in the vicinity of Georgetown, having covered little more than ten miles. Another wasted day put Arnold in a glum mood, but the unexpected appearance of a local patriot, Samuel McCobb, and twenty recruits, all anxious to join the expedition, cheered him. Arnold gladly accepted them. After thirty miles of sailing upriver the next day, the *Broad Bay* reached Colburn's shipyard. By the evening of Friday, September 22, all eleven vessels had arrived at Gardinerston in what Arnold described as "very troublesome" passage.[35]

A nasty problem in logistical preparations now presented itself. The carpenters at Colburn's shipyard, laboring day and night, had produced two hundred bateaux. In meeting the expedition's short deadline, however, they had slapped these flat-bottomed craft together with hastily cut green pine. Arnold doubted they would last long. Fortunately, Colburn and his carpenters had contracted to travel along with the detachment; they would have plenty to do in keeping the bateaux afloat. Arnold also found that, besides being "very badly built," many of the craft were "smaller than the directions given." To compensate, he insisted that twenty additional bateaux be constructed, with guaranteed completion in three days. An apologetic Colburn promised to do his best.[36]

Arnold also focused his attention on intelligence accounts. He pored over the report of two Maine woodsmen, Dennis Getchell and Samuel Berry, who had gone out to scout the wilderness route in early September. Their narrative contained a warning about an Indian, Natanis, who lived near the Dead River and was a reputed "spy" hired by Carleton "to watch the motions of an army . . . daily expected from New England." Getchell and Berry also mentioned "a great number of Mohawks" in the vicinity of Sartigan, the southernmost of the French settlements on the Chaudière River. Fearful the Mohawks "would have destroyed us if we had proceeded," the woodsmen had turned back, having also learned that only seven British regulars were on duty in the Chaudière River Valley. As for the trail itself, the portages around the numerous rapids on the Kennebec and Dead rivers were "pretty passable," since the water level was quite "shoal, on account of the late dry season."[37]

These observations suggested a relatively quick, safe passage to the Canadian border, which eased Arnold's concerns about the feebly built bateaux. He was more skeptical of the warning about warlike Indians near Sartigan. If anything, he reasoned, the Native Americans had gathered in that area to hunt for winter food. Mohawks and "noted villain" Natanis aside, Arnold knew that Carleton had so far failed to gain promises of martial support from potential Indian allies.[38]

Another intelligence source was Samuel Goodwin, who claimed an intimate familiarity with the wilderness route. At Colburn's request, this back-woodsman and surveyor had sketched a more detailed version of John Montresor's crude map. (Arnold carried a copy of Montresor's journal with him.) Goodwin was a key source of "information," but he had little sense of distance. With about forty-five days' worth of provisions for each soldier, Arnold felt he had ample food on hand to sustain his force during the estimated journey of 180 miles to Quebec City (the passage was closer to 350 miles). The march, he calculated, could be accomplished in twenty days. It was to take more than twice that long, with soldiers facing starvation by the time they reached the Chaudière River Valley.[39]

By early Saturday morning, September 23, Arnold was at Fort Western (in modern-day Augusta), about ten miles north of Colburn's shipyard. An active military post during the Seven Years' War, the fort was now little more than a ramshackle frontier trading post atop a bluff on the eastern bank of the Kennebec River. Fort Western served as the final rendezvous and jumping-off point for the wilderness journey.

That day, Arnold officially launched the expedition by sending out two scouting parties. Lieutenant Archibald Steele of Smith's Pennsylvanians led the first group. They were to push hard for Lake Megantic, the source water of the Chaudière River, "to reconnoiter and get all the intelligence" they "possibly could from the Indians." If they ran across Natanis, they were to shoot him if they could not capture him. The second scouting party, headed by a Lieutenant Church, had a more prosaic assignment. They were to measure the "exact courses and distance to the Dead River" so the main column would know how far to travel each day in adhering to the projected twenty-day schedule.[40]

Once the scouting parties were underway, Arnold arranged the companies into four divisions, the idea being to space the troops out so that they would not become entangled at the many portage points ahead. The riflemen, with Daniel Morgan in command, were the first to embark. They headed up the Kennebec on Monday, September 25. They were to move as swiftly as possible and "clear the roads over the carrying places." Arnold had intended to have Lieutenant Colonel Christopher Greene and two New England musket companies travel with the riflemen. Morgan wanted nothing to do with this arrangement, since he would have to report to Greene, and he angrily confronted Arnold. Musketmen would only slow down the riflemen, he bellowed. Further, Washington had assured him that the rifle companies would be subject only to Arnold's orders. Rather than dispute Morgan's word—he was not exactly telling the truth—and perhaps face a mutiny by the riflemen on the verge of entering the wilderness, Arnold judiciously conceded. Greene and three companies of musketmen put their bateaux into the water and moved out on September 26.[41]

The next day at noon the third division under Major Return J. Meigs, consisting of four musket companies, began paddling up the Kennebec. Only three companies, as well as Colburn's carpenters, now remained behind. Arnold had already formed them into a rear-guard division under Lieutenant Colonel Roger Enos. Their duties included rounding up stragglers and carrying reserves of food for the forward companies. The extra weight of crucial provisions would not be greatly burdensome, Arnold believed, because Enos's troops would be passing over portages and trails already hacked out of the wilderness by the first three divisions.[42]

Arnold may have given the rear-guard assignment to Enos because, at the age of forty-six, he was the oldest officer present—and perhaps the least fit to endure a long wilderness march. This veteran had a solid record of service during the Seven Years' War, making him one of Arnold's most experienced subordinates. Enos's military experience, more than his age, was likely the prevailing factor in his selection as rear division commander. Whatever the reason, Arnold had made a regrettable choice.[43]

Enos's troops began to embark from Fort Western on Friday, September 29. Arnold, meanwhile, kept addressing various problems, including the disposition of a young soldier, James McCormick, who had laced himself with alcohol on the evening of September 23, gotten into an argument, and shot one of his comrades dead. A court-martial board ordered McCormick to be hanged. When he approached the gallows, he broke down and begged for clemency. Describing McCormick as "very simple and ignorant" and normally a "peaceable fellow," Arnold took pity on him as "a proper object of mercy." He called off the hanging and made arrangements to have him returned to Cambridge. McCormick later died in the camp prison while waiting for a new trial.[44]

Impatient to move up the Kennebec himself, Arnold set out from Fort Western at noon on September 29. He traveled with Eleazer Oswald and with two or three Indians who served as guides as well as paddlers for his birch-bark canoe. His goal was to regain the head of the column within four or five days; but after a few miles the canoe sprang a leak. The colonel and his party put in at the settlement of Vassalborough, eight miles north of Fort Western, where they obtained a dugout canoe. Soon they were again plunging forward against the current of the Kennebec. Early the next morning they passed Fort Halifax, another decaying military edifice, where the Sebasticook enters the Kennebec. It was from Fort Halifax that Montresor's journal described the passage to Canada via the Kennebec and Dead Rivers.

Montresor had taken only twelve days to travel from the southern end of the Chaudière River to Fort Halifax. Assuming another eight days to reach Quebec City, Arnold had visions of seizing the lightly defended provincial capital before the end of October. If only the weather would hold warm and dry, a stunning rebel triumph was in the offing—and for Arnold, so recently spurned by the patriot cause, great accolades.[45]

VI

During the next three days, Arnold and his small party darted rapidly ahead. "To Quebec and victory," the commander shouted enthusiastically each time he passed through a company of musketmen, often at portaging points where his troops struggled to move their bateaux and supplies around impassable points on the river. At Five Mile Ripples, Arnold contracted with a settler to carry his canoe and equipment around these rapids, which he described as "very dangerous and difficult to pass." Soon he approached Skowhegan Falls, representing a sharp rise of nearly one hundred feet. Again, local settlers provided assistance in negotiating the carrying place. Before the day was out, Arnold proceeded another five miles upriver before lodging at the home of the Widow Warren (near present-day Norridgewock).[46]

By ten o'clock on Monday morning, October 2, Arnold had reached Norridgewock Falls, where the Kennebec rose before him by at least ninety feet over a series of cascading rapids a mile in length. Now at the outer edge of Maine's frontier settlements, he had caught up with Morgan and the riflemen. Having traversed some fifty miles in three days, Arnold should have been exhilarated. His mood, however, was anything but cheery. The expedition was facing serious problems, and he would spend the next week at Norridgewock Falls trying to solve them.

As Arnold had passed through the divisions, he had observed how quickly the bateaux were disintegrating. Well before Skowhegan Falls "our bateaux began to leak profusely," reported Dr. Senter. A swift current, shallow water, and "rocks plenty," he continued, "soon ground out many of the bottoms." The bateaux were so "villainously constructed," declared an irritated Captain Simeon Thayer, that everyone was "always wet," having "to wade half the time." Arnold probably made the best statement. "When you consider the badness and weight of the bateaux and large quantity of provisions, etc., we have been obliged to force up against a very rapid stream," he wrote to Washington, "you would have taken the men for amphibious animals, as they were [a] great part of the time under water."[47]

Other difficulties were manifest as well. Water in the bateaux had ruined a portion of the food supply, including packages of bread and peas. Much of the salted beef had become rancid. Daily rations, henceforth mostly pork and flour supplemented by fish and animal game, would now require careful monitoring. Evening temperatures had started to dip below the freezing mark, causing much discomfort for "amphibious" soldiers who were constantly wet. Captain Thayer's company awoke the morning after they portaged around Skowhegan Falls with their "clothes . . . frozen a pane of glass thick, which proved very disagreeable." Colds, fevers, and even dysentery were stalking the column by the time everyone reached Norridgewock Falls. Within a few days Arnold reported only 950 effectives, with more than 100 troops in poor health.[48]

Arnold buoyed his fatigued column by maintaining a bold command presence. Though concerned about leaky bateaux, food supplies, and worsening weather, he exuded confidence as he walked among his troops. He exhorted them to keep themselves and their equipment as dry as possible and put them to work repairing and caulking their bateaux, a task made easier after Colburn's carpenters arrived at the falls. And he urged everyone forward, around Norridgewock Falls, up the Kennebec, and into the mountains, even as he mistakenly told them how they had already traversed nearly one-third of the distance to Quebec City.

Morgan's riflemen moved out on Tuesday, October 3, with orders to locate the Great Carrying Place, a crucial portaging point. Using this route would allow the expedition to bypass a long, turbulent course of additional water travel up the Kennebec to its west branch, the Dead River, which descended through a series of impassable rapids before emptying into the Kennebec. By comparison, the Great Carrying Place represented a route of about twelve miles that cut overland across three small ponds from the Kennebec to the Dead River. The riflemen were to wield their axes and begin clearing a pathway for the musketmen who followed.

With the assistance of local settlers, the bulk of the column pushed beyond Norridgewock Falls by Sunday, October 8, a day of torrential rains. The soldiers thus passed into the wilderness. They would now have to fend for themselves until they reached the French *habitants* on the Chaudière. Arnold was off and running again on October 9. He marveled at the scenery, including land "in general fertile and tolerably well wooded." Once he had portaged around Carritunk Falls, he described how "mountains begin to appear on each side [of] the river, high and snow on the tops."[49]

Early on October 11, Arnold reached the Great Carrying Place. He learned that Morgan's and Greene's companies had already pushed through to the second pond. At the first pond, the soldiers were gorging themselves on "a prodigious number of fine salmon trout"; some had even dined on moose meat before leaving behind the Kennebec River. Abundant fish and wild game would compensate for shrunken food supplies—another providential sign, Arnold thought. Lieutenant Church also gave him positive news. Having surveyed the length of the Carrying Place, he described the trail to the Dead River as a "bad road but capable of being made good." [50]

Church, as Arnold soon learned, had not taken into account the inordinate rainfall of the past few days. When the musketmen started portaging their bateaux, they found themselves trudging through a spongy quagmire of muck. Private George Morison spoke of "stumbling over old fallen logs, one leg sinking deeper in the mire than the other, then down goes a boat and the carriers with it; a hearty laugh prevails." The trail between the second and third ponds was terrible, not only muddy but "choked up with roots," noted Arnold. As the troops sank into the ground, the roots tore apart their shoes and bloodied their feet. The rebel commander thought the final portage from the third pond to Bog Brook, which twisted and turned for about a mile to the Dead River, was the worst stretch. Already exhausted by their travails, the soldiers now "had a most fatiguing time in getting . . . their bateaux, baggage, etc." up and down a steep hill and across a muddy savanna. [51]

Morale held up, even as Arnold's forceful voice urged the detachment forward. Still, the Great Carrying Place exacted a toll. Strong winds and blinding flurries of snow had followed the heavy rains, which delayed the advance divisions in moving across the ponds. Winds toppled down trees and heavy limbs; and one soldier was crushed to death, the expedition's first casualty. (Arnold expressed amazement that no one had drowned in the Kennebec.)

Several soldiers became incapacitated. Some drank their fill of brackish water from the second pond after consuming heavily salted rations, and they doubled over with stomach cramps. "No sooner had it got down," wrote Dr. Senter, "than it was puked up by many of the poor fellows." Other troops began experiencing "a sad plight with the diarrhea." To provide for the disabled, Arnold ordered the construction of a log hut at the second pond, which the troops called "Arnold's Hospital." This rude structure was "no sooner finished than filled," wrote Dr. Senter. One of the worst cases was a young rifleman from Pennsylvania, who Senter said had the "most violent rheumatism I ever saw," with "every joint in his extremities inflexible and swelled to an enormous size." [52]

Spreading illness forced Arnold to ponder the unthinkable—turning back. To activate that contingency plan, he had a log hut built at the first pond to serve as a depot for reserve provisions. Then he ordered up one hundred barrels of food from Fort Halifax, "that our retreat may be secured in case of any accident." That Arnold would bring up reserves of food, in case of retreat, and provide shelter for those racked by illness conveyed a positive message to his soldiers. He cared about their welfare, and their feelings of respect for his leadership helped keep the column moving toward Canada—at least for the moment.[53]

Each division averaged about a week to get bateaux, supplies, and troops across the Great Carrying Place. For the superstitious among the soldiery, Friday, October 13, was an auspicious day because Morgan's and Greene's divisions finally reached the Dead River. Arnold made it on October 16, and the last companies, those under Enos, left the savanna behind on October 20 in what seemed a herculean triumph over an untamed wilderness and increasingly unfavorable weather. The contest was only beginning.

VII

On that same October 13, Arnold took time to compose a few letters. To General Washington, he wrote with circumspection about problems while admitting to "a very fatiguing time." The detachment still had twenty-five days' worth of rations, he estimated. Based on discussions with Lieutenant Steele, whose scouting party had crossed into Canada and just gotten back to him, he had hopes of reaching the Chaudière River within ten days.[54]

Cut off from information about events in Canada, Arnold next prepared a short summary of his own expedition for General Schuyler. He predicted an appearance before Quebec City within two weeks and asked for intelligence of any kind, "as this detachment was intended to cooperate with your army." He enclosed this dispatch in a letter to John Dyer Mercier, a trusted mercantile acquaintance in Quebec who favored the patriot cause. Claiming an army of two thousand (a purposeful overstatement), Arnold told Mercier that his detachment, in conjunction with Schuyler's, intended "to frustrate the unjust and arbitrary measures of the ministry and restore liberty to our brethren in Canada." He wondered how supportive the populace would be, and he asked for specifics about British troops, warships, and the state of defenses at Quebec City.[55]

If his messages to Schuyler and Mercier happened to miscarry, Arnold realized, British officials in Canada would learn of his expedition and have time to mount resistance. Success, however, depended on obtaining accurate intelligence, so Arnold accepted the gamble. He entrusted the missives to the "faithful Indian[s]" Eneas and Sabatis, both of the St. Francis tribe, as well as to Private John Hall, a British deserter who spoke fluent French but who was to go only as far as the French settlements to gain intelligence. The Indian emissaries made good time in getting through to Quebec, but Mercier never saw the letters. They ended up in the hands of a shocked Lieutenant Governor Hector Cramahé, who quickly initiated efforts to defend the capital city.[56]

Another three weeks passed before Arnold discovered the fate of his letters. Meanwhile, his oarsmen paddled hard on Monday, October 16, against the rapid current of the Dead River, which wound back and forth for what seemed endless miles at the base of a majestic mountain (later named Mount Bigelow in honor of Major Timothy Bigelow). That evening Arnold camped with Greene's division. The news was not good. A frustrated Greene apologized for making so little headway. The river was too swollen from all the rain—and the current too swift—to be easily overcome by his paddling and poling troops. They had taken to grabbing at reeds—indeed, anything along the banks—to help them inch forward. Just as bad, the constant seepage of water into their bateaux had spoiled more rations, and his soldiers even lacked flour. Trout were plentiful, but no one could be sure how long the easy fishing would last. Arnold told Greene to hold his position and set his troops to making cartridges. At daylight, he would send back a squad under Major Bigelow to bring forward some of the extra provisions from Enos's division. Arnold also reluctantly ordered everyone onto half rations.[57]

Then disaster struck. On Thursday, October 19, the rains returned, and they continued unabated the next day. This "prodigious fall of rain," an amazed Arnold recorded, "has raised the river upwards of three feet." On October 21, the floodgates opened, this time accompanied by raging winds, as if, of all things, a late-season hurricane had slammed deep into the Maine wilderness. At 4 a.m. on Sunday morning, October 22, Arnold's party, having sought high ground for a campsite, found themselves rudely awakened by water "rushing on us like a torrent." The Dead River had risen another eight feet and was flooding everything in sight. Grabbing as much of their baggage as they could salvage, Arnold and those with him struggled to yet higher ground.[58]

When morning dawned, the storm had finally abated, but in whatever direction the rebel commander looked he saw water. Arnold could not even be sure where the riverbed was, let alone the correct course for Canada. With "our provisions almost exhausted," he glumly confided to his diary, "we have but a melancholy prospect before us." He had expected to be approaching Quebec City by this date. Yet here he was, far from his goal, supplies dwindling, column submerged in water, and virtually lost in the howling Maine wilderness.[59]

CHAPTER Six

Hannibalian Breakthrough to Quebec

I

Isolated as his detachment was in the Maine wilderness, Arnold knew nothing about the activities of Schuyler's Northern Department army. This expeditionary force had gotten off to a wobbly start back in late August. The poorly trained, ill-disciplined patriot troops first experienced a storm-tossed water journey down Lake Champlain to Canada. After bivouacking on low-lying, swampy Isle aux Noix (Island of Nuts) in the Richelieu River, they twice failed to execute probing actions against British defenders at St. Johns. As for Schuyler, he had entered Canada "much indisposed with a bilious fever." In mid-September, a ferocious attack of rheumatic gout forced him to return south a virtual invalid. The general did recover, and he devoted himself to keeping food supplies and military equipment moving toward Canada. Meanwhile, his talented second in command, Brigadier General Richard Montgomery, a former company-grade regular officer in the British army, took charge of Northern Department operations in Quebec Province.[1]

When Arnold's troops began struggling up the Dead River, Montgomery had the fortress at St. Johns locked in an unbreakable vise. The seven hundred British regulars and Canadian defenders inside the fort doggedly withstood the patriot siege for forty-five days before they surrendered in exhaustion on Thursday, November 2. Two weeks earlier the small British garrison force at Chambly, some twelve miles north of St. Johns, had capitulated with virtually no resistance. Consequently, enemy troops no longer stood between Montgomery's rebels and their primary target of Montreal. Governor Carleton had only a handful of regulars to bolster the Montreal populace, but the citizenry there was not in a fighting mood. On

Saturday, November 11, Carleton fled down the St. Lawrence River for Quebec City, the last bastion of British imperial authority in the province. Two days later, Montgomery's cheering soldiers easily secured Montreal for patriot arms.

The pathway to total victory in Canada now led to Quebec City, both for Montgomery and for Arnold. The question remained, however, whether Arnold's detachment could break through the wilderness. As the rebel colonel scanned the flooded landscape on the morning of October 22, he appreciated that his expedition had reached a critical juncture. To go forward with what little food and supplies remained was to risk death from severe weather or starvation. To retreat was to admit failure and, just as bad from Arnold's perspective, likely meant censorship for him from carping civilian patriots, who could never imagine the travails his soldiers had endured. Arnold feared public ridicule, the kind meted out to his drunken, dying father; yet he had to consider the hundreds of human lives placed in his care. The possible loss of so many worthy patriots could also destroy his reputation, regardless of whether he survived a continued attempt to reach Quebec.

Arnold wanted to press forward, but he kept recalling Washington's instructions: if conditions proved too "hazardous to proceed in your own judgment and that of your principal officers (whom you are to consult) — in that case you are to return." Yet on October 22, a day he and his party spent in "drying our baggage, etc., the whole of which was sometime under water (last night) and very wet," he hesitated to bring his officers together, as if he feared a vote for retreat.[2]

The next morning Arnold's party set out again, only to discover that a number of Meigs's troops had mistakenly followed a swollen branch of the Dead River. Two hours were lost in retrieving them. Once back on the river's main course, Arnold traveled in company with several bateaux. In preparing to portage around yet another set of rapids, seven of these craft suddenly overturned in the rapid current. No troops were lost, but all their equipment and food — guns, powder, ball, bread, and pork — went cascading downstream. This accident forced Arnold's hand; he ordered everyone to make camp and called the officers in the vicinity together for a council of war.[3]

They gathered in Arnold's field tent and listened solemnly as their commander explained the alternatives. The expedition had reached a point of no return, Arnold stated. Should the column continue its advance, food shortages could become acute, especially since the storm and flooding had scattered the wild game and ruined the fishing. The troops were exhausted, and sickness was spreading at an alarming rate. Also of concern, Arnold pointed out, was the absence of any intelligence from Canada. For all he knew,

British troops were now gathering south of Quebec City to finish off the emaciated rebel force.

Even with these foreboding prospects, Arnold wanted to forge ahead. He estimated the distance to Lake Megantic at thirty miles. Once there, the detachment would no longer have to fight against swift-running currents and endless rapids. Soldiers who still had functional bateaux—the number was in rapid decline—could glide forward almost placidly on water rushing northward toward the St. Lawrence River. By sending back all infirm troops, and with strict food rationing, he thought the healthy members of the column could reach the southernmost French settlements before the specter of starvation overwhelmed the column. Whatever their view, Arnold encouraged his officers to speak up and promised to abide by their vote.

The officers sat silently. The cause of liberty demanded personal sacrifice, they knew, including the possibility of death. Then, one by one, they spoke their minds before they overwhelmingly endorsed stouthearted action. They would not turn back, unless ordered to do so by Arnold, since the purpose of their mission fully justified the taking of ultimate risks.

The officers agreed to a series of essential actions. In company with Arnold, Captain Oliver Hanchet of Connecticut and fifty handpicked troops were to move out early the next morning and make a dash for the Chaudière River. When they reached Sartigan, they were to secure food and start moving it back toward the advancing main body. Soldiers weakened by disease were to be sent back to the Maine settlements. Before leaving, Arnold would write to Colonels Greene and Enos, telling them to move forward quickly with "as many of the best men . . . as you can furnish with fifteen days' provisions." Those too "sick and feeble" to continue and obvious shirkers were to receive three days' worth of provisions—with the expectation that additional food supplies would be awaiting them at the Great Carrying Place. By thus streamlining his column, Arnold expected to win the race for survival. He was positive such raw courage would soon revel in the reward of a great victory at Quebec City.[4]

II

Early on Tuesday, October 24, Arnold prepared orders for Greene and Enos, then walked among his troops, as Private Morison put it, "to quiet our fears of *wintering* in the wilderness." "Our gallant colonel," Morison recorded admiringly, "after admonishing us to persevere as we hitherto had done, set out with a guide for the inhabitants in order to hasten the return of provisions." The troops appreciated Arnold's encouragement. Their own survival, they realized, depended on getting to the French settlements as quickly as their wearied limbs and battered bateaux could carry them. So they struggled forth again, on up the Dead River toward the Height of Land and the maze of unknown but dreadful swamps through which they would have to pass before reaching Lake Megantic and the Chaudière River.[5]

Arnold had no idea that Greene's and Enos's divisions were then at loggerheads over the dwindling supply of rations. Despite his orders, Enos had refused to release food reserves, except for two paltry barrels of flour, to Greene's famished soldiers. Either Enos's troops, out of fear of what lay ahead, were hoarding these rations for themselves or water leaking into their bateaux had caused extensive spoilage. Possibly, too, they had more than once gorged themselves while the three advance divisions blazed an easy trail for them to follow. Whatever the explanation, Enos's division hardly moved forward after passing over the Great Carrying Place. Dr. Isaac Senter believed the rear division had contracted a new illness—faintheartedness. Enos's officers, he wrote, "had been preaching to their men the doctrine of impenetrability and non-perseverance."[6]

Lacking virtually any food, Greene's soldiers now faced a serious crisis. Dr. Senter reported on October 24, "I found them almost destitute of any eatable whatever, except a few *candles,* which were used for supper, and breakfast the next morning, by boiling them in water gruel." Making the situation worse, six inches of snow fell that night, adding to forebodings of disaster, as did the invalids sent downstream by Arnold. Some of these disease-ravaged souls exhorted Greene's troops to retreat with them to the Maine settlements. Captain Simeon Thayer helped gather up forty-eight additional invalids from Greene's division, and he observed, "The men are much disheartened and eagerly wish to return. However, I am certain if their bellies were full, they would be willing enough to advance."[7]

Despite glum prospects, Greene got his healthy troops moving forward again on October 25. They covered a grueling three miles before making camp. As they were settling in for the night, Enos and his officers came paddling up the river. Stepping ashore, Enos announced his intention to parley with Greene and his officers. He wanted to discuss whether both divisions should admit defeat and turn back. A highly irregular "council of war," one not authorized by the commanding officer, ensued. Of those in attendance, five (those officers with Enos) voted to retreat and five voted to proceed (Greene and his subordinates). For the official record, Enos hid his true sentiments by casting his ballot to continue on, thereby breaking the tie. As if previously rehearsed to protect Enos's reputation, his officers—Dr. Senter called them "a number of grimacers"—demanded to meet with him privately. A few minutes later Enos announced that, while he personally favored advancing, he could not do so. With his own officers pressing him to return and his troops in an allegedly mutinous mood, duty compelled him to save as many lives as possible. He had decided to lead his own division, along with the invalids, back to the Maine settlements. Meanwhile, he pledged to release four barrels of flour and two of pork, which he described as a generous split of the remaining food, to Greene.[8]

Enos's promise quickly proved to be as deceiving as his official vote at the council of war. The next morning, Greene sent a party under Captain Thayer and Matthias Ogden downriver to get these supplies. They had to beg amid threats from Enos's officers to get even two and a half barrels of flour. Then Enos, "with tears in his eyes," according to Thayer, bid them goodbye, thinking he had taken "his last farewell of me." Greene's troops somehow stretched this paltry supply of flour for more than a week before they ran out of rations and nearly proved Enos's words correct.[9]

Enos's defection cost Arnold about three hundred soldiers. Subtracting another seventy-five or so invalids, the patriot detachment now consisted of no more than seven hundred troops. This loss in strength proved to be a serious handicap when the expeditionary force reached fortress-like Quebec. As such, Enos's craven leadership seriously damaged the patriot plan to conquer that city and see Quebec Province become the fourteenth colony in rebellion.

When Enos and his officers got back to Cambridge, they dwelled on Arnold's foolhardiness in proceeding, the horrible weather, and the reputed scarcity of food supplies. A dismayed Washington had Enos placed under arrest. On December 1, 1775, a court of inquiry, chaired by General John Sullivan, examined Enos's actions. With his subordinate officers rallying to his defense and no one present to testify against him, Enos listened to a paean of praise regarding his skill in getting his troops back to the Maine settlements—on full stomachs no less. The hearing board voted to "acquit him with honor."[10]

Enos saved himself because those who could testify against him were in Canada. In their absence, he could say whatever suited the occasion. Among his statements before the board, he claimed to have had only enough rations for three days, had he chosen to distribute all available provisions among his own division and Greene's. However, he had not presented the same information to Greene and his officers. At the council of war, he had fostered the impression of ample food reserves on which to forge ahead, just hours before he refused to release a bare minimum of provisions. Enos thus played his part selfishly and irresponsibly. No one under his retreating command starved to death, but a few of Greene's soldiers did. Fortunately, Roger Enos resigned from the Continental service shortly after his exoneration, and he never again had the opportunity to rise out of the historical obscurity into which he now so justifiably descended.[11]

Greene's troops, meanwhile, pushed ahead, even as word stretched up the line that Enos and his division had defected. In his journal Captain Henry Dearborn mentioned the "unhappy news," which "disheartened and discouraged our men very much" because "they carried back more than their part" of the provisions. Their retreat, however, had one beneficial effect. Explained Dearborn, "being now almost out of provisions we were sure to die if we attempted to return back—and we could be in no worse situation if we proceeded on our route." In this paradoxical sense Enos's actions helped the expedition, but Dearborn's company had other views. His troops offered up "a general prayer, that Colonel Enos and all his men, might die by the way, or meet with some disaster, equal to the cowardly, dastardly, and unfriendly spirit they" had so obviously manifested "in returning back without orders."[12]

Burdened as Arnold was in keeping his column alive, he kept his thoughts to himself. In a letter to Washington dated November 8, he did mention how "surprised" he was to learn that Enos's troops "are all gone back," but he offered no recrimination. Still, he surely wondered how long the rebellion could hope to endure when less-than-virtuous patriots held vital positions of public trust. Arnold would have many additional opportunities to ponder this subject in the days and months ahead, and in time he would be anything but forbearing in the articulation of his sentiments.[13]

III

On Wednesday, October 25, another day of heavy snow and high winds, Arnold and his party found themselves surrounded by "prodigious high mountains." They were nearing the Height of Land, a point in the Appalachian chain that formed a natural geographic border between Maine and Canada. The next morning, although not completely sure of the trail, Arnold kept moving his company forward until they finally reached the "*Terrible Carrying Place,*" as Private Morison later identified this precarious portage that would bring the column over the Height of Land.[14]

Those troops with Arnold and Hanchet continually slipped and fell as they struggled uphill for two miles over icy, snow-covered stones and rocks. Some lightened their burdens by abandoning bateaux too battered to be of much further use. At dusk, they were cautiously maneuvering themselves and their equipment, including four serviceable bateaux, another two miles down the steep mountainside toward Seven Mile Stream (today known as the Arnold River) at the base of the mountain in Canada. With darkness enveloping them, they set up camp in a "much fatigued" condition, at which point they spied some of the advance scouts of Lieutenants Steele and Church. The scouts briefed Arnold and Hanchet about the trail ahead and the way to reach Lake Megantic without becoming entrapped in a network of treacherous bogs.[15]

Early the next morning (Friday, October 27), Arnold's party soon reached Seven Mile Stream. "Bidding adieu to the southern waters," Arnold moved forward with the four bateaux while Hanchet's company began to walk toward Lake Megantic. Early that afternoon the colonel and his bateauxmen came upon Steele, Church, and a man named Jaquin, whom Arnold had earlier sent to the French settlements to gain intelligence. Jaquin had reached Sartigan, and he reported that "the French inhabitants appear very friendly and were rejoiced to hear of our approach." Nor were British troops blocking the Chaudière water route. Carleton, he also learned, had concentrated his regulars in the vicinity of Montreal to ward off Schuyler's advance. As a result, Quebec was not well defended.[16]

So much welcome news gave new energy to Arnold and his party. They proceeded down the "very crooked" Seven Mile Stream, which held "many obstructions of logs, etc.," before entering Lake Megantic as daylight was fading. Paddling another three miles, they came upon "a very considerable wigwam," where they made camp and waited for Hanchet's company to catch up. Here Arnold wrote a summary of events for Washington. With his trademark determination he declared, "I have been much deceived in every account of our route, which is longer, and has been attended with a thousand difficulties I never apprehended; but if crowned with success, and conducive to the public good, I shall think it but trifling."[17]

One such difficulty was just then playing itself out. Hanchet and his company had tried to follow the water bed of Seven Mile Stream. They walked right into the tangle of bogs that formed several false entrances from the river to Lake Megantic. If they had "kept on the high land" as ordered and headed in a northeasterly direction, stated Arnold, the trail "would have brought them to the lake clear of the sunken ground." Arnold's bateauxmen spent most of the evening extricating Hanchet and his troops.[18]

This incident had two noteworthy consequences. First, Arnold sent back instructions to Meigs and Greene about how to avoid the swampy bogs. He gave these letters to a scout, Isaac Hull, who supposedly understood the problem, and told him to lead the rear divisions around the boggy maze.

Second, Arnold curtly reprimanded Hanchet for not following orders. These two Connecticut patriots had so far worked together harmoniously, but the pouting captain took the chastisement very personally, which ultimately provoked a petty form of retaliation from him.[19]

Arnold's frustrations with Hanchet reflected his concern about further delays. Hundreds of lives depended on reaching the French settlements and securing food supplies. Early the next morning, Arnold and sixteen others "paddled on briskly" and reached the Chaudière (which means "caldron") before noontime. Now they were flowing with a "very rapid" current, but the river was "full of rocks and dangerous." No more than fifteen miles down the Chaudière they encountered a long set of rapids, requiring yet more portaging. As they maneuvered toward shore, three bateaux suddenly overturned in the turbulent water, and two splintered apart as they smashed headlong into the rocks. Everything in the three craft, including baggage and arms, danced madly downstream.

"Happily," Arnold recorded, "no lives were lost although six men were a long time swimming in the water and were with difficulty saved." After everyone tried to dry themselves, Arnold crowded them into the two remaining bateaux and a birch-bark canoe found at the wigwam campsite the previous evening. Now the rebel commander spoke of the "kind interposition of Providence." When "we embarked" again, he explained, "one of the men who was forward cried out a fall[s] ahead, . . . and had we been carried over [we] must inevitably have been dashed to pieces and all lost." The rest of the day the party proceeded "with more precaution than before."[20]

Events were not quite as life-threatening on Sunday, October 29. The river widened and became less tempestuous. By nightfall, having traversed nearly forty miles, Arnold knew he was close to Sartigan. At daybreak the next morning, he got everyone moving again. The party came across two Penobscot Indians, who assisted them around some rapids and explained that Sartigan was close at hand.

Arnold soon joyously spied "the first house on" the Chaudière. By evening he was securing food, and the next morning (Tuesday, October 31) the first consignment, including cattle for slaughter, was moving back up the trail under the charge of Lieutenant Church and some French *habitants*. The lieutenant also carried a note from Arnold to his officers explaining how to distribute the provisions. He closed with these words: "Pray make all possible dispatch." He was also praying that the food would reach his soldiers before it was too late.[21]

IV

Meanwhile, Meig's and Greene's divisions kept struggling forward. Although Dr. Senter admired the rugged, mountainous landscape that "fired" the troops "with more than Hannibalian enthusiasm," their personal thoughts, he knew, lay elsewhere. Food was almost nonexistent, and survival was uppermost on everyone's mind. Two of Senter's recent meals had "consisted of the jawbone of a swine destitute of any covering . . . boiled in a quantity of water." Captain Thayer's soldiers downed equally unappetizing fare when they boiled and ate animal hides originally stowed in their bateaux as material for shoes and moccasins.[22]

Such unsatisfying food gave these starving patriots enough energy to cross the Height of Land. At first the troops wrestled with their bateaux on their shoulders, but they kept crashing to the ground as they lost their traction in ice and snow. Most simply gave up and abandoned their boats, along with their tents and anything else representing unnecessary weight. A few even lost their guns. They were too "feeble from former fatigues" and lack of food to do anything else.[23]

Daniel Morgan exercised more discipline over his woodsmen. He ordered them to carry all their bateaux down the mountainside to Seven Mile Stream. Private John Joseph Henry's heart ached over "the intolerable labors of his fine fellows," some of whom "had the flesh worn from their shoulders, even to the bone." Morgan was soon being labeled as "too strict a disciplinarian," but his troops had a much easier journey until they struck the same rapids that had swamped Arnold's party on the Chaudière. Besides losing valuable equipment and supplies, one soldier drowned in the swirling water.[24]

On October 28, Meig's and Greene's divisions held a general rendezvous on Seven Mile Stream. A few companies pushed on, eager to make headway during daylight. Then Isaac Hull appeared with Arnold's instructions. The colonel had ordered an equal division of all remaining food, which amounted to about five pints of flour per soldier (not enough pork was left to give each of them one ration). Some troops did not exercise good judgment. They quickly consumed the firecakes baked for them from their flour rations. Within a few days, recorded Private Simon Fobes, these patriots "were obliged, in order to sustain life, to eat their dogs, cartridge boxes, old shoes, and clothes."[25]

In trusting Isaac Hull, Arnold had made another error. This scout had little idea about how to avoid the bogs. Early on the morning of October 29, Greene's musketmen and Hendricks's riflemen fell into line behind Hull, who soon led this column right into what Dr. Senter called "the most

execrable bogmire . . . imaginable." Another two days of sloshing through
half-frozen water, snow, and muck passed before these lost patriots reached
the shoreline of Lake Megantic. "Hunger and fatigue had so much the
ascendancy" during this desperate period, wrote Dr. Senter, that some gave
up, sank down in the bog, "nor were heard of afterwards." These soldiers
might have been forever lost had not a young Indian appeared out of
nowhere and showed them the way to the lake. He was an associate of the
reputed villain Natanis, who had been tracking the expeditionary force since
it had entered the Dead River.[26]

The companies that left the rendezvous point before Isaac Hull's arrival
had an easier time of it—but not by much. They, too, struggled through
the bogs. Private Henry was walking behind Mrs. Grier, "a large, virtuous,
and respectable women," when they entered the swamps. His "mind was
humbled, yet astonished, at the exertions of this good woman," who with
"her clothes more than waist high, . . . waded before me to firm ground."
No one snickered or "dared to intimate a disrespectful idea of her."[27]

The troops admired Mrs. Grier's fortitude and courage, just as they felt
compassion for Jemima Warner, whose husband had fallen desperately ill
and could no longer keep up. He died just before his Pennsylvania comrades
went into the bogs. They did not stop, since survival of the group was at
stake. However, she "tarried by him" until the end, Private Stocking wrote.
Since she had "no implements" to dig a grave, "she covered him with leaves,
. . . took his gun, . . . and left him with a heavy heart," then caught up with
the rest of the company some twenty miles ahead.[28]

By the afternoon of Tuesday, October 31, all parties, minus starving and
dying stragglers, were approaching the Chaudière River. On November 1, the
column wobbled forward along the banks of the Chaudière. Captain Thayer
told how he and Captain Topham walked behind, "spurring on the men as
well as we could, although the orders were for every man to do for himself
as well as he could." Dragging themselves up and down steep hills, which
now appeared as "ruthless mountains" to Private Morison, the troops were
becoming delirious. They continually stumbled and fell but fought to get
back up, the instinct for life driving them on. Morison recalled thanking
Providence for having supplied him with "an uncommon degree of strength,"
but still he "staggered about like a drunken man."[29]

At this juncture, the column started consuming anything with even a
remote prospect of providing nourishment, including shaving soap and lip
salve. A few dogs, such as Captain Dearborn's Labrador, had followed their
masters on the expedition. None survived past November 1. Wrote Dr.
Senter, the Labrador succumbed to the blows of some desperately hungry

"assassinators" and "was instantly devoured, without leaving any vestige of the sacrifice."[30]

By the morning of Thursday, November 2, the soldiers, Private Caleb Haskell indicated, were "very much discouraged, having . . . no prospect of anything" to sustain life. Yet they kept forcing themselves forward. Those in the lead, who were still about twenty miles south of Sartigan, thought they were seeing a mirage when they "were blessed," as Matthias Ogden stated, "with the finest sight my eyes ever beheld." First they discerned cattle being herded toward them, and then birch-bark canoes appeared on the Chaudière, loaded with grain, mutton, and tobacco. Arnold had gotten food to them barely in time and had saved hundreds of lives. Like Captain Thayer, many troops "shed tears of joy, in our happy delivery from the grasping hand of death."[31]

The column was spread out by as many as twenty miles, so Lieutenant Church kept the provisions moving upstream. As a semblance of bodily strength returned to those who first received food, they formed search parties and went back to help rescue their fallen comrades. Well into the evening, they kept stumbling across soldiers who had given up and lay on the ground dying. Some were too far gone to be saved; as many as forty to fifty did not survive. When Private Simon Fobes returned home by the same route in the spring of 1776, he "saw their bleaching bones, hair, etc."[32]

Arnold, meanwhile, had continued downstream in search of additional provisions. Before leaving Sartigan, he drafted orders for Major Meigs to distribute "a little pocket money" among the captains "for present use, and to supply their men." Although the *habitants* enthusiastically welcomed *Les Bostonnais,* as they called the soldiers, they also charged dearly for whatever supplies the detachment needed. Arnold did not complain; he was anxious to gain the *habitant's* confidence and allegiance. Likewise, by providing a few extra items for his troops after so harrowing a trek through the wilderness, he was boosting their morale.[33]

As the soldiers recouped, they departed in small groups from Sartigan and proceeded down the Chaudière toward the hamlets of Gilbert and St. Mary (Ste. Marie). As before, the welfare of his troops was Arnold's dominant concern. In the vicinity of St. Mary, for example, Private Henry collapsed with a violent fever. Arnold, who had secured a horse, came riding up to the young man, who sat near the pathway immobilized. Amazingly, Henry wrote, the commander "knew my name and character, and good-naturedly inquired after my health." When Arnold realized how sick Henry was, he "ran down to the river side, and hailed the owner of the house which stood opposite across the water." Just as quickly, he made arrangements for Henry's care, then handed the Pennsylvania private two silver dollars so he could pay the French family for food and lodging while recovering. After Arnold's treason, the aging patriot Henry described his benefactor as "sordidly avaricious" by nature; however, he never indicated whether he returned the two silver dollars to the man who helped save his life in Canada.[34]

V

Once through the wilderness, Arnold focused on getting his column, now representing only about 650 troops, into position to seize Quebec City. He comprehended the difficulty of this challenge, given his diminished numbers and his mounting apprehension that his Indian couriers had "betrayed" his letter to John Dyer Mercier. Arnold had to learn whether he had lost his best weapon, the element of surprise, so he sent a missive from Sartigan to another Quebec contact, again seeking the latest intelligence. He inquired whether "any ships of war are at Quebec," perhaps aligned in a defensive posture on the St. Lawrence River. He also inquired whether "one or two of my friends would meet me on the road, and that you would let me know whether the enemy is apprised of our coming." These confidants, he hoped, could supply him with critical information as well as give advice regarding a feasible plan to capture the city.[35]

During the next few days, Arnold stayed well ahead of his column. He purchased provisions as he traveled down the Chaudière and set up ration stations where the troops could expect to fill their stomachs. Arnold seemed to be luring the soldiers forward with complements of food over the final seventy miles from Sartigan to the southern shore of the St. Lawrence River. He thus kept the detachment moving forward at a tolerable pace while hoping that he had not yet lost the advantage of surprise.

On Saturday, November 4, Arnold paused near the village of Gilbert and parleyed with several Native Americans. Dr. Senter recorded the scene. The natives "addressed the colonel in great pomp," to which he replied in equally embellished terms. Arnold proclaimed King George III a monstrous tyrant who had "now taken up the hatchet against us." He "and his wicked great men" had "sent a great army to Boston" that "killed a great many women and children, while they were peaceably at work." In reaction, New Englanders had "in six days raised an army of fifty thousand men." Then Arnold claimed "the French and Indians in Canada have sent to us" because "the king's troops oppress them and make them pay a great price for their rum, . . . [and] press them to take up arms against the Bostonians, their brethren, who have done them no hurt."

The rebel commander urged the assemblage to join in the patriot effort "to drive out the king's soldiers." He offered bounties, regular pay, and food for all those courageous enough to challenge so wicked an enemy. His performance—and promises—were persuasive, since about forty Indians enlisted for short-term service. Among them was Natanis, no villain at all but an inquisitive friend who had traveled along invisibly with the patriot column. Natanis's small party had twice proffered direct assistance, Arnold eventually found out, first in guiding the division of lost soldiers out of the bogs and then in providing morsels of food and rescuing some of those "forlorn objects" who were too weak to keep walking toward Sartigan.[36]

Up and moving again after the council, Arnold next established his headquarters at St. Mary, about halfway between Sartigan and Quebec. As before, the populace greeted him warmly. They gave him access to the manor home of a local *seigneur,* Gabriel Taschereau, who was away at the time but had recently outraged the villagers by threatening to arrest male inhabitants unwilling to perform militia duty in defense of the province. From this residence, Arnold sent out orders for the rear companies to move up quickly for a final rendezvous at St. Mary before pushing on to the St. Lawrence.

On Sunday, November 5—ironically Guy Fawkes Day—Arnold went to the local Roman Catholic church and, while the parish priest looked on disapprovingly, presented Washington's proclamation of friendship. The villagers seemed pleased, but they ignored every overture to step forth and enlist. Certainly the haggard appearance of Arnold's gaunt, unkempt soldiers in their dirty, ragged clothing did anything but inspire confidence in *Les Bostonnais,* especially when the villagers feared reprisals from the likes of Taschereau and church officials. A messenger carrying unwelcome news for Arnold soon proved the point. The British, he reported, had captured the bearer of the colonel's most recent letter to Quebec. Then this herald of gloom nearly panicked the villagers by telling them how "the English were determined to burn and destroy all the inhabitants in the vicinity of Quebec, unless they came in and took up arms in defense of the garrison."[37]

Arnold now knew he had lost the vital element of surprise. Still, with Carleton and so many British regulars apparently at Montreal, he still hoped to conquer the city before adequate defensive measures could be taken. So Arnold again sent back urgent appeals for all companies to gather at St. Mary. Enough troops were present on November 6 to commence the last leg of their journey, which took them in a northeasterly direction away from the Chaudière to Point Levy (Pointe Lévis) on the southern bank of the St. Lawrence.

For those troops lacking footwear (some of which they had boiled for food in days past), the notion of traveling on established roads held much appeal. Unfortunately, the ground was a sea of muck from unrelenting rain and sleeting sheets of snow. Everyone kept sinking knee-deep into mud, but few complained because this challenge was nothing compared to previous experiences. Dr. Senter even made light of the situation. Exhausted from slogging through the mud, he and Chaplain Spring hired horses, but they still found themselves wallowing around on a "terrible road," with "mud and mire [up] to the horses' belly."[38]

Anticipation now drove the column forward. On Thursday, November 9, scouts assured Arnold that he could safely approach the St. Lawrence River. Through gusts of swirling snow, the troops soon beheld their target. At long last, some two months after signing on for the expedition, they peered out from the bluffs of Point Levy and scrutinized the mighty St. Lawrence, as wide a river as most of them had ever laid eyes on—and across, on the northern shore, resting atop what looked like an insurmountable cliff rising to more than three hundred feet above the river, the walled capital city of Quebec.

Now the question was whether they could get across the St. Lawrence. The task would not be easy, since British officials, once apprised of Arnold's approach, had confiscated or destroyed every form of watercraft they could locate along the southern shore. In addition, a well-armed naval frigate, the *Lizard* (twenty-six guns), and a sloop of war, the *Hunter* (sixteen guns), were in constant patrol, just waiting to assail any rebel band with enough temerity to attempt passage across the river.

Having persevered through so much, Arnold was not about to back off. Suspecting that boats would not be readily accessible, he had ordered Captains Simeon Thayer and John Topham, who were in the rear urging on stragglers and providing for the sick, to secure canoes from *habitants* along the Chaudière. Thayer's and Topham's companies brought up not only ninety-six invalids but twenty canoes as well. Another fifteen to twenty craft, which the British had not found, would be uncovered along the St. Lawrence.[39]

Even as Arnold regarded Quebec through his spyglass, he still had no idea how prepared the British were to defend the city. On the evening of November 7, in grasping for intelligence, he had again written John Dyer Mercier. The Kennebec detachment intended to cross the St. Lawrence River within two or three days, he stated, "and if practicable" to "attack the city." If enemy reinforcements had arrived from Montreal, however, their presence "may possibly put it out of my power." In that case, Arnold planned "to march for

Montreal," where he would link up with General Montgomery and help secure the western sector of the province.[40]

Within a few hours, the patriot colonel knew much more. An informant, most likely an old-subject merchant, crossed the river and offered a detailed report. Lieutenant Governor Hector Cramahé, the ranking British official in Carleton's absence, had gotten hold of Arnold's October 13 letter to Mercier. Despite his reputation as an ineffective, doddering old bureaucrat, Cramahé immediately went into action. He placed the city's population of five thousand on full alert, ordered the Upper Town's gates to be closed each evening, and arranged for the firing of cannons should lookouts spot the rebel detachment. In addition, he notified all able-bodied adult males to muster for militia service. Although many *habitants* and old subjects demurred, more than seven hundred residents had accepted Cramahé's call to arms. The lieutenant governor was also keeping a close watch on suspicious old-subject merchants—he had already arrested and incarcerated Mercier. Then, in early November, the frigate *Lizard* had sailed into Quebec's harbor. The vessel carried an abundant cargo of arms, ammunition, uniforms, and £20,000 in specie from England, all for the defense of the city. Finally, Captain Malcolm Fraser of the Royal Highland Emigrants had just appeared with about 150 recruits from Newfoundland.[41]

Arnold assessed this information in the context of his first communication from Montgomery. In responding, he made no mention of an all-out assault. Instead, he advised Montgomery of his intention to cut the city off from the countryside and keep its defenders "in close quarters until your arrival here, which I shall await with impatience."[42]

Unfortunately for Arnold's rebels, this letter also miscarried—right into the hands of Lieutenant Colonel Allan Maclean, the energetic commander of the Royal Highland Emigrants. A seasoned veteran of the French and Indian War, Maclean had just failed in operations with Carleton to relieve the besieged St. Johns fortress. Ordered by the governor to reinforce Quebec City, Maclean and about 170 of his crack troops were sailing down the St. Lawrence when they alertly snared Arnold's Native American couriers out of the water. Shocked to learn about the patriot column, Maclean determined he had to get Quebec quickly. With gale-force winds blowing from the northeast, the hard-nosed Scottish officer abandoned his slow-moving watercraft, executed a rapid overland march, and reached the capital city on Sunday, November 12, ready to bolster and advise Cramahé, who lacked military experience, in how to withstand the patriot threat.[43]

Had Arnold beaten Maclean to the walls of Quebec, he might have gained a surrender with a bold demonstration of force. Maclean's presence ended any hope of a capitulation without offensive operations, as Arnold soon found out. Meanwhile, the rebel colonel could not even contemplate crossing the St. Lawrence. The same furious winds that caused Maclean to proceed overland kept the patriot force pinned down on the southern shore. Arnold had enough troops in place to attempt a crossing on November 10, but the turbulent waters of the St. Lawrence would have easily sunk the patriot flotilla of small craft. The windstorm persisted until late Monday afternoon, November 13, the day after Maclean reached the protective walls of the Upper Town.

The waiting period was agonizing. With each passing day Quebec City would be more prepared to resist the rebel column. Many troops wondered when Providence would finally repress what seemed a conspiracy among nature's elements to frustrate, if not vanquish, the expedition. Always concerned about flagging morale, Arnold chatted confidently with the soldiers. He kept them busy by ordering the construction of ladders and pikes to scale the Upper Town's thirty-foot-high walls and sweep the ramparts clean of enemy defenders. Arnold even held a formal review, during which he commended the troops for their impressive military appearance, despite their resemblance to emaciated ragamuffins. He gratefully thanked these "famine-proof veterans," as Dr. Senter started calling the soldiers, for risking their all in the cause of human liberty. Victory would surely be theirs, he promised, as a reward for their suffering and sacrifice.[44]

Late on November 12, Arnold circulated word for his officers to gather in a council of war. No matter how daunting, he told the assemblage, the fierce northerly winds could not last forever. He instructed everyone to prepare their troops for crossing the river—under cover of darkness and within the next forty-eight hours, he hoped. Then Arnold presented John Halstead, who operated a gristmill near Point Levy in the employ of Colonel Henry Caldwell, one of Quebec's wealthiest citizens, who had recently taken command of British subjects called to militia duty inside the walled city. Halstead, a New Jersey native, had proved himself a friend by provisioning the rebels with flour from the mill. (Arnold soon named him a commissary.)

As the officers listened, Halstead briefed them on Quebec's defenses and estimated the number of resisters. Counting Fraser's Emigrants, marines from the warships, armed sailors from merchant vessels, and British and French militiamen (he did not know about Maclean's return that day), Halstead expected the rebels to encounter about eight hundred defenders. (The actual number at this juncture, including Maclean's troops, was 1,126.)

At most, Arnold had about six hundred effectives, certainly an unfavorable strength ratio for offensive operations against well-protected defenders. Still, Halstead was sure that Cramahé's militiamen would not stand and fight, since many of them had only reluctantly taken up arms. He thought the patriots still held the advantage, if they could just find the means to breach the Upper Town's walls.[45]

Arnold now posed the central question—whether the column should attempt a preemptive strike if the opportunity presented itself while approaching the city. Halstead had advised him about the apathy of the night guards in closing the city's principal gates, despite Cramahé's admonitions. Further, the defenders had yet to mount a significant number of artillery pieces on the walls, and cannon cartridges were in short supply. If, in addition, the militia were skittish, a lightning-quick assault could prove decisive, Arnold concluded in advocating dynamic action.

Arnold's more aggressive officers, among them Daniel Morgan and Christopher Greene, agreed. Most of the others demurred. They pointed to the enemy's advantage in position and numbers and the possibility of laying a purposeful trap by not appearing to be prepared. The odds were too great, especially since the defenders had abundant knowledge of their presence. The naysayers were in a clear majority, and Arnold reluctantly accepted their verdict. He made no contingency plans for a preemptive attack.[46]

At three o'clock the next afternoon, Arnold reassembled his officers, since the winds were at last subsiding. He had decided to attempt a crossing that night, should sufficient cloud cover blot out the moon's glare. Arnold then ordered Captain Oliver Hanchet to maintain a rear guard with sixty men. When a sulking Hanchet seemed offended about not receiving a place of honor in the van, Arnold ignored him. Hanchet could expect orders to bring over the rear guard within a couple of days, along with the scaling ladders and pikes. The watercraft, Arnold reminded everyone, should be pointed toward Wolfe's Cove, one and a half miles across the St. Lawrence. Near that landing place, where General James Wolfe had debarked his army back in September 1759 before conquering the city, the rebel detachment was to follow the path up the escarpment that the legendary British general had used to get five thousand soldiers onto the Plains of Abraham, immediately to the west of the walled Upper Town.

The weather conditions were at last favorable by 9 p.m. With Halstead serving as guide and Arnold and Morgan in the lead canoe, the first wave of troops shoved off from the southern shoreline. Gliding stealthily through the water, they passed between the *Hunter* and the *Lizard,* as well as barges moving back and forth between the two naval vessels. By four o'clock the next morning, the rebel force had executed three crossings, and Arnold had about five hundred soldiers on the northern shore. Not sure whether another passage could be effected before daylight, and with moonlight occasionally breaking through the cloud cover, he ordered a halt to the evening's work.[47]

Arnold also stopped because of concerns about discovery. On one of the passages, a canoe had broken apart, dumping its human cargo into the river. All but one of the men, Arnold's valuable scout Archibald Steele, scrambled safely aboard other craft. Steele grabbed onto a passing canoe, which dragged him through the frigid water to the shore. His rescuers then assisted the scout, who was shivering uncontrollably, to a vacant cabin near the cove, where they built a fire to warm him and the others who had tumbled into the river. Not long thereafter one of the barge crews, spying the glowing light, rowed close to the shoreline to investigate. Someone fired a musket, and a brief skirmish ensued. Three enemy mariners were shot, Arnold later stated, in this untimely exchange. The barge backed off, and its crew members were soon spreading the alarm about a hostile force on the northern shore.[48]

Arnold had already sent out scouts, among them his Indian allies, and they soon reported back that the pathway up the escarpment was free of resisters. Even before dawn began to break, the detachment was moving furtively onto the Plains of Abraham. Constrained not to initiate an attack, Arnold did nothing when a rumor reached him about one of the town gates being left open and virtually undefended. Evidence about this claim remains flimsy, and such an opportunity likely was a phantom. Allan Maclean was too demanding a military officer to have permitted so fundamental a breach in security. Nevertheless, no British patrol was monitoring Wolfe's pathway, the obvious approach route to the city. Quebec's defenders were still not fully organized, despite the arguments of Arnold's more cautious officers.[49]

Admonishing everyone to proceed in silence, Arnold led his troops to King's Road, which the column followed in moving eastward across the plains. They emerged from woods into snow-covered fields about a mile west of the city's walls and St. Louis Gate. They had reached a few scattered dwellings, in the midst of which was the grand country estate of Colonel Henry Caldwell. With dawn fast approaching, Arnold ordered his officers to seize the houses, post guards, and rest their troops. Relieved to have their long evening's toil over, almost everyone fell asleep. Arnold remained awake. Exhilarated about reaching Quebec City at long last, he was also trying to devise a plan to subdue the provincial capital with so small a force.

VI

During the next few days, Arnold kept probing Quebec and its defenders, looking for some sort of an opening. Having established his headquarters at Caldwell's residence, he regularly sent out scouting parties into the suburbs outside the walled Upper Town. These squads were to confiscate food supplies and other provisions being carried overland to the city. Although lacking in artillery pieces, Arnold's strategy was to keep the Upper Town under a semblance of a siege until General Montgomery covered the 150 miles from Montreal to Quebec with badly needed reinforcements. At that point, further plans could be devised for taking the city.

Near noontime on Thursday, November 14, a flicker of opportunity presented itself—but only for a moment. One of Morgan's men, Private George Merchant, posted to watch St. John's Gate, fell asleep. Some defenders rushed out through the gate, grabbed Merchant, and quickly disappeared back behind the walls with their startled prey. When Arnold heard the news, he decided on a demonstration of force, hoping to tempt his adversaries into an engagement outside the walls. Soon he had his troops spread out across the plains, with his advance companies standing at attention within three hundred yards of the western wall. In turn, hundreds of curious civilians, as well as the Upper Town's armed defenders, began appearing on top of the ten-foot-thick walls. With great bravado, Arnold's troops first unleashed a series of huzzahs in the name of liberty, after which they offered a smattering of musket fire, which in no way threatened their audience because of the distance involved.

If Cramahé seemed worried, Maclean scoffed at this less-than-intimidating performance. He responded with a brief flurry of artillery fire, which did little more than reveal the poor marksmanship of his cannoneers. Through this defiant reply, Maclean stated that rebel blustering would not lure Quebec's defenders into combat outside the walls, even against so feeble-looking a body of soldiers. He was not going to repeat the mistake the Marquis de Montcalm had made when he accepted Wolfe's challenge and marched his troops out onto the Plains of Abraham, where they suffered a crushing defeat. Maclean intended to keep the burden on the rebels, who would have to scale or breach the walls if they wanted to capture the city. Arnold understood and ordered everyone to return to their assigned posts.[50]

Never easily dissuaded, Arnold kept serving up challenges. After pulling back his troops on November 14, he composed a note in which he denounced the "unjust, cruel, and tyrannical acts of a venal Parliament" and demanded the "immediate surrender of the town." He guaranteed no looting of property should Quebec's defenders capitulate immediately. But, he warned, "if I am obliged to carry the town by storm, you may expect every severity practiced upon such occasions." Matthias Ogden agreed to deliver this ultimatum, but as he and a drummer approached St. John's Gate just before sunset with a white cloth held high, a cannon belched forth indignantly, which sent Ogden and his escort scurrying back to rebel lines. The next day Ogden again tried to present Arnold's ultimatum. The results were the same, except for the greater accuracy of the cannon shot. This salvo almost obliterated the Jerseyite.[51]

In this second venture, Ogden carried a hotly worded message from Arnold to Cramahé that referred to the first rebuff as "contrary to humanity and the laws of nations." The cannon shot was unbecoming to Cramahé's "honor or valor" and represented "an insult I could not have expected from a private soldier." It would be "deeply resented" by "the United Colonies." Cramahé and Maclean likely turned up their noses at these words. To recognize in any way a band of rebels so presumptuously questioning imperial authority would have impeached their own reputations as loyal British subjects, especially when they had superior numbers under arms and were in control of a fortress-like stronghold.[52]

Nor did Cramahé and Maclean merely remain passive in their defense. While Arnold was parading his column on November 14, Maclean sent a squad scurrying into the suburb of St. John's with orders to ignite buildings closest to the wall. Before Arnold could react, many structures were in flames and no longer available to the rebels as sites for launching deadly volleys of sniper fire or a full-scale assault over the walls.

Quebec's artillery gunners soon received orders to shell parties of rebels whenever they appeared within cannon range. On Thursday afternoon, November 16, when a squad of Morgan's riflemen were out scouting for food near the St. Charles River just north of the Upper Town, heavy-caliber cannonballs started to rain down on them. They fled for cover, but a careening ball ripped apart the leg of Sergeant Robert Dixon. In an attempt to save his life, Dr. Senter amputated what remained of the mangled limb, but Dixon was too far gone from the loss of blood and died the next morning.[53]

With civilians moving in and out of the city (some fleeing and others seeking British protection), each side gained ample, although often erroneous intelligence. On November 17, Arnold received the exciting news of Montgomery's triumph at Montreal, but then he picked up disquieting reports from informers leaving Quebec. Cramahé and Maclean had called their officers together the previous evening, and they had voted to defend the provincial capital to the last person. An alleged deserter told Arnold early on Saturday, November 18, about a new plan by Maclean to march out of the city with a large, well-armed force to sweep away the rebels. The colonel flinched, since his officers had finally supplied him with a full inventory of weapons. The situation was grievous. Besides lacking cannons and bayonets, many muskets had been lost or rendered useless during the wilderness march; and no more than five rounds of ammunition were available per soldier.[54]

Cramahé and Maclean had employed this person to feed Arnold false information. They never intended to venture beyond Quebec's walls and risk having Arnold outmaneuver them in combat—beyond the lack of rebel artillery, they had no idea how short his column was of weaponry. Moreover, they were fearful that reports of Montreal's capitulation might embolden their adversary in some way, perhaps to the point of attempting an assault. That may explain why the deserter also related to Arnold how great numbers of British soldiers driven from Montreal were rapidly descending the St. Lawrence for Quebec—the actual party consisted of a handful of sailors and Governor Carleton.

Once apprised of his column's shortage of arms, as well as the probable appearance of additional enemy troops, Arnold knew his only real alternative was to pull back from Quebec City. No matter how distasteful he found the notion of retreating, neither he nor his officers could come up with good reasons to keep the detachment located in so vulnerable a position—and possibly subject to annihilation, especially if a strengthened force did come out and challenge them. Certainly, the effort to cut off the flow of provisions into the walled city did not justify holding their ground. Rebel numbers were too few and the city and its suburbs too extensive to prevent a substantial portion of supplies from getting through. Considering every-thing, the "most prudent" course, Arnold stated, was to march upriver where the column could wait in relative safety for Montgomery and reinforcements from Montreal.[55]

To a man, the officers voted to pull back. Before daylight on Sunday, November 19, Arnold's famine-proof veterans ignored the flurries of snow as they set off on yet another journey. This time they had to march only twenty miles before reaching their destination, the quaint hillside village of Pointe aux Trembles (modern-day Neuville) on the northern bank of the St. Law-rence. For Arnold, this day was particularly dispiriting. Nothing was more alien to his temperament than to back off from an adversary. Still, the welfare of his troops as well as long-term prospects for total victory in Quebec Province, he reminded himself, depended on controlling his emotions and making considered decisions.

When *habitants* in and around Pointe aux Trembles warmly greeted the rebel force, Arnold became more cheerful. Once settled in, he spent many evenings socializing with such old-subject refugees from Quebec as Hector McNeill, a seagoing merchant with whom he had traded in years past. During daylight hours, Arnold attended to the needs of his troops. Most pressing, they lacked decent footwear; some were all but barefoot. Arnold purchased a stock of leather and put the column to work making moccasins. Since he wanted to maintain the goodwill of local civilians, he paid for everything out of his supply of hard money; as a result, the *habitants* of Pointe aux Trembles were eager to keep helping *Les Bostonnais*. [56]

Facing critical shortages of all kinds, Arnold wrote to Montgomery and asked him to bring specie, since "my hard cash is nearly exhausted," as well as clothing and blankets. Not knowing whether the general could obtain extra supplies, he also ordered clothing and blankets from mercantile acquaintances in Montreal. Arnold instructed these merchants to charge his personal account if his courier, Matthias Ogden, lacked sufficient funds— an impressive act for a person of such reputed greed. Despite his experiences with the Massachusetts Provincial Congress, Arnold was still willing to use his personal credit on behalf of the cause of liberty, with nothing more than the hope of someday getting reimbursed. He took this risk, he explained, out of compassion for the "brave men" of his command, "who were in want of everything but stout hearts." [57]

As the days passed, Arnold waited with "great anxiety" for Montgomery. A combined force of two thousand troops, he now estimated, would be required to succeed in conquering Quebec City. Even if short of that number, Arnold remained as determined as ever to fulfill that objective. As he explained to Schuyler, too much had already been borne by the Kennebec column, which, "inspired and fired with the love of liberty and their country," had just barely survived "a march . . . not to be paralleled in history." [58]

Only a magnificent victory could alleviate the frustration gnawing at Arnold. "Had I been ten days sooner," he penned to Washington on Monday, November 20, "Quebec must inevitably have fallen into our hands, as there was not a man there to oppose us." Not only had the route of march been twice the distance expected, but delays caused by a cacophony of turbulent winds, flooding rains and heavy snowstorms, and virtually impassable terrain had cost the column those ten crucial days—and more. As a patriot enthusiast anxious to demonstrate his talent and virtue, Arnold found such reflections more than annoying. They were downright maddening, yet they helped propel him forward toward another season of reckoning with the imperial defenders of Quebec. [59]

Seven

Liberty or Death at the Walls of Quebec

I

Guy Carleton was tenacious by temperament. Of middling stock from Northern Ireland, his determination had carried him to impressive heights for a British subject initially devoid of influence at court. As a young man, he secured an ensign's commission in the 25th Regiment of Foot, the beginning of a tedious process of purchasing his way up the officer ranks. His opportunity for significant advancement came when a rising young star in the British army, James Wolfe, befriended him. Wolfe demanded that Carleton serve as his quartermaster general for the campaign against French Canada in 1759. As a result, the future governor was on the Plains of Abraham on September 13, 1759, when Wolfe's force crushed Montcalm's French defenders. Carleton received a slight head wound during the battle, but he quickly recovered—unlike his patron Wolfe, who died that day. Despite the loss of Wolfe, Carleton emerged as a conquering hero of French Canada, which secured his base for political and social advancement. In 1766 he became lieutenant governor of Quebec Province, and he assumed the governor's post a year later. In 1770 he returned to England, where he spent four years lobbying for the Quebec Act. Carleton also gained the rank of major general and won the hand of Lady Maria, daughter of the second Earl of Effingham. With marital ties to one of England's most influential families, he was now a full-fledged gentleman of consequence in the innermost circles of British imperial government.[1]

The tall, slender Carleton maintained a grave, reserved, humorless bearing, befitting a ranking officer in His Majesty's military forces. Shrewd and resourceful, he was much more than just another imperial bureaucrat carefully constructing a pathway to yet loftier offices by trying to mollify everyone in sight. He was fully capable of resolving perplexing problems because he was not afraid to take chances or make hard decisions. In November 1775, the monumental challenge before him was to save Quebec Province from the invading rebel forces of Montgomery and Arnold, a task that would severely test his capacities as an astute military and political leader.

After the capitulation of the fortresses at St. Johns and Chambly, Carleton's prospects looked bleak. With very few regulars still at hand, the governor concluded he could not defend Montreal. His only recourse was to flee down the St. Lawrence River to Quebec, where he could mount a final stand, but he warned Lord Dartmouth, the Secretary for American Affairs, on November 5 that "the prospect at Quebec is not much better." He had just received an ominous report about a rebel force under one "B. Arnold" descending the Chaudière at a time when "we have not one soldier" there and "the lower sort . . . not more loyal than here." [2]

Carleton's immediate objective was to reach the provincial capital and rally the local populace before Arnold's column got into the city. Before leaving Montreal, he ordered the destruction of all military supplies, except for matériel that could be placed on board the vessels designated to sail with him for Quebec. On the evening of Saturday, November 11, Carleton's fleet cast off, even as advance patriot units threatened the gates of Montreal. The next night, the governor's fleet lost its favorable breeze. Strong northeasterly winds—likely from the same storm system that delayed Arnold in crossing the St. Lawrence—stopped the flotilla from making any forward movement. Like Arnold, a frustrated Carleton could only wait apprehensively for improved weather conditions.

The governor's fleet was near the village of Sorel, where the St. Lawrence's main channel passes through a narrow gap between an island and the southern shoreline. The flotilla bobbed helplessly at anchor until startled on November 15 by unexpected cannon fire, at which point the vessels retreated back upriver. None other than Colonel James Easton and Major John Brown, operating under orders from Montgomery, had led Arnold's old Ticonderoga regiment to Sorel. Their assignment was to cut off enemy forces from Montreal that might be trying to move through the tight channel passage.

Carleton refused to accept entrapment. As the principal symbol of imperial authority in Quebec Province, he was sure the *habitants* would not give their full allegiance to the rebel invaders as long as he remained uncaptured and could supervise resistance efforts. When Easton sent a messenger out to the fleet demanding surrender, Carleton decided to risk his own escape. After dark on Thursday, November 16, he dressed in the plain clothes of a *habitant,* complete with wool cap. He then lowered himself over the side of his flagship, the brigantine *Gaspé,* into a whaleboat. To avoid making any sound that might attract attention on shore, the crewmen used their hands as paddles and got Carleton past the rebel blockade point before daylight. Eventually the snow *Fell,* patrolling upriver from Quebec, picked them up and carried the governor to the walled city.

As Arnold and his troops retreated to Pointe aux Trembles on November 19, they spied the *Fell* scampering down the St. Lawrence, but they had no way of knowing the governor was on board. Carleton's return brought "unspeakable joy" to "the friends of government," according to Collector of Customs Thomas Ainslie, and "utter dismay" to "the abettors of sedition and rebellion." Stated Ainslie, "we saw our salvation in his presence." The fifty-one-year-old governor was not quite as sanguine. He wrote to Lord Dartmouth the next day, "I think our fate extremely doubtful to say nothing worse."[3]

II

As Arnold's soldiers neared Pointe aux Trembles, they heard the muffled reverberations of artillery fire emanating from Quebec. The low, rumbling sounds filled them with trepidation. They suspected that Quebec had been reinforced in some way. More than ever during the next few days, Arnold felt the need for decisive action, before the walled city's defenses became too strong. Success depended on the rapid appearance of Montgomery, whose "full possession" of Montreal had given his column new cause for hope. Arnold rejoiced when he received word of Montgomery's planned movement down the St. Lawrence with additional troops and vital artillery pieces, as well as extra muskets and clothing.[4]

On Friday, November 24, four British war vessels—the snow *Fell,* the frigate *Hunter,* and two schooners—appeared off Pointe aux Trembles. Arnold hurriedly dispatched a warning to Montgomery, advising him to send "three or four boats ahead at a proper distance to give you timely notice" of the likely presence of armed enemy craft. He wanted nothing to delay Montgomery, since Quebec's defenders were "very busy in collecting provisions, fixing cannons on the walls, and putting themselves in the best posture of defense." Patriot troops at Pointe aux Trembles, Arnold also remarked, were "as ready, as naked men can be, to march wherever they may be required."[5]

While waiting "with great anxiety" for Montgomery, Arnold regularly sent out intelligence-gathering parties. They obtained a copy of Carleton's November 22 proclamation in which he announced the pending eviction from inside the walled city of all "persons . . . busy in endeavoring to draw away and alienate the affections of His Majesty's good and faithful subjects." In addition, those who refused to muster for militia service and bear arms had four days to remove themselves and their families. They could not take any possessions with them, not even food and clothing, since "the country abounds with the necessaries of life." To neutralize arguments about using power tyrannically in seizing property without due-process proceedings, Carleton consented to offer cash payments for goods left behind, which he planned to use in case of a protracted siege.[6]

Most of the exiles were old subjects, some of them merchants, who resented the Quebec Act and were fully capable of stirring up dissension in support of the rebels. As a result, Carleton's heavy-handed purge did build unity of purpose within the city. By late November, according to Collector Ainslie, the governor had eighteen hundred "men bearing arms," about half of whom were local inhabitants assigned to English- or French-speaking militia units.[7]

Carleton likewise sought estimates about stockpiles of supplies and learned that enough provisions were on hand to withstand a siege for up to eight months—well into the summer of 1776. Key shortages included firewood, oats, and hay, but the governor intended to burn every piece of wood in town for winter fuel and let horses and stock animals starve to death, if need be. Their carcasses could always be dumped over the walls. The unyielding Carleton simply was not going to surrender under any terms, unless somehow overwhelmed in an assault by the rebels before a promised relief expedition of British regulars appeared in the spring of 1776.[8]

While Carleton strengthened his position and Arnold fretted, Montgomery, still back in Montreal, dealt with a host of problems. His subordinate officers and New England troops were particularly troublesome. Typical of the officers was Captain John Lamb, a valuable artillery officer from New York City who complained of "consuming his own property to maintain himself" in the field because his pay was "such a trifle." Montgomery used his considerable charm to convince Lamb to remain in Canada, but he was less successful with the New Englanders. They had spent much of the autumn threatening to return home. Montgomery had prevailed with them about staying until Montreal had fallen. Now he implored them to extend their enlistments into the New Year, since troop shortages could undo "in one day what has been the work of months." He urged them to join him and Arnold's Kennebec column in reducing Quebec, thereby depriving "the ministerial army of all the footing in this important province." His appeals mostly failed. Before the end of November many New Englanders began departing for home, including the bulk of Arnold's old regiment, with Colonel James Easton prominently in the lead.[9]

Despite losing valuable troop strength, Montgomery pushed preparations to link up with Arnold. He borrowed hard money from old-subject merchants and arranged for the purchase of clothing, weapons, and gunpowder. He confiscated a large supply of British uniforms somehow not destroyed before Carleton's flight from Montreal. He met with Roman Catholic clergymen, assuring them that no patriot soldier would attack church property or privileges. To counteract troop shortages, he authorized James Livingston, who lived in Canada and was a distant kinsman of the powerful New York clan of the same name into which Montgomery himself had married, to enlist a regiment of Canadians. Finally, he placed his second in command, General David Wooster, Arnold's longtime New Haven neighbor and sometime adversary, in charge of Montreal. The aging, crotchety Wooster, upset with the Continental Congress for having offered him only a brigadier's commission, had recently come north with a regiment of Connecticut Continentals. All told, Wooster would have about five hundred troops to help him garrison Montreal.

Montgomery appreciated the necessity of getting to Pointe aux Trembles—and before Quebec—as soon as possible. Although exhausted from his herculean labors, he set sail with three hundred troops, all from New York, on Tuesday, November 28. At Sorel his small fleet picked up Arnold's old nemesis, John Brown, and some 160 soldiers who had not followed Easton home. Later, about two hundred Canadian recruits under James Livingston would link up with the Montgomery-Arnold force outside the walls of Quebec.[10]

Arnold, meanwhile, kept sending reports to Montgomery, including one delivered by feisty little Aaron Burr with news that the four British war vessels had sailed back downriver toward Quebec. Montgomery thus would face "no danger in coming down, . . . except that of ice." Arnold went on to recommend volunteer Burr as a person of "great spirit and resolution," just in case Montgomery had an open staff appointment—he did. Late on the morning of Friday, December 1, the advance vessels of Montgomery's fleet hove into view. The two columns had at last come together. Their combined strength would amount to no more than 1,325 soldiers, some seven hundred below Arnold's prescribed number for conquering fortress-like Quebec.[11]

Montgomery and Arnold met for the first time that day, and the colonel

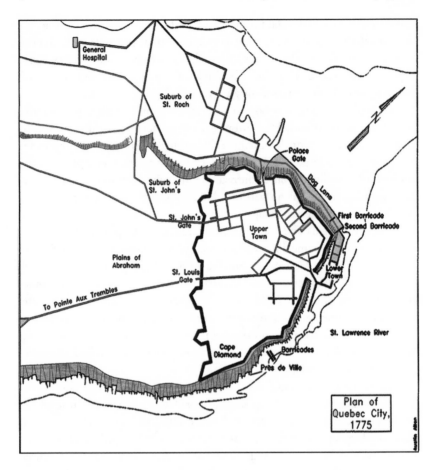

General Hospital

Suburb of St. Roch

Palace Gate

Dog Lane

Suburb of St. John's

First Barricade

Second Barricade

St. John's Gate

Upper Town

Plains of Abraham

St. Louis Gate

Lower Town

To Pointe Aux Trembles

St. Lawrence River

Cape Diamond

Barricades

Près de Ville

Plan of Quebec City, 1775

graciously acknowledged his status as the general's subordinate. Late in the afternoon, Arnold ordered out his detachment for Montgomery's review and inspection. "He made us a short but energetic and elegant speech," recalled Private Henry, "the burden of which was an applause to our spirit in passing the wilderness; a hope that our perseverance in the same spirit would continue; and a promise of warm clothing." Arnold's soldiers replied with a "few huzzahs from our freezing bodies."[12]

Montgomery clearly made a positive first impression. Captain Thayer described him as "a genteel appearing man, tall and slender of make, bald on the top of his head, resolute and mild, of an agreeable temper." The soldiers noticed his pock-marked face, but like Private Morison what struck them most was the general's "easy and affable condescension to both officers and men," which "forbids an improper familiarity, creates love and esteem, and exhibits him the gentleman and soldier." Montgomery's command presence inspired confidence, as did his recent spate of victories.[13]

During his thirty-seven years, Montgomery had gained extensive military experience as a British regular officer fighting in America during the Seven Years' War. His highest rank was a captaincy. In 1772 he sold his commission, migrated to New York, and purchased a modest-sized farm before marrying Janet Livingston, the daughter of powerful and wealthy Robert R. Livingston. His family connections helped him gain a Continental brigadier's commission in June 1775. Still, as he explained to Arnold and others, his only military ambition was to see Canada secured for the patriot cause. He then intended to return home to his beloved Janet, whom he sorely missed; resign the commission; and serve the rebellion in other capacities.[14]

Montgomery possessed a well-tutored military mind. By the time he reached Pointe aux Trembles, he had considered various operational plans for conquering Quebec. Arnold, who was a raw military novice by comparison, eagerly absorbed the knowledge of his more experienced senior. For his part, Montgomery treated Arnold with respect, all of which resulted in harmonious command relations between these two comrades in arms.

On their first evening together, Montgomery and Arnold discussed how they might reduce the walled city. Neither was overly optimistic. Stating that "until Quebec is taken, Canada is unconquered," Montgomery laid out tactical options, which included "siege, investment, or storm." Employing traditional siege tactics was out of the question. Trenches could not be dug in ground so solidly frozen, and the artillery pieces Montgomery had brought along, mostly captured at Fort St. Johns, were not powerful enough "to break walls like those of Quebec," even the weaker sections in disrepair. "Investment" held "fewer objections." To shut off the flow of "necessary supplies of food and fuel" to Quebec's inhabitants was unattainable with so small a force, presuming the defenders had not already gathered in several months' worth of provisions. Without significant reinforcements, Montgomery concluded, the tactics of investment would prove futile, especially with "the enemy's works being very extensive, and offering many avenues to the neighboring settlements."

Only one alternative, "the storming plan," seemed to have merit. Back in 1759, Montgomery pointed out, Montcalm had let "his courage . . . to get the better of his discretion." Carleton fully appreciated the consequences of Montcalm's error. He would not come out onto the plains for a set-piece battle but would stay inside the walls, no matter what, Montgomery reasoned. Thus a key element in any plan had to involve harassing the Upper Town, hoping to "breed discontent" and confusion among Carleton's supporters. The goal would be to wear down Quebec's defenders by keeping them constantly on alert while making them prepare for an attack "at all times and places." Meanwhile, "as master of our secret," the patriot commanders could "select a particular time and place for attack" before the defenders could figure out the actual rebel battle plan. Storming the Upper Town was the only alternative, declared Montgomery, and the assault had to be launched well before springtime when the river would "open and let in supplies and reinforcements to the garrison." [15]

If possible, Arnold pointed out, the strike should come before January 1, 1776, because, as of the New Year, enlistments among the Kennebec troops would be up. Many of them, Arnold warned, were already talking of little else but returning home. Two men, and possibly even more, had recently left Pointe aux Trembles on no one's authority but their own; he expected more desertions in the days ahead. Montgomery understood, based on his experiences at Montreal. If the opportunity presented itself, he promised, the assault would come before the New Year, but only after waging a form of psychological warfare designed to fray nerves as well as foment dissension among Quebec's defenders. [16]

III

A few days after their first meeting, Montgomery paid Arnold a great compliment by calling his detachment "an exceeding fine one," certainly "inured to fatigue," if nothing else. "There is a style of discipline" among his troops, he wrote to Schuyler, "much superior to what I have been used to see[ing in] this campaign." Regarding Arnold, Montgomery referred to him as "active, intelligent, and enterprising." Because he found his subordinate so sagacious, the general was paying "particular attention to Colonel Arnold's recommendations" with respect to reducing Quebec. [17]

These words would have buoyed Arnold, had he read them, since he was having problems with two subordinate officers, Daniel Morgan and Oliver Hanchet. Arnold and Morgan had earlier engaged in a nasty shouting match about shortages of food and supplies for the riflemen, who were regularly conducting scouting missions and gathering intelligence around Quebec City. Arnold finally said he would provision the riflemen more generously, although not at the expense of other troops, an agreement that appeased Morgan.

The rift with Hanchet was more serious. Arnold's earlier problems with this officer had turned Hanchet into an avowed antagonist and fomenter of anti-Arnold animus, all of which started to become clear on Saturday,

December 2. Early that morning, Arnold handed out assignments for moving back to Quebec, and he ordered Hanchet to take charge of three vessels designated to carry the heavier artillery pieces and other vital military goods downriver. The Connecticut captain peremptorily refused, "alleging the danger of such an undertaking to be too imminent." "Enraged" by such insubordination, Arnold "swore he would arrest" Hanchet, then curtly dismissed him. Then he sought out Captains Thayer and Topham, asking if either of them would "perform the said command." Eager to do so, they flipped a coin; Thayer won the "*head or tail*" contest. The next evening he spiritedly led his company in executing what proved a most dangerous assignment. Dodging large chunks of ice while all but blinded by a "prodigious" snowstorm, Thayer's troops helped maneuver the heavily laden craft down the St. Lawrence for unloading near Quebec.[18]

For various reasons, including temporizing counsel from Montgomery and murmurings from Hanchet about marching his company home, Arnold chose not to place his dissident captain under arrest. He did so to maintain as much troop strength and harmony as possible in the face of the formidable challenge ahead. Rather, Arnold concentrated on other matters, such as distributing new clothing, mostly British military uniforms from Montreal. Even if dressed in the garb of enemy soldiers, his troops appreciated having garments that were not rotting off their bodies.

At midday on Monday, December 4, the patriot force began its trek back to the suburbs of Quebec City. The next morning Montgomery established his headquarters at Holland House, a grand French residence about two miles southwest of St. John's Gate. The general located his New York troops to his front and right, out along the Plains of Abraham. He assigned Arnold's musket companies to his left, ordering them to secure the suburb of St. Roch to the northwest of the Upper Town. Finally, he placed Morgan's rifle companies on Arnold's left, in the most exposed position of all. Situated in the lowlands next to the St. Charles River, they were to keep a close watch on the harbor area and Palace Gate, the lone entrance to the walled city from the north.

While refining these dispositions, Arnold had yet another confrontation with Hanchet. When he ordered him to assume an advanced position close to the wall, Hanchet "abruptly refused," claiming the assignment was "too dangerous, as being . . . half a mile exposed to the cannons of the enemy." Recognizing Hanchet for what he had become, a fainthearted malcontent, Arnold again looked the other way and called on ever-cooperative Captains Thayer and Topham to move into the forward positions. They did so with relish, but a few mornings later, the two captains had to question their zeal for hazardous duty when a burst of enemy artillery fire struck their place of lodging. One ball ripped through the bed in which the two captains had been sleeping. "Much to our astonishment," wrote Thayer, the projectile passed cleanly between the two officers, but they maintained their post without complaint to Arnold.[19]

Such unexpected cannonades were part of Carleton's response to the rebel game of harassment. Arnold and Montgomery met frequently to decide on actions for gaining tangible advantages, perhaps even an offer of surrender. One tactic was to spread misleading rumors. They allowed *habitants* to pass through the rebel lines into Quebec, telling the defenders that Montgomery's army was growing daily and soon would number forty-five hundred troops. When informed of this story, Carleton denounced it as a falsehood and reiterated that he would never surrender. Country inhabitants, noted Collector Ainslie, were also relating "that the *Bostonnais* were musket proof, being all covered with sheet iron." This falsehood, he explained, had resulted from confusion over a French word used to describe lightweight clothing. Amazed at how the patriots seemed "insensible of cold and wore nothing but linen in the most severe seasons, the French word *toile* (linen)" somehow got "changed to *tolle* (iron plate)." Most likely, the patriots encouraged such confusion to whittle away at Carleton's base of support among French inhabitants inside the city.[20]

No patriot ruse seemed to work. When a prostitute presented herself at Palace Gate, spoke of rebel soldiers "drunk at her house," and encouraged Quebec's defenders to come out and capture them "without risk," her listeners sent her scurrying away, shouting that they were not stupid enough to fall so easily into "rebel clutches." On Wednesday, December 6, Montgomery asked an elderly woman to carry two messages into town. The first, directed to "friends and fellow subjects," conjured up images of a bloody battle and "the city in flames at this severe season" unless they repudiated "ministerial hirelings" like Carleton and accorded the patriot force a "peaceable admission" into the city. The second, addressed to the governor, spoke of "the absurdity of resistance" against inspired "troops, accustomed to success, confident of the righteousness of the cause they are engaged in, [and] inured to danger and fatigue." Carleton contemptuously ordered an aide to place this missive in a pair of tongs and hold it in a roaring fireplace until consumed by the flames. He then had the woman drummed out of the Upper Town.

The rebels continued to deliver communications any way they could. Montgomery had French translations prepared of his two messages and solicited the same old woman to distribute them inside the city. She did so on December 7, for which brazen act Carleton had her clamped in jail for a few days before again drumming her out of town. When the woman did not immediately return, Montgomery had copies affixed to arrows and shot over the walls by Natanis's Indians, but with no effect.[21]

On Friday, December 15, at 10 a.m., Arnold and Captain John Macpherson, one of Montgomery's aides-de-camp, accompanied by a drummer and carrying a flag of truce, approached the walls and demanded to speak with the governor. Arnold carried a letter with him promising Carleton and Cramahé safe conduct to England, should they choose the wise course of surrender. The governor curtly refused any meeting, stating forcefully that he would never negotiate with rebel scum. When Arnold and Macpherson, after a lengthy wait, received Carleton's reply, they shouted to those on the ramparts, "Then let the general be answerable for all consequences." [22]

So far Montgomery and Arnold had gained nothing, which explains why they looked the other way when some of Morgan's riflemen borrowed *carioles* (sleighs) and went on a plundering expedition to Cramahé's country home. These soldiers seized not only basic supplies—"firkin after firkin of butter, lard, tallow, beef, pork, fresh and salt"—but everything else—paintings, furniture, pillows, and silverware—they could carry away. Nothing escaped "the notice of our cupidity," Private Henry trumpeted. There were only a few such looting excursions, and as Henry explained, "we plundered none but those who were notoriously tories, and then within the walls of Quebec." [23]

The rebel message was not very subtle. Ranking British resisters could expect to have their private property seized or destroyed. Others of wealth, such as old-subject merchants still in Quebec, became quite anxious about losing their possessions, but the rebels avoided plundering the goods of influential citizens whom they hoped would support the cause of liberty. Selective looting was thus a means of fomenting anti-Carleton opposition inside the city. The governor, however, had such firm control that property holders did not confront him with demands for surrender.

Montgomery and Arnold had only two other methods to pressure Carleton into submission, short of an all-out assault. The first was selective sniper fire, most ably performed by Morgan's sharpshooting riflemen. Concealed in buildings outside the walls, they used their long rifles to maim or kill any human target on the ramparts. Wrote an angry Customs Collector Ainslie, rebel snipers were "worse than savages." To "lie in wait to shoot a sentry" would "ever be held in contempt with men of courage." The sniper fire, which killed a few defenders, had the opposite effect of raising "the indignation of our militia," claimed Ainslie. Still, a few days later he prayed "to God that the suburbs be reduced to ashes," since they served only "as a cover from which our enemies tease us continually." The sniper fire, it seems, was taking a psychological toll.[24]

Montgomery and Arnold also hoped for positive results by cannonading the city. After Carleton rejected Montgomery's written demands for surrender, the patriots set up two artillery batteries. The first, consisting of five mortars and two fieldpieces under the direction of Captain Isaiah Wool, operated in Arnold's command zone of St. Roch. Wool kept moving these weapons so that they would not be destroyed by shells from Carleton's more powerful artillery pieces. The St. Roch battery had little effect except in drawing enemy fire, including an instance noted by Dr. Senter in which a French prostitute died from a hurtling cannonball while "in her brothel administering a spirituous potion to one of our lads."[25]

The St. Roch battery unleashed its first "fire pills," as Dr. Senter dubbed the shells, in the predawn hours of Sunday, December 10. The inhabitants, noted Ainslie, initially acted as if every shot "would inevitably kill a dozen or two of people, and knock down some two or three houses." But within a few days they were calling the shells, which varied in weight from 6 to 12 pounds, "bombettes." Even though one woman lost her life during the spurts of rebel cannonading, everyone now "walked the streets laughing at their former fears." The lightness of the rebel artillery buoyed the defenders, who had as many as two hundred ordnance pieces, with some capable of firing shells up to 32 pounds in weight. The real threat, they realized, was the destruction the rebels might inflict with their small arms should they ever get inside the walls. That thought served to stiffen their resolve.[26]

Under the direction of Montgomery's chief artillerist, Captain John Lamb, the patriots located their second—and main—battery about seven hundred yards southwest of St. John's Gate. Since the ground was frozen and little earth could be dug up to form a protective breastwork, Canadian volunteers brought in piles of sticks, which they tied together as fascines and staked to the ground. Then they secured the fascines with makeshift gabions, or bags filled with snow and whatever dirt they could find. Adding straw and additional snow, they carried in buckets of water to pour over the accumulated mass of material. As the water froze, the breastwork soon turned into a wall of ice that blended into the snow-whitened landscape.

To protect themselves from enemy fire, work parties labored only at night, beginning on December 9. Because of the "extreme cold," wrote Major Meigs, "I froze my feet." Many others also experienced frostbite. At last, after five evenings of intense labor, Lamb moved in five cannons and one howitzer—none capable of firing anything heavier than 12-pound balls.

Patriot soldiers regarded the breastwork as an indestructible engineering marvel, but they would soon revise their opinion.[27]

The rebel activity did not go unnoticed by the "Carletonians," as Dr. Senter now labeled Quebec's defenders. Sentries on the ramparts spied the work site on the morning of December 10, but rows of houses in the suburb of St. John's, wrote Ainslie, "hindered our view." Invariably ready with countermeasures, Carleton ordered these buildings burned. The governor did not fret about those still living in St. John's. Since they had not yet taken shelter inside the walled city, he considered them rebel collaborators.[28]

On Friday morning, December 15, the patriot ice battery opened up with a steady barrage of artillery fire. Then Lamb's cannoneers paused while Arnold and Macpherson parleyed at the walls. As soon as they retreated, both sides engaged in a furious exchange of shells. Carleton's more powerful weaponry took an exacting toll. By evening the ice battery, or what Private Simon Fobes now described as "our heap of nonsense," lay in ruins. Patriot cannonading from the two batteries had accomplished virtually nothing. "Their shot had no more effect upon our walls," scoffed Collector Ainslie, "than peas would have against a plank." For so little intimidation the price for the rebels came in casualties, among them Jemima Warner, the dauntless woman who had stayed with her dying husband back on the trail to Quebec, only to be killed on December 11 while on duty at the St. Roch battery.[29]

IV

On December 8, General Montgomery rode in a *cariole* from Holland House to Arnold's headquarters at Menut's Tavern on the edge of St. Roch. As he walked into the tavern, an enemy cannonball obliterated his carriage and decapitated the horse that had just pulled him across the frozen landscape. Survival in war and winning battles, Montgomery appreciated, was sometimes a matter of luck, and he had just been very lucky. Like Arnold, he had hoped for good fortune in effecting a surrender short of combat. After the destruction of the ice battery, the two patriot officers agreed about the necessity, as Montgomery wrote to Schuyler, of making "an effort for the reduction of the town."[30]

Other considerations, besides Carleton's obduracy, gave them little choice. They could not be sure how long the local *habitants* would support their force if they did not act decisively. Even more pressing was the spreading menace of smallpox. Private Henry blamed the outbreak on the "indecorous, yet fascinating arts of the enemy." The disease was taking a toll inside the city, and Carleton apparently sent smallpox victims into the American lines.

Besides this deadly malady, the bitterly cold and snowy weather was a source of distress. Dr. Senter reported from his General Hospital, actually a nunnery near the south bank of the St. Charles River a mile west of St. Roch, that pleurisy, pneumonia, and "other species of pulmonic complaints" were striking down troops at an alarming rate.[31]

Increasing numbers of desertions likewise worried the two patriot leaders, and Captain Hanchet was still causing trouble. When Arnold assembled his officers on December 16 to discuss attacking the Upper Town, a heated debate ensued. Finally a "large majority," wrote Major Meigs, agreed to an assault on the condition that their troops were "provided with bayonets, spears, hatchets, and hand grenades." Leading the minority was Hanchet, who had rallied two other company commanders, Captains William Goodrich and Jonas Hubbard, to his side. As they soon informed Montgomery, they wanted nothing more to do with Arnold's command, and they refused to join the attack unless placed under another field-grade officer, a person who had no doubt kept Hanchet stirred up once he found out about the rift.[32]

Without naming names, Montgomery spoke of a "friend" who was "deeply concerned in this business." The culprit was Major John Brown, who had served effectively with Montgomery during the Montreal campaign but who still felt unremitting enmity toward Arnold. Brown was ambitious for rank and military fame. Garnering in three of Arnold's companies to complement the 160 troops currently under his own command would have given him the makings of a regiment, thereby helping to justify a promotion to a colonelcy, which he would later claim Montgomery had promised him.

Brown's timing was awful. He and Hanchet were purposely stirring up discord when command unity was essential. Montgomery viewed the conflict in terms of petty "resentment against Arnold"; he supported his second in command. To do otherwise "will hurt him so much that I do not think I can consent to it." Although anxious about troop shortages, Montgomery refused the disgruntled captains' offer to extend their enlistments, while encouraging their troops to do the same in return for reassignment under Brown. The malcontents responded by announcing their intention to wait out the few days remaining on their enlistments; they would then lead their companies home.[33]

Montgomery tried to calm everyone down by appealing to patriotic sensibilities. On Christmas Day he assembled Arnold's soldiers and addressed the need to put service to the cause of liberty above personal differences. Arnold kept his own counsel, except in answering a supportive letter from Dr. Senter. After conversations with soldiers in the dissident companies, the physician explained how numbers of these troops wanted to participate in the assault, regardless of their captains' obstinacy. Senter offered to take charge of one of the companies. Acknowledging this "spirited" gesture, Arnold politely refused, reminding the doctor of the vital importance of well-organized medical support. He asked Senter to stand ready to attend to the needs of the wounded.[34]

Arnold penned this note on Wednesday, December 27, shortly after Montgomery had issued orders for everyone to prepare themselves for combat "at the shortest notice." The plan was to strike late at night under the cover of turbulent weather. A heavy snowstorm was then unleashing its fury. To confuse the Carletonians, Lieutenant Colonel Christopher Greene was to lead a diversionary thrust against the Lower Town, which was the center of commercial exchange but also heavily defended. Montgomery and Arnold would direct the bulk of their force in breaking into the Upper Town by scaling the walls near the Cape Diamond bastion. Shortly after midnight, however, the storm suddenly subsided. Moonlight soon was casting a luminous glow on the freshly fallen snow. Scaling the walls without detection was no longer possible. Montgomery called off the assault.[35]

Arnold now fought to keep up his own spirits. In the original battle plan he was to lead the diversion, but at the last moment the assignment went to Greene, who was on good terms with Arnold but a neutral in the Hanchet controversy. Montgomery made the switch with the hope of getting the disaffected captains to place their companies under Greene and join in the feint against the Lower Town. Although Arnold graciously accepted his commander's explanation about the greater importance of leadership at the main point of attack, he knew these words were a palliative.[36]

Despite Montgomery's judiciousness, Arnold could not help feeling somewhat slighted. With the exception of a few sharp words, he had controlled his temper in the face of Hanchet's ongoing slurs and insubordination. Arnold would have liked to call out the three churlish captains and demonstrate to them that they had no good reason to smear his good name. Still, he realized that Montgomery wanted to resolve the dispute in his favor; and as a virtuous rather than selfish patriot, he did not want to jeopardize the conquering of Quebec City in any way. Defending his honor against the likes of Hanchet and Brown would have to be put aside—at least for the moment.

Arnold soon received an unexpected form of comfort. A few fainthearted soldiers had failed to muster for the aborted assault. The next morning, Captains Thayer and Topham encouraged their troops to seize four of these shirkers, as Thayer wrote, and lead "them from place to place with halters around their necks, exposing them to . . . ridicule . . . as a punishment due to their effeminate courage." Topham considered the haltering ceremony a fit form of censure for cowards, "who after entering into the . . . service should refuse to do their duty at such a time as this." He expressed nothing but contempt for patriot enlistees who were "afraid of dying." [37]

Many of the famine-proof veterans interpreted the haltering ceremony, then a common form of public humiliation, as a condemnatory statement about the character of the disgruntled captains as well. The bulk of Arnold's officers and troops saw nothing but merit in their colonel's leadership, and they openly scoffed at Hanchet and his associates. The Pennsylvania riflemen, Private Henry noted, were asking why "the patriotism of the summer of seventy-five" was vanishing so quickly among the New England troops. He wondered whether "the austerity of the winter," "the harshness of the service," or something more deeply ingrained, such as lack of nerve, had caused so many troops to reject pleas about extending their enlistments into the New Year. Some even wondered whether the real problem was cowardice in the face of the enemy among certain New England officers. [38]

Surviving records do not indicate why the disaffected captains developed a renewed sense of duty. Possible reasons include Montgomery's skillful diplomacy and pressure from soldiers who resented being subjected to imputations of timidity solely because they were under the command of the malcontents. Thoughts of plunder may also have entered the equation, since Montgomery had promised his force "the effects" of every defender who was "active" in denying Quebec to "the friends of liberty." As a New Englander wrote home, those who survived the assault "will live well" because they can "take what they please." Whatever the explanation, Hanchet, Goodrich, and Hubbard soon led their companies into combat under Arnold's command. [39]

As Montgomery and Arnold formulated yet another plan of assault, they realized how limited their options were. Making their task especially vexing was the steady flow of detailed intelligence into Quebec. When Joshua Wolf, an employee of Colonel Caldwell, escaped from the rebels on December 22, he told Carleton about the stockpiling of scaling ladders and the imminence of an attack. Two days later, a rebel deserter explained that Wolf's escape had forced Montgomery to delay a planned strike, just in case Carleton had placed Quebec on full alert. After the aborted assault of December 27, a New York sergeant, Samuel Singleton, fled to the enemy and confirmed rumors of an attack on "the first dark night." Such reports confirmed what the governor was hearing from spies planted among the patriot force. [40]

For Carleton, the only element of surprise would be the actual design of attack—he knew that the rebels, with enlistments running out, hoped to strike before the New Year. From Christmas Eve onward, he slept in full military uniform in the Récollet Monastery across the street from the governor's mansion, as did other off-duty officers and soldiers. The Carletonians may have slept, but they did so fitfully, waiting for any sign of an assault. The governor also watched the weather very closely. When an "outrageous" snowstorm, actually a northeaster with "cold wind extremely biting," started unleashing its wrath at sunset on Saturday, December 30, he could almost feel his adversaries making final preparations for battle. Carleton hardly slept at all, especially after midnight when the storm intensified dramatically.

V

Reckoning with the steady flow of information into Quebec, a pensive Montgomery decided to reverse the previous battle plan and attack through the Lower Town. He divided his small army of little more than one thousand effectives into four units. To foment as much confusion as possible among Quebec's defenders, James Livingston's Canadians were to make a feint against St. John's Gate and, if time permitted, Palace Gate, with the intent of setting both on fire. John Brown's soldiers were to form a second diversionary party and create the impression of a major attack at the Cape Diamond bastion.[41]

When Brown's party struck, they were to ignite rocket flares as a signal for Arnold, who was in command of his detachment as well as John Lamb's artillery company (about six hundred troops overall). From St. Roch, Arnold's troops were to proceed along a narrow pathway between the St. Charles River and the imposing bluff jutting straight up to the walled Upper Town. Once in position, they were to storm the barricades below the Sault au Matelot (Sailor's Leap) precipice, a tip of land overlooking the spot where the St. Charles flowed into the St. Lawrence River, and gain access to the Lower Town from its northern end.

Meanwhile, Montgomery and three hundred New York soldiers were to assemble on the Plains of Abraham. They would first descend the pathway leading to Wolfe's Cove, where they were to turn left and follow a treacherously narrow trail for two miles between the escarpment and the ice-clogged St. Lawrence River. Once beneath Cape Diamond, they would have to penetrate two barriers blocking the trail in the area known as Près de Ville before pushing forward into the Lower Town from the southern side.

If all these maneuvers worked, Montgomery's Yorkers were to link up with Arnold's famine-proof veterans near the center of the Lower Town. At this juncture, the two patriot officers planned to stop, consolidate their

gains, and possibly even push forward, with the idea of breaking through the
heavily defended gate near the top of steep, winding Mountain Hill Street,
thereby gaining access to the Upper Town from its eastern side. Private
Henry thought that when the forces "conjoined," Montgomery and Arnold
intended to gather up residents and drive them up Mountain Hill Street as a
human shield "intermingled" among the rebels. Quebec's defenders would
surely lay down their arms rather than shoot down innocent townspeople.
Other troops held that Montgomery's design was to secure the Lower Town
and threaten to destroy everything, particularly the shops and warehouses of
influential merchants. He would then count on civilians desperate to save
their property to pressure Carleton into surrendering. According to Collector
Ainslie, the governor had already considered this possibility. As unyielding as
ever, he declared that he would cannonade the Lower Town into "a heap of
rubbish."[42]

The major rebel problem was to penetrate the Lower Town's well-placed
defenses. Once in the Sault au Matelot zone, Arnold's column would have
to break through two fortified barricades, each defended with light artillery.
The first barrier, more than ten feet high, ran from the bluff to the St.
Charles River and blocked off Dog Lane, the only route into the Lower
Town on the northern side. The second barrier was three hundred yards
beyond the first one, located at the far end of tightly packed buildings lining
Dog Lane. This barricade had to be taken to reach Sault au Matelot Street,
which then ran in a southerly direction parallel to the escarpment toward
Mountain Hill Street.

Montgomery's troops would also confront two barriers, separated by
about one hundred yards, before reaching a fortified two-story log house. If
they could get beyond these Près de Ville defenses, where huge ice chunks
thrown up by the St. Lawrence River left little room for combat maneuvers,
they would then have to march northward for nearly a mile before reaching
Mountain Hill Street, hopefully without confronting heavy enemy resistance.

Although fraught with danger, the battle plan had its advantages. With
four forces striking in orchestrated fashion, the enemy was bound to react in
confusion. Moving out so late at night might catch on-duty defenders asleep
or, considering the ferocious wind and frigid temperatures, tipsy from heavy
drinking. Even though Carleton had nearly twice as many soldiers under
arms, he was lacking in trained regulars and had a huge area to defend.
Montgomery hoped the governor would order his most experienced troops
to reinforce defenders at the western wall, based on his knowledge of the
previous battle plan. Meanwhile, a sudden rout of skittish British or French
militiamen in the Lower Town might well cause enough panic to assure a

patriot triumph before Carleton had time to reverse his initial troop deployments and get his best troops into the major battle sector.

Still, by any reasonable calculation, "to storm a place so strongly defended," as Private Abner Stocking wrote, "was rash and imprudent." Had Montgomery or Arnold known of Stocking's assessment, they might have nodded in agreement but then reminded this soldier of the need for decisive action before the New Year 1776 brought an end to the enlistments of so many New England troops. A steadfast pledge to endure above all else in arms would have permitted greater flexibility in planning. Montgomery could even have postponed the assault—at least to a time when the Carletonians were running short of key supplies or showing signs of nervous fatigue over the continuing threat of a strike. But without a firm sense of long-term commitment on the part of their troops, Montgomery and Arnold had to strike when they did—with prayers for success before their ranks became too thin to achieve their objective of getting Quebec Province fully aligned with the patriot cause.[43]

Arnold and other key officers met with Montgomery in a council of war at Holland House late on the evening of December 30. Dr. Senter described Montgomery as "extremely anxious," if not in a state of "despondency." Others had forebodings of disaster as well, but the officers agreed unanimously to start assembling all available troops at 2 a.m., unless the storm abated. They also decided to have everyone, officers and enlistees alike, attach to their head coverings not only sprigs of hemlock but also pieces of paper with three words—"LIBERTY OR DEATH"—boldly displayed. That way, patriots wearing British uniforms would not confuse their comrades with the Carletonians.[44]

In the early hours of Sunday, December 31, the storm built up to a new crescendo of fury. Arnold had returned to St. Roch and had his troops in position by 4 a.m., the appointed time for the units on the Plains of Abraham to advance. As Montgomery led the Yorkers down to Wolfe's Cove, the two diversionary parties moved to the attack. Shortly after 4:30 a.m., they struck. Livingston's Canadians tried to ignite St. John's Gate, but the driving wind kept snuffing out their torches. Brown's troops began shooting at shadowy figures guarding Cape Diamond bastion. The storm muffled the loud popping of their muskets but did not cover up flashes of powder.

Captain Malcolm Fraser of the Royal Highland Emigrants was in charge of Quebec's guard that night. Gazing westward beyond the ramparts, he thought he saw intermittent flickers of light, perhaps from partially shielded lanterns, perhaps from musket fire. Then two rocket flares blazed skyward from beyond Cape Diamond bastion. Fraser did not react at first but stood still in amazement; then reality sunk in. He had just witnessed a rebel attack signal. Within seconds he started running toward the Récollet Monastery shouting, "Turn Out!" "Turn Out!" "Turn Out!" Carleton, ready for action, met him at the monastery's entrance.[45]

By the time Arnold saw the rocket flares, he was more than ready for action. If any patriot officer or soldier still questioned his capacity for military leadership, he intended to prove him wrong that morning. For as long as he could remember, human conflict had affected his life, and Arnold had learned to thrive and prosper in confrontational situations. Success in the impending battle, he reasoned, would surely establish his virtue as a committed patriot, as well as spread glory upon his tarnished family name. Demonstrating his courage would also show his doubters that Benedict Arnold belonged where he stood at that moment—at the head of his column leading rather than merely ordering his brave troops into battle.

Arnold signaled the twenty-five volunteers who formed the "forlorn hope," or advance party, to follow him. Off they strode into the blinding snowstorm, groping toward the first Sault au Matelot barricade. Immediately behind them was Captain Lamb and his artillery company, using a sled to haul a small cannon capable of firing 6-pound balls. Then came Morgan, the riflemen, and the Kennebec musketmen. Bringing up the rear were the companies of Hanchet, Goodrich, and Hubbard followed by a few Canadians and Indians, among them Natanis.[46]

Out in front, the resolute colonel pushed forward at a brisk pace, proceeding along a pathway so narrow that his troops could only advance single file behind him. The wind raged at Arnold, and stinging snow pelted his face. Soon he was past Palace Gate, at which point he thought he heard a cacophony of noises coming from the Upper Town—church bells pealing, dogs howling, humans shouting, and cannons firing—amid the whistling and hissing sounds of gale-force wind and snow. The rocket flares, he imagined, had startled the enemy into action. He hoped the feints had fooled Carleton into rushing his best-trained troops away from the principal attack zone.

More time passed, and the first barricade loomed ahead. Soon the rest of the forlorn hope came up, and Arnold spread the word to wait quietly until Lamb's artillerists joined them and took aim at the wooden wall with the 6-pounder. Then, unexpectedly, a hailstorm of musket balls cascaded toward the rebels. Before Arnold could react, a ricocheting ball sliced into his lower left leg. Experiencing a burst of pain, he instinctively put weight on the limb but almost fell down. He felt warm blood oozing into his boot.

Arnold's thoughts clouded as the pain spread from his leg into his torso. For a brief moment, he wondered if he might bleed or freeze to death without ever knowing whether the assault succeeded. Leaning against a wall, he soon regarded the large frame of Daniel Morgan lumbering toward him. Lamb's artillerists had fallen behind, the captain reported; they could not keep the 6-pounder moving through the deep snow. They would likely have to abandon the piece, Morgan guessed. The barriers would have to be taken without supporting cannon fire.

Morgan then noticed Arnold's bloodied limb. He called over Chaplain Spring and a rifleman and ordered them to direct their wounded commander to the General Hospital. Arnold protested but was too weak to resist. He wished Morgan Godspeed and watched unsteadily as the Virginian ordered his troops to bring forward scaling ladders. With the chaplain and the rifleman propping him up on either side, Arnold hobbled away. Intensely disappointed, he promised himself that he would have other opportunities to engage the enemy and earn his share of glory, if he somehow survived this terrible wound.[47]

By the time Arnold's helpers had guided him back to the vicinity of Palace Gate, he could no longer walk. He despaired as he watched his troops advance ever so slowly through the blowing snow, even as galling musket fire poured down from the ramparts above. Balls were finding human targets, and a few patriots were already dead or writhing in the snow with serious wounds. Some of the wounded would freeze to death before full daylight. Straining to remain conscious, Arnold, according to Private Henry, "called to the troops in a cheering voice . . . urging us forward." For many, however, the sight of their disabled commander "dampened their spirits." They kept moving toward the barricade but whispered to each other, " 'We are sold.' "[48]

Dawn was breaking when Chaplain Spring and the rifleman, having carried Arnold for a mile after passing beyond Palace Gate, finally reached the General Hospital. A few wounded soldiers were already at the makeshift facility, and the nuns who lived in this convent building were helping to comfort them. When Dr. Senter saw Arnold, he quickly examined his colonel's wound. A musket ball had splintered against "a cannon, rock, stone or the like," the physician surmised, before the larger portion dug through Arnold's left leg. The ball had "entered the outer side of the leg, about midway" between the knee and ankle, before taking an "oblique course" downward and lodging "at the rise of the tendon achilles." Arnold grimaced as Senter probed for the piece of metal and "easily . . . extracted it." Once the bleeding was under control, he bandaged the limb and assured his commander that amputation would not be necessary unless an infection set in.[49]

As more wounded patriots reached the General Hospital, they offered their impressions of the battle. Senter was just finishing with Arnold when Matthias Ogden came in with a slight shoulder wound. He spoke of Morgan leading the way in breaching the first barricade. The attack was not going well, however, and he "gave it as his opinion that we should not be successful." As yet, no one had any information about Montgomery's force. Everyone at the hospital was in a state of "anxious suspense" until, at last, a messenger arrived and presented a gruesome summary of events.[50]

The Yorkers, with Montgomery in the lead, had made their way to the first Près de Ville barricade and cut through it. The general moved forward to the second barrier and helped saw through two of the log posts on the cliffside. Then he and a few others crawled through the opening; they found themselves facing a rude two-story log house not more than fifty yards away. Unbeknownst to them, the handful of defenders, including sailors and militiamen, had heard the muffled, distant sound of church bells indicating an attack. In a panic they had nearly fled the fortified log house, which contained four small cannons capable of firing 3-pound balls. Adam Barnsfare, a sea captain, and John Coffin, a loyalist who had recently removed his family from Boston to Quebec City, refused to run without a token show of resistance. They convinced their comrades to offer a round or two of fire before retreating, should any rebels break through the barriers.

Montgomery and a few others cautiously approached the log house. Standing within point-blank range, the American general unsheathed his sword and waved it above his head, signaling a charge. At that moment, the defenders threw open portholes and fired their cannons and muskets. Flying metal cut through the patriots. Montgomery died instantly, his arm still raised in the air as he crashed backward into the snow, never knowing that the Continental Congress had recently granted him a major generalship for his valorous service in Canada. Two of his aides, Captains John Macpherson and Jacob Cheeseman, were also dead, along with a half-dozen others. Those who survived, among them Aaron Burr, fled back through the barricade in shock and panic.

Colonel Donald Campbell, second in command of Montgomery's column, rushed forward from the first barrier where he was exhorting troops to move up. He listened as a distraught lieutenant described the gory encounter. Beyond the barrier, artillery and musket fire kept emanating in sporadic bursts from the log house. A few of the Yorkers were attempting to shoot back, but their gunpowder was wet, and they could not ignite their muskets. Campbell consulted the panicky officers around him, and they favored a retreat. Rather than probing further to test the enemy's strength, the colonel now "found" himself "under the disagreeable necessity of drawing off the troops . . . at about 7 o'clock" in the morning. Leaving behind their fallen comrades, the Yorkers pulled back to the Plains of Abraham, where they sat out the rest of the battle in the vicinity of Holland House.[51]

Hardly had the mortifying news of Montgomery's death sunk in than a breathless soldier raced into the General Hospital with a report that enemy soldiers were approaching. Since the inception of the attack, a few rebel artillerists under Captain Wool had been firing shells from St. Roch into the Upper Town. Once Arnold's column had moved beyond the first Sault au Matelot barrier, Carleton ordered out a small detachment to silence the battery. These troops quickly accomplished their mission, easily seizing both the weaponry and some of the rebel gunners. Flushed with success, they then decided to attack the hospital.

Wool, who had barely evaded capture, soon appeared at the General Hospital. Arnold, lying prone on his back, asked him to offer resistance. The captain quickly assembled a group of defenders, including some of the less seriously wounded patriots, and ordered them to join him in the roadway. Within minutes they were moving back toward St. Roch with two small cannons in tow. Spying the advancing Carletonians, Wool's party took cover, then engaged them in an exchange of cannon shots. Just as the firing commenced, some of Livingston's Canadians and a few Yorkers, who were making their way from Holland House to the General Hospital, linked up with Wool's makeshift force. Their timing was fortuitous, and they helped drive off the enemy detachment. Wrote Dr. Senter, Wool had "much distinguished himself on this occasion," an otherwise inglorious day for the American rebels.[52]

VI

After Wool's force left the hospital, Dr. Senter and others "entreated" with Arnold "for his own safety to be carried back into the country where" the enemy "would not readily find him," but to "no purpose." Their colonel steadfastly refused. Instead, he "ordered his pistols loaded, with a sword on his bed, . . . adding that he was determined to kill as many as possible if they came into the room." He also insisted that every wounded soldier should have a musket. "We were now all soldiers," proclaimed Senter, with everyone in the hospital prepared "to make the most vigorous defense possible."[53]

By ten o'clock that gloomy morning, as the snowstorm continued to rage outside, the patriots at the General Hospital could no longer detect the sounds of far-distant musket and cannon fire. Most of Montgomery's Yorkers were safe, as were Livingston's and Brown's troops. No one could be sure, however, what had happened to Arnold's Kennebec veterans, whose numbers represented more than half of the rebel command.

Sometime before noon, Arnold composed a letter for General Wooster at Montreal summarizing the "critical situation." He still had not learned the fate of his detachment, but he was "exceedingly apprehensive." Three possibilities existed: "They will either carry the lower town, be made prisoners, or [be] cut to pieces." Although Arnold could not lead any relief effort, he intended to formulate plans for lending assistance to his column, if there was a column left to support. Something, he hoped, could be done under cover of darkness that New Year's Eve night. Meanwhile, he had placed Colonel Campbell in temporary command of the remaining force.

Then the wounded colonel added a postscript in which he stated the obvious: "It is impossible to say what our future operations will be, until we know the fate of my detachment." Those words chilled Arnold as he sealed the letter and handed it to a courier. The reality of the patriot situation was grim. The Northern Department army had suffered a devastating wound, perhaps best symbolized by his own mangled leg; the only question was the extent of the damage and how long it might take the rebels to recover.[54]

Despite tormenting physical pain, Arnold would not back off, and he dismissed any notion of retreat. He vowed to himself to find some means, if means could be found, to complete the conquering of Quebec Province, despite the distressing circumstances now facing the battered patriot force. As soon as his health permitted, he intended to reassume his command. And to sustain himself, he would keep drawing on his abiding faith in the "Providence which has carried me through so many dangers," he stated in a letter to his sister. "I . . . know no fear," Arnold likewise told Hannah, and "I have no thoughts of leaving this proud town, until I first enter it in triumph."[55]

CHAPTER *Eight*

A Winter's Worth of
Making Brick
without Straw

I

Patriot soldiers at the General Hospital had little reason to celebrate the New Year. "The prospect was gloomy on every side," stated Dr. Senter. As the hours dragged by on December 31, everyone became more apprehensive with "no intelligence from the troops in the Lower Town." Arnold did not delude himself with false expectations. He suspected the worst; his famine-proof veterans were either casualties or prisoners of war. Rather than risk the loss of yet more patriots by sending out a relief force, he deployed all those fit for duty in a defensive line running from the hospital to Holland House. With no more than eight hundred troops, including about four hundred Canadians and the sick and wounded, Arnold could only hope that Carleton did not sally forth from the walled city with a sizable detachment. Such an operation, he realized, would surely result in the destruction of his vulnerable patriot band.[1]

The suspense kept mounting as New Year's Day 1776 dawned. In an attempt to relieve the tension, Arnold finally succumbed to the appeals of a soldier who had repeatedly volunteered to go out in search of the lost column. This patriot promised to retrace the trail over which Arnold's column had passed into the Lower Town. Soon he was off, quickly disappearing into another driving snowstorm. He never returned.

Then early on Tuesday afternoon, January 2, more than fifty hours after all guns had fallen silent, the spectral figure of Return J. Meigs approached the General Hospital. One of Carleton's aides accompanied him. Arnold soon learned the major's new status, that of prisoner of war. The governor had extended Meigs a temporary parole so he could return to his rebel brethren and make arrangements to collect the baggage and personal effects of his fellow prisoners.

Arnold's troops had fought gallantly under Morgan's leadership, Meigs stated, but they had not broken through the second Sault au Matelot barricade. Some had died in the battle, including Captain William Hendricks of the Pennsylvania Riflemen. Others had sustained serious wounds, among them Artillery Captain John Lamb, who was barely clinging to life with a portion of his face and left eye blown away by grapeshot. Around four hundred patriots were now incarcerated inside the Upper Town, where, the major indicated, Quebec's defenders had so far treated them humanely.[2]

Responding to Arnold's queries, Meigs explained that the column had reached the second barricade but had lost the initiative while waiting to link up with Montgomery and the Yorkers. Daniel Morgan had led the charge against the first barricade. He called for scaling ladders and had them laid up against the wall. Then he clambered up one of them and peered over the other side. A sudden volley of enemy musket fire threw him backward off the ladder, and he came crashing down into a pile of snow. Morgan lay still for a short time, and some thought him dead. Actually knocked senseless, he slowly regained his bearings, pulled himself up, and blinked uncertainly at the soldiers surrounding him, his blackened face bleeding from gunpowder burns.

Steadying himself, Morgan soon bellowed at his riflemen to follow him. He charged back up the ladder, vaulted over the barricade, and crashed onto a platform supporting two cannons. Fortunately, he landed between their barrels, which protected him from the bayonet thrusts of the startled defenders. Before they could slice him to pieces, other riflemen came hurtling over the barrier. The Carletonians retreated in full panic. Within minutes these defenders, as well as civilians living along the street, were surrendering to rebel soldiers, who were now screaming such phrases as "Vive la liberté!" and "Quebec is ours!" Morgan's troops took more than one hundred prisoners after breaching the first barricade.

A French interpreter at his side, Morgan cantered down the street to reconnoiter the second barrier. To his amazement, no defenders were present. He opened a gate in the barricade and stepped through, only to confirm that all was quiet on the other side. Proceeding some distance up Sault au Matelot Street, the Virginian then returned back through the barrier and urged other officers to gather what troops they could and push into the

Lower Town before enemy resisters appeared. To a person, however, the officers refused. Not enough troops were yet through the first barricade, they stated. If too many patriots advanced, the prisoners might subdue their guards and effectively block any retreat. Their orders were to wait for Montgomery at the second barricade, not to advance beyond it. The officers "were sure of conquest if we acted in caution," Morgan later wrote, and "to these arguments I sacrificed my own opinion and lost the town."[3]

The opportunity to seize at least a portion of the Lower Town soon passed. Up in the walled city, Carleton had long since disregarded the rebels' brief diversionary thrusts along the western wall. Colonel Henry Caldwell, who had initially marched his British militiamen to Cape Diamond bastion, reversed his course and was now, with Carleton's approval, rushing his troops down Mountain Hill Street. Along the way a number of Royal Highland Emigrant regulars linked up with Caldwell, as did a former naval officer named Anderson at the head of some fifty sailors.

Some two hundred militiamen reached the second barricade just minutes before Caldwell's column arrived. Discerning rebel activity on the other side, these defenders seemed hopelessly confused, but Caldwell, who had once held a field-grade commission in the British army, steadied them. He barked out orders and organized the assemblage into two defensive lines with muskets primed and bayonets fixed; and he had artillery pieces hoisted onto a platform set high enough to fire over the barricade.

Morgan, meanwhile, was aware that Carletonians were massing on Sault au Matelot Street, where he had walked less than a half hour before. Ordering up scaling ladders, he planned to assault the second barrier. He kept hoping for assistance from Montgomery's column, which by this time should have been approaching Caldwell's soldiers from the rear. A pincer-like blow from the converging rebel forces might well have caused Caldwell's militiamen to panic and run—or even surrender.

Morgan was lining up his troops for the attack when the gate in the barricade swung open. Out stepped Captain Anderson at the head of a small squadron. Walking forward, the mariner shouted at the patriots to lay down their arms. Morgan raised his long rifle and shot Anderson dead on the spot. Even as Anderson's men scrambled back through the doorway, the rebels surged forward with loud cheers and slammed their ladders up against the barricade. All those who ventured up, Morgan prominent among them, were sent reeling backward from the blistering intensity of enemy fire. Caldwell's troops had stopped the rebel advance.

The coup de grâce came when Carleton decided to effect a pincers maneuver of his own. He ordered Captain George Laws to assemble a force, eventually numbering five hundred troops, and lead them out through Palace Gate to assail the rebels from the rear. Descending to the same pathway Arnold's column had earlier taken, Laws instructed his soldiers to move forward toward the first barricade. At around 8 a.m. they ran into Henry Dearborn's company. Dearborn saw Laws's troops coming and was about "to hail them, when one of them hailed me." Asked to identify himself, the patriot captain proclaimed himself a "friend . . . to liberty." The voice replied, "God damn you." Dearborn primed his musket, but the weapon failed to fire. "Neither I, nor one in ten of my men could get off our guns they being so exceeding wet," he later explained. Seeking cover in nearby houses, they tried to dry their powder and weapons, but to no avail. Now defenseless, Dearborn decided "to surrender after being promised good quarters and tender usage."[4]

Overly excited by Dearborn's capitulation, Laws personally rushed head-long past the first barrier and informed a party of rebels that they were his prisoners. His column had not kept up with him, and Laws temporarily became their captive. In reality, the rebels were entrapped. With Laws's column bearing down on the first barricade, they could not retreat, nor could they advance. Not even the "gigantic stature and terrible appearance" of Morgan, moving "as if he did not touch the earth," could rally them. With galling enemy fire coming at them from front and rear, as well as from the ramparts above, casualties mounted rapidly. Many took cover in houses and shops along the street, but they, too, found their powder and weapons too wet to return much fire. Despite the words attached to their head coverings, surrender or death was now their only viable alternative.[5]

By ten o'clock, the battle was all but over. Morgan was among the last to surrender. According to traditional accounts, he kept slashing his sword at his assailants, even though cornered against a wall, while shouting that he would never submit to armed dupes of the tyrannical British government. Then a priest appeared and offered to accept the Virginian's sword, which allowed Morgan to preserve his honor in laying down his weapon.

Except for life itself, not much else could be saved. Montgomery was dead. Patriot losses stood at fifty-one killed and thirty-six wounded, com-pared to just seven Carletonians dead and eleven wounded. Nearly two-thirds of Arnold's column had become prisoners of war, among them Oliver Hanchet. Captain Thayer, also a captive, effectively encapsulated the battle's outcome when he sardonically described the patriots' rout as a very "bad method to begin the new year."[6]

II

Arnold listened attentively as he received confirmation of his worst fears. He betrayed no feelings of distress but expressed confidence that the patriot cause would ultimately prevail. He readily acceded to Meigs's request to release whatever baggage and personal effects could be found. To help keep up the spirits of those brave souls who had endured so much under his command, now including the indignity of imprisonment, Arnold also provided money, some even from his own purse, so that the officers could make small purchases of necessities for themselves and needy soldiers.[7]

After saying goodbye to Meigs, Arnold prepared a report for General Wooster, who with Montgomery's death had become the ranking Continental officer in Canada. This missive revealed the emotional duress actually felt by Arnold, the product of "excessive pain from my wound (as the bones of my leg are affected)" and the burden of adjusting to so decisive a defeat. He noted how "dispirited" his officers were, and a great many troops were not only "dejected" but "anxious to get home." Dozens of rank and filers were packing up and leaving camp, intending to return to New England via Montreal. Exasperated that these patriots would forsake their comrades, even if their enlistments were up, Arnold implored Wooster "to stop every rascal who has deserted from us, and bring him back again."

The representation of those who had fulfilled their terms of service as craven deserters revealed the depth of Arnold's despondency. An evaporating army low on ammunition, food supplies, and hard money (the lubricant of goodwill with the *habitants*) encapsulated his problems, yet bedridden as he was, he could not even provide leadership in seeking out and exhorting downcast troops to reenlist. In addition, the prospect of Carleton emerging from his lair and wiping out what remained of his rebel band resulted in another frenzied sentence. "For God's sake," he beseeched Wooster, "order as many men down as you can possibly spare, consistent with the safety of Montreal, and all the mortars, howitzers, and shells that you can possibly bring."[8]

The letter to Wooster exposed a rare moment in which Arnold felt all but helpless. Dr. Senter had already informed him that he should confine himself to bed for up to two months to assure proper healing of his wounded leg. Someone had to serve as temporary commander, but various company-grade officers had already objected to Colonel Donald Campbell, blaming him for the precipitous flight of Montgomery's Yorkers. That left two choices, Colonel James Livingston and Major John Brown. Livingston, however, needed to keep recruiting Canadians in rebuilding depleted rebel numbers, and any notion of Brown in temporary command was wholly unacceptable to Arnold.[9]

The other possibility was Wooster, if he would come down from Montreal. This prospect hardly appealed to Arnold, so he could only bring himself to mention that "your presence will be absolutely necessary" in a postscript. Arnold recognized his fellow New Havenite for what he was, an experienced military veteran dating back to King George's War who could be rude and overbearing in manner, especially after heavy bouts of alcohol consumption. Now in his mid-sixties, Wooster correctly suspected that many rebel leaders, Washington and Schuyler prominent among them, viewed him as anything but an "enterprising genius." In retaliation, he let almost everyone have a good taste of his well-developed capacity for abrasiveness.[10]

Although Arnold respected some of Wooster's past deeds, including his leadership in New Haven's Masonic lodge, he recognized in him a person who could as easily alienate as rally the patriot troops still at Quebec. Yet Arnold had vowed to respect his superior officers, and Wooster, for good or for ill, was his senior in Canada. Further, Arnold had rejected various solicitations from his own officers who wanted to pull back into the countryside — perhaps to Pointe aux Trembles — to await reinforcements. Any withdrawal after so devastating a reversal in battle, he responded, might cause the *habitants* to doubt patriot resolve, thereby threatening their local base of material support. Wooster, at least, was obstinate enough to keep pressuring the Carletonians from outside the walls of Quebec.

In pondering whether to give up and pull back, Arnold also considered the confidence Washington and Schuyler had placed in him. He had acknowledged their trust by refusing to accept defeat in the Maine wilderness. Now he would do so a second time by hanging on at Quebec. Nor would he give petty, self-serving patriots back home any reason to accuse him of faintheartedness. He would persist, moreover, out of respect for Montgomery and his other comrades who had fallen in the battle. Further, he could not imagine forsaking the Kennebec veterans imprisoned in the Upper Town. Had he read a letter sent home in mid-January by James Knowles, one of his junior officers from Pennsylvania, he would have endorsed his words. Stated Knowles, "I intend to stand by my undertaking until I see my acquaintances set free from Quebec or lose all. . . . I long to see you all, in the peaceable established enjoyment of liberty." With committed patriots such as Knowles still in camp, the chance remained, however slight, of yet conquering the walled city.[11]

Despite his pain and gloom, Arnold maintained a bold front while providing leadership from his sickbed. He issued instructions to continue blockading the walled city. He strengthened the center of the patriot line by having all remaining cannons placed around a makeshift powder storehouse about halfway between the General Hospital and Holland House. The activity enlivened the troops—a small victory in appearances since Carleton's aides were circulating messages into the countryside with one dominant theme: "We have drubbed the rebels." The Carletonians were also exhorting the *habitants* to rise up and "completely drive away our enemies." Arnold's show of determination was effective. "The country people have come to our assistance," he informed Wooster. "They appear friendly, and concerned for us; many offer to join us who have no arms."

Within a few days Arnold moved to Holland House, where he could rest more comfortably and, even if bedridden, greet local citizens in a manner befitting a military commander still expecting victory. By comparison, the General Hospital, crowded with sick, wounded, and dying soldiers, was a constant reminder of the mortifying defeat of December 31. Getting away from the hospital helped accelerate the pace of Arnold's personal revival, although he still felt "unequal to the task" of command, "considering my present circumstances," when on January 5 he again asked Wooster to relieve him.[12]

As he settled into Holland House, Arnold kept reflecting on Carleton's behavior. The governor's lack of resolution in not finishing off what remained of the rebel force greatly puzzled him. "Had the enemy improved their advantage," he wrote to Washington in mid-January, "our affairs here must have been entirely ruined." Perhaps Arnold had found a weakness in Carleton's otherwise implacable temperament. He wondered whether such circumspection related to the indelible image of the pugnacious Montcalm's fatal miscalculation in engaging the British outside the walled city—and losing everything. Possibly Carleton, that recollection etched in his memory, could not bring himself to take calculated military risks. Perhaps he could be aggressive only when he fully controlled events, such as when he had ordered out the pincers column under Captain Laws. Whatever the explanation, Arnold made note of his opponent's apparent hesitancy, intending to exploit that weakness should the opportunity someday present itself. Meanwhile, the governor's cautious defensive posture allowed the rebels to keep up the facade of their investment of Quebec.[13]

A paper-thin blockade and sporadic acts of harassment, Arnold appreciated, would not seriously threaten the Carletonians. His purpose was to keep his adversaries in a defensive stance until an infusion of patriot troops made a new attack feasible. On Thursday, January 11, he encapsulated his thinking for Congress. He was enduring "a severe fit of the gout" that was slowing his recovery, and he apologized "for the incoherence . . . of my scrawl," a product of trying to write while lying in bed. Arnold reviewed the reasons for conquering Quebec City, still an "object of the highest importance." Then he called for three thousand additional troops to mount a "regular siege" and five thousand if another assault was to occur.

Asking for so many soldiers, especially in the dead of winter from colonies hundreds of miles away, seemed absurd. The troops needed to reach Quebec by the end of March—in well under three months! Arnold based his request on the time left before Carleton could expect reinforcements. The St. Lawrence River would be free enough of ice by mid-May to enable British troop transports to get to Quebec. That left only four months to reduce the walled city, the remaining roadblock "to a firm and lasting union with Canada."[14]

The next day, much to Arnold's relief, Colonel James Clinton, an amiable and competent officer who commanded the 3d New York regiment, appeared at Holland House. Wooster had sent him from Montreal to give Arnold a temporary respite, since the general felt too pressed by problems there to venture forth at this time. Wooster, Clinton reported, had rushed word to Schuyler and Congress about the December 31 debacle. He had likewise called for new troops, and he promised to send two hundred men, one-third of the rebel force at Montreal, to Quebec within a few days. Hundreds more, Wooster expected, would follow when word reached Congress about the failure to seize Quebec.[15]

Clinton's presence allowed Arnold to enjoy some peace, quiet, and rest. He still worried about so many shortages, but Carleton's persistent defensive-mindedness also reduced the need to be on constant alert. The governor, he was sure, wanted to avoid any showdown battle on the supposition that British reinforcements would reach the city before the rebels could muster enough strength to storm the Upper Town. All Arnold could do was hand over the matter of winning the manpower race to the just and benevolent Providence that was at the center of his religious faith. His prayer was that his patriot brethren back in the rebellious colonies would exhibit convincing proof of their commitment to selfless service by enlisting and rushing north-ward with all haste—even in the middle of winter. If they did so, Arnold believed, God's blessings would surely follow as a glorious reward for so undeniable a demonstration of public virtue in the defense of American liberties.[16]

III

Ever since his teenage years in Norwich, Arnold had challenged any perceived form of tyranny in his life. He had refused to submit to the vengeful
Calvinist God that his mother believed had taken the lives of his brothers
and sisters. He had broken free of the Norwichites who had, in effect,
censured his dying, alcoholic father. He had ordered the whipping of reputed
customs informer John Boles and proclaimed the need to resist British trade
policies that he was sure were stifling American commerce. He had dueled
with Captain Croskie over a trivial insult. He had tried to chastise the likes
of the Reverend Samuel Peters for so haughtily supporting imperial rule. His
defiant manner had endowed him with a reputation for pugnacity. For many
of his contemporaries, Arnold was an ambitious, hard-driving, self-assertive
person who never seemed to question himself, only those around him. What
they were not aware of were those periods when he scrutinized his own
deficiencies before again engaging other suspected human demons of tyranny.

The forlorn days of January 1776 represented one such time of personal
reckoning for Arnold. Appreciating his own amateur status as a military
officer, he was uneasy about his capacity to command at so crucial a frontline
position. Personal courage and boldness of purpose, he realized, could not
always make up for his lack of formal training or experience in the art of
making war. He had felt at ease under Montgomery's guiding hand, but this
gallant gentleman was dead. As he pondered matters, Arnold concluded that
a more seasoned commander should be placed in charge of patriot operations
at Quebec. In his January 11 letter to Congress, he asked the delegates to
send forth "an experienced general . . . as early as possible." He did not
presume to offer names, but he was not thinking of Wooster. Three days
later he mentioned Major General Charles Lee in writing to Washington.[17]

Gaunt, unkempt, foul-mouthed Lee possessed what Arnold lacked—a
breadth of military experience. He had held a regular British officer's commission and had fought gallantly at Braddock's defeat and throughout the
Seven Years' War. In 1773, having forsworn his military career, Lee moved to
Virginia, where he became an outspoken advocate of American rights. In
June 1775, congressional delegates named him the Continental army's third-
ranking general officer—behind only Washington and Artemas Ward of
Massachusetts. Many in Congress regarded Lee as the most talented person
in the initial lot of patriot generals. His admirers included Montgomery,
who considered Lee superbly qualified to command in Canada, a fact not
lost on Arnold.[18]

Paradoxically, the day before Arnold admitted his sense of inadequacy to Congress, the delegates, still ignorant of the December 31 debacle, had awarded him the laurel of a brigadier generalship, based on his newfound hero's status. Schuyler, after learning about the travails of the Kennebec column, had written the delegates that "Colonel Arnold's march does him great honor; some future historian will make it the subject of admiration to his readers." Washington was equally effusive. "The merit of this gentleman is certainly great," he proclaimed, and "I heartily wish that fortune may distinguish him as one of her favorites." The commander also sent Arnold a note of appreciation: "My thanks are due, and sincerely offered to you, for your enterprising and persevering spirit." [19]

The news of Arnold's extraordinary achievement spread steadily. Some patriots started comparing him to classical military heroes. In a letter to Boston popular leader Samuel Adams, James Warren described Arnold as "a genius" who had commanded "a march under such circumstances, and attended with such difficulties, as [any] modern story can't equal." Warren "compared" Arnold's feat "with Hannibal's over the Alps, or Xenophon's retreat." In Congress, Thomas Jefferson picked up on the allusion to Xenophon, an Athenian of noble birth who had studied with Socrates before joining a military expedition against Persia in 401 b.c. After losing a major battle, the ten thousand Greek soldiers chose Xenophon to guide them home, a distance of fifteen hundred miles through the harrowing terrain of Asia Minor. For Jefferson, the "march of Arnold's" was undoubtedly "equal to Xenophon's retreat." Since Congress had just elevated Montgomery to a major generalship, Jefferson thought it "probable" that Arnold would be named to the "vacant" post. [20]

Securing a general officer's commission for the patriot equivalent of Hannibal or Xenophon, however, was not that easy. Some delegates complained that Connecticut already had ample numbers of general officers. They put forth the names of other aspirants—gentlemen of influence from their own colonies who had not yet had the opportunity to show their merit but whose local prestige would help solidify public support for the cause. To buttress their arguments, they dredged up unflattering stories about Arnold's fractious conduct at the Champlain forts. They were not averse to having heroes, but they would have more easily embraced patriots with greater political influence, preferably from their own colonies.

To effect the promotion, Arnold needed a persuasive patron in Congress who could sway delegates more absorbed in serving their own local interests than in recognizing proven military achievement. Six months earlier, when Congress first named general officers, no one gave Arnold any consideration.

The Connecticut delegates had pushed the likes of David Wooster, who had the favor of Governor Trumbull and other colony-wide leaders. As for Arnold, his choice was to accept or reject service in the Champlain region under the well-connected but virtually incompetent Benjamin Hinman.

Six months later, the circumstances had changed dramatically. Arnold had since gained the favor of Schuyler and Washington, which netted him a Continental colonel's commission and the opportunity to lead a detached force to Canada. As a reflection of Arnold's success, Washington did more than offer words of praise; in early December 1775, he promised his subordinate a regiment "in the establishment of a new army" for 1776, should his duties in Canada come to an end. The commander hoped Arnold would accept the guarantee of a regimental command as a testament of appreciation for his distinguished service.[21]

Washington also asked Congress to delineate a suitable assignment for Arnold in Canada, presuming the delegates voted to raise "a new establishment" of enlistees for service in Quebec Province. Should Congress bypass Arnold, Washington noted his intention to offer him the opportunity to rejoin the main army at the head of a regiment. The commander was being circumspect because he wanted to avoid charges of tampering with Congress's prerogatives regarding the selection of general officers. In commenting favorably about Arnold, however, he had conveyed his strong endorsement for promotion.[22]

Washington's recommendation might have been lost in the maelstrom of congressional politics had not Connecticut delegate Silas Deane actively sought advancement for his "brave friend." Concluding that only Arnold, as an award for his valiant leadership, should fill the open brigadier generalship created by Montgomery's promotion, Deane showed other delegates "two long letters from . . . Colonel Arnold, which I improved in his favor." Deane also played on classical allusions. His lobbying worked. Wrote delegate Joseph Hewes of North Carolina in early January, Arnold's march "is thought equal [to] Hannibal's over the Alps." That same day, Christopher Gadsden of South Carolina nominated Arnold for the open brigadier's commission— to be held in Schuyler's Northern Department army. On Wednesday, January 10, Congress unanimously approved Gadsden's motion.[23]

Had the delegates known about the ill-fated December 31 assault or Arnold's self-doubts, they might well have elevated some other, less meritorious candidate. Their ignorance came to an end a week later when the "disagreeable intelligence" of defeat finally reached Philadelphia. Like Washington, who also received the "melancholy" news at his Cambridge headquarters the same day, the delegates reacted with genuine shock. They immediately "determined to erect a splendid monument to the memory of the gallant Montgomery and to every other commanding officer bravely fighting and falling in his country's cause." Then they turned to the inescapable task of trying to rescue the Canadian campaign.[24]

IV

Reluctant Revolutionaries in Congress had only begrudgingly gone along with the invasion of Canada. By the end of 1775, the expanding war effort had them fretting about losing any chance of a peaceful settlement of differences with King and Parliament. In December, Congress turned the issue of raising more troops for Canada over to a committee headed by John Dickinson, a leader of the reconciliationist faction. The matter languished there until January 6, when a letter from Schuyler again apprised the delegates of the "indispensable" need to send "a considerable force . . . immediately . . . into Canada." The northern commander's imploring tone gave more radical delegates a leverage point, and they used Schuyler's letter to good effect.[25]

A heated debate ensued and resulted in a resolution mandating nine regiments—about sixty-five hundred soldiers—for service in Canada. Troops under Wooster and Arnold were to form the backbone of two regiments, and James Livingston's Canadians would make up the third, known as the 1st Canadian regiment. The 1st Pennsylvania and 2d New Jersey regiments, already being formed, were to move northward as soon as possible. The delegates called on New Hampshire, Connecticut, New York, and Pennsylvania to raise the four remaining regiments.[26]

Congress had finally authorized a sizable force for Canada, but the reconciliationists remained opposed to rapid mobilization. Then came the appalling news from Quebec. The delegates turned to Samuel Adams, as staunch an advocate of independence as there was in early 1776, to chair a committee charged with formulating further actions. The Adams committee recommended having "the American army in Canada . . . reinforced with all possible dispatch." A majority of delegates agreed. They approved bounty payments and pay advances to encourage rapid enlistments.

The delegates also voted to enlist a second regiment of Canadians as the fastest way to augment troop strength, since recruits from New Jersey and Pennsylvania faced a journey of six hundred miles through the Champlain corridor—in the middle of winter—to reach the rebel front line at Quebec City. Congress named Moses Hazen, a onetime British regular officer who had amassed considerable wealth at St. Johns, to command the 2d Canadian

1. Arnold quickly gained attention in England for his harrowing march in 1775 through the Maine wilderness. An anonymous artist prepared this imagined likeness of Arnold overlooking Quebec City, which London printer Thomas Hart first published in March 1776. *Courtesy, Library of Congress.*

2. In 1854, E. Z. Webster took this heliographic photograph of Arnold's birthplace and boyhood home in Norwich, Connecticut. Local citizens, embarrassed that Arnold was a native of their community, had no interest in preserving this residence, which is no longer standing. *Courtesy, Library of Congress.*

3. Arnold prospered as a merchant in New Haven, Connecticut, and constructed this imposing residence on Water Street in the early 1770s. Confiscated by the Connecticut government after his treason, the home eventually fell into disrepair, as this photograph from the 1890s demonstrates, and was torn down. *Courtesy, Library of Congress.*

ETHAN ALLEN.

To his Grandson, Gen. Ethan Allen Hitchcock, U.S. Army.

4. (LEFT) and 5. (ABOVE) Vermont's Ethan Allen, here depicted in a bust sculpted by
Benjamin Harris Hinney during the 1850s, was Arnold's rival in the taking of Fort
Ticonderoga on May 10, 1775. *Courtesy, American Antiquarian Society.* Allen and his
associates repeatedly vilified Arnold and disparaged his part in securing the Lake
Champlain region for the patriot cause. Allen would have likely endorsed this
misleading nineteenth-century drawing above in which he alone demanded
surrender of the fort from British Captain William Delaplace. Adding Arnold and
replacing Delaplace with Lieutenant Jocelyn Feltham would have made this
rendering of the actual scene more accurate. *Courtesy, Library of Congress.*

6. (ABOVE) and 7. (RIGHT) Lacking inside political connections in Connecticut, Arnold needed influential patrons to champion his Revolutionary military career. Fellow Connecticut merchant Silas Deane *(left)* of Wethersfield worked on Arnold's

Painted by J. Trumbull.   Engraved by T. Kelly

MAJOR GENERAL PHILIP SCHUYLER.

behalf in the Continental Congress during 1775 and early 1776. New York's Philip
Schuyler *(right)*, who was the first commander of the Continental army's Northern
Department, recognized Arnold's military talents, based on his strong performance
on Lake Champlain, and encouraged his advancement. *Courtesy, Library of Congress.*

8. (LEFT) and 9. (ABOVE) George Washington *(left)*, depicted here by the noted Revolutionary era artist Charles Willson Peale, gave Arnold the opportunity to prove his merits in the late summer of 1775 by naming him to lead a detached force into Quebec Province. Washington developed great admiration for Arnold's martial capacities, which disturbed ambitious Horatio Gates *(above)*. Gates and Arnold worked together effectively in defending Lake Champlain during 1776, but Gates resented Washington's preferment of Arnold for a command assignment in Rhode Island and turned against his martial comrade. *Courtesy, Library of Congress.*

10. Arnold's dauntless march to Quebec City took twice as long as planned. Supplies gave out, and a few troops starved to death. In this drawing, artist Sydney Adamson depicted the struggle to portage around Skowhegan Falls in ascending the Kennebec River. That some of Arnold's detachment reached Quebec earned him hero's status as America's Hannibal. *Courtesy, Library of Congress.*

11. (ABOVE) and 12. (RIGHT)
Virginia's Daniel Morgan *(above)* and
New Hampshire's Henry Dearborn
(right) were two of the many
valuable officers who accompanied
Arnold on the expedition to Quebec.
Morgan and Dearborn made many
other significant contributions to the
patriot war effort, including serving
with Arnold at Saratoga during the
1777 campaign season in defeating
John Burgoyne's British-Hessian
force. *Courtesy, Library of Congress.*

13. Conquering fortress-like Quebec City, here shown in a drawing from around 1760, was essential to having the province join the thirteen colonies in rebellion. Off in the distance just to the right of the large vessel is Point Levy, where Arnold's column first viewed the Upper and Lower towns from the south side of the St. Lawrence River. *Courtesy, American Antiquarian Society.*

14. (LEFT) and 15. (BELOW) Guy Carleton *(left)*, the resolute British governor of Quebec Province, refused to yield to the patriot invaders, even though St. Johns and Montreal had fallen to the rebel force under the command of Richard Montgomery *(below)* [first name was not George, as indicated in the picture] in November 1775. Carleton successfully directed the defense of Quebec City during the winter of 1775–76. Montgomery, the ranking patriot officer in Canada, died in the ill-fated patriot assault on December 31, 1775. *Courtesy, Library of Congress.*

George Montgomery Esq.
Major General of the American Armies
Kill'd at Quebec Decr. 31. 1775

17. When Arnold could not continue, Daniel Morgan assumed command but could not convince other rebel officers to advance decisively through the second barrier, located at the entrance to Sault au Matelot Street. As this drawing by Sydney Adamson indicates, British defenders had appeared in abundance before the hesitant patriot force finally assaulted that barrier. Two-thirds of the rebels surrendered to the British before the fighting was over that morning. *Courtesy, Library of Congress.*

OPPOSITE PAGE: 16. Befitting his aggressive leadership style, Arnold was out in front of the patriot troops, as represented in this painting by F. C. Yohn, when they advanced through a driving snowstorm toward Quebec's Lower Town early on the morning of December 31, 1775. Near the first barrier, Arnold suffered a disabling wound that took him out of the battle. *Courtesy, Library of Congress.*

18. (LEFT) and 19. (ABOVE) With Montgomery's death, Arnold's New Haven neighbor David Wooster *(left)* assumed overall command of patriot forces in Quebec Province. Wooster was overbearing and largely ineffective, but he fully redeemed himself in April 1777 when, in conjunction with Arnold, he resisted a British raiding force in western Connecticut and lost his life. Troublesome, ambitious James Wilkinson *(above)* served as an aide to Arnold in Canada but then joined Gates's staff and helped provoke the confrontation between Arnold and Gates at Saratoga. *Courtesy, Library of Congress.*

A View of the New England Armed Vessels, in Valcure Bay, on Lake Champlain, 11th Octor. 1776.

No. 1 Royal Savage 8 Six & 4 fourpounders Burnt 11th. * Revenge Schoor 8 fourpounders, 4 two's, run ashore & burnt 13th. *Lee Cutter, one 12 & one 6 Poundr. taken 13th.* Trumble one 18 one 12 two 9's one 6 & two 4's. Washington arived Somewhat damaged, taken 13 Octor. Congress Genl Waterbury—Burnt 13 Octor. Philadelphia 1 12, 3 9 & 1 6 Burnt 11th. Octr. * New York 12 Pounders—Jersey one 18 one 12 Poundr. Congress and Burnt 13th. Providence and Philadelphia and Gall[e]ys. last Galleon Burnt 13 Octr. Gondola Burnt 11.th — Bixton Sunk 11th. * Up the Leaving Schoor of a Row gally at Turenlaraga, with two Mast. * were taken or Destroyed in this above Boats & carried some humber Sloops of Metal at the Philadelphia — the Above Vessels were Commanded by Benedic Arnold

A View of His Majesty's Armed Vessels on Lake Champlain, October 11, 1776. The Carleton by Valcour Island... [remainder of handwritten caption within image]

20. (ABOVE) and 21. (BELOW) Arnold's dauntless stand at the Battle of Valcour Island on October 11, 1776, revealed the depth of American fighting resolve to Governor Carleton but resulted in extensive patriot criticism, even in the Continental Congress, about expending rather than saving the patriot vessels. Pictured here in water color sketches drawn in 1776 by Charles Randle are Arnold's [c13202] and Carleton's [c13203] squadrons. At the center of the American fleet is the *Royal Savage*, lost on the day of the battle. Arnold's flagship, the row galley *Congress*, is the fourth vessel from the left. Appearing at the left of Randle's rendering of the British squadron is the schooner *Carleton*, which the patriots came close to sinking that day. *Courtesy, National Archives of Canada.*

22. General John Burgoyne, here shown in a portrait by the renowned Sir Joshua Reynolds, thought he could break through the Lake Champlain wilderness and reach Albany with little difficulty. Effective patriot resistance in combination with a resounding defeat at Saratoga on October 7, 1777, forced Burgoyne to surrender his army. *Courtesy, Library of Congress.*

23. No one fought more courageously at Saratoga than Arnold, here shown charging into Breymann's Redoubt on October 7, 1777, in this 1858 painting by Chappel. *Courtesy, Library of Congress.*

24. Arnold suffered another serious wound in this battle and spent several months recuperating. Gates, never near the fighting, won Congress's accolades as the hero of Saratoga. The delegates even honored Gates with a rarely given medal that declared him "the vigorous leader." Drawing of medal from Lossing, *Pictorial Field-Book of the Revolution. Photo by Vic Pennell.*

25. In this painting by John Trumbull, which depicts Burgoyne's surrender on October 17, 1777, the focus is on Gates, as if he were the central figure in achieving this pivotal triumph. *Courtesy, Library of Congress.*

26. (ABOVE) and 27. (RIGHT) That
Gates received so much of the acclaim
had an adverse effect on Arnold's
thinking about the merits of the
patriot cause. After Arnold returned
his allegiance to the British, many
Americans felt compelled to depreciate
his invaluable contributions to the
rebel war effort. The monument to the
boot at the Saratoga battlefield,
located on the site of Breymann's
Redoubt, does not mention Arnold's
name but does admit that he was a
"brilliant soldier" in serving the
American cause. *Monument photos by
James Kirby Martin, reproduced by Vic
Pennell.*

regiment. During the summer of 1775, Hazen had staunchly supported Carleton. Nervous about the confiscation of his property holdings once Montgomery had launched the siege of St. Johns, he suddenly found the cause of liberty irresistible. He cultivated friendly relations with Montgomery and proved himself trustworthy by traveling with the patriot commander and lending his military expertise in planning the assault on Quebec. Hazen was one of the messengers who had carried word of the December 31 debacle to Congress. Within another few months, he would number himself among Arnold's host of enemies.[27]

Congress also called on Washington to release a regiment, if he could "spare one," and "an active able general . . . to take command" in Canada, a reflection of concern about Arnold's incapacitating wound and widespread disaffection with Wooster's capacities. Schuyler had already appealed to Washington for troops, but the commander demurred. "Since the dissolution of the old army [of 1775]," he explained, "the progress in raising recruits . . . for the new [army of 1776] has been so very slow and incosiderable that five thousand militia have been called into the defense of our lines." An extensive recruitment effort, including putting the hard sell on soldiers whose enlistments were up at the end of 1775, had not produced a second patriot rush to arms in the spirit of the *rage militaire.* Hardly anyone, it now seemed, wanted to be a Continental soldier, so much so that a frustrated Washington concluded brusquely, "In short, I have not a man to spare."[28]

The commander in chief fully appreciated the strategic importance of securing all of Quebec Province before British reinforcements arrived, and he carefully considered his options. Congress had authorized him to continue all established regiments and to form thirteen new ones for service with the main army during 1776. Recruiters were even then scurrying about the countryside in search of enlistees. After consulting his general officers, Washington directed the colonels of three fledgling regiments—one each from New Hampshire, Massachusetts, and Connecticut—to wrap up their recruiting, even if regimental quotas remained unfilled, and to move out for Canada with all possible dispatch. He hoped that news of the December 31 setback would rekindle enough popular zeal to provoke a new rush to arms. In this sense "the rebuff" had its "favorable" side, Washington stated. Had Canada "been subdued by such a handful of men," it was "more than probable that it would have been left to the defense of the few, and rescued [taken back] from us in the spring. Our eyes will now, not only be open to the importance of holding it, but the numbers which are requisite to that end."

When the commander learned in late January "that Arnold was continuing the blockade of Quebec" in spite of "the heaviness of our loss there," he considered this news "a fresh proof of Arnold's ability and perseverance in the midst of difficulties." If only the new brigadier could hold on until additional troops arrived, Washington believed that "the entire conquest of Canada this winter" was still possible. Some soldiers were already on their way, coming from the Berkshires and the Green Mountains, the latter group of Boys under the command of Seth Warner. Others would follow in what by late April amounted to a paper commitment, had the units filled their quotas, of some nine thousand troops. Most regiments traveled north well below specified strength, but that could not negate the impressive effort to rescue the Canadian campaign. The *rage militaire* was not yet fully moribund.[29]

Arnold, meanwhile, began hobbling from room to room at Holland House before the end of January, when he decided to reassume command responsibilities. Then, on Thursday, February 1, two companies totaling 150 troops arrived from Montreal. The number was smaller than Wooster had promised, but only because some had deserted on the way to Quebec. Four days later, Arnold gladly welcomed twenty-five volunteers from New England. Their arrival signaled the prospect of receiving necessary reinforcements for an assault before time ran out, which greatly cheered Arnold's band.[30]

V

As February dawned, Arnold had not yet learned about his promotion or hero's status. Nor was he aware that the king's ministers in London now knew his name. To these self-inflated heads of state, Arnold was just another dirty, contemptible, treasonous rebel who had forsaken his proper sense of duty toward the empire. Condescendingly, they wondered how this deluded colonist, "quite simply a horse trader" from Connecticut, a man so lacking in proper breeding or influence that they had never heard his name before, could ever have maneuvered an army through the inhospitable Maine wilderness. They would have scoffed at comparisons to Hannibal or Xenophon, but in time their haughty voices would betray begrudging respect.[31]

What imperial leaders eventually found out was that Benedict Arnold could be "a most persevering hero," as General Horatio Gates wrote in early 1776, especially in the face of extreme adversity. Persistence would denote Arnold's contest of wills with Carleton at Quebec. As Arnold explained to one correspondent toward the end of winter, "we labor under almost as many difficulties as the *Israelites* did of old, obliged to make brick without straw." Despite everything, he kept encouraging his troops with nothing more tangible than the "hope" of events taking "a more favorable turn." [32]

Lack of troops remained the major deterrent to offensive operations. By the end of February, Arnold had welcomed an additional four hundred patriot enlistees and, as he wrote, "many are daily coming in." Before mid-March the manpower pool had risen to 1,794 soldiers; Arnold now had a larger force outside the walled city than before the December 31 assault. By the end of March the muster count reached 2,505, another sizable increase but still only half the number the new brigadier thought necessary to succeed in a second assault.

Further, of these 2,505 soldiers, 786 (31 percent) were unfit for duty. Smallpox had begun spreading to the troops back in early December from inside Quebec, and both the Carletonians and the rebels struggled all winter to contain the ravages of this deadly disease. During February, Arnold noted that one-fourth of some two hundred soldiers "sick and unfit for duty" had smallpox. Fresh troops were no less susceptible. In mid-February, Arnold advised his officers to isolate suspected cases at the General Hospital. "All soldiers who shall know of any persons with that disorder in their private quarters, and do not make immediate complaint thereof to the barrackmaster," he warned, "shall be treated as neglecting their duty, and guilty of a breach of orders." The situation was no better at the end of March. Arnold complained that his quarantine orders, although "repeatedly given," were "repeatedly disobeyed or neglected." Just as bad, Dr. Senter had run out of medicine, and smallpox-ridden soldiers were overcrowding even makeshift hospital space. [33]

Arnold also forbade self-inoculation, a controversial procedure of the era that involved slicing open one's skin—favored places included under fingernails and along thighs—and rubbing in fluids taken from active smallpox pustules. This crude, uncontrolled form of inoculation usually resulted in milder cases, and the death rate was significantly lower in comparison to contracting smallpox the "natural way." [34]

Although a sensible procedure in terms of saving lives, massive self-inoculation, as Arnold observed, rendered fresh units useless for weeks. He complained particularly about short-term volunteers like Seth Warner's Green Mountain Boys, who had enlisted for only three months. As the Boys entered camp, they had themselves inoculated and then used up scarce supplies of food and medicine while recovering. Each was to receive £20 in wages for his brief stint of service, which Arnold estimated at no more than ten days apiece during three months of military duty. Short-termers hardly represented the kind of deeply committed soldiery so desperately needed for investing and conquering Quebec City, let alone resisting the expected onslaught of British regulars.[35]

Brutal winter weather, the worst in years, added to health problems, producing colds, pneumonia, influenza, and frostbite. Private Haskell summarized many a day when he wrote on Monday, January 15, "A bad snowstorm, and so cold that a man can scarce get out without freezing." Two weeks later a Carletonian described temperatures frigid enough "to split a stone." Before dawn that day, a British officer became "very angry" with a sentry who did not respond when "hailed." The indignant officer started shouting at the sentry, who replied, "God bless Your Honor, . . . I am glad you are come for I am blind." The sentry's "eyes had watered with the severity of the cold and . . . his eyelids were frozen together." The officer, now ashamed of himself, led the sentry to the guardhouse "to be thawed." Dozens of soldiers on both sides—indeed, anyone exposed to the unmerciful weather—risked losing fingers, toes, arms, and legs to frostbite.[36]

The most violent snowstorm of the season, a "heavy" northeaster, commenced on the morning of Friday, February 9. This blizzard "increased to a perfect hurricane," stated Collector Ainslie, and pounded away for nearly forty hours, leaving streets so clogged with snow that residents used secondstory windows as doorways. Ainslie reported artillery pieces "deeply buried" in huge drifts along the western wall, "although their muzzles are at least thirty feet from the bottom of the ditch." Had Arnold's soldiers possessed snowshoes, they could have walked through embrasures atop the wall directly into the Upper Town. As soon as the blizzard let up, Carleton ordered out work parties to clear the snow from the upper portions of the wall, a task performed repeatedly as additional storms dumped fresh layers of snow. Even at the end of March after some thawing, Arnold made reference to nearly five feet of unmelted snow, "sufficiently hard to bear a man and horse."[37]

Quebec's inhabitants, even though amply provisioned with food, clothing, weapons, and gunpowder, started running short of firewood by mid-January. Without additional winter fuel, Carleton faced the possibility of losing control of the city's defenders, who would surely submit to the patriot force before freezing to death. To obtain wood—indeed, anything that would burn—the governor dispatched parties of soldiers and woodcutters into the suburbs of St. Roch and St. John's. Arnold ordered his troops to harass the intruders but confessed how weak the rebel position really was by repeatedly warning his officers not to bring on a general engagement.

The Carletonians, typically organized as a reconnaissance force, would venture out through either Palace or St. John's Gate. On Thursday, January

25, for example, a sizable party marched into St. Roch with a 6-pound brass cannon in tow. Carleton himself joined this sortie and even ordered up a few volleys of cannon and musket fire to drive off skirmishing patriots. The woodcutters finished their work without further challenges, returning to the Upper Town at dusk with sleighs weighted down by forty cords of wood.[38]

Since Arnold lacked the troop strength to keep the Carletonians penned up and freezing inside the walled city, his only effective counterweapon was fire. Night after night, as if directly retaliating against each successful woodcutting foray, he ordered buildings in St. Roch set ablaze. The rebels also ignited merchant vessels moored along the western edge of the harbor touching St. Roch. On many a "still and gloomy" evening, Quebec's inhabitants heard "the crackling of burning beams, and a hollow roaring of fierce flames." If they looked outside, they saw "snow loaded clouds" reflecting "an orange tinge" and freshly falling snow that appeared "reddish yellow." By late January virtually every wooden building in St. Roch was gone, but still Carletonian work parties came out to sift through the rubble and bring in "all the boards, fences, etc. fit for firewood they could get."[39]

With St. Roch all but leveled, the contest shifted to the suburb of St. John's. Well-aimed artillery shots kept rebel snipers out of St. Johns during the day, but Arnold's troops assiduously set fires almost every night. Then, on Sunday evening, February 18, the patriots started a general conflagration and "burned down the greatest part" of the abandoned suburb. Buildings were ablaze all day on February 19, and the next night a few daring rebels ignited houses still standing contiguous to St. John's Gate. "Nobody was seen," Collector Ainslie stated, "although the distance from our sentries is not fifty paces." All that was left of the suburb was smoldering rubble.[40]

Ainslie interpreted such demolition as proof of rebel callousness and desperation. Carleton "would have burned both" suburbs "long ago," he claimed, "but in commiseration of the poor proprietors he let the houses stand." From Arnold's perspective, incinerating the suburbs was a necessary investment tactic. His objective was to provoke a mutiny against Carleton, instigated either by persons alarmed about winter fuel shortages or by those who hoped to save their suburban property before it was too late. To encourage the latter group, Arnold initially ordered the burning of only a few buildings at a time. By mid-February, he doubted whether any group would rise up against Carleton's authority. Hence, igniting what remained of the suburbs was the best way to ensure shortages of fuel. If the terrible winter persisted, Quebec's defenders would suffer, but they could also surrender to gain relief.

In addition, the suburbs had ceased to have any protective value for the rebels. Whenever squads got into buildings close enough to the walls to snipe at enemy sentries, salvos of cannon fire quickly drove them off. The Carletonians had at their disposal more than 110 artillery pieces, including cannons capable of firing 32- and 42-pound balls. The patriots had no way of responding effectively with their handful of fieldpieces, only one of which had the capacity to fire 24-pound balls. Thus Arnold's decision to destroy what remained of the two suburbs made good tactical sense.[41]

VI

While convalescing, Arnold busily planned a second assault. In late January he wrote to Congress about making local arrangements for obtaining "shot, shells, etc., all in the month of March." Monsieur Christophe Pelissier, who owned the St. Maurice Forges at Three Rivers, said he could manufacture these vital munitions, but a coal shortage caused him to revise his time frame. He could not promise delivery before May—certainly too late if British reinforcements reached Carleton. Arnold urged Pelissier to spare no effort to assure full production by early April at the latest.[42]

Pelissier was a valuable friend to the patriots. He advised Arnold about ways to control the St. Lawrence River after the ice began to melt, a serious problem with British war vessels moored in Quebec's harbor. Once free to sail, these craft could move upriver and disrupt rebel supply lines to Montreal. As a countermeasure, Pelissier suggested fireships filled with explosives that could be floated into the harbor. With any luck, a collision would set many vessels ablaze, perhaps even warehouses and other buildings in the Lower Town. A general conflagration would represent a splendid diversion for a massed escalade against the western wall, Arnold reasoned. Thus he kept his soldiers busily engaged in constructing more scaling ladders. Even if an assault was not possible, "destroying the ships," he stated, would make it "impossible for the town to hold out until . . . relieved."[43]

Engulfing the harbor in a blazing inferno was a critical component of Arnold's evolving battle plan. To further implement his scheme, he maintained contact with his old-subject mercantile acquaintance Captain Hector McNeill, who was still living at Pointe aux Trembles. Around mid-March, if not before, Arnold asked McNeill to take charge of the patriot naval effort on the St. Lawrence. He even queried his friend about "laying a boom across the St. Lawrence," somewhere in the vicinity of the Island of Orleans (Ile d'Orléans) to the east of Quebec, to delay British troop ships sailing upriver to relieve the city. McNeill apparently thought the notion impractical. Instead, he and Arnold focused on outfitting floating batteries, specifically two flat-bottomed craft armed with a 12-pounder each and smaller arms. These gundalows were to harass enemy warships attempting to leave the harbor.[44]

McNeill also began outfitting two fireships, concentrating first on a trading vessel that had likely run aground along the shoreline of the Island of Orleans the previous autumn. According to Collector Ainslie, this craft belonged to Arnold, which other sources corroborate in referencing the brigantine *Peggy* that had sailed for Quebec back in the summer of 1775. The vessel still contained its cargo of rum, which Arnold's troops gladly unloaded in late January and carted back to the main rebel line. Two months later they refilled the hold with explosives. This newborn fireship, representing a sacrifice of Arnold's personal property for the cause of liberty, was fully armed for action—and destruction—before the end of April.[45]

Arnold thus carefully put the elements in place for a second assault. Working with Captain Wool, who had only twenty matrosses (gunners), "very few of whom know their duty," he devised plans for two major artillery batteries. One would be located on the Plains of Abraham about five hundred yards from the western wall. It contained nine artillery pieces, but none with the size and range to duel with the defenders' heavier ordnance. The second battery would be placed at Point Levy. This position commanded both the Lower Town and the harbor, but not with the three 12-pound cannons and one 8-inch howitzer then available. Arnold ordered the battery's construction anyway, despite harassing enemy fire. Even without additional fieldpieces, gunners at Point Levy could support the launching of fireships, just as the Plains battery could assist a massed escalade of troops along the western wall. Arnold hoped, too, that more powerful artillery pieces would arrive before mid-May.[46]

Ordnance shortages seemed less significant when compared to money problems. By early March, the rebel force had run out of specie. After consulting his officers, Arnold announced in a formal proclamation that *habitants* and other suppliers should henceforth expect payments in "paper money . . . on the universal credit of the United Colonies of the continent." He promised that the "given paper or cardboard money" would be redeemed at face value "in gold or in [other hard] money" within a few months. Arnold also declared that anyone who refused to accept the makeshift currency would "be considered as an enemy of the United Colonies and will be treated as such."[47]

As long as the patriots had specie, local civilians seemed supportive. Paper money, guaranteed to lose all value should the invaders fail to conquer Canada, quickly produced disaffection. As Arnold explained, the absence of "a well furnished military chest" was now causing many *habitants* to shun his force. "To tell you the truth," he wrote in frustration, "our credit extends no farther than our arms." Unfortunately, some rebel soldiers, despite orders, used threats and even physical abuse to obtain goods, which only further damaged civilian relations.[48]

The lack of hard money also undercut efforts to sign up enlistees for the two Canadian battalions. Even after extensive recruiting, Hazen's regiment could muster only fewer than 250 troops, slightly more than one-fourth of its authorized strength. Livingston's numbers were even smaller. Potential recruits wanted specie, not cardboard money, for bounty payments—equivalent to a month's wages—when enlisting. Just as bad, *habitants* already in the ranks started deserting as soon as they received wages in paper money. By late March, Arnold's rebels could no longer depend on most Canadian civilians for support of any kind.[49]

Nor could the patriot brigadier rely on continued service from veteran troops still in camp. The Yorkers talked incessantly among themselves about going home when their enlistments ended on April 15. Others, such as Private Haskell, had grown weary of the "arbitrary rule" of military life. "Looking upon ourselves as freemen," no amount of reenlistment rhetoric was going to keep him—and many other New Englanders—in camp after mid-April. The prospect of losing so many veterans left Arnold vexed and frustrated about ever having enough soldiers to launch a second assault.[50]

If all these "choice of difficulties" were not enough, Arnold had to contend with angry company-grade officers, a number of whom confronted him about not having guaranteed assignments in the newly established army of 1776. They vented their concerns in relation to officers "who deserted the cause and went home last fall" and were now getting, or so they believed, promotions and worthy assignments with Washington's main force. Arnold promised them just treatment. Eventually he was able to tell them about Congress's decision to form two new regiments made up of companies that had remained in Canada for the winter. This news seemed to placate the officers.[51]

Unfortunately, Arnold was not so judicious in handling his perpetual nemesis John Brown. On February 1, he directed a letter to Congress in which he impugned Brown for falsely assuming "the title of colonel, which, he says, the general [Montgomery] had promised him at Montreal." Montgomery apparently had made such a pledge but then reversed himself, according to Arnold, because of "unbecoming" accusations about thievery by

Brown and James Easton at Sorel back in mid-November. After Carleton had escaped downriver, the British flotilla surrendered rather than risk a destructive bombardment. Shortly thereafter, Brown and Easton "were publicly impeached with plundering the . . . baggage" of the captured British officers. Montgomery, Arnold stated, had informed Brown that "he could not, in conscience or honor promote him, . . . until these matters were cleared up."

Arnold postured himself as a disinterested senior officer with a duty to report to Congress. "It would give great dismay to the army," he wrote, to see Brown considered for a colonelcy until a board of inquiry had investigated the charges. By alerting Congress to such potentially damaging allegations, Arnold was making the most of an opportunity to etch a lasting image of Brown and Easton as truly craven patriots. In doing so, he acted as if he had no personal interest in the matter when he sanctimoniously stated in a postscript, "I should despise myself were I capable of asserting a thing in prejudice of any gentleman without sufficient reasons to make it public."[52]

Arnold would have served his own ambitions better by disregarding the likes of Brown and Easton. Tempering his outrage, however, would have defied his confrontational nature. Not surprisingly, Arnold's smearing letter served as a clarion call for these two inveterate adversaries to renew their attacks on his character as the best method to save their own reputations—with damaging consequences for America's Hannibal.

This imprudent letter aside, Arnold, a neophyte at making war, performed like a knowledgeable veteran during the winter of 1776. Beset by so many shortages and problems, he hardly had time to revel in the news about his promotion to brigadier general. On Monday, February 12, he took a few moments to convey to Congress his "respectful compliments and sincere thanks for the honorable mark of esteem" bestowed on him, "which I shall study to deserve." Certainly grateful, the new brigadier did not suddenly overate his capacities; he repeated his request for a more experienced commander at Quebec.[53]

The promotion, along with reports of his hero's status, encouraged Arnold in his unyielding harassment of the Carletonians. On Tuesday, March 5, he authorized the hoisting of a large red flag near the General Hospital in remembrance of the five Boston "massacre" martyrs of 1770. The banner flew as a symbol of self-sacrifice on behalf of liberty, and its unfurling was a sure way to remind homesick soldiers of the necessity for ongoing personal sacrifice. In addition, the flag served as a warning of no quarter in any future assault, which caused sneering among Carleton and his aides.[54]

The governor was just as resourceful as Arnold in devising plans of harassment. In mid-March, he contrived with Roman Catholic clergymen to induce some three hundred *habitants* living downriver beyond the Island of Orleans to ambush rebel soldiers who were trying to procure supplies in their region; then they were to attack and destroy the patriot artillery battery at Point Levy. Arnold got word of the scheme through his intelligence network, and he ordered out troops under Canadian Major Lewis Dubois. Dubois's column entrapped and routed an advance party of these downriver *habitants*, wounding or killing several of them. This decisive action convinced many civilians around Quebec City to accept the rebels' cardboard money.[55]

Arnold's alertness saved his force from disaster on Monday, April 1. Inside Quebec, the famine-proof prisoners had devised a bold plan to seize the Upper Town. In mid-March, after smallpox had run its course through their ranks, Carleton ordered them into the Dauphin Jail, which Private Henry described as "an old French building in the Bastille style" with walls three feet thick. Its location, only 150 yards from St. John's Gate, inspired a committee of sergeants—the officers were in separate quarters—to plot a breakout. Success depended on overpowering their guards, mostly old men and boys. Once free, designated parties were to ignite buildings. Others were to seize the gate and its defenders, swing artillery pieces around and start bombarding the city, and open the gate to admit Arnold and their waiting comrades in arms.[56]

Near the end of March, a volunteer escaped from the jail and informed Arnold of the pending uprising. The prisoners, however, were caught in their final preparations on Sunday, March 31, and "the greatest part of those concerned . . . were put in irons," noted Collector Ainslie. Although angry, Carleton also saw an opportunity to lure Arnold into a trap. At 2 a.m. on April 1, the governor had his whole garrison primed for action. Hundreds of soldiers lined the ramparts surrounding St. John's Gate. At a prearranged signal, they started controlled fires and discharged cannons without shot while groups of English-speaking Carletonians screamed loudly for liberty.[57]

The performance was impressive. Quebec's defenders would have ripped Arnold's troops to shreds had he taken the bait. Displaying the composure of a seasoned general officer, he sensed that something was awry. By checking his natural combativeness and holding his troops back, Arnold averted what could have been a disastrous encounter.

VII

By the end of March, Arnold's health had shown significant improvement, so much so that he overexerted himself. One day he rode fourteen miles and walked five more while inspecting his force's dispositions and reconnoitering Quebec's defensive works and artillery placements. The extended outing, he stated, "fatigued me so much I have hardly been able to walk since." [58]

Never far from Arnold's thoughts was the need for a more experienced commander. Before sunset on April 1, several hours after Carleton's ruse, a superior officer did appear at Holland House. There, standing before Arnold, looking almost imbecilic in his oversized periwig, was not Charles Lee but David Wooster. With no advance warning, the New Havenite had at last come down from Montreal, having left Colonel Hazen in charge there. Wooster, who had repeatedly praised Arnold's leadership that winter, now greeted his neighbor frostily before proclaiming his assumption of command responsibilities at Quebec.

The next morning Arnold took Wooster on a tour of patriot positions. As the two generals rode together, the senior brigadier solicited no information or advice. Treating Arnold as a military rube, Wooster grumbled about almost everything he saw. Clearly his subordinate had not made the bricks properly, despite the shortage of straw. Arnold kept his composure, but his level of annoyance matched the hue of the bright scarlet coat he wore that morning. [59]

After returning to Holland House, Arnold responded to word of a possible Carletonian foray. He rushed outside and mounted his horse. The animal suddenly reared up, lost its balance, and came crashing down "violently" on his "lame leg and ankle." Aides carried Arnold back inside, where he remained bedridden for ten days nursing a massive bruise. Wooster, as supercilious as ever, ignored him, nor did he show any interest in learning about Arnold's battle plan. Thoroughly disgusted, the junior brigadier finally asked for permission to retire to Montreal, where he hoped to make some contribution. Wooster breezily granted his request.

On Friday, April 12, 1776, Benedict Arnold rode quietly away from Quebec. He had obeyed Washington's dictum not to question superior authority, regardless of his apprehension that the rebels, with Wooster now in command, had lost any chance of entering the walled city in triumph. For the first time, Arnold began admitting to himself that the Canadian campaign might fail. If only his Kennebec column had gotten to Quebec City a few days sooner; if only Congress had not dallied but called for reinforcements before the onset of winter; if only he had urged Montgomery to avoid a climactic battle, regardless of unsteady troops refusing to extend their enlistments; if only Montgomery had not lost his life and he had not sustained a disabling wound; if only Wooster had stayed away for another month to six weeks; and if only a more judicious senior commander had appeared before Quebec. These frustrating thoughts only deepened his melancholy as he traveled in personal defeat to Montreal, knowing as he did that a major British counterthrust was sure to happen.[60]

CHAPTER Nine

Reduced to a Great Rabble

I

In early 1776, the benevolent Providence to which Arnold so often attached his personal fate, as well as that of the American rebellion, seemed perplexed about which side to support. For Washington's soldiers besieging Boston, the Almighty was acting as their faithful ally. In late January, they received fifty-nine pieces of artillery originally captured by Arnold, Allen, and others at Ticonderoga. A column under Colonel Henry Knox had hauled this "noble train of artillery" overland through the Berkshire Mountains of western Massachusetts. The Continentals then fortified Dorchester Heights, which commanded Boston from the south. Washington stood ready to bombard that port city into submission, but the British occupying force, now commanded by Lieutenant General William Howe, evacuated Boston by sea on March 17, 1776, rather than face possible obliteration. Howe's flotilla sailed to Halifax, Nova Scotia, and patriots everywhere gratefully praised God for the dislodgment of the king's "bloody lobsterbacks" from New England soil.

Divine Providence seemed much less committed to sustaining the patriot cause in Canada. In late February, Arnold would have discounted so bleak an appraisal. "The many, unexpected, and remarkable occurrences in our favor," he wrote to Washington, "are plain proofs of the overruling hand of Providence, which I make no doubt will crown our virtuous efforts with success." Two months later, he could muster few signs of divine approval. Very soon "we shall have our hands full" with enemy soldiers, but he promised to "do all that can be expected" in offering resistance with "raw troops, badly clothed and fed, and worse paid, and without discipline."[1]

On April 20, shortly after reaching Montreal, Arnold expressed to Schuyler his frustrations regarding the course of the Canadian campaign: "Everything is at a stand[still] for want of . . . resources, and if not obtained soon," he concluded, "our affairs in this country will be entirely ruined." He likewise hinted at a likely culprit. "I cannot help lamenting that more effectual measures have not been adopted to secure this country in our interest," Arnold declared in a circumspect reference to Congress.[2]

After assuming command from Colonel Hazen and settling into his quarters at the elegant Chateau de Ramezay, Arnold held meetings with prominent inhabitants. He heard many complaints, most having to do with Wooster's high-handedness. His New Haven neighbor had spoken grandly of liberation from Britain's arbitrary rule but had very often dramatized the persona of a tyrant in his own decision making. He showed his New Englander's prejudice toward Roman Catholicism by denying Montreal's civilians the right to celebrate mass on Christmas Eve. He arbitrarily imprisoned several prominent Montrealites after the patriot defeat at Quebec. When asked to explain this action, he pronounced his intention to incarcerate anyone whom he suspected of being pro-Carleton. He even had the residents of three Montreal suburbs temporarily disarmed because of unfounded rumors about a plot among them to rise up against his authority.

Grappling with how foolish the patriot quest for liberty looked to Montreal's residents, Arnold said he would make amends. Unfortunately, he lacked every resource except high-sounding words and a bold posture. He spoke of the arrival of additional troops and, even more important, of hard money, the cement to improved relations. While urging patience, he pledged that soldiers and specie would appear just as quickly as the spring floods receded, a serious problem in late April 1776 because of the heavy runoff of water from so much melting snow.

Maintaining an offensive posture, Arnold, as a realist, also began preparing for an orderly retreat from Quebec Province. To assure continued control of the principal escape route, the Richelieu River–Lake Champlain corridor into New York, he asked Hazen, whom he described to Schuyler as "a sensible judicious officer," to take command of the forts at Chambly and St. Johns. Hazen was to secure these posts against any British threat.[3]

Arnold soon had to respond to rumors of a possible enemy strike against Montreal from the west. To protect this flank, he ordered a battalion of four hundred New Hampshirites under Colonel Timothy Bedel to "take post" and "guard against a surprise from the enemy or their Indians" at the Cedars (Les Cedres). This strategic point lay some forty-five miles southwest of Montreal just above a series of dangerous rapids on the St. Lawrence River. Any enemy column moving east from Lake Ontario would likely portage through the Cedars area. Bedel's troops were to finish constructing a stockade there and stand ready to offer resistance.[4]

On Friday evening, April 26, Arnold joyously received a surprise visitor at the chateau. The tall, robust guest was fifty-one-year-old Major General John Thomas, who presented himself as the new commander of patriot forces in Quebec Province. Congress, having initially selected Charles Lee for the Canadian command, had then decided to send him into the southern colonies to rally patriots there against a British force that was about to take direct aim at Charleston, South Carolina.

Thomas, a physician by trade but also a military veteran who had seen service in Canada during the Seven Years' War, brought greetings from Washington. The commander had spoken highly of Arnold, he related, and had advised Thomas to work closely with America's Hannibal. Thomas did not mention that Congress had nearly named Arnold to the Canadian command but reconsidered because of the junior brigadier's wound and requests for a more experienced officer. Nor did he explain how the Massachusetts delegates used the standard aspersions about Arnold's troubles at Ticonderoga (and with their Provincial Congress) to secure the appointment for Thomas, a native son. Rather, he spoke of Washington's concern about Arnold's health. Soothingly, the commander in chief, thinking Arnold still at Quebec, had written how Thomas "will take the burden off your shoulders" so that "you will soon gather strength sufficient to assist in finishing the important work you have with so much glory to yourself, and service to your country, hitherto conducted."[5]

Thomas, who had directed the fortification of Dorchester Heights, shared additional news. With the British evacuation of Boston, Washington was moving his army to New York City, the expected focal point of the main British campaign thrust in 1776—with Canada and South Carolina identified as critical secondary theaters of action. Thomas also estimated that fifteen hundred patriot soldiers were at Ticonderoga and Crown Point, waiting for the ice-clogged, flooded water route north to become passable. With any good fortune, these troops would reach Quebec City by the middle of May.[6]

Arnold did not try to soften reality about the sorry state of rebel affairs, especially with Wooster in command at Quebec. He was not sure the fresh troops could get to the walled city before the expected British relief force arrived. Also of concern, the patriot besiegers had lacked hard money for nearly two months, and food supplies were in precarious shape. Thomas might well have to resort to plundering the countryside, even if that forever ruined relations with the local *habitants*. No matter what, Arnold warned, the choice among difficulties would require judicious decision making.

Thomas asked about possible courses of action. Arnold spoke of his battle plan, mentioning that at least one of the fireships, his own brigantine *Peggy*, stood ready for initiating a second assault, should Thomas decide to risk a general engagement. A sensible alternative plan would involve a temporary retreat and redeployment of patriot troops at Deschambault, about forty miles upriver from Quebec. This quaint French-Canadian village sat atop a 120-foot-high bluff overlooking the Richelieu Rapids, where only a narrow channel allowed vessels to maneuver their way through this hazardous passage point. Arnold had already written Schuyler about Deschambault and requested fifteen cannons (four 18- and eleven 12-pounders) to be placed there. With these pieces firing away in unison and with armed gundalows stationed beyond the rapids, patriot gunners, Arnold believed, could inflict severe damage on British war vessels and troop transports seeking to reach patriot-held positions farther up the St. Lawrence.[7]

Thomas said he would inspect the bluffs at Deschambault on his way downriver to Quebec. Most likely, he would designate this site as a reconcentration point, should a full-scale retreat become necessary. Arnold promised to forward the ordnance pieces as soon as they arrived, and the two generals agreed to have Hazen oversee the construction of four gundalows at Fort Chambly. Then they parted company, but not before Thomas mentioned the congressional commissioners who were coming up from Philadelphia to help oversee patriot martial affairs in Canada. He had traveled with them from Albany to Saratoga. Thomas thought they could be of assistance, especially in dealing with resentful civilians. Arnold asked whether they were bringing hard money. Thomas said no; all they could offer was goodwill. Without specie, Arnold replied, he was not sure how many more days the cause of liberty had left in Canada before succumbing to its own self-inflicted wounds.

II

On Monday afternoon, April 29, curious civilians lined Montreal's river shoreline to watch as Arnold ostentatiously greeted the commissioners. One of Congress's representatives, seventy-year-old Benjamin Franklin, who headed the delegation, was a celebrity in his own right. As a salute of cannon fire boomed, Franklin waved at the assemblage, then shook hands warmly. Less well known were Samuel Chase and Charles Carroll, both from Maryland. Chase had been an activist in mobilizing popular resistance against unwanted imperial taxes before serving in both the First and Second Continental Congresses. Like Chase, Charles Carroll of Carrollton, the scion of perhaps the wealthiest Roman Catholic family in all of North America, was a firm advocate of American rights. Because of his boyhood education in France, Carroll spoke impeccable French, which along with his Roman Catholic faith made him an invaluable person to cajole support from leery French Canadians.

Two other men journeyed north with the commissioners. Father John Carroll, a cousin of Charles, was a Jesuit. He had agreed to work with church officials and local priests to convince them that the patriots were not necessarily intolerant toward Roman Catholicism. (Father Carroll soon learned about Wooster's actions, and he could not help the delegation.) The other traveler was Fleury Mesplet, a Philadelphia printer who was to publish a French-language newspaper full of laudatory commentary about the patriot cause. (His labors likewise bore no fruit.)

Arnold's pomp and circumstance in greeting the commissioners was calculated to impress skeptical Montrealites with patriot resolve. He conducted the commissioners through the streets at the head of a military procession to the Chateau de Ramezay, where he grandly offered toasts to his guests and the Continental Congress while "a very polite, though not a numerous company ... of ladies and gentlemen" looked on. An elaborate formal supper and festive evening followed. If nothing else came of the day's events, Charles Carroll formed "a very favorable opinion of Arnold's good taste and politeness." "An officer bred up at Versailles," he declared, "could not have behaved with more delicacy, ease, and good breeding." [8]

Early the next morning, Arnold brought the commissioners into full contact with reality. They attended a council of war, the purpose of which was to brief them about faltering patriot military affairs in Canada. Arnold summarized his recent conversation with Thomas. Everyone appreciated that time was not on the rebels' side, and the assembled officers voted "to fortify" Deschambault with artillery pieces. Before closing the meeting, Arnold announced his intention to travel to Fort Chambly and assist Hazen in speeding up the construction of the armed gundalows designated for possible combat against the British at the Richelieu Rapids.

Charles Carroll sought out Arnold after the meeting and asked him about the wilderness trek through Maine. His animated "manner of telling" the story was exciting to behold, Carroll wrote before penning this evaluation: "Believe me, if this war continues, and Arnold should not be taken off pretty early, he will turn out a great man. He has great vivacity, perseverance, resources, intrepidity, and a cool judgment." Carroll's only concern was Arnold's noticeable limp, "but his lameness does not prevent him from stirring about, and he may in time get the better of it." For Carroll, the junior brigadier was, indeed, a patriot of heroic proportions.[9]

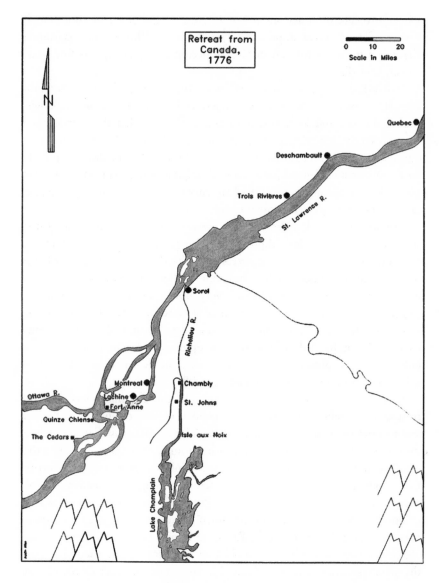

Arnold soon left for Fort Chambly but was back in Montreal a few days later, when he took a few moments to send his compliments to Washington "on the success of your arms against Boston." Unfortunately, he could not reciprocate with "a more pleasing account of our affairs in this country, which wear no very favorable aspect at present." He reported that the gundalows, each capable of carrying three cannons, "are building at Chambly," but he knew that his pathetic little fleet at Montreal, which consisted of an armed schooner, two gundalows, and several bateaux, did not possess the strength to resist any sizable British flotilla that got beyond the rapids at Deschambault.[10]

During the hectic days of early May, Arnold assisted Franklin, Carroll, and Chase in determining the amount of hard money needed to continue the Canadian campaign "with honor." To square current accounts and to support the army for the foreseeable future, the estimated figure was £20,000. Obtaining this sum was essential, the commissioners wrote to Congress, if the patriots were going "to regain the affections of the people, to attach them firmly to our cause, and induce them to accept a free government." Should no specie be available, the commissioners were of the "firm and unanimous opinion" that it would be "better immediately to withdraw" a force viewed as "contemptible in the eyes of the Canadians, who have been provoked by the violences of our military in exacting provisions and services from them."[11]

Concerns about filling the empty Canadian war chest faded quickly when a courier from General Thomas appeared at the Chateau de Ramezay on Friday, May 10. He bore devastating news. The first elements of the British relief force, having sailed through stormy winter weather in the North Atlantic, had reached Quebec early on the morning of May 6. The besieging rebel force had fallen back in disarray and panic to Deschambault. Once there, Thomas had called his officers together and spoken forcefully about digging in and making a stand. Wooster was among the dissenters who outvoted Thomas eleven to three. They favored retreating another seventy miles upriver to Sorel. Even if not so readily defensible, resistance could be more easily mobilized there, they insisted. If not, the rebel force would be in a much safer position to evacuate Canada. Since Thomas still had no artillery pieces, he conceded the argument. Just in case the ordnance was on its way downriver, he would remain at Deschambault with five hundred soldiers; they could begin digging entrenchments for the cannons. Everyone else was to proceed to Three Rivers and await further orders.

News of the possible abandonment of Deschambault deeply disturbed Arnold. A proponent of dynamic military strokes, he asked the commissioners for permission to go to Sorel, where some of the artillery promised to Thomas had recently arrived. Arnold wanted to be nearer the potential zone of combat, where he could influence how the patriots responded. A critical variable was the enemy's troop strength. If the numbers "should be found inconsiderable," he favored a full reconcentration of troops at Deschambault. However, if the British force numbered in the thousands, he did not think it "practicable, if advisable, to keep possession of this part of the country." The commissioners agreed, and they cautioned him against making too bold a stand at Deschambault if enemy numbers were potentially overwhelming. They did not want to lose hundreds of patriot soldiers who could fight another day under more favorable circumstances.[12]

Despite their sage advice, the bad tidings from Quebec disconcerted the commissioners. Franklin announced his intention to return to Philadelphia as soon as possible. Besides suffering from a bout of ill health, the aging patriot believed the commissioners could not "render our country any further services in this colony." Father Carroll decided to join Franklin, but Charles Carroll and Samuel Chase opted to remain in Montreal a few more days. They were certainly not expecting a miraculous reversal in patriot fortunes; appearances were their major concern. The sudden departure of the whole delegation could possibly demolish the morale of patriot forces — and might even spark an uprising by Montrealites anxious to end what many of them perceived as the tyrannical rule of liberty-loving patriots.[13]

As for Arnold, he vowed to do "everything in my power . . . to keep possession of this country, which has cost us so much blood and expense." Even if "the enemy's reinforcements are as considerable as we have reason to think," he wrote to Philip Schuyler on May 11, resolute action was essential to protect "our scattered, sick, starved, and distressed army, as well as . . . our friends in this country, many of whom will lose their all if we are obliged to evacuate it." He now spoke of a modest delaying action at Deschambault that would slow the enemy in its advance upriver and buy valuable time for patriot soldiers and civilian friends to get out of Quebec Province.[14]

Arnold could offer only the cheerless prospect of escape — and refugee status — to the latter group, whose numbers included Christophe Pelissier and Hector McNeill. Deeply concerned about their plight, he took another slap at Congress, this time for its "repeated promises . . . to our friends in this country" about making an all-out effort. Congress had dallied when it should have acted decisively — back in the autumn of 1775 — and had not even sent a farthing's worth of hard money north with the commissioners. In many ways, Arnold felt betrayed by Congress because he had encouraged so many civilians to throw in their lot with the patriot cause. Thus he would also fight to the end for these civilian allies, who deserved a better fate.[15]

III

A swirl of military business kept Arnold pinned down in Montreal until the early hours of Sunday, May 12, when he sailed for Sorel. Providence seemed to ignore his supplications for favorable winds. A blustering gale lengthened the forty-mile journey to almost two days. Once ashore, Arnold reviewed the latest intelligence, which was grim. Thomas, after holding on for a few days at Deschambault, had given in to supply shortages and continued his retreat. His troops, he later reported, were down to "only three pounds of meal per man, and not an ounce of meat." [16]

Arnold could appreciate Thomas's decision, having barely avoided the starvation of his Kennebec column only six months before. He had hoped, however, to proceed to Deschambault on an armed gundalow to see for himself "if there should be any prospect of maintaining our post" there. With Thomas's withdrawal, Arnold was now sure the advancing British relief force could not be stopped. If the rebels made a stand, they would have to do so at posts such as Sorel, which lacked any natural defensive advantage. [17]

Arnold assumed temporary command as the ranking officer present at Sorel. The soldiers, he saw the moment he arrived, were short of supplies and in a state of hopeless "confusion," a reflection of the poor planning, delayed timing, and badly coordinated operational effort that had so often beset the Canadian campaign. Shortly after the British evacuation of Boston, for instance, Congress had instructed Washington to detach troops for service in Canada. In mid-April, some two thousand Continentals began the northward journey from New York City under the command of Brigadier General William Thompson of Pennsylvania. Along with those troops previously delayed at Ticonderoga and Crown Point, Thompson's soldiers were now pouring into rebel posts along the Richelieu River. As Arnold summarized the situation for Thomas, "men indeed we have, but almost every other requisite for war is wanting." [18]

This fresh increment of patriot manpower had lost the race for Quebec City. Thompson's troops were now stuck at the Richelieu posts, and they had already consumed most of their rations. Before going to Sorel, Arnold had alerted Schuyler about food shortages in the region. Food was always more scare at the end of winter, and the *habitants* were hiding what supplies they still had left. Sending forward any additional soldiers, Arnold stated, would only "add to our distress, unless they are supplied with provisions, which must be forwarded on to us immediately." In the interim, he issued an unpopular general order placing the troops on half rations of meat with a slightly larger allowance of bread. [19]

Making the situation worse, Thomas's retreating troops were devoid of supplies. "Most of our men, returned from below, are naked," Arnold reported on May 15. Many of these ghostlike figures were desperately ill, and a number were suffering from smallpox. As they reached Sorel, Chambly, and St. Johns, they carelessly mingled with soldiers coming up from the colonies below, which only accelerated the spread of smallpox. The situation was so dire that Arnold rescinded his standing orders against self-inoculation and worked out a plan with Chase and Carroll whereby whole regiments would be inoculated and then sent off to recover in quarantine camps near Montreal. "We shall have more effective men in four weeks," he calculated, "than by endeavoring to prevent the disorder [from] spreading—a period so near that the enemy will not, with any considerable force, be able to reach this place by that time." [20]

Confronted with so much misery and suffering, Arnold welcomed the assistance of General Thompson, who finally arrived at Sorel late on May 16—he had made a courtesy visit with the commissioners at Montreal. Not long thereafter, an exhausted General Thomas appeared with his rear guard of troops. Rather than taking time to regain his strength, he immediately went to work on supply, health, and defense problems.

As moments allowed, Thomas told Arnold about the headlong retreat from Quebec. The commander had reached the patriot lines before the walled city on May 1 and had first dealt with Wooster, who resented being relieved. Putting up with his bluster was bad enough, but what Thomas found in the form of a patriot force was even more disconcerting. More than two thousand rebel soldiers were at Quebec, but almost half were unfit for duty, many of them having contracted smallpox. Some enlistments had expired, and these troops were pressing to return home. In addition, rumors were rife about British troop and supply transports making their way up the St. Lawrence.

Faced with the imminent relief of Quebec, Thomas explained how on the evening of May 3 he had tried to implement Arnold's battle plan by unleashing the one fireship ready for service. Using a dark night as an ally, Thomas hoped the Carletonians would hold off on bombarding the faintly visible craft, which Quebec's defenders might think was carrying messages from the relief force. When the brigantine did not respond to prearranged signals from shore, Carleton ordered his cannoneers to blast the intruder out of the water. They did so successfully, and Arnold's own *Peggy* disintegrated in a series of explosions some two hundred yards from the entrance to the harbor.

Since the brigantine had failed in its mission, Thomas called off any further action. He met with his officers on May 5, and they voted overwhelmingly to commence an orderly retreat. Those troops infected with disease were to be moved to Three Rivers, and all ordnance pieces were to be shipped upriver to Deschambault. Early the next morning, before the patriots could initiate their evacuation plan, the British war frigate *Surprise* appeared off the Island of Orleans, followed closely by two transport vessels carrying two hundred soldiers from the 29th Regiment of Foot. After this detachment debarked, Carleton forsook his long-standing defensive posture, marched nine hundred of Quebec's defenders out onto the Plains of Abraham, and dared the rebels to stand and fight. Thomas knew better. His troops were too sick or too scattered at various posts to accept the challenge. He ordered an immediate retreat. The scene was shortly one of panic. The patriots fled "in the most irregular, *helter skelter* manner," as aptly described by Dr. Senter, in what Thomas admitted was a humiliating conclusion to the patriot quest to conquer the walled capital city.[21]

The wasted wreckage of his brigantine *Peggy* seemed to Arnold an apt symbol for the futile exertions of so many valiant patriots in Canada. Their virtuous service had apparently gained nothing for the cause of liberty. Now the only reasonable course of action was to avoid further meaningless rebel losses. In declining health, the haggard-looking Thomas agreed. Arnold urged his superior to take better care of himself. Thomas, who was a physician, dismissed these concerns. Even Carroll and Chase advised him that "it will be almost impossible for you to escape catching the smallpox and therefore wish you would immediately inoculate." Thomas did not listen—not with so much pressing military business at hand. By Tuesday, May 21, he was too sick to keep functioning. He asked to be transported up the Richelieu River to Fort Chambly, where he endured the ravages of smallpox for several days before dying on Sunday morning, June 2, still hoping that the patriot effort in Canada could somehow avoid a similar fate.[22]

IV

While at Sorel, Arnold kept up with his command responsibilities at Montreal. Among his concerns was the continued loyalty of Montreal's inhabitants. He warned Carroll and Chase to watch for hostile signs because he was "convinced they are in general our bitter enemies." In the same letter, he optimistically stated that if the latest "intelligence can be depended on, . . . Colonel Bedel is in very little danger at his post." This information was completely wrong. A column of British regulars, French Canadians, and Indians, numbering about three hundred under Captain George Forster of the 8th Regiment, had taken dead aim on the Cedars from the west. Forster intended to liberate Montreal, but he had to deal with Bedel's force first.[23]

Even before Arnold's letter reached Chase and Carroll, they found themselves staring at the figure of Timothy Bedel. They demanded to know why he was in Montreal. He explained that his assigned duties involved more than his command at the Cedars. Arnold had ordered him to stay in touch with the Caughnawagas, the only Indians in the region willing to support the patriots. On the morning of May 15, Bedel had placed his troops under his second in command, Major Isaac Butterfield, and crossed to the southern shore of the St. Lawrence to parley with the Caughnawagas. They warned him about Forster's approach. Rather than returning to the Cedars to alert his troops, Bedel decided to carry the news himself to Montreal and ask for reinforcements.

The commissioners could hardly believe what they were hearing. At best, Bedel had shirked his primary duty to warn his troops; at worst, he had deserted his command in the face of the enemy. Apparently he was still suffering from the effects of smallpox after self-inoculation, and he seemed disoriented and confused. Carroll and Chase quickly made arrangements for a relief column, then complained to Congress that "your commissioners who have neither abilities nor inclination, are constrained to act like generals." On Friday, May 17, plucky Major Henry Sherburne set out in a rush for the Cedars with 140 troops. Carroll and Chase also sent an urgent communiqué to Arnold. The junior brigadier, in many ways relieved to let others deal with the chaos at Sorel, quickly returned to Montreal.[24]

Captain Forster, whose numbers were growing daily as *habitants* joined his column, besieged the Cedars stockade on Saturday afternoon, May 18. Throughout the night desultory musket fire filled the air, as did war cries from Forster's Indians. By early morning Major Butterfield had lost his nerve, even though none of his troops had suffered a serious wound. Panicked by threats of a bloody massacre at the hands of the natives, Butterfield saved little except his troops and the clothes they were wearing in acceding to Forster's terms of capitulation on Sunday, May 19.

Butterfield had no idea a relief force was on its way. On May 18, Sherburne reached Fort Anne (Ste. Anne) on the western end of Montreal Island and crossed the Ottawa River, which flowed to the northwest out of the St. Lawrence. He landed his party at the village of Quinze Chiens (Vaudreuil), about ten miles east of the Cedars. The major's scouts soon picked up jumbled reports of fighting, but with evening coming on Sherburne retreated back to Fort Anne for protective covering until daylight.

Sherburne's caution also reflected his dwindling numbers. Some of his soldiers had not kept up because they had not fully recovered from smallpox. Others simply deserted. The next day the major tried to recross the Ottawa but could not do so against gale-force winds. Finally, he got his remaining one hundred soldiers over to Quize Chiens on Monday, May 20. Sherburne's troops soon came under heavy enemy fire. They had run into the teeth of Forster's advancing column. The patriots suffered twenty-eight casualties before Sherburne, to avoid annihilation, surrendered. Forster's Indians stripped the captives of personal possessions, even in some instances their clothing. Sherburne, a physically imposing man, suffered the ultimate indignity of standing naked before his captors until a French-speaking soldier took pity on him and draped a cape around his beefy body.

Unlike Butterfield, Sherburne had not capitulated without a serious contest of arms. Further, he had sent back news of Forster's likely presence at the Cedars. Arnold, back from Sorel, needed no further intelligence. Knowing that Forster intended to liberate Montreal, he rallied what few troops were still available, no more than 150, and marched them nine miles southwest to the village of Lachine. There he set up the rebel standard and ordered the construction of entrenchments intersecting the main road to Montreal. With soldiers coming in from other posts, Arnold's strength reached 450 by the evening of Friday, May 24, when the distant sound of Indian drums proclaimed the presence of the enemy column little more than two or three miles west of Lachine. Determined to go on the offensive, Arnold urged his fellow officers to launch a surprise attack, but they refused. They would fight, they told their commander, but only from behind entrenchments.

Throughout the night Arnold's uneasy troops prepared for the British onslaught, expected at morning's first light. Nothing happened, however, so Arnold sent out scouts to gather intelligence. Forster, he soon found out, had "made a precipitate retreat" after learning about the entrenched rebels. Only later did he discover why. The British captain had received reports, including information from a trusted Montreal source, that Arnold would soon have twenty-five hundred troops, at least five times his own strength. Further, Forster could not deploy all of his troops, since some of them had to keep guard over nearly five hundred rebel prisoners. If only, Arnold mused, his officers had possessed more resolution and supported an attack, they could have caught Forster preparing to retreat, landed a devastating blow, and gained a notable victory that might have revitalized the faltering patriot effort in Canada.[25]

Knowing only that his adversary was on the run but slowed by so many captives (Forster had divided the prisoners, leaving some at the Cedars and moving the rest across the Ottawa River to Fort Anne), Arnold gave chase. By late afternoon on Sunday, May 26, they reached Fort Anne, where they saw "several of the enemy's bateaux taking our unhappy prisoners off an island at one league distance from us" in the Ottawa River. "Words cannot express our anxiety," Arnold wrote to the commissioners, "as it was not in our power to relieve" the captives.

Unsure whether his troops could catch up with Forster before the enemy column reached the Ottawa River, Arnold had sent a party of Caughnawagas ahead "demanding a surrender of our prisoners." Should they not be freed or if "any of them were murdered," he intended to "sacrifice every Indian who fell into my hands, and would follow them to their towns, and destroy them by fire and sword." The Caughnawagas delivered this message and reported back with Forster's response. If the rebels kept up their pursuit or mounted an attack on Quinze Chiens, where Forster's troops now "were posted," the British captain would let his native allies "immediately kill every prisoner, and give no quarter to any who should fall into their hands hereafter."

Temporarily at least, Forster had checked Arnold. The patriot commander found himself "torn by the conflicting passions of revenge and humanity." On the one hand, he had "a sufficient force to take ample revenge," and he was "raging for action." On the other hand, his concern for the welfare of "500 unhappy wretches, who were on the point of being sacrificed if our vengeance was not delayed," demanded prudence and restraint.

Arnold worked to curb his penchant for aggressiveness. Still, he had to test Forster's resolve, so he ordered about three hundred of his soldiers into the fifteen bateaux available to him at Fort Anne. Within minutes these troops were paddling toward the island, where they "found five unhappy wretches, naked and almost starved." The rest of the prisoners "were all taken off by the savages," Arnold explained, "except one or two, who, being unwell, were inhumanely butchered."[26]

The sight of these men, both living and dead, caused Arnold to forge ahead across the Ottawa River to reconnoiter—and possibly even attack—Forster's column at Quinze Chiens. Daylight was giving out, and the river was "as smooth as a mirror," according to Captain James Wilkinson, who had attached himself to Arnold as an aide. As the patriot bateaux approached the shoreline, Forster's "savages began to yell and fire from one extremity of their line to the other." Their shooting had no effect, since the patriots were not yet within musket range. Forster also ordered up salvos from two cannons he had seized at the Cedars. Wilkinson, never known for his bravery during his long and truly inglorious military career, fretted about these artillery blasts, now "plunging beneath or passing over us." Much to his relief, Arnold soon issued instructions to rest "on our oars," and "the current

... drifted us beyond the range of his [Forster's] shot." The rebel commander, meanwhile, had four Caughnawagas paddling furiously as he "darted about in his canoe." Arnold was evaluating the enemy's defensive alignment and assessing various attack options. He then ordered the bateaux back to Fort Anne, where his exhausted troops debarked well after dark.[27]

As soon as Arnold landed, he called his officers together in a council of war and explained his thinking. He "judged it most prudent" not to launch an amphibious assault but to pursue a no less bold but more judicious plan. Arnold wanted to move by water up the St. Lawrence "a few miles, under cover of the night," to "gain the rear of the enemy, and fall on them at daybreak." Concerned about his officers' lack of initiative at Lachine, he forcefully "asserted the feasibility of the enterprise, and urged it for the deliverance of the captives taken at the Cedars." [28]

Moses Hazen, who had traveled from Fort Chambly to join the column, disputed Arnold's logic. He spoke of "his long acquaintance with the Indian character." Their well-known "vigilance," he insisted, "would prevent surprise, and that the moment of attack would be the signal for the massacre of the prisoners." A strike of any kind was folly, Hazen concluded. Colonel John Philip De Haas of the 1st Pennsylvania Regiment, four companies of which formed the backbone of Arnold's troop strength, sided with Hazen. Others spoke up in turn, tempers flared, and Arnold and Hazen even engaged in "some reproachful language." The junior brigadier likely questioned the depth of Hazen's commitment to the patriot cause, now that events in Canada had swung in favor of the British. The colonel no doubt counterpunched with comments about needlessly risking lives in a senseless operation conjured up by a military amateur, no less, whose sole purpose was to gain personal glory. Close to midnight, the assemblage finally took a vote, which carried against Arnold. "Although highly irritated," he resolved not "to enforce his proposition," which he could have done "on his own authority." Pursuing so risky a combat plan would have been foolhardy with so many officers adamantly opposed.[29]

Arnold and Hazen, in their flurry of insults, abused the gentleman's code for mannerly deportment. Neither tried to heal the breach, although Arnold, in his summary report to the commissioners, sidestepped discussion of the council of war. His silence suggests that he did not want to dwell on the acrimonious scene. Arnold realized that pursuing their differences, including the filing of charges of insubordination against Hazen, would only promote unnecessary divisiveness at a time when harmony among the rebel officers was essential. Hazen did not exercise the same restraint. Convinced that

Arnold had purposely and maliciously slandered him, he would link arms with John Brown and James Easton as yet another vengeful enemy of America's Hannibal.[30]

Near 2 A.M. on Monday, May 27, little more than two hours after the council of war ended, Arnold found himself staring through candlelight at Major Henry Sherburne and Captain Andrew Parke. The two captives had appeared out of the dark bearing a flag of truce from Captain Forster. They handed over a written agreement on prisoner exchange, a cartel worked out by some of the captured rebel officers in concert with the British captain. Forster, Sherburne stated, would not negotiate. Should Arnold not accept all the terms, the captain would turn loose his Indian allies, who were pressing him for an opportunity to slaughter and scalp the prisoners.

Arnold pored over the text. According to one clause, the patriot prisoners, once freed, would "be under an obligation not to take up arms again" during the remainder of the rebellion. Patriot authorities, in contrast, would not only be expected to set free an equal number of British prisoners, but these soldiers would "be at full liberty" to continue fighting against the rebels. Arnold told Sherburne and Parke he would only accept an exchange "on equal terms." Should Forster not delete the offending clause, he would launch an immediate strike, "and if our prisoners were murdered," his force would "sacrifice every soul who fell into our hands."[31]

Parke carried this uncompromising message back to Forster. Arnold clearly was bluffing. Since the bulk of his officers had voted against combat, he might well have accepted the cartel on unequal terms, had Forster pressed the point. The British captain, however, had problems of his own. He was not sure how much longer he could control his Indians, and he did not want to deal with the consequences of a massacre. Therefore he acceded to Arnold's demand. The process of ferrying the patriot prisoners back to Fort Anne commenced early on the morning of May 28 amid menacing taunts from Forster's Indians, some of whom used their muskets to fire balls of mud at the departing rebels.[32]

Late on May 27, Arnold, who felt he should return to Montreal to assist the commissioners, asked De Haas to finish the liberation effort. Arnold went on to express his outrage about the handful of patriot captives "murdered in cold blood" by Forster's Indians and the many others "stripped naked" of clothing and personal belongings. "The king's officers" were no more civilized than the "savages" they employed "to screen them in their butcheries." Retaliation was necessary, he told De Haas, especially to stop the natives west of Montreal from joining any future operations against the patriots. By the terms of the cartel, neither force was to strike at the other for six days. Arnold would accept the letter of that agreement. Once all the prisoners were free, however, De Haas was to destroy Fort Anne and place his troops in a defensive posture back at Lachine. Before he did so, he was to attack and burn the local Indian village of Conosadaga, the home of a number of Forster's Indian allies. When the Pennsylvania colonel seemed to demur, Arnold replied that a village was not an army. De Haas had his orders, and he was to execute them without further questions.[33]

V

Back in Montreal, Arnold found Chase and Carroll in a somber mood. News of the prisoners' liberation cheered them, but everything else, they related, was discouraging. In Sorel, where they had briefly visited, the soldiers were "in want of the most necessary articles—meat, bread, tents, shoes, stockings, shirts, etc." The army was "broken and disheartened, half of it under inoculation or under other diseases, soldiers without pay, without discipline, and altogether reduced to live from hand to mouth, depending on the scanty and precarious supplies of a few half-starved cattle and trifling quantities of flour." Viewing the Canadian campaign as beyond repair, Chase and Carroll had reluctantly decided to return to Philadelphia.[34]

Arnold was hardly surprised. He spoke of the timidity of his officers in twice refusing to engage Forster. They had acted as defeated warriors, wanting only to survive, rather than as virtuous patriots willing to risk their all in daring to defeat the enemy. Keeping alive what little hope was left, he opined, depended on initiating a dramatic action, and he was ready with a plan. With the commissioners' permission, he intended to gather additional troops, return to Lachine to link up with De Haas's regiment, and march for the Cedars with the objective of wiping out Forster's force, which he expected to be much weakened after the destruction of Conosadaga.

Chase and Carroll approved Arnold's scheme. They also spoke with him about other issues. "To prevent a general plunder" of Montreal's citizens by hungry patriot troops, they had consented to the confiscation of flour and other food goods, pledging payment at a later date on "the faith of the United Colonies." Now they authorized Arnold, as they would other general officers, to continue these forced requisitions, rather than let soldiers starve or use the force of their arms to obtain food from the civilian populace.[35]

While at Sorel, they had learned that John Thomas, near death, had asked Wooster to serve as temporary Canadian commander. They could not accept this determination because Wooster, as they had just written Congress, was, "in our opinion, unfit, totally unfit, to command your army, and conduct the war," and they had recommended "his recall" at the earliest possible moment. Chase and Carroll asked Arnold to assume overall command until the appearance of yet another brigadier general, John Sullivan of New Hampshire, who was senior to Arnold and whom they expected to arrive within a few days at the head of an additional three thousand troops on detached duty from the main Continental army.[36]

Arnold may have derived some satisfaction from the censorious commentary about Wooster. Keeping this irascible old general away from posts of major responsibility in the future, he believed, was for the best. Still, he knew that Wooster had tried to serve the cause of liberty, and he was not solely responsible for the patriot fiasco in Canada. Arnold considered the dilatory Continental Congress as the primary culprit and was reluctant to see a military man become a scapegoat for civilian failures. (Congress did recall Wooster. The delegates later exonerated him, but the churlish New Englander received no further command assignments in the Continental service.)

Arnold traveled with the commissioners to Fort Chambly, where on Thursday, May 30, he called a council of war. Even though in command, he accorded Wooster the courtesy of sitting as "president" of the meeting. Chase and Carroll also attended, and they strongly endorsed Arnold's scheme to seek out and destroy Forster's column. Perhaps to avoid embarrassing themselves in front of the commissioners, the assembled officers voted in the affirmative, but they refused to consider additional plans, should Arnold succeed, or to make preliminary preparations for offensive operations in the direction of Deschambault and Quebec.

Two days later, Arnold was back in Montreal making final arrangements to march to Lachine with five hundred troops when a disturbing report reached him from Colonel De Haas. Captain Forster had "made a precipitate retreat" after releasing the rebel prisoners, thereby lessening the possibility of catching him. Worse yet, local *habitants* had filled De Haas's ears with "vague and uncertain" intelligence about a major concentration of Indian warriors, at least seven hundred in number, at Conosadaga. Their alleged purpose was to attack the colonel's force at Fort Anne. In response, De Haas had called together his officers "to determine if he should obey" Arnold's "very positive" orders to destroy Conosadaga. Without hesitation, the officers agreed to retreat to Lachine after razing Fort Anne. A helpless Arnold was furious about this "very extraordinary" rejection of instructions from a superior officer. "A fatality seems to attend every [one] of our enterprises," he wrote the commissioners, and now an opportunity to smash the enemy west of

Montreal—and regain some initiative in Quebec Province—was forever lost.[37]

On Friday, May 31, before learning about the fate of his plan, Arnold had composed a letter to General Horatio Gates in which he spoke of rebel troops "neglected by Congress below; [and] pinched with every want here." With the soldiers reduced to the condition of "a great rabble," he held out little prospect for a return of "good fortune." After learning of De Haas's action, he sent word to Carroll and Chase that he was now "making every possible preparation to secure our retreat." His procuring officers had already seized six tons of powder and lead, and he intended to continue the confiscation of "merchandise" in Montreal. Almost at a loss for words, he sent the commissioners his "esteem and affection," but not before writing in total frustration, "I wish with all my heart we were out of the country. We had much better begin anew, and set out right and methodically."[38]

Arnold penned this personal epitaph to the campaign the same day that John Sullivan, who had arrived at St. Johns the day before, took command. While traveling north, Sullivan had repeatedly insisted that a dash of dynamic generalship—which he, of course, intended to provide—would get the patriot forces in Canada moving forward again. So full of enthusiasm and full of himself, he hardly seemed to notice the ragged, emaciated appearance of the troops all around him. Bold leadership was all these dispirited soldiers craved, and Sullivan, who was sure that nothing could be learned from the likes of Arnold, proclaimed his intention to go back on the offensive and resecure Three Rivers before moving on to and fortifying Deschambault.

A New Hampshire lawyer in civilian life, Sullivan had been a delegate to the Continental Congress, where he maneuvered to gain a brigadier's commission. Like Arnold, he lacked military experience; unlike his Connecticut counterpart, he possessed little military talent. Sullivan was, as Washington stated confidentially after the siege of Boston, "active, spirited, and zealously attached to the cause." Yet he had "his foibles," which he "manifested in a little tincture of vanity, and in an over desire of being popular, which now and then leads him into some embarrassments."[39]

Once at Sorel, Sullivan received intelligence that a detachment of only eight hundred British regulars and Canadians was at Three Rivers. He responded by ordering General Thompson to assemble two thousand troops and seize the town. The patriot column left Sorel on Thursday, June 6. Sullivan was "certain that victory" would come and was particularly annoyed with Arnold for having detained De Haas's regiment near Montreal. He could not comprehend why the junior brigadier was holding back troops to defend that city when the true theater of action was at Three Rivers. He thus faulted Arnold for "some strange kind of conduct . . . directly contrary to repeated orders." Sullivan wanted De Haas's regiment released immediately, since he intended to proceed downriver with more troops in clearing the way to Deschambault—perhaps even to Quebec.[40]

Actually, the time for an orderly retreat and regrouping of the patriot military effort in the Canadian–Lake Champlain theater was at hand, and the Battle of Three Rivers fully established that point. By June 1 the British had landed some eight thousand troops at Quebec. Major General John Burgoyne, whom many considered the most dashing general officer in the British army, was in command of these British regulars and Hessians, subject only to the authority of Governor Carleton. With the long-awaited relief force at last in place, Carleton ordered an advance up the St. Lawrence. Some six thousand troops had already disembarked at Three Rivers when Thompson attacked. The patriots lost nearly four hundred men, over half of whom became British prisoners, including Thompson himself. The remainder reeled backward in shock and panic.[41]

By Monday, June 10, Thompson's thoroughly routed troops were pouring back into Sorel. Now even Sullivan recognized the truth. As Arnold, who was at Chambly that day, wrote to his senior, "the junction of the Canadians with the colonies—an object which brought us into this country—is now at an end." Without trying to offend Sullivan, he queried, "Shall we sacrifice the few men we have by endeavoring to keep possession of a small part of a country which can be of little or no service to us?" Arnold assured Sullivan that "there will be more honor in making a safe retreat than hazarding a battle against such superiority"; and he stressed that his "arguments are not urged by fear for my personal safety: I am content to be the last man who quits this country, and fall, so that my country [will] rise. But let us not fall together." The stunned, deeply embarrassed Sullivan listened this time. He had no other choice.[42]

VI

Arnold, meanwhile, was having more problems with Colonel Hazen, this time over provisions seized on the commissioners' authority "for the use of the army." The junior brigadier sent these goods overland from Montreal on Thursday, June 6, in the care of a small detachment under a Major Scott, who was to turn them over to Hazen for safekeeping. Still smarting over his verbal scuffle with Arnold, Hazen refused to take responsibility for the merchandise. Scott and his detachment could not stand guard, since they had orders to proceed to Sorel. They left the provisions along the banks of the Richelieu; not surprisingly, the "great part" of them, as Arnold later told Schuyler, were "stolen or plundered" by retreating rebel soldiers.

When Arnold learned about Hazen's negligence, he rushed to Chambly and tried to straighten out the mess. Before dispatching the merchandise, he had ordered the packages labeled with the names of the persons, mostly merchants, from whom the goods were taken. He had expected staff officers in Chambly to make a complete list so that these civilians would someday be compensated for their forced contributions to the patriot cause. Now, with so many packages "broken open, . . . mixed together in the greatest confusion, and [in] great part missing," constructing such a record was impossible. Hazen's breach of orders, from Arnold's perspective, caused the rebels, including himself, to look like dishonorable thieves. He wondered how his patriot comrades could expect to gain civilian support in Quebec Province, should they attempt another, better-planned invasion.

After inspecting the litter, Arnold verbally reprimanded Hazen, then ordered him to send what remained of the goods, along with any sick troops and war matériel, upriver to St. Johns in preparation for the final evacuation. Hazen would accede this time, but he informed Arnold that he intended to demand a court of inquiry to prove himself innocent of any wrongdoing. Hazen also promised to show the world what a loathsome, self-serving scoundrel Arnold really was. Facing far more serious problems than Hazen's bruised sensibilities, the junior brigadier shrugged off this challenge. The two of them could settle their differences some other time.[43]

Arnold rode on to St. Johns and focused his energies on the evacuation process, including the movement of hundreds of disease-ridden troops to swampy Isle aux Noix twelve miles up the Richelieu River—just north of the Canadian–New York border. By Thursday evening, June 13, Arnold was back at Chambly, where he jotted a few lines to Schuyler about the need for watercraft of all kinds. "You may expect soon to hear of our evacuating Canada, or being prisoners," he also wrote before traveling back to Montreal early the next morning.[44]

Arnold was aware from intelligence sources that the British, after their crushing victory at Three Rivers, were continuing their advance up the St. Lawrence River. What surprised him was their slow pace. He correctly assumed that Carleton was acting in character and avoiding unnecessary risks, even when so obviously holding the military advantage. The governor was likewise reckoning with provision shortages for his troops, although nothing comparable to the rebels' plight. The British reinforcements had not sailed from England with ample food reserves, normally deemed to be three months' worth of rations per soldier for duty away from supply bases. The king's planners had assumed that Canada's *habitants* would have an abundance of crops but the growing season was only getting underway. In addition, the patriots had picked many portions of the countryside clean. Carleton consequently had to conserve provisions, and he did not want to share rations with the retreating enemy, should his force move too decisively with the effect of overrunning and capturing hundreds of half-starved rebels.

Carleton also appreciated the psychological advantage of driving so many defeated patriots, whom he had taken to calling "mighty boasters" and "plunderers," back into the rebellious provinces. Discouraged and humiliated soldiers would not return to their communities full of braggadocio about the glories of war or their personal martial prowess. They would convey a very different message: Making war against the mighty British military machine epitomized human folly. As such, each rebel exorcised from Quebec Province had the potential to serve as an advocate for settling differences with the parent nation—before the Americans lost everything dear to them as their punishment for having dared to challenge Britain's mighty military forces.[45]

Carleton thus carefully paced the rate at which he allowed his military flotilla to advance. On June 13, rebel troops at Sorel spotted British regulars on the north side of the St. Lawrence. Sullivan consulted his officers and wisely ordered a general retreat. Early the next morning, Carleton debarked four thousand regulars under Burgoyne to give chase. The governor continued upriver, aiming directly at Arnold's small contingent of rebels at Montreal. At this juncture, Providence finally seemed to intervene. The wind that had favored the British fleet vanished, and the vessels could not move forward. On Saturday, June 15, Carleton landed his troops just fifteen miles beyond Sorel, at a point where no adequate road existed to sweep southward and cut off the three hundred patriot soldiers still at Montreal. Warned in time, Arnold effected an evacuation early that same evening in the midst of a driving rainstorm. His column successfully evaded Carleton and "destroyed all the bateaux, . . . and all the bridges in our rear," before reaching St. Johns.[46]

At St. Johns, Arnold allowed his detachment to rest before directing them upriver to Isle aux Noix. On Monday, June 17, Sullivan came in with his rear guard. The British were not far behind, he reported. His troops had set fire to Fort Chambly, seized every boat they could find, and demolished bridges along the way. Sullivan called his ranking officers together to discuss whether the patriots should throw up entrenchments and offer resistance at St. Johns. No one favored that proposition. As Arnold later communicated to

Washington, accepting combat "in our distressed situation," with "one half of the army sick and almost the whole, destitute of clothing and every necessary of life except salt pork and flour," would have been absurd. The officers concurred that a reconcentration of troops within safe proximity of Fort Ticonderoga and Crown Point was their only viable alternative. Sullivan agreed but declared his intention not to remove the rebel army from Isle aux Noix until he received orders from higher authority—specifically Schuyler. He was doing so to protect himself from accusations of faintheartedness.[47]

By arrangement with Arnold, Sullivan concentrated on moving all remaining soldiers, baggage, and ordnance up the Richelieu. Arnold stayed at St. Johns and directed a small detachment in destroying every usable building in the vicinity. By early afternoon on June 18, the work was done, which included putting the home of Moses Hazen to the torch. Arnold did so out of military necessity, and Hazen had agreed that his property should not be spared as a source of succor for the British. With St. Johns smoldering in ruins, Arnold ordered his troops into waiting craft and told them to be off. Then he announced to his aide James Wilkinson that he wanted to reconnoiter the enemy before departing. He asked the young captain to come along, and the two of them rode north until they spied Burgoyne's advance column. Arnold hesitated a few moments, perhaps musing over all the human sacrifice that had gone for naught during the past nine months, before wheeling his mount around and galloping back to St. Johns.

At the shoreline, Arnold stripped the saddle and bridle from his horse and handed them to a soldier in the lone waiting boat. He next removed his pistol from his belt, took aim, and shot his horse dead on the spot before ordering Wilkinson to do the same. The squeamish captain also killed his mount, although "with reluctance," as if failing to understand that America's Hannibal refused to leave anything behind that could assist the enemy. Once on board, Arnold "pushed off the boat with his own hands," which Wilkinson viewed as indulging in "the vanity of being the last man who embarked from the shores of the enemy." Perhaps it was. Except for the dead and the dying, no patriot had contributed more to the Canadian campaign, and no one took the final collapse of that effort more painfully.[48]

Darkness had set in by the time Arnold's craft landed at Isle aux Noix. Scattered everywhere amid the soft glow of flickering candles were "vast crowds of poor distressed creatures," human apparitions who had once been the heart and soul of the northern patriot army. Now there was "scarcely a tent," as a distraught physician described the tragic scene, "but what contains one or more in distress and continually groaning, and calling for relief, but in vain!" One building, a "large barn," was "crowded full of men with this disorder [smallpox], many of which could not see, speak, or walk" but who still had to endure "large maggots" crawling all over their bodies. "No mortal will ever believe what these [troops] suffered unless they were eyewitnesses," wrote the doctor.[49]

Arnold could do nothing to help alleviate the tragic human spectacle on Isle aux Noix. When light came the next day, he watched as fatigue parties dragged the lifeless remains of patriot comrades toward hastily dug burial pits. He did not indict the advancing British for the dispirited, broken, dying soldiery all around him, nor did he condemn his benevolent Providence. He refused to brood but focused his thoughts as best he could on dealing with the southward thrust of thousands of enemy troops. The rebels had to find some means to withstand any British descent into northern New York or face the prospect of a shattered rebellion. Theirs was an unenviable task, indeed.[50]

CHAPTER Ten

Malevolent Spirits in the Summer of 1776

I

General Sullivan was distraught. As he regarded the disease-ravaged and beaten patriot soldiery on Isle aux Noix, he contemplated how much public calumny he would have to endure. He regretted having spoken with such self-assurance—even arrogance—about reviving the patriot effort. Sullivan did not want his name to become synonymous with the collapse of the Canadian campaign. Somehow he had to shield himself from the inevitable process of scapegoating, and that depended on getting someone else— someone like his immediate superior, Philip Schuyler, or perhaps even Washington or Congress—to issue the fateful order to withdraw from Quebec Province.

With that purpose in mind, Sullivan prepared a lengthy missive for Schuyler on Wednesday, June 19. He described the patriot retreat in the face of enemy troops "much more powerful than mine." "Sufficiently mortified" though he was, he disdained accepting any blame for so dreadful an experience—"the grand post was lost before my arrival, and put beyond my power to regain." In a disingenuous puff of modesty, Sullivan claimed "no merit, except in making a safe and regular retreat." As for the hundreds of infirm patriot soldiers on Isle aux Noix, he would evacuate them as bateaux and other watercraft became available. Meanwhile, until he heard from Schuyler he would hold his current position with those troops still "fit for duty" and have them "ready to execute any orders you will please to communicate." This letter, as much a public justification as a private communication, would prove useful, Sullivan hoped, in warding off carping critics who would surely denounce his military capacities and call for his resignation.[1]

To lend a sense of urgency to his supplication for additional orders, Sullivan asked Arnold, rather than a lower-ranking officer, to serve as his messenger. Despite having had only a few hours to rest since reaching Isle aux Noix, Arnold embraced the opportunity to get away from the mosquito-infested island. With the rebels on the run, furthermore, he was anxious to converse with Schuyler about the defense of Lake Champlain. Knowing he could get some sleep while sailing up Lake Champlain, Arnold was soon off with staff aide James Wilkinson. Not finding Schuyler at Ticonderoga, the two officers pressed on for Albany, where near midnight on Monday, June 24, they located the Northern Department commander at his stately residence. Even though recovering from a bout of the ague, Schuyler was still awake and poring over stacks of papers. He greeted Arnold and Wilkinson warmly. He knew what their presence meant. Quebec Province was lost. The news was hardly unexpected.

Arnold handed over Sullivan's epistle, then dismissed Wilkinson so that he and Schuyler could talk freely. The ranking officers in Canada, he stated, had urged the New Hampshirite to withdraw completely to Crown Point. Schuyler could appreciate Sullivan's hesitation. Patriot harpies were everywhere, he replied, always ready to despoil some worthy patriot's good name. He had acquired a legion of critics himself, mostly from New England. They had castigated his attempts to instill sorely needed discipline in that region's independent-minded soldiery. They had described his public demeanor as too haughty, if not openly aristocratic and tyrannical. Scoffing at his physical infirmities, they had accused him of cowardice for not taking direct charge in Canada. They had even derided his unrelenting efforts to obtain provisions, weapons, and other military necessities as purely a way to gain huge profits for himself. They had denounced him because, as a New Yorker, he did not seem sensitive enough to the military needs of New England. Now they would surely delight in excoriating him for issuing the order to pull out of Canada.

Arnold had heard various versions of these accusations but had dismissed them as the grumblings of small-minded patriots. Schuyler could be cold and aloof, a manifestation of his public bearing as a patrician leader and high-ranking military officer. But from Arnold's more intimate knowledge, the man before him possessed a "cultivated mind," "polished manners," and "amiable disposition." Surely, no well-informed person could seriously consider the northern commander to be anything but a model patriot.[2]

At about 1 A.M., Schuyler took a few moments to write Washington. He expressed the "grief" he felt "on the evacuation of Canada" and told the commander in chief of his "wish" that Sullivan had listened to his officers and continued the retreat. Schuyler's major concern was "that the enemy will throw themselves between him and the broad part of Lake Champlain," with the effect of cutting off the patriot force from "a supply of provisions" and other forms of succor from below.[3]

Four hours later, after additional deliberations with Arnold, the northern commander drafted a response for Sullivan. He had already written Washington with the "wish you had complied with the opinion of your council of war, and retreated as far south as Crown Point." Schuyler could not wait for Washington's "pleasure" on the subject—not with entrapment at Isle aux Noix a distinct possibility. So Schuyler formulated these delicately phrased orders: "I am, dear general, so far at least in sentiment with your council of war, that I think and wish you to retire at least into the broad part of Lake Champlain." By affirming the recommendation of Sullivan's ranking officers, Arnold among them, Schuyler, too, was vulnerable to possible allegations of faintheartedness.[4]

Arnold concurred in the wording of Schuyler's "positive orders" and no doubt assisted in their composition. He felt a great sense of debt to his Yorker patron, a man who had helped rescue his military career from virtual extinction a year before. If congressional patriot leaders had to have scapegoats, let them feast on John Sullivan or David Wooster, because neither had brought military honor to the rebel cause or glory to themselves by their performances in Canada.[5]

Arnold's heroic actions, in turn, had assured him Schuyler's trust. As the two generals conversed about the likely course of events, they assumed that Carleton would try to recapture Crown Point and Ticonderoga. Before the year was over, their adversary might also attempt to conquer the rugged, sparsely settled region stretching south from Lake Champlain to Albany. Both appreciated the implications should Carleton's force gain access to the Hudson River and reach Albany. Just 150 miles to the south, in the environs of New York City, the main Continental army was preparing to resist what everyone thought would be the major British military thrust of 1776. Should the king's troops overwhelm Washington's, the port of New York could then serve as a staging area for operations directed up the Hudson River and through the Hudson Highlands region to Albany. To avoid such a junction, Carleton had to be resisted, delayed, and, if at all possible, stopped.[6]

Knowing Arnold's aggressive temperament, Schuyler hardly seemed surprised when his subordinate pronounced himself ready, with the blessings of Providence, to strain "every nerve" in the forthcoming duel with his nemesis Carleton. The Canadian governor, Arnold stated, had three major obstacles to overcome before mounting an effective challenge on Lake Champlain.

First, he had to have adequate reserves of supplies for his troops. As such, he would not feel comfortable about moving his army south until the harvesting season was well underway. Second, the British could not launch their invasion until they constructed a fleet of vessels at St. Johns—beyond the impassable Richelieu River rapids that ran south for about twelve miles from Fort Chambly. Arnold assumed that Carleton was already turning burned-out St. Johns into a shipyard, and he had received reports about Burgoyne's relief force bringing from England the unassembled frames for flat-bottomed boats. Constructing enough watercraft to move ten thousand or more troops, however, would certainly delay any British southward thrust until late summer.

The third point related to Arnold's sense of Carleton's temperament. The governor's strengths were those of a defensive warrior, as demonstrated at Quebec. He would not easily adapt to bold offensive strokes. When he was ready to move, Arnold predicted, Carleton would most likely enter Lake Champlain in a posture of massed strength and with great circumspection.

For all of these reasons, Arnold thought the northern patriot force would have at least two months—perhaps even longer—to prepare its defenses, an essential component of which would involve the "naval armament" of Lake Champlain. The junior brigadier expressed how it was "of the utmost importance" to build "a large number (at least twenty or thirty) of gundalows, row galleys, and floating batteries."[7]

Given his extensive maritime experience, Arnold underscored his desire to play an active part in the construction and command of the fleet. Schuyler was counting on Arnold's assistance. The northern commander had already solicited Washington for naval materials and a small workforce of ships' carpenters. He had also selected Skenesborough, which had the best sawmill capacity in the region, as the site to construct the gundalows and row galleys. Patriot laborers at Skenesborough, located about thirty miles south of Fort Ticonderoga on Wood Creek at the base of Lake Champlain, had assembled the bateaux that had carried hundreds of soldiers northward during the past two months. Familiar with the location and its many advantages, Arnold saw the merits of Schuyler's decision.[8]

As they continued their discussion, Schuyler asked for a favor and issued a warning. Knowing Arnold's high credibility with Washington, he wanted his guest to write the commander and reinforce his own entreaties for naval supplies and shipwrights. Arnold promised to do so, stating that he would ask for at least three hundred carpenters. Then Schuyler addressed the subject of petty-minded patriots. He expected a summer full of needless recrimination, the price of failure in Canada. Just as much as anyone else,

Arnold had the right to defend his reputation from groundless calumnies, but Schuyler advised him to disdain the kind of damaging turmoil that had almost destroyed his prospects in 1775. No matter what happened, Arnold should not engage his critics. If they became too abusive, he could always resign his commission and return to private life, an option Schuyler had begun pondering for himself because of so many slights from his New England antagonists. The rebellion's continued viability, the Yorker emphasized, now depended on the full focusing of energies in containing Carleton's advance, regardless of the demeaning slurs of carping patriots. Arnold said he understood, but he wondered to himself how much forbearance he would be able to muster toward the likes of Moses Hazen or John Brown if their words became too slanderous.

II

Before the two generals parted company to get some rest, Schuyler mentioned one other matter. Congress, he had learned, had voted on June 17 to turn over the Canadian command to Major General Horatio Gates. Arnold counted this officer among his patrons. Back in August 1775, while serving as Washington's adjutant at Cambridge, Gates had spoken favorably of Arnold as a strong choice to lead the Kennebec detachment. These two officers, moreover, had worked well together in preparing the column for its march to Quebec. When writing to Washington later that day, Arnold indicated how "happy" he was "to hear" that Gates was "on his way here." [9]

What Arnold had not yet fathomed was the depth of Schuyler's vexation over Gates's appointment to a command department—all of Quebec Province—separate from his own. By this action the delegates had seriously reduced Schuyler's range of authority, since supplying and directing patriot operations in Canada had represented the Northern Department's primary function during the past year. Now Schuyler's suspicions peaked. Perhaps the delegates, bowing to clamorous New Englanders in their midst, had a hidden agenda. Perhaps they intended to pin on Schuyler the blame for failure in Canada. With Gates coming to the Champlain region but with no army left in Canada to command, they could more easily remove Schuyler without an interruption in leadership.

Schuyler viewed Gates as a serious rival because the former adjutant was then emerging as the darling general of New England delegates in Congress. Born of humble parentage in England, Gates had served in the regular British army during the French and Indian War. By happenstance, he had made George Washington's acquaintance in 1755 while marching with General Edward Braddock toward disaster near the forks of the Ohio River. After the war, Gates sold his major's commission and eventually resettled in Virginia. Named the Continental army's adjutant general (with a brigadier's ranking) in June 1775, Gates quickly showed his talent for effective military administration. While residing in Cambridge, he likewise developed a network of friendships among notable New England patriots.[10]

Gates was ambitious. Service in the Continental army gave him a level of military recognition and personal eminence that lay beyond his grasp in the British army. Because of his commoner's birth, he had lacked the influence and personal income to purchase his way up into the highest field-grade ranks. In the colonies he faced no such castelike restrictions. Drawing on Washington's initial support and his own record as a regular British officer, Gates the American rebel now held military rank well beyond what he could have ever expected in England. He even had notions of becoming a great military leader, should good fortune or astute political maneuvering favor him.

When Samuel Chase and Charles Carroll returned to Congress from Quebec Province, they did not exactly explain the whole truth—that the campaign was moribund. Rather, they spoke of "the many and great abuses and mismanagements in Canada" and claimed that a dynamic, fully experienced commander possessing "the powers of a Roman dictator" might yet revive the patriot effort there. No general officer in Canada, they stated, not even Arnold and certainly not Sullivan, had the qualifications for so critical an assignment. Gates, with his proven administrative capacities, was the obvious choice.[11]

As was too often the case with its Canadian-related decisions, Congress had again acted too late. This time the delegates' decision had the effect of launching a long-term, highly divisive controversy between Schuyler and Gates over the Northern Department command, in which Arnold also became ensnared. Some of the delegates hoped to avoid needless rancor. Samuel Chase told Gates that Schuyler was a man of "integrity, diligence, abilities, and address," who had been "basely traduced" and "injured" by his critics. Above all else, Chase stressed, Gates should treat so well-connected a patriot with respect. Gates understood. Although his own range of influence was expanding, Schuyler was still more powerful, even in the halls of Congress.[12]

When Gates reached Albany, the northern commander greeted him with civility. On Sunday morning, June 30, the two general officers held a formal meeting. Tall, stately Schuyler asked to have an aide present to provide a record of the proceedings. Short, stocky Gates, well known for his guttural language, agreed. Both clung firmly but politely to their respective positions. For Schuyler, the issue was clear-cut: Gates no longer had an army to command, now that the northern force was retreating from Canadian soil. Revealing his own ambitions, Gates asserted his authority over that army regardless of its location. Schuyler proposed a compromise, that Gates function as the senior officer of the northern force in Schuyler's absence, just as Montgomery and Thomas had done. Gates demurred. Schuyler replied that no army could function effectively with two commanders; Washington and Congress would have to resolve the issue. Gates promised to abide by any ruling. Meanwhile, he stood ready to work with Schuyler in resisting Carleton's expected southward thrust.[13]

Congress wrestled with its command dilemma in upper New York on Monday, July 8. The delegates finally voted to inform Gates that they "had no design to vest him with a superior command to General Schuyler, while the troops should be on this side of Canada." This resolution confirmed that the Yorker still had greater influence in Congress than Washington's former adjutant. Gates accepted the verdict, at least temporarily. As for Schuyler, he had maintained the demeanor of a gentleman in defending his military rank and reputation. He had displayed the self-assurance of a wealthy patrician, which Arnold, hardly secure in his own family lineage and legacy, could not so easily replicate.[14]

III

Congress expected Schuyler and Gates to work together "with harmony." The two major generals did so during the summer and autumn of 1776, most likely because they spent so little time together. Arnold served directly under Gates. What proved to be a brief period of goodwill between Schuyler and Gates turned out to be a season full of acrimonious turmoil for Arnold. Fortunately for the cause of liberty, his two superiors held him in the highest esteem. They used their command authority to keep his critics at bay while he concentrated his boundless energy on hindering the British invasion.

Arnold became a target of criticism simply because he had been a general officer in Quebec Province making hard decisions in the absence of adequate resources. Such an individual as Dr. Lewis Beebe, who had traveled to Canada with Connecticut troops during the spring of 1776, repeatedly confided in his daily journal his chagrin about the "poor distressed soldiers." For Beebe, the fault did not lie with Congress but with the general officers in Canada, a disgusting "set of haughty, ambitious, aspiring miscreants, who only [took] pride in promotion and honor." The worst of them, he wrote, was "the great Mr. Brigadier General Arnold," who in his "superior wisdom, which is necessary for a man in his exalted station of life," had treated the troops callously. While pronouncing "his great pity and concern for the sick," he had mandated "that every sick man, together with everyone returned not fit for duty, should draw but a half allowance" in rations. That the army lacked provisions and that Arnold hoped to avoid cases of starvation and to save lives by carefully distributing what food there was made no difference to Beebe. Arnold was a despicable human being.[15]

In his daily entries, Beebe neglected to mention how his negative predisposition toward Arnold related to family and personal connections. The physician had married a sister of Ethan Allen, and one of his Yale classmates was John Brown, with whom he had regular contact in Canada. Beebe's perceptions thus were tainted, but his vituperation was no less real: "I heartily wish some person would try an experiment upon him [Arnold], (viz.) to make the sun shine through his head with an ounce ball; and then see whether the rays come in a direct or oblique direction." Such venomous words were an embarrassing testament to patriot mean-spiritedness, when unity of purpose was essential to saving the patriot cause from collapse.[16]

The wider process of faultfinding for the failed Canadian campaign began in earnest when congressional leaders, who refused to consider their dilatoriness as part of the problem, set up committees to ferret out culprits. The delegates proceeded along three lines of inquiry. Even before they received news of the withdrawal, they had formed a committee to examine the cartel arrangement between Arnold and Captain Forster. Once apprised of the final evacuation, they called on Washington to investigate "the conduct of the officers heretofore employed in the Canada department," with the intent of bringing all those "accused of cowardice, plundering, embezzlement of public monies, and other misdemeanors . . . immediately . . . to trial." Finally, they authorized a special committee to probe "into the cause of the miscarriages in Canada." In each instance, Arnold's name came under scrutiny, if not some form of condemnation.[17]

Regarding the Cedars agreement, Congress walked a fine line between praising and insulting Arnold. In their public resolutions, the delegates explained how the brigadier had been "extremely averse" to signing the cartel and had done so out of "no other motive than that of saving the prisoners from cruel and inhuman death." Still, he had overstepped the bounds of his authority because he had no British prisoners in his "possession" to exchange. He had signed the agreement as "a mere sponsion . . . , he not being invested with powers for the disposal of prisoners not . . . under his direction." Congress alone had that prerogative. Thus, the delegates treated the cartel as an unauthorized arrangement forced on Arnold by Forster, who had allowed his Indian allies, in a few instances, to butcher patriot prisoners. They would not ratify the cartel until Carleton handed over "the authors, abettors, and perpetrators" of these "horrid" crimes for punishment by Congress.[18]

Knowing that Carleton would dismiss this demand, Congress effectively disavowed the cartel while questioning Arnold's decision-making capacities when faced with perplexing choices. "I am fearful his humanity got the better of his judgment," sniffed a New England delegate who apparently had no idea that Arnold was lacking alternatives, since his own subordinate officers refused to risk combat. The resulting impression of Arnold as being overly zealous, if not presumptuous, in the use of military authority reminded many delegates of all the turmoil at the Champlain forts the previous year.[19]

Other commentary also resulted in negative impressions. The committee charged with investigating the reasons for defeat in Canada met sporadically during July and took testimony from a number of "witnesses," including highly respected Canadian refugees. The prominent Montreal merchant James Price referred to Arnold as "vigilant and careful, but not attentive to discipline." He viewed America's Hannibal as no more effective than Wooster: "They give good orders, but take no care to have them obeyed." Arnold's maritime friend Captain Hector McNeill spoke of New York troops at Quebec who were "dissatisfied" with Arnold because he had criticized their less-than-courageous behavior in retreating so precipitously after Montgomery's death. Indeed, Wooster's arrival in early April, McNeill stated, "was lucky, as he kept the men there, which he thinks Arnold could not have done."[20]

Reporting to Congress on July 30, the committee members generally avoided criticizing particular officers. Rather, they identified three factors— short enlistments, the scarcity of hard money, and smallpox—as the principal causes for failure. They did insist upon courts-martial for Colonel Bedel and Major Butterfield; and in a related set of recommendations, they reacted to a flurry of anti-Arnold accusations from John Brown and James Easton.[21]

These two implacable adversaries, employing self-righteous vehemence as their primary weapon, had persistently attacked Arnold's character ever since he had charged them in writing with plundering the personal baggage of captured British officers at Sorel. Easton, as soon as he learned about the letter, petitioned Congress for a hearing. In April 1776 he traveled from Massachusetts to Philadelphia and presented "testimonials" on behalf of his own integrity and that of his regiment. He loudly declared "his innocence," stating "that he neither plundered, nor directed, nor was privy to the plundering of any prisoner or other person whatever." The delegates chose to sidestep the dispute. Easton, they voted, would have to travel to Canada if he wanted a military court of inquiry to investigate the allegations. These proceedings would give him "an opportunity of making his defense, . . . in order that justice may be done to the petitioner, if he has been accused without sufficient reason."[22]

A very disappointed Easton was about to leave for Canada when creditors from Massachusetts caught up with him and had him incarcerated in a Philadelphia jail. Easton was in debt for about £2,400 in "lawful" New York currency. He had already told the delegates that Montgomery had promised him and his regiment financial compensation—a plunder payment—for the public stores they had seized from the British at Sorel. If Congress would only settle accounts with him, he now claimed from jail, he could cover his debts three times over, based on the value of his share in the public stores. Easton thus implored the delegates to "relieve me, consistent with their true dignity," and "liberate" him from both jail and his debts, since "they cannot be losers by me."[23]

Pressed as Congress was, the delegates ignored Easton's pleas for nearly three months. Then, on July 31, Congress's Board of War asked to be "discharged from so much of Colonel Easton's petition, as prays a settlement of his accounts," in favor of a final determination by its Board of Treasury. The next day the delegates granted Easton a colonelcy in the Continental army, with full pay retroactive to July 1775. The delegates expressed their "confidence" in him "for future employment" as a regimental commander, which he would have as soon as he cleared himself of the plundering accusation.[24]

What had transformed Easton's bleak prospects was the advocacy of John Brown, who after the retreat from Canada had hastened southward and reached Philadelphia before the end of June. Brown was a man possessed by one thought: seeking "satisfaction" as a patriot deeply "injured in the highest manner and in the nicest point of honor." His mission was to exonerate himself while demolishing Arnold's reputation. In petitioning Congress, Brown described how "General Arnold and his adherents" had willfully fabricated the outrageous allegation of plunder, which was completely "false, scandalous, and malicious." They had purposely forced Brown to keep "serving in an inferior rank," despite Montgomery's "express order" awarding him a colonelcy. When Brown had demanded a court of inquiry, Arnold "peremptorily refused" the request. Then he further sullied Brown's reputation, and Wooster, the Canadian commissioners, and Schuyler had also rejected his appeals for a hearing. In conclusion, Brown proclaimed that "men and angels, as well as the informer [Arnold]," could never prove "any part of" the charges against him.[25]

Brown was persuasive in personal discussions with congressional delegates, partly because his vision had been damaged by overexposure to the brutal winter weather in Canada. Brown also knew that Arnold, consumed as he was by his military duties more than 250 miles to the north on Lake Champlain, could not dash to Philadelphia to defend himself. Since Brown could say whatever he pleased, he spewed out a scurrilous tale about Arnold operating as a notorious pillager in Canada, all of which, he promised, would soon be demonstrated in court-martial proceedings against Moses Hazen.

With such slurs filling the halls of Congress, the delegates could not be sure whom to believe. Arnold's reputation for impertinence and pugnacity at the Champlain forts had faded in the wake of the heroic march through the Maine wilderness and the assault on Quebec. Now, during the summer of 1776, a variety of complaints and allegations, the most damaging of which were Brown's, again had the delegates wondering about Arnold's true character.

Brown was grateful when Congress confirmed him in the rank of lieutenant colonel, backdated to November 18, 1775—the day Montgomery had apparently promised him higher rank. The delegates had partially vindicated his good name while repudiating Arnold's action. In addition, the delegates prepared instructions for Schuyler to convene courts of inquiry for Brown and Easton so that "any charge against them" would be "determined by trial as speedily as possible, that there may be no delay in justice."[26]

Brown now prepared to travel to Ticonderoga, where he planned to join his assigned regiment, obtain his hearing, and continue his personal vendetta against Arnold. Easton, however, now out of jail, decided to return to Massachusetts. With his creditors only momentarily at bay, he needed to resolve his financial difficulties. A favorable court-martial ruling for Brown, Easton knew, would effectively cleanse his own name as well and allow him to activate his colonel's commission. As for Arnold, he received a telling warning from Samuel Chase. In the wake of Brown's smear campaign before Congress, Chase wrote, "I cannot but request all persons to suspend their opinion, and to give you an opportunity of being heard." Then he added ominously, "Your best friends are not your countrymen."[27]

IV

Traveling together from Albany, Arnold, Gates, and Schuyler reached Crown Point on the evening of Friday, July 5. What they beheld were "the wretched remains of what was once a very respectable body of troops." An estimated five thousand patriot soldiers sent to Canada were now casualties—wounded or killed in battle, missing in action, dead of disease, or captured and imprisoned. Of those still under arms—and optimists placed the number at no more than eight thousand—at least a third were unfit for duty. "That pestilential disease, the smallpox, has taken such deep root," reported an astounded Gates, that Crown Point "had more the appearance of a general hospital than an army formed to oppose the invasion of a successful and enterprising enemy." Almost as bad, he added, was the absence of discipline. Soldiers in good health were regularly getting into arguments and fistfights with patriot comrades from other regions.[28]

Hardly had the three general officers arrived before Schuyler faced a sulking General Sullivan, who was upset about Congress superseding him with Gates. His honor as a patriot and a gentleman would be forever compromised, he exclaimed, unless he departed for Philadelphia at the earliest possible moment and resigned his commission. Trying to assuage Sullivan, Schuyler asked him to remain at Crown Point a few more days. Important decisions had to be made, and he very much wanted the benefit of Sullivan's advice.

Schuyler gathered the general officers on July 7 in a council of war. They approved various plans regarding "the most effectual measures . . . to secure our superiority on Lake Champlain," including "a naval armament of gunda-lows, row galleys, armed bateaux, etc." Most controversial was their decision to abandon Crown Point in favor of a strengthened position at Ticonderoga. As Gates later explained to Washington, "the ramparts" at Crown Point "are tumbled down, the casements are fallen in, the barracks burned, and the whole so perfect a ruin, that it would take five times the number of our army, for several summers, to put it in defensible repair." The best option was to "retire immediately to the strong ground" around Ticonderoga, the design being to construct defensive works on a promontory (soon called Mount Independence) across from the main fort on the east side of the lake. The general officers also agreed to quarantine all "sick and infected" soldiers by sending them to the fort at the base of Lake George. They hoped this action would encourage New England militia to come forward more quickly and join their healthy Continental brethren in resisting the British offensive.[29]

The decision to concentrate the patriot line at Ticonderoga quickly produced contention, since Crown Point had certain defensive advantages. The decaying fortifications faced northward at a geographic location where Lake Champlain narrowed significantly. If the site was properly strengthened by earthworks and artillery pieces, the British would be hard pressed to get beyond the Point without sustaining major losses. Although the lake was also constricted at Ticonderoga, the fortress faced southward, belying its origins as a French citadel standing in the path of northward-moving British columns. Given the direction of the impending invasion, Ticonderoga could not be as easily defended—not without ample fortifications on Mount Independence, a natural geographic position for aiming artillery pieces in a northwesterly direction.

Regimental officers from New England were the primary protesters. Showing little respect for their senior commanders, they fired off a strongly worded "remonstrance" to Schuyler. The abandonment of Crown Point, they argued, would leave that ground open as a base for Carleton's force to strike not only at Ticonderoga but all of New England as well. Schuyler responded with soothing words, but the decision, he stated, was "not only prudent, but indispensably necessary, for a variety of reasons, against which those you have given do not, in my opinion, bear sufficient weight to alter it."[30]

This controversy was a sign of ongoing disharmony in the northern army. Not only had rank-and-file soldiers, in their frustration, taken to defending their particular locale's honor by bloodying each other's faces, but the officers were metaphorically doing the same. When the court-martial of Moses Hazen got underway, Arnold would personally taste the lingering wrath of some of the field-grade officers.

On July 8 the general officers, except for Arnold, left Crown Point. He remained there to manage the evacuation process. Schuyler, Sullivan, and Gates traveled to Ticonderoga and reconnoitered the Mount Independence site, which they concluded was "so remarkably strong as to require little labor to make it tenable against a vast superiority of force." Gates then assumed command at Ticonderoga, and Schuyler and Sullivan headed south for Albany. Sullivan, still determined to offer his resignation to Congress, continued on to Philadelphia. Schuyler soon left for German Flats in the Mohawk Valley, where he sought pledges of neutrality from the Six Nations of Iroquois Indians. Had Iroquois warriors completely aligned themselves with the British (some Mohawks and Senecas had already done so), they could have moved east in great force and severed patriot supply lines running north from Albany to Ticonderoga, thereby rendering any defense of the Champlain region untenable. Schuyler, however, gained the necessary pledges.[31]

Arnold, meanwhile, served as a communications link for scouting parties sent down the lake to seek intelligence about British activities along the Richelieu River. He identified carpenters and other skilled workers among

.the rank and file and directed them to Skenesborough. On Friday, July 12, he told Gates to expect the appearance of all remaining soldiers within a few days, "unless you think proper for part of them to remain here until barracks can be built at the new camp, as many of them are destitute of tents."[32]

With each passing day, Arnold sensed that the enemy was that much closer to launching its invasion. As a result, he almost never rested. On July 14 he asked whether a regiment should remain at Crown Point as an advance scouting force, and a day later he received the welcome news that Brigadier General David Waterbury, a valuable Connecticut militia officer, had appeared with a body of troops at Skenesborough and taken charge of daily boatbuilding operations—with Arnold to provide more general supervision when he was free of his duties at Crown Point. That same day Arnold expressed his "pleasure" about getting back to Ticonderoga, and he stated how anxious he was to put forth "my utmost exertion in forwarding our naval armament, on which I think much depends." Nothing more could have been asked of a person who, despite the aspersions of his critics, was "ever active, and anxious to serve his country," as Gates described him in late July.[33]

V

Arnold got to Ticonderoga sometime before Saturday, July 20, and soon met with an ebullient Gates, who mentioned rumors about a formal declaration of independence. The soldiery, Gates indicated, had received the news "with . . . applause" and with appreciation for "the great benefit America will receive thereby." Morale had definitely improved. Equally important, the king's former colonists now knew exactly what they were fighting for. The declaration, Gates thought, would encourage thousands of uncommitted persons to become involved in the martial struggle for freedom. Arnold was not so sure.[34]

The senior general had made a number of decisions, he informed Arnold, about the command structure at Ticonderoga. The various regiments would be organized into four brigades. Since Arnold was the only other general officer present, Gates would honor him with command of the first brigade, consisting of three Massachusetts regiments under Colonels William Bond, John Greaton, and Elisha Porter and a Connecticut regiment under Colonel Charles Burrall.[35]

Gates promised to keep his own eye on this brigade, since he had other duties in mind for Arnold. Earlier in the year, Schuyler had named a locally prominent Dutchman, Jacobus Wynkoop, to serve as commodore of the patriot Champlain fleet. In the process of moving troops, supplies, and equipment from Crown Point, mostly by bateaux, Gates had come to regard Wynkoop as thick-witted, indecisive, and lazy—virtually incapable of directing the handful of makeshift mariners under him. Confessing his own ignorance of naval matters, Gates wanted "the armed vessels commanded by men of firmness and approved courage." As a first step, he asked Arnold to replace Wynkoop at the head of the Champlain fleet. The junior brigadier fairly leaped at the offer. As Gates later reported to Congress, "Arnold (who is perfectly skilled in maritime affairs) has most nobly undertaken to command our fleet upon the lake. With infinite satisfaction, I have committed the whole of that department to his care, convinced he will thereby add to that brilliant reputation he has so deservedly acquired."[36]

Before Arnold could assume a commodore's role, he needed a fleet worthy of the name. As such, Gates wanted his subordinate to leave as soon as possible for Skenesborough to "give life and spirit to our dockyard." Gates, meanwhile, would focus on reinvigorating and training the northern army at Ticonderoga and seeing to the completion of the encampment and fortifications on Mount Independence.[37]

Gates also discussed Congress's order to conduct courts-martial for officers who had allegedly committed some malfeasance while on duty in Canada. Washington had delegated that "work of difficulty and delicacy" to Schuyler, Gates, and Arnold, asking them to form "some plan" to "comply with" Congress's request. Of those facing courts-martial, Bedel and Butterfield were the most notorious. Hazen, who was then under a form of house arrest, was also to have an opportunity to defend his actions. Gates had already established a hearing board to consist of the five most senior colonels along with the four ranking lieutenant colonels and majors in camp. These officers had postponed the Hazen inquiry so that Arnold would have a few days to prepare his case. He should be aware, moreover, that Hazen was ingratiating himself with these same field-grade officers, as well as spreading allegations of Arnold's peculating behavior during the evacuation from Canada.[38]

Hazen's accusation infuriated Arnold, but Gates urged him to focus on the far more consequential matter of readying the Champlain fleet for service. Arnold said he would do so. For the next week he devoted himself to speeding along construction of the patriot flotilla. On Tuesday, July 23, he traveled to Skenesborough, where he found three gundalows all but finished and another two nearing completion. He reported on the expected appearance of one hundred carpenters from Pennsylvania and Massachusetts and promised to return to Ticonderoga as soon as he had given "proper instructions" to these and other skilled workers. Unfortunately, cordage and sail-cloth were still scarce "though much wanted," but he pressed forward in the search for such items. He prepared requisitions for other essential supplies—anchors; hawsers; linseed oil; paint- and tarbrushes; frying pans; speaking trumpets; spyglasses; fishnets; and grape, canister, and double-headed and chain shot for cannons falling in the 9- to 24-pounder range. Mostly, Arnold was optimistic. "I think we shall have a very formidable fleet" within "two to three weeks," he wrote. Besides supply shortages, the most serious problem was the "want of seamen or marines," which could be solved only by sending urgent appeals to Connecticut and Massachusetts for experienced mariners.[39]

The presence of David Waterbury, who was performing yeoman service in pushing work crews day and night, significantly eased Arnold's burdens. Still, he felt immense pressure. Having lost one race to Carleton, Arnold did not want to taste defeat again, this time because of a failure to get a respectable fleet launched and operating on Lake Champlain. He likewise resented having to waste precious moments on a matter so irrelevant to the current military situation as Hazen's court-martial. Thoughts of that officer, along with too much work and lack of sleep, kept Arnold tense. He was in no frame of mind to be trifled with when he returned to Ticonderoga on Friday, July 26; but trifled with he was going to be by a host of malevolent patriot spirits.

VI

Colonel Elisha Porter, whose regiment now belonged to Arnold's brigade, was in a foul mood on Saturday, July 27. Prominent among those New England officers who had objected to the abandonment of Crown Point, he "did not like" the Mount Independence site. Just as irritating for Porter, he was among the senior field-grade officers whom Gates had called on to conduct courts-martial. A practicing attorney before the war, the Massachusetts colonel now found courtroom duty excruciatingly boring.[40]

Porter did not particularly care for his new brigade commander either. While in Canada, he had heard the grumblings of men like John Brown and Lewis Beebe. Just as bad, Arnold had showed himself a betrayer of New England interests by voting to abandon Crown Point. Nor did Porter think much of Arnold's decisive but at times abrupt manner. On the afternoon of July 27, the junior brigadier had offended the colonel's sensibilities by not siding with him in a trivial dispute over the location of housing for Porter's regiment on Mount Independence. Arnold, who was trying to prepare for Hazen's court-martial, refused to massage the feelings of the ruffled colonel.

Porter was livid; if his superior officer did not support him, he wondered how America's Hannibal could be of much value to the cause of liberty.[41]

The next day, Sunday, July 28, the soldiery at Ticonderoga participated in a formal ceremony and public reading of the Declaration of Independence. The assemblage listened attentively, then broke into enthusiastic cheers amid a thirteen-cannon salute. Yet the celebration did not improve Porter's spirits, since he still found himself "obliged to attend upon court martial again." A heavy, lingering rainstorm further aggravated Porter's disposition; he did not get into a better frame of mind until the next morning, when he learned that court-martial duty had been canceled for that day. His brief respite ended on Wednesday morning, July 31, with the opening of Moses Hazen's hearing. Porter recorded that "nothing extraordinary" occurred at the outset, but that was the only session in which civility prevailed.[42]

Arnold engaged in the proceedings with trepidation. He did not care for a hearing panel made up solely of regimental officers, all junior to him in rank. He worried lest these men would instinctively identify with Hazen, their fellow field-grade officer, and treat the Canadian colonel as an innocent victim of overzealous generalship. Arnold was likewise aware of their smoldering resentment over Crown Point. Just as bad, with so many pressing responsibilities he had not had the opportunity to nurture acquaintanceships with these same regimental officers, yet he had openly irritated the likes of Porter, who could now salve his bruised feelings by embarrassing his senior officer.

Perhaps most disturbing to Arnold, he had lacked the opportunity to curb the bad-mouthing campaign of Hazen, whose prehearing defense consisted of repeating the same thievery tale that Brown had employed before Congress. Hazen had skillfully trumpeted his own sacrifices, including the burning of his estate and the loss of his respected standing as a loyal British subject in Canada. In the same breath, he had painted his adversary Arnold as a self-serving swindler; Arnold's only motive in persecuting Hazen was spite because the goods he had intended to steal for his personal profit had actually, because of the colonel's inaction, done some good for starving, half-naked soldiers. This tale represented little more than a convenient twisting of the pilfering charges leveled against Brown and Easton, but this time with Arnold as the culprit. Clearly, Brown had counseled with Hazen about shifting the burden of accusations onto a man whom they mutually despised.

Despite all these points of potential friction, the atmosphere in the hearing room remained calm through the first day's proceedings. Then, on Thursday, August 1, something akin to hell broke loose. Major Scott, Arnold's source of "principal evidence," presented his testimony, but the hearing board started to peck away at Scott's commentary. Arnold had not given Scott written orders for Hazen; Scott's party had handled the goods "in such a disorderly manner that part of them must unavoidably have been damaged or lost" in transit from Montreal; Hazen had at no time assumed responsibility for the goods, which he could not do because he lacked a "sufficient store room," and which he did not have to do because he had no written orders from Arnold. Since Scott was junior to Hazen in rank, perhaps he should have accepted the judgment of the superior officer before him that the goods could not be accommodated at Chambly.

Scott, rather than Hazen, now seemed the officer on trial. An astounded Arnold offered his assurances, "on honor," that the major "had punctually obeyed my orders." Scott also tried to defend himself, but according to the hearing board's president, Colonel Enoch Poor of New Hampshire, he became "extremely solicitous" in manner and showed "overstrained zeal" in his responses. He acted as if he were the "judge advocate" rather than a mere witness. The board, almost as if by prearrangement, declared all of Scott's testimony "inadmissable" to the proceedings.

With this ruling, Arnold knew that he could no longer prove his case. The field-grade officers seemed determined to find Hazen innocent and impugn their superior officer's character in the process. Feeling entrapped, he dashed off a written statement formally protesting "against their proceedings and refusal as unprecedented, and I think unjust." He also told the hearing board as much, using far more pointed language. Porter considered Arnold's outburst abusive, and his comrades agreed. Arnold's protest, they pronounced, was "illegal, illiberal, and ungentlemanlike." In addition, they asked Poor "to demand satisfaction of the general," which the president did in writing by informing Arnold that "you have drawn upon yourself" the hearing board's "just resentment, and that nothing but an open acknowledgment of your error will be conceived as satisfactory." Hazen was delighted. The court-martial's focus no longer had anything to do with his own alleged insubordination.

Furious, Arnold replied in writing to Poor that he would never "comply with" so contemptible a "demand." The hearing board's actions represented, in his opinion, "ungenteel and indecent reflections on a superior officer, which the nature and words of my protest will by no means justify." Although not fully "conversant with courts martial," he would "venture to say" that "they are composed of men not infallible." "Even you may have erred," Arnold stated bluntly, and he would let "Congress . . . judge between us; to whom I will desire the general to transmit the proceedings of this court." Meanwhile, since he had "injured" the "very nice and delicate honor" of the hearing board officers, he promised each one that "as soon as this disagreeable service is at an end, . . . I will by no means withhold from any gentleman of the court the satisfaction his nice honor may require." [43]

The court-martial thus ended in chaos, but not before Hazen offered the "grossest abuse" to Arnold and then "claimed the protection of the court, and was by them countenanced." Arnold did not indicate what the denigrating remarks were, but Hazen no doubt directly accused Arnold of thievery. One of Hazen's witnesses reported having seen "four or five packages said to be B. Arnold's private property marked B. A." among the goods transported to Chambly. These boxes, Hazen no doubt claimed, did not contain Arnold's personal belongings; the general had obviously pilfered Montreal's merchants with the expectation of reaping handsome personal profits after returning to the colonies below. [44]

Schuyler had warned Arnold about the distorting words and wiles of self-serving patriots. Yet he still seemed stunned by so massive a dose of premeditated calumny. Like his mother's Calvinist God, he thought the hearing board had treated him both arbitrarily and unjustly. Like New Haven's self-righteous old guard, the field-grade officers had acted as if he were nothing more than a grasping, unscrupulous parvenu. As with Captain Croskie, Arnold had challenged these officers—all of them—to more than a duel of words. He wanted satisfaction because they had so maliciously attempted to destroy his good name, a family name he still fully intended to restore to its once-exalted stature.

Arnold also felt aggrieved because of his many personal sacrifices in Canada. He still limped from his leg wound, while putting up with biting rheumatic pains. He had opened his own purse to help provide for the welfare of his troops, including the imprisoned famine-proof veterans, and he had allowed his brigantine to be armed and destroyed as a fireship. He did so without knowing if he would ever be fairly compensated, based on his experiences with the Massachusetts Provincial Congress. Hazen, of course, had sacrificed as well, but Arnold had not covered over insubordinate behavior toward a senior officer by deliberately smearing that person's reputation.

Captain James Wilkinson proclaimed Arnold innocent of thievery at the time—somewhat surprising, since he later adopted Hazen's allegations as if they were gospel and even stated in his *Memoirs* that his superior officer had been very anxious to retreat from Canada because "he was interested in making arrangements for . . . disposal" of the "spoils" of war that he had stolen from Montreal's merchants. Writing from Ticonderoga on Monday, August 5, Wilkinson expressed "effusions of a heart actuated by no partial tie or prejudiced view." He defended "General Arnold's character," which "has been here traduced lately in the most villainous assassin like manner." Having served as his aide during those last, hectic days in Canada, Wilkinson had closely "observed" Arnold's "exertions where the public interest was concerned," and he had "always found" his senior to be an "intrepid, generous, friendly, upright, honest man." That Wilkinson forgot about this letter and adjusted his own story was not solely a function of his own well-earned reputation as a scoundrel; his later rendition reflected the pattern of adjusting Arnold's life history to fit posttreason stereotypes. To make Arnold greedy to the point of wanton thievery more easily matched the myth of a man destined to become entangled in the clutches of Satan.[45]

In the summer of 1776, Arnold's objective was anything but petty personal gain. His immediate—and consuming—goal was to thwart Carleton's expected invasion. If there was a fault, it lay in his inability to circumvent rather than engage persons like Hazen. Still, the issue was not solely his to determine. The Canadian colonel had demanded a court of inquiry to clear his name, and Congress had also insisted on courts-martial for those officers charged with some malfeasance while in Canada. Hazen, still angry after his verbal contretemps with Arnold during the Cedars operation, had clearly acted in an insubordinate fashion; but none of that really mattered to fellow field-grade officers like Poor and Porter. They were defending one of their own, and they embraced Hazen's version of reality, probably even before the court-martial began. As such, Arnold never had a fighting chance, which provoked his loss of composure.

Gates and Wilkinson understood, but they saw something more—natural human jealousy by the field-grade officers toward a person who was their superior not only in rank but in martial accomplishments as well. "Is it for men, who can't boast more than an easy enjoyment of the Continental provision," Wilkinson queried immediately after the hearing, "to blast the reputation of him [Arnold], who having encountered the greatest perils, . . . [and] fought and bled in a cause which they have only encumbered?" He answered, "No, forbid it honor, forbid it justice." Gates was less pontifical and more blunt. "I am astonished at the calumnies that go to Congress against General Arnold, and more astonished they should be one moment attended to," he wrote to Schuyler. Then he offered this thought: "To be a man of honor, and in an exalted station, will ever excite the envy in the mean and undeserving." The Ticonderoga commander was "confident," however, that "Congress will view whatever is whispered against General Arnold as the foul stream of that poisonous fountain, detraction." Gates was on the mark about why some officers of ordinary capacities had sided with Hazen, but he was mistaken in assuming the greater perspicacity of Congress.[46]

The court-martial board exonerated Hazen on Friday, August 2, but decided to meet again the next day. The field-grade officers, as "sensible men of rank" who deserved to be treated "with delicacy," wanted their own form of satisfaction. Arnold had insulted and perhaps even frightened them, having referred to an accepted method—the *code duello*—for settling personal disputes among honorable gentlemen. Given Arnold's challenge, the officers preferred "to punish insults offered to us" by trying their adversary on charges of contempt of court. "Justice to the army and to our country requires it of us," they sanctimoniously proclaimed.[47]

Gates denied their supplications. He recognized what the regimental officers could not see about themselves: Their partisanship toward Hazen had befuddled their capacity to offer justice of any kind. They now wanted only to manipulate their own court proceedings to legitimize their own behavior. To mollify them, Gates accepted their verdict regarding Hazen's innocence, which, according to Porter, resulted in a dinner celebration on Saturday, August 10, that included not only members of the court-martial board but even Hazen himself. Apparently, the field-grade officers saw no evidence of bias in this action. Two days later, these same men gathered again as a hearing panel and ordered Arnold's arrest. Gates responded by dissolving the court.[48]

In a summary statement to John Hancock, the wealthy Massachusetts merchant patriot who was then serving as president of Congress, Gates explained why he had acted so "dictatorially." Although "the warmth of General Arnold's temper" had pushed him beyond "the precise line of decorum to be observed before and toward a court martial," the junior brigadier was not the only party at "fault." "Too much acrimony" toward Arnold had denoted the hearing board's behavior. Gates then asked Hancock to "represent this affair in the most favorable light to Congress," since "the United States must not be deprived of that excellent officer's service at this important moment." The Board of War investigated and dismissed Hazen's charges of thievery by Arnold in the spring of 1777.[49]

VII

Gates said it all. Neither he nor Congress nor the cause of liberty could afford to lose Arnold's varied abilities. The most obvious evidence came in the form of Gates's decision to have his talented brigadier command the patriot Champlain fleet. When Schuyler learned about Arnold's elevation, he pronounced himself "extremely happy" and "relieved . . . from [a] very great anxiety under which I labored on that account." Washington likewise professed pleasure, stating that if Gates "assigned" the fleet to Arnold, "none will doubt of his exertions." [50]

Even in far-off London, the British ministry had come to appreciate the junior brigadier's martial capacities. "I am sorry Arnold escaped" from Canada, wrote Lord George Germain, the powerful Secretary for American Affairs, to General John Burgoyne. "I think he has shown himself the most enterprising man among the rebels," even though he doubted that Arnold's "military knowledge will distress you" in pushing south across Lake Champlain. Germain might have been more cautious with his words had he really reckoned with Arnold's record for tenacity in the face of adversity. [51]

Back at Ticonderoga, the field-grade officers were upset with Gates for having protected their quarry. They gathered yet again and sent an unctuous remonstrance to Congress along with a "naked and unadorned" transcription of the court-martial proceedings. They declared themselves "under no apprehensions of censure," since their motive in asking the delegates to investigate the "impropriety" of Arnold's conduct was to protect the sanctity of courts-martial as well as "the good of our country and the discipline of our army." They did so as well because Arnold had asked Gates to lay "the whole proceedings . . . before Congress." Most of all, they did not want the delegates to think of them as anything short of truly virtuous patriots. [52]

On Tuesday evening, August 6, Arnold returned to Skenesborough, not only because of the urgency of getting the fleet to sail but because Gates wanted to keep his valued subordinate away from the field-grade officers. Like Gates, Arnold still understood who the real enemy was, so he poured himself into launching the naval squadron. Still, in the days ahead he could not forget the charges leveled against him. When he received Chase's warning about the damaging effects of Brown's pilfering tale, he could not quite believe his friend's haunting words: "Your best friends are not your countrymen." [53]

Truly mortified, Arnold articulated for Gates the depth of his injured feelings in early September. "I cannot but think it extremely cruel," he related, "when I have sacrificed my ease, health, and a great part of my private property, in the cause of my country, to be calumniated as a robber and thief—at a time, too, when I have it not in my power to be heard in my own defense." As a devoted officer anxious to earn the patriot community's lasting respect, Arnold would still serve the Revolution; but the frustration in his words suggests something else. Subconsciously, at least, he had begun to ask himself whether the cause of liberty, with all of its grand-sounding rhetoric, was more hollow than genuine—and perhaps not worthy of his continued sacrifice.[54]

Eleven

A Most Tenacious
Naval Commander

I

When Horatio Gates found some quiet moments on Wednesday, August 7, he put the finishing touches on a series of "orders and instructions" for his newly designated naval commodore. Securing "the northern entrance into this side of the continent, . . . from further invasion" was a "momentous" assignment, yet under no circumstances was Arnold to consider offensive operations. "It is a defensive war we are carrying on; therefore, no wanton risk or unnecessary display of the power of the fleet is at any time to influence your conduct," the orders stated. Within the parameters of this restriction, Gates expected Arnold to employ "your courage and abilities" in "preventing the enemy's invasion of our country," which stood as "the ultimate end of the important command with which you are now entrusted."

Arnold received authorization to sail as far north as Isle aux Têtes just above the New York–Canadian border, if he deemed it safe to get that close to Carleton's forces. Whether there or farther south, he was to align his vessels across one of Lake Champlain's narrow points, so as to challenge any enemy naval squadron moving south from the Richelieu River. Should the British offer battle, Gates expected Arnold to "act with such cool, determined valor, as will give them reason to repent their temerity." If Carleton's fleet proved too large or too powerful to engage, the patriot vessels were to "retire" promptly to Ticonderoga, where Gates hoped to have his growing numbers of troops ready to repel any enemy assault.[1]

Before Arnold left for Skenesborough on August 6, he and Gates discussed the orders in some detail. Once removed from Ticonderoga, the junior brigadier's mood became more buoyant. Thanks to the exertions of David

Waterbury and the "very industrious and spirited" laborers under his supervision, construction of the fleet had not lagged, despite bedeviling shortages of "plank and iron." The new commodore now anticipated having a respectable fleet under sail before the minions of Carleton entered Lake Champlain.[2]

The patriot fleet, Arnold indicated to his superiors, would include nine gundalows—flat-bottomed, single-masted craft that carried fixed square sails and could cruise effectively only with the wind. Windward movement depended on the muscle power of crew members pulling at oars. About forty to fifty feet in length, each gundalow could comfortably handle a crew of forty-five men as well as a small number of artillery pieces, including a 12-pounder in the bow, two to four 9-pounders amidships, and up to eight swivel guns. Arnold expected the gundalows—christened the *Boston, Connecticut, Jersey, New Haven, New York, Philadelphia, Providence, Spitfire,* and *Success*—to be available for service very soon.[3]

Also in the Champlain squadron were three row galleys, very maneuverable craft that averaged seventy to eighty feet in length. They had two short masts, fore and main, each rigged with triangular-shaped lateen sails that swiveled before the wind, thus facilitating tacking to the windward. They were also easier to handle in rough water because of rounded bottoms that drew deeper drafts, although each galley carried oars in case of becalmed conditions. Row galleys had quarterdecks and cabins for ranking officers as well as space for up to eighty crew members. Each could hold ten to twelve artillery pieces, ideally consisting of a 12- and an 18-pounder in the bow, three to four 6-pounders along each side, two 9-pounders in the stern, and up to sixteen swivel guns—significantly more firepower per craft than the gundalows could accommodate.[4]

Arnold would have preferred a full fleet of row galleys; but with time running short, he had to make do with the craft then available. Besides the nine gundalows and the three row galleys—the *Congress, Trumbull,* and *Washington* (a fourth galley, the *Gates,* would not be outfitted in time for service that season)—the patriot fleet included one smaller vessel, the cutter *Lee,* no larger than the gundalows but mounting lateen sails; the sloop *Enterprise,* which Arnold had captured the year before in his raid on St. Johns; and three schooners: the *Liberty,* seized at Skenesborough from loyalist Philip Skene at the time of the rebel triumph at Ticonderoga; the *Royal Savage,* taken during Montgomery's siege at St. Johns; and the *Revenge,* likewise appropriated at St. Johns. The schooners represented a cross of sorts between the gundalows and row galleys. They could accommodate crews of up to fifty men and a variety of lighter artillery pieces—2-, 4-, and 6-pounders—and as many as ten swivel guns each.[5]

One of the row galleys, Arnold informed Schuyler and Gates, was already in the water and ready for final outfitting at Ticonderoga. He was pushing hard to have the other galleys "launched in ten days or a fortnight," and he had ordered Waterbury to focus the labors of every shipwright on meeting that deadline.[6]

The lake fleet, as it came together, had serious shortcomings. Arnold had envisioned up to thirty vessels, but he would have only seventeen at his disposal. The nine gundalows had virtually no capacity to maneuver quickly in battle or to outrun the enemy. Just as bad, Carleton's naval force was likely to have superior firepower, including a number of 24-pounders. Since Arnold's largest pieces were 18-pounders, of which he would have only four, he had to reckon with a distinct disadvantage in both the weight and volume of munitions fired, as well as distance carried.[7]

Compounding his problems, Arnold would have to accept crews virtually devoid of sailing experience. Entreaties to New England seaboard communities did not produce a rush of mariners, since skilled seamen could easily sign onto privateering vessels that offered premium wages and prospects of sharing in prize money for every captured British vessel. Arnold's fleet offered neither, only standard army pay and the abstract satisfaction of having sacrificed immediate pecuniary gain for the cause of liberty.

Patriotic appeals produced few willing volunteers for naval duty among the Continentals at Ticonderoga. No matter how bad camp conditions were, the inherent dangers of turbulent lake weather and fighting the enemy on water seemed greater. New England militia units that appeared at Skenesborough provided most of Arnold's makeshift sailors — the marines and gunners largely came from Continental regiments. The bulk in each category were those who lost when drawing lots for lake service or whose officers rated them as undesirables. Arnold was sure, by comparison, that Carleton's lake fleet, representing the maritime muscle of Britain, would have a full complement of experienced mariners, as well as trained marines ready to board and capture whatever patriot craft enemy cannoneers did not blow out of the water.[8]

Once again, Arnold found himself attempting to make bricks without sufficient straw. His best hope was to play on Carleton's lack of military aggressiveness, which explains why he and Gates decided on a ploy. Gates had advised his commodore not to disclose to anyone "the limits beyond which you are not to" sail. Publicly and in front of crew members, however, Arnold loudly proclaimed his determination to attack St. Johns. Should British spies be around (and they were), they could convey to Carleton an attitude of reckless boldness. The governor then might well hold back on entering Lake Champlain, in anticipation of an easy rout of the pugnacious rebels on the Richelieu River. Any delay would permit Arnold the opportunity to offer some naval training to his neophyte crew members and to scout the lake carefully in selecting the most advantageous site for combat, should a full-scale battle prove necessary.[9]

After Arnold's return to Ticonderoga on Saturday, August 10, he kept talking about audacious offensive operations. Hazen's following of field-grade officers quickly condemned America's Hannibal as a madman. Even admirers such as Matthias Ogden, who had taken part in the Kennebec expedition, wondered about Arnold's judgment. "He says he will pay a visit to St. Johns," Ogden wrote before observing, "I wish he may be as prudent as he is brave."[10]

Arnold had no intention of violating his actual orders. His objective was to delay the enemy as long as possible from reaching Ticonderoga, at least until Gates had established a solid enough defensive line to dissuade Carleton from attempting a breakthrough to Albany; and he had to do so with a squadron grossly deficient in the key elements of naval fighting. Because of the high probability of failure, Arnold's was an assignment few military leaders would have relished, but he energetically accepted the challenge. The cause of liberty would endure, he believed, only if some patriots were willing to take great risks under "the protection of that Power upon whose mercy we place our hopes of freedom here, and of happiness hereafter."[11]

II

On Thursday, August 15, Arnold sailed for Crown Point, the final staging area for launching the fleet. He arrived "a little feverish, but [with] no ague fit." Refusing to rest, he took "a dose of the physic," which he hoped "will set matters in order." He was anxious to cruise northward with the craft then available. Once outfitted, the remaining gundalows and row galleys could join the fleet at the northern end of the lake.

Arnold wanted to establish enough of a presence near Canada to impress Carleton with the vigor of rebel activity. He had to curb his impatience, as he explained in a note to Gates on August 16, for various reasons, among them the unavailability of a physician. He aired his frustration with a sarcastic play on words regarding the lethal reputation of surgeons. Arnold would accept any practitioner willing "to kill a man *secundum artem* [according to his skill]," since he could easily "procure a case of capital instruments for him here" with which to start butchering crew members.[12]

Arnold remained at Crown Point for eight more days. In the interim, he addressed a situation more absurd than humorous. Just past midday on August 17, Colonel Thomas Hartley, who commanded the lone advance regiment at Crown Point, told Arnold troubling news. A company of Hartley's troops, charged with providing cover for oar makers who were searching for wood seven miles down the lake, had ignited a bonfire, the signal for the approach of a hostile force. Arnold instructed Hartley to go out with troops aboard the *Revenge* and the *Liberty* to provide transportation and artillery cover for the exposed soldiers and workers. As the schooners were getting under sail, an indignant Jacobus Wynkoop, the elderly Dutchman who still fancied himself "commodore of Lake Champlain," strode out of his cabin on the *Royal Savage* and ordered a volley of cannon fire shot across the bows of th advancing vessels. The vessels hastily retreated to their moorings.

Flabbergasted by this baffling act, Arnold charged onto the *Royal Savage* and demanded to know why Wynkoop had so brazenly decided "to contradict my orders." The agitated Dutchman announced just as bluntly that he still held a commission from Schuyler designating him "commodore" of the fleet. This "appointment . . . cannot be superseded," declared Wynkoop. He would determine when vessels were to sail, and in the future, he informed Arnold, he expected any instructions regarding the fleet's disposition to meet with his prior approval.

Arnold was incredulous. He had long since "acquainted" Wynkoop with Gates's orders, at least those portions meant for public consumption, and he had also offered him the reduced responsibility of serving as captain of the *Royal Savage*. Trying to remain calm, especially with an alarm at hand, Arnold asked why Wynkoop had heretofore "received and executed" his orders. Then he stated, "You surely must be out of your senses to say no orders shall be obeyed but yours." He directed Wynkoop to inform the captains of the schooners to proceed at once. If the Dutchman failed to do so, Arnold would "be under the disagreeable necessity of . . . immediately arresting you." Wynkoop reluctantly complied.

The alarm related only to the presence of a small British-Indian scouting party. Once Arnold was sure that a larger enemy force was not present, he wrote to Gates for advice and let Wynkoop enclose a statement as well. For the Dutchman, the issue related to his prior commissioning and prerogative of rank. Schuyler had guaranteed him, Wynkoop insisted, "that no one should have it [the command] but me." He would accept "general orders to sail" only from Schuyler, and he expected to have full authority "to give orders to the captains of the fleet when I receive them from the commander in chief." Anything less was unacceptable, "for I am resolved to go under the command of no man," Wynkoop declared.[13]

Gates was nonplussed. Like Arnold, he thought Wynkoop understood his more circumscribed duties, and he was in no mood to tolerate insubordinate behavior from a man whom he regarded as virtually incompetent. Gates fired off a missive to Arnold in which he ordered Wynkoop's arrest and return to Ticonderoga.[14]

Arnold, meanwhile, found time to hear Wynkoop out. The Dutchman was contrite but perplexed. As Arnold explained to Gates, "I believe the commodore was really of [the] opinion that neither of us had authority to command him." His commission, after all, bore the signature of Schuyler, the ranking officer in the Northern Department. Further, no one had given Wynkoop written notification of his demotion, which he now viewed as an intentional slap at his personal honor. Had someone in authority been polite enough to do so, Wynkoop told Arnold, he would have resigned immediately and accepted an earlier request from the New York Provincial Congress to assume command of a frigate then under construction on the Hudson River north of New York City.

As they talked, Arnold felt compassion for the Dutchman. Humiliating a doddering old man for having tried to serve the rebellion was too cold-hearted, Arnold thought, especially since Wynkoop now was "sorry for his disobedience of orders." He deserved a better fate than formal arrest. "If it can be done with propriety," Arnold recommended to Gates, Wynkoop should "be permitted to return home without being cashiered" from the service.[15]

Gates acceded and sent Wynkoop on "my pass to go at liberty to Albany" to meet with Schuyler. Under no circumstances, Gates stated, was the Dutchman to "be sent back here," since Wynkoop's "refractory disposition" could "in some serious moment" cause "the entire ruin of our maritime affairs." Schuyler admonished the Dutchman for his "want of subordination and discipline" and told him not to expect further assignments relating to the defense of Lake Champlain.[16]

Feeling more aggrieved than ever, Wynkoop sent a wordy petition to Congress in which he was silent about Arnold's munificent behavior. Rather, he demanded "such relief as he is in justice entitled to" for having put up with the insults of such ill-informed senior officers as Arnold and Gates. Had they been patriots of solid judgment, they would have realized that Wynkoop had halted the schooners, as he had come to rationalize, only out of fear "that some design had been formed by the captains . . . or their crews to go over to the enemy."[17]

Since Congress held Wynkoop in no particular esteem, the delegates ignored his petition. Most had already welcomed the news about Arnold taking command of the fleet, rating him "a good sailor," as Thomas Jefferson stated. Some delegates, however, would remember the Dutchman's allegations, regardless of their substance, in light of the current swirl of damning commentary about Arnold's rectitude, temperament, and judgment.[18]

III

Arnold finally obtained a physician on Friday evening, August 23. "I . . . am very happy at his arrival," he wrote Gates, "as I was determined to have sailed the first fair wind, even without a surgeon." That wind, a pleasant southerly breeze, sprang up under partly cloudy skies the next afternoon. Arnold instructed his captains "to get all hands on board and prepare for getting under sail." Near sunset, the Champlain commodore boarded his designated flagship, the *Royal Savage,* and ordered sails hoisted on all craft. As the sun sank behind the mountains to the west of Crown Point, the fleet, consisting of ten vessels but as yet no row galleys, finally began its northward cruise. Everyone cheered—even Arnold, who understood better than most what harrowing dangers lay ahead.[19]

Arnold's launching of the fleet, even without his most mobile, warlike craft, reflected the pressing need to perform a naval reconnaissance in force. Intelligence was scanty, so the commodore still lacked a clear sense of the potential size and firepower of the British squadron. At the same time, if Arnold could effect a bold enough exhibition of patriot martial resolve at the northern end of Lake Champlain, Carleton might decide to use the lateness of the season—biting autumn and early winter weather were not far away—as a rationalization for postponing a southward offensive until the spring of 1777.

Any delay, even a few weeks, would offer the growing American force at Ticonderoga valuable time to strengthen defenses and collect a full storehouse of munitions. More vessels, including row galleys, could be constructed to add greater muscle to the patriot fleet. Just as important, Arnold and his captains would be able to train their crews in basic nautical skills and the art of waging naval warfare.

On the latter count, Arnold recognized the danger of inexperienced artillerists on board. In early August, for example, the gundalow *Providence* had practiced firing its cannons. Discharging the first round went smoothly, but then Captain Simonds, trying to approximate combat conditions, ordered each weapon loaded, aimed, and fired a second time. One green crew member, Solomon Dyer, "sponged the bow gun" and proceeded "to ram down the cartridge." Unfortunately, "there being fire in the gun" from the first shot, the weapon belched forth its contents while Dyer "was standing before the mouth of the cannon." Dyer never knew what hit him. Not only did the explosion blow off his hands, but "the sponge rod part or all of it went through the left part of his body at the root of his arm [and] blew him overboard." Two days later crew members finally found what remained of Dyer, and they "buried him decently" with the honors of war.[20]

Unseasoned mariners, for their part, placed severe limitations on how Arnold could offer battle. He would have to avoid a running engagement because his landlubbing crew members had no training in how to outmaneuver or board enemy vessels. Should battle come, he would have to fight from a fixed position, and he would need to have at least one or two skilled artillerists aboard each vessel to orchestrate the gun crews in properly aiming and firing their weapons.

Further, Arnold could not let his gun crews do much training with live ammunition. His supply of powder and ball would be barely sufficient if a battle of any consequence occurred. Just as bad, he had very little grape or chain shot. The latter was useful for shredding enemy sails and rigging and for shattering masts; the former would be crucial, should Carleton's vessels get close enough to threaten boarding. Gates had promised to send out grape and chain shot as soon as it reached Ticonderoga. In the interim, the fleet had to rely on its meager supply of round shot.

The matter of inadequate shot related to an even more vexing problem. Arnold was among the few officers who knew just how scarce munitions supplies, especially gunpowder, were at Ticonderoga. Should the Champlain fleet fail to slow down or block Carleton's advance, at least until Gates's troops received shipments of powder and ball from New England and elsewhere, Ticonderoga's defenders would have to flee or surrender after firing only a few opposing shots. Thus Arnold carried the additional burden of possibly having to invite battle, despite green crews and missing row galleys, if Gates did not soon receive several tons of gunpowder; and he would have to create a vivid enough sensation of patriot fighting tenacity to help dissuade Carleton from quickly launching an assault on munitions-starved Ticonderoga.[21]

All of these worrisome matters lay behind Arnold's objective of getting close enough to the Canadian border to make Carleton aware of the rebel fleet. Considering the handful of vessels currently at his disposal, Arnold did not assume his squadron would make much of an impression, but still he would try. And while sailing northward, he intended to study inlets, bays, and landforms. In case combat became necessary, he would at least have the advantage of choosing a favorable site.

As Arnold viewed the passing landscape through his spyglass, nature's elements prepared to gang up on his fleet. On Monday, August 26, the vessels, cruising smoothly on a gentle southerly breeze, had reached Willsborough, not quite halfway to Canada. Then, to the northeast, Arnold observed a "violent storm" bursting over the horizon. With gale-force winds and monsoon-like rains about to strike, he issued orders for a southward retreat. The signal came at 1 P.M. One of the gundalows, the *Spitfire,* did not react in time, and surging waves started to push the craft landward. When Arnold saw what was happening, he jumped into a small boat and directed his frightened oarsmen to row him toward the endangered gundalow. Bouncing through the raging water, which he later described as "an amazing sea," he got near enough the *Spitfire* to make himself understandable through a speaking trumpet, and he screamed out directions for trimming the sails properly. Soon the *Spitfire* swung about, thereby avoiding certain destruction.

Arnold did not mention this deed in his correspondence; his obligation as commodore was to provide for the fleet. But those manning the patriot vessels had witnessed a remarkable act of bravery. They had seen firsthand Arnold's reputed fearlessness, and many crew members now regarded their commander as the kind of charismatic military leader who deserved their best efforts, even unto death in battle.

By 5 P.M., the fleet had reached the protection of Buttonmould Bay on the lake's eastern shore. Only the *Spitfire* was missing. Arnold "expected to hear the gundalow was foundered or driven on shore," but the captain had simply dropped anchor to ride out the storm, since his amateur crew could not control the vessel in the turbulent water. To everyone's joy, the *Spitfire* sailed into the bay near sunset on Wednesday, August 28. Although battered and needing repairs, the whole fleet had survived its first harrowing test.[22]

Genuinely thankful, Arnold, seeking to promote camaraderie among his officers, invited his captains and lieutenants to join him on shore the next afternoon for a celebration. As recorded by Bayze Wells, a lieutenant serving on the gundalow *Providence,* the festivities began at 3 P.M. when the officers gathered for a marksmanship contest with small arms. Then followed a "most genteel feast of a roast pig, good wine, some punch, and good old cider." Soon the officers were offering toasts. They first drank to the health of Congress and then to Arnold's, and they honored their commodore by proclaiming the spot on which they stood "Arnold's Point."[23]

The commodore responded by addressing the challenges ahead and encouraging his officers to give their all in confronting the enemy. Then everyone returned to their vessels, few having noticed Arnold's anxious bearing. As the fleet lay dormant in Buttonmould Bay, the commodore kept recalling how another storm had kept his Kennebec column stymied for several crucial days on the southern shore of the St. Lawrence River when Quebec City was ripe for the taking. Now he worried lest the tempest just past had stolen the precious days he needed to reach the Canadian border and make a statement of patriot defiance. If the British were already ascending the lake in the wake of the storm, then his partially assembled fleet would have to reckon with even greater failure than his Kennebec column had experienced—and this time with potentially catastrophic consequences for the rebellion.

IV

Taking advantage of a southerly breeze, the fleet commenced sailing northward again on Sunday, September 1. Early the next morning, intelligence reached Arnold regarding a sizable enemy force about four miles ahead. Sure that his worst fears were about to be realized, he "sent his boat through the fleet to be ready for action at a minute's warning." He also dispatched a warning back to Ticonderoga; but as the squadron continued on, no adversary could be found. Two days later the vessels "arrived safe" at their northern destination, Windmill Point, a neck of land jutting out from the eastern shore close to where the waters of Lake Champlain flowed into the Richelieu River. Still about six miles south of Isle aux Têtes, where the British had an advanced outpost, Arnold was as near to enemy defenses as he intended to get. He soon sent out scouting craft and then ordered the fleet into battle-line formation extending across the lake.[24]

The reconnoitering parties found no evidence that the British were ready to come up the lake. This news allowed Arnold to relax for the first time in days. Taking pen in hand, he forwarded congratulations through Gates to Arthur St. Clair, a ranking colonel at Ticonderoga. Congress had recently promoted this Pennsylvania officer to a brigadier generalship. Once again displaying his penchant for playful sarcasm, he also commented on the latest information regarding John Sullivan. When that officer appeared before Congress, the delegates had feted him as a conquering hero. Not only had they refused his attempted resignation, but they had absolved Sullivan's sense of despoiled personal honor by raising him to the rank of major general. Meditating about Congress's generosity toward a general officer more mediocre than meritorious, while musing about his own standing with that body, Arnold commented to Gates, "When the enemy drives us back to Ticonderoga, I have some thoughts of going to Congress and begging leave to resign. Do you think they will make me a major general?" The junior brigadier had no idea that he had just foreshadowed—up to a point—events in his own future.[25]

The Champlain commodore also briefly indulged himself in the thought that "the enemy will not dare attempt crossing the lake" so late in the season, especially if the soul of the patriot squadron, the row galleys, arrived expeditiously. A few days later, the appearance of the cutter *Lee* and the gundalow *Jersey* brought Arnold's strength to twelve vessels; however, as he pointed out to Gates, the row galleys were likely the key to impressing Carleton with the patriot fleet's potential to mount serious resistance.[26]

Lacking complete intelligence, Arnold could only speculate about what his fleet might face in combat. He was sure the British had a great number of bateaux that they could fill with marines "whenever they think proper to attack." The danger, Arnold told Gates, was that "our vessels are so low" to the water "that numbers [of enemy marines] could carry them" easily. As a countermeasure, he ordered his captains to send crews "on shore to cut fascines"—in this instance, bundles of branches "to fix on the bows and sides of the gundalows, to prevent the enemy's boarding and to keep off small shot."

For mutual protection, the crews of every vessel were to approach the shoreline as a massed body early on Friday morning, September 6. As Arnold related, however, "one of the boats went on shore, contrary to orders, before the others were ready." A party of Indians and British regulars ambushed these overeager patriots. Arnold quickly ordered up cannon fire to help drive off the small enemy detachment, but three crew members lost their lives and another six were wounded.[27]

Arnold used this incident to vent some of his frustrations with the crews assigned to the fleet. "We have but very indifferent men in general," he wrote to Gates. He implored his senior to send him a minimum of "three or four good gunners" and "fifty seamen" who were true mariners as replacements for crewmen who were sick and waiting for transportation back to Ticonderoga. Two weeks later, Arnold was even more pungently critical. Those drafted out of the Ticonderoga regiments "are a miserable set," he declared. "The men on board the fleet . . . are not equal to half their number of good men."[28]

Negligence in performing duties was as much a problem as lack of training. Wherever Arnold stationed his squadron, he insisted on the vigilance of sentries. He did not want any British craft, not even a lone bateau, slipping through his line of vessels either to get information about Ticonderoga or to report back to Carleton after a close inspection of the fleet. On one gundalow alone, as representative of breaches of duty during

September, two crewmen were caught fast asleep at their sentry posts. Each received a whipping of "twelve strokes on his naked buttocks" in front of his assembled comrades—a clear warning that excruciating physical pain awaited shirkers, whose irresponsible behavior might threaten the safety of the fleet or of the patriot defenders at Ticonderoga.[29]

In early September, allegations of plundering by his crews upset Arnold. While the fleet lay anchored in Buttonmould Bay attending to repairs, various hands went ashore to look around, and some supposedly took to scavenging. According to William Gilliland, a seemingly trustworthy local settler, these troops "wantonly and wickedly committed great destruction on several of my plantations," executing "every villainy in the most insolent and licentious manner." They trampled under or dug up fields full of corn, potatoes, and peas and stole everything from tools to furniture. Just as bad, Gilliland noted, "these things could not possibly have all been taken on board without the knowledge of the officers."[30]

Arnold assembled his captains and denounced such conduct. Stealing from civilians would only convince them to collaborate with the enemy. The chastened captains denied seeing looted articles on their vessels. They questioned Gilliland's honesty, but they agreed not to allow crewmen ashore in the future without officers present.

Arnold soon discovered that Gilliland was lying. "The whole stuff that was brought off was not worth forty shillings," he reported to Gates. Worse yet, Gilliland was "a most plausible and artful villain." He had not vacated his freehold as had other settlers, who feared devastation from warfare in the region, because he was apparently selling information to British spies. To compound his crimes, he was now trying to fleece the patriots out of money in compensation for crops and personal goods never stolen. Arnold ordered Gilliland's arrest and had him sent to Ticonderoga.[31]

Learning the truth about this enemy collaborator did not temper the commodore's worries about his crew members. He still considered them an ill-disciplined lot, a poor reflection of the glorious cause they were representing. They were like the hundreds of heedless rebel troops who had so recently engaged in unauthorized looting and seriously eroded vital civilian support in Quebec Province. As long as Arnold was in command, he refused to tolerate any form of unscrupulous behavior that might rend the delicate fabric of continued civilian loyalty to the patriot cause.

This thought reignited Arnold's outrage over Hazen's allegations of thievery. More than once during September he addressed these charges when transmitting information to Gates. Trying to soothe his valued commodore's bruised sensibilities, Gates wrote on Thursday, September 12, about sending a "public letter" to Congress "upon the subject you so earnestly mentioned." The Ticonderoga commander reassured Arnold that "when my letter is received, the Congress and your friends will be convinced that every report to your prejudice is founded in calumny, and should meet with the contempt and disregard it so justly deserves." In response, Arnold thanked Gates "for the friendly notice you have taken of me in your public letter, which, I make no doubt, will have the desired effect."[32]

Gates's letter did not really help Arnold much. Having reviewed documents on Hazen's court-martial, Congress's Board of War presented its findings to the assembled delegates on Wednesday, September 18. The board could not "approve the behavior of Brigadier General Arnold toward the court martial," yet it did not specifically admonish him. Nor did it condone the actions of Colonel Poor and the other field-grade officers. Rather, the board, reflecting the influence of its New England members, used the occasion to heap praise on Gates for having put "an end to so dangerous an altercation (which appears to have been too warm on both sides)." He truly deserved "the thanks of Congress" for his "vigilance, prudence, and activity . . . in composing differences" and in "removing jealousies and animosities" from among the quarreling officers of the Northern Department army.

The delegates voted to postpone consideration of these resolutions, not out of newfound affection for Arnold but because they did not want to offend Schuyler in so blatant a panegyric to Gates's virtue. They also left the matter of Arnold's "conduct" dangling for nearly a week before they referred the dispute to Washington. Aware of the esteem the commander had for America's Hannibal, the delegates were effectively shielding Arnold from his critics. As much as anything they did so out of expediency, since they did not want to precipitate Arnold's resignation at so critical a martial juncture. They could always investigate his reputed misdeeds at a later date, if pressures to do so still existed, but only at a time when his military talents were not so pivotal to keeping the cause of liberty alive.[33]

The delegates were functioning as pragmatic gentleman-politicians, which Arnold did not appreciate when he eventually learned of their ruling. He was indignant about what he viewed as an unjustified congressional slap at his personal honor and integrity. Also among his resentments was the seeming blindness of Congress to his steadfastness as a virtuous patriot, committed first and foremost to resisting the imperial enemy. His sense of duty had so far kept him from rushing to Philadelphia to defend his reputation when others, such as John Sullivan and John Brown, had done so at their personal pleasure, regardless of the military exigencies of the moment. Arnold thus began to ask himself how long the Revolution could endure when its fate rested on the judgment of civil leaders who could not discern the difference between truly meritorious patriots and those who only acted the part when personally convenient.

V

While in command of the Champlain fleet, Arnold could do nothing to shield himself from the barbs of noisome personal adversaries. He controlled his feelings by concentrating on the other, more immediately threatening enemy in Canada. Having aligned his vessels across the mile-and-a-quarter-wide channel near Windmill Point, he had fulfilled the objective of displaying the fleet's presence. The British soon responded with more than ambushing scouting parties. On Saturday evening, September 7, patriot sentries heard faint human voices and saw occasional flickers of light along both shorelines. The British "were erecting batteries," Arnold stated, "and their design was doubtless to have attacked us by land and water at the same time." Not thinking "it prudent to run any risk, as it could answer no good purpose," he ordered the fleet to sail some eight miles south to a point on the lake two miles wide near Isle la Motte. "I think the station we are in the best in the lake to stop the enemy," he wrote to Gates—an opinion he would soon revise.[34]

On Monday, September 9, yet another gundalow, the *Philadelphia,* hove into view. Aboard was Colonel Edward Wigglesworth, whom Gates described as "a good seaman" of "unimpeached . . . character." In addition, this Massachusetts colonel had extensive experience with artillery, having served as a captain of matrosses (cannon support crews) early in the conflict. Arnold likewise had a "good opinion" of Wigglesworth, who was to serve as the fleet's third-ranking officer. Gates had also decided to have Waterbury join the squadron as second in command. He would sail down the lake with one of the galleys, hopefully in no more than a week's time.[35]

After the two officers exchanged greetings, Wigglesworth handed Arnold a long missive from Gates. The first paragraph contained a garbled account of a major battle in the vicinity of New York City. The king's troops had moved onto Long Island and "attacked our lines, but were repulsed with loss." Gates reported three thousand British casualties as compared to two thousand for the patriots, a gross exaggeration for both sides. The Ticonderoga commander did state with obvious apprehension, "We wait with impatience for more particulars."[36]

Arnold tried to frame his reaction in the most positive light. Even though patriot casualties were high, such horrendous losses for the British, he responded to Gates, "must so much weaken and discourage them that they will hardly make another attack this season." As such, "time must gain us a victory." With his faith in a generous Providence unshaken, Arnold still had "no doubt the Almighty will crown our virtuous struggles with success." [37]

In the days ahead reports did not improve materially. By eighteenth-century standards, the combined British land-naval assault force was massive in size, numbering some forty-five thousand soldiers and sailors. Army Commander in Chief William Howe first assembled his redcoats and Hessians on Staten Island, then landed fifteen thousand of them at Gravesend, Long Island, on August 22. He soon had Washington's badly outnumbered and inexperienced soldiers on the run. Setback after setback followed as summer gave way to autumn. The Continentals first escaped from Brooklyn Heights. Then they retreated northward through Manhattan Island. Howe pursued at a plodding pace, inflicting many wounds along the way. Those few patriot warriors who were left standing with Washington eventually escaped across New Jersey and finally into Pennsylvania in early December. Only the Delaware River and the winter season stopped Howe, who concluded that his regulars could easily finish off what remained of Washington's all-but-beaten band the next spring.

Arnold knew none of this. Throughout September he could not even get an accurate account of the Battle of Long Island. He assumed the British intended to reconquer as much territory as possible before frigid winter weather ended the campaign season, even if they could not bring their two armies together in executing the Hudson Highlands strategy. In addition, Arnold conjectured that Carleton would have to make some demonstration of force before wintertime or likely lose the confidence of his superiors back in England. A reasonable goal would be to establish naval dominance on Lake Champlain, thereby setting the stage for the final crushing of the rebellion during the 1777 campaign season.

From the time he received Gates's letter, Arnold believed that Carleton would come out of his Canadian lair before the middle of October, if the governor were to have any chance of recapturing Fort Ticonderoga before winter. He also guessed that Carleton would not attack Ticonderoga until he had regained complete control of the lake, which depended on sweeping aside the patriot fleet. Arnold thus pushed himself, his officers, and his crew members to prepare the kind of dramatic greeting that would favor the patriot fleet. After much consultation with Wigglesworth, Arnold revealed his thinking. "I design making a remove to the island Valcour, until joined by the three galleys," he apprised Gates on Sunday, September 15. Valcour

Island has "a good harbor, and if the enemy venture up the lake, it will be impossible for them to take advantage of our situation."[38]

Lying not quite halfway between Crown Point and St. Johns, a distance of 120 miles, Valcour Island represented a natural defensive site. Vessels approaching from the north could not see the bay, since it lay on the southwestern side of an island about two miles long and one mile wide, with a topographical rise on heavily wooded ground up to a height of 180 feet. Separated from the New York shoreline by a half mile, shoal water would block any but the smallest craft from slipping between the island and the mainland.

Under the most likely scenario, Carleton's vessels would sail along the main channel well past the island before spying their adversary. Presuming the enemy would be riding a northerly breeze, Carleton's flotilla would be hard pressed to reverse its course and beat to the windward. Still, the governor would have to engage. He could not just continue south and allow the rebel squadron to stand between his own fleet and Canada. With such an opportunity, Arnold could easily move north to disrupt Carleton's extended supply line, as well as attack thousands of unprotected British regulars trailing behind in lightly armed bateaux.

The more Arnold considered making a stand at Valcour Bay, the more the idea appealed to him. By September 18 he had gained enough intelligence to be sure that the British fleet would be sizable and almost certainly more muscular than his own. One enemy ship, still under construction, had the capacity alone to mount twenty cannons in the 9- to 12-pounder range. In itself, the likely presence of this powerful vessel caused Arnold to consider offering battle from a naturally strong defensive position. Already thinking of possible tactics, he told Gates that Valcour's "good harbor" would offer "the advantage of attacking the enemy in the open lake," but "if they are too many for us we can retire" toward Ticonderoga.[39]

On Thursday, September 19, Arnold had the fleet sail south about ten miles from Isle la Motte into Bay St. Amand along the western shore. He did so because of suspected British raiding parties in the vicinity, and he wanted to get closer to Valcour Island. Before weighing anchor, he instructed the schooner *Liberty* to scout northward. The *Liberty* found no signs of the enemy on Isle la Motte. Returning along the New York shoreline, the crew soon spotted a French-looking subject waving frantically at them. Captain Premiere maneuvered in for a closer look, at which point the Frenchman plunged into the water, "making believe he was in distress and wanted to come on board." Premiere suspected a ruse and backed off, at which point about three hundred Indians under the command of a British officer emerged from the woods and opened fire. The *Liberty's* crew responded in kind but suffered five casualties before the schooner got away. Just as ominous, as the *Liberty* made for Bay St. Amand, the vessel passed a band of more than two hundred Indians with birch canoes resting along the bank. These raiding parties, Arnold wrote to Gates, could select ambush sites during the night and attack unsuspecting craft that were performing daytime scouting missions. Their presence also indicated that the British fleet would soon be coming south.[40]

Bay St. Amand was a convenient stopover on the way to Valcour Island. The bay likewise proved to be a fortuitous location for riding out "an exceeding hard gale . . . and a prodigious sea," Arnold stated to Gates. "A more windy night I scarce ever knew," Lieutenant Bayze Wells confided to his diary. The vessels sustained little damage. Determined to proceed as soon as weather conditions permitted, Arnold got his favorable northerly breeze on Monday, September 23. He ordered the squadron to make sail for Valcour Bay, where he nestled the craft closely together in a half-moon formation. In so doing, he assumed a battle line "in such a form that few vessels can attack us at the same time, and those will be exposed to the fire of the whole fleet." Arnold had already requested Gates's authorization to wait for the enemy at Valcour, but "if not, I will return to any of my former stations."[41]

VI

As the rebel fleet lay snugly anchored in Valcour Bay, Arnold kept fretting about the fleet's shortcomings, and his written communications to Gates took on an increasingly petulant tone. Just about everything bothered him. With the appearance of the gundalow *Success* on September 11, he had fourteen craft at his disposal. Yet, ten days later, he remained "greatly at a loss [over] what could have retarded the galleys so long . . . ; the want of those galleys may decide the contest against us." As September neared its end, none of the row galleys had yet arrived. "I expect them every minute," he wrote Gates on Saturday, September 28, since "the time is elapsed" when they should have reached Valcour. Without the row galleys, he stated almost frantically, any decision to offer battle would be irresponsible. A stiff northerly breeze that day—"a fine wind for the enemy to come down"—made him especially nervous. Should Carleton's squadron suddenly materialize, he would have to abandon the bay and "retire until I meet the galleys."[42]

Arnold also persisted in complaining about his "wretched motley crew." Before reaching Valcour, he described his marines as "the refuse of every regiment" at Ticonderoga; his seamen were equally useless, since "few of them" had ever been "wet with salt water." Once at Valcour he was less critical, although he kept pleading for qualified mariners.[43]

The commodore's more sanguine tone related to the positive response of crew members to what little training they received. Arnold had initially ordered his captains to see that "the men are daily trained to the exercise of their guns"; but with powder and ball in such short supply, he could not "afford" to let them practice with live shot. Once at Valcour, he relented. For three days in late September, Arnold permitted his artillerists to fire "one round each . . . about one mile at an empty cask anchored" in the bay. The target was set at a distance the commodore hoped the cannon crews could consistently strike in dueling with any attacking British fleet. Much to his surprise and pleasure, the gun crews performed their duties respectably.[44]

Arnold's mention of ammunition shortages caused Gates to remind his subordinate that "the powder written for so long ago, is not even in part received at Ticonderoga; so economy is the word." This comment appeared in a note in which Gates asked Arnold to stop pleading for the row galleys. "You cannot be more anxious to have all the galleys with you, than we are to send them. Be satisfied more cannot be done than is done to dispatch them," Gates said as gently but forcefully as possible.[45]

This missive traveled north aboard the row galley *Trumbull*, which reached Valcour Island late on the day of Monday, September 30, amid a brief but joyful exchange of cannon salutes. Had Gates's letter reached him under any other circumstances, Arnold might well have lost his composure. As it was, he was soon complaining again. Although the *Trumbull* was "a considerable addition to our fleet," the craft was "not half finished or rigged." Worse yet, he grumbled, "her cannons," including one 18- and one 12-pounder as well as two 9- and four 6-pounders, were "much too small" to help offset expected British firepower advantages.

Just about everything else was wrong as well, Arnold declared, bursting forth with a geyser of complaints. He had ordered cordage for eight row galleys back in July, but not even the *Trumbull* had adequate rigging. Food supplies were barely adequate, and a "great part of my seamen and marines are almost naked." Increasingly exposed as they were to "continual gales of wind" and freezing temperatures at night, they desperately needed additional clothing and blankets. Clearly exasperated, he scribbled angrily, "I hope to be excused . . . if with 500 men, half naked, I should not be able to beat the enemy with 7,000 men, well clothed, and a naval force, by the best accounts, near equal to ours." Congress, he concluded, was responsible for so many shortages: "I am surprised at their strange economy or infatuation below. Saving and negligence, I am afraid, will ruin us at last."[46]

Arnold, no matter how hard he tried, could not get the central patriot government out of his mind. The lack of timely and effective congressional support, he believed, had undermined patriot operations in Canada. Yet this body had piously refused to assume its rightful share of blame. Instead, the delegates had nosed around everywhere else for likely culprits, even as they willingly listened to the slurs of Brown, Easton, and Hazen—and possibly now even Wynkoop.

Congress, from Arnold's perspective, had fallen into the bad habit of projecting its own inadequacies onto dedicated, sacrificing patriots such as himself. Should Lake Champlain's defenders fail to stop Carleton, Congress would likely engage in another flurry of faultfinding. The delegates would use him as a scapegoat rather than admit to their own inability to supply their forces with essential resources to achieve victory.

If Arnold had learned nothing else from the Ticonderoga and Canadian campaigns, he had come to appreciate the importance of personal vigilance in protecting his reputation. As a means of doing so this time, he drafted a long "memorandum of articles which have been repeatedly written for, and which we are in the most extreme want of," that he sent to Gates along with his frenzied letter of Tuesday, October 1. Among a host of essentials, the fleet needed 1,740 rounds of double-headed, grape, and chain shot for its artillery pieces; three hundred pounds of musket balls; fifty swivel guns; three hundred grenades filled with powder and armed with fuses; one hundred real seamen ("no landlubbers"); "rum, as much as you please"; and "clothing for at least half the men in the fleet, who are naked."[47]

Arnold knew that Gates, with severe arms and powder deficiencies of his own, could not provide the munitions. The commodore was not trying to embarrass his superior; rather, he was establishing a record, to be shared publicly if necessary, regarding critical shortages facing his fleet on the eve of combat. If need be, he would use this ledger to defend himself against the accusations of small-minded patriots, including leaders in Philadelphia. The list would stand as an indictment of congressional incapacity, if not ineptitude, in support of those persons who were giving their all to the rebellion.

One possible ray of hope remained, however. Arnold reported in his October 1 missive that a scout had just returned from the vicinity of Isle aux Noix. The British, although "exerting every nerve to augment their navy," had not as yet begun to move southward in force. Arnold still thought their "design" was "to cross the lake this fall," but the ever-deliberate Carleton may have decided to delay his invasion until the spring.[48]

VII

Arnold did not delude himself with false expectations. His instincts kept warning him that a major battle was nearing. In this northern clime the brightly colored leaves of autumn were already tumbling down, leaving branches bare and the landscape bleak. The first heavy snow had fallen on the night of Thursday, September 26; five days later, Lieutenant Wells noted how "all this day we could see snow on the mountains."[49]

If Carleton was coming this campaign season, he had to do so soon, and the daily grind of waiting wore at Arnold. Nothing seemed to relieve his precombat nervousness. He was furious with a courier who missed the fleet at Valcour Bay and then "stupidly destroyed" the letters charged to his care, including one from Arnold's sister Hannah, just before the schooner *Revenge*, which he mistook for an enemy craft, rescued him. The offending sergeant had "deprived" Arnold of a letter from Gates and possible "particulars of the affair at New York," which he had for "a long time anxiously waited for." He wanted any additional news about "our army and friends below," and he speculated that if Carleton's forces "hear in time that Lord Howe is in possession of New York, they will doubtless attempt a junction with him" before the end of the current campaign season.[50]

Not even the appearance of two more row galleys, the *Congress* and the *Washington,* on Sunday, October 6, seemed to ease Arnold's apprehensions. He ordered these craft saluted with five cannon shots each and gladly welcomed General Waterbury, his second in command. Waterbury announced that he had brought a barrel of rum for each vessel, which Arnold had distributed to the delighted crew members. Arnold did appreciate Waterbury's presence and the enhanced firepower the row galleys gave the fleet. The *Congress,* in fact, carried two 18-pounders. After viewing the new vessels, Arnold decided to move from the *Royal Savage* and take direct command of the *Congress,* which he duly designated as the fleet's flagship.[51]

The commodore asked Waterbury for news about Washington's army. The general replied that matters were not going well. Early the next morning, Arnold erupted in condemnatory words about the resolve of his fellow patriots. "It appears to me our troops or officers are panic struck," he wrote to Gates, "or why do 100,000 men fly before one quarter of their numbers? Is it possible my countrymen can be callous to their wrongs or hesitate one moment between slavery or death? What advantage can we derive by blockading the enemy when they are in possession of a part of the country sufficient to support them? It appears to me coercive measures should be adopted."

Why Arnold used such fanciful estimates of troop strength in the respective armies is not entirely clear. Both he and Waterbury were aware that Howe had Washington heavily outnumbered, which may have been Arnold's point. This outburst reflected his mounting concern about the unwillingness of American civilians to rise up massively in arms when political slavery was their alternative. Was not death a more noble reward? he queried. Arnold surely believed so, but the lack of popular commitment when Washington's army was facing obliteration greatly bothered him. How could the cause survive in the absence of public virtue? he kept wondering. To allay his apprehensions, and his sense of futility in standing up to Carleton with such an inadequate force, Arnold turned over his worries to "that Being in whose hands are all human events," who "will doubtless turn the scale in favor of the just and oppressed." [52]

When the *Liberty* returned that morning with clothing and blankets, Arnold was appreciative, even though these supplies were far short of what his crew members actually needed. He also reveled in some soothing words from Gates. The Ticonderoga commander, trying to settle the frayed nerves of his commodore, spoke of Arnold's "zeal for the public service," knowing that he would again give his all for the cause that he represented and not abandon the bay at Valcour "one moment sooner than in prudence and good conduct you ought to do it." The compliment pleased Arnold, even if he had to swallow hard at Gates's admonition to "be satisfied, when you do not hear all you wish" about the military situation around New York City. "It is because all you wish is not come to my knowledge," the Ticonderoga commander wrote pointedly. [53]

Arnold would have swallowed harder—and perhaps laughed—had he known of a letter sent from Congress to his patron Silas Deane, now serving as an American commissioner to the French government. "We are formidable on the lakes, in galleys, boats, and gundalows under command of your friend Arnold," and the army at Ticonderoga was "better provided than the others so that we do not seem to apprehend any danger in that quarter at present," the communiqué claimed. Arnold would have called such commentary ludicrous, even if the purpose was to encourage material aid from France. [54]

Had Arnold known of another letter, penned on October 5 by James Easton for the eyes of Congress, he would have challenged him to a duel or possibly slammed him with the flat side of his sword. Having temporarily pacified his creditors in Massachusetts, Easton had traveled to Albany and joined John Brown in pressing Schuyler for a court of inquiry. Because of Arnold's crucial assignment on Lake Champlain, the northern commander again put off these two officers. Easton wrote Congress immediately, complaining that Schuyler's actions had nothing to do with military necessity but represented willful collusion. "It's evident General Arnold will evade the trial, if possible," because "there appears not the least spark of evidence against us." Then, with an oblique reference to Hazen's imputations of thievery, Easton alleged that "a general complaint among officers of all ranks as well as soldiers, is heard against him [Arnold], and it's hoped he will, ere long, meet the just demerits of [his] deeds." Even though Easton would never "desert this cause, nor think it a bad one, because I have been abused by General Arnold and others," he stood ready to accept "an honorable discharge and my pay, and quit the service"—unless, of course, Congress granted him satisfaction against Arnold.[55]

The delegates noted Easton's complaints on Monday, October 21, but not even they could call the Champlain commodore to account. Ten days before, on Friday, October 11, Arnold had proved he was doing something more than riding the waves on Lake Champlain to evade facing up to charges of dishonesty and thievery. As daylight broke that morning, Arnold saw impressions of snow on the mountains to the west of Valcour Bay. Just a few more days, he was sure, and Northern Department forces would not have to reckon with Carleton this year, not with the winter season fast approaching. Then he felt the northerly breeze, the kind the British fleet needed to sail southward on the lake.

For the past three days, Divine Providence had seemingly favored the patriots by offering only gusty southerly winds. Near 8 A.M. a scouting craft cut between Valcour Island and the New York mainland, rushing headlong toward the tightly formed fleet. As Lieutenant Wells reported, the vessel "fired an alarm and brought news of the near approach of our enemy." The frustrating wait was over. Carleton's flotilla was finally at hand.[56]

Arnold experienced a sense of calm as he ordered the hoisting up of a white pennant, announcing a council of war. As captains and their crews started hustling about, Arnold regarded the pennant and watched it flap strongly toward the south. He remembered his three young sons and how his sister Hannah had characterized them in a recent letter he had pored over during so many days of apprehensive waiting. "The little boys are well," she had written, and Harry, now four years old, wanted his "papa" to buy him "a little horse and a pair of pistols," since "he thinks himself big enough for the cavalry." "As far as courage goes," he was very much like his father and was "a little loving pup too; he gives me twenty kisses a day for papa."

Arnold had not seen his sons or his devoted sister for more than a year. With combat almost at hand, he rejoiced in the thought of someday again being in their loving company, should he survive. Still, whether he lived or died that day, the boys were going to be proud of their papa and the family name he and they bore in common. As they grew older, his sons, he hoped, would come to appreciate their father for the selfless patriot he aspired to be, a man who, despite harping critics, had not yet flinched in the face of the enemy. Arnold also recollected his sister's closing words: "Our cause is just and to the great Disposer of all events we must commit the issue. We all want to see you, but whether that happiness is again to be repeated to us, God only knows." Now fully composed, Arnold vowed to himself and Divine Providence to serve tenaciously that day; and as he greeted his captains, he exuded absolute confidence that the looming battle, no matter how unpropitious the odds were for victory, would bring martial glory to them, to their crews, and to the cause of American liberty as well.[57]

CHAPTER Twelve

The Valiant Defense of Lake Champlain

I

The council of war aboard the *Congress* took place in a hushed, almost meditative atmosphere. The brisk wind from the northwest made the morning air chilly, so the assemblage took comfort in the warmth generated by crowding so closely together in Arnold's tiny cabin. As the row galley creaked and bobbed about on the choppy waves rolling across the bay, Arnold's reassuring words and self-possessed manner helped steady everyone's taut nerves. The commodore opened the meeting by speaking about his orders from Gates. The fleet was to provide a "resolute but judicious defense of the northern entrance" into the rebellious states and was to retreat only after having "discovered the insufficiency of every effort to retard" the enemy's "progress" toward Ticonderoga. Quite simply, Gates's instructions were to engage in combat, if necessary; the only question was in what manner, since intelligence reports had convinced Arnold that the British squadron was stronger in almost every way than their own.[1]

Waterbury stood virtually alone in advocating an alternative to engaging the enemy within the restricted confines of Valcour Bay. "I gave it as my opinion that the fleet ought immediately to come to sail," he later wrote, "and fight them on a retreat in [the] main lake." Since Carleton's fleet was "so much superior to us in number and strength," Waterbury feared entrapment, especially because the British "with their small boats" had the capacity "to surround us on every side, as I knew they could." The only hope for survival, he argued, was to try to outsail the enemy for Ticonderoga, where the fleet could coordinate its combat response with the main body of rebel defenders.[2]

Arnold thanked his second officer. He had given serious consideration to this option but now judged it undesirable. With so many unseasoned sailors, no effective defensive formation could be maintained while on the run, he explained. The more powerful British fleet, with its trained mariners and a favoring northerly wind, would easily run down and annihilate the retreating patriot vessels long before they reached Ticonderoga. Nor did the patriot fleet have enough row galleys to shield the slow-moving gundalows. Should the wind suddenly shift and start blowing from the south, these flat-bottomed craft would be virtually immobilized, even with oarsmen pulling hard at their sweeps. Whether pursuing from the windward or leeward, the commodore concluded, Carleton's vessels would be able to use their superior mobility and firepower to destroy the patriot fleet in detail.

Arnold repeated to everyone that his orders enjoined him to employ "every effort to retard" the enemy's "progress" before considering retreat. He hated to disagree with Waterbury, a dedicated patriot whom he greatly admired. Fighting from a fixed position made greater sense, and Arnold considered Valcour Bay an especially strong position from which to challenge and perhaps even achieve an impressive victory over Carleton.[3]

With these comments as prologue, Arnold presented his own, admittedly unconventional battle plan. As long as the wind held its northerly course, the British vessels, to get at the rebel squadron after passing around the east side of Valcour Island, would have to turn to their starboard side in leaving the main channel and beat up into the bay against strong headwinds. Even for well-trained mariners, sailing to the windward would inhibit their efforts to form and hold a battle line. The enemy craft would not be able to strike at the sixteen patriot vessels in unison. (The schooner *Liberty* was not present but currently on a run to Ticonderoga for supplies.) As such, their superior strength and firepower would be neutralized, thereby giving the Americans a chance, however slim, to seize the laurels of victory.

To facilitate a coordinated patriot defense, Arnold intended to keep his fleet facing southward in its current tightly packed, crescent-shaped formation, just waiting for isolated enemy vessels to beat up against the wind and square off in combat. When they did, patriot gunners could concentrate their artillery fire and, with the blessings of Providence, inflict enough wounds for the unaggressive Carleton to back off and perhaps even order a retreat into Canada.

Arnold paused and waited for reactions. Hearing no dissent, he reminded his officers to look to him aboard the *Congress*—at the center of the patriot line—for overall instructions. General Waterbury on the *Washington* would direct the fleet's right wing, and Colonel Wigglesworth on the *Trumbull* would have charge of the left wing. With these command dispositions in place, Arnold reminded the captains to have wet blankets placed over their powder magazines as protection against accidental explosions from flying sparks or red-hot metal. They were also to have sand spread over their decks to help crew members avoid slipping in pools of human blood.[4]

The grim-faced officers, bidding each other godspeed, returned to their vessels and started barking out orders. As for Arnold, he made himself plainly visible by striding back and forth on the *Congress*'s quarterdeck. As he did so, he kept reviewing his battle plan. Although he had doubts about his fleet's capacity to defeat Carleton, he thought his vessels could inflict enough damage to prompt the governor to proceed to Ticonderoga with extreme circumspection. Trying to execute Waterbury's proposed race up the lake, in contrast, would only draw the British in magnet-like fashion to the main patriot line, where rebel defenders, with powder and ball still in short supply, could not make an effective stand. Stout resistance by the patriot fleet might even cause Carleton to blink and retreat back into Canada for the winter. As such, Arnold's landlubbing crews, even if badly mauled at Valcour Bay, could celebrate a strategic triumph. Everything, however, depended on the fervor with which they acquitted themselves in the pending engagement.

As the Champlain commodore paced the quarterdeck that cold morning of Friday, October 11, he savored the notion of getting another chance at Carleton. Still, he was conscious of at least two flaws in his otherwise resourceful battle plan. Should the wind turn against him, Carleton's flotilla could rush into the bay and ravage his fleet. Arnold had to make sure the British accepted battle before their vessels simply dropped anchor and waited a day or two for a southerly breeze. To guarantee an engagement on his terms, he would have to initiate the action. Arnold likewise appreciated Waterbury's concern about the lack of a convenient escape route. Valcour Bay might well prove a death trap that would forever shame his name; but he had to take that chance, he believed, to help the cause stay alive beyond the 1776 campaign season.

Not wanting to let his apprehensions loose again, Arnold put these problems out of his mind. He was ready to fight to the death, so he held up his spyglass to watch the waters beyond the southern tip of Valcour Island. At any moment he expected to get a glimpse of enemy scouting boats, but none appeared. Apparently the British were flaunting their self-assurance or being downright careless in not probing for the location of their adversary. The absence of scouting craft cheered Arnold. His fleet stood a much better chance of good fortune against so overconfident or oblivious an opponent.

II

Carleton did not enter Lake Champlain with much enthusiasm. Back in March 1776, Lord George Germain, the American secretary, had drafted instructions for the governor: Once the king's forces had driven the rebels from Canada, Carleton was to "endeavor to pass the lakes as early as possible, and in your future progress to contribute to the success of the army under General Howe." When Germain received the governor's May 14 report on the liberation of Quebec, he responded with compliments and then up-braided Carleton for his "silence . . . as to your own intended operations." The governor replied on July 8, informing the American secretary that "the operations of the army against the rebels must now be suspended for some time." He hoped Germain could comprehend the "great difficulties . . . in transporting provisions, artillery, stores, etc., overland from Chambly to St. Johns and providing the boats and armed vessels necessary for Lake Champlain." [5]

Carleton was reckoning with frustrating circumstances. His superiors in London expected him to move swiftly in pushing through the Champlain region, but they had scant appreciation for the host of logistical obstacles he had to overcome. For Germain, the highest priority was to destroy the rebel will to fight, preferably by no later than the end of the 1776 campaign; Carleton's was to restore order in Quebec Province. Since the governor was already maintaining a backbreaking work schedule, he exhibited little desire to proceed with offensive warfare. The rebels, if need be, could wait. From his perspective, it was only a matter of time—and a few more embarrassing defeats—before these "unhappy subjects" regained their senses, cast aside the demagogues "who kindled the flames of rebellion in America," and accepted "the king's mercy and benevolence" that was "still open to them." [6]

Carleton made a good-faith effort to act as if his heart were in military operations. After driving the rebels back into New York, he established his military headquarters in Montreal, from which he directed overall prepara-tions for a southward offensive. Besides redressing supply shortages for an army that numbered thirteen thousand by September, including some five thousand Hessians under Major General Baron Friedrich von Riedesel, Carleton addressed the equally vexing task of assembling a naval fleet at St. Johns.

Unlike the patriots at Skenesborough, the British had an abundance of skilled shipwrights and raw materials, besides a number of imposing vessels on the St. Lawrence River. The challenge was to get some of these craft around the turbulent, shallow, impassable Richelieu River rapids that ran southward from Fort Chambly to St. Johns. From there the water route was navigable all the way to the upper end of Lake Champlain near Skenesborough, some 150 miles away. Because of its location above the rapids, St. Johns served as the hub of fleet construction. Carleton charged Brigadier General William Phillips, a proficient artillery officer, with daily management of shipbuilding operations. Phillips executed his duties with aplomb and the valuable assistance of talented young officers in the Royal Navy. Carleton, meanwhile, went on to Quebec to see to the full restoration of civil government before returning to Montreal in mid-August.

Phillips's first task was to establish a functioning shipyard. By mid-July the shoreline was bustling with activity, and by the end of August an impressive naval squadron was taking shape. Captain Charles Douglass, one of the assisting naval officers, spoke about "the prodigies of labor which have been effected . . . in creating, recreating, and equipping a fleet of above thirty fighting vessels of different sorts and sizes, and all carrying cannons." Much of the work involved disassembling craft north of the rapids at Chambly before hauling the pieces, large or small, overland for reassembly at St. Johns. Even mariners from Royal naval vessels and merchant ships on the St. Lawrence "exerted themselves to the utmost on this great and toilsome occasion." Douglass viewed these seamen as "truly patriotic"; some two hundred of them, he noted, "impelled by a due sense of their country's wrongs," had agreed "to serve in our armed vessels during the expedition" onto Lake Champlain.[7]

By early September, Carleton had plenty of seasoned mariners and artillerists as well as a respectable squadron in place. The heart of his fleet consisted of four square-rigged vessels, including two schooners, the *Carleton* and the *Maria*, the former carrying twelve 6-pounders and the latter, named for the governor's wife, fourteen 6-pounders; the radeau *Thunderer*, a bargelike craft that resembled a floating battle wagon with its complement of six 24-pounders, six 12-pounders, and two howitzers; and the gundalow *Loyal Convert*, originally built near Quebec under Arnold's aegis but seized after the patriot retreat and now armed with seven 9-pounders. Also ready to sail were twenty gunboats, ten of which had come in numbered pieces from England for reassembly at St. Johns, and twenty-eight longboats. Each gunboat mounted one artillery piece, ranging from a 24-pounder to a howitzer, and each had a well-trained artillery crew. Four of the longboats were to carry fieldpieces on gun carriages for shore battery duty, and the other twenty-four stood ready to haul provisions of various kinds.[8]

When Carleton learned about the presence of Arnold's vessels at Windmill Point, he hesitated. He could not be sure whether his own squadron was decisively superior. Since his first military objective was to eliminate rebel naval resistance on Lake Champlain before moving thousands of troops southward in bateaux, he decided to keep his fleet at anchor until yet another vessel, a three-masted, 180-ton sloop of war, could be reassembled at St. Johns. Workers relaid the keel of this monster craft, at least by the standards of inland waterways, on Friday, September 6, three days after the patriot squadron had reached Windmill Point. Twenty-eight days later the *Inflexible*, mounting eighteen 12-pounders, was ready for service.

Carleton now had a squadron with the capacity to rip the rebels to shreds—or better yet, from his perspective, force them into submission without a gruesome battle. He had 670 experienced mariners to guide his twenty-five fighting craft, as well as a company of soldiers from the 29th Regiment assigned to each of his four largest vessels and a half company to the gundalow *Loyal Convert*, all to act as marines. In total, he had a naval assault force of well over one thousand crew members, plus about four hundred Indian warriors standing ready to paddle south in birch-bark canoes under the command of his younger brother, Major Thomas Carleton.[9]

The British armada was formidable, indeed, in comparison to Arnold's. Still, the ever-prudent governor had lost an important round to his adversary. Even before the British fleet moved up the Richelieu River and past Isle aux Noix on Friday, October 4, Carleton had decided to limit his campaign objectives. "Unfortunately the season is so far advanced that I dare not flatter myself we shall be able to do more . . . than to draw off their [the rebels'] attention and keep back part of their force from General Howe," he explained to Germain.[10]

Thus, despite the great storm at the end of August, the ever-tenacious Arnold had reached the northern end of the lake in the nick of time. The presence of the small patriot flotilla, which Carleton described as "a considerable naval force," had an intimidating effect on the governor and helped delay British offensive operations for a critical month. When Carleton finally sallied forth onto the lake on Saturday, October 5, he did so with a decidedly superior squadron but with a circumscribed mission. And if the governor was not sure how hard he should press the rebels, Arnold and nearly eight hundred patriot officers and crew members were waiting at Valcour Island, ready to show him the depth of patriot fighting capacities.[11]

III

At last underway, the British fleet seemed to move forward by inches because of contrary southerly winds. Carleton was aboard his designated flagship, the

Maria, along with the young and zealous Royal naval officer Captain Thomas Pringle, whom the governor had named fleet commander. Carleton had warned Pringle that "horse jockey" Arnold was an astute, relentless opponent. Like so many British officers, however, the presumptuous Pringle could not imagine a worthy rebel adversary.

Before dropping anchor between Long Island and Grand Island, some fifteen miles north of Valcour Island, late on Thursday, October 10, Carleton and Pringle received intelligence regarding the near presence of the American fleet. Early on October 11, however, Pringle threw caution aside in taking advantage of the strong northerly breeze. He did not send out scouting craft, since he assumed his fleet, especially with the impressive firepower available on the *Inflexible* and the *Thunderer*, could easily pulverize Arnold's vessels, regardless of where they were hiding.[12]

Just after 10 A.M., Arnold saw the lead British vessels, oblivious to his presence, sailing past the southern tip of Valcour Island. Patiently he waited for the enemy to spy his fleet, which finally occurred when the van of the British squadron was nearly two miles south of his position. When his adversary began hauling into the wind, Arnold delivered his invitation to combat. At about 11 A.M. he put the *Congress* under sail and ordered the other two row galleys and the *Royal Savage* to do the same. With the wind favoring them, these four vessels rushed toward the disorganized enemy fleet while firing scattered cannon salvos, which the British soon returned.

Arnold had calculated correctly. He had counted on British impetuosity and overconfidence as the best lures to combat. The bait having been offered, the Battle of Valcour Island now began. Had Carleton exercised the same level of deliberateness in agreeing to engage the patriot fleet that he had shown in preparing enter the lake, he could have swiftly gained the upper hand. He should have ordered Pringle to form an extended battle line blocking off the southern end of the bay, then to drop anchor and wait for a favorable southerly breeze. As it was, Pringle was anxious to get on with what he and his fellow naval officers expected to be an easy conquest.[13]

Once sure he had hooked his adversary, Arnold signaled the other three craft to rejoin the tightly packed rebel line. Employing their lateen sails, the galleys tacked easily against the wind. Crew members also used their sweeps to regain their assigned positions. The *Royal Savage* never got back because of what Arnold described as "some bad management" in sailing. As the schooner hauled into the wind, enemy shots cut into its rigging and seriously damaged one of its masts. Lacking sweeps, the square-rigged vessel started drifting to the leeward and soon ran aground near the southern tip of Valcour Island. Its gunners kept firing their 4- and 6-pounders, but enemy

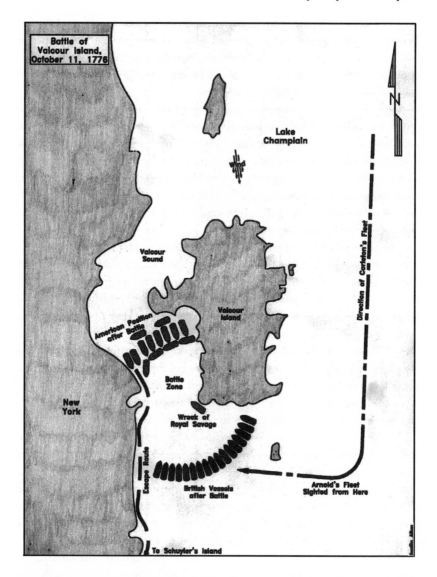

Battle of
Valcour Island,
October 11, 1776

Lake
Champlain

Valcour
Sound

Valcour
Island

American Position
after Battle

Battle
Zone

New
York

Wreak of
Royal Savage

Escape Route

Direction of Carleton's Fleet

British Vessels
after Battle

Arnold's Fleet
Sighted from Here

To Schuyler's Island

gunboats, a few carrying 24-pounders, quickly maneuvered into range and blasted away at the hapless schooner. Captain David Hawley's crew finally abandoned ship and got back safely to the rebel fleet with only a few casualties.[14]

The disablement of the *Royal Savage* spurred the British on, convincing them the kill would be almost effortless. Grouping like a pack of hungry jackals, the gunboats used their sweeps to form a semblance of a battle line.

With the exception of the schooner *Carleton,* however, the larger British craft struggled futilely against the wind and played little part, except for offering largely ineffective long-range artillery fire, in the ensuing battle.

The *Carleton* had just sailed past the island's southern end when the British squadron first discovered the rebels. The commanding officer, Lieutenant James R. Dacres, succeeded in hauling his vessel into the wind. The schooner closed to within seven hundred yards of Arnold's fleet by shortly after noontime. Out in front of the gunboats, the *Carleton* kept crawling forward to about 350 yards, at which point Dacres ordered the anchor dropped, but not before having his crew attach a spring line to the anchor cable. Heaving on this line, his sailors quickly maneuvered the *Carleton* into a position broadside to the American line. Working in concert with several swarming gunboats, Dacres already had his gun crews aiming and firing the schooner's complement of 6-pounders.[15]

"The engagement," Arnold reported, now "became general, and very warm." The acrid smell of burned gunpowder and billows of smoke soon enveloped the vessels, even as the blaring, discordant sounds of incessant artillery fire reverberated in loud claps off the steep banks of Valcour Island. As the battle built in intensity, splinters from shattered wood filled the air. Both sides started to sustain casualties. A large piece of debris knocked Dacres senseless, but the rebels were getting somewhat the worst of the action at this juncture.

Aboard the *Congress,* Arnold shouted out instructions to concentrate the fleet's firepower on the *Carleton.* His half-trained artillery crews tried as best they could, even though, as he later wrote, "we suffered much for want of seamen and gunners." Like Dacres, Arnold made himself highly visible as a source of encouragement. He continued to bark out orders and proffer words of admonition and praise. Because of the inexperience of his artillery crews, Arnold was also "obliged . . . to point most of the guns on board the *Congress,* which I believe did good execution." Like those of his comrades, his face and uniform became blackened by spent gunpowder and rising smoke.[16]

The commodore occasionally looked over his shoulder at the high bluffs of Valcour. British redcoats and their Native American allies had swarmed onto the island, and others were positioning themselves along the bay's western shoreline. Even though encircled, Arnold had positioned his vessels far enough from any shore to reduce the effects of musket fire and arrows. The fascines that his crews had tied to their vessels also worked to deflect enemy shots. As a result, the patriots did not have to worry about getting caught in a wicked cross fire.

In the course of the afternoon, Arnold and the rebels fought valiantly, even as they experienced moments of elation and despair. They cheered lustily when one of their cannon shots sent a ball careening into the powder magazine of a Hessian-manned gunboat, causing a massive explosion. Other scurrying gunboats rescued survivors before the lurching, smoking craft sank. Another patriot shot severed the *Carleton's* spring line, and the schooner started to drift aimlessly in the water with its bow swinging toward the rebel firing line. Arnold ordered the fleet's gunners to pour on the shot, and the *Carleton,* suddenly reeling from several hits along her bow and sides, began to lean and roll, as if it might keel over and sink.

With the British schooner foundering, the Americans seemed to have the makings of a stunning combat triumph. Seeing the *Carleton's* awkward movements, however, Pringle spoke with Carleton, and they called off the schooner. At first, nothing happened. Dacres was unconscious, and his second officer had lost an arm. Yet there were courageous warriors on both sides that afternoon, and one of them now came to the fore. He was a nineteen-year-old midshipman named Edward Pellew, who in later years became the renowned naval admiral Viscount Exmouth, one of Britain's most magnificent fighting seamen. Youthful Pellew decided to take charge. With rebel shot flying all around him, he raced for the bow, clambered onto the bowsprit, and struggled to swing the jib sail over to the windward side. Pellew's dramatic performance rallied the *Carleton's* crew and kept them fighting. Finally, two longboats maneuvered into position and pulled the listing schooner, now bogged down with two feet of water in its hold, away from the fire of Arnold's fleet.[17]

Now the British gunboats assumed the brunt of the battle. Each of these craft carried about eighty rounds of ammunition, including thirty rounds of largely ineffective round shot. Until about 5 P.M. "they continued a very hot fire," Arnold later wrote, before retiring to about seven hundred yards. Having all but expended their supplies of grapeshot, the gunboats continued to lob intermittent blasts of round shot at Arnold's fleet. At the same time, the radeau *Thunderer* had worked close enough to the patriot line for its gun crews to unleash a flurry of heavy shot from their 24-pounders. The radeau then backed off, admitting that the engagement was over for the day, since darkness had begun to envelop the bay.[18]

IV

The Battle of Valcour Island might fairly be called a standoff. Neither side had overwhelmed the other. Captain Pringle admitted to somewhat fewer than forty casualties, besides the loss of a gunboat and heavy damage sustained by the *Carleton*. By comparison, Arnold counted about sixty casualties. All of the officers on board the gundalow *New York,* except Captain Reed, had sustained wounds. On the row galley *Washington* a lieutenant was dead, and the captain and shipmaster were among the injured. The patriot vessels had likewise taken a beating. Enemy shots had so hulled the gundalow *Philadelphia* that it sank about an hour after the engagement ended. Also lost was the *Royal Savage*. During the height of the engagement a party of rebels had reboarded the schooner, but the British eventually drove them off. Shortly after dark, an enemy detachment got aboard the schooner and set the hapless craft ablaze.

As the flames rose, Arnold considered his own negligence. He had left most of his clothing as well as valuable papers, including his financial records, aboard the *Royal Savage* after moving over to the *Congress*. His clothing could be replaced, but his papers were apparently forever gone. The crackling timber and rising ball of fire were also symbolic warnings of just how precarious the rebel position had become. The northerly wind had begun to die down at day's end, and the enemy squadron was forming a solid line across the mouth of Valcour Bay. The British still had regular troops and Indian allies deployed on every piece of land surrounding the American fleet. They were also massing dozens of bateaux to facilitate the boarding of the patriot craft, which they would certainly attempt the next day, barring another strong blast of unfavorable wind.[19]

Compounding problems was the damage suffered by his squadron's vessels, as well as a dwindling supply of ammunition, which Arnold stated was "nearly three-fourths spent." British and Hessian gunners had battered the gundalows. The *Congress* had taken seven balls "between wind and water" and had been "hulled a dozen times." The *Washington* had also been "hulled a number of times" and had its "mainmast shot through," Arnold noted. As a result, these two craft were "very leaky, and want repairing." Only the *Trumbull* among the row galleys had emerged from the engagement relatively unscathed.

Arnold appreciated that his fleet was all but entrapped, as did his senior officers. His battle tactics had worked up to a point, since the enemy had failed to marshal the full strength of its fleet. Tomorrow, however, or perhaps the next day, whenever the wind shifted, the British would get what their young naval officers had expected all along: unconditional surrender or annihilation of the patriot fleet. Either way, Carleton would regain control of Lake Champlain, the critical first step in vanquishing patriot resistance in the northern theater.

Some dramatic maneuver had to be devised. Sometime before 7 P.M., Arnold met with Waterbury, Wigglesworth, and the other officers. Low on ammunition and facing the full weight of an "enemy greatly superior to us in ships and men," the assemblage voted to risk a breakout. Since a heavy fog was then enshrouding the bay, they could take advantage of British blindness. They did not think they could pilot their vessels through the rocky, shoal water gap to the north of them between Valcour Island and the mainland. They had noticed that Pringle, to make sure none of his craft ran aground, had left a small opening between the left end of his blockade line and the New York shoreline. With oars muffled under cover of a thick fog, the patriot fleet could attempt to slither its way past the enemy line and make a dash for Crown Point. However dangerous, the alternatives were obliteration or surrender.[20]

Arnold ordered wounded crew members moved into cabins on the row galleys so that British lookouts could not hear their groans. As agreed, Wigglesworth on the *Trumbull* took the lead, hugging close to the New York shore. Each vessel had mounted in its stern a lantern with the sides covered to block any telltale flickers of moving light. In single file, each craft followed the faint glow emanating from the vessel ahead. The *Washington,* with Waterbury on board, was the second to last in line, and Arnold on the *Congress* brought up the rear. The oarsmen did not let their muffled sweeps splash the water; and near midnight, having rowed beyond the sounds of British soldiers and Indians on shore and the creaking of enemy vessels, the patriots had passed beyond the British line. Before daylight the fleet, now with bilge pumps running to keep some craft afloat, had reached Schuyler's Island, about eight miles south of the enemy. In writing to Gates that morning, Arnold called the escape "very fortunate"; and he expressed "great reason to return our humble and hearty thanks to Almighty God for preserving and delivering so many of us from our more than savage enemies."[21]

The race for Crown Point, still thirty-five miles to the south, had just begun. Back at Valcour Bay, Carleton, Pringle, and the whole British fleet watched closely as the fog slowly lifted a little after 8 A.M. Officers and crew members alike were dumbfounded to see the empty body of water before them. Carleton was furious. He instructed Pringle to get under sail immediately, and the British squadron, after sending out scouting boats to check north of Valcour Island, started cruising southward. The angry governor then remembered that he had not issued orders for the movement of his supporting land forces. He told Pringle to return the fleet to the bay, where he informed his army officers to push south behind the fleet.

Carleton's delay helped the retreating patriots, but only briefly. At Schuyler's Island, Arnold surveyed the extent of the fleet's damage. The gundalows *New York* and *Providence* were no longer seaworthy, while a third gundalow, the *Jersey*, was so full of water that only the rocks on which the craft now rested kept it afloat. Arnold ordered the ordnance pieces moved to other vessels and then had the first two gundalows towed into deeper water and sunk. An attempt to burn the stranded *Jersey* failed, since it was so water-logged. This gundalow became the first British prize.

The *Congress* and the *Washington* were also in bad shape. While work crews labored to patch holes, fix masts, and mend sails, Arnold conferred with his officers. The fleet, or what was left of it, he stressed, had to reach Crown Point. To facilitate that intent, he wanted the *Trumbull*, with Wigglesworth in command, to serve as a shepherd for the nine remaining vessels. In turn, the *Congress* and the *Washington* would perform rear-guard duty. He and Waterbury would do whatever was possible to delay the enemy. That way a portion of the Champlain fleet would survive and serve as evidence to Carleton that he had not yet achieved naval dominance on the lake.[22]

After everyone had consumed a hastily prepared meal, their first food in a day, Wigglesworth's vessels got underway, even as repair work continued on the two row galleys. Not long thereafter, at about 2 P.M., enemy sails appeared on the horizon, pushing against a southerly breeze. The *Congress* and the *Washington* weighed anchor as "the enemy came hard against us," in the words of Lieutenant Bayze Wells.[23]

That wind, in combination with intermittent squalls of sleet and rain, made progress difficult for both sides. The gundalows fell behind the *Trumbull*, even with oarsmen pulling robustly at their sweeps. Toward evening the wind calmed down, and the patriots kept ahead of the enemy by rowing all night. Early morning light on Sunday, October 13, revealed that the patriots were astride Willsborough, still twenty-eight miles north of Crown Point. After sixteen hours of sailing and rowing, Arnold's crews had traversed only seven miles. Carleton's fleet had not gained on them.

Later that morning the wind intervened, this time on behalf of the British. A stiff breeze swirled out of the northeast and filled the sails of Carleton's squadron long before the same gusts reached the *Congress*, the *Washington*, and the lingering gundalows. With hardly any passage of time, the schooner *Maria*, with Carleton and Pringle on board, along with the sloop of war *Inflexible* and the heavily patched *Carleton* slightly astern, were closing in on the patriots. An alarmed Waterbury, his badly damaged row galley lagging behind the *Congress*, requested permission to "run my vessel on shore, and blow her up." Arnold, however, preferred to fight. He wanted to offer the other vessels time to catch the northerly breeze and get away, so he ordered Waterbury "to push forward to Split Rock," astride a narrow point in the lake where Arnold intended to make a stand.[24]

Waterbury did reach Split Rock, but with the three British vessels pressing in for the kill. He struck his colors and surrendered "after receiving a few broadsides." Arnold did not fault Waterbury's decision. Rather, he said the general had no viable alternative, given the *Washington*'s "shattered condition" and "so many men killed and wounded" on board. By comparison, Waterbury, worried about charges of faintheartedness, blamed Arnold for his vessel's capture. When he sought permission to scuttle the *Washington*, he later claimed, Arnold countered by promising to "draw the fleet in a line, and engage them again" at Split Rock. "When I came to Split Rock, the whole fleet was making their escape as fast as they could, and left me in the rear, to fall into the enemy's hands," at which point Arnold "with four gundalows, ran ashore, and blew up the vessels ahead of me."[25]

Waterbury's statement conveyed the impression that Arnold had purposely sacrificed the *Washington* to assure himself an honorable escape rather than a prisoner's status. No evidence supports this damning allegation. Back at Schuyler's Island, Arnold had stipulated that the two row galleys were to act to defend the rest of the fleet. Certainly Waterbury understood his assigned role, which was to offer combat if at all possible, regardless of the battered condition of his vessel. Stated differently, Waterbury's surrender freed Carleton's vessels to concentrate on the *Congress*. Arnold could have used the loss of the *Washington* to strike his own colors, but he chose to fight, not with any hope of saving his own craft but with the goal of facilitating the escape of the rest of the fleet.

When Arnold engaged the swarming British vessels, he did so for much longer than Waterbury's implied few brief moments. Totally outmanned and outgunned, the commodore and his crew put on a virtuoso performance. Having reached Split Rock near noontime, Arnold ordered his helmsmen to haul into the wind. The British now took dead aim on the *Congress*. For something over two hours, Arnold and his crew engaged the three enemy craft, "two under our stern, and one on our broadside, within musket shot" range and possessing combined artillery firepower at least five times greater than that of the *Congress*. "They kept up an incessant fire . . . with round and grape shot," Arnold later wrote, but his crew fought back "briskly." Methodically, the British tried to eradicate the *Congress*, but Arnold refused to strike his colors. Even with casualties mounting, he knew that every moment his crew members held on, they were helping to save some of the fleet. By two o'clock "the sails, rigging, and hull of the *Congress* were shattered and torn to pieces," and the galley was foundering. Four more enemy craft had since come up to join in the unmerciful hammering. Still Arnold refused to yield.[26]

The young British naval officers relished the pounding. Their opponent deserved a severe mashing, they thought, because colonial rebels were nothing more than rude, treasonous upstarts without proper training in the art of naval warfare. Arnold, however, after years of plying the West Indies trade, was no rube in handling ships, and he now taught his adversaries a lesson in outwitting self-assured opponents. Even in the mayhem of combat all around him, Arnold kept surveying the eastern shoreline, looking for a point of escape. All the while he kept a close eye on four waterlogged gundalows, incapable of retreating farther up the lake. They hovered nearby, but the British ignored them, knowing their crews would surrender as soon as the *Congress* sank or Arnold gave up the fight.

As the Split Rock engagement built to its crescendo, Arnold kept the *Congress* moving toward the eastern shoreline. Then, at the right moment, he ordered his crew members to man their sweeps. As oars met water, the galley lurched to the windward and escaped through a small opening between two British craft. With sweeps also churning, the gundalows followed the *Congress* into Ferris Bay, just south of Buttonmould Bay and at an awkward enough angle that the larger British vessels, now having to haul into the wind, could not quickly pursue.[27]

The startled enemy continued to heave sporadic cannon shots into the cove even as the patriots ran their vessels aground, grabbed their small arms and their wounded comrades, and quickly disembarked. Arnold bellowed out orders to spread out gunpowder and ignite the five craft, which were soon consumed in flames and explosions. Most accounts credit Arnold with being the last person to abandon ship after personally firing the *Congress* but refusing, in a final act of defiance, to strike the row galley's colors. What can also be verified is that he nearly ran his sword through a gunner after learning that this soldier had refused to help one of the *Congress*'s seriously wounded officers escape from the burning vessel. The officer's body flew high in the air as the galley exploded, resulting in later accusations, popular in British circles, that Arnold had mercilessly sacrificed the lives of up to thirty of his wounded crewmen along with the five vessels.[28]

None of the surviving crew members reported so callous an act, but they did commend their commodore for his courageous leadership that day and for getting them safely to Crown Point, located ten miles to the south on the opposite shore. Carleton's Indians had paddled their canoes up the lake and "waylaid the road" along the eastern shoreline in anticipation of an ambush. As Arnold stated, however, his party "very luckily escaped the savages" by taking a more circuitous route to Chimney Point, just across the lake from Crown Point.[29]

Once at Chimney Point, Arnold and his crewmen sighted the four surviving vessels hovering around the *Trumbull*. Soon transported over to Crown Point, they took part in the general retreat to Ticonderoga, where they blended back into the regiments from whence they came. Arnold arrived before his Champlain veterans, having rushed ahead to report in person to Gates. He appeared out of the dark at 4 A.M. on Monday, October 14, feeling "exceedingly fatigued and unwell, having been without sleep or refreshment for near three days."[30]

V

Gates listened intently as Arnold summarized the fighting of the past three days. The junior brigadier calculated total patriot casualties at "eighty-odd." Those aboard the *Congress* had endured the worst of it, with "twenty-odd men killed and wounded." In addition, Arnold estimated that 110 men had fallen into the hands of Carleton with the capture of the *Washington*, meaning an overall casualty rate of nearly 25 percent. Of the vessels engaged, only one unidentified gundalow was left, besides the row galley *Trumbull*, the sloop *Enterprise*, and the schooner *Revenge*. Although the row galley *Gates*, not outfitted in time to join the fleet, and the schooner *Liberty* were also available for service, the hard fact was that Carleton's squadron had attained naval superiority on the lake. Further resistance would now have to come from the patriot troops at Ticonderoga.[31]

Arnold felt frustrated because he had not accomplished more with the limited human and material resources available to him, but he was confident about having made a powerful impression on Carleton. If the battle at Valcour Island had not fully demonstrated patriot resolve, he believed his defiant stand off Split Rock had fulfilled that purpose. Should the governor, having experienced firsthand rebel determination, hold off in attacking Ticonderoga that autumn, then the patriots would have accomplished their objective—gaining further time to strengthen their northern defenses. Along this line, Arnold urged the construction of more vessels, especially row galleys. He also favored building a patriot sloop of war that could hold its own against the *Inflexible*.[32]

Gates agreed but wondered whether Congress could marshal the resources to construct additional vessels or even support the Northern Department war effort more adequately. Although militia troops were pouring into

Ticonderoga, raising Gates's manpower pool to some fourteen thousand with about nine thousand effectives, critical infusions of gunpowder, ball, and other munitions had still not arrived from below. Carleton's fleet could still easily take Ticonderoga, but he had to attack. Gates, too, hoped that Arnold's determined resistance, in combination with the lateness of the campaign season, would cause the governor to remain deliberate rather than bold in his decision making.

Gates advised Arnold to rest and regather his physical strength, and he promised him a new assignment and place of honor at Ticonderoga. On Saturday, October 26, the commander announced that Arnold would take charge of all troops assigned to the redoubts north of the old stone fortress, the point at which any British assault force would likely strike first. He was also to continue his duties as commodore, with all remaining craft now assigned to guarding the boom connecting the western shore with Mount Independence.[33]

As Arnold rested during his first day back at Ticonderoga, a curious incident occurred. Near sunset, several small British craft approached the fortress. Under a flag of truce, they unloaded Waterbury and the other rebel prisoners, all of whom had accepted parole terms. They were now free to mingle with their comrades, although they had also agreed not to take up arms against the British until their names appeared on prisoner exchange lists. Once on shore, the erstwhile prisoners spoke affirmatively about Carleton's treatment of them. A worried Gates decided that 110 men loitering in camp and talking so positively about the enemy might dampen the resolution of other troops. He quickly ordered Waterbury and the other parolees to proceed to Skenesborough, where they could rest before returning home. Waterbury quietly accepted this banishment, but once back in Connecticut he penned his spurious portrayal of Arnold's behavior at Split Rock. He sent this after-action report to Congress, and his self-absolving words soon became further evidence for some delegates of Arnold's lack of sound judgment.[34]

Carleton's clemency represented a means to save rations while spreading doubt and dissension among enemy soldiers at Ticonderoga. He also expected the officers accompanying Waterbury's party to evaluate the strength of the defensive works and numbers of troops there. The patriots, not having to reveal their munitions shortages, looked imposing. Even before Carleton paroled the prisoners, he had written Germain from Crown Point to announce that "the rebel fleet upon Lake Champlain has been entirely defeated in two actions." After briefly describing the "gallant behavior" of his naval force, he stated, "The season is so far advanced that I cannot yet pretend to inform your lordship whether anything further can be done this year." The muscular impression of the rebels at Ticonderoga, along with Arnold's stouthearted defense of the lake, convinced Carleton that an all-out assault would be unwise so late in the season.[35]

Gates and Arnold were not sure what Carleton was thinking, and they experienced some anxious moments. Gates did send an urgent note to Schuyler in which he described himself as "distressed to the last degree" over the ongoing shortage of munitions. Three tons of lead had just arrived, but the Ticonderoga commander needed several more tons, given the "the defeat and almost total ruin of the fleet." At the same time, Gates issued orders for regiments to be "well acquainted with their alarm posts" and "alert in marching to support the works they are severally intended to defend." He fully expected some sort of a contact with the enemy and was counting on the "bravery and fidelity" of the soldiers "when called to action."[36]

By the time Carleton got his British regiments—most of the Hessians remained in Canada—to Crown Point, Ticonderoga's defenders had received enough powder and ball to offer something more than token resistance. The governor's military advisers, especially Burgoyne, kept pushing for a massed assault or siege operations. Carleton, however, allowed only a reconnaissance in force. On Monday, October 28, the rebel resisters heard an alarm gun from a small scouting boat down the lake. Soon cannons started booming along the American line, all warning of the enemy's approach. The British landed troops on the western side of the lake, but far out of range of the patriots. Two gunboats moved ahead and unleashed a few salvos, but patriot artillery fire kept them at a safe distance after one shot killed two British crew members. For the rest of the day Ticonderoga's defenders stayed in their lines, and the British intruders, in the words of Lieutenant Bayze Wells, "disappeared" toward nightfall "and as we supposed returned to Crown Point."[37]

Four days earlier Gates had written Schuyler, reporting that he had scouting parties "continually down both sides of the lake" to watch Carleton's force at Crown Point. "I . . . expect this stillness will be succeeded immediately by a grand attack," he stated. "Heaven grant he [Carleton] may be defeated. The army here . . . think only of victory." The expected assault, however, never materialized. On Saturday, November 2, Carleton began withdrawing his forces from Crown Point. As Arnold explained to Washington, "they give out their intention is to return to Canada, and pay us a visit in the spring." The winter season, he hoped, "will effect as much as a victory" in getting ready for the onslaught that was sure to come. What Arnold left unstated was that Carleton's withdrawal was its own form of patriot triumph, a handsome prize for the campaign that he had helped spearhead in denying the British a military foothold in northern New York during 1776.[38]

Carleton seemed satisfied with his accomplishments. Back in England, George III had recently dubbed him a Knight of the Bath in recognition of his defiant stand against the rebel invaders at Quebec City. He would now be known as Sir Guy Carleton and, in time, gain full peerage status as Lord Dorchester. Lord Germain, however, was most unhappy after learning the results of Sir Guy's invasion effort. He felt compelled to identify a ranking military leader who both appreciated larger strategic considerations and would fight. That person, Germain decided, was General John Burgoyne.[39]

VI

At first, Arnold received accolades for his performance on Lake Champlain. Gates, in his general orders of October 14, thanked "General Arnold, and the officers, seamen, and marines of the fleet for the gallant defense they made against the great superiority of the enemy's force. Such magnanimous behavior will establish the fame of American arms throughout the globe." In writing Schuyler, he expressed gratification that "it has pleased Providence to preserve General Arnold. Few men ever met with so many hairbreadth escapes in so short a space of time." A few days later, Gates signified how "it would have been happy for the United States had the gallant behavior and steady good conduct of that excellent officer been supported by a fleet in any degree equal to the enemy's. As the case stands, though they [the British] boast a victory, they must respect the vanquished."[40]

When word of the Champlain fleet's defeat reached Philadelphia, the reaction among delegates was initially favorable toward America's Hannibal. Wrote delegate Benjamin Rush of Pennsylvania, "General Arnold . . . has conducted himself like a hero. Like Francis I, he has lost all save honor and the honor of the states." More generally, Virginia's Richard Henry Lee spoke of how "our people bravely maintained the unequal contest, conducting themselves with a valor that has extorted applause even from their enemies, and which certainly deserved a better fortune."[41]

The British did offer some generous words. The rebel retreat up Lake Champlain "did great honor to General Arnold," wrote a British officer who commanded a gunboat in Carleton's fleet. Such praise would be reiterated in the highest circles in England. One widely read publication commended Arnold's "desperate resistance." As the rebel fleet's commodore, he had greatly added to "that renown which he had acquired on land in the Canada expedition." He had "not only acted the part of a brave soldier, but . . . also amply filled that of an able naval commander." Not even "the most experienced seaman could . . . have found a greater variety of resources . . . to compensate for the want of force, than he did." Arnold had, this publication concluded, "raised his character still higher than it was before with his countrymen."[42]

The tide of patriot opinion, however, quickly turned against Arnold, at least among a handful of well-placed patriot leaders. One source of negative commentary was New Jersey's recently elevated Brigadier General William Maxwell, who was at Ticonderoga where he spent much of his time objecting to Congress's decision to promote Arthur St. Clair ahead of him. Maxwell sent a blistering "private" communication to his state's chief executive, Governor William Livingston. He castigated Arnold as "our evil genius to the north" who "has, with a good deal of industry, got us clear of all our fine fleet," which, "by all impartial accounts, was by far the strongest." Losing so many vessels, Maxwell sarcastically opined, was a "pretty piece of admiralship" that had left Ticonderoga completely exposed to attack. The army, he claimed, had no higher "opinion of his [Arnold's] abilities by land than water."[43]

Maxwell was a retired British field-grade officer who, in writing with such premeditated hostility, betrayed obvious jealousy toward his far more celebrated comrades, Arnold and Gates. That he should question expending rather than saving the fleet was a matter of military judgment. Possibly Carleton would have remained just as irresolute in approaching Ticonderoga had Arnold violated Gates's orders and avoided combat. However, the fleet's appearance at the northern end of the lake did influence the governor's decision to delay the invasion for a month. Arnold's willingness to fight at Valcour Island and Split Rock conveyed a strong but misleading impression (in the absence of sufficient munitions) that patriot defenders would not retreat from Ticonderoga without a major bloodletting. What Maxwell also failed to grasp was that reconquering Lake Champlain gave Carleton enough of a sense of victory to justify pulling back into Canada without striking at the old French fortress. As such, Arnold's naval operations had kept the British from fully regaining the strategic advantage in the Champlain region, which rendered their tactical triumph against the patriot fleet virtually meaningless.

Maxwell was not thinking in strategic terms. His purpose was to enhance his own credibility by faulting Arnold for "bantering" the enemy "for two months or more, contrary to the opinion of all the army." Maxwell had apparently believed Arnold's braggadocio about attacking St. Johns. He was among those who charged the commodore with willfully violating Gates's orders, as James Wilkinson also claimed several years later, by putting "no limits to his cruise." Arnold had done so, Wilkinson insisted, out of "excess of rashness and folly" in a vain quest for personal glory and "to exalt his character for animal courage, on the blood of men equally brave, which he was bound to spare, by the strongest obligations of duty and humanity."[44]

Evidently Wilkinson, who had jumped over to Gates's staff as a brigade major, had not yet gained the close confidence of the Ticonderoga commander. In responding to Arnold's regular reports from the fleet, Gates at no point questioned the disposition of the fleet. When Arnold suggested that the approaching winter season might force him to redeploy the rebel squadron closer to Crown Point, Gates replied on October 12, before he had learned about the previous day's engagement, "I . . . am pleased to find you and your armada ride in Valcour Bay in defiance of the power of our foes in Canada." During the autumn of 1776, at least, Gates never indicated that Arnold did anything in breach of orders regarding the defense of Lake Champlain.[45]

Arnold's critics, most notably Maxwell, saw matters otherwise. His thoughts soon reached Congress, where they reinforced Waterbury's indictment. The notion that Arnold had exercised faulty judgment by seeking combat rather than retreating and saving the fleet, as Waterbury had suggested, in conjunction with vague innuendos about disobeying Gates's orders and wasting human lives in an "absurd and desperate" defense of the lake, all to gain personal military fame, only further damaged Arnold's reputation. In early November, Richard Henry Lee, whose praise was initially effusive, revealed the changed attitude when he accorded Arnold the derisive testimonial of having acted as a "fiery, hot, and impetuous" commander, who, "without discretion, never thought of informing himself how the enemy went on, and . . . had no idea of retiring when he saw them coming, though so much superior to his force!"[46]

Arnold's valiant defense of Lake Champlain thus became misshapen and took on the form of self-aggrandizing glory hunting, which seemed to resonate with the allegations of Brown, Easton, and Hazen, as well as the court-martial board of regimental officers who had demanded his censure. America's Hannibal seemed much less heroic now than only a few months before. What he needed was an influential patron in Congress, someone who could take the place of Silas Deane, someone who could articulate his strengths and defend his integrity as a virtuous patriot amid so many personal assaults. Unfortunately for Arnold, no such person was present among the congressional delegates in late 1776.

VII

As Arnold went about his assigned duties at Ticonderoga, he had no idea what grave difficulties lay ahead in regard to preserving his good name. At the moment, reports confirming Carleton's pullback to Canada gratified him. At the same time, disquieting news about continuing setbacks for Washington's army kept him uneasy. He appreciated that the campaign effort—and the rebellion as well—could still be lost should Washington's Continentals be crushed by the powerful enemy force of William Howe.

In mid-November, another problem also became a focal point of concern. After Carleton's evacuation of Crown Point, Gates and Schuyler released the militia from further service. This decision stirred up the Continental troops at Ticonderoga. Since the British were no longer in the vicinity, these regulars threatened not to "re-engage unless they had furloughs granted them to return home" immediately. To resolve the dispute, Schuyler asked Arnold, Gates, and James Brickett, a brigadier general of Massachusetts militia, to meet with him at his summer residence at Saratoga (now Schuylerville). The generals gathered on Thursday, November 21, and voted unanimously to grant furloughs, since most enlistments extended only through December 31 anyway. The generals did so with the condition that when the Continentals returned home, they would encourage friends and neighbors to enlist—a "prudent" method to augment the army's ranks for upcoming campaign seasons.[47]

The general officers were not putting Ticonderoga at risk. There was no likelihood of a sudden British advance—not with Carleton in command, with snow already falling heavily in the Champlain region, and with ice building on the lake. By the end of November, Gates had reduced the troop strength at Ticonderoga to about fourteen hundred soldiers. They would act as a skeleton garrison force under the command of Colonel Anthony Wayne of Pennsylvania until springtime necessitated a new buildup in manpower.

Washington's army, meanwhile, was in full retreat across New Jersey. Fearing the rebel cause was on the verge of collapse, the commander in chief sent urgent pleas to the Northern Department for assistance. Fortunately, Schuyler had decided to furlough the Continentals at Ticonderoga through Albany. Once aware of Washington's plight, he ordered these troops to hold themselves in readiness, just in case they might be needed "to succor the southern army," in the words of Gates. By Sunday, December 1, Gates was sailing down the Hudson River with vessels carrying eight Continental regiments. Before leaving Albany, he wrote how "anxious" Arnold was, "after his very long absence, to see his family, and settle his public accounts."

Sixteen months had passed since the junior brigadier had left New Haven, and he was not sure whether he would recognize his growing sons. Still, Gates stated, his fighting subordinate felt a deep commitment to assist Washington at so perilous a moment. The senior general strongly suspected that Arnold's "zeal for the service will outweigh all other considerations, and induce him to take the route that leads to" the enemy.[48]

Gates was correct. Torn between family and the cause of liberty, Arnold postponed his long-awaited trip home and soon traveled down the Hudson River. He could not leave Albany with Gates, however, because of yet another niggling complaint lodged by Hazen, who now charged Arnold with slander—specifically, of accusing Hazen of stealing rum for personal profit during the patriot retreat from Canada. Determined to gain satisfaction, Hazen insisted on a court of inquiry on this point alone. Hoping to keep the Canadian colonel at bay, Schuyler asked Arnold to defend himself.

The hearing took place on Monday, December 2. Hazen produced a receipt for the purchase of thirty kegs of rum plus 150 pounds of tobacco for the rebel garrison at Chambly. On the back of this document, Arnold had later scribbled that some of the rum "was delivered to a Frenchman who kept [a] tavern at Chambly." Then, in an intentional slur, he also wrote, "Colonel Hazen can best tell how much he sold." After reviewing the evidence, the court ruled that Arnold's words represented "an aspersion of . . . Hazen's character," since the junior brigadier had no proof that the colonel had personally pocketed any money. Hazen, thinking that he had finally gotten some satisfaction, was dumbfounded when the hearing panel, even after declaring his "complaint just," disbanded without recommending any form of reprimand for Arnold.[49]

America's Hannibal offered no comment on the proceedings. His mind was on rushing southward to catch up with Gates. Near Newburgh, the two generals debarked the Continentals and marched them overland through mountainous terrain, in the face of driving snow and sleet, for Bethlehem, Pennsylvania, which they reached by Sunday, December 15. Now only about fifty miles north of Washington's camp in Bucks County along the western shore of the Delaware River, Gates offered the exhausted troops a few days of rest before finishing their journey. Washington started welcoming the Ticonderoga regiments to camp on Saturday, December 21, just four days before launching his daring Christmas evening assault on Hessian-held Trenton back across the Delaware River.[50]

Traveling ahead of the troops, Arnold reached Washington's headquarters before December 21. Along the way, a courier caught up with him and handed over a nearly week-old letter from the commander himself. Much to

Arnold's surprise, Washington had ordered him to make haste for New England, where the British had recently invaded Rhode Island. At last by dint of military necessity, Arnold had a valid reason to return home, but not before visiting briefly with Washington and offering positive counsel on the commander's proposed counterattack against British outposts in New Jersey.

On Sunday, December 22, Arnold began an overland journey that brought him back, at least for a few days, to New Haven and the loving arms of his three boys and sister Hannah. Traveling by horseback, he had many hours to consider the new military crisis that he would soon confront and how he would work "in conjunction with" aging and largely inert Major General Joseph Spencer, also from Connecticut, in taking "such measures," according to Washington's instructions, "as in your opinion will be most likely to give opposition to, and frustrate the intents of the enemy." As he rode, he also pondered the possible implications of his most recent encounter with Hazen. Arnold still had no firm sense of the vicissitudes of his reputation in Congress, nor could he imagine that his most threatening critic was about to emerge in the personage of his trusted military comrade, patron, and friend, Horatio Gates.[51]

CHAPTER *Thirteen*

Fundamental Matters of
Military Rank and
Personal Honor

I

Shortly before Arnold's brief visit to Washington's Bucks County headquarters, the commander in chief wrote in despair, "*I think the game is pretty near up.*" After so much initial enthusiasm for war in 1775, the patriot martial effort was now in woeful shape. Washington's army—what remained of it—was in shambles and all but vanquished from a series of devastating losses that culminated in a headlong flight across New Jersey. Except for Arnold's defense of Lake Champlain and Carleton's retreat into Canada for the winter, rebellious Americans had little to give them hope as "the affrighted remains of Mr. Washington's army," to draw on the taunting words of a British general, sought to regain its virtually shattered equilibrium in eastern Pennsylvania.[1]

Patriot fighting commitment had reached an alarming low point. Thomas Paine thought so when writing about "the times that try men's souls," and when castigating "the summer soldier and the sunshine patriot" who "will, in this crisis, shrink from the service of their country." The *rage militaire* of 1775, conjured up in so many vibrant images of virtuous patriots selflessly uniting as one, had proved illusory when tested against superior enemy forces. Even with Paine's poignant reminder that "tyranny, like hell, is not easily conquered," the pivotal question in late 1776 was whether the Revolution could survive. A dramatic military triumph was paramount for rallying popular support, Washington indicated when describing to Arnold his plan to strike at British outposts in New Jersey. America's Hannibal would have been out of character had he spoken up for caution rather than resourceful action.[2]

Not so with General Gates. Preferring defensive operations, he implored Washington to continue retreating, all the way west across the Susquehanna River and into the mountains of central Pennsylvania if necessary. There he could rebuild his force and march eastward at a more propitious time. Washington respectfully rejected Gates's advice. He knew that General Howe considered the main rebel force beaten. Now was the most propitious time to strike boldly, when an overconfident foe would least suspect further patriot actions. Gates, in virtual disgust but using the guise of illness, refused to assist and left camp. His unsupportive behavior left Washington wondering why he had not selected Gates for detached duty in New England, since congressional delegates from that region had clamored for him. Washington would have been better served had he kept Arnold with him and given the New Englanders the officer they preferred.[3]

Severe adversity had failed to produce unity of purpose among ranking Continental officers. Gates had just received a missive from Major General Charles Lee, whom Washington had instructed to move his force of seven thousand troops from the Hudson Highlands region to eastern Pennsylvania. Lee did so at a suspiciously lackadaisical pace. As he dawdled at a crossroads tavern in north-central New Jersey on Friday morning, December 13, his luck gave out. A small British squad captured him, but not before he had penned an imprudent letter to Gates questioning Washington's competence. "A certain great man is damnably deficient," Lee wrote, and his inept generalship during the recent campaign had "unhinged the goodly fabric we had been building." Someone with much greater military perspicacity—no doubt Lee had himself in mind—had to assume command of the Continental army before everything was lost.[4]

General Sullivan took command of Lee's troops, now hardly more than two thousand effectives in the wake of desertions and the ravages of disease, and got them across the Delaware River. There they joined other units coming into camp, including Pennsylvania militia and the regiments under Gates and Arnold. As a result, Washington had minimally acceptable numbers, about six thousand troops, to launch his counteroffensive on a snowy Christmas evening. The outcome was his much-celebrated rout and capture of some one thousand Hessians who were garrisoning the advance British outpost at Trenton.

In conjunction with a second successful clash at Princeton on January 2, 1777, Washington's dazzling display of resourceful generalship caused the British to pull in their outposts much closer to their main base in New York

City and allowed the scanty patriot army to reclaim substantial portions of western New Jersey. The commander could now begin reconstructing his army some thirty miles west of New York City at Morristown, nestled snugly in the Watchung Mountains of north-central New Jersey. Just as significant, Washington had demonstrated, as had Arnold on Lake Champlain, the importance of daring action when facing overwhelmingly unfavorable circumstances. The Trenton and Princeton victories, in conjunction with the resistance effort on Lake Champlain, had stifled the British high command's strategic objectives for 1776.

Meanwhile, Gates's decision to forsake the army for the company of Congress made Washington wary of the ambitions of his former adjutant general. For his part, Gates never effectively explained why he was so anxious to seek out congressional leaders, who had voted on Thursday, December 12, to adjourn to Baltimore out of concern—and in a virtual panic—that Howe's advancing minions might overrun Philadelphia and capture them.[5]

Why Gates, on no one's authorization but his own, rushed to Baltimore, where he arrived "in a very poor state of health" on Saturday, December 28, has served as a source of much speculation. One argument runs that Gates was so physically ill by the time he reached Washington that he had to leave camp for medical help (as if none existed in the army). Gates did suffer from persistent bouts of dysentery, but if he were so debilitated, he surely could have gotten more assistance in Philadelphia, the largest city in North America, than in the much less populous Chesapeake Bay port town of Baltimore. Traveling another one hundred miles beyond Philadelphia to reach Baltimore made no sense for a person in such allegedly ill health.[6]

Something else spurred Gates southward. One possibility is that, fearing total disaster from Washington's planned counterstroke, he intended to show the delegates Lee's derisive letter and urge his New England partisans to demand the repudiation of Washington in favor of a new commander in chief—perhaps even himself, since Lee had become a British prisoner. If that was his purpose, Gates had to set aside this plan, at least for the time being, because of the electrifying news of Washington's Trenton victory.

Baltimore proved quite salubrious to Gates's health. He soon was socializing with the delegates while relying on his New England advocates to help him realize his principal objective: replacing Schuyler. Wrote Samuel Adams on Thursday, January 9, in an unguarded moment, "Congress is very attentive to the northern army. . . . General Gates is here. How shall we make him head of that army?" When answering queries from delegates, Gates kept coming up short in articulating complimentary words for Schuyler. Nor, for the first time, was he supportive of Arnold. Had his fighting comrade known of the contents of a petition—another one of John Brown's damning indictments—that Gates had carried to Congress, or that his trusted friend had come to view him as a serious rival for military preferment, Arnold would not have ridden with such fervency of purpose to yet another war zone, this time in Rhode Island.[7]

II

Even as Gates scurried toward Baltimore, Arnold pushed hard for New Haven. He had crossed the Hudson River and reached Fishkill by Saturday, December 28, hoping to get to New Haven before New Year's Day 1777. Once home, Arnold rejoiced in the company of his sister and sons. The boys greeted their father with the hugs and kisses so often promised him in letters from Hannah. Little Ben, his namesake, was now almost nine years old; Richard, seven; and lively Harry, four. As Arnold expressed amazement at how much they had grown since he had last seen them, he wondered when he might find the time to look for a new spouse for himself and stepmother for the boys.

Noticing their father's limp, his sons wanted to know everything about his war adventures. So, too, with the inhabitants of New Haven, at least those who considered themselves patriots. They welcomed Arnold home as a military veteran of heroic stature. Besides his experiences, they asked about Washington and other ranking military officers. Arnold graciously described them all as truly selfless persons, and he urged his listeners never to forget those patriots who had given their all, men such as Dr. Joseph Warren, who had helped launch his military career with a Massachusetts colonel's commission, and General Richard Montgomery, who had died so bravely a year ago at Quebec.

The community veneration thrilled Arnold. Somehow his neighbors no longer cared whether he was from one of New Haven's old families. Through their attentiveness, he glimpsed in the Revolution the opportunity to break free of the traditional deferential values that had permitted community patriarchs, whether personally meritorious or not, to dominate political and social relationships. The Revolution held the promise for something far better, a republic organized on the principle that ability, achievement, and virtuous service should be the measure of every citizen's worth. Arnold could envision a bold new world in which an "aristocracy of talent" could rise from obscurity to the pinnacle of community respect. If any Connecticut patriot had helped shape the meaning of public virtue during the past year and a half, surely it was Arnold. He now believed more than ever that the ideals of the Revolution would undergird his quest to return his family name to its once-exalted stature.[8]

Arnold did not crave glory solely for himself. Acting as a virtuous patriot, he supported the careers of other meritorious officers. Back in November, he had written Washington to request that "particular notice" be taken of three of his captured Kennebec veterans, Daniel Morgan, John Lamb, and Eleazer Oswald, who had "lately returned on their parole" from Quebec. These dedicated soldiers, who had already "distinguished themselves for their bravery and attachment to the public cause," should be "among the first who are exchanged" for British prisoners, Arnold urged.[9]

Washington responded positively. In January 1777, all three were officially exchanged. Morgan received a colonel's commission and was soon organizing his famous regiment of Virginia riflemen. Lamb, who had survived his disfiguring face wound, also gained a colonel's commission, with orders to establish the 2d Continental Artillery Regiment. Oswald agreed to serve as a lieutenant colonel in the same unit. Lamb soon discovered that Congress would not appropriate funds for cannons, horses, and other accoutrements. When Arnold learned of the situation, he personally underwrote the formation of Lamb's new artillery corps. Knowing there was scant likelihood of repayment, he told Lamb to call on his sister Hannah for a draft of £1,000 in the form of a loan. Deeply appreciative, Lamb named his benefactor's brother-in-law, Samuel Mansfield, one of his captains.[10]

At the same time, Arnold did not just freely disburse his private funds without any reference to supporting his family and himself. In early January, he sat down with Hannah and reviewed his financial accounts. The disruption in trade had taken its toll. Back in September, Hannah had written to him how she had sold virtually every commodity on hand to cover various debts. Because her brother no longer had an inventory of goods for market, she gloomily explained to him that "if you ever live to return you will find yourself a broken merchant."[11]

Since Arnold rarely received wages due him for his Continental service, he had to search for alternate sources of income. Like other New England merchant-traders, he started to invest in privateering ventures. Working through Hannah, he apparently was already employing his brigantine *Polly* in this legalized form of piracy against British supply vessels. Then, in mid-January, he sent a letter to Hector McNeill, seemingly unaware that this mercantile friend from Canada had criticized him before a congressional committee. McNeill had since moved to Boston, where he was organizing privateering ventures. "If there is any stout private ship of war fitting out, that you can recommend," Arnold stated, "I should be glad to be concerned as far as £500, or £800." Thus, even as he shared his financial resources with the Revolutionary cause, he risked his shrinking assets to avoid destitution.[12]

III

Because of the uncertain military situation in Rhode Island, Arnold spent little more than a week in New Haven. As he rode off for the town of Providence, he felt refreshed and as physically fit as ever. Almost thirty-six, he was, even with his slight limp, very much "a fine spirited fellow, and active general," as Nathanael Greene had recently described him to Governor Nicholas Cooke of Rhode Island; and he was once again ready to engage in the dangerous game of rebellion against mighty Great Britain.[13]

Arnold was also conscious that next to his fellow New Havenite David Wooster, he was now the senior brigadier general in the Continental army. If he performed with his usual vitality in Rhode Island, Congress might even advance him in rank. Yet as Arnold guided his mount across the frozen, bleak New England landscape, he also focused his mind on the reality of his detractors. Back in Albany, Gates had warned him that John Brown was still angrily demanding a court of inquiry to clear his name of Arnold's "unjustifiable, false, wicked, and malicious accusation" about the alleged pilfering of captured British officers' baggage. Brown had met with Gates and stated that he would no longer tolerate the "expensive dance from generals to Congress, and from Congress to generals," in efforts to clear his name. The press of military business, Gates rejoined, was why Brown had not had a formal hearing, not some evil plot to deny him justice. In response, Brown asked Gates to carry a petition to Congress calling for Arnold's arrest and court-martial. The Ticonderoga commander agreed to do so—at that juncture with the purpose of stopping Brown from pestering him.[14]

The petition consisted of a litany of thirteen alleged "crimes" committed by Arnold, which Brown was "ready to verify." Besides "endeavoring to asperse your petitioner's character" and "unwarrantably degrading and reducing the rank" conferred on him by Montgomery, Brown denounced Arnold for such abhorrent acts as making a "treasonable attempt" to escape to the enemy in June 1775 after resigning his Massachusetts colonel's commission to the Spooner committee; for allowing smallpox to spread through the camp outside Quebec City by "promoting" inoculations; for "depriving" the army of its "usual" sustenance by reducing rations; for "interfering and countermanding" orders from ranking officers; for "plundering the inhabitants of Montreal"; for issuing "cruel and bloody orders, directing whole villages to be destroyed . . . by fire and sword, without any distinctions to friend or foe, age or sex"; for signing an "unwarrantable, unjustifiable" cartel agreement at the Cedars; and for misusing "his command of the Continental fleet on Lake Champlain, which occasioned the loss thereof." [15]

Even in a sympathetic light, these accusations represented a highly distorted interpretation of reality. A less charitable explanation would suggest that Brown's dogged vendetta against Arnold had become too consuming, perhaps to the point of mental instability. Brown sent a copy of his petition to Theodore Sedgwick, a rising young lawyer in western Massachusetts who had served as General Thomas's military secretary in Canada. He glibly described the document as something "for your amusement," as if his relentless campaign was some form of sport. Brown also wrote confidentially, "You will find some names of witnesses in the margins of the complaint which you are not to communicate lest advantage be taken by the defense." These names certainly included Easton, Hazen, and the field-grade officers who had allowed Hazen's court-martial to degenerate into an assault on Arnold's honesty. [16]

Gates had not shown Brown's condemnatory petition to Arnold, apparently to keep his aggressive subordinate concentrating on military matters during the critical days of December 1776. Had Arnold known the contents, he might not have taken the Rhode Island assignment; instead, he might have gone to Congress to defend his reputation. As it was, even as he rode for Providence, he still held tight to his belief that steadfast service to the cause of liberty was his most profound and rewarding obligation, which bolstered his fighting resolve as he was about to reengage the enemy.

IV

Despite the legends swirling about Arnold, he was not invariably impetuous or incautious as a military leader. A more accurate description would have him taking calculated risks only after evaluating his opponents and concluding that combat might produce a positive outcome. Washington respected Arnold's judicious form of aggressiveness, and that was among the reasons he had ordered America's Hannibal to Rhode Island. The commander needed an astute general officer there, one who would not act too quickly and foment a martial disaster but who was not afraid to harass and possibly even engage the British should circumstances justify military action.

Had Washington thought less of Arnold, he would not have instructed Major General Joseph Spencer to "cooperate with" rather than direct his junior colleague in achieving what was "most conducive to the public good" in Rhode Island. For reasons of protocol, Washington felt bound to call on

Spencer, a brigadier general of Connecticut militia before the rebellion, to assume command in Rhode Island. When first appointing general officers in June 1775, Congress had offered the sixty-one-year-old Spencer a brigadier's commission. The delegates did so after naming one of his militia subordinates, Israel "Old Put" Putnam, to a major generalship. Thoroughly insulted, Spencer sulked at home for a while, letting everyone know how deeply Congress had wounded his pride, before assuming his duties with Washington's army. After a year of ordinary service, Congress, seemingly to make amends, accorded him a major generalship. In ordering Spencer to Rhode Island, Washington may have been reminding New England's congressional delegates that militia preferment and political connections in pre-Revolutionary times bore no necessary relationship to proven martial talent. At the same time, the commander did not leave that region bereft of dynamic generalship, since he had also directed the less well connected but far more capable Arnold to provide leadership "in conjunction with" the higher ranking Spencer.[17]

On Sunday, December 8, a British invasion force of seven thousand under General Henry Clinton had easily captured Newport and the surrounding territory on Rhode Island. Beyond that, the enemy did nothing. Clinton refused to venture north and seize an almost defenseless Providence. Part of the reason was the onset of winter weather; the other was Clinton's lack of enthusiasm about the seaborne offensive against Rhode Island. He was unhappy with his superior, William Howe, for deciding to disperse British forces late in the autumn of 1776, rather than concentrating them on finishing off Washington's army.

Clinton was diffident in personality, once describing himself as "a shy bitch." Although capable of strategic insight, he too often held back in arguing forcefully for his own ideas. One such instance was in November 1776, when he recognized an easy opportunity to level a potentially fatal blow at the rebellion by sailing a detached force up the Delaware River to get behind and entrap Washington's fleeing army. Howe listened instead to his brother, Admiral Richard, Viscount Howe, who was in charge of British naval operations. Swarthy looking "Black Dick," as he was known, thought crushing the rebels could wait a few months. He preferred deploying a land-naval force against Newport, Rhode Island, to obtain additional winter anchorage and a strong foraging base from which his war vessels could also mortify New England privateering vessels. William Howe gave the command assignment to Clinton, who finally acceded after threatening to resign and gaining permission to return to England for a winter's leave.[18]

Arnold, meanwhile, arrived in Providence on Sunday, January 12, where he greeted Spencer. The next day, after securing lodging and reviewing intelligence reports, he sent a report to Washington. Clinton was preparing to depart for England, and the enemy soldiers, about "one half foreigners," had "orders to hold themselves in readiness to embark at a minute's notice, perhaps for New York." They were not planning to attack Providence— welcome news because available patriot strength amounted to about two thousand troops, or one-third the number ordered out by the New England states for emergency duty. "The others are on the march, and expected in, in a few days," the senior brigadier stated. His "hope" was that "we shall be able to give a good account" in dislodging the British.

Arnold's optimism sprang from the victory at Trenton, "a most happy stroke," he noted in complimenting Washington, that had "greatly raised the sinking spirits of the country." He assumed that virtuous New Englanders "in high spirits" would now heed the call to arms in Rhode Island. No popular rush to arms occurred during the winter and spring of 1777, either toward Spencer and Arnold at Providence or toward Washington at Morristown.[19]

Having endured the frustrations of keeping patriot troops in the field during the Canadian invasion, Arnold now gained experience in the equally daunting task of getting civilians to come out and fight in the first place. On Friday, January 31, he described to Washington a battle plan for retaking Newport that was markedly similar to the one he had devised for capturing Quebec. His design was to propel fireships into the British transports in Newport's harbor while maneuvering two large detachments into position to strike at Newport from its land side. "We are making every necessary preparation of boats, artillery, etc.," he explained, with "nothing . . . wanting but men." Arnold's plan required about eight thousand troops, since "a superior force" was necessary to surmount the "great difficulty of coming at the enemy" in control of substantial territory beyond the town. However, only four thousand soldiers, "chiefly raw militia," were then in camp at Providence with "not more than 1,000 more (of the six ordered) . . . expected" to appear. Because of this shortfall, Arnold concluded, "I believe your Excellency will not think it prudent for us to make a general attack."[20]

Washington responded promptly. He was "sorry to find the forces now assembled . . . are not competent to the projects you have in view," and he affirmed the path of discretion. "If the attack" promised "certainty of success," then such "a favorable issue would be productive of the most valuable and important consequences," Washington counseled, but "a miscarriage would lead to those of the most melancholy nature."[21]

Arnold understood. He once again had to accept the frustrating reality of insufficient troop strength, knowing that his battle plan would most likely not be tested. In addition, as he told Washington, the militiamen in camp lacked training in the manual of arms and were serving only on renewable monthly enlistments. They were soldiers "on whom little or no dependence can be placed," since they would most likely flee the field of combat the moment they faced concentrated British firepower, if they did not rush home on the eve of an attack. What Arnold and Spencer needed were seasoned Continentals committed to long-term service, but very few were available to them—or to Washington for that matter.[22]

On Monday, February 10, Arnold again wrote to Washington with mixed news. Spencer had just returned from Boston, where he had convinced Massachusetts officials to send forward one thousand Continentals. Unfortunately, the general had received only a trifling sum, £1,000 in local currency, to provide wages for these troops. Connecticut had already "been applied to in vain" for funds, without "which every wheel in this department moves slow." Once again, Arnold found himself agonizing over shortages of every kind while wondering how, in the absence of widespread public support, to keep making war against superior numbers of highly disciplined, well-supplied enemy troops.[23]

Much to Arnold's relief, he received an unexpected respite from his daily labors. Spencer asked him to continue his effort "to raise a few Continental battalions for our intended attacks." Arnold soon rode east to the vicinity of Boston, where he found himself feted as he had been in New Haven. Local leaders sought him out, wanting to meet America's Hannibal. Well-to-do hosts and hostesses were eager to have him attend their social gatherings. Basking in the adulation, Arnold decided to cut a more stylish figure. He contacted an old acquaintance, Paul Revere, and asked for assistance in obtaining a "sword knot, sash, [and] two belt apparatus," as well as "one dozen silk hose," to wear with his dress uniform, all of which he promised to pay for immediately.[24]

Although Arnold maintained a stylish wardrobe, he had a special reason to be impeccably dressed while in Boston. He intended to make a favorable impression on young Elizabeth De Blois, the attractive daughter of a wealthy loyalist merchant who had fled Boston with the British army back in March 1776. Virtually nothing is known about "Betsy" De Blois, making her a source of many fanciful tales. Her only claim to something more than historical anonymity rests on Arnold's infatuation with her. He apparently met Betsy at a Boston social gathering, and he decided she should become his wife.[25]

Because of his acquaintance with Washington's talented artillery chief,

Henry Knox, Arnold asked Knox's wife, Lucy Flucker, also the daughter of a wealthy loyalist merchant, to present his case to "the heavenly Miss De Blois." Relishing the role of matchmaker, Lucy delivered a letter to Betsy along "with the trunk of gowns, etc." provided by Arnold. He hoped that Betsy would accept these gifts as well as his desire to court her. Until he heard from Lucy, he would "remain under the most anxious suspense," he wrote in a romantic flourish, caused by "the fond anxiety, the glowing hopes, and chilling fears, that alternately possess the breast of . . . your obedient and most humble servant."[26]

Arnold was back in Providence by Friday, March 8. He could not justify staying in Boston, he explained to Schuyler, because Washington had pre-empted his search for troops and money by ordering all Continental regiments then in Massachusetts to Ticonderoga. Since the commander had also authorized smallpox inoculations for Connecticut's Continental enlistees, they would not be readily available for duty. In a near-exasperated tone, Arnold told his Yorker patron that defensive operations were the only option in Rhode Island. As such, Arnold had begun to wonder about his own field assignment for the upcoming campaign season. He was hoping Schuyler would request his presence in the Northern Department, thereby rescuing him from what he thought would remain an inactive war zone in 1777.[27]

A few days later, Arnold shared another complaint with Nathanael Greene. "The wise assembly of this state," he wrote sarcastically, had publicly chastised Spencer and him for leaving the British too "long unmolested" at Newport. Since the two general officers seemed so unassertive, the Assembly had instructed Spencer "to attack . . . immediately." Poor, intimidated Spencer, hoping to "avoid the anathemas of the great and general assembly," was toiling to get the militia troops ready for a strike. Arnold could not believe the obliviousness of the local legislators regarding the human and material resources needed to dislodge the British, and he would keep urging Spencer to ignore so insensible an order.[28]

Arnold's admonitions for military sanity helped settle down a rattled Spencer. No offensive operations took place in Rhode Island that spring, which was fortunate in a way for Arnold, who was about to face a profoundly disturbing crisis.

V

Amid the combat blows of 1776, Washington had called for "a respectable army," one in which Continental enlistees committed themselves to long-term service, defined as three years or the duration of the martial contest.

These troops, unlike the short-term Continental recruits of 1775 and 1776 or militia more generally, had to become the kind of hardened warriors, based on rigorous training and discipline, who could hold their own against enemy musket and cannon fire or bayonet charges. The commander also coveted meritorious officers—specifically, virtuous patriots of demonstrated talent who could work together harmoniously while inspiring the confidence of their troops.[29]

Without such a regular force of long-termers, Washington doubted whether the rebellion could be sustained against superior British arms. Congress was reluctant to concede the point. Most delegates held fast to the ideal of a citizens' army, with the ranks filled by liberty-loving, property-holding patriots. They eschewed any form of standing army, which conjured up images of automaton soldiers loyal only to the commands of their officers. Such military forces, historical experience seemed to confirm, could become destroyers of basic rights and liberties, should soldiers and officers become disenchanted with the polity they had initially pledged to serve under arms. As a consequence, Samuel Adams stated in January 1776, every standing army was a potential source of destructive "power" and "should be watched with a jealous eye."[30]

Military necessity in the wake of the massive British land and sea offensive of 1776 forced Congress to vote in favor of expanding and regularizing the Continental army. After 1776, long-term Continental service became the preserve of unpropertied and unfree inhabitants in Revolutionary America. Like rank-and-file soldiers of European armies, these men and women had little or no economic or political stake in society. As such, they represented the human cannon fodder characteristic of standing armies. At least in theory, they seemed like the very kind of soldier-automatons that Samuel Adams feared might rend the fabric of the new republic, should their officers decide to challenge civil government—even to the point of overthrowing republican institutions in favor of a military dictatorship.

Because of these concerns, congressional leaders after 1776 became more exacting about maintaining the superiority of civil authority over the Continental army. Indeed, the delegates who regathered in Baltimore acted like a chastened group because they had just failed to do so. When they bolted from Philadelphia in December 1776, they had conveyed virtual dictatorial powers to Washington. Congress quickly reasserted itself as the political master of the Revolution. Even before the delegates learned about Trenton and Princeton, they were already constricting the powers conveyed to Washington. Among other limitations, he was not to appoint or discharge general officers, a key prerogative if Congress intended to monitor and control a more respectable but also more latently dangerous army. Always sensitive to keeping the military subordinate to civil authority, Washington readily acceded.[31]

In late January 1777 the commander wrote Congress from Morristown to request an expansion of the general officer corps, since the delegates had long since committed themselves—on paper—to a greatly enlarged Continental force. The expanded army, Washington indicated, needed at least three lieutenant, nine major, and twenty-seven brigadier generals. Washington assumed that seniority in one rank would be the prevailing criterion for promotion to the next. Suddenly assertive, the delegates were not going to let their temporary dictator advise them too closely. They quickly dismissed his proposal for lieutenant generals. Too many ranks and titles seemed very unrepublican, a throwback to the finely graded but artificial distinctions of European aristocracies and military institutions. Furthermore, basing promotions only on seniority would effectively deprive the delegates of the capacity to appoint and promote general officers as they saw fit, which they interpreted to mean in the best interests of the republic.[32]

Also in reaction to Washington's request, the delegates engaged in what North Carolinian Thomas Burke called a "perplexed, inconclusive, and irksome" weeklong debate over "fixing a rule of promotion" for general officers. On Wednesday, February 19, they finally resolved "that in voting for general officers, a due regard shall be had to the line of succession, the merit of the persons proposed, and the quota of troops raised, and to be raised, by each state." By applying these three standards, Congress hoped to be fairminded and "judicious" in its appointments. In reality, however, virtually no patriot, no matter how deserving, could measure up on all three counts. Thus the delegates were free to do as they pleased. Under the guise of the third criterion, that of state troop quotas, they attempted to balance off competing local interests, or what a New York delegate called "colonial prejudices." The result was a glorious triumph for political parochialism at the expense of assuring the most capable leadership for the Continental army.[33]

By the first measure, seniority in rank, Wooster and Arnold were at the top of the list of brigadier generals. By the second, merit, Arnold could easily claim a superior record among the current group of brigadiers, even when discounting the persistent and damaging commentary of his detractors. By the third, troop quotas, Connecticut had done more than its fair share early on in the war. Now what mattered were future manpower allotments. Since

Connecticut already had two major generals, Israel Putnam and Joseph Spencer, that state did not seem to deserve a third, regardless of Arnold's seniority or merit.[34]

The delegates selected five new major generals before finishing their deliberations on February 19. Senior brigadier Arnold was not among them. William Alexander (Lord Stirling) of New Jersey, Thomas Mifflin and Arthur St. Clair of Pennsylvania, Adam Stephen of Virginia, and Benjamin Lincoln of Massachusetts were the delegates' preferences. Only one, Alexander, had arguably performed at something above a pedestrian level; and Lincoln was not even in the Continental service. Although he had shown his competence as a major general of militia, the bulk of Lincoln's experience related to the training of troops.[35]

The promotion proceedings appalled delegate Thomas Burke. Since he "knew nothing of the merit of any officers in nomination," he "did not choose to give a vote . . . for which he could give no reason." He also claimed that Congress, once having adopted promotion guidelines, took "no notice" of them in their deliberations, except in some unfathomable relationship to assigned troop quotas. Thus, even as John Adams spoke glowingly on behalf of Lincoln, the Connecticut delegation only "mentioned" Arnold and Wooster "on the first two principles."[36]

Several factors thwarted Arnold's candidacy. Among them was Congress's determination to keep the general officers subordinate to civil authority. Washington had mentioned "some persons" who warranted promotions—Arnold was likely among the names—"as a hint to Congress," indicated delegate Francis Lewis of New York. Paying too close attention to the commander's recommendations, argued John Adams, might compromise Congress's prerogatives. Although Adams thought Washington a most worthy person, he was merely a servant of Congress in his military post. "In this house I feel myself his superior," Adams proclaimed, and he chided delegates who were so "disposed to idolize an image which their own hands have molten." The "superstitious veneration" of the commander in chief had to stop in the name of upholding civil authority. As such, Arnold's close identification with Washington worked against him in Congress's deliberations.[37]

Exclusive of the matter of seniority, Arnold's best case rested on sustained meritorious service. He had earned a hero's portion of gratitude from Congress, but denigrating allegations about his judgment and integrity kept descending on the delegates. Then, in a matter of bad timing for Arnold, John Brown had conveniently encapsulated many of these aspersions in his defaming petition, which Congress had received from Gates little more than a month before its deliberations. America's Hannibal thus seemed to possess too many flaws for some delegates, especially those who were pushing favorites from their own states.

Nor did the Connecticut delegation offer much support. Roger Sherman, who had years before fined Arnold for thrashing the informer Peter Boles, was mostly apathetic about his fellow New Havenite's fate. When Sherman finally reported on the promotions to Governor Trumbull, he did so as an afterthought in a letter announcing that Congress had returned to Philadelphia. Wrote an indifferent Sherman, "Connecticut had more general officers than in proportion to the number of troops furnished by that state."[38]

One influential person who could have spoken up on Arnold's behalf was Horatio Gates. Before responding to orders from Washington and leaving Baltimore in mid-February to take command of militia units at Philadelphia, the Ticonderoga commander made favorable references to general officers like Arthur St. Clair. Yet Gates apparently did not rebut Brown's petition, nor did he make any effort to commend Arnold.

Gates's silence related directly to Washington's December decision about selecting general officers for the Rhode Island command. A cadre of New England delegates had vigorously besought Washington to name Gates or Greene. Having already chosen Arnold and Spencer, the commander declined their request. Washington intended no slight to Gates; rather, he was thinking of how much the main army could benefit from that officer's return to the adjutant's post. Gates's displeasure in not obtaining what he most craved, an independent line command like the Rhode Island assignment, helped provoke his headlong rush to Baltimore to press his own case for advancement.

As for Arnold, Gates now viewed him as a serious competitor for major command appointments. The former British major was not about to advocate the promotion of an officer whom Washington had so recently preferred over him. By not supporting his newfound rival, Gates had conveniently served himself and his own grand ambitions. Before the turbulent year of 1777 was over, he would endeavor to destroy Arnold's military career.

For a host of reasons, then, the delegates passed over Arnold. After wheeling and dealing among themselves and balancing off conflicting local and state interests, the delegates acted as if their determinations were sacrosanct. If neglected officers complained about their sullied honor, they should be disregarded as unworthy patriots, stated John Adams. "I have no fears from the resignation of officers if junior officers are preferred to them," he declared during the debates. "If they have virtue they will continue with us. If not, their resignation will not hurt us."[39]

Curiously, two days after Congress passed over Arnold, Adams was grum-
bling that nonmeritorious officers—he named Major Generals Philip
Schuyler, Israel Putnam, Joseph Spencer, and William Heath—were already
too prevalent in the army's highest ranks. These four gentlemen, he went on
to assert, were "thought by very few to be capable of the great commands
they hold." Then he declared, "I wish they would all resign." Adams neglected to mention that Congress was responsible for these appointments in
the first place, largely to gratify noisome, if not powerful, local interests
Almost disingenuously, he chose to ignore that the delegates, in their naming
of additional general officers in February 1777, had only sustained their
pattern of shortsighted decision making.[40]

Delegate Burke said it all when he indicated that Congress had again
acted as it pleased, by which he meant the delegates had bowed first and
foremost to parochial influences. In the process, Arnold had lost out, predicated on the convenient rationalization that Connecticut, based on state
troop quotas, already had its fair number of major generals in Putnam and
Spencer, whom Adams himself stated had shown themselves incapable of
"heroic deeds of arms."[41]

VI

Washington wrote to Arnold with the distressing news on Monday, March
3. He began his letter with a reference to military business, again cautioning
against any attack on Newport unless "you can reasonably promise yourself
a *moral certainty* of succeeding." Then he addressed the vexing matter of
promotions, stating that he was "at a loss whether you have had a preceding
appointment, as the newspapers announce, or whether you have been omitted through some mistake." Apparently even newspaper editors were incredulous about Congress's actions, so they repeated an erroneous rumor about
an earlier promotion for Arnold. The commander promised to investigate.
Meanwhile, he stated solicitously, "I beg you will not take any hasty steps in
consequence of it; but allow proper time for recollection, which, I flatter
myself, will remedy any error that may have been made."[42]

Three days later, Washington sent a carefully phrased note to Richard
Henry Lee, his old and close Virginia friend in Congress. He was "anxious
to know whether General Arnold's non-promotion was owing to accident or
design." Then he stated his own sentiments rhetorically: "Surely a more
active, a more spirited, and sensible officer, fills no department in your
army." Washington went on to express great "uneasiness" that Arnold, "being
the oldest brigadier," would not "continue in service under such a slight."

Just as worrisome, the commander suspected that other valuable officers might resign when they learned that seniority and merit carried so little weight with Congress.[43]

Arnold, meanwhile, opened and read Washington's letter at Providence, most likely on Monday, March 10. The commander's tactful prose represented the first notification about his denial of promotion. The words stunned America's Hannibal. He considered Schuyler's warnings about pretended patriots who would promote their own petty careers by belittling those who were truly virtuous. These artists of calumny—the Browns, Eastons, and Hazens—had indeed succeeded with Congress, Arnold quickly concluded. He hardly seemed surprised, since he had grown wary of that body's competency to support the war effort properly.

As Arnold wrestled with his wrathful feelings, he ruminated about his June 1775 confrontation with the Spooner committee at Crown Point. Then he had peremptorily resigned, but he had acted too rashly, he had come to realize, and almost ruined any further chance to serve the patriot war effort. Only good fortune and the patronage of Washington, Schuyler, and Gates had resulted in a second chance. Now he would proceed more rationally. Should his resignation become necessary, he would leave the army with his personal dignity intact, and only after making every effort to reclaim his honor as a patriot who had tried to serve the Revolutionary cause with distinction.

Allowing his fury to subside, Arnold waited until the next day to respond to Washington. As had the commander in chief, he first discussed the local military situation. He remained "fearful" that launching a "general action" without "our new levies ... in a manner complete" would "end in our disgrace." Then Arnold turned to his own situation. He generously thanked Washington "for interesting yourself so much on my behalf," before stating that "Congress have doubtless a right of promoting those, whom, from their abilities, their long and arduous services, they esteem the most deserving." However, by elevating "junior officers" over him, the delegates had chosen "a very civil way of requesting my resignation, as unqualified for the office I hold." Since they had "conferred unsolicited" to him his brigadier's commission, which he had "received with pleasure only as a means of serving my country," he would "with equal pleasure ... resign it, when I can no longer serve my country with *honor*."

Arnold had cut to the heart of the issue: Promotions were a sign of community favor and should rightfully come as a reward for virtuous service. "When I entered the service of my country," he explained, "my character was unimpeached. I have sacrificed my interest, ease, and happiness in her cause." In his "zeal for the safety and happiness of my country, in whose cause I have repeatedly fought and bled, and am ready at all times to resign my life," he thought he had demonstrated his merit. Congress, however, had recast his personal reputation as an object unworthy of the community's admiration. Because he felt so aggrieved, he, like every other gentleman, had an obligation to defend his personal honor from such obvious censure. "The person who ... will tamely condescend to give up his rights, and hold a commission at the expense of his reputation, I hold as a disgrace to the army," he concluded, "and unworthy of the glorious cause in which we are engaged."

Arnold could not "in justice, therefore, to my own character, and for the satisfaction of my friends," continue to hold his commission without "a court of inquiry into my conduct" that investigated and cleared his name of every false allegation. Still, even though he "sensibly" felt "every personal injury" to his reputation and "the ingratitude of my countrymen," he promised not to do anything "to injure my country" by taking "any hasty step." He promised not to "leave this department," not with a dangerous enemy force still lodged in and around Newport, until his departure could be effected without "any damage to the public interest."[44]

Subscribing as he did to the gentleman's code, Arnold held his sense of ravaged honor in check so that he did not somehow injure the cause that was now treating him so capriciously. He wanted to show himself more worthy than the likes of John Sullivan, who had forsaken the Champlain region out of pique over losing his command to Gates. As Arnold had then sarcastically observed, the New Hampshire general had secured from Congress a promotion to a major generalship as a seeming reward for abandoning the field. He was sure the delegates would not treat him so graciously, based on their repudiation of his claim to promotion. Arnold's primary objective had therefore become that of cleansing his own name of the calumnies he assumed had caused his nonpromotion. Once he had accomplished that purpose, he would decide whether to continue in the service, depending on how Congress responded to the findings of the court of inquiry.

These thoughts only made Arnold more anxious to besiege Congress; yet in a striking display of dedicated officership and maturity of temperament, he held himself in check. As he had previously demonstrated, he took his duties too seriously to leave his command post with the enemy just over the horizon. He also held back out of respect for his patron Washington, who had promised to make inquiries on his behalf.[45]

For two weeks, Arnold struggled to contain his instinctive impatience. On Tuesday, March 25, he finally vented some of his pent-up indignation in a revealing letter to Gates, whom he did not yet recognize as a duplicitous patron. Arnold made three points, the first of which was that he considered Congress nothing more than "a body of men who seem to be governed by *whim and caprice.*" Their actions had "surprised and mortified" him. When he had accepted his brigadier's commission, he had no idea the delegates, in what he considered "extremely cruel" behavior, had elevated him "for their sport, or pastime, to displace or disgrace when they thought proper, without sufficient reason, and giving me an opportunity to be heard in my defense."

The apparent whimsy of Congress, Arnold next declared, would have disabling long-term effects on the war effort. "I think it betrays want of judgment, and weakness, to appoint officers and break, or displace them, on trifling occasions," he stated. The danger was that "if this plan is pursued, no gentleman who has any regard for his reputation will risk it" for the cause of liberty: "Had I been content with barely doing my duty, I might have remained at ease and in safety, and not attracted the notice of the malicious, or envious." The Revolution seemed destined to fail, he was saying, unless Congress mustered the courage to recognize and advance its most illustrious officers.

Arnold's third point, based on his assumption that Congress lacked sound judgment, was that he was surely the victim of "some villain" who "has been busy with my fame and basely slandered me." In response to those who had so persistently defamed him, he contended categorically, "I am conscious of committing no crime since in the public service that merits disgrace, except it be a crime to have sacrificed my interest, ease, and happiness in the public cause." Acutely feeling "the unmerited injury my countrymen had done me," Arnold concluded in a flurry of suppressed rage, "By heavens I will have justice, and I'm a villain if I seek not a brave revenge for injured honor."

Throughout this tormented communication, Arnold revealed the depth of his anguish while beseeching his comrade for assistance. He specifically asked for copies of Gates's August 7 orders relating to the command of the Champlain fleet, as well as their correspondence while he served on the lake. (Arnold had lost his copies with the capture and burning of the *Royal Savage.*) He needed these materials for the court of inquiry he had requested, since he could not "think of drawing my sword until my reputation, which is dearer than life, is cleared up." [46]

In a momentary release of so much aggravation, Arnold stated that he would first resign his commission before participating in a court of inquiry. He did not, however, make the same statement in writing to Washington the next day. He first expressed concern over a report that "your Excellency was exceedingly ill with a fever." Then he addressed the military situation in

Rhode Island, mentioning that "we now confine ourselves to a defensive position only." Finally, he briefly spoke of Congress's "implicit impeachment of my character," pointing out that when conditions permitted, he would vacate his post with the intention of getting on with a court of inquiry and acquitting "myself of every charge malice or envy can bring against me."[47]

Composed within a day of each other, these letters were strikingly different in tone. Arnold was very formal with Washington. Respecting the commander's request for patience, he made no reference to a possible early resignation. To Gates he revealed his inner torment. Arnold obviously felt a close personal bond of friendship with Gates. They had campaigned together, and they had shared moments of despair and elation in resisting Carleton's movement out of Canada. By comparison, Arnold had met with Washington on only a few occasions. He did not feel comfortable sharing the depth of his emotional turmoil with the distant, reserved, imposing commander in chief. What Arnold did not yet fully appreciate was that Washington genuinely cared about his dilemma—and wanted to help him. By comparison, Gates, his putative brother in arms, never responded to his appeal for assistance.

Each day seemed to drag by for Arnold as he met with Spencer and dealt with the problems of supplying and strengthening the patriot force at Providence. As rumors reached Providence about Congress's decision to predicate new major generalships on state troop quotas, Arnold pondered his personal predicament of being trapped below more favored men like Spencer, who had gotten where they were because of influence, not military talent. Still, Arnold did not evidence any ill will toward this aging, phlegmatic officer. His correspondence indicates that he kept working harmoniously with him.

Certainly Arnold respected Spencer's seniority, since that criterion represented one basis for his own claim to higher rank. At the same time, he asked himself whether demonstrated merit in the performance of public service would ever become the basis for advancement in the newly formed republic. The Revolution, he believed, could not endure without proper community recognition for virtuous service. He now felt nothing but indignation toward civilians in Congress who did not appreciate or respect that precept. With such myopic leadership, he wondered just how long devoted patriots like himself should continue to serve a cause lacking the fortitude to realize its own ideals. The distasteful sensation of being used—and abused— left an empty feeling and caused Arnold to ponder, as he had not done before, the Revolution's essential integrity.

As March gave way to April and the New England landscape showed the first vernal signs of spring, Arnold heard again from Washington. The commander lauded the senior brigadier for staying at his assigned post before mentioning that he had asked General Greene, who had been in Philadelphia, to look into what "principle" Congress had used in selecting general officers. The response was in "proportion . . . to the number of men" furnished by each state. Since "Connecticut had already two major generals, . . . their full share," the delegates had passed over Arnold. "I confess this is a strange mode of reasoning," Washington admitted, but "it may serve to show you, that the promotion which was due to your seniority, was not overlooked for want of merit in you."[48]

These comments did nothing to appease Arnold. Congress, he realized, could insist that seniority and merit were also essential criteria on which to award promotions—but now, apparently, only for officers who were fortunate enough to live in more populous states, since enlistment quotas directly reflected population distribution. Should there be no senior officers who had evidenced real military talent from more populous states, then Congress, to appease noisome leaders from these polities, would of necessity have to advance persons of ordinary accomplishments over those of undisputed merit from less populous states, as the delegates had essentially done in February 1777. Public rewards in the form of military promotions now were apparently to be more a function of one's place of residence than one's record of service. Such a system, Arnold reasoned, seemed just as arbitrary as Britain's, which gave every advantage to favored bloodline aristocrats, regardless of ability. He found this prospect appalling and personally stifling, especially for a Revolution devoted, at least on a rhetorical plane, to recognizing and rewarding true talent and merit.

Washington also pointed out that "public bodies" of governance "are not amenable for their actions" and "can place and displace at pleasure," a statement that made Arnold wonder about the purpose of the Revolution in the first place. Had he been duped, he wondered, into exchanging one form of tyranny for another? In addition, since Congress denied the influence of slanderous comments in passing over him, Washington did "not see upon what ground you can demand a court of inquiry." In short, with "no particular charge . . . alleged against you," Arnold could not even formally defend his honor. What Washington asked was that his valued subordinate gracefully accept his bedeviling set of circumstances, knowing that "when . . . overlooked" he could rest secure, "if innocent" of any wrongdoing, with "a consciousness that he has not deserved such treatment for his honest exertions."[49]

Arnold could not bring himself to abide by Washington's temperate advice. He would never submit to petty, self-serving despots, whether they came in the form of Brown, Easton, Hazen, or leaders in Congress. He would never bow before the capricious will of such persons, because for him they were no different from his mother's vengeful Calvinist God or the Norwichites of his youth who had been so full of harsh judgment at the time of his father's tragic descent into an alcoholic's death. As Arnold had promised himself long ago, he would always resist despotic power. So he now determined, as he soon informed Washington, to travel to Philadelphia, resign his commission, persist in his demand for a court of inquiry, and exact "brave revenge for injured honor," to draw on his words to Gates.

VII

Arnold bid farewell to Spencer in mid-April. He directed his horse to New Haven, where he planned to comfort himself with the adoring family fellowship of his sons and sister before proceeding on to Philadelphia. Likewise, he wanted to review his languishing business affairs, since after two years of active military campaigning, he might well soon be returning to his life as a civilian merchant-trader.

By the time Arnold reached New Haven, news had caught up with him about "the heavenly" Betsy De Blois. Lucy Knox had sent word to her husband that "Miss De Blois has positively refused to listen to the general, which with his other mortification will come very hard upon him." Various stories range from Betsy accepting the injunctions of her strong-willed loyalist mother, who refused to let her daughter have anything to do with a rebel general, to her falling in love with a Boston stay maker of no particular means, with whom she nearly eloped. At the moment, however, Arnold had scant time to fret over Betsy's rejection, since a far more stinging form of "mortification" had befallen him.[50]

One of Arnold's goals in going to Philadelphia was to settle his financial accounts from the previous campaign season. Many of the records were lost to him because of the destruction of the *Royal Savage*. He dreaded having to present his case without key documents, especially with accusations of plunder hanging over him. Until he had better evidence, which he still hoped to obtain from Schuyler and Gates, to prove his expenditures, he would not press Congress too hard for a settlement.

As Arnold planned for his journey, he thought about his three military patrons—Washington, Schuyler, and Gates. Most of all, he felt wrongheadedly aggrieved about Washington's apparent lack of vigorous support. He failed to appreciate that the commander wanted to avoid any appearance of dictating to Congress, which could have ruined Arnold's case. During April, Washington was still encouraging Richard Henry Lee to speak with other delegates about preventing "the loss of so good an officer" as Arnold. The commander did more than intimate his own feelings this time. "I could wish to see Arnold promoted to the rank of major general, and put in his proper place," he told Lee before concluding, "It is by men of his activity and spirit the cause is to be supported, and not by H[eat]h, Sp[ence]r, etc." Lee promised to "exert" himself on Arnold's behalf.[51]

Arnold was likewise unaware that Washington had stood up to the fulminations of John Brown, who had appeared at Morristown in mid-February. Washington listened patiently as Brown angrily described Arnold's putative sins and pressed for an immediate court of inquiry. The commander explained that Brown's adversary was again executing a critical military assignment, this time in Rhode Island. Military necessity, not some pernicious plot by ranking general officers, had kept Arnold on duty in the field. Washington refused to offer any form of appeasement to Brown, who a month later defended his own honor by resigning his commission.[52]

Had Arnold placed greater confidence in Washington, he would have held himself at bay in dealing directly with Congress. Then, on Saturday, April 26, even as he was making final preparations to depart for Philadelphia, a courier galloped into New Haven with shocking news. A large, menacing British detachment had landed the previous evening near Norwalk, Connecticut, some thirty miles to the west. At last report this column was marching inland, presumably toward Danbury, the site of a major patriot supply depot. Arnold hardly hesitated as he pondered whether he would still fight for the cause of liberty. He prepared himself for combat.

Fourteen

The Humiliating Part of a Faithful Soldier

I

Benedict Arnold bore a grimly tenacious expression as he rode through the jagged hills of western Connecticut on Saturday, April 26. Accompanying him was a small band of New Haven neighbors, among them David Wooster. As they pressed northwestward, they sent out pleas for local citizens to come out and join them. By the time they reached Redding, some eight miles south of Danbury, darkness had fallen. Soaking wet from heavy spring downpours, they were a dejected lot, as only about one hundred militiamen had responded to their supplications for assistance.

Local militia General Gold S. Silliman was already at Redding, along with some five hundred citizen-soldiers whom he had mustered from communities directly in the path of the invading force. The three generals exchanged greetings, and Silliman briefed his New Haven comrades on the day's events. The British raiding column had marched twenty-three miles inland and reached Danbury late that afternoon. Truculent William Tryon, New York's defrocked royal governor who had recently taken command of loyalist troops attached to William Howe's main army, was in command of about two thousand troops, including some fifteen hundred light infantrymen and a battalion of five hundred loyalists.

Silliman provided additional details, based on reports from Continental troops stationed at Danbury. When word of the approaching enemy force first reached these soldiers, who numbered about 150 men, they hid what few supplies they could. Then, as the thudding cadence of the marching British column drew within earshot, they scattered in all directions. Once in the village, Tryon ordered his troops to destroy everything—food, clothing, shoes, medicines, and various camp equipage, including seventeen hundred tents. Nor did the raiders let the rain prevent them from setting fire to some forty homes and outbuildings, a few of which also held patriot supplies. By day's end, they had methodically destroyed Danbury.

Tryon, Arnold commented, believed in employing both fire and sword, even against civilians, as a tactic to shatter patriot morale. Somehow the enemy column had to be given a severe thrashing, if for no other reason than to bolster the languishing resolve of the pusillanimous among Connecticut's inhabitants. Arnold could envision thousands of lukewarm patriots renouncing the Revolution and readopting their former British allegiance out of fear that future sorties like Tryon's might result in the loss of their families and property.

Hoping for some sort of psychological turnabout, Arnold encouraged his fellow officers to approach Danbury with the idea of more closely monitoring the enemy. The others agreed, and the militiamen were soon trudging through mud toward Bethel, just two miles southeast of Danbury. They reached that hamlet near 2 A.M. on Sunday, April 27, and they could now make out a faint glow along the horizon from the smoldering ruins of Danbury. The generals told their troops to dry their powder and weapons and get some rest. They could expect to move out sometime after dawn.

Initially, Arnold conjectured that Tryon would lead his raiders southwestward through the rugged terrain of Westchester County, New York, most likely toward Tarrytown, where British vessels would be waiting on the Hudson River to retrieve them. He had already sent a message to Brigadier General Alexander McDougall, who was in command of a detachment of Continentals at Peekskill, about fifteen miles north of Tarrytown, asking him to cut off Tryon's force. The Connecticut column, Arnold promised, would focus on harassing the enemy's flanks and rear.[1]

McDougall soon had twelve hundred Continentals on the move, but to no avail. Tryon, having seen how easily his column had "proceeded with very little opposition" so deeply into Connecticut, decided to march back from whence he came. As a precautionary move, he selected an alternate route, one that would take his column through the town of Ridgefield, not quite a third of the way to the coastline. Prepared for this contingency, the patriot generals agreed that Wooster should annoy the enemy's rear with two hundred men. Arnold and Silliman were to march cross-country with the remaining four hundred troops for Ridgefield, where they would form a defensive line and directly challenge the enemy.[2]

Near 9 A.M. on April 27, with rain showers still lingering, Tryon ordered his column to evacuate Danbury. Once sure the enemy was marching south,

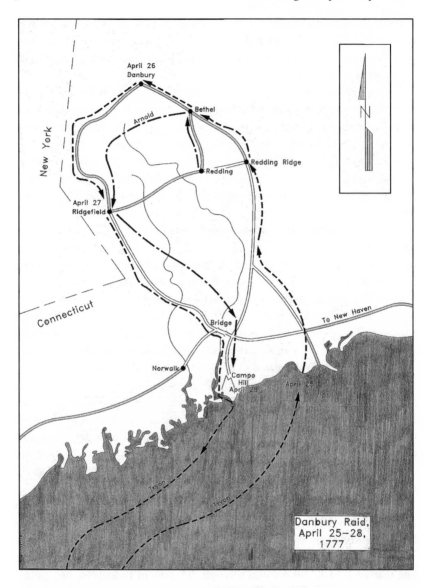

the rebel force divided into two columns. As Arnold and Silliman moved toward Ridgefield, another one hundred or so militiamen joined them. They now had five hundred citizen-soldiers with whom to intercept two thousand of His Majesty's troops. Unfavorable ratios, commonplace for Arnold, could not deter so determined a warrior. Once in Ridgefield, he and Silliman selected an easily defensible position, a narrow point in the road flanked on one side by a rocky ledge and on the other by a farmhouse and outbuildings. The troops entrenched themselves in a line across the road, and Arnold kept reassuring one and all that the day, with the blessings of Providence, would be theirs.

As the hour approached 11 A.M., even before Arnold and Silliman reached Ridgefield, Wooster's troops struck at Tryon's rear guard. The raiders responded quickly, and they were soon upon the Americans. Intending to keep punching and running, Wooster ordered a retreat just as an enemy musket ball tore into his groin. He was thrown to the ground, stunned and bleeding; his distraught son tried to assist him up. Enemy troops charged forward, and when Wooster's son refused to ask for quarter, a soldier ran him through with a bayonet, killing him instantly. Not interested in taking prisoners, they ignored Wooster who, having been recalled from Canada in virtual disgrace less than a year before, died five days later at the age of sixty-six, having given his life and his son's to the cause of liberty.[3]

Wooster's attack momentarily delayed the British column, effectively purchasing valuable time for Arnold and Silliman. Before mid-afternoon, their citizen-soldiers were waiting nervously behind a breastwork of earth, stone, logs, and wagons. Near three o'clock, Tryon's column marched into view. Arnold cautioned everyone not to waste their fire, even as the British launched a frontal attack. Heavily outnumbered, the patriot line held steady, much to Tryon's amazement. In response, he ordered out flanking parties. When one company reached the top of the ledge, they opened up with disrupting enfilade fire.

The citizen-soldiers started to break and run. In desperation, America's Hannibal brandished his sword and rode back and forth, trying to form a rear guard to protect his fleeing column. Suddenly Arnold's horse collapsed. Having been hit by nine musket balls, the tortured animal, thrashing in death throes, had his rider pinned to the ground. An enemy soldier, climbing off the ledge, rushed forward with bayoneted musket in hand. Supposedly he shouted, "Surrender! You are my prisoner!" "Not yet," was Arnold's alleged reply as he deftly retrieved a pistol from his saddle holster, took aim, and leveled his adversary with one shot. Freeing himself from the flailing horse, Arnold hobbled off toward a nearby swamp, with enemy musket balls flying all around him. His hairbreadth escape was a testament to what England's *Annual Register* of 1777 called his "usual intrepidity." A British officer on the scene conceded only that Arnold, like Wooster before him, had "opposed us with more obstinacy than skill," a statement of begrudging respect.[4]

Arnold's impertinent stand at Ridgefield caused Tryon to halt his march.

Besides suffering from postbattle fatigue, his raiders had sustained several casualties, and they were still more than fifteen miles from the coastline, too far to traverse before darkness enveloped them. Posting sentries, the British tended to their wounded and buried their dead while resting that night near the Ridgefield battle site.

Since the outset of his expedition, Tryon had worried about provoking massive patriot resistance comparable to the outpouring at Lexington and Concord. He was not taking much of a gamble in stopping for the evening, he was sure, because his rout of Wooster's force and easy victory at Ridgefield would serve to dampen any additional surge of patriot opposition. Should resistance continue, Tryon felt he could more safely move his column to the coastline during daylight hours, as long as he deployed wide-ranging flanking parties to drive off possible gatherings of pesky patriots along his route.

Arnold, meanwhile, worked feverishly throughout the night to reassemble his force. Locating two guides, he rode through the surrounding countryside, according to one officer, "in order to stir up the people and collect them so as to make a stand." By early morning on Monday, April 28, he had raised the rebel standard two miles north of Norwalk at a geographic point where Tryon would have to follow one of two roads to the coast. No matter which way the enemy column turned, Arnold planned to attack its flanks and rear. As one participant noted, he had "made the best disposition possible of his little army." Exhausted and still hopelessly outnumbered, Arnold was now ready for further combat, "as much as circumstances would permit." [5]

At daybreak, Tryon ordered his troops to continue their southward march. Local loyalists told him where Arnold was concentrating his citizen-soldiers, so he instructed his detachment to turn left toward the Saugatuck River, just north of the patriot position. By the time Arnold learned about Tryon's maneuver, he could not redeploy his force quickly enough to strike effectively at the enemy column. Alternatively, he employed hit-and-run tactics while the British crossed the Saugatuck and swung southeastward toward Compo Hill, overlooking Long Island Sound. By late afternoon, the British column had reached that advantageous position. With troops from the waiting transport vessels now reinforcing his raiders, Tryon decided to send a detachment of four hundred soldiers back down the hill to disperse the marauding patriots.

Arnold, meanwhile, had been in the thick of the fighting. An amazed witness described how the senior brigadier constantly "exposed himself, almost to a fault," and repeatedly "exhibited the greatest marks of bravery, coolness, and fortitude" under fire. Just as Tryon launched his countercharge, Arnold "rode up to our front line" and, ignoring "the enemy's fire of musketry and grape shot," exhorted the troops "by the love of themselves, posterity, and all that's sacred not to desert him, but . . . all to no purpose." The "nerves" of these citizen-soldiers "were unstrung" as the unflinching enemy advanced toward them, and they quickly broke and ran. During this flurry of combat, a musket ball ripped through the collar of Arnold's coat, and he had another horse shot out from under him. The animal had taken a ball in the neck. As at Ridgefield, Arnold escaped with only bumps and bruises and the frustration of knowing that he had again failed to deflate the British raiders, whom Tryon easily evacuated after the countercharge at Compo Hill.[6]

That evening Arnold sent another letter to McDougall, this time advising him of Tryon's successful escape from Connecticut. He did not relate his own deeds but commented favorably on "many of the officers and men" who had "behaved well." Not only was he thinking of Wooster, who he mentioned was nearing death, but also of John Lamb and Eleazer Oswald, who had managed to get a few artillery pieces into service that day. Poor Lamb, blind in one eye from his wounds at Quebec, had suffered another mangling injury when enemy grapeshot struck his side and back. Unlike Wooster, he survived.[7]

Arnold's real disappointment was the citizenry of Connecticut. The militia had acted with its "usual" ineffectiveness. "I wish never to see another of them in action," he stated, thinking of how he had "found it impossible to rally them" at Ridgefield or Compo Hill. They had not passed the test of public virtue or demonstrated much capacity for self-sacrifice, even with an enemy force in their midst. Such a pitiful showing kept Arnold "complaining," noted a congressional delegate, about "the supineness of the country [Connecticut] which suffered such an insult without resistance or proper revenge." He was indeed asking just how long the Revolution could survive with the "languor" that "prevails everywhere," as Washington more generally characterized the public mood in the spring of 1777.[8]

II

Members of Congress quietly absorbed the news of Tryon's Danbury raid. Some even felt momentarily embarrassed about having denied Arnold a promotion, at least until one delegate suggested on Friday, May 2, that the Continental army could surely use another major general. Others nodded approvingly, and "the ballots being taken, Brigadier General Benedict Arnold was promoted to the rank of major general." Congress thus disclaimed its allegedly pivotal criterion of state troop quotas and advanced Arnold, according to John Adams, because of "his vigilance, activity, and bravery in the late affair at Connecticut." His behavior was "highly approved of by Congress," stated congressional president John Hancock in conveying the tidings to Washington.[9]

The delegates had acted as much out of expediency and embarrassment as out of a sense of justice. A major concern of Congress was the slow rate of new enlistments, a legacy of "the unfortunate events of the last campaign," John Adams stated, as well as the devastation caused by smallpox and other killer diseases in military camps. Equally bad was "the unhappy state of our finances," which meant that supplies and wages for soldiers were invariably deficient. Another deterrent to enlistments, opined Adams, was "the prevalence of dissipation, debauchery, gaming, profaneness, and blasphemy" among those troops in the service. Virtuous families should not be expected to subject their loved ones "to the dangers of the sword" when they were shuddering "at the thought of exposing them to what appears to them, the more destructive effects of vice and impiety."

To overcome so many problems, the Continental army, Adams went on to assert, needed more chaplains, firmer discipline, and truly courageous officers who could inspire the patriot populace to enlist and fight. The Massachusetts delegate underscored his point by speaking of "the utility of medals" that celebrated the deeds of authentic heroes. These medallions would appeal to the "pride, ambition, and . . . vanity" of all citizens, since they, too, if their efforts were truly remarkable, could expect to receive enshrinement as public heroes. "For my own part," Adams concluded, "I wish we could make a beginning, by striking a medal with a platoon firing at General Arnold, on horseback, his horse falling dead under him and he deliberately disentangling his feet from the stirrups and taking his pistols out of his holsters before his retreat." Then, on the back side, Arnold "should be mounted on a fresh horse, receiving another discharge of musketry, with a wound in the neck of his horse." Adams believed the world had seen "few such scenes" of such boundless courage.

The idea of casting such a honorific medal was not far-fetched. Congress had already done so in 1776 to celebrate Washington's efforts in driving the British from Boston. The delegates would do so seven more times during the war. Mitigating circumstances negated any serious discussion of a medal celebrating Arnold, among them the ongoing attacks on his personal character. Such a medal could also be viewed as too much fawning over an officer whom Congress had so recently passed over for promotion. If only "Arnold did not unfortunately belong to Connecticut," Adams declared, he would have been more useful to the Revolutionary cause and could have even made "his fortune for life" because of his remarkable opposition to Tryon's force.[10]

The delegates also fretted about making too damaging a breach in the application of their own criteria for promotion. Arnold should gladly accept his major general's commission, they reasoned, as recognition for his recent feats of bravery. As such, they did not authorize a medal, nor would they restore his seniority over the five officers so recently promoted over him.

Washington received the news of the promotion with "much pleasure." In responding to Congress, he again stressed that Arnold had demonstrated "in every instance where he has had an opportunity, much bravery, activity, and enterprise." The commander was reminding the delegates that Arnold was not a newfound hero. Selecting his words carefully, he queried, "But what will be done about his rank? He will not act, most probably, under those he commanded but a few weeks ago." Washington was urging Congress to be judicious about the matter of restoring Arnold's seniority.[11]

Still hoping to heal Arnold's lacerated sensibilities, Washington sent his fighting subordinate a congratulatory note on Thursday, May 8. He was "happy to find that a late resolve of Congress . . . has restored you to the Continental army." The commander then referred to the increased "importance" of the Continental supply depot at Peekskill. He wanted Arnold to take command there until "a general arrangement of the army can be effected, and the proper province of every officer assigned" for the upcoming campaign. Washington promised a more consequential post after the focus of British operations became clear.[12]

Arnold did not receive the commander's missive at New Haven. He was already on his way to the army's main encampment at Morristown, intending to visit with Washington and obtain permission to proceed to Philadelphia. When Arnold appeared unexpectedly at headquarters on Monday, May 12, the commander put other matters aside. He greeted his comrade enthusiastically and complimented him by mentioning the latest intelligence reports, which had the British describing Arnold as exhibiting "the character of a devilish fighting fellow" in resisting Tryon's raiders.[13]

Arnold could not hide his agitation, explaining that he had repeatedly risked his life because of his patriotic convictions, not to gain praise from Congress or the British. He then solicited Washington's indulgence about the Peekskill assignment. To his own detriment in the past, Arnold emphasized, he had remained in the field while detractors played havoc with his reputation. With no military emergency at hand, he had to, once and for all, prove false the unending calumnies "propagated" to destroy "his character as a man of integrity." The best way to do so was to present his own case to Congress, and he was also "anxious to settle his public accounts, which are of a considerable amount."[14]

To support his case, Arnold showed Washington a public handbill printed the previous month at Pittsfield, Massachusetts. Jeremiah Wadsworth, a fellow Connecticut merchant and a future commissary general of the Continental army, had sent him a copy of this "very extraordinary production." The handbill, Arnold pointed out, represented the most vicious assault yet on his reputation and had convinced him that he must go to Philadelphia without further delay.[15]

Washington studied the handbill in amazement. The document bore the imprimatur of John Brown and reprinted his multiple accusations of the previous December, as well as his demand for Arnold's arrest. Brown again charged America's Hannibal with employing "every possible art to prevent a trial." As a result, he had never had the opportunity to show the world that Arnold's "character was not worth a sixpence." The reference to money was purposeful. Brown was emphasizing his most damaging allegation: Arnold's alleged thievery in Montreal. In case the handbill's readers missed his point, Brown spelled out exactly what he meant: "Money is this man's god; and, to get enough of it, he would sacrifice his country."[16]

Washington evinced exasperation and recalled for Arnold his brief meeting with Brown back in February, after which that gentleman had resigned his commission. Arnold replied with words that he had recently sent to Wadsworth. Brown was a malicious troublemaker, "as infamous a gallows' bird as ever escaped, . . . who will ere long grace a gallows if he has his deserts." His "scandalous reflections . . . can injure no man," Arnold also insisted, "but will rather serve to establish his character. Whenever I have an opportunity of seeing him, he shall no longer have reason to complain for want of satisfaction." He "shall have more than he chooses," an unvarnished invitation to settling differences over a brace of pistols.[17]

Cautioning Arnold against precipitous behavior, Washington did not try to dissuade him from going to Philadelphia. The commander said he would look elsewhere for a Peekskill commander, and he reiterated his opinion that the delegates had not passed over Arnold because of pernicious slurs; the primary reason had to do with state troop quotas. Congress, Washington also observed, had acted in good faith by promoting Arnold to a major generalship for his valorous performance in western Connecticut.

Arnold disagreed. Men such as Brown, Easton, and Hazen had cast a damaging pall over his reputation. Only Congress could repair his sullied honor, by restoring his seniority in rank and by condemning Brown's handbill and punishing that "scoundrel as he deserves." Without these gestures, Arnold intended to offer his resignation, since he would never knowingly compromise his honor as a patriot and a gentleman.[18]

Eager to keep his best fighting general in the ranks, Washington closed their meeting by promising to prepare a letter for John Hancock. Later that day, he took up his pen and carefully explained that Arnold did "not consider the promotion . . . sufficient to obviate the neglect arising from their having omitted him in their late appointments to major generals." Nor was he prepared "to be commanded by those, who had been inferior to him" in rank just a few months ago. Washington encouraged Congress to address these concerns, since "it is universally known" how Arnold had "always distinguished himself, as a judicious, brave officer, of great activity, enterprise, and perseverance."[19]

The next morning, Washington handed his fighting general the sealed letter and wished him well. He counseled Arnold to remain composed at all times, but he stopped short of telling him what he suspected might happen. In the name of their prerogatives, the delegates would not yield to America's Hannibal in any contest between the inviolable civil authority of Congress and the sacred personal honor of a virtuous general officer.

III

"G[en]. Arnold is in town," wrote an enthusiastic Charles Carroll of Carrollton on Friday, May 16. The Maryland delegate helped his friend secure lodging at the same boardinghouse where he was residing. Like Washington before him, he also advised Arnold to tread carefully with the hypersensitive Congress. Arnold said he would and, in company with Carroll, spent the weekend mingling with delegates on a social basis. In the words of Benjamin Rush, these leaders noticed "his face handsome" and his muscular appearance as a man "low" in height "but well made." The delegates seemed impressed with the congenial gentleman before them. After all, he was the military celebrity of the moment because of his fearless deeds against Tryon's column.[20]

On Monday, May 19, Arnold went to the Pennsylvania State House, which some patriots were now calling Independence Hall, and turned over Washington's letter. The next morning he submitted a statement of his own, as well as a copy of John Brown's handbill. "I am extremely unhappy to find after having made every sacrifice of fortune, ease, and domestic happiness to serve my country," he stated, that "I am publicly impeached . . . of a catalogue of crimes . . . which, if true, ought to subject me to disgrace, infamy, and the just resentment of my country." Indisputably "conscious of the rectitude of my intentions (however I may have erred in judgment)," Arnold requested a court of inquiry to clear his name. He likewise asked to have his public accounts settled. He avoided any hint of resigning, since such a threat would have been impolitic before Congress had an opportunity to respond.[21]

The delegates acted the very same day, but not quite as Arnold had expected. Offering him public thanks for his recent acts of heroism, they turned his case over to the Board of War. As compensation for the two horses shot out from underneath him, Congress voted to have the quartermaster general "procure a horse, and present the same, properly caparisoned, to Major General Arnold, . . . as a token of their approbation of his gallant conduct." The delegates hoped the newly outfitted animal would mollify him somewhat, especially for having endured the slurs of John Brown. Stated Richard Henry Lee, "one plan, now in frequent use, is, to assassinate the characters of the friends of America in every place, and by every means." Lee's proof was Brown's "audacious attempt" to ruin the reputation of "the brave General Arnold."[22]

Arnold accepted the caparisoned horse, but this gesture of recognition meant little to him in comparison to the matter of cleansing his reputation. During meetings with various delegates over the next few days he evoked much sympathy, largely as a result of Brown's handbill. On Wednesday, May 21, he spent the evening with John Adams after a session with the Board of War. The Massachusetts delegate took pity on Arnold as a worthy gentleman "basely slandered and libeled." Adams went on to declare in a letter to his wife Abigail, "The regulars say, 'he fought like Julius Caesar.'" Then, in reference to Arnold's problems with Brown, as well as to other feuds such as that between Schuyler and Gates, Adams could not have been more acerbic when he told Abigail, "I am wearied to death with the wrangles between military officers, high and low. They quarrel like cats and dogs. They worry one another like mastiffs, scrambling for rank and pay like apes for nuts."[23]

The compassion of Congress clearly had narrow limits. With Washington and Gates as the only exceptions, the delegates were of the persuasion, at least during the spring of 1777, that no ranking officer, not even a brilliant fighter like Arnold, was indispensable. Only those who accepted the absolute authority of Congress over the Continental army would be tolerated—a lesson that Arnold had yet to learn.

The Board of War met again with Arnold on Thursday, May 22, and pored over various documents relating to his accounts. Charles Carroll served on the war committee, and he verified for any doubters that Arnold had not functioned as a thief while in Montreal. The next day the board expressed its "entire satisfaction . . . concerning the general's character and conduct, so cruelly and groundlessly aspersed in the publication" of John Brown. Congress agreed with "the said report" and ordered its findings published. Neither the board nor the full assemblage of delegates, however, chose to address the manifest issue of Arnold's seniority.[24]

Arnold kept trying to nurture his credibility with the delegates. Such blatantly obsequious behavior was not easy for him, since he was hardly an admirer of Congress's record in directing the rebel war effort. He had endured too many shortages in the field, for which he held the delegates responsible. The public recognition of receiving a newly caparisoned horse also bothered him, the implication being that he might succumb to flattery and compromise his claim to higher rank. No true gentleman would ever consider such an unbalanced exchange. Only the restoration of his seniority, Arnold believed, would fully vindicate his reputation.

At the end of May, Arnold let loose with his frustrations for a moment in writing to Jeremiah Wadsworth about Congress's unanimous dismissal of John Brown's "scurrilous paper." "The liberty of the press I hold sacred," he declared almost sanctimoniously; still, he wanted the Pittsfield printer to make amends for having produced so "false, cruel, and malicious" a handbill. The printer could do so by publishing and distributing at his own expense Congress's affirmation of Arnold's integrity. "I wish not to have him censured," he insisted, but "whoever takes an unbecoming liberty with my character, I shall take an opportunity of calling to account." As an enemy of arbitrary power and subscriber to the gentleman's code, Arnold would, in time, have to consider calling Congress to account as well, should the delegates not fully exonerate his good name by restoring his seniority in rank.[25]

IV

Arnold was not singular among general officers who were questioning Congress's decision-making capacities during the spring of 1777. Philip Schuyler, having used his political influence to get the New York Provincial Congress to name him a delegate to Congress, had been in Philadelphia since early April. At his persistent request, the delegates had named a committee to review his conduct as Northern Department commander. By the time Arnold reached Philadelphia, Schuyler was on the verge of obtaining complete vindication.[26]

Arnold and Schuyler quickly renewed their patron-client relationship, commiserating together about the vilification they both had endured over the past year. Schuyler pointed out that New England remained the epicenter of his difficulties. So many of the charges lodged against him, ranging from war profiteering to losing Canada, had emanated from that region. Delegates from New England clearly wanted to replace him with their darling general, Horatio Gates. They had helped him sidestep an order to return to Washington's army as adjutant general. At their urging, Congress had designated a committee to consult with Gates about preparations for the 1777 campaign season, with special reference to the northern theater. Less than two weeks later, Schuyler added, the delegates had at last honored his request to name a general officer to take command at Ticonderoga and provide temporary leadership in the Northern Department while he attended Congress. They had chosen Gates, and once again, as they had done the year before, they used the kind of ambiguous terminology that implied a command independent of Schuyler's.[27]

The Yorker also recounted how Gates had rushed northward and, despite instructions "to repair to Ticonderoga," had gone no farther than Albany. Setting up his standard in Schuyler's home community, Gates began cultivating the impression that his assignment was permanent. Congress almost appeared to accept this posturing when it approved Gates's advice to have Arthur St. Clair take command at Ticonderoga.[28]

Schuyler reminded his comrade that Congress consisted of fallible, prideful men who deftly employed rhetorical flourishes to cover over their self-serving political agendas. Many New England delegates found Gates attractive because, unlike himself, they thought they could manipulate and control him. So they were now blaming lagging New England enlistments on Schuyler's "undemocratic" manner while claiming that only Gates could rally that region's liberty-loving populace to arms—yet another reason to make him Northern Department commander. Gates, in turn, was using them to satisfy his own inordinate military ambitions. Arnold, Schuyler warned, should be very much on guard in any dealings with that gentleman.[29]

In response, Arnold noted that events of the past few months had shown him how capricious political bodies could be. His own plan, he indicated, was to act judiciously and give Congress ample time to resolve the seniority issue. He also mentioned that Gates had neither replied to his distressed letter of late March nor supplied him with copies of the crucial documents he had requested. Arnold had to keep in mind that without Gates's cooperation, he might never obtain a fair financial settlement. Still, he would heed Schuyler's advice, having already begun to wonder himself whether he should continue to think of Gates as a fully trustworthy comrade in arms.

Arnold also bristled at the thought of Congress naming St. Clair, one of the five officers elevated over him, to the Ticonderoga command. He considered this Pennsylvania officer honest but unimaginative, a man who had obviously attached his star to Gates. In response, Schuyler said he planned to work with St. Clair. The Pennsylvania delegation, he explained in offering Arnold yet another lesson in the wiles of congressional politics, was supporting him in his own drive for vindication.

Arnold saw the practicality of this stratagem when Congress voted to exonerate Schuyler on Thursday, May 22, by only five states to four, with Pennsylvania in the affirmative. The delegates then directed him to resume his duties as Northern Department commander. Gates, in turn, would have to choose whether to serve under Schuyler at Ticonderoga or assume duties as Washington's adjutant general. Temporarily, at least, the Yorker had again prevailed in a contest over command that seemed to bear out John Adams's words about officers incessantly "scrambling for rank and pay like apes for nuts." What Adams did not admit, however, was that politicking members of Congress were as much a cause of the scrambling as were the officers themselves.[30]

V

Schuyler left for Albany at the end of May, but Arnold remained doggedly in Philadelphia under the guise of settling his accounts. With Schuyler gone, Arnold was the ranking Continental officer in Philadelphia, and he took command of the immediate region. Getting back to military matters stirred his blood. He reestablished communications with Washington, who was waiting for General Sir William Howe to emerge from his winter's hibernation in New York City. Based on good intelligence, Washington expected Howe to aim his main force at eastern Pennsylvania. What no one yet knew was exactly when or by what route the British would move.

Howe's puzzling delay in commencing offensive operations had John Adams predicting in early June that "we shall have an unactive campaign— that Howe will shut himself up, in some impregnable post, and lie still." Other patriot leaders guessed that the British commander could not bring himself to end what rebel rumormongers had depicted as a most spirited— and often ribald—winter social season in New York City. Sir William had certainly set a whirlwind pace. He reveled in his newfound status as a Knight of the Bath, a reward for his triumph on Long Island back in August 1776; and he grandly entertained ranking officers, wealthy loyalists, and assorted hangers-on. He also indulged his well-developed gambling habit and continued his liaison with Mrs. Joshua Loring, his attractive blonde consort whose greedy husband had chosen to ignore his wife's profligacy in exchange for easy profits from the highly lucrative post of commissary of prisoners.[31]

Indecision, more than social diversions, lay at the root of Howe's slowness in getting into the field. Although the British commander would never admit it, Washington's stunning victories at Trenton and Princeton had confounded him. Whenever Sir William looked across the Hudson River at New Jersey's ashen winter landscape, he recalled how "Mr." Washington, who lacked formal military training and the kind of family stature to have influence at court, had both outgeneraled and embarrassed him.

By mid-January 1777, Howe began contending that the only sure way to snuff out the rebellion quickly was to entice Washington into a climactic battle and destroy the main rebel force. Should the American commander eschew all-out combat, Sir William would then invade Pennsylvania, where, even if he accomplished nothing else, he could humiliate the rebels by capturing Philadelphia. Washington, furthermore, would surely attempt to protect the capital city. He might even get his army entrapped and have to engage in a fatal battle.[32]

Howe's reasoning was at odds with the home government's intention of proceeding with the Hudson Highlands strategy, which called for synchronized operations between Sir William's troops and the expeditionary force scheduled to invade New York through the Champlain region. Caught as he was between discordant operational plans, Howe seemed to retreat into a state of mental immobility. He kept debating whether he could vanquish Washington's force and still have time to offer proper support to the army coming out of Canada. Once convinced that he could accomplish both objectives, Howe appeared in the field. Had he commenced his operations a month or so sooner, he might well have succeeded.[33]

With each passing week, as Sir William stewed during the spring of 1777, Washington's army slowly regained strength. By early June the American commander had about ten thousand troops in his ranks, but fewer than seventy-four hundred were actually present and fit for duty. Washington was still far short of the numbers he needed to wage serious combat, yet he had received firm pledges of support from Jersey militia units. Although the commander justifiably had little confidence in the fighting prowess of militiamen, they could help harass and disrupt the enemy's supply lines, should Howe attempt to march his force across New Jersey for Pennsylvania.

In late May, Washington broke camp at Morristown and moved his Continentals some twenty miles southeastward, where they took up a strong defensive position at Middlebrook Heights on the first Watchung Mountain (above modern-day Bound Brook). Once nestled into these heights, which overlooked the most advanced British outpost at New Brunswick some seven miles to the east, Washington could respond intelligently to almost any enemy movement.

On Saturday, May 31, General Sullivan, who had command of a small detachment at Princeton some seventeen miles south of New Brunswick, sent Arnold an urgent message. Howe was at last showing signs of activity by concentrating additional troops at New Brunswick. Sullivan was not sure whether the British intended to march toward Philadelphia or attack Washington's force. "Apprehensive the former is their intention," he promised to keep "up a free and constant communication" with Arnold.[34]

Arnold displayed his military sagacity in politely disagreeing with Sullivan. He could not fathom the British "being so imprudent, as to march to Philadelphia and leave General Washington in their rear." As such, Arnold had "no doubt the enemy will soon open the campaign, by attacking our army." He also suspected that Howe's real intention was to transport his force—"I doubt if the enemy will entirely abandon New York"—by sea "into the Delaware [River] to make a feint, if not [a] real attack."[35]

Arnold's thinking paralleled Washington's. Based on reports that "a fleet is upon the point of sailing from New York," the commander considered the troop buildup in New Brunswick as likely a ruse to tie down his force in central New Jersey. He thus enjoined Arnold to give him "the earliest possible" notice if he was "certain that the [enemy] fleet is in the bay" of the Delaware River. The commander also warned about the danger of false cannon signals from lookout posts along the river, "which I am told have been fired several times without any grounds for so doing," especially since "a move of this army upon a false alarm might prove fatal."[36]

This admonition reflected Washington's own lack of surety about Howe's campaign plans. The American commander consequently clung to his position at Middlebrook Heights and waited, certain that his adversary would soon make one of three telling advances. Should Howe use his brother's fleet to move troops up the Hudson River, which Washington considered the least likely prospect, he would march his army northeastward with all haste. Should the British sail out to sea and around New Jersey, he would lead his troops southwestward toward Philadelphia. Should Howe enjoin him to battle in central New Jersey, he would not engage unless the British attacked his mountainside entrenchments. Most of all, Washington was not going to let his undersized army get ensnared in a decisive confrontation on the enemy's terms.

Howe arrived in New Brunswick on Monday, June 9, at last ready to

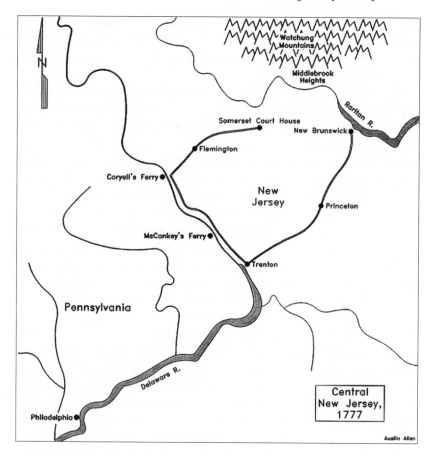

flaunt before Washington a sizable field force of eighteen thousand. His purpose was to draw the Americans onto flatter ground, more suited to traditional open-field combat. Sir William had decided to allow only two weeks to entice Washington into battle. Should the rebels cling to their mountainside defenses, he would pull all British forces back toward New York City. Richard, Lord Howe, was even then beginning to assemble a fleet of more than 260 vessels to transport some fifteen thousand soldiers by sea to Pennsylvania.

Showing his disdain for superstitions, Howe ordered his troops to march westward from New Brunswick on Friday, June 13. He might have been more attentive to that date had he known how poorly the 1777 campaign would turn out for British forces in North America. A disaster was already in the making because of his colossal blunder in not providing a sizable detachment of soldiers to move up the Hudson River in support of the British army dropping out of Canada under General John Burgoyne, whose force was already in position to push southward onto Lake Champlain.

On the same day that Sir William appeared in New Brunswick, Arnold learned just how badly he had failed in rallying the support of Congress. Garrulous Thomas Mifflin, an adept Pennsylvania politician and one of the five officers elevated to a major generalship over him, appeared in Philadelphia that day. Because of rapidly developing military circumstances, Arnold stated that as a dutiful patriot, he would work closely with Mifflin, "with whom I shall concert measures, for the more effectually rendering all their [British] schemes abortive." [37]

In what he meant as an unselfish act, Arnold stood ready to subordinate his own sense of damaged personal honor by offering to serve with—but not under—Mifflin. Congress, however, used the Pennsylvanian's presence as an excuse to order the junior major general back into the field. Many of the delegates were glad to get rid of Arnold, and they handled the matter rather crudely. When he sent them recommendations on Tuesday, June 10, for strengthening the river forts below Philadelphia, they replied by directing him "immediately to repair to Trenton, and there conduct himself agreeable to the orders of the commander in chief." Their message was clear. With one of their preferred general officers now available to counsel them, they no longer needed the services of the heroic but politically uninfluential officer from Connecticut. [38]

Having left himself vulnerable, Arnold felt grossly insulted. Grappling to keep his composure, he waited two days before sending a carefully worded response to Congress on June 13, the same day Howe directed his troops westward from New Brunswick. Arnold observed that only a smattering of militiamen and Continentals were in the vicinity of Trenton. So few soldiers would hardly "form a brigadier general's command," let alone a major general's; yet he would "cheerfully submit to the orders of Congress, being determined at this critical juncture to sacrifice my own feelings and every consideration of rank to the safety and happiness of my country." Arnold promised to do his best with this "handful of men." Then he exhorted the delegates to remember how they had "deprived of his rank in the army a person who since the commencement of the present war, has strenuously endeavored to act the part of a faithful soldier, and who is not conscious of having committed any offense or neglect of duty, which should induce your honorable body to pass an implied censure on his conduct." [39]

Arnold rode out of Philadelphia in a downcast frame of mind. He felt the irony of sitting astride the caparisoned horse that denoted his bravery while being shuffled off to a virtual noncommand assignment at Trenton, thirty miles to the northeast. As soon as circumstances permitted, he vowed to himself, he would put an end to such blatant mockery of his good name by returning to Philadelphia, placing his resignation before Congress, and insisting that his financial accounts be settled.

The prospect of getting at the enemy soon relieved Arnold's gloom. By the time he crossed the Delaware River on Saturday morning, June 14, he had received reports that Howe was on the move. He then learned that Sullivan's detachment at Princeton had pulled back toward Coryell's Ferry (modern-day New Hope, Pennsylvania) on the Delaware River, so as not to be cut off from Washington's force. Arnold waited several hours in Trenton for any message from Sullivan. As dusk fell, he found out that Howe's column had taken a westerly course. Concluding that the British might also be aiming for Coryell's Ferry, he rode some fifteen miles northward to that same point.

Once at Coryell's Ferry, where the patriots kept enough boats to move up to three thousand soldiers at a time back and forth across the Delaware, he met with Sullivan before the New Hampshire general marched his detachment off to Flemington, New Jersey, twelve miles to the northeast. On Sunday, June 15, Arnold reported to Mifflin that Sullivan's numbers were approaching five thousand, thanks to a healthy outpouring of Jersey militia, and he stated that "troops who arrive here are immediately sent after him." With the rebel manpower base increasing so rapidly, Arnold was actually "fearful the enemy will retire to Brunswick" before additional patriot soldiers arrived. Characteristically, he was priming himself for combat. "For fight them we must," he exclaimed to Mifflin, as if also reflecting on his thinking about Congress, because "when all our reinforcements are in we cannot avoid it with honor." [40]

John Adams admired Arnold's aggressiveness, as long as the junior major general was directing his fervor toward the enemy. On Wednesday, June 18, he wrote Abigail that "Arnold, you see will have at them, if he can." He also described Washington as "our Fabius," who "will be slow, but sure." Adams portrayed both generals correctly. Howe's advance column under Charles, Lord Cornwallis, had marched only about nine miles west to Somerset Court House before halting. The British still had their line firmly anchored in New Brunswick. Washington remained convinced that Sir William's objective was "to draw us down from the heights we occupy along his whole front." No matter how much the American commander ached to fight, he appreciated the necessity of restraint. He would not allow the British any opportunity "to give a severe blow to this army," he advised Arnold, "with the most ruinous consequences" for the Revolution.[41]

Washington could not envision Howe attempting to march his force overland toward Philadelphia. The British had "come out as light as possible," he reported to Arnold, "leaving all their baggage, provisions, boats, and bridges at Brunswick." Should they continue their westward thrust, however, he expected Arnold to link up with Sullivan and Mifflin and engage them before they approached the Delaware River. The commander promised to "keep close upon their heels" and come crashing in from the rear.[42]

Squashing Howe with hammer-and-anvil tactics would have delighted both Washington and Arnold, but Sir William was not a military novice. He did not intend to move beyond Somerset Court House. On Thursday evening, June 19, he ordered his troops back to New Brunswick, then abandoned the latter post and marched for Perth Amboy and Staten Island. Howe hoped the rebels would come rushing down from Middlebrook Heights to attack his rear guard, which was ready and waiting. Wanting to maintain nominal contact with his adversary, Washington did move most of his troops onto flatter terrain closer to Perth Amboy. Early on Thursday morning, June 26, Howe directed two columns to cut off the patriots before they could retreat to safety, but the Americans, after an intense engagement, got themselves untangled from the enemy. Sir William, having failed to generate a conclusive battle, ordered the abandonment of the region, except for Staten Island, which his troops accomplished by July 1. The British commander now turned to the next page of his campaign plan—the seaborne invasion of Pennsylvania.

The prospect of combat had temporarily infused Arnold with a sense of purpose, and he lamented the news of Howe's swift pullback to New Brunswick. On Tuesday, June 24, he reluctantly returned to Philadelphia. Because he so desperately wanted to stay in the army, to serve the cause of liberty, to achieve martial glory, and to restore the faded luster of his once-ascendant family name, Arnold talked himself into trying one more time to retrieve his seniority. Still, the thought of again fawning over congressional leaders repulsed him, and the controversies of the next few days only strengthened his growing sense of hostility toward the Revolution's civilian leadership.

VI

Buffeted as they were by so many issues, members of Congress were courteous but perfunctory in greeting their fighting general. They were no more encouraging to him than was Betsy De Blois, or so Arnold reasoned when he heard from Henry Knox that his wife Lucy was wondering what should be done with the rejected trunk of clothing. Lucy, who felt fond affection for Arnold, had asked "to have a scarf which is in the trunk," and Nathanael Greene's wife Catherine had expressed interest in a dress. Whether Arnold accommodated these requests is unclear, since he had not completely dismissed the idea of winning over Betsy's heart, just as he had not yet accepted Congress's apparent rebuff of his bid for restored seniority.[43]

Then, in early July, a disquieting confrontation between three of Washington's generals and Congress finally convinced Arnold to stop pressing for satisfaction. The dispute centered on Philippe Charles Tronson de Coudray, a French officer who had recently arrived from Europe waving a Continental major general's commission before the delegates. Arnold's friend and patron Silas Deane was the source of the dilemma. As a commissioner to France, his duty was to secure whatever support he could for the rebellion. Coudray was a colonel in the French army who had written extensively on the use of artillery, and he had useful connections at the court of Louis XVI. Hoping to exploit Coudray's contacts, Deane offered him a military commission dated August 1, 1776, which the Frenchman readily accepted. When Coudray presented himself to Congress in May 1777, he expected confirmation as General of Artillery and Ordnance in Washington's army.

The delegates found themselves in a perplexing bind. Should they repudiate Coudray's commission, he could storm back to France and damage the commissioners' efforts to secure essential material largesse as well as formal diplomatic recognition from the powerful French nation. Should Congress send the haughty Coudray into the field, they would be inviting the wrath of ranking Continental officers. In seeking a solution to the predicament, the delegates kept stalling Coudray while playing to his boundless sense of self-importance. More than once Arnold attended gatherings at which delegates fawned over Coudray, who unlike himself had contributed nothing to the patriot war effort yet would outrank him if Congress confirmed his commission.

Arnold kept his own counsel; other general officers did not. At first, Washington's ranking lieutenants grumbled among themselves. Then an illusive story reached them in late June, even as Howe was completing his withdrawal from New Jersey, that Congress was about to send the Frenchman into the field. Since Coudray would supersede Henry Knox as Chief of Artillery and outrank Nathanael Greene and John Sullivan, based on his August 1, 1776, commission date, these three generals cried foul in unison, although each directed his own statement of protest to Congress. In the words of Knox, "I wish to know . . . whether this information be true; if it is I beg the favor of a permission to retire, and that a proper certificate for that purpose be sent me immediately."[44]

Arnold appreciated the outrage of the three general officers. Losing their services would represent a staggering blow to the army's morale at the most critical of times—the outset of a campaign season. Many other useful officers, Arnold was sure, would submit their resignations in support of Greene, Knox, and Sullivan. The result would be chaos in the Continental army's command structure, all of which could destroy any unity of purpose in resisting British offensive operations that summer.

Arnold hoped the delegates would handle the complaints of Greene, Knox, and Sullivan prudently while finding some way to get rid of Coudray. Neither happened. On Monday, July 7, Congress instructed its president, John Hancock, to forward the letters of protest to Washington "with directions . . . to let those officers know" that the delegates considered their words "an attempt to influence their decisions, and an invasion of the liberties of the people, and indicating a want of confidence in the justice of Congress." They expected the officers to apologize and "make proper acknowledgment for an interference of so dangerous a tendency." Should Greene, Knox, and Sullivan not accept "the authority of Congress, they shall be at liberty to resign their commissions and retire."[45]

Congress's resolution was the handiwork of a beleaguered body. The delegates had acted as if any military officer who dared to complain about their actions were a veritable Oliver Cromwell, bent on destroying free republican government. Arnold could not fathom how Congress could conjure up so distorted an image of dedicated military leaders who had repeatedly displayed their public virtue and who in return had asked only not to have their personal honor impugned. If the delegates would not treat the likes of Knox, Greene, and Sullivan with consideration and respect, then there was surely was no hope for him. The time had come to prepare his own a letter of protest in asking Congress to accept his resignation.

Had Arnold been prescient, he might have held back. In early July, however, he had no way of knowing that Washington would corral his three lieutenants, that they would choose to ignore Congress's resolution, or that the delegates would soon devise a way to resolve the Coudray dilemma. In August they designated the Frenchman a "staff" major general in charge of the inspection of ordnance and other weapons. Coudray would have only advisory duties and no authority over any "line" general officer. On September 15, Coudray found his own way to settle the problem. Dismissing the advice of those traveling with him, he rode rather than walked a spirited young horse onto a ferryboat about to cross the Schuylkill River. The skittish animal bolted forward, straight into the water. Coudray drowned before he could get himself disentangled from his stirrups.

Coudray's "strange" death, John Adams confided to his diary, was a "dispensation" that "will save us much altercation." In the case of Arnold, however, nothing had been resolved. After so many weeks of watching Congress in action, he had run out of patience with civilian politics and delegates who so readily deferred to some martial leaders while treating others as if their existence was a manifest threat to preserving the liberties of the republic.[46]

Among the politically favored officers, Gates came sprinting back to Philadelphia in mid-June after learning that Congress had sustained Schuyler in the northern command. He had no intention of again serving under the Yorker or as Washington's adjutant general. Nor did Gates seem to care that the main Continental army was on full military alert in New Jersey. Based on his actions, his singular concern was his own advancement over Schuyler.

Frothing with self-righteousness, Gates angrily presented himself to his New England friends as a man cruelly deceived by congressional allies. A chastened Roger Sherman cleared the way for Gates to be admitted to the floor of Congress on Wednesday, June 18, to present a report on military affairs in upper New York. To the delight of Schuyler's supporters, Gates soon lost his composure. He got into a shouting match with New York delegate James Duane, a close friend of Schuyler who took umbrage at the general's rambling commentary, which mostly had to do with Gates's sacrifices. The general eventually withdrew in a huff, even as pro- and anti-Schuyler delegates hurled insults at each other.[47]

Attempting to regain their dignity, the delegates stated that any further communications from Gates should be in writing. That they did not vote to censure him as a general officer trying to influence their judgments, as they soon did with Knox, Greene, and Sullivan, was not lost on Arnold. What Congress had revealed was its own double standard. The delegates did not hold officers with significant political influence to the same punctilio of compliant behavior as those who lacked a strong base of congressional support. Arnold knew that if he had acted so indecorously, the delegates would have quickly called him to account. At no point, however, did Congress so much as hint that Gates should consider resigning, even though he had exhibited as much impertinence toward that body's decision-making prerogatives as had Knox, Greene, and Sullivan.

Worse yet from Arnold's perspective, the delegates chose not to enforce their earlier resolution to have Gates join Washington's army. Instead, they allowed him to stay on in Philadelphia, where he continued to lobby for the Northern Department commander's post. Eventually, those unfriendly toward Gates marshaled enough votes for a resolution on July 8 that ordered him "to repair to headquarters, and follow the directions of General Washington." Gates responded by announcing his intention to return to Virginia for a long-delayed visit with his family.[48]

Even with such conspicuous defiance of a congressional mandate—in the midst of the rapidly unfolding campaign season no less—the delegates avoided any reprimand of Gates. Congress's forbearance smacked of hypocrisy to Arnold. Some delegates, he guessed, were of the sentiment that "amateur" American officers could never measure up in the performance of their duties to professionally trained Europeans such as Coudray and Gates. Another aspect of the problem too, he was sure, related to the shortsighted political decision making of ever-manipulating gentleman-politicians who, despite their rhetorical flourishes, had no understanding of truly selfless public service. They could not recognize and reward what they did not comprehend. Whatever the reason, the delegates, Arnold concluded, would not restore his seniority, especially when they were so cavalier in their treatment of such worthy martial servants as Knox, Greene, Sullivan, and even, as he liked to think, so devoted an advocate of liberty as himself.

VII

In early July, Arnold met a few times with Congress's Board of War. Because he had led an invasion force through the Maine wilderness and had extensive maritime experience in sailing the trade routes to the West Indies, the board wanted his "sentiments" about a plan calling for a patriot strike against Pensacola and Mobile in British West Florida. Colonel George Morgan, a prominent Philadelphia merchant, land speculator, and sometime Indian agent, had proposed the scheme, which called for the movement of twelve hundred troops from Pittsburgh down the Ohio and Mississippi rivers, as well as the deployment of three or four Continental frigates to sail around East Florida to support of the intended assault.

After a lengthy meeting with Morgan during which Arnold "carefully examined the map of the country," he offered a mixed endorsement. If Morgan's objective was only to seize war-related goods at these British posts, he did not feel "capable of judging of the propriety of it." If the purpose was significantly larger and included "the destruction of those places (the trade of which has become very considerable and important to Great Britain)," then he thought the plan "an object of importance, not only as an acquisition of territory" but also as a potential opening of "a door for a very considerable and lucrative trade, with the Spaniards and Indians."

Arnold liked these prospects, but he decided not to comment on "the minutiae of the affair." He also encouraged the board to rely on Morgan, whose "intimate acquaintance with the country" made him "the best judge" of the proper time to launch such an expedition. What Arnold left unstated was his concern that Congress would foolishly engage in yet another far-ranging military enterprise destined to fail because of insufficient logistical support.[49]

Had his own circumstances been different, Arnold might have expressed more enthusiasm about Morgan's plan. His mind, however, was elsewhere — on the resignation. His indifference reflected his own forlorn sense of personal defeat. With each passing day he came closer to drafting the letter that, above all else, he did not want to write. Finally, on Thursday, July 10, he put words to paper. Upon his honor as a gentleman, Arnold was not offering his resignation "from a spirit of resentment (though my feelings are deeply wounded.)" Instead, his words arose "from a real conviction that it is not in my power to serve my country in the present rank I hold," because of the "implied impeachment of my character and declaration of Congress that they thought me unqualified for the post that fell to me in the common line of promotions." Still anxious to "enjoy my highest ambition, that of being a free citizen of America," he stood ready to continue sacrificing, even if that involved life itself, but he would not do so "in my present disgraceful rank in the army," quite simply because any such acquiescence might permanently mar his reputation. In closing he thus stressed, "Honor is a sacrifice no man ought to make, as I received [it] so I wish to transmit [it] inviolate to posterity."[50]

Arnold could hardly believe his military career had to come to so humiliating an end, when he had done everything in his power to play the virtuous part of a faithful soldier. He now longed to get away from Philadelphia, to return to New Haven and the loving embraces of his sons and sister, and to reconstruct his life as a once-prospering civilian merchant.

On Friday, July 11, Arnold entered the Pennsylvania State House and handed over his letter of resignation. Feeling debased and dishonored, he maintained his outward aplomb and acted as if his only concern were whether he might somehow get his accounts settled within the next few days. If not, he would come back to Philadelphia at a later date. Then he turned and walked out of the State House, still limping slightly from his wound at Quebec. He did not know that Congress had just received an urgent communiqué from Washington asking for the services of "an active, spirited officer." The commander had specifically enjoined the delegates to send him Benedict Arnold.[51]

CHAPTER Fifteen

An Unsettled Return to the Northern Theater

I

George Washington had just received a garbled report from the northern theater that Fort Ticonderoga had fallen to the British. This news, he hoped, would prove "premature and groundless." Yet, he continued, "we cannot doubt but General Burgoyne has come up the lake, determined, if possible, to carry his point, I mean, to possess himself of our posts in that quarter and to push his arms further." With "Continental levies ... so deficient," the commander also stated, "our security and safety will require that aids from the militia should be called forth in cases of emergency." Arnold, he believed, could help rally New England's populace in checking "Burgoyne's progress or the most disagreeable consequences may be apprehended." [1]

Some congressional leaders expressed surprise that Washington had not asked for Gates, so often touted as a general truly adored by the people of New England. The commander had plenty of reasons, not the least of which was the matter of trustworthiness; and Gates, whatever his motivations, had not stayed—or stood—with the army in the critical hours before Trenton. In addition, Washington had no idea whether Gates could set aside his own ambitions and work harmoniously with General Schuyler at so momentous a juncture in Northern Department affairs. Arnold, by comparison, had repeatedly displayed his capacity for intrepid leadership in combat. Washington wanted a true fighting general whose known strengths would complement the logistical talents of Schuyler.

Congress had little time to second-guess Washington. The rumored loss of Ticonderoga forced the delegates to disregard Arnold's resignation. They ordered him "immediately to repair to headquarters, and follow the orders of General Washington." The next day, Saturday, July 12, President John Hancock confirmed this resolution in a note to Arnold, to which the chastened junior major general immediately replied. He reiterated his desire to have his resignation accepted, despite "the late advices from Ticonderoga." Still, he would travel to Washington's headquarters and execute any orders "respecting the militia, with whom I shall be happy as a private citizen to render my country every service in my power." America's Hannibal thus was willing to keep serving the patriot cause, but not under the authority of Congress—not unless that body restored his seniority in line of command.[2]

Arnold left Philadelphia early on Tuesday, July 15, but not before he asked a few trusted delegates to press for a formal vote on the seniority issue. By the time he reached Washington's headquarters on the west bank of the Hudson River near the New Jersey–New York border, he had cast the wiles of congressional politics from his mind. Now focusing on repelling the ominous military challenge being offered by "Gentleman Johnny" Burgoyne, Arnold even indulged himself by imagining, at long last, a definitive patriot victory in the northern theater after two long years of grueling but inconclusive campaigning.

Washington greeted his fighting general on the evening of July 17, then briefed him. The enemy was advancing in massed strength down through the Champlain corridor; General St. Clair had decided to abandon rather than defend Ticonderoga; and the northern army was in apparent flight. Schuyler had to receive a major infusion of troops, especially an outpouring of militia from New York and New England. Because of Schuyler's tainted reputation in the latter region, Washington hoped that Arnold could effect a large turnout. The commander expected him to take command of all available militia units while assisting Schuyler in thwarting Burgoyne's southward drive toward Albany.

Washington also discussed St. Clair, one of the five officers elevated over Arnold. His precipitous retreat would surely result in an investigation and court of inquiry to afford that general "an opportunity," as the commander stated, to give "the reasons for his sudden evacuation of a post, which, but a few days before, he, by his own letters, thought tenable at least for a while." For the sake of unity of command, Washington asked Arnold to waive, "for the present, all dispute about rank" and, if need be, to accept St. Clair's seniority should the two of them find themselves working together. Arnold acceded "generously" and promised to set "aside his claim." "Although he conceives himself, had his promotion been regular, superior in command to General St. Clair," Washington wrote to Schuyler, he would "create no dispute should the good of the service require them to act in concert."[3]

The commander thanked Arnold and promised to send north whatever soldiers and war matériel he could spare. Unfortunately, muster rolls showed that Washington's own troop base had not grown appreciably since the end of May. Further, the commander was still not sure in which direction Howe intended to move. Knowing that British control of the Hudson-Champlain corridor could prove devastating to the rebellion, Washington had his army camping along the Hudson River. He thus had his troops in position to offer resistance if the enemy sailed up the Hudson with the fifteen thousand regulars General Howe had recently ordered onto transport vessels. Should the British force, as intelligence reports kept indicating, proceed to Philadelphia by water, he would then march his soldiers across New Jersey to defend the rebel capital.

Washington noted that he had already dispatched General John Nixon's brigade of New Englanders—about six hundred effectives—to Albany in response to Schuyler's pleas for additional manpower. Badly outnumbered himself, the commander could not spare additional troops until his own strength increased. To help in the meantime, he promised to circulate a communiqué imploring New England's patriots to muster in force for militia service against Burgoyne.

While Arnold rested and prepared to continue his journey, Washington saw to the drafting of an appeal to all militia commanders in western Massachusetts and New Hampshire. They were to rally as many citizen-soldiers as possible in "this time of trial," since Continental troops were not sufficient in number to "check the progress of the enemy." Washington also announced that "General Arnold, who is well known to you all, goes up at my request to take the command of the militia in particular." Like Arnold, he doubted the fighting prowess of militia. The two generals had no other manpower resource, however, which caused the commander to thank Congress for having sent him Arnold, who had repeatedly demonstrated his aptitude for innovation in the face of insuperable obstacles. "From his activity and disposition for enterprise," Washington declared, "I flatter myself, his presence and assistance in that quarter, will be attended with happy consequences."[4]

Late on the afternoon of Friday, July 18, the commander in chief again said goodbye to his fighting subordinate. Arnold wanted to travel through the night rather than delay even a few more hours reaching the front line. This small act of resolution represented further assurance to Washington that he had not misplaced his confidence in Arnold, an officer he was sure would use "his utmost exertions . . . to baffle the enemy's views."[5]

II

General John Burgoyne has often been portrayed as ambitious, pretentious, and vain, a person with enough intelligence to perceive the weaknesses of others but too shallow to appreciate his own. Born in 1723 to common family stock, he had the advantage of a gentleman's education. At Westminster School he developed a close friendship with James Smith-Stanley, eldest son and heir of the politically powerful eleventh Earl of Derby. In Smith-Stanley, later known as Lord Strange, Burgoyne had found his patron; and when his parents scraped together enough money to purchase their son a low-ranking officer's commission, he had found his primary calling. When, in 1751, Burgoyne eloped with Strange's sister, Lady Charlotte Stanley, he briefly infuriated Lord Derby, but he also secured impeccable social credentials for himself.

Burgoyne was able to purchase his way up the officers' ranks, and he gained recognition for heroic feats while fighting in Portugal against the Spanish during the Seven Years' War. He also earned his nickname, "Gentleman Johnny," because of his conviction that common soldiers should not be treated like curs to ensure their proficiency in close-order combat. After the war, Burgoyne pursued his aspirations as an actor and playwright, and he earned quite a reputation as a gambler, often risking large sums in the most fashionable London clubs. He also won election to Parliament, where he supported the king's legislative agenda. In 1772 he received his reward for loyal political service in the form of a major general's commission.

Because of his high military rank, Burgoyne joined William Howe and Henry Clinton in sailing for Boston in late April 1775. Before landing, the generals learned that the rebels had Thomas Gage's troops under siege, the news of which reputedly caused Gentleman Johnny to exclaim, "What! Ten thousand peasants keep five thousand of the king's troops shut up! Well, let *us* get in, and we'll soon find elbow-room." If Burgoyne had offered the colonists only a portion of the respect he had demanded for British regulars, he would not have so glibly underrated his opponents. The patriots mocked his flamboyant words by dubbing him General "Elbow Room." [6]

Nothing about the colonies appealed to Burgoyne's sophisticated tastes. Proclaiming American winters even more unbearable than the crude provincial populace, he sailed back to England in late 1775. Indulging himself in London's winter social season, he also worked with Lord Germain in pulling together the relief force that sailed for Canada in the early spring of 1776. Burgoyne had command of the troops, but he was to operate under Carleton's authority and was soon unhappy about the governor's lack of aggressive-

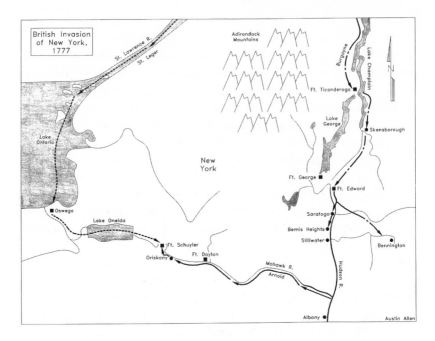

ness in seeking out and crushing the annoying but hardly dangerous rebel yokels.

Once again, Burgoyne found American winters intolerable—or life in London preferable. Reaching England in early December, he faced the painful task of settling Lady Charlotte's personal estate; she had died the previous June. He likewise met with Germain, ostensibly to present Carleton's supplication for four thousand additional troops for the 1777 campaign. Burgoyne knew the American secretary detested Carleton and was looking for ways to embarrass or recall him. When Germain kept raging about the troop request, George III tried to settle the matter. Carleton would remain as Quebec's governor, but a more spirited officer, none other than Burgoyne himself, would direct the 1777 martial effort emanating from Canada—an assignment Gentleman Johnny later claimed was both "unsolicited and unwelcome."[7]

Burgoyne had finally grasped what he longed to have: a chance at martial immortality. Still, he failed to get all the resources he wanted. He requested at least 8,000 regulars; Germain allotted him 7,173, "together with as many Canadians and Indians as may be thought necessary for this service." Some 3,770 British regulars and Hessians were to be retained in Quebec Province under Carleton to "secure Canada from external attacks." Burgoyne asked for the option, should circumstances warrant, of marching straight into New England from Lake Champlain to rendezvous with the king's forces in Rhode Island. Germain's orders offered him no flexibility. His assignment was "to pass Lake Champlain . . . by the most vigorous exertion of force" and "to proceed with all expedition to Albany and put himself under the command of Sir William Howe."

A component of Burgoyne's plan involved sending a diversionary force up the St. Lawrence River to Lake Ontario and thence to Oswego, with the idea of rallying the loyalist populace throughout the Mohawk Valley. Germain assigned 675 troops, including tories, to this column, plus "a sufficient number of Canadians and Indians," all under the command of Lieutenant Colonel Barry St. Leger. Once in the valley, St. Leger was to sweep eastward toward Albany and strike at the side or rear of any remaining rebel force trying to impede Burgoyne's progress. Ideally, the British forces would crush patriot resistance in the northern theater once and for all as they converged on Albany—and thereby open up New England for final subjugation.[8]

When Burgoyne disembarked at Quebec City on May 6, 1777, he handed Carleton a rather officious letter from Germain. According to General Simon Fraser, the governor reacted like "a Roman dictator" and was uncooperative with Burgoyne. Gentleman Johnny stated otherwise. Carleton, he indicated, offered him with "assiduity and zeal . . . all the assistance in his power," so much so that Burgoyne had elements of his army moving southward from St. Johns by mid-June. Some five hundred natives—mostly Hurons, Abenakis, and Algonquins—also joined the expeditionary force. The only disappointment was that so few Canadians, probably no more than 150, came forward to bear British arms.[9]

By Monday, June 23, Burgoyne's Advance Corps of fifteen hundred under Fraser was approaching Crown Point. Within another four days the whole British force—some ten thousand souls, counting mariners, victualers, and women and children—was making camp there. Some women were in the ranks and performed auxiliary services, everything from cooking to nursing. Others were camp followers, including prostitutes but also a few aristocrats, such as the Baroness von Riedesel. Her husband, Major General Baron Friedrich Adolphus von Riedesel, was the ranking German officer. He commanded 3,025 Hessian troops, mostly Brunswickers, who made up about 40 percent of Burgoyne's soldiery.

Assuming the rebels would never engage so formidable a force, Burgoyne indulged his capacity for pompous prose in a public proclamation, dated Sunday, June 22, 1777, that exhorted the rebels to lay down their arms or suffer the most dire of consequences. The imperial government, he pronounced, had "called forth" its "military servants" with "the sole purpose of restoring the rights of the [British] Constitution." His army intended to end the "the present unnatural rebellion" that rested on "the most complete system of tyranny, that ever God in his displeasure suffered for a time to be exercised over a forward and stubborn generation." Should foolhardy rebels continue their "frenzy of hostility," Gentleman Johnny could only hope that "I shall stand acquitted in the eyes of God . . . in . . . executing the vengeance of the [parent] state against the willful outcasts." For all the good these words did him, he should have signed the proclamation "General Elbow Room."[10]

At Ticonderoga, Burgoyne encountered a hopelessly outnumbered and unprepared patriot force. To defend the fortress area and Mount Independence properly, St. Clair, who had arrived only on Thursday, June 12, needed several thousand troops; however, he had about twenty-two hundred and could not supplement that number because of limited food supplies. Camp equipment such as tents, he wrote, were "in general, very bad." The fleet of bateaux were "in ruin for want of pitch and tar," and heavy rain showers had damaged his stores of gunpowder because the magazines were so leaky. Just as bad, St. Clair had to report that "we have no cartridge paper," meaning that loading the proper amount of powder and ball into muskets was problematic at best.[11]

Nor did St. Clair have adequate intelligence. In a fretful letter to Schuyler of Wednesday, June 18, he stated, "I am at a loss to form a judgment of the design of the enemy." That same day he explained his precarious prospects to a Pennsylvania confidant and then concluded, "My dear friend, if you should not hear from me again, . . . remember that I have given you this account of our situation, and do not suffer my reputation to be murdered after having been sacrificed myself."[12]

Burgoyne was soon ready to launch a massive assault. On Monday, June 30, he decreed absolutely that "this army must not retreat." His Advance Corps was already in motion toward Ticonderoga, and the next morning the main army commenced its southward processional by water. The sight was spectacular, wrote a junior-grade officer, with "the music and drums of the different regiments . . . continually playing . . . to make the scene and passage extremely pleasant." By Friday, July 4, Burgoyne's army was squeezing in on the defending Americans.[13]

The next afternoon, the patriots spied enemy activity high atop Sugar Loaf Hill. Rising 750 feet above Lake Champlain just to the southwest of the old stone fortress, this promontory commanded the patriot works below—

only fourteen hundred yards to Ticonderoga and fifteen hundred to Mount Independence. The rebels had left the peak undefended because they thought no one could haul large cannons up the heavily wooded mountainside. Burgoyne's artillery officers believed otherwise. Stated General William Phillips, Burgoyne's second in command and artillery chief, "Where a goat can go a man can go, and where a man can go he can drag a gun." What St. Clair's troops were witnessing was the construction of a cannon battery that gave Burgoyne's matrosses the potential to bombard the rebels into oblivion.[14]

St. Clair called an emergency council of war, and the assembled officers wisely decided that "a retreat ought to be undertaken as soon as possible," noting "that we shall be very fortunate to effect it." Under cover of darkness early on Sunday, July 6, St. Clair's troops withdrew by land and water. At daylight the British gave chase. By four o'clock that afternoon, one detachment had closed in on about five hundred patriots who had sailed southward for Skenesborough. The Americans first set fire to buildings at Skenesborough before retreating eleven miles up Wood Creek, where they at last paused and rested at Fort Anne. The next morning they skirmished with a British pursuit party before again burning whatever they could, including the small stockade, and retreating another twelve miles to Fort Edward on the east bank of the Hudson River, where Schuyler had recently raised the patriot battle standard.

St. Clair, meanwhile, led the bulk of his fleeing soldiery overland into Vermont territory. At dawn on Monday, July 7, Fraser's Advance Corps caught up with the patriot rear guard at Hubbardton, twenty-four miles southeast of Ticonderoga, and a bloody battle ensued. Camping six miles ahead at Castleton, St. Clair's main body of troops heard the echoing bursts of musket fire and got away. Five days later they also reached Fort Edward. St. Clair, having encountered a vastly superior enemy force at Ticonderoga, had acted in exemplary fashion. He had saved most of his soldiers; they could stand and fight yet another day—under far more favorable circumstances.[15]

Only twenty-three miles away from Fort Edward at Skenesborough, Burgoyne savored his "several successes." He stated categorically to Germain that "I am confident of fulfilling the object of my orders," before adding with feigned modesty, "The instruments I have to employ are so good that my merit will be small." Then he requested "a discretionary leave" to return to England once the campaign was over, reminding him that "my constitution is not fitted for an American winter." Burgoyne was likely dreaming of a hero's welcome back home. Even before taking Ticonderoga, his "great apprehension," according to Fraser, "was that the rebel army would go off, and the conquest would not have been rendered sufficiently brilliant by [capturing] a great number of prisoners, or a large quantity of stores."[16]

After driving back St. Clair's small force, Gentleman Johnny became even more contemptuous of his provincial bumpkin adversaries. They would keep retreating in disarray, he was positive, rather than risk full-scale combat against the destructive power of concentrated British arms. Burgoyne had finally gained his elbow room, or so he thought; and he now intended "to risk nothing without being sure of success." His lack of bold initiatives in the days ahead gave the rebels exactly what they had to have: time to rally around the likes of Benedict Arnold.[17]

III

Arnold rode into Albany on Monday, July 21, with little fanfare. One local citizen saw no purpose in his appearance, since he had not brought troops. "Generals without men are not what we want, we have generals of every specie," he sneered. Although this observer had underestimated Arnold's value, the fundamental problem in the Northern Department remained inadequate troop strength.[18]

Arnold reached Fort Edward, some forty-five miles north of Albany, on July 22. Schuyler greeted his fighting comrade warmly and offered a full briefing. On paper, the northern force showed modest strength. A muster roll of July 20 listed 6,359 troops, including 3,925 Continentals and 2,434 militiamen. Interminable rain had repeatedly soaked the soldiery, which was lacking in tents. Because of fevers, colds, and assorted camp maladies, some nineteen hundred troops were unfit for duty. The 4,467 soldiers who could muster arms faced weapons, ammunition, and clothing shortages. With only two functioning fieldpieces, Schuyler could not even assemble a respectable artillery company. What his force could do was harass the enemy and keep falling back as Burgoyne advanced, while at the same time imploring Washington and civilian leaders in New York and New England to send forward more troops, arms, and supplies.[19]

Unaccountably but fortunately, Schuyler also reported, the British had remained stationary at Skenesborough. As Burgoyne himself later explained, he had rejected any "retrograde motion" of his troops back to Ticonderoga as part of a general advance up Lake George and across sixteen miles of rugged countryside from Fort George to Fort Edward. Rather, he kept the bulk of his troops at Skenesborough while General Phillips directed the southward movement of gunboats, bateaux, artillery, and heavy supplies over the Lake George water route. What Gentleman Johnny did not foresee was how much time—three valuable weeks—would be lost in dragging this equipment uphill through the nearly impassable three-mile portage from Ticonderoga to Lake George, a body of water more than two hundred feet higher than Lake Champlain. The British transport vessels and gunboats did not reach Fort George, which the rebels had abandoned several days earlier, until Monday, July 28, and these supplies still had to be hauled to Fort Edward.

Burgoyne was correct about one point. Had he pulled back from Skenesborough and attempted to move his whole force by the Lake George route, the rebels "would have destroyed the road from Fort George to Fort Edward." By remaining almost inert at Skenesborough, however, he allowed Schuyler to send hundreds of Massachusetts and New York militiamen into the swampy, hilly, heavily wooded terrain separating the two armies. Their task was to make the landscape as difficult to traverse as possible. With axes flying, they blocked the main pathway by felling huge trees. They destroyed every bridge along the way as the trail twisted back and forth across Wood Creek. They rolled huge boulders into fordable sections of the stream. Taking advantage of heavy rain showers, they hacked out ditches from waterlogged swamps, thereby flooding low-lying sections of the route.[20]

Despite their efforts, Schuyler indicated that advance enemy units—and their Indian allies—had reached Fort Anne late on Sunday, July 20. Very soon, he thought, his patriot force would have to begin retreating down the Hudson River, hoping to gain strength so it could make a stand before reaching Albany. If those increased numbers were exclusively militia, Schuyler did not know if Burgoyne, once back in full motion, could be stopped. The militiamen at Fort Edward, one of his aides stated, were "a most disorderly set." The northern commander had already "dismissed" some who had pressed to go home "to reap their harvests." Others had recently "deserted by whole companies," most likely because they feared being butchered should they make contact with Burgoyne's best light shock troops, his Native Americans.[21]

Schuyler did not expect Arnold to focus completely on militia matters. Delaying the enemy's advance was the first order of business. The Yorker had already selected a site on Moses Creek, five miles south of Fort Edward, as more defensible, and he intended to pull back the next day. Meanwhile, he asked Arnold to take command of a squad of Continentals and militiamen who would function as pickets, stay close to Fort Edward, and relay intelligence on Burgoyne's movements. Arnold willingly took the assignment.

While Schuyler's force retreated south on July 23, Arnold established an advance outpost at Snook Hill, about halfway between Fort Edward and Moses Creek. The two generals communicated regularly. Most of the news from Arnold was not encouraging. "The want of salted provisions" for his "badly clad and armed" troops, Arnold wrote to Washington, "prevented our sending out any considerable parties of men on scout, by which reason we have been deprived of intelligence, . . . except such as is very vague and uncertain." Worse yet, scouting parties out seeking the enemy's whereabouts were "daily insulted by the Indians." In a few instances, Burgoyne's native allies ambushed, killed, and scalped rebel pickets. However dangerous, such duty was vital to protecting Schuyler's main force from being overrun in what Baron von Riedesel had proudly taken to calling "the march of annihilation" from Canada.[22]

On the morning of Sunday, July 27, a particularly vile incident occurred. Arnold had established a picket line of one hundred troops at Fort Edward. Suddenly, a column of British regulars and Indians—Arnold estimated the number at one thousand—emerged from the woods and sent the patriot scouts scurrying back to Snook Hill. The fleeing Americans sustained ten casualties, including one lieutenant and five privates "killed and scalped," according to Arnold's account. During the melee, a party of Wyandot Indians captured two civilian women, both loyalists, in a nearby house. The younger of the two was Jane McCrea, better known as "Jenny," often described as ravishingly beautiful with long, flowing locks of golden hair. According to one version of the story, twenty-three-year-old Jenny was waiting to meet her betrothed, Lieutenant David Jones, a loyalist officer in Burgoyne's army. While escorting Jenny and the older woman back to the regulars, an argument erupted over which Wyandot held claim to Jenny as a war prize. Shots rang out and struck down Jenny, at which point, according to Arnold, the natives "scalped, stripped, and butchered" her "in the most shocking manner." After learning of this horrible deed, Arnold ordered out pickets for an attack, but a "heavy shower of rain . . . wet their arms and ammunition and gave the enemy time to retire."[23]

Arnold's description of the slaying of Jenny McCrea bore directly on one of the most talked-about events of the Revolutionary War. The tale of her murder spread far and wide, becoming more embellished with each retelling, to the point of including ghastly descriptions of unmerciful torture and even rape by besotted, lustful savages. Jenny's name supposedly became a rallying cry to arms for thousands of New England militiamen who feared that Burgoyne's marauding army, if not checked in its wanton butchery, might maim and kill their own families. Jenny McCrea, however, was a loyalist, which hardly endeared her to New England's rebel populace. Certainly as pertinent, if not more so, to the militia turnout were the setbacks suffered by Burgoyne's troops in August 1777. Only then, after the British force was in serious trouble, did New England's militiamen rush into the field in large numbers, and they were hardly buzzing about the horrible death of Jenny McCrea when they finally arrived in the upper Hudson River Valley.[24]

Despite his nasty encounters with the enemy in late July, Arnold was still optimistic. In writing to Washington, he mentioned Seth Warner's success in gathering seven hundred militiamen at Bennington in the Hampshire Grants and the appearance of Brigadier General John Glover's 750 Massachusetts Continentals at Albany. If Daniel Morgan's regiment of riflemen came north, Arnold felt the necessary troops would be in place to challenge Burgoyne "with all his infernals on any ground they might choose." He was also "very anxious to know the destination of General Howe," and he would have danced with joy had he known that Sir William had put out to sea for Philadelphia on July 23. Even without that information, Arnold wrote confidently, "I believe we shall be able to manage General Burgoyne." Then he appended words of praise for Schuyler, who "has done everything [a] man could do in his situation. I am sorry to hear his character so unjustly aspersed and calumniated."[25]

Schuyler could do nothing about his noisome New England critics. Outmanned and outgunned on the front line, he stayed with his strategy of retiring before the enemy, usually after heavy skirmishing between Arnold's pickets and advance enemy units. Schuyler abandoned Moses Creek on Thursday, July 31; crossed to the western bank of the Hudson River at Saratoga four days later; and then marched his force another twelve miles south to Stillwater. There he paused for ten days before renewing his southward retreat and reaching the northern bank of the Mohawk River, nine miles above Albany, on Sunday, August 18. Meanwhile, Fraser's Advance Corps broke through to Fort Edward on Tuesday, July 29. Two days later, Burgoyne's main body of troops reached that post, after which they focused on transporting their heavy equipment and supplies from Fort George. Even as the two armies maintained a loose form of contact, the Continental Congress was also acting—and not in a manner that would simplify the martial task of vanquishing Burgoyne's expeditionary force.

IV

The delegates wanted a scapegoat for the loss of Ticonderoga. They were not about to blame themselves for deficient troop levies or wholly inadequate provisioning. Nor were they going to fault Horatio Gates, who had ignored the Ticonderoga command assignment they had bestowed on him earlier that spring. Certainly they were not about to criticize, in the words of Connecticut delegate William Williams, the "pure, uncorrupt, and well founded" people of New England, even though so few of these virtuous folk had enlisted for Continental service in recent months. New Englanders had exercised sound judgment, said John Adams, by disdaining military duty under Schuyler, whom he now described as an "evil genius" to his congressional colleagues. The only way to reverse the tide of defeat and rally the populace, insisted the New England delegates, was to replace Schuyler with Gates.[26]

Leaders like Adams thus seized on the Ticonderoga debacle to get what they had sought for months. The New England delegates did not resort to repeating the widespread—and ludicrous—rumor about Burgoyne's soldiers firing silver musket balls and cannonballs into the fortress for the traitor St. Clair to gather up and share with the money-grubbing loyalist Schuyler. They dwelled on Gates's alleged popular appeal and how he had masterfully—and apparently single-handedly—"collected [the] shattered remains of [the] army last year," then "reduced it to order" and "repulsed the enemy."[27]

The New Englanders likewise adhered to procedural niceties. On Tuesday, July 29, they pushed through a resolution calling for a formal inquiry "into the conduct of the general officers who were in the Northern Department at the time of the evacuation" of Ticonderoga. The wording was important, since Schuyler was not at the fortress when it fell. Three days later, Congress instructed Schuyler—they did the same with St. Clair—to "repair" to Washington's headquarters for a court of inquiry. The delegates also "directed" Washington "to order such general officer as he shall think proper, to relieve Major General Schuyler"—a curious action since they had not consulted him about removing the Yorker.[28]

Washington had just arrived in Philadelphia. He was in the process of marching his force into southeastern Pennsylvania to contend with Howe's army, once Sir William landed his troops. Had Washington been free to select a northern commander, he would most likely have named Nathanael Greene. Not trying to restrain themselves, however, the New England delegates were precise about their preference. Their man was Gates, who "stands high in the esteem of the eastern states and troops," they wrote to Washington on Saturday, August 2. Since Gates was no longer very high in the commander's esteem, he wanted no part in appointing him to the northern post. Thus Washington asked Congress to be "excused" from the assignment.[29]

Two days later, the New Englanders finally obtained their objective when Congress accorded Gates command of the Northern Department. To make sure Washington was not questioning their judgment—which he was—the delegates "directed" him to order Gates northward. Washington did so, but with an intentional play on words: he informed Gates that Congress has "destined you" for the Northern Department command and that he should "proceed to the place of your destination" with all possible haste. The commander would let the delegates take the credit or the blame for that general's performance.[30]

John Adams, by comparison, was ecstatic. He sent the tidings to Abigail, pointing out that Generals Arnold and Lincoln were also in the northern theater. "These three I believe will restore our affairs in that department," he stated, perhaps recalling how effectively Arnold and Gates had worked together the previous summer. He never considered that voting against restoring Arnold's seniority, which he did in another few days, would help provoke a terrible tempest between America's Hannibal and the darling general of the New England delegates, even as they engaged in combat with Burgoyne.[31]

In late July, Arnold received a communication from a friendly delegate warning him not to expect satisfaction. His adherents in Congress could not muster enough votes to move him up on the seniority list of major generals. Shortly thereafter, Arnold met with Schuyler, expressed his frustration, and "asked . . . to retire" from the field. The Yorker "advised him to delay," pointing out that should St. Clair be "ordered down" by Congress, the Northern Department would have a shortage of senior officers. He also served up a generous helping of flattery, and Arnold, after further reflection, promised to stay with the army, but only as long as Burgoyne's minions were a threat.[32]

Schuyler may also have forewarned Arnold that his own days with the Northern Department were likely numbered. Little else could account for Arnold's decision to send Gates a long, newsy letter, dated Tuesday, August 5, that reads like a briefing document. He began disingenuously by apologizing for "my long silence," blaming the crush of military business. Then Arnold described the current disposition of British and patriot troops. The greatest problem was dealing with Burgoyne's "infernal savages," a source of terror throughout the countryside. "Painted like furies," they were "continually harassing and scalping our people and the miserable defenseless inhabitants." Arnold also claimed to have evidence about persons being "roasted alive in [the] presence of the *polite and humane British army.*" The patriot force, "including boys and invalids," was at Stillwater "with a view of making a stand" and "expecting to be reinforced, of which there is some little probability." Without additional troops, however, the army would likely "retire" to the Mohawk River, "whose passage we shall dispute at all events."

Arnold also tried to evoke sympathy for his personal plight over rank. He conceded the "embarrassment" of his position and then mentioned a rumor that Congress might possibly accept his resignation. "No public or private injury or insult," he expounded in a statement that contradicted what he had indicated to Schuyler, "shall prevail on me to forsake the cause of my injured and oppressed country until I see peace and liberty return to her, or nobly die in the attempt." [33]

Perhaps Arnold thought Gates might reverse his disdainful course of recent months and assist him with Congress. At the same time, he offered only words that his erstwhile patron and friend could not twist against him, since he had good reason to be wary of Gates. Perhaps, too, Arnold was extending an olive branch on behalf of comradeship in the field, since Gates would surely become the Northern Department commander if Schuyler did, indeed, fall from Congress's grace. That Gates made no attempt to reply to this letter, even with a brief acknowledgment, was not an auspicious sign for command unity.

On Friday, August 8, Congress got around to debating and voting on the question of restoring Arnold's seniority. An amendment to justify the change "on account of his extraordinary merit and former rank in the army" failed to pass. Sixteen delegates then voted against the original motion, as compared to only six in favor. Since each state possessed an equal voice in congressional decisions, the official tally was seven states in the negative as compared to four (New Hampshire, Rhode Island, Connecticut, and Georgia) in Arnold's favor. Despite his close association with Schuyler, the New York delegation eschewed him, and he received no support from Massachusetts, New Jersey, and Pennsylvania, home states of the officers elevated over him. Arnold did not even gain the vote of Marylander Samuel Chase, ostensibly one of his friends and admirers. Thus, in spite of two months of personal effort and his unusual record of meritorious service, he had failed to muster a sympathetic alliance of congressional delegates. [34]

Outspoken James Lovell of Massachusetts felt Congress had wasted too much time on Arnold's case. "It was really a question between monarchical and republican principles put at a most critical time," he contended, as if Arnold's pleas for just treatment represented some sort of praetorian assault on civil authority. Had Lovell and other New Englanders held Horatio Gates to the same standard, such a grand-sounding rationalization would not have reverberated with hypocrisy. [35]

A new delegate from South Carolina, Henry Laurens, who had just arrived in Philadelphia but did not vote, viewed matters very differently. He called Congress's mode of "reasoning on this occasion . . . disgusting" and stated that Arnold "was refused not because he was deficient in merit or that his demand was not well founded but because he asked for it and that granting at such instance would be derogatory to the honor of Congress." Laurens also expressed concern that the decision would "deprive us" of the "good old servant General Arnold," as well as have "further ill effects in the army."[36]

Delegates like Lovell, by comparison, did not seem to care. Arnold was "at liberty to quit" if he would not submit to the superior judgment of Congress. Should he resign, he would forever be known as a man "who leaves a patriotic exertion because self-love was injured in a fanciful right incompatible with the general interest of the union." What Lovell did not admit was that political influence, much more than meritorious service, had become the one sure key to congressional preferment. This reality was particularly irksome to Washington's most talented lieutenants, especially when the delegates so obviously played favorites with the likes of Gates or even Benjamin Lincoln, whom Congress had elevated over Arnold primarily because he resided in Lovell's home state of Massachusetts.[37]

From Arnold's perspective, civilian leaders such as Lovell were little more than ciphers. They were the kind of pretend patriots who were always ready to shout republican platitudes about selfless public service when the words happened to reinforce their own parochial interests—in Lovell's case those of Massachusetts. Such congressional ilk, Arnold also concluded, had removed Schuyler to divert attention from their own incapacities as war leaders while proudly proclaiming themselves true servants of the people by elevating the likes of Gates—or more properly an officer, unlike Schuyler, whom they believed they could manipulate for their own petty purposes.

By its vote, Congress provoked as nothing else could Arnold's sense of debased personal honor. From his point of view, the delegates had at last revealed their flagrant disregard, if not blatant contempt, for so fundamental a standard of community recognition and approbation as demonstrated public virtue. They had shown themselves as unworthy stewards of republicanism in America. Thus for Arnold, Congress no longer deserved the respect of truly selfless patriots.

Congress's denial of so "fanciful" a plea for justice, as Lovell sneeringly wrote, represented a major turning point in Arnold's life. No longer would he bow and scrape with the hope of earning Congress's favor and preferment, as he had done from May to July in Philadelphia. Now the key issue was whether Arnold could keep his deeply scorched feelings from igniting while serving under the command of Gates.

V

Burgoyne was still extremely confident when he reached Fort Edward in late July. He scoffed at "the perseverance of the enemy in driving both people and cattle before them as they retreat," which he dismissed as "an act of desperation and folly." Although patriot resistance could "retard me for a time," he admitted to Germain, "it cannot finally impede me." A week later, he predicted with certainty that his army would complete its "successful progress" toward Albany by no later than Saturday, August 23.[38]

Even as he penned these words, a host of debilitating blows were shredding Gentleman Johnny's plans. His Native American allies were one source of problems. "There is infinite difficulty to manage them," Burgoyne wrote on Wednesday, August 6. "My effort has been to keep up their terror and avoid their cruelty," he also stated in self-congratulatory fashion, claiming that "they scalp the dead only and spare the inhabitants."[39]

Actually, Burgoyne had lost control of his Indian allies. When he ordered the arrest of Jane McCrea's alleged murderer, the tribal chiefs threatened to return to Canada unless the general spared the warrior's life. Burgoyne acquiesced, but a few days later the Indians suddenly "wished to have . . . leave to return home," insisting they had not agreed to serve beyond August 5. Burgoyne quickly assembled the chiefs, and "with the promise of a little rum attended with the usual ceremonies," they declared that the "knife should not be sheathed" until their warriors had redressed all rebel wrongs against their English father King George. The alcohol soon wore off, however, and groups of Indians started to disappear from camp. By the end of August, Burgoyne had fewer than one hundred warriors at his disposal. His expeditionary force no longer had its primary instrument of terror to keep rebel scouting parties at bay or to intimidate—if not butcher—non-loyalist settlers.[40]

Burgoyne's Native Americans were not his only manpower problem. After securing Ticonderoga, the general called on Carleton to garrison that post as well as to protect his ever-lengthening supply line back to Montreal. The governor refused to provide any assistance, despite the presence of some three thousand troops in Canada. He could not help, he claimed, out of "obedience to the orders" sent him by Lord Germain, who had "taken the conduct of the war entirely out of my hands" by mandating that these soldiers remain in Quebec Province. Carleton was using a literal reading of Germain's instructions to embarrass the American secretary, which forced Burgoyne to leave about nine hundred British and Hessian troops behind at Ticonderoga. In addition, Burgoyne had to garrison other key posts, such as Fort George, as his army pushed farther south.[41]

Lack of forward movement, some of which related to bringing up supplies, was a third problem. Burgoyne's army lingered for several days in the vicinity of Fort Edward, waiting on the delivery of bulk food and heavy war matériel from Lake George. The crude pathway from the lake was "in some parts steep and in others wanting great repair," Burgoyne advised Germain. No more than a third of the horses (some five hundred of fifteen hundred) secured "by contract in Canada" had arrived, although the army did have fifty teams of oxen—confiscated from local settlers—to help with the transportation of supplies. "Exceeding heavy rains" likewise caused interminable delays in moving up artillery pieces and rations.[42]

To proceed decisively for Albany, which at forty-five miles distance was no more than two to three days of hard marching away, Burgoyne wanted his army to have at least thirty days' worth of provisions, a textbook figure. Without full provisioning, he was willing only to move his army eight miles south to Fort Miller along the east bank of the Hudson River, which he had accomplished by mid-August.

Gentleman Johnny preferred not to dwell on such problems. The general devoted himself, stated the Baroness von Riedesel, to "having a jolly time" by "spending half the night singing and drinking and amusing himself in the company of the wife of a commissary, who was his mistress and, like him, loved champagne." He was sure, based on the patriot flight from Ticonderoga, that his regulars could sweep away the rebel vermin whenever he ordered them to do so. He did not even evidence concern when in early August he at last received word from Howe about moving by sea for Philadelphia. Sir William did not promise any assistance whatsoever to the northern force, not even a diversionary movement up the Hudson River.[43]

Burgoyne kept Howe's message secret while he pondered how to keep advancing without expected succor from below. Finally, he consulted with Baron von Riedesel, who had earlier asked that a raiding party go into Vermont territory to seize horses for his Hessian dragoons; most of them lacked mounts. Burgoyne now decided on a more elaborate sortie "to disconcert the councils of the enemy, . . . and to obtain large supplies of cattle, horses, and carriages." This plunder would help replenish provisions, so that his force could proceed without further delay. Once at Albany, Burgoyne planned to take a defensive posture until reinforced with enough troops from New York City or elsewhere to conduct additional operations—assuming that rebel resistance did not collapse during his final march to Albany.

Riedesel warned against too elaborate an operation, but Burgoyne refused to listen. On Saturday, August 9, he drew up orders for Lieutenant Colonel Friedrich Baum, who commanded the Brunswick dragoons, to lead some 750 soldiers into Vermont. Baum was to spread the word that he was leading an advance corps of Burgoyne's army, now preparing to shift course and move into New England to link up with British troops coming overland from Rhode Island. The ruse would keep the rebels on their heels, thought Burgoyne, and afford Baum's detachment the time to seize needed supplies without much resistance.[44]

Neither Baum nor his troops, nearly half of them Hessians and the remainder mostly Canadians, plus a few loyalists and Indians, had any idea that they were marching into a virtual death trap. General John Stark and nearly fifteen hundred New Hampshire militiamen were waiting at Bennington. Unlike Arnold, Stark had resigned his Continental colonel's commission the previous March, after Congress had elevated officers junior to him into brigadier generalships. Then, in July, the New Hampshire assembly offered him a militia generalship. He accepted the commission, then quickly convinced hundreds of local citizens to join him in resisting Burgoyne. When his column arrived in Vermont, Benjamin Lincoln, whom Schuyler had now placed in charge of militia operations, ordered Stark to join the Yorker's Continental force. He refused; he was a general of the people, not of Congress, he informed Lincoln, and his plan was to strike at Burgoyne's flank and rear.

The battle that ensued at Bennington on the sweltering afternoon of Saturday, August 16, saw Stark's force, augmented by about 350 Green Mountain Boys under Seth Warner, rout Baum's troops, as well as a relief column of about 550 Hessians. The patriots sustained only light casualties, about sixty killed and wounded. By comparison, 207 of Baum's soldiers, including the colonel himself, were slain, and countless more were wounded. Stark's troops took about seven hundred prisoners. These losses reduced Burgoyne's fighting strength by about 15 percent.

Wrote Burgoyne to Germain, "I yet do not despond." But Gentleman Johnny now seemed perplexed, and he began to blame others for the difficulties besetting his army. Riedesel, he claimed, "had repeatedly pressed" him to get horses or he would not have sent out Baum's detachment, a less-than-straightforward rendering of events. Shrewdly, however, Burgoyne had not endangered his "best troops," obviously British regulars, but had wasted only lesser folk—Hessians, Canadians, loyalists, and Indians. He admitted that Vermont territory "now abounds in the . . . most rebellious race of the continent and hangs like a gathering storm upon my left." Another "most embarrassing circumstance" was "the want of communication with Sir William Howe," and for the first time Burgoyne faulted Carleton for not garrisoning Ticonderoga. "Had I latitude in my orders," he also announced, he would consider a temporary retreat to protect his flanks. Lacking discretionary authority, Burgoyne intended to collect twenty-five day's provisions; cross the Hudson, where "all safety of communication ceases"; and press for Albany, despite the presence of "an army superior to mine"—another exaggeration at this point in time. His major source of hope lay with Barry St. Leger, whose diversionary force, from what Burgoyne then knew, had Fort Schuyler at the upper end of the Mohawk Valley under siege. Gentleman Johnny, however, had not yet learned that Benedict Arnold was leading a relief column westward with orders to drive off St. Leger's detachment.[45]

VI

Schuyler's strategy of slowly giving way before Burgoyne's army, while straining the enemy's ever-lengthening supply line, was working. His reward for these labors was the letter he received from Congress on Sunday, August 10, ordering him to proceed to Washington's headquarters for an inquiry into the loss of Fort Ticonderoga. Even though effectively sacked, Schuyler was too selfless a patriot to quit in a huff. "I thought it my duty to remain with the army," he would reply to Congress.[46]

Among the most pressing matters was how to deal with the menacing diversionary force of Barry St. Leger. Lieutenant colonel of the 34th Regiment, St. Leger had fought in the French and Indian War and gained a reputation for being well versed in frontier warfare. The core of his column consisted of about 750 regulars, Hessians, and Sir John Johnson's loyalist "Royal Greens." Johnson was crucial to the expedition, since his late father, Sir William, had been the highly effective Northern Department Indian agent based in central New York. Sir John had convinced many local frontier settlers to stand with King George. He also had a legacy of family connections with the Six Nations of Iroquois, whose hatchets and scalping knives British planners deemed crucial to the expedition's success.

In late June, St. Leger's force departed from Montreal. Moving ahead more quickly, Sir John reached Oswego on the southern shore of Lake Ontario in mid-July. He met with a large gathering of Iroquois Indians, mostly Mohawks, led by the powerful war chief Thayendanegea (Joseph

Brant). Thayendanegea employed his dazzling oratory to help convince between eight hundred and one thousand of his fellow Iroquois warriors to join St. Leger, in return for weapons as well as scalps lifted and goods plundered from rebel settlers.

St. Leger mistakenly assumed that Fort Schuyler (known before the war as Fort Stanwix), the most important military facility blocking his planned advance through the Mohawk Valley, was both dilapidated and lightly garrisoned. The fort stood at the upper end of the valley, some 110 miles west of Albany, at a key portaging point running between the Mohawk River and the water pathway running northwestward toward Oswego and Lake Ontario. Back in April, Schuyler, suspecting an enemy incursion into the valley, had ordered Colonel Peter Gansevoort's 3d New York Continentals, about 550 soldiers, to refurbish and garrison the fort. Gansevoort and his able lieutenant colonel, Marinus Willett, diligently executed the assignment. They also received six week's worth of provisions, along with two hundred additional soldiers, just a few days before St. Leger's Indian allies reached the fort on Saturday, August 2.

St. Leger came up with his column of regulars two days later, and he quickly demonstrated that he was much more a textbook British officer than a skilled frontier combatant. He could have bypassed the fort and raided down through the valley toward Albany, but he made camp and launched a formal siege, even though he lacked artillery pieces powerful enough—his largest cannon was a 6-pounder—to breach the walls. He likewise paraded his full force before the defenders, which only intensified their resolve to hold out rather than face possible butchery from the Iroquois if they surrendered. Next St. Leger issued a demand for capitulation, written with a pomposity that only Burgoyne could have admired. Gansevoort and Willett did not respond; they preferred to gamble that their supplies would last until relief arrived. By accepting the siege, they were also keeping St. Leger from pillaging friends and families farther down the Mohawk Valley and reaching Burgoyne.

News of the enemy's approach reached rebel militia general Nicholas Herkimer, one of hundreds of Palatine Germans in the valley, in late July. He issued orders for all patriots to muster at Fort Dayton, about thirty miles below Fort Schuyler. On Wednesday morning, August 6, some eight hundred militiamen, supported by Oneida and Tuscarora allies, marched into a trap near the Indian village of Oriskany, some six miles short of Fort Schuyler. As they proceeded through a narrow ravine, Sir John's Royal Greens and Brant's Indians ambushed them. Seriously wounded, Herkimer rallied his troops, who warded off enemy thrusts while he sat at the base of a tree smoking his pipe and bleeding profusely from his wounds. After several hours of intermittent but intense combat, Brant's Indians withdrew. They had sustained too many casualties, including about thirty killed and forty wounded, among them some principal chiefs. The mortally wounded Herkimer, with about 150 of his troops killed and wounded plus another 50 captured, some of whom would be tortured to death, led the battered survivors back to Fort Dayton. The bloodletting at Oriskany seemed to dash any immediate prospect of relief for Gansevoort's troops.

A harried Schuyler learned about the battle at Oriskany on Friday, August 8. Should the fort's defenders decide to surrender, he realized, nothing could stop St. Leger's force from rampaging through the Mohawk Valley to Albany. Besides the devastation, such a stroke would place his own army at Stillwater in a precarious position if Burgoyne's army altered its dilatory conduct, moved across the Hudson River, and marched decisively southward.

The critical question was whether to send a Continental detachment westward to relieve Fort Schuyler, thereby dispersing patriot troop strength with Burgoyne likely to move any time, or to leave Gansevoort to his own fate. Schuyler presented these two unattractive alternatives to a council of war on Tuesday, August 12. Except for Arnold, those in attendance favored conventional military wisdom. They exhorted Schuyler to keep his outmanned force of about forty-five hundred soldiers concentrated at Stillwater. The Yorker favored the unorthodox option. He did not see how his army could withstand concurrent blows from the west and north. Decisively checking St. Leger would enable the patriots to contend more easily with Burgoyne, regardless of whether a sizable British detachment began ascending the Hudson River from New York City.

As the meeting progressed, Schuyler became visibly angry when one officer muttered words about intentionally weakening the northern army in the presence of the enemy. If need be, the Yorker replied sharply, he would lead the relief column westward, since none of his brigadiers apparently had the fortitude to do so. Arnold then spoke up and offered to take on the assignment. Schuyler would have preferred a lesser-ranking officer, but no one was more resourceful than Arnold.

Arnold's orders called for him to proceed up the Mohawk River at the head of Brigadier General Ebenezer Learned's brigade of nine hundred Continentals. The latter officer would serve as his second in command. Arnold was to rally as many Tryon County militiamen as he could before marching "with all convenient speed" to Fort Schuyler. He was likewise to encourage the participation of such Iroquois allies as the Oneidas and Tuscaroras. Meanwhile, as authorized at another council of war on August

13, the northern army would pull back twelve miles from Stillwater to the Mohawk River, a preferable base from which to challenge Burgoyne, should his force become active, or St. Leger, should Arnold fail in his assignment. Six days later, Schuyler gracefully performed the ceremonial task of turning over his command to Horatio Gates on Van Schaick's Island at the mouth of the Mohawk River.[47]

Arnold was not yet aware of Congress's negative vote on his seniority claim when he began his westward trek. Using forced marches, he got his troops to the German Flats area near Fort Dayton by Thursday, August 21. There an express letter from Horatio Gates caught up with him, formally notifying Arnold of Congress's decision "to appoint me to the command in the Northern Department." Gates then stated a theme that dominated his messages over the next few days: "As soon as you have put a happy finishing to our affairs to the westward, I desire you will immediately return to the main army with all the force you carried with you, the artillery, and as many of the militia as you can collect." Arnold understood that Gates, an officer steeped in traditional military logic, was exceedingly nervous about Schuyler's decision to disperse troops with Burgoyne hovering in the vicinity. Still, Gates did "rejoice . . . for the very great success of our arms at Bennington," and he asked Arnold to "signify" to Nicholas Herkimer and the Tryon militiamen "how much I think the United States are obliged" to them for "the glorious victory they obtained over the savage enemies" at Oriskany.[48]

The tone of Gates's words was neither chilly nor friendly. Arnold responded in kind, informing Gates of Herkimer's death, then promising to "return your thanks to the other gentlemen" involved in the battle. Now in contact with a small detachment of Continentals at Fort Dayton, Arnold intended to march very soon for Fort Schuyler with twelve hundred soldiers and "a handful of militia." Trying to reassure Gates, he wrote, "Nothing shall be omitted that can be done to raise the siege. You will hear of my being victorious, or no more; and as soon as the safety of this part of the country will permit, I will fly to your assistance." Arnold did offer one prickly comment: "I beg leave to congratulate you on our late success over the enemy by the troops commanded by General Stark."[49]

Arnold also wrote Schuyler later that day and offered the same congratulations, but this time "heartily." This missive was also more candid, since Arnold was communicating with a respected military steward and friend, as compared to a person he no longer trusted. Somehow a copy of this letter, in what appears to be Arnold's handwriting, made its way to Gates. That Arnold would take the time in the midst of a crisis to prepare a copy for his new commanding officer makes no sense. Possibly a messenger accidentally—or even purposely—delivered the original to Gates. More important, the affectionate tone toward Schuyler was certainly evident, perhaps enough to increase Gates's suspicions about where Arnold's personal loyalties lay.[50]

At that moment, the dilemma facing Arnold was how to reckon with St. Leger's force. Not surprisingly, he favored a direct overture to combat—an unappealing prospect for his subordinate officers, who envisioned another bloodletting like that at Oriskany. On August 21 they asked Arnold for a council of war. At the outset of the meeting, a party of Oneidas recently in contact with St. Leger's troops testified to the enemy's superior strength— probably double Arnold's. Marinus Willett, who had managed to sneak through St. Leger's lines to seek help, verified this estimate. After much discussion, the officers voted "not to hazard our little army"—Arnold's words—until more troops and Indians were available.[51]

A frustrated Arnold decided not to defy his officers. He had no guarantee that Learned's troops would follow him. Quick action, however, was essential. Then, late that evening, Arnold received an unusual offer. He agreed to meet with the mother and brother of a local loyalist, Hon Yost Schuyler. They pled for Hon Yost's life, since Tryon County officials had ordered his execution because he had recruited tory soldiers for St. Leger's detachment. Arnold could do nothing, he explained; but the imploring mother convinced him to speak with her condemned son. Hon Yost proved to be a rather enigmatic fellow who was allegedly a half-wit; he also claimed to be a distant relative of General Schuyler. Staring death in the face, the Dutchman said he would help drive off St. Leger in return for his freedom. His idea was to spread panic among the Britisher's native allies by rushing into their camp and warning them that a rebel column of two thousand or more troops was bearing down on them, with the infamous "dark eagle" General Arnold in command.

Hon Yost claimed to know Thayendanegea's Indians well. Apparently he had lived among them, and they had always treated him respectfully. Because of his reputedly addled brain, the Iroquois supposedly accorded him special status as a prophet from the Great Spirit, able to foretell the future. More likely Hon Yost, anything but half-witted as he bargained for his life, told Arnold of the mounting discontent among St. Leger's Indians. In undertaking a European-style siege, St. Leger had failed to consider the Native American mentality regarding drawn-out military operations. The Indians had found the siege tactics boring; they had lost too many valuable chiefs and warriors at Oriskany; and they had gotten very little booty and few scalps since joining the British column. The right kind of spark might inflame the Indians and cause them to renounce St. Leger and flee.

Short on alternatives, Arnold authorized the scheme. He incarcerated Hon Yost's brother (by some accounts also his mother) to make sure the Dutchman carried through in spreading the alarm among St. Leger's warriors. He likewise sent along a trusted Oneida scout, both to keep an eye on Hon Yost and to help with the deception. The Dutchman added his own theatrical touch by shooting holes in his clothing, thereby creating the impression of having barely escaped Arnold's clutches. On the afternoon of Friday, August 22, Hon Yost, looking bewildered and frightened, darted into the Indian camp near Fort Schuyler and breathlessly related his tale.

In a report to Carleton five days later, St. Leger articulated what he believed had happened. Already trying to keep his Indian allies calm because of intelligence about a rebel relief column of one thousand gathering at Fort Dayton, the Britisher referred to "scouts" who suddenly "came in with the account of the first number swelled to 2,000; immediately after a third, that General Burgoyne's army was cut to pieces and that Arnold was advancing by rapid and forced marches with 3,000 men." Suspecting "cowardice in some and treason in others," St. Leger gathered the native leaders in council, only to learn that some two hundred Indians had already "decamped." The chiefs "insisted that I should retreat or they would be obliged to abandon me." In their panic the Indians "grew furious." Some even "seized upon the officers' liquor and clothes in spite of the efforts of their servants and became more formidable than the enemy we had to expect." With his numbers suddenly cut by more than half, St. Leger's only choice was to end the siege and retreat northward for Oswego.[52]

An amazed but delighted Gansevoort sent out a note early that evening. He reported that "St. Leger with his army was retreating, with the utmost precipitation." He had met with Hon Yost, who had related even to him the tale of a relief column of two thousand troops. Arnold had already launched a march to Fort Schuyler, based on intelligence that St. Leger was about to overrun the fort. By digging a series of parallel trenches, the British were within two hundred yards of the defenders. The prospect of Gansevoort's troops being overrun had overcome the officers' lack of aggressiveness. Once Arnold had the colonel's message, he engaged in "a forced march," hoping to catch the enemy's "rear [guard], and securing their cannons and heavy baggage." When convinced that Fort Schuyler was secure, he would, as he wrote to Gates, move his troops back down the Mohawk River with "great dispatch."[53]

Arnold reached Fort Schuyler early on Sunday evening, August 24, and he offered Gansevoort and his soldiers "great applause for their spirited conduct and vigorous defense." Then he prepared for a quick thrust at "harassing the enemy" but also noted that Gansevoort had "anticipated my design by sending out a small party" to bite at the heels of the retreating British force. Four days later, Arnold was back at Fort Dayton busily making arrangements to transport twelve hundred troops by bateaux down the Mohawk River, since he was sure "there is nothing to be feared from the enemy in this quarter at present." He was right. St. Leger's column continued its flight back into Canada, leaving Burgoyne to his own devices. The once-confident British general would now have to make additional elbow room on his own.[54]

VII

Gates never thanked Arnold in writing for his part in driving off St. Leger's force. Perhaps that was because no one person deserved complete credit. Gates did, however, rush an express message to Congress noting "the defeat and disgrace with which the enemy have been obliged to retreat from Fort Schuyler," which, in combination with the "brilliant victory gained by General Stark and Colonel Warner at Bennington, gives the brightest luster to American arms, and covers the enemies of the United States with infamy and shame." Apparently Gates did not feel threatened enough by Stark or Warner to withhold their names.[55]

Not surprisingly, Washington was more generous in offering words of commendation. He declared to Congress that if Arnold had arrived sooner, "it is probable the enemy would have suffered considerably in their retreat." Washington's orders of the day, issued at Wilmington, Delaware, on Monday, September 1, noted specifically how "the approach of General Arnold with his detachment" was crucial to breaking the siege of Fort Schuyler.[56]

Unlike Gates, Washington repeatedly acknowledged the contributions of his key lieutenants. Indeed, if anyone, including members of Congress, had looked at Northern Department affairs objectively, they could have easily discerned that Gates played no part in positioning Burgoyne for possible defeat. Despite the initial patriot setback at Ticonderoga, the likes of Schuyler, Arnold, and Stark and their patriot soldiers had struggled against adversity and successfully taken advantage of the enemy's sluggish form of opportunism in the field. Gates appreciated his nonexistent part all too well, which only whetted his determination to claim for himself any glory emanating from the pending confrontation with Burgoyne.

With Gentleman Johnny's army nearby, Gates also needed the services of Arnold, his most tenacious and dynamic officer. Thus the form of public praise Gates offered—he had little choice because of Arnold's military rank—came by placing his fighting subordinate in charge of the northern army's left wing. In such a position, the new northern commander could take full advantage of Arnold's martial talents while at the same time closely watching his behavior. He could even rein in Arnold, should he attempt to perform heroics that would cast doubt on Gates's own congressionally endorsed role as savior of the Northern Department. He was not going to let America's Hannibal overshadow him in the days ahead—certainly not after Washington had favored the junior-ranking Arnold for the joint command assignment in Rhode Island and more recently scorned Congress's request to certify Gates's "destiny" as a creditable replacement for Schuyler.

When Arnold reported to Gates's headquarters on Van Schaick's Island late on Saturday, August 30, the new commander greeted him with civility. Gates said he would meet soon with his ranking officers in a council of war to "settle a fixed plan for our future operations." Both officers appreciated that Burgoyne, after the serious woundings at Bennington and Fort Schuyler, would soon have to press forward for Albany. Arnold, meanwhile, was to begin readying his division, now gathering at Loudon's Ferry on the north bank of the Mohawk River, for an advance northward. He would do so with his usual steadfastness of purpose. "Our people are in high spirits, and wish for action," he wrote to another old comrade, Colonel John Lamb, on Friday, September 5. "I heartily wish your regiment [was] with us, as a few days, in all probability," he accurately predicted, "will determine the fate of General Burgoyne's army, or that of ours." [57]

Still, Arnold was less than fully ebullient because he now knew about Congress's denial of his supplication for restored seniority. That decision had him seething with anger and put him in a defiant mood, perhaps reflected in his decision to appoint one of Schuyler's chief aides, Henry Brockholst Livingston, to his own staff. By doing so, he seemed to be needling both Gates and Congress. He also intended to demonstrate, once and for all, the depth of his virtue as a worthy patriot. To restore his personal honor, he intended to harvest his own share of glory from any engagement with Burgoyne's army. In seeking a hero's portion, Arnold had placed himself on a collision course with both Gentleman Johnny Burgoyne and Horatio Gates.

Sixteen

The Battles of Saratoga

I

For two years, Arnold had endured a series of martial failures against British forces in the north. Now he felt the decisive battle coming, and he longed both to purge his personal frustrations and to earn the laurels of public gratitude that would follow with the vanquishing of Burgoyne's army. Focusing his energies as never before, he refused to accept any diversions, even when he learned of Gates's decision to assign him as a brigade commander Enoch Poor, his old antagonist from the Hazen court-martial tempest. Arnold strove to resolve his differences with Poor, certainly the wise course on the verge of facing the real enemy, Burgoyne's army. Poor would directly supervise three New Hampshire Continental regiments under Colonels Joseph Cilley, Nathan Hale, and Alexander Scammell, as well as two New York regiments under Colonels Philip Van Cortlandt and Henry Beekman Livingston.

These Continental units formed the backbone of Arnold's wing. In addition, he welcomed the presence of Colonel Daniel Morgan, his comrade from the Canadian invasion, who had just marched north with 331 riflemen on orders from Congress and Washington. Morgan's regiment arrived in camp on August 30, only hours before Arnold returned from Fort Schuyler. Within a few days another famine-proof veteran, Major Henry Dearborn, who was serving under Scammell, accepted command of a special unit of 250 Continentals "drafted from the several regiments" to serve as light infantrymen "in conjunction with Colonel Morgan's corps of riflemen." Since Gates and Arnold did not yet know about the mass defection of Burgoyne's native allies, the plan was to have the troops of Morgan and Dearborn act as pickets to probe the enemy force and to ward off guerrilla-like Indians sorties. Morgan and Dearborn, nominally under Arnold's com-

mand, also had access to Gates's headquarters, a bifurcated reporting relationship with potential for problems.[1]

While organizing his wing, Arnold took time to secure additional horses
for himself, reflecting his anticipation of all-out battle, and to expand his
personal staff. When traveling north back in July to join Schuyler, he had
asked eighteen-year-old Matthew Clarkson, the scion of a renowned New
York mercantile family, to become his aide-de-camp. The Clarksons had
close ties with Schuyler, and one of young Matthew's first cousins, Major
Henry Brockholst Livingston, the nineteen-year-old son of New Jersey's
Governor William Livingston, was then serving as an aide to Schuyler. With
the Yorker's downfall, Livingston was looking for a new assignment. Arnold,
at the prompting of Clarkson, offered "Cousin Harry" duty as a staff aide.[2]

In addition, Arnold made twenty-four-year-old Lieutenant Colonel Richard Varick, Schuyler's former military secretary and Deputy Commissary
General of Musters for the Northern Department, visibly welcome at his
headquarters. He may have considered how the presence of these young
officers, all connected to Schuyler, might bother Gates, but from his perspective, they were deserving patriots anxious to serve the Revolutionary cause.
If Arnold was being callous toward the feelings of Gates, who did view their
presence as evidence of his subordinate's greater loyalty to Schuyler, he was
being no more small-minded than the northern commander, who had only
a few days before shown little regard for Arnold's sensitivities by assigning
him Enoch Poor as a brigade commander.

Adding to points of tension in early September, Arnold stood out as an
advocate of bold offensive action during Gates's councils of war. He favored
luring the weakened enemy force into a climactic battle. Gates, Arnold soon
realized, could conceptualize upcoming operations only in defensive terms.
The new commander was willing to march the northern army twelve miles
north to Stillwater, but Gates's preferred operational strategy was to erect a
strong line of entrenchments and let Burgoyne assault the American force.

Belying the patronizing conceptions of his British military training, Gates
seriously doubted whether American rebels, even the kind of battle-hardened
Continentals now forming the backbone of his force, could take the offensive
and engage the king's regulars successfully in open-field combat. Despite his
alleged admiration of patriot Americans under arms, he had little faith in
their fighting competence. He believed the patriots could prevail in combat
only if they had vastly superior numbers and fought from behind strong
defensive entrenchments. Thus he was doing everything possible to effect a
large turnout of New England militia with appeals that emphasized the
murder and mutilation of Jane McCrea.

Given Burgoyne's increased vulnerability, Arnold could hardly hide his contempt for Gates's defensive-mindedness. Many factors, he suspected, were keeping his superior from adopting an aggressive operational strategy. As Arnold knew, Gates's exalted rank had resulted from political favoritism, not from leading patriot troops in combat. Inexperience made Gates unsure of his own capacity for resourceful martial leadership, meaning that he would likely avoid risks that might jeopardize his standing with the civilians who had quenched his thirst for high command. Arnold even guessed that Gates might let the British force escape back into Canada—perhaps accomplishment enough to impress congressional delegates but an unthinkable outcome for America's Hannibal. His goal was nothing less than the obliteration of Burgoyne's army.

Because of his calls for offensive-minded warfare, Arnold started to feel like "a cipher" whenever he was at Gates's headquarters. Then, on Wednesday, September 10, his temper flared as he read the general orders of the day. A trickling of New York and Connecticut militia had recently come into camp. Gates had asked Arnold to assign these troops to appropriate brigades, but now he read of their posting with General John Glover's troops on the army's right wing. Charging over to headquarters, Arnold spoke to Gates about being "placed . . . in the ridiculous light of presuming to give orders" when "I had no right to do so, and having them publicly contradicted." Gates apologized for the mistake and said he would correct the error "in the ensuing orders." He never did so, however, most likely because he was upset with Arnold for having taken on Livingston as a staff aide the previous day.[3]

Arnold also employed the moment to protest his exclusion from the inner counsels of Gates's headquarters. He even named the person whom he believed most responsible for causing needless tension between the two senior officers. The "designing *villain*" was James Wilkinson, now a lieutenant colonel and Gates's hand-selected deputy adjutant general for the Northern Department.[4]

Twenty-year-old Wilkinson had long since attached his fortunes to the rising star of Gates. As an inordinately ambitious sycophant, "Wilky," as Gates affectionately called him, tried to mollify the uncertainties of his chief. As a born master of petty intrigue, he regularly questioned Arnold's loyalty, invariably disparaging Clarkson, Livingston, and Varick as that "New York gang." Their presence was proof of Arnold's true allegiance to Schuyler. Readily consuming Wilky's divisive brew, Gates would truckle with Arnold only as long as he needed his talents.

Gates dismissed his subordinate's concerns, which served as proof to

Arnold that he truly had no standing at headquarters. Having to deal with Gates as northern commander—and the scheming likes of Wilkinson as well—caused Arnold to resent Congress that much more. That body, after all, had recalled Schuyler, a general who no doubt would have turned him loose at the right moment to wreak havoc on Burgoyne's beleaguered force.

Despite his aggravation with Gates, Arnold maintained his equanimity. He would not be diverted from his primary target. The Anglo-German force was still out there, and he rejoiced when the patriot army, somewhere between six thousand and seven thousand strong and mostly Continentals, began its trek back to Stillwater on Monday, September 8. Arnold was among those who concluded that the Stillwater site would be difficult to defend because of the broad expanse of lowland separating the Hudson River from hills to the west. He rode north with the talented Polish engineer Thaddeus Kosciuszko in search of more easily defensible terrain. They did not have to go far. Some four miles ahead they found hills rising to a height of three hundred feet and stretching in a westerly line from the river's edge. This elevation was known as Bemis Heights, named after Jotham Bemis, who kept a tavern on the river road below. If Burgoyne's troops followed that pathway, they could be barraged from the heights; if they swung sharply west to outflank the Americans, they would become engulfed in heavy woods and rugged terrain interlaced with deep ravines; and if they directly attacked Bemis Heights, they would have to march uphill into withering musket and cannon fire. Kosciuszko and Arnold had found a prime defensive site.[5]

On Friday, September 12, the northern army moved forward to Bemis Heights and began digging trenches and constructing breastworks. Besides placing entrenchments across the river road, the main defensive line atop Bemis Heights resembled a squared-off semicircle, roughly three-quarters of a mile long on each side. The rear, abutting a protective ravine, was left open for escape, if necessary. On the right was General John Glover, and on the left was Arnold. Outside the entrenchments, covering a few stumpy fields and even higher terrain to the west, were Morgan's riflemen and Dearborn's light troops. Gates located his headquarters in the center. He directed operations from a tiny, ramshackle structure—better quarters were not available—with the brigade of General Ebenezer Learned camping around him. This humble abode was anything but pleasant, especially with the heavy rain of the past few days. It would become even more unpleasant once Arnold and Gates launched their own battle of Saratoga.

II

Burgoyne was running out of time. In the absence of strong diversionary support from New York City, he had two choices: call off the expedition and return to Canada or cross to the western side of the Hudson River and push ahead for Albany. The excoriation of Carleton for pulling back from Crown Point the previous year negated any serious contemplation of retreat. Burgoyne really had no choice. He had to lead his depleted force—in mid-September, Gentleman Johnny had fewer than five thousand combat-ready effectives out of a total strength of 6,588—across the Hudson, then straight south toward what intelligence sources told him was a rapidly growing enemy force.[6]

On Friday, September 12, the same day Gates's army moved up to Bemis Heights, Burgoyne had at last secured his ordnance pieces from Lake George and had minimal provisions in place. "The army will be ready to move tomorrow," he announced in fateful orders. His troops crossed the Hudson just north of the village of Saratoga, where General Schuyler had extensive property holdings. Once the force was on the west bank, the temporary bridge of boats "was broken up, and floated down the river," as one officer wrote, "and all communication with Canada [was] voluntarily cut off." Although Burgoyne was not yet sure where he could expect to encounter the Americans, he "burned with impatience to advance on the enemy," stated Baron von Riedesel. The rebels, he soon learned, were placing entrenchments about eight miles south of Saratoga.[7]

Just getting over the Hudson took nearly two days. While completing the crossing, Burgoyne rested his advance units on and near Schuyler's ripening fields. The troops methodically denuded the "plantation" of crops; they used Schuyler's mill to grind grain for extra bread, and corn became fodder for the army's horses. Exclaimed one officer, the rebel general's holdings were quickly "reduced to a scene of distress and poverty! What havoc and devastation is attendant on war!"[8]

On Monday, September 15, the British force began marching southward but made little headway because of the necessity of repairing bridges that Schuyler's retreating rebels had destroyed. On Wednesday evening, September 17, the army had reached Sword's farmhouse, about four miles north of Bemis Heights. Here American deserters, in return for hard money, explained to Burgoyne the exact rebel dispositions. The general now realized that he would have to fight for additional elbow room if he wanted his army to reach Albany.

As the British force moved southward, small-scale skirmishes erupted.

When Gates called together his general officers that same Wednesday, Arnold virtually begged for orders to let his wing go out and assess the enemy's strength. Gates could not deny the need for accurate intelligence. He finally acceded to Arnold's proposed reconnaissance in force, but only after sternly warning his fighting subordinate not to initiate a general engagement. Should Burgoyne do so, Arnold was to keep the British pinned down in the river's lowlands until Gates could move up with additional troops.

Arnold's column, perhaps three thousand soldiers, set out at dawn the next morning and swung in a northeasterly arc to approach the encamped Anglo-Hessian army from the west. When "the enemy appeared in considerable force," Burgoyne later wrote, he believed their purpose was "to obstruct the further repair of bridges and . . . to draw on an action where artillery could not be employed." In response, he kept his soldiery on full alert in camp, except for pickets assigned to fend off the molesting fire that Arnold's soldiers directed at enemy fatigue parties performing bridge repairs.[9]

Around noontime, a company of rebel skirmishers attacked several unarmed redcoats and women scavenging a potato field near Burgoyne's main camp. The action was short and bloody. The Americans killed or wounded fourteen and took a few prisoners before a relief force drove them off. An appalled British officer described the action as "cruel and unjustifiable conduct" that "serves greatly to increase hatred and a thirst for revenge." Arnold would have scoffed at such sentiments, stating that Burgoyne's Indians— when he still had substantial numbers of them—had shown little mercy for unarmed patriot civilians.[10]

At no point did Arnold try to force a battle. Late in the afternoon, he pulled his troops back to Bemis Heights and reported the results of the day's events to Gates. Arnold's opinion was that the enemy would attempt an assault on Bemis Heights within forty-eight hours, most likely by a flanking attack against his own left wing. Gates shrugged off his subordinate. Burgoyne would concentrate his movements along the river road, he was sure, giving the Americans the advantage of fighting from well-entrenched high ground. Gates thus saw no reason to seize the initiative.

III

How much Burgoyne intended to accomplish on Friday, September 19, remains shrouded in mystery. After a heavy ground fog lifted on that crisp, autumn-like morning, he put his whole force in motion. His primary objective was to maneuver his army into position for a full-scale assault on Bemis Heights. Given his penchant for deliberate maneuvers, however,

Burgoyne most likely planned to launch his main attack on September 20 or 21, as reflected in his decision to issue rations for three days. Most of all, he did not expect the "contemptible" rebels to come forward from their defensive works and square off in a "regular engagement." Should they be so foolish as to do so, he was sure that his highly disciplined British regulars would rout them.[11]

Burgoyne's troop deployment for advancing on Bemis Heights replicated his plan for approaching Ticonderoga. He divided his army into three columns. The right wing under General Fraser was to march westward along a ridge before angling south and securing the high ground flanking Bemis Heights from the west. Fraser's Advance Corps had performed similar duty at Ticonderoga and had found the way to Sugar Loaf Hill. Fraser's wing now contained the light infantry and grenadier companies of Burgoyne's ten British regiments, as well as Colonel Heinrich Breymann's Hessian riflemen and fifty British sharpshooters. Fraser also had command of the 24th Regiment's musket companies and all the Canadians (fewer than 125), loyalists (not quite three hundred), and Indians (no more than ninety) still present and fit for duty. In total, there were about twenty-three hundred soldiers in his column, plus four 6- and four 3-pounders.

Burgoyne placed Generals Phillips and Riedesel in charge of his left wing—Riedesel had the same assignment in moving against Ticonderoga. This column consisted of three Hessian infantry regiments (Rhetz, Riedesel, and Specht); the Hesse Hanau artillery company, with an allotment of six 6- and two 3-pounders; the Hesse Hanau infantry; the remnants of Colonel Baum's regiment (about fifty men); and six musket companies from the British 47th. Phillips and Riedesel were to move forward along the river road, repairing bridges and guarding the army's store of provisions, being carried in wagons or floated down the Hudson in some two hundred bateaux. The makeup of this force, which numbered between eleven hundred and twelve hundred soldiers, suggests that its function was to divert the Americans into thinking that Burgoyne intended to punch through the rebel defenses at the narrow stretch of land between Bemis Heights and the river.

Burgoyne rode along with the third, or center, column—he had done the same in approaching Ticonderoga. His line commander was Brigadier General James Hamilton, whose force consisted of the musket companies of the 9th, 20th, 21st, and 62d regiments, around eleven hundred soldiers. That these troops were exclusively British was no accident. Because of the allegedly poor performance of the Hessians at Bennington and the flight of St. Leger's native allies at Fort Schuyler, Burgoyne purposely concentrated his British regulars in this line. Their route of march would place them in the most

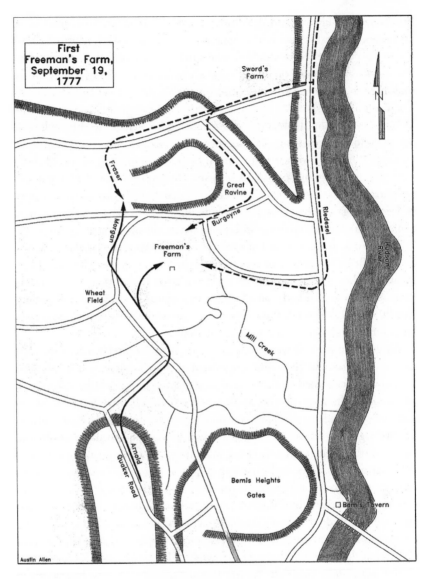

advanced position, should the Americans come forward from their entrenched lines and attempt a general engagement.

Should the patriots hold to their defenses, as Burgoyne expected, he
would then undertake the second phase of his plan. He would have Phillips
and Riedesel's left wing and Hamilton's regulars launch diversionary attacks
against the rebel center and right, while Fraser established himself on the

high ground northwest of Bemis Heights. Then Burgoyne would commence a classic turning movement to his right as his own cannons and enfilading artillery fire from Fraser's guns ripped into the Bemis Heights defenders. With the rebels caught in a cross fire, he would release Fraser's troops to crash into the American left, which was Arnold's position. As the Americans broke and ran, the British troops would press them up against the Hudson River, at which point they would conduct mopping up operations against the broken, entrapped rebel force before proceeding on to Albany.

Burgoyne longed for a momentous victory, the kind of glorious triumph denied him when St. Clair evacuated Ticonderoga. Gentleman Johnny could still envision British subjects at home celebrating his brilliance as the conqueror of the bumpkin American rebels. Circumstances, however, had changed since early July. Burgoyne's decisive advantage in troop strength was gone, and he would have to reckon with pugnacious officers such as Arnold and Morgan who, unlike the English-born Burgoyne and Gates, had esteem for the fighting prowess of hardened Continental veterans. Indeed, Burgoyne's plan had its best chance of success only if Gates kept his troops bottled up on Bemis Heights, which would let the British general determine the course of battle.

Near 10 A.M. a British cannon issued a round of artillery fire, rattling the foliage on trees showing the first bright hues of autumn. As the low, rumbling sound reached Bemis Heights, the three British columns commenced their forward movement. Phillips and Riedesel moved out along the river road while Fraser marched his column due west along a narrow, rutted wagon road. Burgoyne, riding with Hamilton's "British line" brigade, followed Fraser's troops before turning south and crossing over what came to be called "the Great Ravine" at a point where the rebels had not yet destroyed a bridge. By noontime or shortly thereafter, Hamilton's regiments had scrambled up the south bank of the ravine. They were still in heavy woods but not far from the farm of reputed loyalist John Freeman.

Freeman's farm consisted of nothing more than a tiny log shack for a home, some ramshackle outbuildings, and about fifteen to twenty acres of cleared land still dotted with tree stumps. The oblong field extended about 350 yards from east to west and sloped to the south, with great stands of timber on all sides. These same trees blocked any view of the field from lookouts on Bemis Heights, more than a mile to the south.[12]

Back in the woods touching the northern edge of Freeman's field, Burgoyne formed Hamilton's troops into a battle line. Fraser, meanwhile, had marched two and a half miles west, had also gotten across the Great Ravine, and had turned south along another crude pathway leading directly to Bemis

Heights. Each column now waited for a prearranged report of cannon fire to indicate that the advance should continue.

Gates, meanwhile, had received intelligence about pending British movements from patriot pickets stationed across from Sword's farm on the east bank of the Hudson River. The commander remained inert. Let the enemy come was his attitude, but Arnold "urged, begged, and entreated him" to seize the initiative. Fearing a powerful flanking attack from the northwest, Arnold wanted Morgan and Dearborn to probe the large column seen moving west from the river; and he requested permission to send out some of his musket regiments, should the riflemen need covering support. Arnold likewise expressed concern about the enemy getting cannons placed too close to Bemis Heights. Well-directed artillery fire, he warned, could breach the patriot defenses. Take advantage of American fighting skills, harassing the enemy from the cover of trees and woods, he argued. Most of all, America's Hannibal yearned to disrupt Burgoyne's battle plan. He dreaded the consequences of letting the Anglo-German force dictate the contest.[13]

Arnold persisted in his appeals. Gates, who seemed almost paralyzed by indecisiveness, finally relented, but probably only to stop Arnold from pestering him. He would allow Morgan and Dearborn go out with backup support. The riflemen were only to probe the enemy, avoiding an all-out engagement. Should they get too entangled in combat, Arnold could expect no relief from the center or right wings. These troops, Gates pronounced, would remain anchored in and around Bemis Heights for the expected onslaught from Burgoyne's left and center columns.[14]

Having secured permission to act, Arnold mounted his horse and, for the first time, acted as a field commander charged with coordinating his units. He soon had Morgan's riflemen and Dearborn's light infantrymen fanning out and moving northward to determine exactly what the enemy column was attempting in its westward march. Arnold rode back and forth along the wagon-rutted pathway passing to the left of Freeman's farm. As such, he maintained contact with Morgan and Dearborn while moving forward Cilley's and Scammell's New Hampshire regiments, the first musketmen to advance.

A little after noontime, in the midst of this activity, Arnold listened to the reverberations of cannon fire. The British columns had reached their assigned destinations and were ready to continue their advance. Shortly thereafter, Arnold heard the "smart firing of small arms." Having swept northward through the woods, Morgan's and Dearborn's troops had made contact with Canadian, loyalist, and Indian pickets. The Americans rushed forward, stopping only to aim their long rifles and shoot down their adversaries. The fleeing pickets suddenly ran into flying musket balls when British regulars under Hamilton "commenced a fire without orders (by which many of our own people were killed in retreating)," according to British artillery officer James Hadden.[15]

Hamilton's officers quickly regained control of the troops and, in synchronization with Fraser's column, directed a sharp volley of fire into the onrushing Americans. Morgan, who had moved forward behind the center of his irregular line while orchestrating the advance with a series of whistles and turkey calls, seemed stunned. According to Wilkinson, who claimed to be in the field, Morgan "burst into tears" and was shouting, "I am ruined, by God! . . . And my men are scattered God knows where." More likely, Morgan was shouting out a string of epithets while employing his calls to reassemble his overly exposed riflemen.[16]

To ease the pressure on Morgan and Dearborn, Arnold tried to outflank the left side of Fraser's column with Cilley's and Scammell's regiments. The skillful British brigadier quickly wheeled his troops to their right and drove back the attackers. Arnold and his officers had now located the enemy's position. Fraser held "a very advantageous height" to the right of Hamilton, whose regulars were posted along the northern edge of Freeman's farm.[17]

Looking north from the southern end of Freeman's field, Arnold detected a significant gap between the two British columns. Taking advantage of a lull in the fighting, he carefully aligned his troops to assault that opening, with the goal of smashing through and rolling up the two enemy lines in detail. Around two o'clock, Arnold launched the first charge, but the patriots failed to effect a breakthrough. He then shifted the weight of the American effort to the right and concentrated on trying to shatter Hamilton's British line. For more than three hours, in half a dozen charges and countercharges, the two forces fought back and forth across Freeman's increasingly bloodied field.[18]

Arnold's activities during the afternoon engagement have been a subject of debate. The evidence indicates that he was everywhere coordinating patriot movements. Although General Poor "did not see him once," he learned from Scammell that "Arnold rushed into the thickest of the fight with his usual recklessness, and at times acted like a madman." Scammell also recounted how Arnold "did not seem inclined to lead alone"; whenever "a prominent object among the enemy showed itself, he would seize the nearest rifle-gun and take deliberate aim." Years later one of Dearborn's officers, Captain Ebenezer Wakefield, stated that Arnold, "inspired by the fury of a demon," led at least one of the patriot charges. "Riding in front of the line, his eyes flashing, pointing with his sword to the advancing foe, with

a voice that rung clear as a trumpet," he "called upon the men to follow him
... , and ... he hurled them like a tornado on the British line." To
Wakefield, "nothing could exceed the bravery of Arnold on this day. ...
There seemed to shoot out from him a magnetic flame that electrified his
men and made heroes of all within his influence." [19]

Whether Arnold actually led his troops in one or more assaults cannot be
definitively proven. If he did, his behavior was imprudent for a field commander whose primary duty was to provide overall direction to the patriot
combat effort. Arnold likely spent the bulk of his time only on the edge of
harm's way, moving up yet more troops and aligning them for combat. [20]

Burgoyne had deployed Hamilton's British line so that the 21st was on the
right, the 62d in the middle, and the 20th on the left (with the 9th in
reserve). When Arnold ordered the charge into the gap between Fraser and
Hamilton, the 21st Regiment swung to its right, which formed a salient and
subjected the 62d to a deadly cross fire. As the fighting continued, the
Americans put more and more pressure on the British left, resulting in heavy
casualties in that area as well. Burgoyne, who played Arnold's coordinating
part for the British, had Fraser hold his position to stop the Americans from
overrunning Hamilton's right flank. Also at his commander's orders, Fraser
occasionally sent over companies of troops to shore up the increasingly
battered line of British regulars.

By late afternoon, Arnold had engaged the whole of his wing, some three
thousand troops. Gazing through the billows of gun smoke rising from
Freeman's field, he thought the British line could not withstand another
charge. Burgoyne recognized the same reality. He rushed a message for relief
to Riedesel. (Phillips had long since come over to direct Burgoyne's artillery
fire.) The Hessian general responded speedily. After splitting his column and
enjoining the troops he left behind to defend the army's train of wagons and
bateaux with their lives, Riedesel marched about five hundred soldiers up
and over a steep hill—directly west toward the American right flank a mile
and a half away. [21]

Arnold likewise sought additional troops. Unlike Burgoyne, he did not
have the advantage of overall command. He had to cajole Gates, whose only
oversight that afternoon came in the form of determined inactivity. When
Arnold reached the Bemis Heights defenses and implored Gates to release
more soldiers, the northern commander demurred. He had told Arnold
earlier in the day not to expect additional support. After more entreaties,
Gates finally relented and ordered elements of Learned's brigade to join in
the fight.

As the two general officers were parting company, Deputy Quartermaster

General Morgan Lewis came riding up and reported to Gates on "the indecisive progress of the action." Arnold, worried about the loss of critical momentum, dug spurs into his horse and shouted as he bolted away, "*By God I will soon put an end to it.*" His meaning was obvious. He intended to go out in front and lead his wing in one last dramatic charge before losing the opportunity for a smashing victory. Too risky for the tastes of Lewis, he warned Gates, "You had better order him back, the action is going well, [and] he may by some rash act do mischief." The northern commander hesitated, then looked at a nodding Wilkinson before telling his deputy adjutant to go after Arnold and bring him back to camp.[22]

Gates had just made one of four conspicuous tactical blunders as the First Battle of Freeman's Farm was reaching its crescendo. He had reined in his field commander, thereby leaving his combat units leaderless at the height of the battle. Yet he still sent out a portion of Learned's brigade, even though no ranking officer was present to guide these troops into the patriot line. They marched too far north, bypassed the main combat zone at Freeman's farm, and ended up colliding with Fraser's column. Quickly repulsed, Learned lost thirty-five—ten killed, sixteen wounded, and nine missing—a pointless waste of human beings, since these troops were not in place to help neutralize the appearance of Riedesel's soldiers.

Gates had already missed an obvious opportunity to block any portion of the Phillips-Riedesel river-road column from participating in the Freeman's farm engagement. Had he shown some initiative, he would have released one or two regiments from Bemis Heights to harass this body of troops, which might well have prevented Riedesel from joining the battle. After the Hessian general marched westward, Gates should have come crashing down on the much-weakened river road column. Even without all of Learned's brigade, his Bemis Heights force still had ample superiority in numbers— nearly four thousand against no more than seven hundred of the enemy. Had he acted resolutely, Gates could have easily disemboweled the whole of Burgoyne's army by capturing or destroying its baggage train and reserves of provisions and supplies.

These tactical botches spoiled the patriot prospect for total victory on September 19. Instead, Riedesel's huge gamble in dividing his column paid off when his relief force came careening into the right side of the American line at Freeman's farm. The patriots wavered, tried to recover, and then pulled back toward Bemis Heights as twilight gave way to darkness in the upper Hudson River Valley.

By maintaining the field at the end of the day, Burgoyne had won a technical victory, but at a grisly price. His casualty rate amounted to roughly

22 percent of the twenty-five hundred Anglo-German soldiers (556 killed, wounded, or missing) actually engaged in combat. His vaunted British regulars under Hamilton had taken the worst of the beating, suffering over 350 casualties among the eight hundred troops committed to battle from those regiments. The 62d, caught in the cross fire in the salient, had been all but annihilated, with a staggering casualty rate of over 80 percent.[23]

Patriot losses, by comparison, were modest: 63 killed, 210 wounded, and 38 missing, or 56 percent of Burgoyne's total. The heavier British losses supported Henry Dearborn's pride in the fortitude of his fellow troops. "We . . . had something more at stake than fighting for six pence per day," he declared, "and I trust we have convinced the British butchers that the cowardly Yankees can and when there is a call for it, will, fight." A nonplussed British officer concurred: "The courage and obstinacy with which the Americans fought were the astonishment of everyone." The rebels had shown they were not the "contemptible enemy we had hitherto imagined them, incapable of standing a regular engagement" while fighting only from "behind strong and powerful works."[24]

"No fruits, honor excepted, were attained by the . . . victory" of September 19, Burgoyne later confessed to Germain. In trying to explain the reasons why to Parliament in May 1778, Gentleman Johnny noted his expectation that "Gates would receive the attack in his lines," thus permitting his own troops to establish "a position he could have maintained." When "Arnold chose to give rather than receive the attack," he went on to state, the rebel general effectively disrupted the overall battle plan. But he did not do so alone; Burgoyne also commended the rebels' "perseverance in the attack on his lines" at Freeman's farm. As a result, he lost his opportunity to initiate the second phase of his battle plan and sweep hard into Bemis Heights.[25]

The static operational strategy of Gates, which Burgoyne had counted on, affected the flow of the battle and gave the British their technical victory. Had the northern commander left Bemis Heights and viewed the engagement for himself, he would have seen how capably his own troops were fighting. He might have supported Arnold, secured a "complete victory" (in the words of Varick), and avoided additional, needless bloodshed in the days ahead. By remaining at Bemis Heights and by not supporting Arnold, who seemed to Captain Wakefield and so many other rebel combatants as "the very genius of war" that day, Gates now appeared incapable of either recognizing or seizing the main chance. The British expeditionary force, moreover, was still alive and potentially dangerous.[26]

Burgoyne decided to hold his position and ordered the construction of a line of entrenchments and redoubts anchored on the north side of Freeman's farm. Meanwhile, he sent out detail parties after dark to bring in the wounded and bury the dead. Because the rebels were nearby, these crews did their work hastily. They "left heads, legs, and arms above ground" after throwing dirt over mass graves, and they accorded "no other distinction . . . to officer or soldier than that the officers are put in a hole by themselves." Such was the final grim scene of what Dearborn called "one of the greatest battles that ever was fought in America." This first Saratoga engagement, however, was only the beginning.[27]

IV

Gates's bridling of Arnold was reminiscent of Congress's removal of Schuyler. Both had to endure the frustration of having set the stage for victory only to have that triumph snatched from them by higher authority. In responding, self-assured Schuyler chose the gentleman's course. Rather than obeying Congress's order to proceed to Washington's headquarters, he stayed in Albany and devoted himself to helping supply the northern army. In doing so, he had the personal satisfaction of refurbishing—on his own terms—his reputation as a virtuous patriot. Arnold, unfortunately, was not far removed from his adversary. His own quarters were only about a half mile from Gates's, and he refused to back off in demanding aggressive action—especially from a general whom he now believed, after being peremptorily recalled from the battlefield, was at best a liability to the success of American arms.

Arnold knew how badly the rebels had stung Burgoyne's army. He called for a full-scale assault "on the 20th while the enemy was in confusion." He wanted to strike before the British could erect entrenchments strong enough to cost hundreds of American lives in breaching them. Staying in character, Gates refused to initiate any action; yet there was a noticeable difference in the northern commander's demeanor. He hardly pretended to listen to his subordinate. Arnold found himself ignored more than ever at headquarters, with "little or no attention paid to any proposals I have thought it my duty to make for the public service."[28]

At a minimum Gates and his staff, with James Wilkinson in the lead, were being uncivil, if not intentionally rude. Both they and Arnold knew why. The battle on September 19 had magnified the latter's fighting reputation among the soldiery while lowering that of Gates. The northern commander "seemed to be piqued that Arnold's division had the honor of beating the enemy," wrote Richard Varick. Because Arnold "alone is due the honor of our late victory," added Henry Brockholst Livingston, he had emerged as "the life and soul of the troops," enjoying "the confidence and affection of his officers and soldiers. They would, to a person, follow him to conquest or death."[29]

This commentary, communicated as it was to Schuyler by two former staff aides, cannot be accepted uncritically. Both Varick and Livingston detested Gates, not only because he had helped engineer the downfall of Schuyler but for other reasons as well. Varick had loathed the general since the previous November; Gates, who was still in command at Ticonderoga, had not punished another officer who had tried to stab the unarmed Varick during an argument. Livingston had more recently refined his bad feelings. Schuyler had selected him to carry the tidings of the Bennington victory to Congress. Following prescribed ritual, he asked the delegates to show their approval of the triumph by offering a mark of favor to his talented staff officer. Such recognition normally involved a promotion. This time the New Englanders, as part of their ongoing crusade against Schuyler, defeated the resolution to make Livingston a lieutenant colonel and then had any reference to the motion expunged from the official record. They thereby showed this stunned, embarrassed staff officer how small-minded Gates's proponents could be. Now, to see the northern commander grasping for his army's respect gave Varick and Livingston no amount of personal satisfaction.[30]

Still, their observations cannot be dismissed. Captain Wakefield of Dearborn's light infantry had no direct ties with any of the principals, yet he sustained the assertions of Varick and Livingston. "Arnold was not only the hero of the field" on September 19, "but he had won the admiration of the whole army," stated Wakefield. Gates, by comparison, had cost his own force the opportunity to "have utterly routed the whole British army" by not backing Arnold and sending out enough troops in timely fashion. Wakefield said that "this belief," a commonly held perception among officers and soldiers, was "so damaging to Gates, that as an excuse to save himself from reproaches coming from every side he gave out as the reason that the store of powder and ball in the camp was exhausted, and that the supplies of ammunition from Albany had not arrived." Concluded a skeptical Wakefield, "no one could dispute this, yet no one believed it."[31]

In actuality, the northern commander and his staff were so unnerved by Gates's sudden loss of popularity that they now prepared to assault the soldiers' hero, Benedict Arnold. How extensively Gates involved himself in the scheme to belittle and defame America's Hannibal cannot be stated precisely, but he neither halted nor condemned the actions of Wilky. Perhaps more than anyone else at Bemis Heights, Gates was aware of Arnold's acute sensitivities about his honor and reputation—and how upset he could become when any person dared to challenge his good name. Arnold's reputation would be the point of attack that began on Monday, September 22.

The opening salvo, fired behind Arnold's back, came the day before when Wilkinson sent a letter to former Gates ally Arthur St. Clair, then in Philadelphia trying to restore his own reputation in the wake of losing Ticonderoga. Wilky first described the battle on September 19, naming some of the principal officers involved. Then he categorically pronounced, "*General Arnold was not out of camp during the whole action.*" After denying Arnold's well-documented involvement, the adjutant casually noted that "General Gates despises a certain pompous little fellow" before proceeding into a flurry of flattery about how much the northern commander missed St. Clair's services. The letter was masterfully dishonest in smearing Arnold and making him look like a troublesome—and useless—impediment to Gates's brilliant quest to vanquish Burgoyne's army. Wilkinson hoped that St. Clair, as an unwitting messenger of sorts, would pass along this message to key leaders in Congress.[32]

The second and third salvos came the next day. As if there were some serious problem in "staff duties as well as general details," and "in perfect ignorance" of possibly upsetting Arnold, Wilky disingenuously asked Gates to clarify the reporting line of Morgan's regiment. The northern commander appreciated his adjutant's concerns and announced in his general orders on September 22, "Colonel Morgan's corps not being attached to any brigade or division of the army, he is to make returns and reports to headquarters only, from whence alone he is to receive orders." The public implication was that Arnold had not performed his duties correctly; therefore, Gates had to intervene and directly supervise a portion of his wing commander's troops.[33]

The major fusillade was in the form of Gates's after-action report to Congress. The northern commander carefully etched a most favorable portrait of himself; he had "immediately" countered Burgoyne's movements and had quickly "reinforced" Morgan. He had done so with such great success "that the enemy suffered extremely in every quarter where they were engaged." Gates likewise appreciated the "general good behavior" of the patriot soldiers, who acted like "the most veteran army." Then, in a sentence that was at odds with well-established custom in such reports, Gates chose not to single out for special recognition any division, regiment, or officer, except for two men who were slain. "To discriminate in praise of the officers would be [an] injustice," he concluded, "as they all deserve the honor and applause of Congress." The intended impression was that Gates and the troops who apparently so admired him were equally worthy of commendation.

Gates added a postscript. He included correspondence from Lincoln, charged with commanding militia on the east side of the Hudson and disrupting Burgoyne's long—and currently broken—communications line back to Canada. Lincoln, who had about twenty-five hundred troops at his disposal in mid-September, had called on Arnold's old nemesis, John Brown, now performing militia service, to lead five hundred citizen-soldiers in a surprise attack on the British troops garrisoning Fort Ticonderoga. The day before Freeman's Farm, Brown's column struck from the Lake George side. They destroyed two hundred bateaux and captured three hundred prisoners but fell short of retaking the fortress. Gates specifically named Lincoln and Brown and cited their deeds in at last holding "a fair prospect of the Northern Department soon freed from those violent enemies" threatening New York, all of this after disdaining any mention of the key officers— Morgan, Dearborn, Poor, and Arnold—at Freeman's Farm.[34]

Curiously, Gates revealed only part of the story about militia activity north and east of Saratoga. Before September 19 he had approved Lincoln's plans, since "Burgoyne had totally neglected his rear." Then, as the battle raged at Freeman's farm, Gates suddenly reversed himself. Claiming "it is the opinion of all the generals that I have consulted with," he ordered Lincoln to pull his militiamen all the way back to Stillwater, where they were to await further instructions. "Not one moment should be lost in your marching them thither," Gates wrote, as if he were about to be overwhelmed on Bemis Heights by enemy troops. An astonished Lincoln ceased his operations, thereby ending an encircling campaign with the potential to so isolate Burgoyne that he would have had to consider surrendering without additional fighting—or bloodshed for that matter.[35]

Gates's orders to Lincoln suggest a state of panic in the face of the enemy, even though the Bemis Heights defenses never came close to being threatened that day. Arnold ignored the issue, but he hardly appreciated the public commemoration ordered by Gates on Sunday, September 21, to extol Brown's success. This celebration helped divert the Bemis Heights Continentals from their grumblings about Gates. To keep himself calm, Arnold focused on essential duties of the moment. He directed the strengthening of defensive positions extending westward from Bemis Heights and regularly sent out riflemen under Morgan and Dearborn to direct sniper fire at Burgoyne's troops.

Although thoroughly frustrated by the events of September 19, Arnold kept his composure until the two salvos of September 22 struck home. At first dumbfounded, he recalled Washington's admonition, born of differences with Ethan Allen and others at Ticonderoga, not to dispute the authority of his superior officers. He had rigorously done so; but now he had to contemplate whether the actions of Gates were provocative enough to violate Washington's dictum. He had to consider whether a counterassault on Gates would deprive him of the opportunity he craved to destroy an enemy force that in its various forms had so often defeated him.

Arnold likewise pondered the paradox of Gates attacking him when that same officer lacked the mettle to go on the offensive against Burgoyne. Such thoughts maddened him. The salvos had indeed wounded him to an extent that would "mortify a person with less pride than I have and in my station in the army." Because of all his points of discontent, Arnold could no longer contain himself. With the vitals of his reputation as a virtuous patriot at stake, he accepted this latest call to battle.[36]

Having "pocketed many insults" and "repeated indignities" during the past few days "for the sake of his country, which a man of less pride would have resented"—to use the words of Livingston—Arnold "waited on" Gates early at night on September 22. More accurately, the rebels' fighting general charged into Gates's small hut and engaged in a shouting match with his former friend, now turned mortal enemy. "Matters were altercated in a very high strain," wrote Livingston. Both men used "high words and gross language," echoed Wilkinson. Gates was "rather passionate and very assuming" in comparison to Arnold, insisted Livingston. Wilkinson thought Gates was only defending himself against Arnold's "arrogant spirit and impatience of command" by maintaining a posture of "official presumption and conscious superiority."[37]

Arnold was wrathful about Gates's self-serving report to Congress. He demanded "justice" in the form of proper public recognition for his "division as well as particular regiments or persons." Gates, in response, "ridiculed" his subordinate. He questioned his status as a major general, since Arnold had given his resignation to Congress. Further, Gates roared, Arnold had performed his duties as a wing commander poorly (in reference to having Morgan report to headquarters). He intended to place Lincoln in charge of the left wing, because Arnold was really of no value to the army anyway. Cut to the very bone, the junior major general finally "retired in a rage" (Wilkinson's description), but not before he requested a "pass to Philadelphia with my two aide-de-camps and their servants, where I propose to join General Washington, and may possibly have it in my power to serve my country."[38]

Storming back to his own quarters, Arnold tried to calm himself down but was "so much offended" that Varick wondered whether a challenge might be issued for a duel "as soon as the service will admit." After settling down, Arnold drafted a carefully worded letter to Gates summarizing his grievances before formally asking for a pass, since "I am thought of no consequence in this department."[39]

Gates, meanwhile, prepared for bed, but not before writing an informative letter to his wife. He did not mention his altercation with Arnold, yet he reveled in self-pity. "The fatigue of body, and mind, which I continually undergo, is too much for my age and constitution," he wrote. His difficulty was that "a general of an American army must be everything, and that is being more than one man can long sustain"—a peculiar but revealing statement when he was then encouraging his most competent subordinate to leave camp. "This campaign must end my military labors," Gates continued, but he could not help noticing Washington's major battlefield setback at Brandywine Creek—southwest of Philadelphia on Thursday, September 11—by General Howe's army. Gates wanted "to know the truth of matters to the southward; I wish we had not been again outgeneraled in that department." By comparison, he envisioned a quick triumph over Burgoyne: "One week more will determine the great business of this campaign. . . . The enemy will either retire, or by one violent push, endeavor to recover the almost ruined state of their affairs."[40]

That Gates would consider letting the "almost ruined" British army retreat to Canada indicates a lack of strategic insight, an inability to comprehend the vital importance of gaining an overwhelming victory to help revive and refresh the debilitated American cause. Such a retreat was not going to damage Gates's reputation, however, since he could take credit for driving off the enemy. Risking the offensive in battle, by contrast, might turn out as badly for him as Washington's decision to engage Howe at Brandywine Creek. Combat, then, would come only if Burgoyne made a "violent push" toward Bemis Heights, where Gates felt that his ever-growing throng of combatants could hold their own against a damaged enemy force. Either way, Gates would take no risks, which he believed was the best way for him to emerge from "the great business" at hand with an enhanced reputation.

Gates's growing confidence in an easy triumph lay behind Arnold being so "extremely ill-treated," stated Schuyler to Varick. "Perhaps he [Gates] is so very sure of success that he does not wish the other to come in for a share of it," concluded the Yorker. Varick agreed. "I believe you are not much in the wrong in your conjectures," he responded, "that Gates was sure of success, and wished to ascribe all the honor to himself." With Burgoyne in serious trouble after Freeman's Farm, Gates no longer needed Arnold, who, as a natural risk taker, had caused his commander to look so ineffective in the eyes of the troops.[41]

Gates was not above reproach because these accusations emanated from the New York gang. Along with Wilkinson, he had belittled rather than treated Arnold with respect, and his after-action report was inexcusable in choosing not "to discriminate in praise" of key officers and units actually engaged at Freeman's Farm.

The contretemps, however, reflected on other issues as well. As stated by Livingston to Schuyler, "the reason for the present disagreement between two old cronies is simply this—*Arnold is your friend.*" Certainly, Arnold's decision to place Livingston on his staff—and to welcome the presence of Varick—was not politic. These acts signaled an attitude of inconstancy toward Gates, who, for better or worse, was now in charge of the Northern Department. The presence of Varick and Livingston clearly roused Gates's ire, but it was still Arnold's virtuoso performance on September 19—and open rumblings in camp about Gates's irresolute generalship—that actually triggered the salvos from headquarters.[42]

Arnold had held out an olive branch to Gates in early August when he sent his lengthy report about conditions facing the northern army. Gates ignored this gesture, and Arnold was sure he knew why. Washington recognized his fighting subordinate for what he was, a natural military leader—which Gates was not. Here was the true source of Gates's resentment. Arnold was what the older, more senior general, one formally trained in the art of war no less, wanted to be; but Gates's fumblings on September 19 and his baiting salvos hurled at Arnold, even while Burgoyne's army was digging in at Freeman's farm, bore out the soundness of Washington's judgment.

Arnold and Gates understood the underlying reason for their personal battle. Thus, when Arnold asked for a pass for Philadelphia, he stated his intention to join and assist Washington (his source of preferment); and when Gates responded on September 23, he gave his adversary permission only to go to Congress (his base of support). Gates also refused to answer Arnold's letter, stating that his response would be "transmitted" to the president of Congress. Arnold shot back in reply, "I thought myself entitled to an answer," since he could not imagine being "guilty of any crimes deserving such treatment" and expected "an opportunity of vindicating my conduct." Nor would Arnold accept a pass to Congress. Gates still refused to put anything in writing, claiming that he had no idea what Arnold meant by purposeful "insult or indignity." The proposed pass represented "the civilest method I could devise of acquainting Congress with your leaving the army," words full of meaning in which Gates may have revealed his true objective—driving America's Hannibal from the army altogether. However accomplished, Gates wanted Arnold out of camp, so he finally issued a "common pass," thereby clearing the way for his antagonist to go running off to Washington. The northern commander was sure he could handle explanations required by congressional delegates.[43]

As the two generals continued their personal brawl, their dispute became public, with unexpected consequences for Gates and Wilkinson. "Arnold's intention to quit this department is made public, and has caused great uneasiness among the soldiers," wrote Livingston on Wednesday, September 24. Deeply concerned Enoch Poor, of all persons, "proposed an address" from the general officers and colonels to thank Arnold "for his past services, and particularly for his conduct during the late action," while "requesting him to stay" in camp. The plan went awry, however, when Learned's officers balked out of fear "of giving umbrage to Gates." Poor and others next appealed to Lincoln, who had recently arrived at Bemis Heights, "to bring about a reconciliation" between Arnold and Gates. The Massachusetts general said he would try, since he, too, was "anxious" about Arnold's pending departure.[44]

The effect of this groundswell of support caused the Gates camp to modify its tactics. Wilkinson began to insinuate that Livingston and Varick represented the real problem. They had "poisoned and prejudiced" Arnold's "mind" about Gates. Ever-machinating Wilky thus proposed "some overtures" of conciliation in the form of Arnold severing his ties with these two gentlemen. He even went so far as to send an emissary, Major Leonard Chester, a militia officer from Connecticut and a Gates staffer, to Arnold "to open a way for accommodation." Livingston and Varick had already expressed their willingness to return to Albany if that action would keep Arnold at Bemis Heights, but he was adamant in their defense. He "despised the reflection" on his capacity to think for himself and angrily sent Chester packing. Arnold also stated crisply "that his judgment had never been influenced by any man, and that he would *not sacrifice a friend to* please the 'face of clay.' "

That Gates and Wilkinson had employed Chester as an intermediary galled Arnold, since that officer had recently engaged in a duel with Livingston after making derogatory comments about the latter's failure to obtain a promotion from Congress. What pleased Arnold, however, were the kind words from the general officers, who drafted their own statement beseeching him "not to quit the service at this critical moment." Only Lincoln did not sign. Most likely he chose not to do so after speaking with Gates about a reconciliation and sensing just how much the northern commander wanted to get rid of Arnold. Gates may also have warned Lincoln about avoiding any appearance of sympathy, especially since he might be chosen as Arnold's successor to command of the army's left wing.[45]

The general officers' appeal worked. Livingston grandly announced to Schuyler on Friday, September 26, "It gives me great pleasure to inform you that General Arnold intends to stay" with the army. Still, Arnold had reached no "accommodation" with Gates, who had muffed his objective by not quickly issuing a common pass and getting his competitor out of camp before other officers rallied to his support. Having made yet another tactical blunder, Gates recovered. He took full advantage of a foolishly impertinent act by Arnold, who, on September 24, thought he spied Lincoln giving orders to troops on the left wing. He confronted the Massachusetts general and rashly pronounced a sentence of "certain death" for anyone who, without written instructions from Gates, tried to assume control of his division. The northern commander announced in his general orders the next day that Lincoln would henceforth have command of the army's right wing; Gates himself would take charge of the left wing. If Arnold objected, he could be arrested for insubordination.[46]

Outmaneuvered, humiliated by the loss of his wing assignment, and cut off from headquarters, Arnold did as he said he would—he stayed in camp. Gates chose to ignore him. On Wednesday, October 1, Arnold took pen in hand and stated bluntly to the northern commander, "I have every reason to think your treatment proceeds from a spirit of jealousy." He then urged Gates "to improve the present time" against Burgoyne, advice which he hoped his superior would interpret not as "a wish" by Arnold "to command the army, or to outshine you," but as an expression of "my zeal for the cause of my country in which I expect to rise or fall."[47]

Gates again ignored Arnold's words. He and Wilkinson thought they had won this battle of Saratoga, but they should have read Arnold's letter more thoroughly. "I am determined to sacrifice my feelings," he had declared, "to the public good, and continue in the army at this critical juncture, when my country needs every support." Shorn of his dignity and personal honor, Arnold thus would not leave. No person—certainly not Gates—was going to deny him the opportunity to achieve a crushing victory over Burgoyne. For that climactic confrontation, Arnold was already devising his own plan of action.[48]

V

Burgoyne wanted to assault the Americans the day after Freeman's Farm, but his army was too exhausted. Instead, he focused his soldiers on the construction of entrenchments. On Sunday, September 21, he was still contemplating a strike when a courier arrived from General Henry Clinton. The brief message greatly cheered Gentleman Johnny. Clinton, who had command of the British base in New York City while Howe was off campaigning in Pennsylvania, had finally committed to diversionary operations. He now promised to launch attacks against Forts Montgomery and Clinton (the latter named after New York's Revolutionary governor, George Clinton), located below West Point in the Highlands region of the Hudson River about forty miles north of New York City. Clinton thought he could "make a push ... in about ten days" with two thousand troops, assuming he received long overdue reinforcements from England.[49]

With a relief column possibly even then moving up the Hudson, Burgoyne decided to hold to his defenses. He would wait to assess the effects of Clinton's diversion, hoping the assault would draw off some or all of Gates's force. Calculating how long his provisions, especially food, would last, Burgoyne concluded that he could hold his army in place until Sunday, October 12. Then his force would have to push hard for Albany or face the prospect of disintegrating—perhaps even beginning to starve—as rations gave out.

The two weeks that followed severely tested the morale of Burgoyne's soldiers. Besides putting up with harassing fire from rebel sharpshooters during daylight hours, sleep proved difficult. "Large droves of wolves," wrote a British officer, howled every night as they scavenged the battlefield and dug into the shallow graves. "When they approached a corpse," he noted, "their noise was hideous until they scratched it up." On Friday, October 3, Burgoyne had to reduce rations, to which his troops "submitted with the utmost cheerfulness"—or so he hoped. Just as discouraging, reconnaissance reports indicated a dramatic increase in patriot strength. Levies of militia were appearing in large numbers, as if these citizen-soldiers instinctively knew when to show up for the easy kill. By early October, Gates could muster some ten thousand troops, twice Burgoyne's number. Lacking further word about Clinton's intended expedition, Gentleman Johnny knew he had to act—and soon.[50]

Unbeknownst to the Anglo-German force, Clinton's much-delayed reinforcements, about two thousand British and Hessian regulars, did not reach New York harbor until late September. On the same day that Burgoyne ordered a cut in rations, Clinton finally began his operations. Deploying more than three thousand soldiers, he directed a well-orchestrated feint against the patriot supply depot at Peekskill on the east side of the Hudson River, successfully drawing off many of the rebels stationed at the two forts overlooking the river's west bank. Then, on Monday, October 6, Clinton's force attacked and routed the remaining patriot defenders at the forts. A day later the British fleet broke through rebel defenses at West Point. These actions satisfied Clinton, who sailed back to New York City after ordering a reduced detachment of seventeen hundred to keep carefully picking its way upriver.[51]

Clinton's little campaign thrust accomplished virtually nothing. A despairing Burgoyne had taken action by the time he received news of the feint. On Saturday evening, October 4, he gathered his principal officers in a council of war. He argued for a massed assault against the rebels' left wing. The Americans were now too strong, Riedesel responded, and he proposed retreating back across the Hudson. Then the army could reestablish communications with Canada while waiting for relief from Clinton. Burgoyne, who considered any "retrograde movement . . . disgraceful," would not "hear of it," according to Riedesel. Among other considerations, he wanted to avoid the criticism lodged the previous winter against Carleton for not having fully tested the enemy lines at Ticonderoga before pulling back into Canada. Gentleman Johnny finally approved a large-scale reconnaissance mission, as he later stated, "to discover whether there were any possible means of forcing a passage" through the American line. This probe was "also to cover a forage of the army which was in the greatest distress on account of the scarcity" of provisions. If no possible breakthrough point could be found, Burgoyne agreed to pull back toward Fort Edward, but he would not march so far north as to leave "at liberty such an army as General Gates's" to rush southward (another alleged Carleton error from the previous campaign) and "act against Sir William Howe," which "might possibly decide the fate of the war" against Britain. Gentleman Johnny set Saturday, October 11, as his withdrawal date, unless some fortuitous turn of events intervened.[52]

Heavy rains on October 6 dampened Burgoyne's spirits. Then Tuesday, October 7, dawned brightly. The glistening sun exposed the autumn foliage in glorious color, a reminder that biting blasts of winter weather would soon become another enemy of the immobilized British army. The sunshine made this day seem ideal for a reconnaissance in force, so Burgoyne made up his troop dispositions. On the right, Major Alexander Lindsay, the Earl of Balcarres, assumed command of British light infantry troops and the 24th Regiment; in the center, Riedesel gathered together soldiers drawn from the

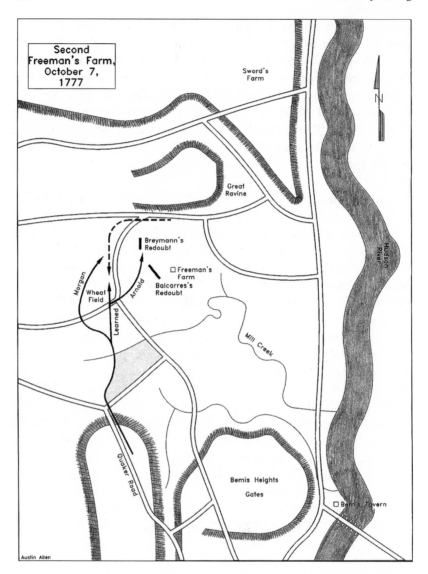

Hessian battalions; and on the left, Major John Dyke Acland took charge of a body of British grenadiers. The whole detachment consisted of fifteen hundred British and Hessian regulars and about six hundred Canadian and American provincials and Indians, who, under Captain Alexander Fraser, were to sweep far to the west "by secret paths in the woods to gain the enemy's rear," as Burgoyne described their assignment, "and by showing themselves there to keep them in check." [53]

The force moved out from Freeman's farm at a little before 11 A.M. It advanced southwest until Burgoyne, who rode with Riedesel, ordered everyone to halt on a rise of terrain in a wheat field. He was hoping to observe the rebel entrenchments some three-fourths of a mile ahead, but thick woods blocked the view. Gentleman Johnny instructed his officers to spread the troops in a thin line across the field while Phillips positioned ten artillery pieces (six 6- and two 12-pounders and two howitzers) among the ranks. Once deployed, the soldiers sat down to await further directions. Burgoyne also released Captain Fraser's troops to begin their attempted circuit around the American left and ordered pickets to cover the southern edge of the field so that foraging parties could cut the stubble of wheat for much-needed fodder.

Even though patriot pickets kept reporting the British advance to headquarters, Gates seemed unresponsive. According to Wilkinson, the commander asked him to reconnoiter the enemy force and recommend appropriate measures. Much more likely, a perturbed fighter such as Morgan stepped forward and played Arnold's part in beseeching Gates to act. Whatever the scenario, the northern commander at last advised Morgan "to begin the game" (Wilkinson's words). The time was now approaching two o'clock in the afternoon.[54]

The first phase of the battle commenced around 3 P.M. The plan was for Poor's brigade to engage the British left; for Learned's to hit the center; and for Morgan and Dearborn's troops to move quietly through the woods and attack the enemy's right. Having the least distance to travel, Poor's Continentals struck first. While evading a few blasts of cannon fire, they carefully positioned themselves in the woods. Acland's grenadiers unleashed a musket volley downhill before charging forward with bayonets fixed. Poor held his troops in check, then called for two volleys of musket fire. When the heavily outnumbered, onrushing British line wavered, Poor ordered an advance. The British were soon in full flight, leaving dozens of dead and wounded grenadiers behind. Among them was Major Acland, with wounds in both legs, now an American prisoner.

As this clash reached its peak, Morgan's troops cut off Captain Fraser's party and forced them back through the woods. Morgan kept circling to the left so that his riflemen could assault the right and rear of Balcarres's light infantrymen. The frontiersmen struck in near perfect coordination with Dearborn's troops, who were not far behind them. When Balcarres adjusted his line to the right to fend off Morgan's attack, Dearborn's troops ensnared their foe in a wicked cross fire. A stunned Balcarres ordered a retreat to more protective cover behind a rail fence.

Hardly an hour had passed since the first smattering of cannon and musket fire, but the reconnaissance mission was in serious trouble. Witnessing a potential military disaster, Burgoyne sent forward an aide, Sir Francis Clerke, to instruct his regimental commanders to start pulling back toward their Freeman's farm entrenchments. The message went undelivered when Clerke sustained a serious rib and abdominal wound. Meanwhile, the focal point of combat now rested on Balcarres's reformed line and Riedesel's Hessians in the center, where Learned had just mounted an unsuccessful charge against the dauntless Hessian combatants.

Benedict Arnold led this assault. He had appeared out of nowhere, on no one's authority but his own. He wore the buff-and-blue uniform and epaulets befitting his rank as a Continental major general. Astride a muscular dark brown horse, he looked especially calm, almost reflective, even though some later swore they detected a burning rage in his eyes. As Arnold rode forward to reconnoiter the battlefield, he passed through Colonel John Latimore's regiment of Connecticut militia. "Whose regiment is this?" he asked authoritatively. "Colonel Latimore's, sir," answered a soldier. Arnold replied, "Ah, my old Norwich and New London friends. God bless you! I am glad to see you. Now come on, boys; if the day is long enough, we'll have them all in hell before night." The soldiers cheered as Arnold spurred his mount forward.[55]

Arnold quickly located Learned, who graciously acceded to his request to take command. The unsuccessful charge, in turn, only whetted Arnold's appetite for additional combat. The rebels' fighting general artfully maneuvered his horse to and fro in aligning the troops for a second attack. Then he suddenly swept to the left in seeking out Morgan, whose riflemen had become locked in a vicious firefight with Balcarres's soldiers. The two veterans regarded a British officer who was riding back and forth on a gray horse while steadying Balcarres's light infantrymen. According to one witness, Arnold advised Morgan to "direct the attention of some of the sharpshooters" at that officer. Morgan concurred and whistled for one of his prime marksmen, Timothy Murphy. This hardened fighter climbed up a tree, took careful aim, and on his third shot leveled General Simon Fraser, who would die the next morning. The sudden deprivation of so respected a commander knocked the fighting wind out of Balcarres's troops. They began to retreat, leaving the Hessians to their left exposed on both flanks. Riedesel now had to pull back to protect his soldiers from a deadly cross fire. As Burgoyne later stated, his "hard pressed" detachment began withdrawing "in good order" toward Freeman's farm.[56]

Arnold stayed out in front of the patriots, brandishing his sword and shouting exhortations to press the advantage. Burgoyne likewise was riding back and forth, issuing orders to cover the retreat. When he reached his lines at Freeman's farm, he found musket-ball holes in his coat and hat, and his horse was bleeding profusely. Gentleman Johnny had no idea whether the rebels would assault his entrenched position, but he exhorted his regiments to brace themselves for an onslaught. The patriots kept surging forward, even as their numbers grew with the infusion of fresh militia units, but no one—certainly not Arnold—had orders from Gates, who was still safely ensconced at Bemis Heights, to engage the Anglo-German force in its stronghold. Given Gates's lack of initiative, no orders could be expected, which caused some hesitation as the Americans closed in on the British line.

Arnold had little use for such words as "hesitation" or "caution." Since the battle had become his engagement, he intended to finish matters with the British northern army. As he ordered the brigades of Generals John Glover and John Paterson into battle formation, he sized up the enemy's defenses. Directly before him across the open field—and not far from Freeman's log hut—was Balcarres's Redoubt, which anchored the British line. About a half mile to the northwest, atop a slight knoll, was another imposing breastwork known as Breymann's Redoubt, designed to protect Burgoyne's right flank. In between were two small, heavily stockaded log buildings meant to cover the gap between the two redoubts. This position had heretofore served as the campsite for Canadian and loyalist auxiliaries. From his vantage point, Arnold could clearly decipher Balcarres's Redoubt, and he decided to lead an assault against that fortified breastwork.

By moving so quickly and decisively, Arnold hoped to take advantage of the enemy's confusion. In doing so, he committed a tactical blunder. The survivors of Burgoyne's reconnaissance force had fallen back to Balcarres's Redoubt, the closest entrenchment in their line of retreat. There officers, at Burgoyne's urging, hastily formed them into combat units. When the Americans charged, they ran into withering blasts of grapeshot and musket fire from this massed strength of the enemy.

Still the patriots came forward, as if pulled along by Arnold in the lead. Although a highly visible target astride his horse, America's Hannibal seemed impervious to flying metal. Waving his sword, he exhorted his troops not to flinch but to smash through the enemy line. Those keeping up with him soon reached the abatis jutting out from the redoubt, but the hailstorm of British fire was too intense. The Americans had to pull back amid horrible carnage. The charge had failed, and the two sides now settled into a steady exchange of weapons fire.

Then Arnold spied the movement of Learned's brigade off to his left. He suddenly appreciated his mistake. He had attacked the enemy's strongest point. Digging spurs into his horse, he bolted straight into the neutral ground, no more than 120 yards wide, between his own troops and those of the enemy. Arnold wheeled his horse to the left and galloped toward Learned's column. Incredibly, he and his mount emerged unscratched in passing through a gauntlet of gunfire coming from both sides.

The sheer bravado of this perilous—and seemingly foolish—act caused one patriot soldier to fault Arnold for behaving "more like a madman than a cool and discreet officer" that afternoon. Others thought him drunk, but he had swallowed down only one "dipperful" of rum before entering the field, no more a quantity of alcohol than other patriot fighters had imbibed to steady their nerves. Indeed, one British participant, amazed at the fighting ardor of the American combatants, wrote, "The rebels were in general drunk, a piece of policy of their general [officer] in order to make them fight." [57]

Arnold's fearlessness reflected the intensity of purpose with which he approached combat. Once engaged, he had the capacity to block out any concern for his own safety and focus on the sole consideration of finding some means to defeat the enemy. When he spurred his horse into the neutral zone, his only thought was to correct his tactical error by getting to Learned's troops along the shortest route and attacking the enemy's weakly defended right flank. Should he succeed, the day would belong to the patriot force, as well as to the cause of American liberty and to himself.

Arnold had evaluated the situation correctly. Burgoyne, in assembling his reconnaissance force, had left the gap between the two redoubts inadequately defended. In addition, about three hundred of Breymann's Hessians had joined the expedition, which reduced the German colonel's strength in the redoubt to about two hundred defenders. After fleeing the wheat field, Breymann's troops did not return to their assigned position. They ended up in Balcarres's Redoubt, where they helped fend off Arnold's charge. As such, the opportunity was there for the Americans, if they could get themselves organized, to penetrate the right flank and roll up the whole British line.

Sensing an overwhelming victory, Arnold drove his panting horse forward at breakneck speed. When he reached Learned's troops, he pointed with his upraised sword toward the two log huts. The enemy had no time to react. The rebels poured into the gap behind Arnold and easily overran the smattering of enemy troops trying to hold this position. This critical maneuver isolated the Hessians still with Breymann, who could now be attacked from all sides before the rebels threw their full weight against the outflanked defenders of Balcarres's Redoubt. The only real obstacle to a complete rout of the enemy was the lateness of the day. The hour was past 5 P.M., and lengthening shadows had started to envelop the battlefield.[58]

Impending darkness made Arnold even more frenetic. He rode back to the point where he had caught up with Learned's troops, only to make contact with four more regiments, including Morgan's, moving forward. Somehow horse and rider became entangled in the melee of troops. Trying to break free, Arnold accidentally bladed Captain Frederick M. Ball, one of Dearborn's officers, in the head, an act for which he later apologized after confessing that he had no recollection of the incident. His mind was else-where—on taking out the Hessian redoubt. He and Morgan set their dispositions. The plan was for Arnold to get behind the redoubt with about two hundred troops. Once he had his column in position, Morgan was to attack the front of the works from the west while Arnold's column swept in from the southeast through the sally port, thereby ensnaring the Germans in a deadly cross fire.[59]

The attack began just as the sun began to set. Morgan's troops moved forward toward the palisaded breastwork, some two hundred yards across its front. Breymann, a hard-nosed disciplinarian, railed and slashed at his own soldiers to keep them from fleeing. In trying to hold them in place, he allegedly killed or wounded four of them. When the onrushing Americans were within fifty yards of their target, Breymann's cannoneers unleashed a mighty fusillade. One patriot had his head blown off. Flying fragments from his shattered skull tore into the head of a second soldier, who fell unconscious on top of the twitching remains of the first man. Inside the redoubt, the frightened defenders began to break and run. One of them apparently shot "Butcher" Breymann dead just before Arnold, with troops from the Massachusetts regiment of Lieutenant Colonel John Brooks not far behind, charged in through the redoubt's sally port.

Arnold's sudden presence startled the fleeing Hessians. They stood frozen for a moment as he loosened the reins of his panting, exhausted horse and surveyed his surroundings. Then he raised his sword, ready to charge and drive these soldiers and the rest of Burgoyne's army straight into hell. As he had done all afternoon, Arnold would attack in the name of his famine-proof veterans and the stouthearted Montgomery. He would strike on behalf of all those suffering patriots who had died so horribly at such places as Isle aux Noix or while serving in his Champlain fleet. He would charge for Washington and Schuyler, patriots leaders who had offered him encouragement and respect, but in defiance of the likes of Ethan Allen, James Easton, John Brown, and Horatio Gates, who had treated his reputation and his devoted service to the cause of liberty with ridicule. He would smite the enemy before him for his own glory and the restoration of his family name.

Just as Arnold started to charge, a platoon of retreating Hessians leveled their weapons and launched a final volley of fire in his direction. A musket ball ripped into his left leg, the same limb wounded during the ill-fated assault on Quebec. Other balls struck his horse. The animal reared upward before crashing to the ground. Arnold had no time to react and went down with the dying horse. His wounded leg hit the ground at an odd angle, splintering with multiple fractures as the full weight of the horse smashed him into the redoubt's earthen floor.[60]

From his prone position, Arnold kept issuing orders as Morgan's troops clambered up and over the palisaded wall. Pursue was his message, but he called off one soldier who was about to bayonet a Hessian, now wounded, who had fired at the fighting American general. The German lad was only doing his duty, Arnold shouted, even as other rebel soldiers came up and "assisted in extricating" their fallen leader from underneath the lifeless horse. Dearborn "asked him if he was badly wounded," to which Arnold allegedly "replied, in the same leg, and wished the ball had passed his heart," before nearly passing out from wrenching pain.[61]

VI

Among those who appeared in Breymann's Redoubt was Major John Armstrong, a staff aide from Gates who had been searching for Arnold. He carried a message for the intractable subordinate to return to his quarters before he "might do some rash thing!" If rashness is the appropriate word, then Arnold's intervention in this second—and decisive—Battle of Freeman's Farm represented a spectacular performance. Forsaking his own welfare, America's Hannibal had led charge after charge against Burgoyne's soldiery. Unlike Gates, he believed that patriot troops, even if poorly trained by the standards of European regulars, could do more in combat than merely fight from behind entrenchments. What they needed was charismatic leadership in the field, and that is what Arnold gave them on September 19 and October 7. By his own fearless example, he emboldened them. He roused their spirits to the point of overcoming instinctive fears about their own safety, and he inspired them to acts of great courage. He thus helped the northern patriot soldiery achieve—well out in front of the protective works of Bemis Heights—a truly momentous military victory.

The scale of the triumph was not yet clear when darkness finally halted the battle—not long after Arnold went down. During the night Burgoyne, with his defenses breached, pulled his troops back across the Great Ravine. There his force hung on for a day in the face of annoying rebel fire before commencing a withdrawal that ended with formal surrender near the village of Saratoga on Friday, October 17.

While in retreat, Burgoyne reckoned with his losses from the October 7 engagement. His army had suffered 618 casualties—94 killed, 134 wounded, and 390 captured. During the whole of the campaign, his expeditionary force lost a total of 2,591 (not including St. Leger's casualties), or more than one-third of the troops who had entered Lake Champlain so self-confidently just four months earlier.[62]

American losses from Second Freeman's Farm were slight. The patriots sustained an estimated 130 casualties, or about 21 percent of Burgoyne's number. For some reason, Gates never got around to compiling an official list. Military business was too pressing, he claimed, even though he could make time—at the height of the October 7 battle no less—for such matters as engaging "in a warm dispute" with Sir Francis Clerke over the merits of the American Revolution. Having captured the seriously wounded Clerke, patriot soldiers escorted him to Gates's headquarters where the northern commander, who had no interest in going near the battle, invited Sir Francis to rest in his bed. Even as Arnold was launching his strikes against Burgoyne's redoubts, Gates was also on the attack in contesting Clerke's assertion that the Americans had been plotting for years to gain their independence. Gates ultimately "became quite incensed," and he asked Wilkinson whether he "had ever heard so impudent a son of a bitch." The deputy could not think of anyone, but the name Benedict Arnold may have crossed his mind.[63]

Clerke's wounds were mortal, and he died a few days later. Arnold survived. Carried on a makeshift stretcher from Breymann's Redoubt, he tried to hide his agony as he spoke with admiring soldiers who showed their appreciation by offering words of thanks and encouragement. Then he endured the long, slow ride south in a medical cart that carried him to Albany for long-term convalescence.

Gates ignored Arnold. Nor did he send a written inquiry about his health, in which he could have thanked him personally for his valiant performance at Second Freeman's Farm. Certainly the northern commander's praise was something short of fulsome in his October 12 after-action report to Congress. Gates did describe Arnold's conduct as "gallant" in referencing the assault on Breymann's Redoubt. Had his subordinate's wounds not already become a subject of widespread public concern, he most likely would have chosen to ignore—and once again possibly deny—Arnold's invaluable contributions. Years later, Wilkinson articulated what Gates and his staff wanted others to believe, that Arnold on October 7 "neither rendered service, nor deserved credit that day." These deceitful words were nothing more than a modification of the earlier fabrication about a "pompous little fellow" who remained in camp during the September 19 engagement. Somehow these slights and slurs had the desired effect. Despite Arnold's shining brilliance in outgeneraling Burgoyne, Gates has come down to posterity as "the hero of Saratoga."[64]

Seventeen

A Violated Right Not
Fully Restored

I

In December 1815, sixty-four-year-old Henry Dearborn, then living in Boston, jotted down some reminiscences about the Saratoga campaign. Thirty-eight years had passed since this Revolutionary War veteran had charged into Breymann's Redoubt. Still, he could recall vividly Arnold's statement to him—wishing "the ball had passed his heart"—as the stricken major general lay convulsed with pain after suffering so terrible a leg wound. Reflecting backward through the prism of treason, others have lamented that Arnold survived his Saratoga wounding. Had America's Hannibal been among the slain, he would have come down to posterity not as a nefarious villain but as a remarkable military hero—a personally ambitious and overly sensitive martyr, but also an archetype of selfless public virtue fully deserving of the community's highest respect.[1]

Had Arnold somehow avoided the volley of Hessian musket fire, he could have remained in the field, secured the great prize of defeating Burgoyne's army, and completely cleansed his sullied reputation. But his debilitating wound changed all that. Just as he had arrived before the walls of Quebec a few days too late, at Saratoga he fell in battle just a few steps short of a great personal victory. A ball in the heart would have spared him the agony of reckoning with just how close he had come to defeating the enemy. Now he could only imagine from his hospital bed the likes of Horatio Gates easily maneuvering Burgoyne's broken army into surrender and winning for himself the glory that so many others—Schuyler, Morgan, and Stark, besides Arnold himself—actually deserved.

Such thoughts tortured Arnold. An extended, five-month confinement at the Continental army's General Hospital in Albany only aggravated his frustration and despondency. Whereas Dr. Senter in early 1776 had depicted Arnold as a model patient at Quebec, he was now exceedingly churlish. Army surgeon Dr. James Thacher spent the evening of Saturday, October 11, with him. The "celebrated" general was "very peevish, and impatient under his misfortunes, and required all my attention during the night," Thacher recalled. In December, Dr. James Browne compared Arnold to another ranking patient, Benjamin Lincoln, who had sustained a bad leg wound the day after Second Freeman's Farm in a skirmishing action against the British. Wrote Browne, Lincoln's "character . . . united the resolution of the soldier; the politeness of the gentlemen, the patient philosopher, and pious Christian." But "not so the gallant Arnold." His continued "peevishness would degrade the most capricious of the fair sex," Browne declared before mentioning that "he abuses us for a set of ignorant pretenders and empirics."[2]

Part of Arnold's irritability related to his very slow rate of physical recovery, for which he regularly chastised his doctors. Browne stated that Arnold's wound was "less dangerous in the beginning than Lincoln's" but not "in so fair a way of healing" more than two months after the battle. Browne and other army surgeons justifiably worried about gangrene. Repeatedly they asked Arnold for permission to amputate. He disdained "such damned nonsense." He would rather die, he kept replying angrily, than submit to their surgical forms of human butchery. To help straighten his splintered limb, the doctors could offer only a wooden fracture box. This crude cast forced Arnold to lie fully immobilized—endlessly and uncomfortably—on his back, which only further demoralized this heretofore vibrantly active patriot.[3]

Comrades and friends came to visit, among them Richard Varick, who optimistically reported in late October that "General Arnold is growing better very fast." His wound apparently on the mend, he hoped soon to join Schuyler when the Yorker traveled to Pennsylvania to defend himself in a court of inquiry regarding the loss of Ticonderoga. A few days later Arnold's health had declined; his wound, Varick observed, was not healing properly. Another three days passed, and the general seemed much better. Then, on Sunday, November 16, Varick found Arnold in a particularly petulant mood, despairing whether his leg would ever heal. Two weeks later he was still very sick. These fluctuations in his health persisted into the New Year.[4]

By mid-January 1778, Arnold finally felt strong enough to write an occasional letter. In one of his first missives since Second Freeman's Farm, he scribbled a note to Henry Laurens, who had succeeded John Hancock as president of Congress. He mentioned shortages of heavy ordnance in the northern theater before adding in a postscript, "I am so far recovered of my wounds, as to be able to sit up, and hope in a few weeks with the help of a crutch, to hobble out of my chamber." In early March, even as hints of milder spring weather had started to brighten the ashen winter landscape, Arnold was still not ambulatory. Determined, though, to break free of his long hospital confinement, he arranged for transportation back to Connecticut. Wherever the cart stopped for the evening, he had to be carried back and forth to his lodgings in a litter.[5]

Arnold had long since come to appreciate how much more devastating this wound was than the one he had sustained at Quebec. During 1776 his injured limb had slowly regained its strength, to the point where his limp was hardly noticeable. This time his muscle tissue atrophied too much, and the compound fracture left his leg shortened a good two inches. Even with the aid of a special shoe having a built-up heel, a crutch, and later a cane, pain shot through his body whenever he put too much weight on his damaged limb. The once agile, athletic Arnold had become a hobbling cripple in the service of his country.

II

As Arnold lay restlessly in the hospital, he continually demanded war-related news. He greatly regretted missing the surrender ceremonies at Saratoga on Friday, October 17. The battered remains of Burgoyne's army, reduced to fewer than four thousand effectives after the October 7 engagement, had retreated eight miles north to Saratoga. Gates carefully pursued, even as his army's strength pushed toward eighteen thousand, the result of eager militia units still joining his ranks. With such a sizable advantage, the northern commander had few problems closing off possible avenues of escape toward Ticonderoga and Canada.

Burgoyne acknowledged his entrapment when, at a council of war on Monday, October 13, he asked his ranking officers whether "capitulating" would be "justifiable upon the principles of national dignity and military honor." His subordinates replied "that the present situation justifies a capitulation upon honorable terms." Negotiations ensued over the next three days. Gates and his principal bargaining agent, James Wilkinson, finally acceded to a "convention" arrangement whereby Burgoyne and his army would be allowed to march to Boston, board transport vessels, return to England, and sit out the remainder of the war on parole.[6]

When Arnold learned of the agreement, he was contemptuous. He "thinks we might have caught them on more advantageous terms than we have,"

Varick told Schuyler in a masterful understatement. So did many others, including Washington and a majority in Congress. With Burgoyne's force completely bagged, Gates had again exhibited his cautionary style of conducting warfare by overreacting to the phantom threat posed by Clinton's diversionary maneuvers up the Hudson. Initially demanding unconditional surrender, he and Wilkinson had granted Gentleman Johnny pretty much anything he wanted, as long as the Anglo-German army quickly laid down its arms. Burgoyne took full advantage of Gates's incertitude. Rather ironically, he measured up to the mocking name the rebels had given him and secured enough elbow room for his conquered troops to remain useful in the war effort, since their return to England would free up other soldiers guarding Britain's home front for military service in America.[7]

Easily grasping what would happen, Congress used technicalities to disavow Gates's handiwork in January 1778. The delegates allowed Burgoyne and two aides to sail back to England, but they eventually ordered the captured troops to march south from New England to the interior of Virginia, where most—some enlisted in the Continental army—sat out much of the remainder of the war.[8]

Despite his flawed negotiations, Congress neither reproved the northern commander nor faulted him for his dilatoriness in moving his victorious Continental units southward to bolster Washington's beleaguered force. By late September, Howe's army had occupied Philadelphia. Worse yet, Washington's unsuccessful assault of Saturday, October 4, on British troops stationed at Germantown, a few miles north of the rebel capital, had resulted in nearly eleven hundred patriot casualties—this on top of losing an estimated nine hundred soldiers less than a month before at Brandywine Creek.

As Washington's troops nursed their wounds, the commander appealed to Gates and Congress for assistance. The delegates were in disarray, having just fled westward from Philadelphia for first Lancaster and then York in Pennsylvania's interior. That the northern commander kept "detaining the troops" under his command resulted in strong "censures" from Arnold, who suspected the worst. He envisaged purposeful conniving by a person whom he was sure had no scruples when engaged in the pursuit of elevated military rank and personal glory. Gates was holding back on Washington, Arnold guessed, in the hope of seeing the commander in chief stumble once too often in battle and lose complete favor with Congress. At this point the delegates would likely call on the New Englander's darling general to replace the oft-defeated Virginian at the head of the Continental army.[9]

Arnold invariably spoke of Gates in contemptuous terms. He even labeled him *"the greatest poltroon in the world"* in conversation with the Marquis de

Lafayette. Congress obviously had a different view, publicly according Gates not a coward's but a hero's portion of gratitude for the momentous Saratoga victory. The delegates did so in early November, despite the bizarre antics of Wilkinson. Gates had decided to honor his adjutant by allowing him to deliver the convention agreement to Congress. In a covering letter, the northern commander followed prescribed ritual by recommending a promotion, to a brevet brigadier generalship no less: "The honorable Congress will believe me when I assure them, that from the beginning of this contest I have not met with a more promising military genius than Colonel Wilkinson." [10]

Wilkinson displayed his "genius" by meandering through the countryside. He took eleven days to travel from Albany to York, a distance of 285 miles that he could have covered in half that time. After rendezvousing with his fiancée for a couple of days in Easton, Pennsylvania, he also loitered at Reading, there talking in less-than-discreet terms about replacing Washington, who, he was quick to point out, had not tasted a great victory in 1777 as had the triumphant Gates. On Friday, October 31, Wilky finally reached York, where he faced angry delegates who demanded to know why he had taken so long to get to them. He smiled and fawned and complained about terrible weather and moments of ill health related to a pesky "convulsive colic." Compulsive cipherism would have been a more accurate diagnosis. [11]

Having made a less-than-dazzling first impression, Wilkinson used the weekend to socialize with Gates-friendly delegates. They warned him that many in Congress, having received descriptions of the Saratoga convention, had frowned at the agreement as overly generous. The New Englanders cautioned Wilky to stress how dexterously Gates had maneuvered Burgoyne into surrender terms, despite Clinton's supposedly menacing maneuvers in the Hudson Highlands.

On Monday, November 3, Wilkinson performed marvelously before Congress. Even skeptical delegates remained silent. The next day, they joined the Gates enthusiasts in applauding the capture of Burgoyne's army "upon terms honorable and advantageous to these states." The same resolution offered "the thanks of Congress" to Lincoln and Arnold, along with the rest of the northern army, but to Gates went the most fulsome praise when the delegates voted to cast "a medal of gold" as a symbolic representation of eternal gratitude from "the American Congress to Horatio Gates, the gallant leader." Henry Laurens also expressed the unqualified admiration of his colleagues when he conveyed the resolution to Gates with these words: "Your name sir will be written in the breasts of the grateful Americans of the present age and sent down to posterity in characters which will remain indelible when the [medal's] gold shall have changed its appearance." [12]

Having anointed Gates as the official hero of Saratoga, the delegates could not sidestep, as most would have preferred, his entreaty to honor Wilkinson with a brevet brigadier's commission. Back in August, they had rejected Schuyler's request to promote Henry Brockholst Livingston, who had delivered them tidings of the Bennington victory. The Yorker had shown poor judgment in stirring up yet more "foolish rashness about rank," James Lovell had sneered. Then, when Major Robert Troup, who bore Gates's report on the first Saratoga engagement, reached Congress, such promotions suddenly made more sense, since Gates had requested a lieutenant colonelcy for Troup. With New Englanders like Lovell leading the charge, they both applauded and approved this recommendation. Not to appear unduly hypocritical or consciously petty toward Schuyler, they then belatedly elevated Livingston to the same rank. Now, it seemed, the delegates could do no less for Wilkinson, as they demonstrated on Thursday, November 6, when they advanced this "promising military genius" to general officer status.[13]

Gates's entreaty to elevate Wilkinson, a junior-ranking lieutenant colonel, over so many deserving field-grade officers senior to him hardly bore witness to the northern commander's good judgment. The New Englanders rationalized that a brevet brigadier's commission held little consequence unless Wilkinson actually took command of troops on some special assignment. Still, they were not happy with Gates for having placed them in so awkward a position. Some vented their exasperation by making jokes; Samuel Adams and John Hancock suggested presenting Wilkinson "with a horsewhip and a pair of spurs."[14]

For field- and general-grade officers, Wilkinson's promotion was no laughing matter. Nathanael Greene was among those who openly expressed displeasure. "Military rank being conferred upon people of all orders so lavishly," he wrote a Rhode Island delegate, "has rendered its value of much less importance than formerly. It was once considered a jewel of great value, but it now begins to be held in light esteem." An unfortunate consequence of Wilkinson's preferment, Greene stressed, was that many officers were asking themselves whether Continental military service was worth the ongoing personal sacrifice.[15]

Combined with Congress's glorification of Gates, Wilkinson's promotion validated Arnold's worst conceptions of Congress. The delegates had reconfirmed their true mettle as ignoble civilian leaders who, in their myopia, had again manipulated the truth and made a mockery of the Revolutionary ideal of public virtue. Local influence such as Gates had with the New Englanders, not merit or exceptional service, was all that mattered with Congress. How else, an indignant Arnold asked himself, could the delegates explain their apotheosis of Gates or their promotion of so egregious a sycophant as Wilkinson when they still denied him, the officer who had rendered critical combat leadership at Saratoga, the seniority in rank that should have been his since February 1777?

Arnold's disgust likely played a part in his physical deterioration after mid-November. Into the New Year, nothing seemed to cheer him. When stories reached Albany about Burgoyne publicly crediting Arnold "for the successes obtained over him," he seemed indifferent. What did it matter? Congress had crowned Gates with the gold medal of victory. As for himself, his reward was a painful, life-threatening wound and confinement in the putrid atmosphere of a military hospital.[16]

As November blended into December and the New Year dawned, deep and bitter resentment was infusing Arnold's troubled soul. As he grappled with the prospect of life as a virtual cripple, he kept asking himself what it had all been for, why the personal sacrifice when his only reward was defamed personal honor. With time passing so slowly, Arnold kept searching for reasonable answers to his question, but he could not find them. Indeed, he never found them.

III

New Jersey's governor William Livingston, writing in late 1777 under the pseudonym of a French gentleman named "De Lisle," publicly lauded Arnold for his performance at Saratoga. His "character is well known in Europe," and "he is said to possess what we call, in our country, the 'rage militaire.'" Not only that, Arnold's crucial part at Second Freeman's Farm had "gained" him "immortal honor."

As with Burgoyne's tribute, these words failed to salve America's Hannibal, in this instance because of two major qualifications. First, the Jersey governor pointed out that Arnold's "countrymen accuse him of too much impetuosity," which had likely been "the case" in his dealings with Congress. Second, Livingston eulogized Gates, whose "glory is as yet unrivalled in the annals of America," but with no accompanying criticism. Gates, concluded De Lisle, was the great champion of the moment because he had "humbled the pride of the haughtiest nation in the world" by capturing Burgoyne's army.[17]

This kind of commentary, coming as it did from the father of Arnold's Saratoga staff aide, Henry Brockholst Livingston, only inflamed the wounded general's personal torment. Charges of "impetuosity" toward Congress particularly upset him, especially when Arnold had made so strenuous an effort to conduct himself as a gentleman while lobbying "the case" for restored seniority. From his point of view, impulsive behavior was a congressional attribute. The delegates had rejected Washington's supplication on Arnold's behalf but then later rushed to approve Gates's petition for Wilkinson. True, Gates had made his recommendation in the context of Burgoyne's surrender, but Washington had offered his sentiments shortly after his critical turnabout victories at Trenton and Princeton. That the delegates would so readily accede to Gates's appeal while evading—and then formally dismissing—Washington's was proof enough for Arnold of the obtuseness of Congress.

In formally rejecting Arnold's appeal for restored precedence, the delegates had presented him with two choices. To remove the corrosive stain on his reputation and family name, he could carry through on his threatened resignation or challenge their judgment. He selected the latter option with his fearless—and defiant—display of military courage at Saratoga. As such, Congress, within the framework of the gentleman's code, owed him some form of an apology. The delegates could have admitted their error by publicly approving his seniority, which would have effectively reestablished his reputation as a fully meritorious patriot, thereby bringing this matter of personal honor to a mutually acceptable resolution.

The delegates came close to extending a full apology, but in the end their dignity as the civilian masters of Continental armed forces held them back. They decided to offer only a perfunctory—and oblique—form of satisfaction when on Saturday, November 29, they resolved to have "General Washington regulate the rank of Major General Arnold." This vote came more than three weeks after Wilkinson's promotion and was not to be interpreted as recognition for Arnold's heroics at Saratoga. The delegates acted, or so they publicly maintained, solely because they had recently adopted a new policy designed to end all the haggling among so many ultrasensitive field- and general-grade officers over precedence in rank.[18]

Back in the summer, a nasty dispute had erupted among Pennsylvania's field-grade officers regarding seniority in rank. One consequence was the breakdown of much-needed cohesion among that state's regiments at a time when Washington was preparing to challenge Howe's expeditionary force south of Philadelphia. Anxious for harmony, Washington impaneled a board of general officers, headed by Nathanael Greene, to examine the conflicting claims. Except in cases of promotion for extraordinary merit, Greene's board favored the establishment of precedence within each rank according to each officer's seniority in his former rank. On Wednesday, November 12, with Washington's encouragement, Congress adopted this policy recommendation—"rank or precedence of officers according to that standing they held in the army immediately before their present commissions." Now the pathway was open for Arnold, who had been a senior brigadier back in February 1777, to gain seniority in his current rank. Since the appointments of Benjamin Lincoln, Thomas Mifflin, Arthur St. Clair, Adam Stephen, and Lord Stirling bore the date February 19, Washington was to have Arnold's commission "called in and cancelled" in favor of a new one dated February 17, 1777.[19]

Congress's November 29 resolve did not at first include Arnold. By late September, rumors had reached Congress about Gates's removal of his fighting subordinate from command. The pro-Gates delegates took delight in this news. Bellowed Lovell, "I fear Arnold has taken for his motto, aut Caesar aut nulles [either Caesar or no one], and yet is only an instrument in the operations of S[chuyle]r." Such statements cast America's Hannibal in the image of a potential military tyrant and an ignorant dupe in the schemes of Gates's "known enemy" Schuyler. Wilkinson, when he finally got to York, added his own fantasied version of reality by denying Arnold any consequential part at First Freeman's Farm. Evidence to the contrary, declared Wilky, was but part of a devious plot by Schuyler "to stab" Gates in the back.[20]

All of the backbiting did little to boost Arnold's case for restored seniority. The delegates had no sure way of knowing how crucial a combat leadership role he had played at Saratoga. They had, however, received grim reports about his wound, which provoked much sympathy. A number of delegates also harbored doubts about Gates's perspicacity, in light of the surrender terms and his strong advocacy of Wilkinson for a brevet generalship. On November 29, consequently, while considering the disputed precedence of two Virginia brigadiers, Charles Scott and William Woodford, someone suggested an adjustment for Arnold as well. Lovell and the other pro-Gates delegates objected. They did not want to see Congress generate yet more problems by possibly insulting the generals initially elevated over Arnold. Despite their dissent, the resolution carried on a voice vote.[21]

Henry Laurens, as Congress's new president, transmitted a copy of this action to Arnold. Since the delegates had not considered his record of service, Laurens appended his own words of praise. "Permit me to assure you sir," he stated, that "I respect your character as a citizen and soldier of the United States of America, that I rejoice at your recovery from the dangerous wounds which you lately received in the defense of your country, [and] that I wish you perfect health and a continued succession of honor."[22]

Laurens's communication reached Albany in mid-December. The news did nothing to improve Arnold's health or spirits, as confirmed by Dr.

Brown's notation of his patient's continued "peevishness." Arnold dismissed Laurens's flattery, since these words did not reflect the sentiments of Congress as a whole. By passing the actual obligation of promotion to Washington, the delegates, he thought, had cast him in the mold of just another aggrandizing officer, not that of a twice-wounded, dedicated champion of liberty. Even more important, by not admitting their mistake they had denied him what they most owed him—the full restoration of his reputation along with his rank.

Arnold thus believed that Congress had defrauded him not only of his right to public vindication but of the requisite respect due him for his resolute service and personal self-sacrifice. These profoundly disturbing reflections caused Arnold to wait for three weeks before responding to Laurens with a perfunctory note. He did not offer even a courtesy statement of thanks. He did not owe anyone, he believed—most certainly not Congress's small-minded leaders—an expression of gratitude because he felt none.[23]

IV

On Wednesday, December 17, Arnold asked an aide to compose a message for Lucy Knox, who had earlier extended him best wishes for renewed good health. He now returned "his sincere thanks," then indicated his determination to make another attempt at winning the hand of Betsy De Blois. Recalling Lucy's solicitation of a scarf from the parcels of clothing he had purchased for Betsy, Arnold explained that he could not "part with any part of the contents of the trunk," at least not until he was well enough to travel to Boston. Should he again fail in capturing Betsy's heart, he promised Lucy full "preference" with regard to the trunk's contents.[24]

This letter contains a revealing glimpse of the consequences of Arnold's self-reckoning since Second Freeman's Farm. For over two and a half years, he had neglected his family, mercantile business, and personal ease and comfort to devote himself completely—and enthusiastically—to the martial needs of the Revolution. Now, almost imperceptibly, he was disclosing a rearranged set of priorities. Taking care of his own needs and interests, as in the matter of finding a new marriage companion, would increasingly dominate Arnold's concerns, especially since the patriot cause now seemed so flawed to him.

Thoughts of wooing Betsy also reflected the terrible loneliness Arnold felt while recuperating. He longed to return to New Haven and the familial love of his three sons and sister Hannah; but his mangled leg had him penned up like an untamed animal. Arnold could not go home, nor could he jump on a horse, seek out his detractors, and call them to account for their continuing disparagement of his name. No matter how aggravating, he had to endure what seemed like a never-ending confinement.

As the New Year beckoned and his thirty-seventh birthday approached, Arnold's physical health finally showed some improvement. He remained clouded in melancholy, however. When he had strapped on the sword of war in 1775, he had done so as a patriot deeply committed to demonstrating his public virtue. Like so many others, his motivations were not wholly pure. In terms of his personal goals, he sought through his military adventures public acceptance and acclamation, if not enduring fame, for the name that he bore. He wanted to earn the rebel community's recognition and lasting gratitude for his efforts. This mixture of selfless and self-serving impulses was not unusual except for the intensity of purpose that characterized Arnold's actions.

Arnold's fervor related directly to the bifurcated legacy of his childhood. His father, Benedict IV, had imbued him with strong ambitions to return the Arnold family name to the once-exalted position of Benedict I, the early governor of Rhode Island. Yet Benedict IV, in succumbing to mind-numbing bouts of alcoholism, had almost ruined his son's ability to do so. The community of Norwichites had stripped Arnold's namesake father of his good name and reputation, almost to the point of excommunication from the First Church. Young Benedict thus entered adulthood with an unsteady sense of self-esteem and a consuming desire to redeem his father's disgrace and family name.

In adulthood Arnold relentlessly pushed himself, first in amassing sub-stantial wealth and then in making war against the British imperial enemy. He invariably displayed an unflinching vision, a boldness of purpose, and a willingness to take huge risks, always depending on his keen intelligence to pull himself through threatening situations. As an amateur citizen-soldier, he would prove himself a military genius. Even as a neophyte officer, he could conceptualize war in strategic terms, as shown in his advocacy of invading Canada as the key to maintaining control of the Lake Champlain–Hudson River corridor—and the New England region. He could display tactical brilliance in combat, as at Valcour Island. According to the conventions for making war in his era, he fully appreciated the necessity of leading rather than merely ordering soldiers into combat. He was never fearful of hazarding his own life, which resulted in instances of uncommon personal bravery—and for which he twice sustained terrible wounds, the second of which left him feeling so bereft, alone, and unappreciated at the General Hospital in Albany.

His zeal and determination gained him deserved accolades as a war hero. Patriots called him America's Hannibal and Xenophon and Washington's fighting general, but members of Congress were hesitant to reward him, largely because he did not have connections or influence among Connecticut's upper tier of Revolutionary leaders, except when Silas Deane was in Congress. Not even the patronage of Washington and his own brilliant record could overcome Arnold's lack of strong local support in February 1777, when Congress promoted over him other, far better connected but certainly less militarily competent individuals.

In addition, Arnold too often appeared overly aggressive, if not too combative—a strength when properly dispensed in making war but a weakness when not carefully regulated in everyday human relations. Since his public reputation meant everything to him, for which he was hardly unique among his peers, he was invariably sensitive to slights of any kind. Had he possessed stronger self-esteem, he might have shown the dignified reserve of Schuyler when falsely accused of despicable deeds or demeaned by the partisan dealings of Congress. Arnold could control himself, as he did during his lengthy stay in Philadelphia while trying to make his case for restored seniority. Too often, however, he could not check his truculent impulses, and his confrontations with Ethan Allan, James Easton, John Brown, Moses Hazen, and Horatio Gates, among others, had a long-term, corrosive effect on his ambitions. Had Arnold been less passionate about protecting and defending his honor and good name, he might well have avoided falling into the abyss of embittered resentment that plagued him after his battles with the British and Gates at Saratoga.

During his childhood, Arnold's Calvinist mother Hannah had repeatedly told him how her vengeful, Old Testament God Jehovah had capriciously struck down his siblings. In time he rejected his mother's unforgiving deity and vowed to stand up against every perceived manifestation of arbitrary power. He most obviously did so when he went to war against the imperial tyrant Great Britain, only to have to reckon with what for him was a new kind of capricious ruling authority in the form of the Continental Congress. He grew to despise Congress, not only for failing at times to support the war effort adequately but also for letting parochial political influences, rather than meritorious service, determine its advancement of officers in the Continental military hierarchy. Arnold's ordeal with Congress was particularly vexing, since he had almost nowhere else to turn if he rejected the authority of that body—the central political agency of the Revolution—as he had earlier done with Jehovah and King George and Parliament.

By the end of 1777, Arnold was trying to decide if the patriot political system, conceived in reaction to alleged political tyranny and dedicated to the republican ideal that virtuous service, rather than bloodline connections, represented the appropriate source of personal advancement and community recognition, was really not very ennobling in actual operation. He was asking himself whether the colonists had thrown off one set of arbitrary rulers for another group, whose high-sounding rhetoric bore no relationship to the reality of their actions. He would come to conclude that Congress had corrupted the ideals of the Revolution, and the overwhelming proof lay not just in his own case for seniority but in the deification of Gates as the hero of Saratoga. Arnold, having so fervently given so much to the cause of liberty, even if not always perfectly given, felt utterly betrayed. This sensation was the most mortifying of them all as he convalesced in Albany.

V

With so many afflictions besetting the main Continental army, Washington was slow to communicate with his fighting subordinate. His most pressing assignment was settling his ill-clad, half-starved force of eleven thousand soldiers into winter quarters at Valley Forge. Another enervating concern related to what Washington believed was a serious challenge to his own continuance in command. Even before Congress had ordered the regulation of Arnold's precedence in rank, Washington had grown deeply suspicious of a plot—the Conway Cabal—to have Gates supplant him at the head of Continental forces.[25]

The magnitude of the cabal remains a point of debate, but this much is known. A few of Washington's subordinates—most visibly the Irish-born Thomas Conway, a respected officer in the French army who had sailed to America and secured a Continental brigadier's commission in May 1777—along with some congressional leaders, among them James Lovell, had become advocates of replacing the "loser" Washington with the "winner" Gates. Conway suggested as much to Gates when he wrote indiscreetly, "Heaven has been determined to save your country; or a weak general and bad counselors would have ruined it." In late October, ever-conniving Wilkinson had repeated some version of Conway's statement at Reading while on his way to York. When Washington heard about Wilky's comments, he and his most trusted staff officers took the offensive. In time the commander called both Conway and Gates to account, with the latter officer vigorously denying any desire to supersede Washington. By the late winter of 1778, the Conway Cabal had pretty much played itself out.[26]

On Tuesday, January 20, 1778, Washington finally found some moments to write to Arnold. He apologized for not having sent through a new commission sooner, explaining that "the situation of my papers and the want of blank commissions prevented me [from] doing it before." He asked Arnold "whether you are upon your legs again, and if you are not, may I flatter myself that you will be soon?" No one, Washington continued, "wishes more sincerely for this event than I do, or ... will receive the information with more pleasure." Then the commander expressed an "earnest wish to have your services [in] the ensuing campaign," and he promised Arnold "a command which I trust will be agreeable to yourself and of great advantage to the public."[27]

Washington was not just being solicitous. He viewed Arnold as an invaluable officer whom Congress had treated unfairly. He stated as much in his next letter, which he addressed to Benjamin Lincoln, who, like Arnold, was still recuperating in Albany from a leg wound. Concerned that Lincoln might take umbrage at Arnold's newfound precedence over him, Washington appealed to this worthy officer's sense of "justice and generosity ... to see every man in the possession of his rightful claim." The commander hoped that Lincoln would "cheerfully acquiesce in a measure calculated" to restore Arnold's "violated right, ... the restitution" of which "will be considered by every gentleman concerned, as I am sure it will by you, as an act of necessary justice."[28]

Washington hoped his fighting general would view the new commission as fully vindicating his reputation, and he was anxious to have Arnold wield his sword once again on behalf of the cause of liberty. Unfortunately, what the commander in chief could not discern was the depth of Arnold's resentment toward those patriots whom he believed had made a mockery of his name and the ideals of the Revolution.

Arnold was not quick to reply to Washington's letter. He finally did so on Thursday, March 12, writing from Middletown, Connecticut, where he rested for several weeks with friends on his journey home. Arnold asked for Washington's indulgence in "neglecting so long to answer it which I should have done sooner." His delay—indeed his reason for staying so long in Middletown—had to do with his limb. The wounds had "closed" but had recently "broke out again, occasioned by some loose splinters of bone remaining in the leg, which will not be serviceable, until they are extracted." According to his surgeon, the cleansing process "will be a work of time, perhaps two, and possibly five or six months." With the "utmost regret," then, Arnold could not form "any judgment" regarding when he might "repair to headquarters and take the command your Excellency has been so good as to reserve for me."

So far Arnold had not indicated any sign of his mental turmoil, but then he offered up this comment: "It is my most ardent wish to render every assistance in my power, that your Excellency may be enabled to finish the arduous task, you have with so much honor to yourself and advantage to your country, been engaged in, and have the pleasure of seeing peace and happiness restored to your country on the most permanent basis." The intimation was there. The cause was Washington's, but not necessarily Arnold's. Nor was the Revolution even worthy of his usual hopeful flourish about the favor of Divine Providence. A disenchanted patriot, Arnold would now do for himself first, letting the course of future events dictate how he should most appropriately care for his family and his own interests.[29]

VI

As the Revolutionary War continued to unfold, the lack of discernment in certain congressional judgments, especially with regard to commissioning and promoting general officers, became more and more obvious. By war's end the delegates had compiled a very mixed record, as demonstrated by the subsequent careers of the five more-favored gentlemen elevated over Arnold in February 1777. Two of them were virtual failures; one became a casualty of insuperable circumstances; and two were modestly successful. None ever achieved the kind of martial stature that Arnold had already earned.

Virginian Adam Stephen turned out to be an embarrassment for Congress. He was court-martialed and convicted of dereliction of duty—"unofficerlike behavior" and "drunkenness"—for his dubious performance at the Battle of Germantown. Washington accepted this verdict and announced the sacking of Stephen from the Continental service on November 20, 1777, a decision Congress sustained. He returned home, revived his medical practice, speculated successfully in land deals, and worked for the ratification of the Constitution of 1787. He died a respected patriot in 1791.[30]

Charming, garrulous Thomas Mifflin of Pennsylvania also proved a disappointment. He started out a promising officer in 1775 as Washington's quartermaster general and also employed his oratorical skills to persuade many patriot soldiers to stay in the ranks after the *rage militaire* had faded. Once promoted to major general, Mifflin faltered dramatically. Angry that Washington would not accept his every idea and upset at public charges about personally profiting from his quartermaster generalship, he all but stopped functioning in that post and linked arms with those who viewed Gates as a potential savior of the Revolution. Congress gladly accepted his resignation in 1779, after which he returned to politics. Before his death in

1800, Mifflin served three terms as Pennsylvania's governor. Later generations would remember him as the Continental general whose negligence helped cause the indefensible shortages of supplies—and consequent suffering—at Valley Forge.[31]

Another Pennsylvanian, Scottish-born Arthur St. Clair, had the misfortune of holding command at Ticonderoga when Burgoyne's army struck the "impregnable" fortress in early July 1777. Although a court of inquiry cleared St. Clair of any wrongdoing, no one chose to entrust him with an significant command assignment for the remainder of the war. As the first governor of the Northwest Territory, St. Clair led an expeditionary force against hostile Miami Indians in the Ohio country and suffered a crushing defeat on November 4, 1791. He resigned his military commission rather than endure another court of inquiry, but he remained in the governorship until 1802, when President Thomas Jefferson removed him for defying efforts to bring about Ohio's statehood. An indignant St. Clair spent his remaining years— he died in 1818—defending his unimposing military and political record.[32]

New Jerseyite William Alexander, better known as Lord Stirling, kept rendering useful service. Caught in a British pincers movement at the Battle of Long Island in August 1776, Stirling was captured while dauntlessly attempting to extricate his troops. Soon exchanged, he fought valiantly at Trenton and performed solidly at the battles of Brandywine (September 11, 1777) and Monmouth Court House (June 28, 1778). Notorious for his heavy drinking, Stirling was not always effective in executing the details of assignments, the last of which began in October 1781 when he took command of the all-but-inactive Northern Department. In January 1783 he succumbed to a devastating attack of the gout while on duty in Albany.[33]

As with Stirling, Benjamin Lincoln of Massachusetts had noteworthy moments, mostly during the Saratoga campaign. He was upset with Washington for making Arnold his senior and made noises about resigning his commission. In September 1778, an apologetic Congress placed him in charge of the army's Southern Department. Lincoln went to Charleston, South Carolina, where he failed to check a major British onslaught in the spring of 1780. On May 12 he surrendered his force of fifty-five hundred, the only patriot army lost to the British during the war. A sympathetic Congress chose not to investigate possible failures in Lincoln's actions at Charleston. Serving as Washington's second-ranking officer at Yorktown, he accepted the symbolic sword of submission on October 19, 1781, from General Charles O'Hara, who, as Lord Cornwallis's second, substituted for his "indisposed" commander at the surrender ceremonies. Soon thereafter Congress named Lincoln its Secretary of War, a post he held until late 1783. His last military action came in early 1787, when he took command of a local subscription army in Massachusetts that marched west from Boston and crushed a poorly armed band of angry backcountry farmers protesting oppressive state taxes. Lincoln garnered little glory in stamping out Shays's Rebellion, and he struggled to get by financially while serving as collector of port duties in Boston before retiring in 1809 and dying a year later.[34]

Among Arnold's Ticonderoga rivals, Ethan Allen contributed little else to the war effort. In late September 1775 the British captured him during his foolhardy attempt to seize Montreal. They shipped him to England in irons, only to send him back to America a year later after deciding not to hang him. Formally exchanged in 1778, Allen became Vermont's major general of militia, but he mainly used his command authority to drive off Yorkers wanting to settle in the Green Mountain region. He also employed a variety of tactics, including threats about rejoining the British empire, to pressure Congress into designating Vermont territory as the fourteenth state. Allen died in 1789, two years before his beloved Vermont achieved statehood.[35]

Tavern keeper James Easton returned from Albany to Pittsfield, Massachusetts, during the autumn of 1776 after drafting and sending his final damning comments about Arnold to Congress. Whether he ever successfully satisfied his creditors is not known. Easton never again served in the Continental army, and Congress canceled his colonel's commission in 1779. He later died in obscurity.

Fellow Pittsfield resident John Brown died in combat. After the Saratoga campaign he returned to his law practice, became a common pleas court judge, and won election to the Massachusetts General Court. As a local militia colonel, Brown again took up arms during the summer of 1780 in response to Indian-loyalist raiding forays in the Mohawk Valley region. He was killed in a skirmish near Stone Arabia on October 19, 1780, less than a month after his supposed prediction of Arnold's apostasy had come true.[36]

Moses Hazen survived into the nineteenth century. Fully committed to a second invasion of Canada in 1778, he helped formulate plans for an assault that never took place. In November 1780, Hazen faced another court-martial on charges that included stealing from his regiment. Once again he was more persuasive than his accusers, in this case his immediate subordinates. Borrowing from his earlier confrontation with Arnold, Hazen preferred charges of peculation and unmilitary behavior against his primary challenger, Major James Reid. This time Hazen actually got satisfaction when a hearing board declared Reid guilty and sentenced him to a public reprimand for not having treated his regimental commander with proper respect.

A few months after this bizarre sequence, Congress awarded gentlemanly, self-righteous, loquacious Hazen a brevet brigadier generalship. Still not paying that much attention to meritorious service, the delegates had just recently lost the services of the heralded but unrefined Colonel Daniel Morgan, after repeatedly denying him a brigadier's commission. Morgan returned briefly to duty in the South and on January 17, 1781, effected a tactical masterpiece in routing an attacking British column under "Bloody" Banastre Tarleton at Hannah's Cowpens in South Carolina. By comparison, Hazen's last service was unexceptional at Yorktown. Retiring from the service in January 1783, Hazen died heavily in debt twenty years later, having focused his energies as a land speculator on various schemes that produced endless litigation. Morgan became wealthy, and as a greatly admired planter and landholder in western Virginia, he even served a term in the new national Congress before his death in 1802.[37]

Revered community status was hardly the lot of James Wilkinson, who led the life of a loutish scoundrel. In the spring of 1778 he turned on Gates, who had rebuked his young protégé for leaking the contents of Conway's letter. A deeply insulted Wilky came close to fighting a duel with his erstwhile patron. Likewise disgusted by the complaints of numerous officers about his sudden elevation in rank, he resigned his commission. Congress still had not had enough of him, however; the delegates named him clothier general for the Continental army in July 1779, only to remove him in March 1781 amid charges of having embezzled public funds.

Wilkinson's career after the war included a variety of self-serving schemes, mostly based in the trans-Appalachian West. During the 1780s he took payments from Spanish officials in return for encouraging western settlers to renounce their allegiance to the United States in favor of Spain. In the early 1800s he served as an accomplice of Aaron Burr in the latter's convoluted plot to create a new southwestern empire separate from the United States. Wilky eventually turned on Burr and helped expose the scheme. Somehow he managed to maintain enough credibility to revive his military career. In 1792 the new federal Congress, not knowing about his dealings with the Spanish government, commissioned him a brigadier general. During the War of 1812, Major General Wilkinson proved himself a spectacular failure after taking command of a force charged with invading Canada. Soon recalled, he evaded the wrath of a court of inquiry and gained an honorable discharge in 1815. During his last years he maneuvered to obtain a large land patent in Texas from the government of Mexico, but his death in 1825 cut short this venture. Wilkinson succumbed either to excessive drinking, which had become a chronic problem for him, or to an overdose of opium.[38]

Horatio Gates did nothing to enhance his hero's reputation after Saratoga.

In June 1780, Congress, in the wake of Lincoln's surrender at Charleston, called on him to resuscitate military resistance in the Southern Department. The delegates did so without consulting Washington, whom they were sure would not sanction Gates. Their prized general rushed southward and gathered a smattering of troops at Hillsborough, North Carolina. Against the wishes of his ranking officers, Gates quickly marched his ill-prepared force of three thousand toward what he thought was a lightly defended British outpost at Camden, South Carolina. In the early morning darkness of August 16 he ran into the unexpected: a sizable enemy column under Lord Cornwallis. Rather than pull back, Gates engaged. The Battle of Camden quickly became a bloody rout for the Americans, who suffered some 750 casualties. Before the engagement was even over, Gates was riding hard northward, allegedly in search of assistance. By late evening he was back in North Carolina, more than sixty miles north of the battle site. Not surprisingly, critics accused him of cowardice in the face of the enemy. Arnold had used the term "poltroon," a characterization that had gone unnoticed by Gates's admirers in Congress.

Why the hero of Saratoga accepted battle at Camden remains an open question. Perhaps he hoped to overcome impressions of his indecisive generalship at Saratoga by proving that he, too, was capable of resolute action. Perhaps he had come to believe Congress's platitudes about his capacity for "gallant" leadership. Regardless of the explanation, an embarrassed Congress recalled Gates and asked Washington to name a new Southern Department commander. His choice was Nathanael Greene, who brilliantly outdueled Cornwallis in the months preceding Yorktown.

Gates kept pestering Congress for a court of inquiry to clear his name of wrongdoing. The disenchanted delegates ignored these requests but finally ordered him to report to Washington, where by virtue of his seniority in rank he became second in command at Newburgh, the site of the Continental army's final cantonment during the winter of 1782–1783. Before springtime, caballing officers, deeply concerned about promised postwar pensions, fused their interests with nationalist-minded congressional leaders. The latter group did not see how the central government could endure without some power of taxation, and they turned to Gates when Washington refused to employ the army as an instrument of force in strengthening the authority of Congress.

What has been called the "Newburgh Conspiracy" played itself out in mid-March 1783 when Washington confronted the army's restive officers, who had begun to rally around Gates. The commander masterfully squelched the threatened uprising by exhorting the officers not to jeopardize the principles of liberty for which they had so unselfishly sacrificed themselves during eight years of war. This successful defusing of an open mutiny and potential military coup against civilian authority marked Washington's finest hour as commander in chief. The same could not be said for the hero of Saratoga.[39]

Gates soon returned to Virginia, where his beloved wife Elizabeth was dying. A few years later he married again, this time to a wealthy Maryland spinster, Mary Vallance. He and Mary eventually moved to an estate on Manhattan Island near New York City, where Gates repeatedly showed generosity toward old comrades in arms who were down on their financial luck. Unlike so many former Continental officers, Gates played virtually no part in the politics of nation making after the war, and Washington as president saw no reason to offer a political post to this overly ambitious, untrustworthy comrade. The hero of Saratoga did not seem to mind; he had earned his place in history. He died quietly, at peace with himself and the world, in 1806.[40]

Philip Schuyler was among those postwar political leaders who felt nothing but contempt for Gates. In October 1778, a court-martial hearing board exonerated Schuyler of any blame for the loss of Ticonderoga. Resigning his military commission six months later, he devoted much of his time to politics. Schuyler served in the Continental Congress, the New York State Senate, and the United States Senate after ratification of the Constitution of 1787. He maintained close ties with his family, including his son-in-law Alexander Hamilton, whose financial plans as Washington's first Secretary of the Treasury he actively supported. During the late 1790s, Schuyler's physical ailments beset him again. He retired from politics and concentrated on managing his extensive business and landholding interests. After the death of his beloved wife Catherine in 1803, he seemed to lose his will for life. Schuyler passed away in November 1804, knowing that his reputation as a valued patron and servant of the new American republic was completely whole.[41]

VII

Back in 1775, Schuyler and Washington were among the first to recognize Benedict Arnold's natural aptitude for waging war. The commander in chief was again thinking of his fighting general on Thursday, May 7, 1778, when he wrote Arnold an encouraging note. He explained how "a gentleman in France" had "very obligingly sent me three sets of epaulets and sword-knots, two of which, professedly to be disposed to any friends I should choose."

Washington had decided to honor Arnold by giving him a set of these emblems "as a testimony of my sincere regard and approbation of your conduct" in serving the American cause. He likewise stated how much he was looking forward to Arnold's return to the army, but he cautioned his subordinate not to "hazard" his health by "coming out too soon."[42]

Much to Washington's astonishment, Arnold materialized at Valley Forge two weeks later. His unexpected appearance was a source of "great joy to the army," according to Henry Dearborn, who had endured the deadly winter season at that hallowed cantonment. Washington enthusiastically greeted Arnold, wondering to himself what kind of a command assignment he could bestow on a ranking officer who could not stand on one leg, let alone walk or ride a horse—Arnold had traveled from New Haven to Valley Forge in a carriage. Still, there before him was his fighting general, gamely holding himself up by leaning heavily on a crutch. There he was, looking as if he was again ready to risk his all at the outset of a new campaign season, despite his shattered left leg.[43]

What Washington thought he beheld was a patriot of unyielding spirit and dauntless courage. What he as yet had no way of assessing was the heart and soul of the troubled officer before him, a person who in actuality felt deeply betrayed by the cause he had so eagerly tried to serve. Even as the commander in chief welcomed Arnold back to the army on that spring day, he had no way of knowing how little America's Hannibal would appreciate the gift of epaulets and sword knots. He had no idea how much Arnold felt defrauded by a cause that had left him lame and nearly lifeless, compromised in sacred honor and debilitated in personal fortune. The elements of Arnold's tragic descent into treason were already congealing, as a shocked Washington would eventually learn at Robinson's House on September 25, 1780. When he did, this heretofore admiring patron took the lead in casting Benedict Arnold out of the pantheon of Revolutionary heroes. What was left was the enduring image of a corrupted villain, so "*vile*" and "*treacherous*" as to be forever "*leagued with Satan.*"[44]

Epilogue

The Current Coinage
of Ingratitude

When George Washington received official news of the Franco-American alliance, he proclaimed "a day of rejoicing throughout the whole army." On Wednesday, May 6, 1778, he jubilantly held a review of the full body of troops at Valley Forge amid thirteen celebratory rounds of cannon fire, a *feu de joie* of musket fire, and loud huzzahs for "the king of France," "the friendly European powers," and "the American states." The next day he wrote to Arnold about honoring him with a set of epaulets and sword knots. Given the timing, Washington was recognizing not only his fighting general's long record of invaluable service but also his critical field leadership at Saratoga, a major triggering event in generating formal military and diplomatic relations with France.[1]

In many ways the alliance had been in the making since the mid-1760s, when French policy makers began monitoring the growing rift between Britain and its progeny in North America. Having just lost Canada to the British, they welcomed the prospect of the much-hated English-speaking empire stumbling and falling in some inglorious manner. As the American rebellion gained momentum, France's aggressive foreign minister, Charles Gravier, Comte de Vergennes, convinced King Louis XVI that to support the patriots with covert aid. The French government also began a military buildup, in the event that formal intervention somehow seemed justified. Since the French system was monarchical, assistance to the republican cause had little to do with some abstract love of liberty. The objective was to restore Europe's balance of power, tilting so heavily in imperial Britain's favor in the wake of the Seven Years' War.[2]

Reports about the vanquishing of Burgoyne's army and Washington's bold but unsuccessful bid to crush Sir William Howe's redcoats at Germantown, Pennsylvania, convinced Vergennes the time was ripe to consummate a formal alliance that would assure the Americans a steady flow of desperately needed financial, material, and martial resources. As part of the alliance, the French government also recognized American independence, the indicator of legitimacy as a sovereign political entity among the nations of the world.

When a naval battle erupted between British and French war vessels in the English Channel on June 17, 1778, declarations of war followed. The American rebellion now would assume the dimensions of a world war. The French had powerful land and naval forces, and they could strike when they pleased at such valued possessions as the British sugar islands in the West Indies—and even at the island kingdom of England itself. A serious strategic consequence for the British was that they could no longer concentrate their military resources against the rebellious Americans. They had to dilute their strength by dispersing some of their forces to other vulnerable points around the globe. They would do so to counter not only the French but also the Spanish and the Dutch, who became belligerents in June 1779 and December 1780, respectively.[3]

Having failed to crush the rebellion before going to war with other European powers, the best British hope for retaking the colonies after 1777 lay in the collapse of the patriot cause from the inside, and collapse it nearly did. Languishing popular support was a serious problem that infuriated Washington's officers. Penned one Continental general in March 1780, "It really gives me great pain to think of our public affairs; where is the public spirit of the year 1775? Where are those flaming *patriots* who were ready to sacrifice their lives, their fortunes, their all, for the public?" Stated another ranking officer in July 1780, "I despise my countrymen. I wish I could say I was not born in America. I once gloried in it, but am now ashamed of it. . . . The insults and neglects which the army have met with from the country beggars all description." Proclaimed Arnold less than two weeks before his flight to the British, "It is a matter much to be lamented that our army is permitted to starve in a land of plenty." There was a "a fault somewhere," and he wanted "its authors . . . capitally punished."[4]

Arnold did not focus his disgust on an indifferent populace. From his perspective, the real culprits in despoiling the Revolution were the small-minded, self-serving civilian leaders seated in the halls of Congress—and in some state governments. They had turned the American cause and its ideals into a sham. Not by coincidence, these were the selfsame persons he blamed for his personal travails over military rank and personal honor.

Since Arnold was still too physically incapacitated to take an active field assignment after returning to the army in May 1778, Washington named him the military commander of Philadelphia in anticipating the British evacuation of June 1778. In trying to be supportive of Arnold, the commander in chief made a poor choice for his disillusioned, resentful, embittered subordinate by stationing him where he would have regular contact and likely conflict with self-possessed civilian leaders in Congress—and even the Pennsylvania state government.

Arnold assumed his new command post with a withering sense of service to the cause of liberty. Had he been reasoning with his usual clarity of purpose and strategic insight, he would have realized how the Franco-American alliance had seriously undercut British prospects of ever regaining the colonies—despite widespread popular apathy and instances of flawed civilian leadership. He would have appreciated how his own audacious generalship and the success of more than two years of campaigning in the northern theater, with the capstone triumph at Saratoga, had established the conditions that would make winning the War for Independence a distinct possibility. Instead, Arnold, as he dwelled on being used and abused, began to lose his broader vision. Having served the cause of liberty so well, he would increasingly put the emphasis on serving himself first—with the long-term consequence of everlasting infamy.

Consumed as he had become by his own damaged sensibilities, Arnold stood ready to challenge—and even embarrass—Congress when that body moved back from York to Philadelphia. No longer would he present himself as the deferring officer who the year before had asked for the delegates' indulgence in seeking to restore his seniority in rank. Rather, he would function as an acrid critic with the intention of exposing the ingratitude of civilian leaders toward those selfless patriots—such as himself—who had sacrificed so greatly for the Revolution.

Ever the offensive-minded warrior, Arnold assailed Congress by dwelling on the destitute circumstances of the widow and children of Dr. Joseph Warren, the much-admired Massachusetts patriot leader who had fallen in battle at Bunker Hill. In July 1778, Arnold explained how he had learned "that my late worthy friend General Warren [had] left his affairs unsettled, and that, after paying his debts, a very small matter, if anything, would remain for his children." Arnold found it galling that Warren's family had "been entirely neglected by the state" of Massachusetts and that civilians there felt no obligation to provide for the progeny of so commendable a patriot, who had given his life with the hope of ensuring their liberties.[5]

Embracing the cause of Warren's widow and children, Arnold pushed hard with Congress for a special pension. He did so at a time when the delegates were trying to sidestep a more general demand from Washington's officers about providing for their families, should they become incapacitated or die while serving the patriot community. The delegates cared neither for Arnold's badgering nor for his announced intention to conduct a private subscription drive on behalf of Warren's family. They knew that he was casting them in the mold of hypocrites, who preached the republican ideal of virtuous service but who offered nothing in compensation for those who made the ultimate sacrifice of giving life itself. In championing Warren's widow and children, Arnold was likewise verifying his own experiences with Congress. The delegates, he thus reconfirmed for himself, were not worthy of a true patriot's respect.

Arnold persisted in his private subscription effort, and he gave the Warren family at least $500 out of his own purse. Because of his harassing tactics, Congress, in the summer of 1780, finally granted the half pay of a major general to Warren's family until the youngest child reached majority status. The delegates from Massachusetts actually split their vote and abstained, which led Arnold to observe, "Charity, urbanity, and the social virtues seem swallowed up in the tumult and confusion of the times, and [the] self wholly engrosses the nabobs of the present day." He penned these biting words less than two months before returning his allegiance to the British.[6]

Even more than hypocrisy, Arnold convinced himself that ingratitude was everywhere evident as he carried out his duties in Philadelphia. Once in the city, he immediately had problems with republican-minded state leaders over the handling of citizens suspected of collaborating with Howe's occupation force. These zealous patriots insisted on severe punishments, even including hangings. Arnold would not cooperate with them; he favored a policy of conciliation in restoring order to the badly divided Philadelphia community.

The local republicans soon started charging Arnold with high-handedness and pomposity—emblems of a potential military dictator. They also accused him of currying favor with Philadelphia's affluent families, some of whom had indeed collaborated with the enemy. They gave knowing looks to each other when Arnold, having failed again to win the favor of Betsy De Blois, began courting Margaret "Peggy" Shippen. She was the intelligent, vivacious, and attractive daughter of wealthy neutralist Edward Shippen, whose disinterest in supporting the rebellion rankled Pennsylvania's republican enthusiasts. Something had to be done, they insisted, to free their community of this puffed-up military commander, and they moved to get rid of Arnold even before he married Peggy on April 8, 1779.

Most of Arnold's local opponents were active in the Constitutionalist party, actually an organized political faction of radical-minded Pennsylvania Revolutionaries. They were sure they knew how best to bring the blessings of liberty to the people and were invariably quick to slander anyone with the epithet "tory" whose viewpoints were at odds with their own. Resenting Arnold's military authority as they did, they publicly—and purposefully—smeared his name in February 1779 by proffering charges of eight alleged abuses of his powers. When he learned about these accusations, he wrote despairingly to his bride-to-be, "I am heartily tired with my journey, and almost so with human nature. I daily discover so much baseness and ingratitude among mankind that I almost blush at being of the same species."[7]

Determined to redeem his good name, Arnold demanded a court of inquiry. Delay after delay ensued, however, as his Constitutionalist party adversaries kept insisting they needed additional time to collect evidence that would prove their case. In May 1779, Arnold sent Washington a frantic letter, fairly begging him to get on with the proceedings. "I want no favor; I ask only for justice," he stated in exasperation. Then he composed these revealing words: "Having made every sacrifice of fortune and blood, and become a cripple in the service of my country, I little expected to meet the ungrateful returns I have received from my countrymen; but as Congress has stamped ingratitude as the current coin, I must take it." A few days later Arnold, using his young wife's contacts with Major John André, whom she had gotten to know during the British occupation of Philadelphia, penned his first treasonous letter.[8]

The allegations of misusing his military authority leveled by his Pennsylvania accusers served as additional proof to Arnold that the cause was no longer worth serving—or even saving. When he finally received a military hearing in January 1780, Arnold could not believe the results. The board declared him guilty of dereliction of duty on two counts: permitting a trading vessel, the *Charming Nancy*, in which he had become an investor, to clear the port of Philadelphia when other merchant craft could not, and employing public wagons for the purpose of moving private goods. Congress instructed Washington to reprimand America's Hannibal, which the commander did in temperate terms. To an astounded Arnold, now even his patron Washington had seemingly rejected him. If he was harboring reservations about continuing his liaison with the British, they now vanished.[9]

Washington's reprimand stood as the ultimate proof for Arnold that thanklessness was all he could expect to receive from the Revolution, despite his monumental labors and sacrifices. He would never gain the enduring respect of the community of Revolutionary patriots, he concluded; rather, for him, his reward was a crushing sense of rejection—and even disgrace—

at the behest of that community. These conclusions, which Arnold expressed with the word "ingratitude," only strengthened the embittered feelings already pulsating through his soul.

While confined to the military hospital in Albany, Arnold had rated himself naive and foolish for having so neglected his own interests while playing the part of a virtuous patriot. By the time he arrived at Valley Forge, he had consciously decided to place much higher priority on attending to his own needs. He would do so, he told himself, because he had already sacrificed so much. He would do so to repair his disintegrating financial position and better provide for his three sons and his sister Hannah; he would do so to fulfill his quest to win the hand of a desirable, loving spouse; he would do so to relieve himself of the accumulated burden of strain placed on his personal honor and reputation; and he would do so to rebut the ingratitude shown him by civilian leaders who could not "admire or reward the virtue they cannot imitate," as he described matters just seventeen days before his flight from Robinson's House.[10]

In a way, what had reawakened in Arnold was the spirit of acquisitive, self-serving commercialism to which he had subscribed as a young merchant seeking to get ahead in New Haven. Service to the Revolutionary community would henceforth come only after he had first addressed his own needs and interests, which were no longer in full harmony with those of the cause of liberty. As such, Arnold actively engaged in questionable mercantile dealings while in command at Philadelphia, and he left himself open to formal charges of peculation, however magnified in content by the Pennsylvania Constitutionalists.

As Arnold's commitment to virtuous service eroded, he began to lose his earlier strategic vision for American victory in the War for Independence. He failed to discern the significance of the French alliance, specifically in distracting Britain's martial efforts away from the colonists. Arnold's larger vision was completely gone by August 1780 when Washington, in seeking to make amends with his chastened but still valued fighting general, offered him the honored position of commanding the Continental army's left wing. Instead, America's Hannibal would accept only the West Point command— and what turned out to be his rendezvous with treason.

Because of his feelings of ingratitude and his perception of rejection by the Revolutionary community, an embittered Arnold thus forsook the cause to which he had given so much of himself. Just as he had done so many times before, he stood in defiance of those persons whom he felt had falsely wronged him and rejected the movement they represented in favor of returning his allegiance to the British empire, an entity that he had deemed completely tyrannical only a few years before. In doing so, Arnold provided handsomely for his family, more than amply recovering what he had sacrificed financially. Still, he failed miserably in his other objective of becoming the pied piper of reconciliation with the parent nation.[11]

The British commissioned Arnold a brigadier general in the regular British army, but they were hesitant about cashing in on their investment. Even if he was America's fighting general, he was still a mere provincial— and one who irritated many British officers because he was not bashful about telling them how they had mishandled the war effort.

In December 1780, on orders from Commander in Chief Henry Clinton, Arnold led a force of sixteen hundred troops by sea to Virginia. The resulting raids and capture of Richmond reduced the flow of patriot supplies southward into the Carolinas for use by Nathanael Greene's Southern Department troops as they dueled with British units under Lord Cornwallis. When the earl himself moved into Virginia in May 1781, ultimately to become entrapped by combined Franco-American forces at Yorktown, Clinton recalled Arnold to New York City.[12]

In late summer, Sir Henry asked Arnold to mount a strike against New London, Connecticut, at the mouth of the Thames River and little more than a dozen miles south of Arnold's Norwich birthplace. The idea was to divert Washington from going after Cornwallis and to take out a bothersome nest of patriot privateering vessels. Arnold struck with about seventeen hundred troops on September 6. One of his columns, attacking Fort Griswold on the east side of the river, barbarously murdered many rebel defenders after they had surrendered. Fires set by troops with Arnold in New London resulted in massive destruction and earned the British brigadier a new epithet as America's Nero, besides much patriot damnation as a vengeful butcher.[13]

In December 1781, Arnold sailed for England, hoping to convince imperial leaders not to give up, despite the loss of Cornwallis's army at Yorktown. Once in London, he had meetings with ranking cabinet officials as well as George III, and they spoke highly of his vigor of martial purpose. Arnold even presented a plan designed to bring about a reunited empire, predicated on Britain's "willingness to carry on the war." As at Quebec, however, he had arrived too late. Because of so many enemies and setbacks on so many fronts, peace sentiment was ascendant. Negotiations were already getting underway to end the war and concede American independence.[14]

Arnold initially made a home for Peggy and their growing family in London, but he soon decided to return to North America, where he resumed his mercantile ventures operating out of newly founded loyalist communities in the province of New Brunswick, Canada. Showing the same financial generosity that had denoted his patriot military career, he made loans to various individuals struggling to reestablish themselves economically. Some of these obligations went unpaid. When Arnold became short of cash and finally attempted to collect what was due him, one or more of these loyalist debtors organized a crowd that visited the Arnold residence in St. John to denounce his alleged avarice. In an ironic twist for American friends of the king, the protestors carried an effigy of Arnold that bore the appellation "Traitor!" [15]

In 1792, Benedict and Peggy again relocated in London. Arnold focused on the West Indies trade and performed temporary military service as a volunteer officer in the islands. With the French Revolution producing yet more rounds of warfare, Arnold pressed hard with the ministry for a command assignment. Although he had the patronage of Sir Henry Clinton and Lord Cornwallis, he lacked the social credentials and range of influence to secure a meaningful post. Finally, he turned to privateering, but he fared poorly in these ventures, even as his health was giving out. Besieged by asthma, the gout, and torturous pain in his twice-wounded leg, Arnold struggled to keep himself going. He died after "a week's severe illness" and "great suffering," in the words of Peggy, on Sunday morning, June 14, 1801. [16]

Back in the thriving young American republic, few seemed to notice Arnold's passing. One of those who did may have been the source of yet another tale in which the apostate general, as he lay dying, begged God's forgiveness for forsaking the American cause, then asked to be dressed in his Continental uniform. Such penitent behavior would have been out of character for Arnold. If he felt remorse for his actions, he kept these thoughts to himself; but that subject is part of another story—the American villain as opposed to a warrior hero of the Revolution.

What Arnold quickly came to appreciate was the intense hatred his erstwhile patriot brethren felt toward him. Allegedly, during his raiding expedition to Virginia, he asked a subordinate what his fate might be if local patriots captured him. That officer replied, "They will cut off that leg of yours wounded at Quebec and at Saratoga, and bury it with all the honors of war, and then hang the rest of you on a gibbet." [17]

Failing to exact retribution, America's Revolutionaries could only pass their wrathful sentiments and tales on to succeeding generations. Their descendants carried forward in their tradition, some even denying Arnold's pivotal significance as a once-magnificent servant to the cause of American liberty. Parents eschewed naming their sons Benedict because they feared any identification with "such a tainted blot" of a human being like Arnold, the handiwork of Satan. Many could not even bring themselves to speak his name.[18]

Even in our own time, visitors to the Saratoga battlefield may regard a monument, first erected in 1887, that shows only an officer's left-footed boot. The inscription on the back side contains these lines: "In memory of the 'most brilliant soldier' of the Continental army, who was desperately wounded on this spot, the sally port of Burgoyne's 'Great Western Redoubt', 7th October 1777, winning for his countrymen the Decisive Battle of the American Revolution. . . ." That momentous contribution has endured, even if given by the unnamed person who was later "reduced . . . to ashes . . . in the sight of all who were watching." [19]

Notes

Archives and Journals

AAS	American Antiquarian Society, Worcester, Massachusetts
APS	American Philosophical Society, Philadelphia
BeA	Berkshire Athenaeum, Pittsfield, Massachusetts
BPL	Boston Public Library
CHR	*Canadian Historical Review*
CHS	Connecticut Historical Society, Hartford
CSL	Connecticut State Library, Hartford
DLAR	David Library of the American Revolution, Washington Crossing, Pennsylvania
HLHU	Houghton Library, Harvard University, Cambridge, Massachusetts
HM	*Historical Magazine*
HSP	Historical Society of Pennsylvania, Philadelphia
JSH	*Journal of Social History*
LC	Library of Congress, Washington, D.C.
MAH	*Magazine of American History*
MdHS	Maryland Historical Society, Baltimore
MH	Magazine of History
MHS	Massachusetts Historical Society, Boston
MNHP	Morristown National Historical Park, Morristown, New Jersey
NA	National Archives, Washington, D.C.
NHCHS	New Haven Colony Historical Society, New Haven, Connecticut
N-YHS	New-York Historical Society, New York City
NYPL	New York Public Library, New York City
NYSA	New York State Archives, Albany
PMHB	*Pennsylvania Magazine of History and Biography*
PML	Pierpont Morgan Library, New York City
PUL	Princeton University Library, Princeton, New Jersey
RUL	Rutgers University Library, New Brunswick, New Jersey
RULQ	*La Revue de l'Université Laval, Québec*
SCL	Smith College Library, Northampton, Massachusetts
USMA	United States Military Academy Library, West Point, New York
WMQ	*William and Mary Quarterly*
YUL	Yale University Library, New Haven, Connecticut

Sources

AA	*American Archives.* Edited by Peter Force. 4th ser., 6 vols. 5th ser., 3 vols. Washington, D.C., 1837–1853.

CAR   *Correspondence of the American Revolution: Being Letters of Eminent Men to George Washington.* Edited by Jared Sparks. 4 vols. Boston, 1853.

DAR   *Documents of the American Revolution, 1770–1783 (Colonial Office Series).* Edited by Kenneth G. Davies. 21 vols. Shannon, Ireland, 1972–1981.

JCC   *Journals of the Continental Congress, 1774–1789.* Edited by Worthington C. Ford et al. 34 vols. Washington, D.C., 1904–1937.

LDC   *Letters of Delegates to Congress, 1774–1789.* Edited by Paul H. Smith et al. 24 vols. to date. Washington, D.C., 1976– .

MQ   *March to Quebec: Journals of the Members of Arnold's Expedition.* Edited by Kenneth Roberts. New York, 1938.

NDAR   *Naval Documents of the American Revolution.* Edited by William Bell Clark, William James Morgan, et al. 10 vols. to date. Washington, D.C., 1964– .

Paps. NG   *The Papers of General Nathanael Greene.* Edited by Richard K. Showman et al. 9 vols. to date. Chapel Hill, N.C., 1976– .

Paps. GW   George Washington Papers. 8th ser. Library of Congress (microfilm edition).

Paps. GW, RWS   *The Papers of George Washington: Revolutionary War Series.* Edited by Philander D. Chase et. al. 6 vols. to date. Charlottesville, Va., 1985– .

PCC   Papers of the Continental Congress. National Archives (microfilm edition).

Writings GW   *The Writings of George Washington from the Original Manuscript Sources, 1745–1799.* Edited by John C. Fitzpatrick. 39 vols. Washington, D.C., 1931–1944.

For purposes of consistency, I have modernized spelling and capitalization in all quoted materials.

P R O L O G U E : *Treason! Treason! Black as Hell*

     1. Reminiscence of Samuel Downing, quoted in Isaac N. Arnold, *The Life of Benedict Arnold: His Patriotism and His Treason* (Chicago, 1880), 29.

     2. Ibid., 29, offers three physical descriptions from BA's contemporaries. Curiously, one said that Arnold had a florid, as opposed to a dark, complexion. Regarding BA's height, Willard M. Wallace, *Traitorous Hero: The Life and Fortunes of Benedict Arnold* (New York, 1954), 1, refers to his subject as a "stocky little man." The implication is that stocky little men have Napoleonic complexes about power. Whatever his faults, BA did not have the opportunity to display much political ambition, and not all short men unconsciously lust after power, or military glory for

that matter, out of a presumed sense of inferiority about their height. BA may have appeared more diminutive than he actually was because of his stoutness; however, he was not much shorter than the average among his peers. Furthermore, his height had little or nothing to do with the frustrations and psychological turmoil that built up in him over the years.

3. Among the documents in BA's handwriting were orders regarding the disposition of the artillery corps "in case of an alarm," dated Sept. 5, 1780; a detailed statement on redoubts making up the West Point defenses, with numbers of troops assigned to each; and various passes prepared by BA to permit Mr. John Anderson to pass over to enemy lines. The originals reside in the NYSA.

4. McHenry's description, dated Robinson's House, Sept. 26, 1780, *Diary of the American Revolution,* comp. Frank Moore (2 vols., New York, 1860), 2:324–25. The archetypal assessment of Peggy Shippen as intimately involved in Arnold's treachery may be found in Carl Van Doren, *Secret History of the American Revolution* (New York, 1941), 193–95, 200–202, and 302–6, among other pages. However, Lewis Burd Walker, "The Life of Margaret Shippen, Wife of Benedict Arnold," *PMHB,* 24 (1900): 257–66, 401–29; 25 (1901): 20–46, 145–90, 189–302, 452–97; and 26 (1902): 71–80, 224–44, 322–34, 464–88, serves as a family denial of Peggy's complicity. For a valuable summary, consult Cynthia Lee Thomas, "Margaret Shippen Arnold: The Life of an Eighteenth-Century Upper-Class Woman" (M.A. thesis, University of Houston, 1982), 98–129.

5. *The Arnold Memorial: William Arnold of Providence and Pawtuxet, 1587–1675, and a Genealogy of His Descendants,* comp. Elisha Stephen Arnold (Rutland, Vt., 1935), 9–39. Some biographers have commented on the seeming irony in relation to the meaning of BA's family name; however, they have not reckoned with the central importance of the concept of family and personal honor to BA in its eighteenth-century context. Clare Brandt, *The Man in the Mirror: A Life of Benedict Arnold* (New York, 1994), 3, stated that Arnold in early German meant "the eagle's power." My use of the term derives from the family's roots in medieval England. On the concept of public virtue as related to BA, see Charles Royster, " 'The Nature of Treason': Revolutionary Virtue and American Reactions to Benedict Arnold," *WMQ,* 3 ser., 36 (1979): 163–93.

6. *Heath's Memoirs of the American War,* ed. Rufus Rockwell Wilson (New York, 1904), 268–69. A more apocryphal-sounding version of Lurvey's words appears in James Thacher, *Military Journal of the American Revolution* (Hartford, Ct., 1862), 472, in which Lurvey caustically replied to BA, "No, sir, one coat is enough for me to wear at a time."

7. BA to GW, On Board the *Vulture,* Sept. 25, 1780, *The Papers of Alexander Hamilton,* ed. Harold C. Syrett et al. (27 vols., New York, 1961–1987), 2:439–40.

8. BA (J. Moore) to John André (John Anderson), n.p., July 12, 1780, Van Doren, *Secret History,* 463–64.

9. James Kirby Martin and Mark Edward Lender, *A Respectable Army: The Military Origins of the Republic, 1763–1789* (Arlington Heights, Ill., 1982), 158–65;

Richard H. Kohn, "American Generals of the Revolution: Subordination and Restraint," in *Reconsiderations on the Revolutionary War: Selected Essays*, ed. Don Higginbotham (Westport, Ct., 1978), 104–23; and James Kirby Martin, "Benedict Arnold's Treason as Political Protest," *Parameters: Journal of the US Army War College*, 11 (1981): 63–74.

10. BA (J. Moore) to John André (J. Anderson), n.p., July 12, 1780, Van Doren, *Secret History,* 463.

11. Alexander Scammell to Nathaniel Peabody, Orangetown, N.Y., Oct. 3, 1780, *HM*, 2 ser., 8 (1870): 145.

12. Frost Orderly Book, USMA. This statement appeared in many other orderly books and apparently originated with NG. See NG's General Orders, Headquarters, Orangetown, Sept. 26, 1780, *Paps. NG*, 6:314; and Thacher, Sept. 26, 1780, *Military Journal,* 215–16. For a sampling from other orderly books, consult that of Col. Philip Van Cortlandt, 2d New York Regiment, Sept. 23–Oct. 1, 1780, N-YHS.

13. Sebastian Bauman to Henry Knox, West Point, Sept. 26, 1780, Bauman Paps., N-YHS; William Beaumont to Samuel Daggett, Tappan, N.Y., Sept. 27, 1780, N-YHS.

14. For a discussion of thinking among Revolutionaries regarding the subject of God's blueprint for a liberated America in an absolutist world, see Charles Royster, *A Revolutionary People at War: The Continental Army and American Character, 1775–1783* (Chapel Hill, 1979), 13–24, among other pages. See also Catherine L. Albanese, *Sons of the Fathers: The Civil Religion of the American Revolution* (Philadelphia, 1976), 81–111.

15. Alexander Scammell to Meshech Weare, Orangetown, Oct. 1[3 or 4?], 1780, Weare Paps., MHS.

16. Words taken from a woodcut reproducing the scene of the Philadelphia parade, Sept. 30, 1780. Description in *Pennsylvania Packet* [Phila.], Oct. 3, 7, 1780, and "Procession in Honor of Arnold," *HM*, 1 ser., 5 (1861): 276–77.

17. Return J. Meigs to John Sumner, Middletown, Ct., Oct. 9, 1780, Sol Feinstone Coll., DLAR [the Feinstone Coll. is located in the APS in Philadelphia but is owned by the DLAR, Washington Crossing, Pa.]; Joshua Ladd Howell to John N. Cumming, Gloucester, N.J., Sept. 30, 1780, Howell Paps., Stewart Coll., Glassboro State College Library, Glassboro, N.J.; *Connecticut Gazette* [New London], Oct. 17, 1780; *Pennsylvania Packet,* Jan. 16, 1781. See also Moore, comp., *Diary Am. Rev.,* 2:323–51, for miscellaneous contemporary commentary.

18. NG to Elihue Greene, Tappan, Oct. 2, 1780, *Paps. NG*, 6:327–28; "Publius," *Pennsylvania Gazette* [Phila.], Oct. 18, 1780; *Connecticut Courant* [Hartford], Oct. 31, 1780; Marquis de Lafayette to Comte de Vergennes, Harrington, N.Y., Oct. 4, 1780, *Facsimiles of Manuscripts in European Archives relating to America, 1773–1783,* ed. Benjamin F. Stevens (26 vols., London, 1889–1895), vol. 17, no. 1627. In *Lafayette in the Age of the American Revolution: Selected Letters and Papers, 1776–1790,* ed. Stanley J. Idzerda et al. (5 vols., Ithaca, N.Y., 1977–1983), 3:191, "rascality" is translated from the French as "villainy."

19. *New Jersey Gazette* [Trenton], Jan. 24, 1781, *Documents Relating to the Revolutionary History of the State of New Jersey*, 2 ser., 5 (1917): 178; *Independent Chronicle* [Boston], Dec. 8, 1780, Moore, comp., *Diary Am. Rev.*, 2:333–35.

20. Alexander Scammell to Nathaniel Peabody, Orangetown, Oct. 3, 1780, *HM*, 2 ser., 8 (1870): 145; "An Acrostic—On Arnold," Oct. 1780, Misc. BA Paps., MHS; verse taken from woodcut cited in note 16 above; NG to Elihue Greene, Tappan, Oct. 2, 1780, *Paps. NG*, 6:327.

21. Weds., Oct. 4, 1780, *JCC*, 18:899; James Lanman to Jared Sparks, Norwich, Apr. 7, 1834, and James Stedman to Jared Sparks, Norwich, Apr. 8, 1834, Sparks Paps., HLHU, for example, have served as major sources with regard to BA's allegedly wanton youth. Sparks incorporated the stories of these venerable but not very well informed Norwichites into his *Life and Treason of Benedict Arnold* (New York, 1847), and other BA biographers have chosen to repeat these stories. For nineteenth- and twentieth-century literary representations of BA, see David R. Johnson, "Benedict Arnold: The Traitor as Hero in American Literature" (doctoral dissertation, Pennsylvania State University, 1975), *passim*.

22. Ezekiel 28:12–17 [New International Version].

O N E : *A Childhood of Legends*

1. See Martin and Lender, *A Respectable Army*, 171–209, and Royster, *Revolutionary People at War*, 331–68, for divergent interpretations.

2. Many of the BA tales were the product of local folk legend and emanated from eastern Connecticut. Typical storytellers were the two aging Norwichites, James Lanman and James Stedman, who responded to queries about BA's childhood from historian Jared Sparks, then making plans to write a biography of Arnold. The two Norwichites captured the essence of the local tales in Lanman to Sparks, Norwich, Apr. 7, 1834, and Stedman to Sparks, Norwich, Apr. 8, 1834, Sparks Paps., HLHU. Stedman's letter in particular conveys the didactic flavor of the tales. Another important written source for the stories is Frances M. Caulkins, *History of Norwich, Connecticut: From Its Possession by the Indians to the Year 1866* (2d ed., Hartford, 1866), 409–13. Caulkins did more than repeat Lanman and Stedman; she compiled other BA tales, as noted below, which she based on legends about young BA that still lingered in the byways of nineteenth-century Norwich. For related stories, see the handwritten copy of Anonymous [Samuel Peters?], "Some Account of Benedict Arnold, Brigadier General in the British Army," *European Magazine and London Review* (1783), unpaged, Tomlinson Coll., YUL. Disgruntled loyalist Peters, whom BA helped to drive from Connecticut in 1774, was likely this essayist, based on the similarity of misinformed tales contained in his "Genuine History of General Arnold, by an Old Acquaintance, . . . ," *Political Magazine* of London, 1 (1780): 690, 746–48, *The Works of Samuel Peters of Hebron, Connecticut . . .* , ed. Kenneth Walter Cameron (Hartford, 1967), 163–65. Although more oriented toward BA's adulthood, see also materials in Johnson, "Benedict Arnold," 6–7, *passim*.

3. Mason L. Weems, *The Life of Washington,* ed. Marcus Cunliffe (Cambridge, Mass., 1962, based on Weems's 9th ed., 1809), 10–12. Sparks, *Life and Treason of Arnold,* 5–6, as reprinted almost verbatim from Stedman's letter. Carrying forward from Sparks, later biographers simply repeated such BA tales. See, for example, George Canning Hill, *Benedict Arnold: A Biography* (Boston, 1858), 13–15; Malcolm Decker, *Benedict Arnold: Son of the Havens* (Tarrytown, N.Y., 1932), 14; and Wallace, *Traitorous Hero,* 7. In some instances, biographers made up their own stories, as in Charles Coleman Sellers, *Benedict Arnold: The Proud Warrior* (New York, 1930), 13, in which readers learn that little BA "had stolen poultry and tied tin buckets to the tails of the farmers' cattle." By comparison, James Thomas Flexner, *The Traitor and the Spy: Benedict Arnold and John André* (New York, 1953), recognized the BA cruelty tales as the stuff of legend and did not retell them.

4. Caulkins, *Norwich,* 411. In the new republic's developing national lore, young GW became a natural leader among his youthful peers—but always virtuously in juxtaposition to BA. According to Weems's legend-riddled account, young GW never encouraged but always stopped potential fisticuffs among his schoolmates, and he constructively trained these same lads in the art of war. GW "was a boy of an uncommonly warm and noble heart," Weems declared. See Cunliffe, ed., *Life of Washington,* 19–21. See also Barry Schwartz, *George Washington: The Making of an American Symbol* (New York, 1987), 2–4, 200–204, among other pages.

5. Caulkins, *Norwich,* 412, was apparently the first to publish the constable's tale. In various forms it has been repeated by Arnold, *Arnold,* 27–28; Sellers, *Arnold,* 13–14; Decker, *Arnold,* 12–13; Flexner, *Traitor and Spy,* 6–7; Wallace, *Traitorous Hero,* 10; and Willard Sterne Randall, *Benedict Arnold: Patriot and Traitor* (New York, 1990), 23, 29. Young BA "was not a bully," wrote Randall (p. 29), as did Flexner (p. 6) before him. According to Randall, youthful BA stood out as a leader because he was "able to rivet other little boys with his dark-eyed gaze." Apparently, he also wore a "scarlet cloak" during wintertime when directing other Norwich striplings in various youthful activities (p. 23). Brandt, *Man in the Mirror,* 4, likewise agrees that BA was "a natural leader of his group" but has little else to say about his childhood except for possible parental influences.

6. Caulkins, *Norwich,* 412, called the suitor a "young foreigner." Arnold, *Arnold,* 27–28, referred to him a "French adventurer," and most others have followed his lead. See Sellers, *Arnold,* 14; Decker, *Arnold,* 20–21; Flexner, *Traitor and Spy,* 12; Wallace, *Traitorous Hero,* 16; and Randall, *Arnold,* 39–40. Only Isaac Arnold doubted the veracity of this story; Randall, following Arnold's lead, questioned the dueling incident.

7. Caulkins, *Norwich,* 411–12, was an initial source of this anecdote. See also Arnold, *Arnold,* 22; Decker, *Arnold,* 12; and Wallace, *Traitorous Hero,* 10.

8. Arnold, *Arnold,* 22. This tale apparently originated with Stedman and has been regularly repeated. See Sparks, *Life and Treason of Arnold,* 6; Hill, *Arnold,* 14; Sellers, *Arnold,* 13; Decker, *Arnold,* 12; Flexner, *Traitor and Spy,* 6; Wallace, *Traitorous Hero,* 10; and Randall, *Arnold,* 29.

9. Caulkins, *Norwich,* 412. The thunderstorm tale has varied greatly with the retelling. Compare one account in Decker, *Arnold,* 14, with that of Flexner, *Traitor and Spy,* 9–10, the more standard version. According to an outraged Decker, the story goes like this: "Ah, but let the lightning flash over the steeple of the Meeting House and he [Arnold] will show you how to play his real role, 'blaspheming God while the thunder roars'—this smug little Congregationalist." See Sparks, *Life and Treason of Arnold,* 5, for the general character assessment.

10. Caulkins, *Norwich,* 409–10. BA's biographers have modeled BA's mother on these descriptions, the first being the phrase that appeared on Hannah's tombstone. Only Brandt, *Man in the Mirror,* 4, suggests that Hannah's piety was so rigid that it undermined little BA's "budding self-confidence."

11. L[ydia] H[untley] Sigourney, *Letters to Mothers* (6th ed., New York, 1845), 14–15, 35–38. The first edition of this highly successful advice manual appeared in 1838. Sigourney (1791–1865) was born in BA's Norwich, and she became very well known as the "sweet singer of Hartford" for her poetry and other writings. Her father, a common laborer and gardener for Daniel Lathrop when a young man, was also a Revolutionary War veteran and may have known BA slightly. Sigourney heard various versions of the BA tales from her father and other old-timers while growing up in Norwich. See her posthumous memoirs, *Letters of Life* (New York, 1867), 12–18; and Ann Douglas, *The Feminization of American Culture* (New York, 1977), 53–54, 87–88, 247–48, among other pages. In contrast, a children's book from this time period with no identifiable author, *Stories about Arnold, the Traitor, André, the Spy, and Champe, the Patriot . . .* (2d ed., New Haven, 1831), does not repeat the childhood tales in fulfilling its intention to warn America's youth about BA's wanton ways.

12. On the role of "republican motherhood" assigned to women in the nurturing of children, especially sons, as dutiful citizens, see Linda Kerber, "Daughters of Columbia: Educating Women for the Republic, 1787–1805," in *The Hofstadter Aegis: A Memorial,* ed. Stanley Elkins and Eric McKitrick (New York, 1979), 36–59; and Kerber, *Women of the Republic: Intellect and Ideology in Revolutionary America* (Chapel Hill, 1980), 269–88.

13. Arnold, comp., *Arnold Memorial,* 44–49.

14. Ibid., 51–56, 71–73, 88–90, 132–33. Other versions of BA's genealogy, such as Leonard Wilson Arnold and Ethel Zwick Luckey, *Arnold-Luckey Family Ties* (New York, 1931), 17–18, 28–29, assume that Benedict II, rather than Benedict III, was BA's grandfather. Certainly, Benedict III was obscure. That he did not outlive his own father may have added to the confusion and skipping of generations. Given the date of Benedict III's marriage (1705), Benedict IV was probably born before 1710, making him slightly younger than his future wife, Hannah Waterman King, whose birth most likely occurred in 1706 or 1707. John Ward Dean et al., *Genealogy of the Family of Arnold in Europe and America* (Boston, 1879), 3–16, does not help clarify the issue. However, whether BA was a fifth- or sixth-generation New Englander is not the central point. The essential issue is that the Benedict Arnolds who preceded BA had

experienced a dramatic decline in community status until BA's father tried to reverse the downslide in family fortunes.

15. Up until Benedict III, the Arnolds adhered to the common Puritan practice of naming eldest sons after fathers (and eldest daughters after mothers). According to ibid., 71–72, 88–89, Benedict III varied the pattern by calling his first son Caleb. A possible explanation is that Benedict III, actually a younger son who received his forename because his firstborn brother had died (using necronyms was common among Puritan families), had a younger brother Caleb who had died in 1700, just a few years before his own marriage. Benedict III may have been paying respect to his deceased brother's memory or honoring an illustrious grand-uncle (1644–1730), who was a physician and prominent political leader in Newport, or possibly both. On naming practices among New England Puritans, see notes 20 and 21 below.

16. On overcrowding, see Kenneth A. Lockridge, "Land, Population, and the Evolution of New England Society, 1630–1790," *Past and Present*, 39 (1968): 62–80. On apprenticeships as an alternate form of inheritance, see Douglas Lamar Jones, *Village and Seaport: Migration and Society in Eighteenth-Century Massachusetts* (Hanover, N.H., 1981), 86–121.

17. Bruce C. Daniels, *The Connecticut Town: Growth and Development, 1635–1790* (Middletown, Ct., 1979), 38–43, 54–59, 146–49, among other pages. More generally, see Robert J. Taylor, *Colonial Connecticut: A History* (Millwood, N.Y. 1979), 90–107.

18. Caulkins, *Norwich*, 206–8, 217–19, 306, 409–10, which also contains a brief genealogy of the Watermans from whom BA's mother was descended.

19. Ibid., 223, 276, 306. Benson J. Lossing, *The Pictorial Field-Book of the Revolution* (2 vols., New York, 1851–1852), 1:604–5. On Norwich merchants more generally and the economic milieu in which they worked, see Daniels, *Connecticut Town*, 38–40, 54–59, 146–49.

20. Arnold, comp., *Arnold Memorial*, 105; *Vital Records of Norwich, Connecticut*, Part 1 (Hartford, 1913), 153. On infant mortality, see David E. Stannard, *The Puritan Way of Death: A Study in Religion, Culture, and Social Change* (New York, 1977), 44–71; and Maris A. Vinovskis, "Mortality Rates and Trends in Massachusetts before 1830," *Journal of Economic History*, 32 (1972): 184–213. Generally speaking, less populous areas did not suffer such devastation from killer epidemics in late colonial New England. See the findings on rural Deerfield, Mass., in R. S. Meindl and A. C. Swedlund, "Secular Trends in Mortality in the Connecticut Valley, 1700–1850," *Human Biology*, 49 (1977): 389–414. On the matter of parents maintaining emotional distance from infants because of the tragic reality of so many childhood deaths, see Lawrence Stone, *The Family, Sex, and Marriage in England, 1500–1800* (New York, 1977), 113–14, 173–74, 206–15, 246–53; Daniel Blake Smith, "The Study of the Family in Early America: Trends, Problems, and Prospects," *WMQ*, 3 ser., 39 (1982): 3–28; and David Hackett Fischer, *Albion's Seed: Four British Folkways in America* (New York, 1989), 111–16.

21. By the Julian Calendar, BA was born on Jan. 3, 1740/41, the date given in *Vital Records of Norwich*, 1:153. During the early 1750s, the British empire changed to

the more accurate Gregorian calendar, which had the effect of moving dates ahead by eleven days. Under the Gregorian calendar, the New Year commenced in January instead of March. Thus by modern reckoning, BA was born on Jan. 14, 1741. Whenever possible, dates have been adjusted to conform to the Gregorian calendar system. On Puritan naming patterns, see Daniel Scott Smith, "Child-Naming Practices, Kinship Ties, and Change in Family Attitudes in Hingham, Massachusetts, 1641 to 1880," *JSH*, 18 (1985): 541–66; and Fischer, *Albion's Seed*, 93–97. As in the case of Benedict III and Benedict V, necronyms were used for an estimated 80 percent of all New England infants whose older siblings had died. This practice was not exclusive to the Puritans. However, Puritan parents, up until about 1740, were unique in their overwhelming selection of biblical names for their children. John, Thomas, Samuel, David, and Joseph were among the most common Puritan male forenames in Hingham. Also, Smith found that about two-thirds of Hingham's parents who were married before 1721 named first sons and daughters after themselves. As with BA's parents, they kept a genealogical chain of name identity going, thereby stressing the importance of family lineage. The forename Benedict was rare, most likely because it was not biblical in origin. It was derived from the Latin word *benedictus,* referring to a benediction, or prayerful spiritual blessing, a rather incongruous meaning when associated with the reputation of BA. See also Bertram Wyatt-Brown, *Southern Honor: Ethics and Behavior in the Old South* (New York, 1982), 118–25, for some psychological implications of patriarchal naming patterns for sons.

22. First Congregational Church of Norwich Records, 2:115, CSL. Stannard, *Puritan Way of Death,* 47–61. For additional information on the First Church, see Caulkins, *Norwich,* 315–24; J. M. Bumsted, "Revivalism and Separatism in New England: The First Society of Norwich, Connecticut, as a Case Study," *WMQ,* 3 ser., 24 (1967): 588–612; and William G. McLoughlin, *Isaac Backus and the American Pietistic Tradition* (Boston, 1967), 3–30.

23. Hannah Arnold to BA, Norwich, Apr. 12, 1754, Arnold, *Arnold,* 23. On the central importance of patronage as the key to socioeconomic and political mobility in the hierarchical late colonial world, see Gordon S. Wood, *The Radicalism of the American Revolution* (New York, 1992), 57–77.

24. On the diversity of imperial-colonial problems and tensions growing out of the Louisbourg expedition, see Douglas Edward Leach, *Roots of Conflict: British Armed Forces and Colonial Americans, 1677–1763* (Chapel Hill, 1986), 63–75. On Connecticut's involvement in King George's War, see Harold E. Selesky, *War and Society in Colonial Connecticut* (New Haven, Ct., 1990), 74–96.

25. One fanciful story, which even BA's most condemnatory biographers have judiciously ignored, has the Captain being thrown in debtors' prison not long after the end of King George's War for failure to pay his creditors. Benjamin Franklin may have been the source of this misleading tale, as related in Anonymous [Samuel Peters?], "Some Account of Benedict Arnold," *European Magazine and London Review* (1783), unpaged, Tomlinson Coll., YUL. In reality the Captain's credit must

have been basically solid into the early 1750s, since he purchased goods from Simon Lathrop in June 1750 and promised to pay him £139 in Connecticut bills of credit by September. Lathrop would surely have avoided such a business arrangement had the Captain's financial status been too shaky. See Benedict Arnold IV to Simon Lathrop, June 6, 1750, Gratz Coll., HSP.

26. *The Autobiography of Benjamin Rush: His 'Travels through Life' Together with His* Commonplace Book *for 1789–1813,* ed. George W. Corner (Princeton, N.J., 1948), 158. BA likely made this comment while visiting Philadelphia during the spring of 1777 when petitioning the Continental Congress for a restoration of seniority in military rank.

27. Richard L. Bushman, *From Puritan to Yankee: Character and the Social Order in Connecticut, 1690–1765* (Cambridge, 1967), 147–82; Bumsted, "Revivalism and Separatism," *WMQ,* 3 ser. (1967): 589–600; and First Church of Norwich Records, 2:7–12, CSL, for various church covenants. In actual numbers, fewer than one in five Norwichites with halfway membership became full members of the First Church between 1717 and 1740.

28. First Church of Norwich Records, 2:81–148, CSL, contain a full list of baptisms and admissions between 1717 and 1760. For specific notations on the Arnolds, see ibid., 2:211–12. Bumsted, "Revivalism and Separatism," *WMQ,* 3 ser. (1967): 596, 600, contains summary tabulations that are slightly lower than my own (ninety-one as opposed to ninety-six full admissions) for the 1741–1744 period, an inconsequential difference. Regardless of the count, full church admissions jumped dramatically when compared to earlier or later periods. For instance, there were only ten full admissions to the First Church in the 1745–1750 period, a time of heated post-Awakening contention in the Norwich community.

29. Hannah Arnold to BA, Norwich, Apr. 12, 1754, Arnold, *Arnold,* 23–24; and Hannah Arnold to BA, Norwich, Aug. 9, 1754, PML.

30. Hannah Arnold to unknown [probably Dr. Jewett of Montville, Ct.], c. 1749, Charles Biddle Paps., HSP.

31. Bushman, *From Puritan to Yankee,* 164–220; Bumsted, "Revivalism and Separatism," *WMQ,* 3 ser. (1967), 601–8; Caulkins, *Norwich,* 318–24; and McLoughlin, *Isaac Backus,* 15–40.

32. On the ways in which outwardly harmonious New England communities dealt with conflict, see Michael Zuckerman, *Peaceable Kingdoms: New England Towns in the Eighteenth Century* (New York, 1970), *passim*; and Bushman, *From Puritan to Yankee,* 235–88.

33. John Duffy, *Epidemics in Colonial America* (Baton Rouge, La., 1953), 118–22. Even though diphtheria represents the most likely culprit, any one of a number of the killer diseases described by Duffy, such as smallpox or yellow fever, could have claimed this Benedict.

34. Arnold, comp., *Arnold Memorial,* 105; *Vital Records of Norwich,* 1:153. Biographers have not always agreed on the number of BA's siblings, and his mother Hannah may have borne one or two children by her first husband, Absalom King. If

she did, these children died quite young. Flexner, *Traitor and Spy*, 5, gives the number of seven children; and Randall, *Arnold*, 17, comes up with eleven, most likely based on the error in *Arnold Memorial*, 105, in which Hannah is credited with having three additional children by virtue of confusing the death dates of Absalom, Mary, and Elizabeth with the birth dates of new children. As a result, Randall (p. 26) has Hannah bearing a new daughter Mary on the very same day young Mary died.

35. Hannah Arnold to BA, Norwich, Aug. 13, 1753, *HM*, 1 ser., 4 (1860): 18; and Hannah Arnold to BA, Norwich, Aug. 30, 1753, *MH*, 3 (1906): 258.

36. Ibid. Most biographers have ascribed these deaths to yellow fever. However, Hannah Arnold twice used the term "distemper" in her vividly descriptive letter of Aug. 30, and the colonists usually referred to diphtheria as the "throat distemper." See Duffy, *Epidemics*, 113–26. Duffy (160–61) notes that yellow fever was uncommon outside the southern colonies during the 1750s; however, there may have been isolated outbreaks of this disease, which attacks the mouth and throat and often results in the vomiting of blood. A third possibility is dysentery, which struck in New London during the early 1750s. Given the virulence of diphtheria epidemics throughout New England during the 1750s, this disease should be considered the leading culprit in the deaths of two of BA's sisters in 1753.

37. Sparks, *Life and Treason of Arnold*, 4, described the Captain as a man "of suspicious integrity, little respected, and less esteemed. . . . by degrees he sank into intemperance, poverty, and contempt." See also Decker, *Arnold*, 6; Flexner, *Traitor and Spy*, 4; Wallace, *Traitorous Hero*, 6–7; Randall, *Arnold*, 24, 28; Brandt, *Man in the Mirror*, 6–8; and the psychological profile of the Captain and BA in Kenneth S. Lynn, *A Divided People* (Westport, 1977), 5–7. According to this category of explanation, the Captain was a weak man who obviously produced a corrupt son.

38. Hannah Arnold to BA, Norwich, Aug. 9, 1754, PML.

39. Arnold, *Arnold*, 24. The Rev. Cogswell was apparently a distant relative of the Arnolds. The Captain's mother was a Cogswell, and Hannah spoke of the minister in very familiar terms. For instance, she wrote in a postscript to her Apr. 12, 1754, letter: "Your father and aunt join with me in love and service to Mr. Cogswell and lady, and yourself." See ibid., 24; and Arnold, comp., *Arnold Memorial*, 88. Cornelius Nepos was a Roman historian (100–25 B.C.) who wrote a history of the world, besides preparing sketches about the lives of eminent Romans. Among BA's alleged youthful crimes was that of defacing books, "which the New England mind was trained to revere, both from scarcity and a sense of their value." See Sigourney, *Letters of Life*, 14–15. Most commentators have likewise assumed that little BA was a very undisciplined student.

40. Hannah Arnold's mother was a Lathrop. See Caulkins, *Norwich*, 77, 86, 206–8, 217, 219, 327, 412. On the prosperity of the Lathrop brothers, see Sigourney, *Letters of Life*, 144–49; and Flexner, *Traitor and Spy*, 7–9.

41. James Stedman served as a principal source of these stories in his letter to Jared Sparks, Norwich, Apr. 8, 1834, Sparks Paps., HLHU. For various versions, see Sparks, *Life and Treason of Arnold*, 6–8; Hill, *Arnold*, 15–19; Arnold, *Arnold*, 24–26;

and Decker, *Arnold,* 14–17. Van Doren, *Secret History,* 145, accepts this material uncritically as the only necessary proof necessary to condemn young BA.

42. Wallace, *Traitorous Hero,* 11–13; and Randall, *Arnold,* 32–34, who closely echoes Wallace's version. The words on Hannah's gravestone, as reprinted in Caulkins, *Norwich,* 409, list her date of death as Aug. 15, 1758, not 1759. If Hannah died in 1758, then this motive for BA's alleged desertion makes no sense. In contrast, the First Church of Norwich Records, 2:211, CSL, give the year of Hannah's death as 1759, the date I have chosen to use. The point is moot, however, since BA neither enlisted in nor deserted from Captain Holmes's company.

43. *Muster Rolls of New York Provincial Troops, 1755–1764,* Colls. of the N-YHS for the Year 1891, vol. 14 (New York, 1892), 96–97, 176–77, 324–45, 522–23.

44. Description in Weyman's *New York Gazette,* May 21, 1759, ibid., 522. These descriptions are both general and vague. For instance, another deserter, Charles Williams, was also "18 years of age" and had a "dark complexion, light eyes, and light hair." The only variation from the BA depiction was the color of hair. Wallace, *Traitorous Hero,* 9, states that BA was not more than five feet seven inches tall but accepts these records as those of the future traitor, even though the 1760 muster roll listed the person in question as five feet nine inches tall. Randall, *Arnold,* 29, also adopting this description, notes that BA was "tall for the times," a description that disregards every contemporary comment about BA's height.

45. Flexner, *Traitor and Spy,* 410, was the first BA biographer to unravel the mysteries surrounding BA's putative desertion. Among Flexner's most telling points were those related to the Lathrops and the trust they continually placed in their young apprentice and future business partner.

46. Ibid., 8–9. On militia turnout in response to Montcalm's advance up Lake George, see Selesky, *War and Society,* 109–10, who states that about five thousand Connecticut males, or 25 percent of Connecticut's available militia force, mustered for duty in August 1757. More generally, see Francis Jennings, *Empire of Fortune: Crowns, Colonies, and Tribes in the Seven Years War in America* (New York, 1988), 312–22; and Ian K. Steele, *Betrayals: Fort William Henry and the "Massacre"* (New York, 1990), esp. 78–148. James Fenimore Cooper immortalized the Fort William Henry siege and massacre in *The Last of the Mohicans* (1826).

47. Flexner, *Traitor and Spy,* 10–11; Wallace, *Traitorous Hero,* 13.

48. Fischer, *Albion's Seed,* 114, argues that Puritans "even prayed that their grief" in losing loved ones "would 'never wear off.' " If that was Hannah's case, then her deep emotional sense of loss may have contributed to her own death. At the same time, BA's mother was much more than the caricature of the "dour," "stern" Puritan woman presented in Randall, *Arnold,* 26, and Brandt, *Man in the Mirror,* 4–5. She was invariably warm and affectionate toward her only surviving son. Wrote Sigmund Freud, "A man who has been the indisputable favorite of his mother keeps for life the feeling of a conqueror." In adulthood BA never seemed to doubt his ability to meet and overcome challenging obstacles of any kind. BA appears to have had an affectionate relationship with his father as well, at least before the mid-1750s;

however, the Captain may also have withheld some feelings as a way to maintain his son's respect. See Wyatt-Brown, *Southern Honor*, 131–32, who quotes Freud.

49. Warrant issued by Isaac Huntington, Norwich, May 26, 1760, *PMHB*, 22 (1898): 124–25.

50. First Church of Norwich Records, 1:46–47, CSL. First Church members were not necessarily being harsh with the Captain. Early New England congregations functioned as frontline sources of peer discipline and therapy to assist drunkards in their plight. In June 1756, for instance, First Church members accepted the confession of Jabez Lathrop, who "had been shamefully and sinfully overcome with strong drink." In November 1766, Stephen Totman was chastised for drunkenness; whether he repented before the church body is unclear. See ibid., 1:43, 47, and 2:34. See also Mark Edward Lender and James Kirby Martin, *Drinking in America: A History* (rev. ed., New York, 1987), 9–21; and Wyatt-Brown, *Southern Honor*, 128–29.

51. BA to Margaret Mansfield Arnold, n.p., n.d., N-YHS.

T W O : *A Person to Be Reckoned With in New Haven*

1. Daniels, *Connecticut Town*, 140–51; Rollin G. Osterweis, *Three Centuries of New Haven, 1638–1938* (New Haven, Ct., 1953), 5–21, 100–105.

2. Christopher Collier, *Roger Sherman's Connecticut: Yankee Politics and the American Revolution* (Middletown, 1971), 28–31; Osterweis, *Three Centuries of New Haven*, 85–117.

3. Bushman, *From Puritan to Yankee*, 267–88; Osterweis, *Three Centuries of New Haven*, 67–76; Collier, *Roger Sherman's Connecticut*, 37–38.

4. Ibid. Floyd M. Shumway, "Early New Haven and Its Leadership" (doctoral dissertation, Columbia University, 1968), 250–65, lists these "new" men among the most prominent mercantile and civic leaders of pre-Revolutionary New Haven. BA was on Shumway's business but not on his civic list.

5. Caulkins, *Norwich*, 412. Solomon Smith was an apprentice who overlapped with BA. He may well have been the person the Lathrops set up in Hartford. On New Haven as a dynamic "central place" of regional economic activity, see Daniels, *Connecticut Town*, 140–70.

6. Caulkins, *Norwich*, 411, denied that the Lathrops invested money in BA, presuming of course that they would have been too wary of his unruly habits to do so. However, there was no other way for BA, who had no financial inheritance, to establish himself, and the £500 figure is a safe estimate. Flexner, *Traitor and Spy*, 10, refers to this subsidy or loan as a gift. That likely would have been the case only if BA had failed in business.

7. The Rev. Samuel Peters probably initiated this tale. For one version, see "Some Account of Benedict Arnold," *European Magazine and London Review* (1783), unpaged, Tomlinson Coll., YUL. Although evidence is lacking to confirm Peters's allegations, Flexner, *Traitor and Spy*, 11–12, repeated the story. Most likely this tale

represented a confused, misdated version of BA's close brush with financial insolvency in 1767, discussed below.

8. BA's store sign, NHCHS. Caulkins, *Norwich,* 413, offers the standard interpretation of "sibi totique" as it related to BA. She wrote, "The first part, *for himself,* is pointedly appropriate. The motto has been rendered by a free translation, *wholly for himself.*"

9. BA advertisement, Arnold Coll., NHCHS. See also BA's Account Book, representing an impressive array of books purchased from London, Feb. 23, 1763–Mar. 6, 1764, HSP; and Thomas Longman to Bernard Lintot, London, July 7, 1766, HSP, in which Longman authorized Lintot to pursue BA for delinquent payments. On this latter subject, see notes 33–37 below.

10. For samples of Arnold's business dealings, see BA Misc. Accounts, 1761–1774, as well as his Minute Book (June–Aug. 1768) and Waste Book (Apr. 1773–Mar. 1780), Arnold Coll., NHCHS. See also Thomas R. Trowbridge Jr., "Ancient Maritime Interests of New Haven," *Papers of the New Haven Colony Historical Society,* 3 (1882): 112–13. Among various tales were those that stressed the perspicacity of old-line New Havenites in immediately recognizing Arnold as a self-serving scoundrel. One version, emanating from "one of the oldest and most prominent citizens," dwelled on Arnold's lack of proper "social standing." When asked how his father treated Arnold, the elderly gentleman stated, "My father bowed to him whenever they met and said: 'Good morning, Captain Arnold.'" The interviewer queried whether reputable folk thought the young merchant worthy enough to invite to their homes. At this, the ancient inhabitant retorted, "My father invite Arnold to his house? No, sir; the extent of their acquaintance was 'Good morning, Captain Arnold.'" See *History of the City of New Haven to the Present Time,* comp. Edward E. Atwater (New York, 1887), 43.

11. Atwater, comp., *History of New Haven,* 43. Rum trade dealings particularly stand out in BA Misc. Accounts, 1761–1774, Arnold Coll., NHCHS.

12. Deed from Daniel Lathrop to BA, Oct. 4, 1763, Dreer Coll., HSP. BA purchased the family homestead for £300 local currency and resold it for £700 to Captain Hugh Ledlie of Windham on Mar. 31, 1764. On the second transaction, see Caulkins, *Norwich,* 410.

13. BA also shared this delayed inheritance with Hannah, but she allowed her brother to invest her portion. He likely used some of the sale profits to acquire trading vessels in partnership with Adam Babcock, a connection that apparently began after BA sold his homestead. For an example of Babcock-Arnold mercantile activity, see Invoice, dated New Haven, Mar. 2, 1766, for the shipment of goods on the brigantine *Fortune,* Emmet Coll., NYPL. On the transition from landed to mercantile wealth, see Jones, *Village and Seaport,* 55–69, 86–97; and on the importance of landed wealth in denoting trustworthy as opposed to pretending gentlemen, see Wood, *Radicalism of the Revolution,* 24–39, 210–12, among other pages.

14. Very little is known about BA's sister HA. Only a select few of her highly

informative letters have survived. Most descriptions are based on Arnold, *Arnold,* 27–29. That HA never married may have reflected the absence of a sizable dowry or even a desire to remain single as much as anything else.

15. Mss. Letter from the Rev. J. S. Leake, n.p., n.d., quoted in Arnold, *Arnold,* 29; Comments of Rutherford Cook, who claimed to be a cousin of Arnold's, in John Jay and Benjamin Franklin Reminiscence, Paris, July 19, 1783–Apr. 17, 1784, *John Jay: Unpublished Papers, 1745–1784,* ed. Richard B. Morris (2 vols., New York, 1975–1980), 2:712–13.

16. On the general theme, see James Kirby Martin, *Men in Rebellion: Higher Governmental Leaders and the Coming of the American Revolution* (New Brunswick, N.J., 1973), *passim.* For the connecting relationship between ambition and honor, see Wood, *Radicalism of the Revolution,* 39–42.

17. On the British decision to garrison troops in peacetime America and on colonial reactions, see John Shy, *Toward Lexington: The Role of the British Army in the Coming of the American Revolution* (Princeton, N.J., 1965), 45–83, 140–63.

18. Imperial acts and orders affecting the colonists for the 1763–1765 period have been reprinted in *English Historical Documents,* vol. 9: *American Colonial Documents to 1776,* ed. Merrill Jensen (New York, 1955), 635–58.

19. Thomas Whately, *Considerations on the Trade and Finances of This Kingdom, and on the Measures of Administration . . . since the Conclusion of the Peace* (London, 1766), 144; Grenville quoted in Stanley Ayling, *George the Third* (London, 1972), 137.

20. Daniel Dulany, *Considerations on the Propriety of Imposing Taxes in the British Colonies for the Purpose of Raising a Revenue by Act of Parliament* (New York, 1765), 17–18. On the parent-child metaphor, see Edwin G. Burroughs and Michael Wallace, "The American Revolution: The Ideology and Psychology of National Liberation," *Perspectives in American History,* 6 (1972): 167–306.

21. Lawrence Henry Gipson, *American Loyalist: Jared Ingersoll* (New Haven, 1920; reprint, 1971), 149–94. See also Oscar Zeichner, *Connecticut's Years of Controversy, 1750–1776* (Chapel Hill, 1949), 60–70; and Edmund S. and Helen M. Morgan, *The Stamp Act Crisis: Prologue to Revolution* (rev. ed., New York, 1962), 280–300.

22. *Connecticut Gazette* [New Haven], Feb. 7, 14, 21, 1766. The New Haven customs house reopened for business in Jan. 1766, despite the Stamp Act, and it cleared ships without stamped papers. On the day Boles visited the customs office, BA wrote to Dr. John Dickinson, "I am in want of some good genteel shipping horses, in three, or four weeks. If you can supply me with one or two I will pay you in West India goods or drugs at cash prices, a fresh assortment of which I have lately received." See Stewart Kidd, *Autograph Letters* (1930), 7, Am. Mss. Colls., AAS.

23. For smuggling activities, consult John W. Tyler, *Smugglers and Patriots: Boston Merchants and the Advent of the American Revolution* (Boston, 1986), 3–23. See also William M. Fowler Jr., *The Baron of Beacon Hill: A Biography of John Hancock* (Boston, 1980), 68–87. Ebenezer Richardson of Boston was the most universally despised customs informer of them all, as described in Hiller B. Zobel, *The Boston Massacre* (New York, 1970), 54–55, 173–79, and 222–26, among other pages.

24. *Connecticut Gazette,* Feb. 14, 1766. BA wrote this newspaper account. He apparently also composed the confession that Boles was forced to sign.

25. Ibid. See also Gipson, *Jared Ingersoll,* 233–36; and Zeichner, *Connecticut's Years of Controversy,* 64–66.

26. Grand Jury Indictment, by T. Blakeslee and J. Wise, Jan. 31, 1766, Warrant for the Arrest of Arnold and the Others, by Roger Sherman, Jan. 31, 1766, and Arrest Notices of Jan. 31. and Feb. 3, 1766, by Jonathan Mix, constable, Sherman Coll., NHCHS. BA was arrested on Feb. 3.

27. Gipson, *Jared Ingersoll,* 235. Gipson suggests the date of Jan. 30, 1766, for this crowd demonstration, but this action much more likely occurred in the immediate aftermath of the indictments.

28. New Haven Town Meeting Minutes, Feb. 3, 1776, quoted in ibid., 234–35.

29. *Connecticut Gazette,* Feb. 14, 1766.

30. BA was not unusual in defining the public good within the parameters of his own private concerns. That practice was common among popular leaders, of whom Samuel Adams was the preeminent example. The Boles affair gained some newspaper coverage outside of New Haven. The *Connecticut Courant* [Hartford], Feb. 10, 1766, reported the whipping of Boles, and the *Pennsylvania Gazette,* Feb. 20, 1766, reprinted portions of the deliberations at the Feb. 3 New Haven town meeting.

31. Act Repealing the Stamp Act, Mar. 18, 1766, and the Declaratory Act, Mar. 18, 1766, Jensen, ed., *English Historical Documents,* 9:695–96.

32. Gipson, *Jared Ingersoll,* 252–60; Zeichner, *Connecticut's Years of Controversy,* 81–83; and Collier, *Roger Sherman's Connecticut,* 66–73. For a valuable general analysis of the postwar depression, consult Marc Egnal, *A Mighty Empire: The Origins of the American Revolution* (Ithaca, 1988), 126–49.

33. Book dealer Thomas Longman of London was among the merchants who retained Lintot. On June 6, 1766, he certified that BA owed him £408.14.11, and on July 7, 1766, he had a legal agreement drawn up in London to have Lintot represent his claims against BA, Soc. Colls., HSP.

34. BA's List of Debts and Effects, New Haven, May 5–6, 1767, Arnold Coll., NHCHS. Arnold "made oath that the above and foregoing lists of debts and effects which he owes and has in hand is the full amount of what he owes."

35. Indenture Agreement, New Haven, May 9, 1767, Ingersoll Paps., NHCHS. See also Ingersoll's statement that he had received one set of bills worth five thousand livres from BA for payment to Lintot, dated New Haven, July 11, 1767, YUL, and Lintot's acknowledgement of the same, New Haven, July 13, 1767, Ingersoll Paps., NHCHS.

36. Bernard Lintot to Jared Ingersoll, New Haven, Aug. 11, 1767, Ingersoll Paps., NHCHS. Like any other provincial merchant, BA was quite adept at manipulating currencies for his own advantage. In 1765, for example, he paid Jeremiah Pennuston in various French currencies for a large order of cordage. Once Pennuston established the value of these currencies, he concluded that BA had seriously shortchanged him.

He sued, and the two merchants reached a settlement satisfactory to Pennuston in 1770. See *Pennuston v. Arnold*, Ingersoll Paps., NHCHS.

37. An early source of the debtors' prison anecdote was Anonymous [Samuel Peters?], "Some Account of Benedict Arnold," *European Magazine and London Review* (1783), unpaged, Tomlinson Coll., YUL. BA's modern biographers have generally eschewed this tale.

38. BA to Dr. William Jepson, New Haven, Dec. 6, 1763, Carnegie, *Catalogue* no. 225 (1958), 3, American Mss. Colls., AAS; Daniel and Joshua Lathrop to Thomas Mumford, Norwich, Sept. 8, 1765, Ford Coll., NYPL. David Atwater to Thomas Mumford, Groton, Sept. 10, 1765, Ford Coll., NYPL, acknowledges Mumford's timely settlement.

39. BA to John Remsen, New Haven, Mar. 26, 1768, Misc. BA Paps., MHS; BA to John Remsen, New Haven, Apr. 21, 1768, MdHS. In Mar. 1766, Babcock and Arnold shipped goods worth slightly over £108 to Remsen on the brigantine *Fortune*. This sum was apparently the amount of money in dispute. See Invoice, New Haven, Mar. 2, 1766, Emmet Coll., NYPL.

40. Wallace, *Traitorous Hero*, 24; and Dorothy Ann Lipson, *Freemasonry in Federalist Connecticut* (Princeton, N.J., 1977), 46–58. Chartered in 1750 through the efforts of DW, who, like BA, had migrated to New Haven, Hiram Lodge no. 1 was the oldest Masonic chapter in Connecticut. As an example of trading ties most likely strengthened through mutual Masonic membership, Dr. William Jepson, an apothecary and lodge activist in Hartford, regularly did business with BA.

41. Ibid. See also Steven C. Bullock, *Revolutionary Brotherhood: Freemasonry and the Transformation of the American Social Order, 1730–1840* (Chapel Hill, 1996), 50–108; and Wood, *Radicalism of the Revolution*, 222–25.

42. *The Descendants of Richard and Gillian Mansfield Who Settled in New Haven, 1639, . . .* , comp. H. Mansfield (New Haven, 1885), 24–25; and Donald Lines Jacobus, *Families of Ancient New Haven*, vol. 5 (Rome, N.Y., 1929), 1137–40. Published genealogies favor the date of Feb. 27, 1767, for the marriage. Many BA biographers, however, apparently drawing on Arnold, *Arnold*, 27, state that the date was Feb. 22, 1767. I have chosen to follow the genealogies; the discrepancy is inconsequential.

43. Ibid. Agreement between Andrew Thomson and BA, n.p., Feb. 17, 1764, and Agreement between Abraham Beach and BA, n.p., Feb. 17, 1764, PML. Beach was a nephew of DW and a fellow Mason who eventually established himself as a merchant in Hartford. He may have gotten BA involved in Hiram Lodge no. 1. See Lipson, *Freemasonry in Connecticut*, 53n. The first evidence of joint Arnold-Mansfield trading ventures may be found in BA Misc. Accounts, June 4–July 7, 1765, Arnold Coll., NHCHS. Anonymous [Samuel Peters?], "Some Account of Benedict Arnold," *European Magazine and London Review* (1783), unpaged, Tomlinson Coll., YUL, asserted that BA, fresh out of debtors' prison, "insinuated himself into the good graces of" Peggy with the purpose of gaining access to Mansfield family money to resume his mercantile career. To guarantee his success, BA allegedly impregnated Peggy but

quickly promised to marry her, the act of which reconciled an angry "Papa" Mansfield to having the scoundrel BA in his family. Since nearly twelve months passed between the marriage date and the birth of their first child, Benedict VI, this tale is obviously lacking in merit. In a curious recent variation, Randall, *Arnold*, 64, claimed that BA wed Peggy so that High Sheriff Mansfield could provide legal protection in case BA faced prosecution for his illicit trading activities. Randall does not explain how Mansfield could have done so through a local office with duties unrelated to running down and prosecuting suspected smugglers.

44. BA to Margaret Arnold, Quebec, Oct. 5–7, 1773, Dreer Coll., HSP.

45. BA to Margaret Arnold, Martinique, June 25, 1768, MHS; BA to Margaret Arnold, St. Christopher, July 14, 1768, and July 16, 1768, and St. Eustatius, July 18, 1768, Lloyd W. Smith Coll., MNHP.

46. BA to Margaret Arnold, St. Croix, Aug. 8, 1768, and Aug. 13, 1768, Dreer Coll., HSP. See also BA to Margaret Arnold, St. Eustatius, July 20, 1768, YUL.

47. BA to Margaret Arnold, Barbados, Apr. 23, 1769, SCL.

48. BA to Messrs. Campbell and McKenzie, New Haven, Jan. 1771, Arnold Coll., NHCHS. A second letter virtually repeating the contents of the first but to an unidentified correspondent, dated New Haven, Jan. 1771, is also in the Arnold Coll., NHCHS. Arnold appears to have attributed the rumor to a Captain Fobes. See Gipson, *Jared Ingersoll*, 233n.

49. Ibid. In the second letter, BA substituted "girl" for "whore."

50. According to Isaac N. Arnold, the Croskie story came from Thomas Waterman, a descendant of BA's mother. See Arnold, *Arnold*, 30–32.

51. BA to Daniel and Isaac Bourdeaux, New York, Nov. 30, 1770, Arnold Coll., NHCHS; and BA to Benjamin Stout, New Haven, Sept. 25, 1772, BPL.

52. BA to Margaret Arnold, New York, Sept. 25, 1768, Sol Feinstone Coll., DLAR [APS]; BA to Margaret Arnold, Boston, Sept. 4, 1772, Charles De F. Burns, *Catalogue of Autographs* (1884), 1, Am. Mss. Colls., AAS.

53. Charles Chauncey to Thomas Lee, New Haven, Dec. 30, 1774, Chauncey Paps., YUL. Given BA's prosperity, he would not have had to borrow "to the hilt to build" this elaborate residence, as asserted in Brandt, *Man in the Mirror*, 16. For the interior design of BA's new home, consult the description, dated circa 1772, Arnold Coll., NHCHS. The home resided on land either given by or purchased from "Papa" Mansfield. BA also purchased land and constructed his own wharf, another sign of his substantial prosperity, during the early 1770s. See deed of land sale from Pierpont Ball and others to BA, August 1772, N-YHS.

T H R E E : *Irrepressible Acts of Martial Resistance*

1. Revenue [Townshend Duties] Act of 1767, June 26, 1767, Jensen, ed., *English Historical Documents*, 9:701–2. Secondary works informing this chapter include Michael A. Bellesiles, *Revolutionary Outlaws: Ethan Allen and the Struggle for Independence on the Early American Frontier* (Charlottesville, 1993), 104–23; Richard Buel, Jr.,

Dear Liberty: Connecticut's Mobilization for the Revolutionary War (Middletown, 1980), 3–53; Allen French, *The First Year of the American Revolution* (Boston, 1934), 129–59, and French, *The Taking of Ticonderoga: A Study of Captors and Captives* (Cambridge, 1927), *passim*; Robert McConnell Hatch, *Thrust for Canada: The American Attempt on Quebec in 1775–1776* (Boston, 1979), 17–42; Charles A. Jellison, *Ethan Allen: Frontier Rebel* (Syracuse, N.Y., 1969), 84–140; J. Robert Maguire, "Hand's Cove: Rendezvous of Ethan Allen and the Green Mountain Boys for the Capture of Fort Ticonderoga," *Vermont History,* 33 (1965): 417–37; James Kirby Martin, *In the Course of Human Events: An Interpretive Exploration of the American Revolution* (Arlington Heights, 1979), 40–91; Justin H. Smith, *Our Struggle for the Fourteenth Colony: Canada and the American Revolution* (2 vols., New York, 1907), 1:90–165; George F. G. Stanley, *Canada Invaded, 1775–1776* (Toronto, 1973), 19–36; and Christopher Ward, *The War of the Revolution,* ed. John Richard Alden (2 vols. New York, 1952), 1:63–72.

2. Tea Act, May 10, 1773, *Colonies to Nation, 1763–1789,* ed. Jack P. Greene (New York, 1967), 196–97. See also Benjamin Woods Labaree, *The Boston Tea Party* (New York, 1964), 58–79.

3. For North's full text, dated Mar. 14, 1774, and delivered on behalf of George III, see *The Parliamentary History of England . . . ,* comp. William Cobbett and T. C. Hansard (36 vols., London, 1806–1820), 17:1163–67. For the texts of the so-called Coercive Acts—Boston Port Act, Mar. 31, 1777; Massachusetts Government Act, May 20, 1774; Administration of Justice Act, May 20, 1774; and Quartering Act, June 2, 1774—see Jensen, ed., *English Historical Documents,* 9:779–85.

4. Zobel, *Boston Massacre,* 180–205, among other pages; Shy, *Toward Lexington,* 303–20.

5. BA to B. Douglas, St. George's Key, June 9, 1770, *HM,* 1 ser., 1 (1857): 119.

6. Continental Association, Thurs., Oct. 20, 1774, *JCC,* 1:75–80.

7. In one conciliatory move, the First Congress prepared "The Declaration of Colonial Rights and Grievances," which implored the home government to recognize American liberties. For the draft text, see Fri., Oct. 14, 1774, ibid., 1:63–74. Otherwise, this gathering's actions were largely confrontational and not designed to settle differences amicably.

8. Samuel Peters, *General History of Connecticut . . . ,* ed. Samuel Jarvis McCormick (London, 1781; reprint, New York, 1877), 260–63.

9. Ibid., 267–68.

10. Ibid., 268–69.

11. Ibid., 269–70.

12. Samuel Peters, "Genuine History of Arnold, by an Old Acquaintance, . . ." *Political Magazine of London,* 1 (Nov.–Dec. 1780): 690, 746–48, *The Works of Samuel Peters of Hebron, Connecticut,* ed. Kenneth Walter Cameron (Hartford, 1967), 163–65. The tone, style, and contents of this condemnatory essay are very similar to Anonymous, "Some Account of Benedict Arnold," *European Magazine and London*

Review (1783), unpaged, Tomlinson Coll., YUL, suggesting that Peters or a plagiarist was the author of this latter essay.

13. George III to Lord North, Kew, Sept. 11, 1774, and George III to Lord North, Queens House, Nov. 18,1774, *The Correspondence of King George the Third, from 1760 to December 1783,* ed. Sir John Fortescue (6 vols., London, 1927–1928), 3:131, 153.

14. Earl of Sandwich, in the House of Lords, Thurs., Mar. 16, 1775, *AA,* 4 ser., 1:1681–83.

15. Earl of Dartmouth to Thomas Gage, Whitehall, Jan. 27, 1775, *The Correspondence of General Thomas Gage, . . . 1763–1775,* ed. Clarence Edwin Carter (2 vols., New Haven, 1931–1933), 2:179–83.

16. David Hackett Fischer, *Paul Revere's Ride* (New York, 1994), *passim,* masterfully discusses Lexington and Concord.

17. Atwater, *History of New Haven,* 40–42, 649–50; Lossing, *Pictorial Field-Book of the Revolution,* 1:421–22; Gipson, *Jared Ingersoll,* 337–38; Zeichner, *Connecticut's Years of Controversy,* 190.

18. Regarding provincial American martial values on the eve of the Revolutionary War, see Lawrence Delbert Cress, *Citizens in Arms: The Army and the Militia in American Society to the War of 1812* (Chapel Hill, 1982), 3–50; on the *rage militaire,* see Royster, *Revolutionary People at War,* 25–53; and on rapid collapse of popular enthusiasm, see Martin and Lender, *A Respectable Army,* 48–78.

19. Despite modern-day stereotypes, colonists, especially in the older seaboard settlements, rarely had muskets hanging over their fireplaces. Most were unprepared to defend hearth and home. Hence, small arms and powder and ball were in very short supply at the outset of the war, at least until France started to provide covert material aid after mid-1776. Although BA's soldiers promised to furnish their own weapons, the only readily available supply of arms was stored at New Haven's central powder magazine, where militiamen went to receive weaponry in case of some military emergency. Thus BA and his Footguards had to gain access to the storehouse if they wanted an amply supply of arms.

20. Atwater, *History of New Haven,* 42, credits BA with these words but offers no source. BA's words may have been apocryphal, but his forceful confrontation with New Haven's old guard leaders was not.

21. Buel, *Dear Liberty,* 36–38, states that 3,716 Connecticut volunteers marched for Cambridge, Mass., within a week of hearing about Lexington and Concord. Some 46 of 72 Connecticut towns sent troops to Massachusetts in the first days of the contest. Gipson, *Jared Ingersoll,* 338n., estimated that about one thousand New Havenites took up arms on behalf of the rebel cause at some point during the war.

22. Agreement Subscribed by Captain Arnold and His Company, n.p., Apr. 24, 1775, *AA,* 4 ser., 2:383–84. Apparently merchant SD, about to represent Connecticut in the Second Continental Congress, drew up this covenant for Connecticut companies to sign. See SD to Capt. John Chester and the Volunteers from Wethersfield, Apr. 24, 1775, *Collections of the Connecticut Historical Society,* 2 (1870): 214–17.

23. On the colonists' sense of providential calling, see Royster, *Revolutionary People at War,* 13–24. On the realities of long-term commitment, see Martin and Lender, *A Respectable Army,* 54–126.

24. Samuel Holden Parsons to Joseph Trumbull, New London, June 2, 1775, *Colls. Ct. Hist. Soc.,* 1 (1860): 181–84.

25. Journal of Captain Edward Mott, ibid., 1 (1860): 165–67.

26. Arnold, *Arnold,* 36; BA to Mass. Committee of Safety, Cambridge, Apr. 30, 1775, *AA,* 4 ser., 2:450; Minutes Mass. Committee of Safety, Cambridge, Apr. 30, 1775, ibid., 4 ser., 2:749–50.

27. JB to Boston Committee of Correspondence, Montreal, Mar. 29, 1775, ibid., 4 ser., 2:240–41.

28. Minutes Mass. Committee of Safety, Cambridge, May 2, 1775, ibid., 4 ser., 2:750; Orders to BA, Cambridge, May 3, 1775, ibid., 4 ser., 2:486; Journal Mass. Provincial Congress, Watertown, May 4, 1775, *NDAR,* 1:268.

29. French, *Taking of Ticonderoga,* 13–18, 37–38.

30. For recruiting efforts, see BA to Gentlemen of the Southern Towns, Ruiport [Rupert], Vt., May 8, 1775, William Williams Paps., BeA; Thomas Allen to Seth Pomeroy, Pittsfield, May 9, 1775, *HM,* 1 ser., 1 (1857): 108–9; Edward Mott Journal, *Colls. Ct. Hist. Soc.,* 1 (1860): 167–69.

31. Born in October 1744, JB was twenty-six when he graduated from Yale, about eight years older than the average graduate of his time. Since Oliver Arnold, who was Rhode Island's attorney general (1766–1770), died in 1770, JB most likely studied law with him before matriculating at Yale, an inverted pathway for professional training in those times. For laudatory JB and JE commentary amid negative flourishes about BA, see *The History of Pittsfield, (Berkshire County), Massachusetts, from the Year 1734 to the Year 1800,* comp. J. E. A. Smith (2 vols., Boston, 1869), 1:211–42.

32. Edward Mott Journal, *Colls. Ct. Hist. Soc.,* 1 (1860): 169–71.

33. Ibid., 171–72. See also Edward Mott to Mass. Provincial Congress, Shoreham, May 11, 1775, *AA,* 4 ser., 2:558–59.

34. BA claimed that he and EA agreed to "issue further orders jointly," which was likely a gesture of courtesy by EA. See BA to Mass. Committee of Safety, Ticonderoga, May 11, 1775, ibid., 4 ser., 2:557.

35. Jocelyn Feltham to Thomas Gage, New York, June 12, 1775, quoted in French, *Taking of Ticonderoga,* 55. Feltham noted that nine regulars and ten women and children were captured at Crown Point on May 12. They represented the whole garrison.

36. Elisha Phelps to Ct. Assembly, Skenesborough, May 16, 1775, *Colls. Ct. Hist. Soc.,* 1 (1860): 174–75; Edward Mott Journal, ibid., 169. Phelps was also a member of the "committee of war."

37. According to the memoirs of Nathan Beman, who claimed to be EA's guide that morning, BA was not with the assault party. This account represents a thoroughly discredited posttreason tale. See B. F. De Costa, "Nathan Beman vs. Benedict

Arnold," *HM,* 2 ser., 3 (1868): 273–74. EA claimed that before approaching the fortress, he made a great patriotic speech that fired the assault group with zeal for combat. See *A Narrative of Colonel Ethan Allen's Captivity, . . .* (Philadelphia, 1789), in *Ethan and Ira Allen: Collected Works,* ed. J. Kevin Graffagnino (3 vols., Benson, Vt., 1992), 2:3. But "Veritas," Ticonderoga, June 25, 1775, *AA,* 4 ser., 2:1086, stated that an irresolute EA refused to approach the fortress until all the troops had crossed the lake. In this pro-BA version, perhaps even written by BA himself, BA finally persuaded EA to proceed with the eighty-three men at hand before the advantage of a surprise attack under cover of darkness was lost.

38. *Narrative Ethan Allen's Captivity,* Graffagnino, ed., *Allen Collected Works,* 2:3–4.

39. Jocelyn Feltham to Thomas Gage, New York, June 11, 1775, quoted in French, *Taking of Ticonderoga,* 44. See also ibid., 84; and Smith, *Struggle Fourteenth Colony,* 1:139.

40. Jocelyn Feltham to Thomas Gage, New York, June 11 and 12, 1775, quoted in French, *Taking of Ticonderoga,* 44, 53–55.

41. BA to Mass. Committee of Safety, Ticonderoga, May 11, 1775, *AA,* 4 ser., 2:557; "Benedict Arnold's Regimental Memorandum Book," May 10, 1775, *PMHB,* 8 (1884): 366; Edward Mott to Mass. Provincial Congress, Shoreham, May 11, 1775, *AA,* 4 ser., 2:559.

42. "BA's Regimental Memorandum Book," May 10, 1775, *PMHB* (1884): 366; Barnabas Deane to SD, Albany, June 1, 1775, *Colls. Ct. Hist. Soc.,* 2 (1870): 247.

43. EA to Jonathan Trumbull, Ticonderoga, May 12, 1775, *NDAR,* 1:319; Smith, *Struggle Fourteenth Colony,* 1:143–45.

44. BA to Mass. Committee of Safety, Crown Point, May 19, 1775, *AA,* 4 ser., 2:646, included an inventory that listed 111 artillery pieces at Crown Point and 86 at Ticonderoga. In addition, there were four brass howitzers "in the edge of the lake" at Crown Point that were "covered with water, [and] cannot be come at present."

45. BA to Mass. Committee of Safety, Ticonderoga, May 14, 1775, ibid., 4 ser., 2:584–85.

46. Ibid.; "BA's Regimental Memorandum Book," May 14, 1775, *PMHB* (1884): 367; BA to Mass. Committee of Safety, Crown Point, May 19, 1775, *AA,* 4 ser., 2:645; Eleazer Oswald Journal on Lake Champlain, May 11, 1775, *NDAR,* 1:312.

47. "BA's Regimental Memorandum Book," May 14–17, 1775, *PMHB* (1884): 367–68; Eleazer Oswald Journal, May 13[14]–May 16[17], 1775, *NDAR,* 1:327, 330, 340, 344, 358. BA claimed to have captured six brass cannons, but Oswald's figure of "two fine brass field pieces" is likely more accurate. BA may have confused the firing weight (6-pounders) of the cannons with the number taken in his memorandum book, since he mentioned only two pieces in BA to Mass. Provincial Congress, Crown Point, May 19, 1775, *AA,* 4 ser., 2:645.

48. Ibid.; see also BA to Albany Committee of Safety, Ticonderoga, May 22, 1775, ibid., 4 ser., 2:839–40.

49. BA to Mass. Committee of Safety, Crown Point, May 19, 1775, ibid., 4 ser.,

2:645; "BA's Regimental Memorandum Book," May 17, 1775, *PMHB* (1884): 367; Eleazer Oswald Journal, May 18, 1775, *NDAR*, 1:358.

50. "BA's Regimental Memorandum Book," May 21, 1775, *PMHB* (1884): 368. For other descriptions, see GC to Lord Dartmouth, Montreal, June 7, 1775, *DAR*, 9:157–58. EA apparently thought he could upstage BA by capturing Montreal. He wrote to friendly merchants there and demanded various provisions, including an ample supply of hard liquor. See EA to James Morrison and Other Merchants, St. Johns, May 18, 1775, ibid., 7:344. Fortunately, the Boys had not gotten any alcohol and were not drunk when the British attacked them. By the time EA and the Boys got back to Ticonderoga, they were famished. BA generously accommodated their need for food but provided no hard drink. See "BA's Regimental Memorandum Book," May 21–23, 1775, *PMHB* (1884): 368–69; and BA to John Stephens, Ticonderoga, May 21, 1775, *NDAR*, 1:501–2.

51. BA to Mass. Committee of Safety, Ticonderoga, May 14, 1775, *AA*, 4 ser., 2:584–85; BA to Mass. Committee of Safety, Crown Point, May 19, 1775, ibid., 4 ser., 2:645–46.

52. Ibid.; BA to Ct. Assembly, Crown Point, May 23, 1775, ibid., 4 ser., 2: 840.

53. Ibid.; BA to Mass. Committee of Safety, Crown Point, May 23, 1775, ibid., 4 ser., 2:694; BA to Noah Lee, Crown Point, May 23, 1775, ibid., 4 ser., 2:841; "BA's Regimental Memorandum Book," May 23, 1775, *PMHB* (1884): 368–69.

54. Eleazer Oswald Journal, May 23, 1775, *NDAR*, 1:513.

55. BA to Mass. Committee of Safety, Crown Point, May 26, 1775, *AA*, 4 ser., 2:714–15; BA to Mass. Committee of Safety, Crown Point, May 29, 1775, ibid., 4 ser., 2:735.

56. GC to Lord Dartmouth, Montreal, June 7, 1775, *DAR*, 9:157.

57. On the matter of British attitudes, see Martin and Lender, *A Respectable Army*, 19–20. For the deeper background, see Leach, *Roots of Conflict*, 107–33, among other pages.

58. BA to Mass. Committee of Safety, Crown Point, May 19, 1775, *AA*, 4 ser., 2:645–46.

F O U R : *The Provincial Politics of Rebellion*

1. EA to Albany Committee of Safety, Ticonderoga, May 11, 1775, *AA*, 4 ser., 2:606. Secondary works informing this chapter include Bellesiles, *Revolutionary Outlaws*, 112–25; French, *First Year of the Revolution*, 143–59, 274–93; Don R. Gerlach, *Philip Schuyler and the American Revolution in New York, 1733–1777* (Lincoln, Neb., 1964), 1–62, 279–86, 315–22; H. James Henderson, *Party Politics in the Continental Congress* (New York, 1974), 45–61; Jellison, *Ethan Allen*, 131–42; Jerrilyn Greene Marston, *King and Congress: The Transfer of Political Legitimacy, 1774–1776* (Princeton, 1987), 131–79; Jonathan Gregory Rossie, *The Politics of Command in the American Revolution* (Syracuse, 1975), 1–44; and Smith, *Struggle Fourteenth Colony*, 1:166–92.

2. EA to Mass. Provincial Congress, Ticonderoga, May 11, 1775, *AA*, 4 ser., 2:556.

3. Edward Mott to Mass. Provincial Congress, Shoreham, May 11, 1775, ibid., 4 ser., 2:557–60.

4. "BA's Regimental Memorandum Book," May 10, 1775, *PMHB* (1884): 364–65; BA to Mass. Committee of Safety, Crown Point, May 19, 1775, *AA*, 4 ser., 2:645–46.

5. BA to Mass. Committee of Safety, Ticonderoga, May 11, 1775, ibid., 4 ser., 2:557.

6. BA's May 11 letter to the Mass. Committee of Safety did not reach the Provincial Congress until Monday, May 22, five days after JE's appearance. See Mass. Provincial Congress Journal, Watertown, *NDAR*, 1:502.

7. Mass. Provincial Congress Journal, Watertown, Wednesday, May 17, 1775, ibid., 1:349–50.

8. EA apparently did not specifically raise the issue of command rights for himself until June 10. On May 29, 1775, for example, BA, writing to the Mass. Committee of Safety from Crown Point (*AA*, 4 ser., 2:735), stated that EA "has entirely given up the command." Nor does BA in his Memorandum Book make mention of any such EA claims. EA, perhaps still embarrassed by the fiasco of his "invasion" of Canada, remained at Crown Point until June 3, at which point he returned to Ticonderoga. Perhaps it was here that he again linked up with JE, who then told him about the Mass. Provincial Congress's ruling. See note 25 below for further information about the BA/EA/JE confrontation of June 10–11, and "BA's Regimental Memorandum Book," *PMHB* (1884): 368, 370, 373.

9. On the full range of issues over which members of the Second Congress wrestled during the spring and summer of 1775, see Henderson, *Party Politics*, 45–61; and Marston, *King and Congress*, 131–79. For more detail on military-related issues, see Rossie, *Politics of Command*, 1–30.

10. Thurs., May 18, 1775, *JCC*, 2:55–56; George Read to Gertrude Read, Phila., May 18, 1776, and George Read to Nicholas Van Dyke, Phila., May 18, 1776, *LDC*, 1:359–60.

11. Thurs., May 18, 1775, *JCC*, 2: 55–56.

12. BA to Continental Congress, Crown Point, May 29, 1775, *AA*, 4 ser., 2:734–35. BA also expressed his concerns in a note to the Mass. Committee of Safety, Crown Point, May 29, 1775, ibid., 4 ser., 2:735.

13. Mass. Provincial Congress to Jonathan Trumbull, Watertown, May 29, 1775, ibid., 4 ser., 2:736–37. See also EA to Continental Congress, Crown Point, May 29, 1775, *NDAR*, 1:561–62. This missive, written without BA's knowledge, favored retention of the forts, no doubt because EA, who herein claimed to have captured the British sloop at St. Johns, was seeking Congress's permission to invade Canada with the intent of capturing Montreal. In masterfully confusing BA's efforts with his own, EA also suggested that he and the Boys were responsible for the patriot success at St. Johns.

14. BA to Ct. Assembly, Crown Point, May 23, 1775, *AA*, 4 ser., 2:840; BA to Mass. Committee of Safety, Crown Point, May 23, 1775, ibid., 4 ser., 2:693–94.

Trumbull's letter to the Connecticut delegates apparently has not survived, but in Ct. Delegates to Jonathan Trumbull, Phila., May 31, 1775 (*LDC,* 1:422), SD, Eliphalet Dyer, and Roger Sherman mentioned the governor's letter of May 27 and its salubrious effects, along with BA's, on Congress. Jonathan Trumbull to His Brother, Hartford, May 29, 1775, *AA,* 4 ser., 2:728–29, mentions "a little of politics" in using BA's letter to encourage Congress to take a more aggressive stance in the Champlain region.

15. Weds., May 31, 1775, *JCC,* 2:73–74.

16. Ironically, BA, acting on his own initiative, had already asked Connecticut to send fifteen hundred troops to the Champlain forts. See BA to Ct. Assembly, Crown Point, May 23, 1775, *AA,* 4 ser., 2:840. In Jonathan Trumbull to His Brother, Hartford, May 29, 1775, ibid., 4 ser., 2:729–30, the governor mentioned the appointment of Hinman in anticipation of the proper response from the Continental Congress. See also Jonathan Trumbull to N.Y. Provincial Congress, Hartford, May 29, 1775, ibid., 4 ser., 2:847. In Apr. 1775, Hinman was the fourth-ranking officer in Connecticut's militia establishment. His three seniors—DW, Joseph Spencer, and Israel Putnam—already had received Continental commissions. BA rated only a captaincy in DW's 1st Regiment. See *Public Records of the Colony of Connecticut,* ed. J. H. Trumbull and C. J. Hoadley (16 vols., Hartford, 1850–1890), 14:423–30.

17. Joseph Hawley to Mass. Committee of Safety, Watertown, May 26, 1775, *AA,* 4 ser., 2:716. Hawley chaired a Mass. Provincial Congress committee looking into the alleged problems with BA. See also Mass. Provincial Congress to BA, Watertown, May 22, 1775, ibid., 4 ser., 2:676, in which the delegates make it clear that they want Connecticut to lead the way in garrisoning the Champlain forts; and Mass. Committee of Safety to BA, Cambridge, May 28, 1775, ibid., 4 ser., 2:726–27, in which that group informed BA that he should accept future orders from the Mass. Provincial Congress.

18. Instructions to Joseph Henshaw, Watertown, May 27, 1775, and Mass. Provincial Congress to BA, Watertown, May 27, 1775, ibid., 4 ser., 2:723.

19. Minutes of Joseph Henshaw's Journey to Connecticut, and Joseph Henshaw to BA, Hartford, May 31, 1775, ibid., 4 ser., 2:724.

20. BA to Mass. Committee of Safety, Crown Point, May 23, 1775, ibid., 4 ser., 2:694.

21. Mass. Provincial Congress to BA, Watertown, June 1, 1775, ibid., 4 ser., 2:1882–83.

22. Minutes Henshaw's Journey to Connecticut, ibid., 4 ser., 2:724. See also Jonathan Trumbull to Mass. Provincial Congress, Hartford, May 29, 1775, *NDAR,* 1:560–61. Trumbull's letter resulted in the expansive words sent to BA even before Henshaw returned to Watertown with the same information.

23. On Congress's decision of Weds., June 14, 1775, to assume responsibility for a Continental army, see *JCC,* 2:89–90. See also Virginia Delegate to Unknown, [Phila.], June 14, 1775, *LDC,* 1:486; and Martin and Lender, *A Respectable Army,* 40–44.

24. "BA's Regimental Memorandum Book," *PMHB* (1884): 371–73. The scouting expedition left Crown Point on June 4, with BA and his small fleet returning to the Champlain forts six days later after proceeding to within a mile of St. Johns, having made only casual contact with the enemy.

25. June 10, 1775, ibid., 373.

26. June 11, 1775, ibid., 373; and "Veritas" essay, Ticonderoga, June 25, 1775, *AA*, 4 ser., 2:1087.

27. Albany Committee of Correspondence to BA, June 1, 1775, *Minutes of the Albany Committee of Correspondence, 1775–1778 . . .*, comp. James Sullivan (2 vols., Albany, 1923–1925), 1:59. As soon as the Albany Committee learned about Congress's decision to have Governor Trumbull appoint a commanding officer, it deferred to that ruling. See N.Y. Delegates (James Duane, Francis Lewis, Philip Livingston, Lewis Morris, PS, and Henry Wisner) to Albany Committee of Correspondence, Phila., June 6, 1775, *LDC*, 1:449–50; and Barnabas Deane to SD, Wethersfield, June 5, 1775, *Colls. Ct. Hist. Soc.*, 2 (1870): 260.

28. BA to Continental Congress, Crown Point, June 13, 1775, *AA*, 4 ser., 2:976–77.

29. EA and others to Continental Congress, Crown Point, June 10, 1775, ibid., 4 ser., 2:957–58; and Tues., June 27, 1775, *JCC*, 2:108–10. Unlike BA, EA and friends had no plan of operations.

30. After selecting GW as commander in chief on Fri., June 16 (ibid., 2:91–92), Congress proceeded to name four major generals, as well as other general officers. Artemas Ward (Mass.) was the ranking major general, followed by Charles Lee (England and Va.), PS (N.Y.), and Israel Putnam (Ct.). PS was the logical choice to command the Northern Department. See Sat., June 17, and Mon., June 19, 1775, ibid., 2:96–100.

31. "BA's Regimental Memorandum Book," June 17, 1775, *PMHB* (1884): 374. On Thurs., June 1, 1775, Congress resolved "that no expedition or incursion ought to be undertaken or made . . . against Canada," a position the delegates reversed on Tues., June 27, 1775 (*JCC*, 2:108–10).

32. Mass. Provincial Congress Journal, Watertown, Tues., June 13, 1775, *NDAR*, 1:667–68.

33. Crown Point Committee Report to Mass. Provincial Congress, Cambridge, July 6, 1775, *AA*, 4 ser., 2:1596–97; "BA's Regimental Memorandum Book," June 23, 1775, *PMHB* (1884): 375.

34. Even as BA mulled over his resignation, he wrote or had someone like Eleazer Oswald, his secretary, prepare a summary report on the necessity of maintaining the Champlain forts, according to the "order" of the Spooner committee. See BA to Continental Congress, Ticonderoga [?], June 23, 1775, *AA*, 4 ser., 2:1066–67.

35. BA to Spooner Committee, Crown Point, June 24, 1775, ibid., 4 ser., 2:1598–99.

36. "BA's Regimental Memorandum Book," June 23, 1775, *PMHB* (1884): 375.

37. June 24, 1775, ibid., 376.

38. Crown Point Committee Report to Mass. Provincial Congress, Cambridge, July 6, 1775, *AA*, 4 ser., 2:1595. See also Walter Spooner to N.Y. Provincial Congress, Springfield, July 3, 1775, and Walter Spooner to Jonathan Trumbull, Springfield, July 3, 1775, ibid., 4 ser., 2:1539–41.

39. Edward Mott to Jonathan Trumbull, Albany, July 6, 1775, ibid., 4 ser., 2:1085–88. Contemporaries did not take Mott's tale seriously, but it is still being repeated, as in Bellesiles, *Revolutionary Outlaws*, 121–22.

40. "Veritas" essay, Ticonderoga, June 25, 1775, *AA*, 4 ser., 2:1085–88.

41. BA to Spooner Committee, Crown Point, June 24, 1775, ibid., 4 ser., 2:1599. BA took on no further "small" debts on behalf of Massachusetts. Rather, he acknowledged receipt of various goods and signed over the burden of payment to the Mass. Provincial Congress. See BA, Bought of Benjamin French, Stone Arabia, July 3, 1775, and BA to Zachariah Ourmouth [?], Crown Point, July 4, 1775, SCL.

42. To BA from the Inhabitants of Lake Champlain, Lake Champlain, July 3, 1775, *AA*, 4 ser., 2:1088. BA had earlier covenanted with the local settlers to preserve American liberties. See General Association, Crown Point, June 15, 1775, *MAH*, 8 (1882): 129–30.

43. BA to Lake Champlain Inhabitants, Crown Point, July 4, 1775, *AA*, 4 ser., 2:1088.

44. Barnabas Deane to SD, Albany, June 1, 1775, *Colls. Ct. Hist. Soc.*, 2 (1870): 247. Barnabas Deane was on a three-person committee appointed by the Connecticut assembly on May 17, 1775, to investigate activities and make recommendations for possible further involvement by Connecticut at the Champlain forts. BA noted that the committee members arrived at Crown Point on Wednesday, May 24, 1775. See "BA's Regimental Memorandum Book," *PMHB* (1884): 369.

45. PS to SD, New York City, June [July?] 3, 1775, *Colls. Ct. Hist. Soc.*, 2 (1870): 252.

46. Rossie, *Politics of Command*, 38–40, states that Congress named PS's staff officers, except for adjutant general. Congress decided to let the N.Y. Provincial Congress recommend some suitable person for that post. Thus SD could not help secure the adjutant's position for BA. The N.Y. Provincial Congress first chose William Duer, who had helped contain the June 24 mutiny at Crown Point. Duer had accused BA of "unaccountable pride" for resigning his Massachusetts commission, yet when he learned that BA was PS's first choice, Duer contracted the same prideful disease and refused the assignment. In the end, the rather obscure Edward Flemming assumed the post.

47. Gerlach, *Philip Schuyler*, 6–14, 43–52, 279–86. Gerlach estimates PS's landholdings in the early 1760s at between ten thousand and twenty thousand acres, placing him among the major landholders in the colony.

48. Benjamin Hinman to PS, Ticonderoga, July 7, 1775, *NDAR*, 1:837.

49. Smith, *Struggle Fourteenth Colony*, 1:190. The extent of Hinman's prior military experience is unclear. He was a prominent resident of Litchfield County, where he held a commission as a justice of the peace. No doubt he was a member of

Governor Trumbull's inner circle of political favorites, which hardly qualified him for so important a command assignment.

50. BA to SD, Albany, July 10, 1775, Mrs. Archibald Crossly Coll., Misc. Mss., LC. PS most likely told BA about his message to Deane regarding the adjutant generalship. He may even have encouraged BA to write SD as a way of nurturing his support.

51. BA to Continental Congress, Albany, July 11, 1775, *AA,* 4 ser., 2:1646–47. See also PS to Continental Congress, Albany, July 11, 1775, ibid., 4 ser., 2:1645–46.

52. BA to SD, Albany, July 10, 1775, Mrs. Archibald Crossly Coll., Misc. Mss., LC.

53. Ibid.; HA to BA, New Haven, June 1775, Arnold, *Arnold,* 47–48; Mansfield, comp., *Descendants of Richard and Gillian Mansfield,* 1140.

54. BA to SD, Albany, July 10, 1775, Mrs. Archibald Crossly Coll., Misc. Mss., LC.

55. HA to BA, New Haven, June 1775, Arnold, *Arnold,* 47–48.

F I V E : *Into the Howling Maine Wilderness*

1. HA to BA, New Haven, June 1775, Arnold, *Arnold,* 47–48. Secondary works informing this chapter include French, *First Year of the Revolution,* 274–93, 376–414; Hatch, *Thrust for Canada,* 1–17, 62–81; Don Higginbotham, *Daniel Morgan: Revolutionary Rifleman* (Chapel Hill, 1961), 1–26; James A. Huston, "The Logistics of Arnold's March to Quebec," in *Military Analysis of the Revolutionary War: An Anthology by the Editors of Military Affairs* (Millwood, 1977), 106–20; Gustave Lanctot, *Canada and the American Revolution,* trans. Margaret M. Cameron (Cambridge, 1967), 17–61; Justin H. Smith, *Arnold's March from Cambridge to Quebec: A Critical Study* (New York, 1903), 1–146, and Smith, *Struggle Fourteenth Colony,* 1:193–271, 492–552; Stanley, *Canada Invaded,* 3–19; Ward, *War of the Revolution,* 1:135–49, 163–75; and George M. Wrong, *Canada and the American Revolution: The Disruption of the First British Empire* (New York, 1935), 222–77.

2. BA to James Price, New Haven, July 25, 1775, Emmet Coll., NYPL. To protect himself in case his letter should be intercepted, BA wrote as if the voyage were being undertaken by an acquaintance. See also HA to SD, New Haven, Feb. 1, 1776, *Colls. Ct. Hist. Soc.,* 2 (1870): 358, in which she stated that BA "is likely to lose a vessel and cargo at Quebec."

3. Ibid., 2:356–57; and HA to BA, New Haven, June 1775, Arnold, *Arnold,* 47–48. Because BA did not return to New Haven after attempting to settle his accounts with the Mass. Provincial Congress, the cargo denoted for the West Indies was never shipped.

4. Mass. Provincial Congress Journal, Aug. 1, 5, 7, 18, 19, 1775, *AA,* 4 ser., 3:298, 312, 313, 343, 344. For BA's listing of expenses, see The Honorable Provincial Congress of the Massachusetts Bay [due] to B. Arnold, [July 1775], Andre deCoppett Coll., PUL.

5. Mon., Jan. 22, 1776, *JCC,* 4:77–78; SD to HA, Phila., Jan. 24, 1776, *Colls. Ct. Hist. Soc.,* 2 (1870): 354–55.

6. When BA had his first meeting with GW is not entirely clear. After the Continental Congress adjourned for a month on Tues., Aug. 1, 1775, some delegates traveled to Cambridge to meet with GW and see the army. Among this group was SD. He may well have arranged the initial meeting after pointing out that BA could brief the commander on the military situation in the Champlain region. He likely also explained that PS thought very highly of BA and had wanted him to join his staff. GW knew about the stock of lead at the Champlain forts by Monday, Aug. 14, 1775 (see GW to PS, Cambridge, *Paps. GW, RWS,* 1:306–7), an indication that the first meeting took place before that date. For SD's opinion that BA deserved the detached command, see SD to PS, Cambridge, Aug. 20, 1775, *LDC,* 1:704–5.

7. On Brewer, see *Paps. NG,* 1:103n. See also Smith, *Struggle Fourteenth Colony,* 1:498; and Ward, *War of the Revolution,* 1:163–64. Brewer composed his letter sometime between April 23 and July 19, 1775, most likely before the Battle of Bunker Hill on June 17.

8. Journal of Lt. John Montresor, 1761, *MQ,* 5–24. Departing from Canada, Montresor took twelve days to travel from Lake Megantic to Fort Halifax in Maine. Departing from Maine, BA's column traversed the same distance in twenty-eight days.

9. GW to PS, Cambridge, Aug. 20, 1775, *Paps. GW, RWS,* 1:332–33.

10. SD to PS, Cambridge, Aug. 20, 1775, *LDC,* 1:704–5. I have assumed that SD used these same points in supporting BA with GW. BA's associate Eleazer Oswald carried both GW's and SD's letters to PS, an indication that GW was already favorably disposed toward BA.

11. HG to BA, Cambridge, Aug. 25, 1775, *HM,* 1 ser., 16 (1857): 372; BA to HG, Watertown, Aug. 26, 1775, *Francis P. Harper, Catalogue 109* (1904), 4, Am. Mss. Colls., AAS; GW to Lund Washington, Cambridge, Aug. 20, 1775, *Paps. GW, RWS,* 1:335.

12. BA to Thomas Walker, Ticonderoga, May 20, 1775, and BA to Thomas Walker, May 24, 1775, *DAR,* 7:344; BA to James Price, New Haven, July 25, 1775, Emmet Coll., NYPL. See also Lanctot, *Canada and the Revolution,* 26–32, 43–49, 60–63.

13. Quebec Act, June 22, 1774, *English Historical Documents,* vol. 10: *1714–1783,* ed. D. B. Horn and Mary Ransome (London, 1957): 787–91.

14. Letter to the Inhabitants of the Province of Quebec, Weds., Oct. 26, 1774, *JCC,* 1:111–12. This document also encouraged the Canadians to send delegates to the Continental Congress. As is common practice, I have used the term "Canadian" throughout this text in referring specifically to the inhabitants of Quebec Province.

15. Address to the People of Great Britain, Fri., Oct. 21, 1774, *JCC,* 1:88.

16. GC to Lord Dartmouth, Montreal, June 7, 1775, *DAR,* 9:158–59. For a description placing less interpretive emphasis on gubernatorial and clerical intimidation, see Lanctot, *Canada and the Revolution,* 49–56.

17. To the Oppressed Inhabitants of Canada, Mon., May 29, 1775, *JCC,* 2:68–70.

18. BA to Continental Congress, Crown Point, June 13, 1775, *AA,* 4 ser., 2:976–77; Tues., June 27, 1775, *JCC,* 2:109–10.

19. On GW's capacities and judgments as commander in chief, see Don Higginbotham, *George Washington and the American Military Tradition* (Athens, Ga., 1985); John Ferling, *The First of Men: A Life of George Washington* (Knoxville, Tenn., 1988), 111–41; Ferling, "George Washington and the American Victory," in *The World Turned Upside Down: The American Victory in the War of Independence,* ed. John Ferling (Westport, 1988), 53–70; and Dave Richard Palmer, *The Way of the Fox: American Strategy in the War for America, 1775–1783* (Westport, 1975), 95–178.

20. BA to Reuben Colburn, Watertown, Aug. 21, 1775, *Paps. GW, RWS,* 1:409–10.

21. PS to GW, Albany, Aug. 27, 1775, ibid., 1:367–69.

22. Instructions to Nathaniel Tracy, Cambridge, Sept. 2, 1775, ibid., 1:404–5; Joseph Reed to Nathaniel Tracy, [Cambridge], Sept. 7, 1775, ibid., 1:405n; Instructions to Reuben Colburn, Cambridge, Sept. 3, 1775, ibid., 1:409; General Orders, Cambridge, Sept. 5, 1775, ibid., 1:414–15. Although Congressional delegates such as SD knew of the expedition's likelihood, GW did not officially inform Congress until after the detachment was on its way to Canada. See GW to JH, Pres. Congress, Cambridge, Sept. 21, 1775, ibid., 2:27–28.

23. GW to PS, Cambridge, Sept. 8, 1775, ibid., 2:436–37.

24. General Orders, Cambridge, Sept. 5, 1775, ibid., 1:414–15. On BA's aversion to the Green Mountain Boys, see BA to Continental Congress, Crown Point, June 13, 1775, *AA,* 4 ser., 2:976–77, and BA's Memorandum for Supplies for March to Quebec, [Cambridge], [Sept.] 1775, PCC, microfilm reel 179, item 162: 4, NA.

25. BA and HG selected the troops and their officers on Sept. 6–7, 1775. See General Orders, Cambridge, Sept. 8, 1775, *Paps. GW, RWS,* 1:431–32, which advised that those who now made up BA's column were "to be forthwith taken off the role of duty" of the main army for detached service.

26. According to Pr. John Joseph Henry, who vividly described the demeanor of the riflemen at the outset of the expedition, it was also their "silly fashion . . . to ape the manners of savages" (*MQ,* 301). On problems with the riflemen, see NG to GW, Prospect Hill, Sept. 10, 1775, *Paps. NG,* 1:117–18; General Orders, Cambridge, Sept. 11 and Sept. 13, 1775, *Paps. GW, RWS,* 1:449–50, 454–55.

27. JH to GW, Phila., July 19, 1775, *Paps. GW, RWS,* 1:132–33. Ogden kept a record of his experiences, which he titled "Journal of Gen. Matthias Ogden, While Serving as a Volunteer in Arnold's Campaign against Quebec," Lloyd W. Smith Coll., MNHP. On Burr, see Milton Lomask, *Aaron Burr: The Years from Princeton to Vice President, 1756–1805* (New York, 1979), 36–63, which reviews Burr's undistinguished Revolutionary War military career. See also Burr's Declarations of Military Service, New York, Feb. 11, 1829, and New York, Apr. 5, 1834, *Political Correspondence and Public Papers of Aaron Burr,* ed. Mary-Jo Kline (2 vols., Princeton, 1983), 2:1193, 1223–24.

28. "Observations of Benjamin Thompson (afterwards Count Rumford)," *Report*

on the Manuscripts of Mrs. Stopford-Sackville, of Drayton House, Northamptonshire, Historical Manuscripts Commission (2 vols., London, 1904–1910), 2:15. On Nov. 4, 1775, Thompson wrote from Boston that GW's troops were "most wretchedly clothed, and as dirty a set of mortals as ever disgraced the name of a soldier. They have had no clothes of any sort provided them . . . except the detachment . . . that are gone to Canada under Col. Arnold, who had each of them a new coat and a linen frock served out to them before they set out." See also GW to James Warren, Cambridge, Sept. 10, 1775, *Paps. GW, RWS,* 1:446; and Ephraim Squier Diary, Sept. 11, 1775, and James Melvin Journal, Sept. 14, 1775, *MQ,* 619, 435.

29. Journal of Colonel Benedict Arnold, [Newburyport, Sept. 15, 1775], *NDAR,* 2:106. These passages were actually composed by BA's secretary, Eleazer Oswald, on behalf of BA.

30. Ibid. To avoid slowing himself up, BA hired a teamster to haul the blankets and ginger to Newburyport. See also Simon Fobes Narrative, n.d., *MQ,* 58.

31. GW to BA, Cambridge, Sept. 14, 1775, Instructions to BA, Cambridge, Sept. 14, 1775, and Address to the Inhabitants of Canada, n.p., c. Sept. 14, 1775, *Paps. GW, RWS,* 1:455–56, 457–59, 461–63.

32. Peters, "Genuine History of Arnold," *Political Magazine of London* (1780), 746, Cameron, ed., *Works of Samuel Peters,* 164. None of BA's officers mentioned the visit to Whitefield's tomb, which renders Peters's version somewhat suspect. See also Royster, *Revolutionary People at War,* 23–24. On parading before the Newburyport community, see Abner Stocking Journal, Sept. 17, 1775, *MQ,* 546.

33. GW gave BA fourteen separate instructions. The second covered this matter. See Instructions to BA, Cambridge, Sept. 14, 1775, *Paps. GW, RWS,* 1:457.

34. Stocking Journal, Sept. 19, 1775, *MQ,* 546; Eleazer Oswald Journal, Sept. 19, 1775, *NDAR,* 2:146–47; Fobes Narrative, n.d., *MQ,* 581.

35. BA to Nathaniel Tracy, Fort Western, Sept. 28, 1775, ibid., 68; BA to GW, Fort Western, Sept. 25[–27], 1775, *Paps. GW, RWS,* 2:40–41.

36. Ibid., 40.

37. Dennis Getchell and Samuel Berry to Reuben Colburn, Vassalborough, Sept. 13, 1775, *AA,* 4 ser., 3:961–62.

38. BA to GW, Fort Western, Sept. 25[–27], 1775, *Paps. GW, RWS,* 2:41.

39. Samuel Goodwin to GW, Pownalborough, Oct. 17, 1775, *AA,* 4 ser., 3:1083–84. Goodwin wanted GW to approve the concept of laying out a road to Quebec Province, from which he would benefit as a speculator in Maine lands.

40. BA to GW, Fort Western, Sept. 25[–27], 1775, *Paps. GW, RWS,* 2:41; Eleazer Oswald Journal, Sept. 25, 1775, *NDAR,* 2:200. Wrote Volunteer Aaron Burr to Sally Burr Reeve from Fort Western, Sept. 24, 1775 (Burr microfilm edition, Burr Family Coll., YUL), "In three weeks or less we expect to be in Quebec."

41. BA to GW, Fort Western, Sept. 25[–27], 1775, *Paps. GW, RWS,* 2:41. BA asked GW for "particular instructions" regarding DM's claim, so "that I may give satisfaction to the field officers with me." GW had no recollection of making such a

promise. See Joseph Reed to BA, Cambridge, Oct. 4, 1775, ibid., 2:44n, which contained advice for DM to accept his place in rank. Realizing the value of the riflemen, BA did not press the point with DM. Greene's three musket companies were those of Captains Jonas Hubbard, Simeon Thayer, and John Topham.

42. Meigs's musket companies were under Captains Henry Dearborn, William Goodrich, Oliver Hanchet, and Samuel Ward. Enos's companies were under Captain Samuel McCobb, a Captain Scott (his first name is not known), and Captain Thomas Williams.

43. On Enos, see Horace Edwin Hayden, "General Roger Enos: A Lost Chapter of Arnold's Expedition to Canada, 1775," *MQ,* 631–48. See also BA Journal, Sept. 27–29, 1775, ibid., 45; and BA to Roger Enos, Fort Western, Sept. 29, 1775, ibid., 68–69.

44. BA to GW, Fort Western, Sept. 27, 1775, *Paps. GW, RWS,* 2:57; BA to Captain Moses Nowell, Fort Western, Sept. 27, 1775, *MQ,* 67–68; See also Squier Diary, Sept. 26–28, 1775, ibid., 620–21. Squier not only mentioned the gallows incident with McCormick but also the flogging of six other patriots for allegedly stealing, presumably from their comrades.

45. BA Journal, Sept. 29–30, 1775, ibid., 45–46. For Montresor's Journal, see note 8 above. A reproduction of Montresor's map appears in ibid., 4.

46. BA Journal, Sept. 30–Oct. 2, 1775, ibid., 46–47.

47. Isaac Senter Journal, Sept. 29, 1775, ibid., 200–201; Simeon Thayer Journal, Sept. 30, 1775, ibid., 250–51; BA to GW, Second Portage from Kennebec to the Dead River, Oct. 13, 1775, *Paps. GW, RWS,* 2:155–56.

48. BA Journal, Oct. 3–8, 1775, *MQ,* 47–49; Thayer Journal, Sept. 30, 1775, ibid., 250; BA to GW, Second Portage from Kennebec to the Dead River, Oct. 13, 1775, *Paps. GW, RWS,* 2:155.

49. BA Journal, Oct. 3, Oct. 8–10, 1775, *MQ,* 47–49.

50. BA Journal, Oct. 11, 1775, ibid., 49.

51. George Morison Journal, c. Oct. 9–12, 1775, ibid., 514; BA Journal, Oct. 14–16, 1775, ibid., 51–52.

52. Senter Journal, Oct. 15–16, 1775, ibid., 205–6. This record is especially valuable in summarizing the health and medically related misfortunes of BA's detachment.

53. BA to Col. Farnsworth, Second Carrying Place, Oct. 14, 1775, ibid., 73.

54. BA to GW, Second Portage from Kennebec to the Dead River, Oct. 13, 1775, *Paps. GW, RWS,* 2:155.

55. BA to PS, Dead River, Oct. 13, 1775, *MQ,* 70–71; BA to John Manir [John Dyer Mercier], Dead River, Oct. 13, 1775, ibid., 69–70.

56. Ibid.; BA to Lieut. Archibald Steele, n.p., Oct. 13, 1775, ibid., 71. Before sending these letters, BA consulted with his officers regarding whether the risk of disclosing his column's presence was worth the possible gains in intelligence about defensive preparations at Quebec City. See BA Journal, Oct. 13, 1775, ibid., 51.

57. BA Journal, Oct. 17–18, 1775, ibid., 53; BA to Roger Enos, Dead River, Twenty Miles above the Portage, Oct. 17, 1775, ibid., 74–75; BA to Maj. Timothy Bigelow, n.p., Oct. 17, 1775, ibid., 75.

58. BA Journal, Oct. 19–21, 1775, ibid., 53–54.

59. BA Journal, Oct. 22, 1775, ibid., 54–55.

s i x : *Hannibalian Breakthrough to Quebec*

1. PS to GW, Ticonderoga, September 20, 1776, *Paps. GW, RWS,* 2:17–21. Secondary works informing this chapter include Charles Bracelen Flood, *Rise and Fight Again: Perilous Times along the Road to Independence* (New York, 1976), 5–42; French, *First Year of the Revolution,* 415–42; Hatch, *Thrust for Canada,* 101–20; Huston, "The Logistics of Arnold's March to Quebec," *Military Analysis Revolutionary War,* 106–20; Lanctot, *Canada and the Revolution,* 62–75; 92–107; Smith, *Arnold's March,* 147–257, and Smith, *Struggle Fourteenth Colony,* 1:304–36, 431–91, 553–606, 2:1–35; Stanley, *Canada Invaded,* 28–76; Ward, *War of the Revolution,* 1:150–62, 176–80; and Wrong, *Canada and the Revolution,* 278–97.

2. Risk taker that BA was, he still faithfully followed GW's orders, dated Cambridge, Sept. 14, 1775. See Instruction 13, *Paps. GW, RWS,* 1:459. BA Journal, Oct. 22, 1775, *MQ,* 55.

3. BA Journal, Oct. 23, 1775, ibid., 55.

4. BA Journal, Oct. 23–24, 1775, ibid., 55–56; BA to Roger Enos, Dead River, Oct. 24, 1775, ibid., 75–76; BA to Christopher Greene, Oct. 24, 1775, ibid., 76–77; BA to Col. Farnsworth, Dead River, Oct. 24, 1775, ibid., 76.

5. BA to Roger Enos, Dead River, Oct. 24, 1775, ibid., 76; Morison Journal, Oct. 24, 1775, ibid., 517.

6. Senter Journal, Oct. 25, 1775, ibid., 210. On the earlier efforts of Bigelow to obtain reserve supplies from Enos, see Thayer Journal, Oct. 21, 1775, ibid., 254–55.

7. Senter Journal, Oct. 24–25, 1775, ibid., 209–10; Thayer Journal, Oct. 25, 1775, ibid., 256.

8. Senter Journal, Oct. 25, 1775, ibid., 210–12, along with Thayer Journal, Oct. 25, 1775, ibid., 256–57, provide the most detailed description of Enos's unauthorized council of war. Thayer had the council taking place on the evening of Oct. 25; Senter said it met that day. I have followed Thayer's account.

9. Senter Journal, Oct. 25, 1775, ibid., 211–12; Thayer Journal, Oct. 25, 1775, ibid., 257. Enos's troops were responsible for a larger proportion of provisions than the advance divisions. According to Senter (ibid., 211), the lead companies had no more than "two or three barrels of flour with several of bread, the most in small proportion." Enos's companies averaged "fourteen of flour and ten of bread." Explained Senter, "the advantage of the arrangement was very conspicuous, as the rear division would not only have the roads cut, rivers cleared passable for boats, etc., but stages or encampments formed" along the way. Thus Enos's troops, although carrying more weight, had less work to perform in penetrating the wilderness. They func-

tioned as a mobile commissary unit but also apparently squandered rather than conserved some of the food supplies assigned to them. See also Huston, "The Logistics of Arnold's March to Quebec," *Military Analysis Revolutionary War*, 114–16.

10. For an unconvincing explanation of Enos's actions, see Hayden, "General Roger Enos," *MQ*, 631–48. Hayden was a direct descendant of Enos.

11. Either Enos was lying at the council of war meeting on Oct. 25, or he was grossly negligent of his duties in not actually knowing the state of his reserve food supplies, for which BA had made him responsible. Just as bad, Enos knew that his division did not really need five days' worth of rations to make it back to the Maine settlements. BA had long since ordered up all reserve food supplies to the Great Carrying Place, in case of a general retreat. Even if the rations were not there (as it turned out, they were not), Enos could assume that these provisions were in transit. Further, by any reasonable estimate, his troops could easily have descended to the Maine settlements in five days, and they could have done so on half rations. In sum, Enos's only rapid movements on the march were toward the rear and at the expense of far more intrepid patriot brethren whom he forsook for his own comfort as well as that of his officers and division. See also Squier Diary, ibid., 619–28. Squier, a member of Enos's division, does not mention any problem with hunger after turning back. He took fewer than five days to get back to the edge of the Maine settlements, based on his diary entries of Oct. 26–30, 1775, ibid., 624–26.

12. Henry Dearborn Journal, Oct. 27, 1775, ibid., 137.

13. BA to GW, Point Levi [Levy], Nov. 8, 1775, *Paps. GW, RWS*, 2:326–27.

14. BA Journal, Oct. 24–26, 1775, *MQ*, 55–58; Morison Journal, Oct. 27, 1775, ibid., 522.

15. BA Journal, Oct. 26, 1775, ibid., 58.

16. BA Journal, Oct. 27, 1775, ibid., 58–59.

17. Ibid.; BA to GW, Chaudière Pond [Lake Megantic], Oct. 27 [–28], 1775, *Paps. GW, RWS*, 2:244–45. Earlier that day, BA had advised the abandonment of the bateaux, which many of the exhausted soldiers had already done. BA saw no reason for the troops to keep enduring the weight of their ravaged bateaux when they could move just as fast by walking to the Chaudière River. See BA to Christopher Greene and Others, 2 1/2 Miles on the Great Carrying Place, Oct. 27, 1775, *MQ*, 77.

18. BA Journal, Oct. 27, 1775, ibid., 59.

19. BA to the Field Officers and Others, Chaudière River [Lake Megantic], Oct. 27, 1775, ibid., 79. Virtually nothing is known about Hanchet. Also from Connecticut, he may have been better connected among Connecticut's gentleman-politicians or may have had more extensive military experience than BA. Whatever the case, he began to resent and ultimately disparaged BA's leadership before the end of the year.

20. BA Journal, Oct. 28, 1775, ibid., 59–60.

21. BA Journal, Oct. 29–30, 1775, ibid., 60–61. This valuable document ends here in mid-sentence. BA made a promise to GW to maintain a daily record of the journey to Quebec. Unfortunately, so many difficulties most likely diverted BA from keeping his journal going, unless, of course, portions dated after Oct. 30 were

somehow lost. The extant portion of BA's journal represents an imposing record of personal determination in the face of adversity. See also BA to Officers of the Detachment, Sartigan, Oct. 31, 1775, ibid., 80, in which he relates his success in obtaining food and advises everyone to expend this supply "as sparingly as possible, that the whole may meet with relief."

22. Senter Journal, Oct. 27, 1775, ibid., 213; Thayer Journal, Oct. 28, 1775, ibid., 258.

23. Morison Journal, Oct. 27, 1775, ibid., 522–23. BA issued instructions on this date to abandon the bateaux. See note 17 above.

24. John Joseph Henry Memoir, Oct. 28, 1775, ibid., 335–436. For reports of Morgan's wreck on the Chaudière, see Senter Journal, Oct. 31, 1775, ibid., 218; Melvin Journal, Oct. 30, 1775, ibid., 439; Stocking Journal, Oct. 31, 1775, ibid., 554–55.

25. Senter Journal, Oct. 27–29, 1775, ibid., 214–15; BA to the Field Officers and Others, Chaudière River [Lake Megantic], Oct. 27, 1775, ibid., 79. BA's promise in this letter "in six days from this time to have provisions half way up the river" may have caused some soldiers to be wasteful with these rations. Had BA not delivered on time, many more would have starved to death. See also Thayer Journal, Oct. 28, 1775, ibid., 258–59; Henry Memoir, Oct. 28–29, 1775, 335–36; Fobes Narrative, n.d., ibid., 585.

26. Senter Journal, Oct. 29–30, ibid., 215–17. Fobes Narrative, ibid., 584, mentions the young Indian guide who helped save these soldiers. See also Smith, *Arnold's March*, 196–216.

27. Henry Memoir, Nov. 1, 1775, ibid., 337–38.

28. Stocking Journal, Nov. 2, 1775, ibid., 555–56; Henry Memoir, Nov. 1, 1775, ibid., 337–38. Stocking and Henry may have been reflecting on experiences in the log zone, which would have occurred before Oct. 31.

29. Thayer Journal, Nov. 1, 1775, ibid., 260; Caleb Haskell Diary, Nov. 2, 1775, ibid., 478; Morison Journal, Oct. 31–Nov. 2, 1775, ibid., 524–28.

30. Senter Journal, Nov. 1, 1775, ibid., 218–19. Senter also mentioned that diarrhea had been a constant curse for the soldiers. Now such unappetizing fare resulted in serious cases of constipation, "which continued for many days." Regarding the consumption of dogs, see Dearborn Journal, Nov. 1, 1775, ibid., 139; Thayer Journal, Nov. 1, 1775, ibid., 261; Melvin Journal, Oct. 31, 1775, ibid., 440; Haskell Diary, Oct. 31, 1775, ibid., 478; Morison Journal, Nov. 1, 1775, ibid., 527; and Stocking Journal, Nov. 1, 1775, ibid., 555. The comparative record suggests a total of three or possibly four dogs being consumed. Acts of human cannibalism might have ensued, had BA not delivered food on time.

31. Haskell Diary, Nov. 2, 1775, ibid., 478; Ogden Journal, Lloyd W. Smith Coll., MNHP, 12; Senter Journal, Nov. 2, 1775, *MQ*, 219; Thayer Journal, Nov. 1 [2], 1775, ibid., 261.

32. Fobes Narrative, n.d., ibid., 585–85. The estimate of those who did not

survive is mine. See also Huston, "The Logistics of Arnold's March to Quebec," *Military Analysis Revolutionary War,* 116.

33. BA to Maj. Return J. Meigs, Sartigan, Nov. 1, 1775, *MQ,* 81. Many soldiers complained about exorbitant prices charged by the *habitants,* but none reported incidents of plundering in retaliation. Under the circumstances, the column behaved meritoriously by not alienating the civilian populace, which would have defeated a major purpose of the expedition—to win over the French *habitants* to the cause of liberty. BA was particularly sensitive about this "hearts and minds" issue in scrupulously executing GW's orders. See Instructions 5 and 11, GW to BA, Cambridge, Sept. 14, 1775, *Paps. GW, RWS,* 1:458–59.

34. Henry Memoir, Nov. 6–7, 1775, *MQ,* 346–48. On BA as a money grubber, see Henry's statement, 301.

35. BA to [Capt. Gregory?], Sartigan, Nov. 1, 1775, ibid., 80–81. BA's suspicions were accurate. Mercier may never have seen BA's Oct. 13. letter. Lt. Gov. Cramahé sent an intelligence report to Lord Dartmouth, dated Quebec, Nov. 9, 1775, in which he enclosed a copy of BA's Oct. 13. letter, along with BA's to PS of the same date. See *DAR,* 10:117–18; and Hugh Finlay to Anthony Todd, Quebec, Nov. 1, 1775, ibid., 11:171–72. Wrote Finlay from inside the walled city, "Their intention must be to enter the city by assault, for what else can they pretend to do without cannons." Finlay could only have known about the absence of artillery pieces if Eneas and Sabatis had told Cramahé. GC had learned about BA's march before Nov. 5. See GC to Lord Dartmouth, Montreal, Nov. 5, 1775, ibid., 11:173.

The vessel that carried Cramahé's report to England included among its occupants EA, who was captured on Sept. 25, 1775, in the midst of executing an ill-designed, unauthorized attempt to seize Montreal. Apparently EA thought he could use the element of surprise to repeat his Ticonderoga triumph. Debating whether to hang EA, the British decided to return him to America in 1776 for exchange as a prisoner of war.

36. Senter Journal, Nov. 4, 1775, *MQ,* 220–21; Henry Memoir, Nov. 4, 1775, ibid., 344–45. Senter thought that about fifty Indians enlisted. Ogden Journal, n.d., Lloyd W. Smith Coll., MNHP, 15–16, stated that thirty-two enlisted but only after promises of not having to perform garrison duty. BA to RM, St. Marie [Mary], Nov. 8, 1775, *MQ,* 83, indicated that the number was forty.

37. Senter Journal, Nov. 5, 1775, ibid., 222.

38. Senter Journal, Nov. 7, 1775, ibid., 222.

39. Thayer Journal, Nov. 7–8, 1775, ibid., 262–63. Apparently Natanis's party of Indians were helpful in securing canoes from the local Native American populace.

40. BA to John Manir [John Dyer Mercier], St. Mary's [Mary], Nov. 7, 1775, ibid., 81–82.

41. BA described his visitor as "a friend from Quebec" in his letter to RM, dated St. Marie [Mary], Nov. 8, 1775, ibid., 82–84. The visitor may well have been John Halstead, described below. For conditions in Quebec City, see *Canada Preserved: The*

Journal of Captain Thomas Ainslie, ed. Sheldon S. Cohen (New York, 1968), 20–24. Collector of Customs Ainslie recalled BA as "the master of a vessel trading from New England to this place, and from hence to the West Indies with horses" (21). The British were already denigrating BA as a "horse jockey," or merchant of no consequence. Americans also started using this phrase after the treason incident. See Henry Memoir, Nov. 15, 1775, *MQ,* 355.

42. BA to RM, St. Marie [Mary], Nov. 8, 1775, ibid., 84; BA to GW, Point Levi [Levy], Nov. 8, 1775, *Paps. GW, RWS,* 2:326–27.

43. On Maclean's movements before returning to Quebec, see GC to Lord Dartmouth, Montreal, Nov. 5, 1775, *DAR,* 11:173. On Maclean's crucial reappearance at Quebec City, see Ainslie, *Canada Preserved,* 22. The exact location on the St. Lawrence River where Maclean intercepted BA's letter is not clearly known.

44. Senter Journal, Dec. 31, 1775, *MQ,* 232. On activities while delayed on the southern shore, see Morison Journal, Nov. 8–13, 1775, ibid., 531–32; and Stocking Journal, Nov. 8, 1775, ibid., 558.

45. Thayer Journal, Nov. 12, 1775, ibid., 264. Although no one referred to a briefing by Halstead, such a presentation fits the evidence. On the actual troop strength in Quebec City, see Ainslie, *Canada Preserved,* 23–24. The number of defenders under arms, whether enthusiastic or reluctant, reached eighteen hundred by Nov. 30.

46. In his Nov. 8 letter to Montgomery from St. Marie [Mary], *MQ,* 82–84, BA indicated that he would besiege the city, based on intelligence that Cramahé's numbers were superior to his own. What he wanted on Nov. 12 was permission to take advantage of favorable circumstances, but a majority of his officers preferred the cautionary course. See BA to RM, Point Levi [Levy], Nov. 14 [13], 1775, ibid., 85–86; and BA to GW, Point Levi [Levy], Nov. 14 [13], 1775, *Paps. GW, RWS,* 2:358.

47. Dearborn Journal, Nov. 13, 1775, *MQ,* 141–42, and Senter Journal, Nov. 13, 1775, ibid., 224–25, provide descriptions of the crossing. See also BA to RM, Colvil [?] Place, Nov. 14, 1775, ibid., 87–88.

48. Senter Journal, Nov. 13, ibid., 225, stated that patriot troops fired on the barge "contrary to orders." Thayer claimed that he, BA, and four others hailed the barge, as if they intended to capture the craft and its crew (Thayer Journal, Nov. 13, ibid., 264). See also BA to Capt. Oliver Hanchet, n.p., Nov. [14?], 1775, ibid., 88.

49. Henry Memoir, Nov. 15, 1775, ibid., 352–53, was the source for the story about St. John's Gate being open. Henry stated that DM was anxious to attack but that no one, not even BA, would listen. Senter, more in touch with BA's officers, wrote that any preemptive strike would have been impossible early on Nov. 14. "The gates were all closed, cannons in order, etc.," which Senter attributed to the presence of Maclean. See Senter Journal, Nov. 13, 1775, ibid., 225, and the explanation by editor Kenneth Roberts, 225 n. 17.

50. Henry Memoir, Nov. 15, 1775, ibid., 354–55, had no idea what the outmanned and outgunned BA was trying to accomplish; he considered the demonstration of force nothing other than a "vain desire to gratify" BA's ego. Henry likewise wrote,

"Having no obtained power, he [BA] became anxious to display it in the face of those who had formerly despised and condemned him." Henry apparently had no idea about the tactics of intimidation, which in this case failed miserably for BA.

51. BA to Honble. H. T. Cramahé, Camp before Quebec, Nov. 14, 1775, ibid., 89–90; Ogden Journal, Nov. 14–15, 1775, Lloyd W. Smith Coll., MNHP, 46–50.

52. BA to Honble. H. T. Cramahé, Camp before Quebec, Nov. 15, 1775, *MQ,* 88. Included with Cramahé's report to Lord Dartmouth about defending the city, dated Quebec, Nov. 19, 1775, *DAR,* 10:133, were copies of BA's two letters. BA thus found some other way to get these messages into the city.

53. Return J. Meigs Journal, Nov. 16–17, 1775, *MQ,* 183; and Thayer Journal, Nov. 18, 1775, ibid., 265, among other accounts. Henry claimed to have been with Sgt. Dixon when he was shot. In cracker-barrel fashion, he claimed that the mortally wounded Dixon, when offered tea by a solicitous local housewife, replied, "No, madam, it is the ruin of my country." See Henry Memoir, Nov. 16, 1775, ibid., 356–60.

54. Senter Journal, Nov. 18, 1775, ibid., 226; and Thayer Journal, Nov. 19, 1775, ibid., 265–66, among other accounts. See also BA to RM, Point[e] aux Trembles, Nov. 20, 1775, ibid., 90–92; and BA to GW, Point[e] aux Trembles, Nov. 20, 1775, *Paps. GW, RWS,* 2:403–4.

55. BA estimated the defenders of Quebec at 1,870, including four hundred neutrals and six hundred of no description. He guessed that about six hundred of the defenders would lay down their arms and join the rebels, if given the opportunity. He also stated that cannons could not breach the walls but that mortars would be effective in "throwing shells" over the walls and "would soon bring them to compliance." A successful assault, he guessed, would require two thousand troops. See BA to RM, Point[e] aux Trembles, Nov. 20, 1775, *MQ,* 90–92. A strength report from inside Quebec, dated Nov. 16, 1775, indicated that 1,311 persons were under arms. This figure is only slightly lower than BA's estimate, since he included four hundred neutrals not yet under arms. See Return of Men for Defense of Quebec, *DAR,* 10:135.

56. On BA's friendship with McNeill and his family, see BA to Capt. Hector McNeill, Holland House [near Quebec], Jan. 18, 1776, *NDAR,* 3:840–41.

57. BA to RM, Point[e] aux Trembles, Nov. 20, 1775, *MQ,* 92; BA to Messrs. Prince [James Price] and Haywood, and BA to Jos[eph] Terry, Point[e] aux Trembles, Nov. 20, 1775, ibid., 94; BA to [James Clinton?], Point[e] aux Trembles, Nov. 25, 1775, ibid., 96–97.

58. BA to [PS?], Point[e] aux Trembles, Nov. 27, 1775, ibid., 97–99.

59. BA to GW, Point[e] aux Trembles, Nov. 20, 1775, *Paps. GW, RWS,* 2:403.

SEVEN: *Liberty or Death at the Walls of Quebec*

1. Although deserving of a full-scale biography, GC has not yet received such a treatment. Paul R. Reynolds, *Guy Carleton: A Biography* (Toronto, 1980), 1–88, provides a summary of GC's life into the Revolutionary years. Perry Eugene Leroy,

"Sir Guy Carleton as a Military Leader during the American Invasion and Repulse in Canada, 1775–1776" (2 vols., doctoral dissertation, Ohio State University, 1960), focuses on GC as a military commander and administrator but takes little notice of his life (see 1:112–27, for material relating to this chapter). Other secondary works informing this chapter include Flood, *Rise and Fight Again*, 43–69; French, *First Year of the Revolution*, 595–620; Hatch, *Thrust for Canada*, 121–36; Isaac Q. Leake, *Memoir of the Life and Times of General John Lamb* (Albany, 1850), 123–30; Hal T. Shelton, *General Richard Montgomery and the American Revolution* (New York, 1994), 116–50; Smith, *Struggle Fourteenth Colony*, 2:76–132; Stanley, *Canada Invaded*, 77–98; Ward, *War of the Revolution*, 1:181–96; and Wrong, *Canada and the Revolution*, 297–303.

2. GC to Lord Dartmouth, Montreal, Oct. 25 and Nov. 5, 1775, *DAR*, 11:165–66, 173.

3. Ainslie, *Canada Preserved*, 22; GC to Lord Dartmouth, Quebec, Nov. 20, 1775, *DAR*, 11:185–86.

4. Dearborn Journal, Nov. 20, 1775, *MQ*, 143, and Senter Journal, Nov. 20, 1775, ibid., 227, note the receipt of official news about RM's capture of Montreal. See also RM to PS, Montreal, Nov. 19, 20, 22, 1775, *AA*, 4 ser., 3:1682–84.

5. BA to the Officers . . . on the Way from Montreal to Quebec, Point[e] aux Trembles, Nov. 24, 25, 1775, *MQ*, 95; BA to RM, Point[e] aux Trembles, Nov. 15, 1775, ibid., 96. See also Journal of H.M.S. *Lizard*, Nov. 23, 1775, *NDAR*, 2:1124. With advancing winter weather, the British vessels quickly returned to Quebec harbor to assure themselves safe dockage until springtime.

6. BA to [Col. James Clinton?], Point[e] aux Trembles, Nov. 25, 1775, *MQ*, 96; A Proclamation by His Excellency Guy Carleton, *AA*, 4 ser., 3:1639–40.

7. Ainslie, *Canada Preserved*, 22–24. Among those prominent citizens who left Quebec were Udnay Hay, who joined the patriot force as a quartermaster; John Bondfield, as a commissary; and Edward Antill, as chief engineer.

8. Before GC returned, leaders attending a council of war called by Cramahé on Nov. 16 discussed the state of provisions, a copy of which was attached to a letter from Cramahé to Lord Dartmouth, dated Quebec, Nov. 19, 1775, *DAR*, 10:133. See also *A History of the Organization, Development and Services of the Military and Naval Forces of Canada from the Peace of Paris in 1763, to the Present Time*, ed. Ernest Cruikshank (2 vols., Ottawa, n.d.), 2:128–30, which contains the council of war minutes. Allan Maclean said the provisions were inadequate to withstand a long siege in writing to Viscount Barrington, dated Quebec, Nov. 20, 1775, ibid., 2:132–33. Capt. John Hamilton, who commanded the *Lizard*, stated otherwise to Vice Adm. Samuel Graves, dated Quebec, Nov. 20, 1775, *NDAR*, 2:1074. He thought the provisions could last until nearly May 15, roughly six months. Collector Ainslie, *Canada Preserved*, 24, gave the most optimistic projection—about eight months. Quebec's leaders were hoping to be relieved by the end of May or early June 1776 at the latest.

9. RM to PS, Montreal, Nov. 20, 1775, *AA*, 4 ser., 3:1684; Recruiting Appeal,

signed James Van Rensselaer, Nov. 15, 1775, ibid., 4 ser., 3:1683–84; RM to PS, Montreal, Nov. 17, 1775, ibid., 4 ser., 3:1633.

10. RM to PS, Montreal, Nov. 19, 1775, ibid., 4 ser., 3:1682–83; RM to PS, Montreal, Nov. 24, 1775, ibid., 4 ser., 3:1694–95.

11. BA to the Officers . . . on Their Way from Montreal to Quebec, Point[e] aux Trembles, Nov. 30, 1775, *MQ,* 101; BA to RM, Point[e] aux Trembles, Nov. 30, 1775, ibid., 101. BA's troop returns, dated Nov. 29, 1775, show 675 officers and soldiers under his command. RM had about 650 troops with him. BA enclosed a copy of his return (see GW Paps., microfilm reel 34, 4 ser., LC) in a letter to GW, dated Before Quebec, Dec. 5, 1775, *Paps. GW, RWS,* 2:495. In this letter, BA said that RM arrived on Dec. 3. Most diarists (see note 13 below) agree that RM got to Pointe aux Trembles on Dec. 1, although Smith, *Struggle Fourteenth Colony,* 2:87, 577, claimed that Dec. 2 was the date. Had that been the case, BA would have not had his confrontation that day with Hanchet, since BA was executing RM's orders (see note 18). Nor would the row galleys have been available, since they helped transport RM and his force.

12. Henry Memoir, Dec. 1, 1775, *MQ,* 363. In GW to BA, Cambridge, Dec. 5, 1775, *Paps. GW, RWS,* 2:494, GW reminded BA that he was not to question but to accept RM's command authority.

13. Thayer Journal, Dec. 2, 1775, *MQ,* 270; Henry Memoir, Dec. 1, 1775, ibid., 363; Morison Journal, Nov. 20, 1775, ibid., 534.

14. Shelton, *Richard Montgomery,* 8–115.

15. Conversation based on RM to Robert R. Livingston, Montreal, Nov. 1775, *AA,* 4 ser., 3:1638–39.

16. Thayer Journal, Nov. 22, 1775, *MQ,* 268. Desertion became a serious problem over the next month, particularly with regard to rebel troops who turned themselves over to British authorities in Quebec and revealed what they knew about patriot plans for harassing and storming the city.

17. RM to PS, Holland House near the Heights of Abraham, Dec. 5, 1775, *AA,* 4 ser., 4:188–90.

18. Thayer Journal, Dec. 2–4, 1775, *MQ,* 269–71.

19. Thayer Journal, Dec. 7–8, 1775, ibid., 271.

20. Ainslie, Dec. 2–3, 1775, *Canada Preserved,* 25.

21. Ainslie, Dec. 6, 1775, ibid., 26; RM to English Merchants, Holland House, Dec. 6, 1775, and RM to GC, Holland House, Dec. 6, 1775, Cruikshank, ed., *Military and Naval Forces,* 2:136–38 (*AA,* 4 ser., 4:289–90, misdated RM's Dec. 6 communication to GC as Dec. 16); GC to William Howe, Quebec, Jan. 12, 1776, ibid., 4 ser., 4:656; Extract of a Letter from a Gentleman in the Continental Service, Quebec, Dec. 16, 1775, ibid., 4 ser., 4:290.

22. Ainslie, Dec. 15, 1775, *Canada Preserved,* 29; Extract of a Letter from Lt. Van Wagenen, Before Quebec, Dec. 16, 1775, *AA,* 4 ser., 4:290.

23. Henry Memoir, Dec. 12, 1775, *MQ,* 364–68. Henry apparently did not see

any inconsistency in condemning BA as a lover of filthy lucre while admitting to his own plundering of the enemy's private property. Still, Henry was refreshingly honest; no other chronicler admitted to pillaging activities.

24. Ainslie, Dec. 8, 1775, *Canada Preserved,* 27. See also Ainslie's entries for Dec. 12 and 18, 1775, ibid., 28, 30.

25. Senter Journal, Dec. 9, 1775, *MQ,* 228.

26. Ibid.; Ainslie, Dec. 11, 1775, *Canada Preserved,* 28.

27. Meigs Journal, Dec. 11, 1775, *MQ,* 186. For descriptions of the ice battery, see Senter Journal, December 14, 1775, ibid., 229; Henry Memoir, Dec. 15, 1775, ibid., 369; and Fobes Narrative, n.d., ibid., 589.

28. Ainslie, Dec. 10, 1775, *Canada Preserved,* 27–28. See also Senter Journal, Dec. 10, 1775, *MQ,* 228–29, who thought another reason for "this *incineration* was to prevent our troops making a lodgement in them, and facilitating the operation of a general storm upon the city, which they had too much reason to apprehend."

29. Fobes Narrative, n.d., ibid., 589; Ainslie, Dec. 14, 1775, *Canada Preserved,* 29. On Warner's death, see Haskell Diary, Dec. 11, 1775, *MQ,* 483. About fifteen patriots were killed or wounded as a result of the various artillery exchanges. The number of casualties inside Quebec could not have numbered more than five. The destruction of the ice battery convinced RM and BA that only a full-scale assault could reduce the city to submission. See RM to DW, Headquarters before Quebec, Dec. 16, 1775, *AA,* 4 ser., 4:288–89.

30. Ainslie, Dec. 8 and 24, 1775, *Canada Preserved,* 27, 32; RM to PS, Headquarters before Quebec, Dec. 26, 1775, *AA,* 4 ser., 4:465.

31. Henry Memoir, Dec. 24, 1775, *MQ,* 374; Senter Journal, Dec. 17–23, 1775, ibid., 230; Haskell Diary, Dec. 16–Dec. 31, 1775, ibid., 484–85. Haskell missed the Dec. 31 assault because he was still recovering from smallpox.

32. Meigs Journal, ibid., 187. Meigs either was aligning himself with the Hanchet dissidents or playing the role of a mediator. See his entries of Dec. 17 and 23, 1775, ibid., 187. Goodrich and Hubbard were from western Massachusetts and likely knew John Brown.

33. RM to PS, Headquarters before Quebec, Dec. 26, 1775, *AA,* 4 ser., 4:464–65. No one named JB as the primary agitator, but the weight of evidence points toward him.

34. Dearborn Journal, Dec. 25, 1775, *MQ,* 148; Meigs Journal, Dec. 25, 1775, ibid., 186–87; Senter Journal, Dec. 27, 1775, ibid., 230–31, which also contains a copy of BA's note to Senter.

35. RM laid out this plan in writing to DW, dated Headquarters before Quebec, Dec. 16, 1775, *AA,* 4 ser., 4:288–89. See also Thayer Journal, Dec. 27, 1775, *MQ,* 273. To keep up morale afterward, Montgomery prepared a statement expressing his "pleasure in seeing the good disposition with which the troops last night moved to the attack." However, too many lives would have been lost had the escalade proceeded. The patriots were to remain on alert, knowing that he was waiting only for

the first "favorable opportunity" to storm the city. See Dearborn Journal, Dec. 28, 1775, ibid., 148.

36. Whether Hanchet and the other dissidents participated in the feint is not clear. More than likely they did. If they sat by idly, then the haltering ceremony described below had even greater cogency. Thayer Journal, Dec. 27, 1775, ibid., 273, remains the only record of troop dispositions.

37. Thayer Journal, including John Topham entry, Dec. 28, 1775, ibid., 273–74. BA may have helped inspire or initiate this public ceremony; he maintained cordial relations with these two captains, who always seemed eager to support him.

38. Senter Journal, Dec. 31, 1775, ibid., 232; Henry Memoir, Dec. 24, 1775, ibid., 374.

39. General Orders, Holland House, Dec. 15, 1775, Ainslie, *Canada Preserved*, 93–94. RM's frustration in not getting GC to surrender short of an all-out attack came out in his letter to DW, Headquarters before Quebec, Dec. 16, 1775, *AA*, 4 ser., 4:288–89, written after BA's Dec. 15 rebuff by the Hanchet dissidents and the demonstrated uselessness of the ice battery.

40. Ainslie, Dec. 22, 23, 24, and 30, 1775, *Canada Preserved*, 31–33. Henry Memoir, Dec. 24, 1775, *MQ*, 373–74, mentioned Singleton's defection as well as the inappropriate behavior of his own company commander, Capt. Matthew Smith. Smith knew the details of the planned assault for Dec. 27 but talked too much. Henry noted under Jan. 1, 1776, that Smith missed the assault for "particular causes" (p. 375). Apparently, Smith was too drunk to participate, and his indiscreet mouthing of secret plans no doubt reflected his inability to remain sober. RM was much more careful in guarding the details of his revised plan after Dec. 27.

41. The account that follows is based on "General Daniel Morgan: An Autobiography," *HM*, 2 ser., 9 (1871): 379–80; Ainslie, Dec. 31, 1775, *Canada Preserved*, 33–38; and *MQ* chroniclers: Dearborn Journal, Dec. 31, 1775, 149–55; Meigs Journal, Dec. 31, 1775, 189–92; Senter Journal, Dec. 31, 1775, 232–35; Thayer Journal, Dec. 30, 1775, 189–92; Henry Memoir, Jan. 1, 1776, 375–83; Melvin Journal, Dec. 31, 1775, 442; Haskell Diary, Jan. 1, 1776, 485–86; Morison Journal, n.d., 535–38; Stocking Journal, n.d., 562–66; and Fobes Narrative, n.d., 589–91. For some reason, Capt. Jacob Brown, JB's younger brother, led the Cape Diamond diversionary operation. JB's whereabouts during the battle are not clearly known.

42. Ainslie, Dec. 31, 1775, *Canada Preserved*, 37–38; Henry Memoir, Dec. 24, 1775, *MQ*, 374.

43. Stocking Journal, n.d., ibid., 562. In the immediate wake of the battle, Col. Donald Campbell, who was with RM, wrote, "Thus you have the four attacks . . . *which was, in many respects, hurried,* from the circumstance of the enlistment of the troops under Colonel Arnold, whose service expires this day." To DW, Holland House, Dec. 31, 1775, *AA*, 4 ser., 4:481 (italics mine).

44. Senter Journal, Dec. 31, 1775, *MQ*, 232–33.

45. Ainslie, Dec. 31, 1775, *Canada Preserved*, 33–34.

46. The accounts indicate a variety of alignments regarding the order of battle, certainly not a significant issue, since BA's column proceeded along the pathway single file. A few of Lamb's artillerists, operating under Capt. Isaiah Wool, remained in St. Roch and fired cannon shots into the Upper Town. Their objective was to create additional confusion among the Carletonians.

47. DM, "Autobiography," *HM*, 2 ser. (1871): 379, stated that he was part of the forlorn hope. Most accounts have DM starting out at the head of the riflemen, immediately behind Lamb's artillerists. BA implied that he participated in the breakthrough before being shot. See BA to DW, General Hospital, Dec. 31, 1775, *MQ*, 102. This comment indicated his confusion and frustration immediately after being wounded, which forced BA to leave the scene of action before fully engaging the enemy. Statements in Dearborn Journal, Dec. 31, 1775, ibid., 149, seem to support BA's intimation about not retiring until after the first barrier was breached.

48. Henry Memoir, Jan. 1, 1776, ibid., 376–77; Fobes Narrative, n.d., ibid., 590, had BA imploring: "Rush on, brave boys." Fobes also spoke of "strict orders, before we marched, not to stop for the wounded or the dying" (590–91). BA thus was an exception; if orders had been followed in his case, he likely would have died in the snow.

49. Senter Journal, Dec. 31, 1775, ibid., 233–34.

50. Senter Journal, Dec. 31, 1775, ibid., 234.

51. Donald Campbell to DW, Holland House, Dec. 31, 1775, *AA*, 4 ser., 4:480–81. None of the diarists was with RM, but a few (see Henry Memoir, Jan. 1, 1776, *MQ*, 385–88) offered after-action details. See also Ainslie, Dec. 31, 1775, *Canada Preserved*, 36. Maj. Meigs, as a ranking officer among those captured, was asked to view and identify RM's remains. He stated that RM was shot through the head and both thighs (Meigs Journal, Dec. 31, 1775, *MQ*, 191). For what is likely John Coffin's account, see Extract of a Letter from a Gentleman in Quebec to Nathaniel Legge, Quebec, May 13, 1776, *The Manuscripts of the Earl of Dartmouth*, Historical Manuscripts Commission (3 vols., London, 1887–1896), 1:405–7.

52. Senter Journal, Dec. 31, 1775, *MQ*, 234.

53. Senter Journal, Dec. 31, 1775, ibid., 234–35.

54. BA to DW, General Hospital, Dec. 31, 1775, ibid., 102–3; Donald Campbell to DW, Holland House, Dec. 31, 1775, *AA*, 4 ser., 4:480–81.

55. BA to [HA?], Camp before Quebec, Jan. 6, 1776, *MQ*, 108–9.

EIGHT: *A Winter's Worth of Making Brick without Straw*

1. Senter Journal, Dec. 31, 1775–Jan. 1, 1776, *MQ*, 235. BA's biographers have skimmed over the three and a half months covered, which are critical to appreciating BA's education as a military commander. Secondary works informing this chapter include Allan S. Everest, *Moses Hazen and the Canadian Refugees in the American Revolution* (Syracuse, 1976), 15–36; Flood, *Rise and Fight Again*, 69–80; French, *First Year of the Revolution*, 686–93; Hatch, *Thrust for Canada*, 136–48; Charles Henry

Jones, *History of the Campaign for the Conquest of Canada in 1776: From the Death of Montgomery to the Retreat of the British Army under Sir Guy Carleton* (Philadelphia, 1882), 1–32; Lanctot, *Canada and the Revolution,* 105–23; Leake, *Life of John Lamb,* 130–45; Rossie, *Politics of Command,* 46–60, 78–95; Doyen Salsig, ed., *Parole: Quebec; Countersign: Ticonderoga: Second New Jersey Regimental Orderly Book, 1776* (Rutherford, N.J., 1980), 29–74; Shelton, *Richard Montgomery,* 116–71; Smith, *Struggle Fourteenth Colony,* 2:132–207, 245–93; Stanley, *Canada Invaded,* 98–108; and Ward, *War of the Revolution,* 1:196–201.

    2. Ainslie, Dec. 31, 1775, *Canada Preserved,* 37–38, stated that 426 rebel prisoners were taken prisoner, of whom 44 were wounded. *The Toll of Independence: Engagements and Battle Casualties of the American Revolution,* ed. Howard H. Peckham (Chicago, 1974), 11, presents a more conservative figure of 387 captured.

    3. DM, "Autobiography," *HM,* 2 ser. (1871): 380. For accounts of the battle, see chapter 7, note 41. See also "Journal of the Siege from 1st Dec., 1775," Dec. 31, 1775, and "Journal of the Principal Occurrences during the Siege of Quebec . . . in 1775–1776," Dec. 31, 1775, in *Blockade of Quebec in 1775–1776 by the American Revolutionists (Les Bostonnais),* ed. Fred C. Würtele (Quebec, 1905; reprint, Port Washington, N.Y., 1970), 17–19, 66–70; and John F. Roche, "Quebec under Siege: The 'Memorandums' of Jacob Danford," Dec. 31, 1775, *CHR,* 50 (1969): 72–74. These commentators admirably complement Ainslie's account.

    4. Dearborn Journal, Dec. 31. 1775, *MQ,* 150–51.

    5. Morison Journal, Dec. 31, 1775, ibid., 538.

    6. Thayer Journal, Jan. 1, 1776, ibid., 278. On the rebel casualty figures, see Peckham, *Toll of Independence,* 11. British casualties are based on estimates in GC to WH, Quebec, Jan. 12, 1776, *AA,* 4 ser., 4:656.

    7. Return J. Meigs to BA, Middletown, [Ct.], July 29, 1776, "Documents sur l'Invasion Américaine," *RULQ,* 2 (1948): 643. BA apparently offered funds from his own purse as temporary loans without interest. However, BA had no way of knowing if he would ever be repaid, since the famine proof veterans were prisoners of war. Whether BA ever received much in the way of repayment is unclear.

    8. BA to DW, General Hospital, Jan. 2, 1776, *MQ,* 103–6; Donald Campbell to DW, Headquarters before Quebec, Jan. 2, 1776, *AA,* 4 ser., 4:670.

    9. BA to GW, Camp before Quebec, Jan. 14, 1776, *Paps. GW, RWS,* 3:81–83. BA had earlier indicated that he would turn the command temporarily over to Campbell. See BA to DW, General Hospital, Dec. 31, 1775, *MQ,* 103. BA changed his mind after several officers, in looking for a scapegoat, denounced Campbell. At no point, however, did BA directly condemn Campbell in writing. Campbell had earlier assumed responsibilities as RM's quartermaster, and he technically outranked BA. He was a junior British officer during the Seven Years' War, after which he sold his commission. Somehow he convinced the Crown to deed him twenty thousand acres in the Champlain region of New York before fleeing to America to evade pressing financial obligations. Campbell had nothing to lose by joining the patriot cause, since his major British creditors had placed a lien on his New York property. All the

reproachful talk about Campbell after the patriot defeat at Quebec effectively ended his patriot military career.

10. BA to DW, General Hospital, Jan. 2, 1776, *MQ,* 106. BA again wrote DW from Holland House on Jan. 4 and Jan. 5, 1776, in much less frenzied fashion. He apologized for the "incorrectness" of his Jan. 2 letter, which he was "obliged to write lying on my back" (Jan. 4), and then indicated (Jan. 5) that "I am anxious to see you here." See ibid., 106, 108. BA no doubt understood that he may have insulted DW's sensibilities; however, he showed his true feelings when he urged GW to send someone such as Maj. Gen. Charles Lee to Quebec. See note 17 below. For GW's doubts about DW's capacities, see his letter to Joseph Reed, Cambridge, Jan. 23, 1776, *Paps. GW, RWS,* 3:173. For DW's clashes with PS, see Rossie, *Politics of Command,* 45–56.

11. James Knowles to His Wife, Camp before Quebec, Jan. 15, 1776, Sol Feinstone Coll., DLAR [APS].

12. Message signed by Charles de Lanaudière, Jr., [Quebec], Jan. 4, 1776, contained in BA to DW, Holland House, Jan. 5, 1776, *AA,* 4 ser., 4:854–55.

13. BA to GW, Camp before Quebec, Jan. 14, 1776, *Paps. GW, RWS,* 3:81.

14. BA to Continental Congress, Camp before Quebec, Jan. 11, 1776, *MQ,* 109–13. BA correctly assumed the British would send a large force to Canada that spring, not only to drive off the patriots but also to invade the rebellious colonies from the north in an effort to cut off New England. On Britain's overall strategy for 1776, see Martin and Lender, *A Respectable Army,* 48–63; James Kirby Martin, "The Continental Army and the American Victory," in *The World Turned Upside Down: The American Victory in the War of Independence,* ed. John Ferling (Westport, 1988), 19–34; and Piers Mackesy, *The War for America, 1775–1783* (Cambridge, 1964), 57–80.

15. BA to Continental Congress, Camp before Quebec, Jan. 12, 1776, *MQ,* 113. See also BA to GW, Camp before Quebec, Jan. 14, 1776, *Paps. GW, RWS,* 3:81–83.

16. BA to GW, Camp before Quebec, Feb. 27, 1776, ibid., 3:381. For similar comments about the protective hand of Providence, see BA to [HA?], Camp before Quebec, Jan. 6. 1776, *MQ,* 108–9.

17. BA to Continental Congress, Camp before Quebec, Jan. 11, 1776, ibid., 111; BA to GW, Camp before Quebec, Jan. 14, 1776, *Paps. GW, RWS,* 3:83.

18. On the enigmatic Lee, see John Shy, "American Strategy: Charles Lee and the Radical Alternative," in *A People Numerous and Armed: Reflections on the Military Struggle for American Independence* (New York, 1976), 133–62. See also Rossie, *Politics of Command,* 78–95.

19. PS to JH, Pres. Congress, Ticonderoga, Nov. 22, 1775, *NDAR,* 2:1100; PS to GW, Ticonderoga, Nov. 22, 1775, *Paps. GW, RWS,* 2:417; PS to GW, Albany, Dec. 9, 1775, ibid., 2:523–24; GW to PS, Cambridge, Dec. 5, 1775, ibid., 2:498; GW to BA, Cambridge, Dec. 5, 1775, ibid., 2:493–94.

20. James Warren to SA, Watertown, Dec. 5, 1775, *The Warren-Adams Letters,* MHS *Collections,* ed. Worthington C. Ford (2 vols., Boston, 1917–1925), 2:428; Thomas Jefferson to John Page, Phila., c. Dec. 10, 1775, *The Papers of Thomas*

Jefferson, ed. Julian P. Boyd et al. (26 vols. to date, Princeton, 1950–), 1:270–71. See also NG to Samuel Ward, Prospect Hill, Mass., Dec. 18, 1775, *Paps. NG,* 1:165; and Samuel Ward to Deborah Ward, Phila., Dec. 25, 1775, *LDC,* 2:519. Wrote Ward, "Arnold's march is considered here as the greatest action done this war. Some say it equals Xenophon's retreat from Persia, others that nothing greater has been done since the days of Alexander."

21. GW to BA, Cambridge, Dec. 5, 1775, *Paps. GW, RWS,* 2:494. In General Orders, Cambridge, Dec. 28, 1775, ibid., 2:615, GW named BA a regimental commander for the 1776 campaign season. Lieut. Col. John Durkee took command of BA's 20th Continental Regiment in BA's absence. See Jonathan Trumbull to GW, Lebanon, Ct., Jan. 1, 1776, ibid., 3:9–10. For the alignment of regiments, see General Orders, Cambridge, Jan. 24, 1776, ibid., 3:176–77.

22. GW to JH, Pres. Congress, Cambridge, Dec. 31, 1775, ibid., 2:622–23; and GW to BA, Cambridge, Jan. 12, 1776, ibid., 3:72.

23. SD to Elizabeth Deane, Phila., Jan. 13, 1776, *LDC,* 3:89–90; SD to Thomas Mumford, Phila., Jan. 25, 1776, ibid., 3:151; Joseph Hewes to Robert Smith, Phila., Jan. 8, 1776, ibid., 3:58; Richard Smith Diary, Phila., Jan. 8, 9, 10, 1776, ibid, 3:60, 72, 80; and Weds., Jan. 10, 1776, *JCC,* 4:47. Taking advantage of BA's enhanced reputation before Congress, SD also secured for BA a favorable financial settlement for Ticonderoga. See SD to HA, Phila., Jan. 24, 1776, *Colls. Ct. Hist. Soc.,* 2 (1870): 354–55.

24. Richard Smith Diary, Phila., Jan. 17, 1776, *LDC,* 3:108–9; Naval Committee [Joseph Hewes, Stephen Hopkins, and SD] to Esek Hopkins, Phila., Jan. 18, 1776, ibid., 3:111–12; Council of War, Cambridge, Jan. 18, 1776, *Paps. GW, RWS,* 3:132–34. Congress issued a public statement regarding the Dec. 31 defeat. See Weds., Jan. 24, 1776, *JCC,* 4:83–84.

25. PS to JH, Pres. Congress, Albany, Dec. 26 and Dec. 31, 1775, *AA,* 4 ser., 4:463–64, 480.

26. Mon., Jan. 8, 1776, *JCC,* 4:39–40; Richard Smith Diary, Phila., Jan. 8, 1776, *LDC,* 3:60.

27. Everest, *Moses Hazen,* 30–36; Thurs.–Weds., Jan. 18–24, 1776, *JCC,* 4:65–84. The other messenger was Edward Antill, whom BA dispatched from Quebec shortly after the Dec. 31 repulse. Antill apparently reported to Congress on Jan. 18. Four days later, the delegates awarded Antill a lieutenant colonel's commission to serve as second in command of what became Moses Hazen's 2d Canadian Regiment, which Congress had established on Jan. 20.

28. JH to GW, Phila., Jan. 20, 29, 1776, *Paps. GW, RWS,* 3:152–53, 210–11; PS to GW, Albany, Jan. 13, 1776, ibid., 3:78–79; GW to PS, Cambridge, Jan. 18, 1776, ibid., 3:141–42. See also GW to JH, Pres. Congress, Cambridge, Jan. 19, 30 [31], 1776, ibid., 3:146–48, 214–15.

29. GW to Joseph Reed, Cambridge, Jan. 31, 1776, ibid., 3:228. See also DW to Seth Warner, Montreal, Jan. 6, 1776, *AA,* 4 ser., 4:588–89; and DW to GW, Montreal, Jan. 21, 1776, *Paps. GW, RWS,* 3:164–66.

30. BA to Continental Congress, Camp before Quebec, Jan. 24, 1776, *MQ,* 117–19; BA to JH, Pres. Congress, Camp before Quebec, Feb. 1, 1776, ibid., 119–20; Haskell Diary, Feb. 4, 1776, ibid., 489.

31. Count de Guines to Count de Vergennes, London, Jan. 12, 1776, *NDAR,* 3:504–5. De Guines regularly reported to Vergennes on the thoughts and activities of the British ministry. He also repeated the latest rumors, such as this wild story, contained in his letter to Vergennes, dated London, Feb. 23, 1776 (ibid., 3:928): "Mr. Montgomery's father-in-law [Robert R. Livingston], a man who displayed much zeal and held a leading position in the rebel party, hanged himself following the events of the first of January."

32. HG to [?], Cambridge, Jan. 30, 1776, *NDAR,* 3:1047; and BA to [possibly HA or SD?], Holland House, Mar. 26, 1776, *AA,* 4 ser., 5:512. Just in case his letter somehow fell into the hands of the enemy, as had happened to him during the autumn of 1775, BA revealed only selected elements of his plan.

33. BA to GW, Camp before Quebec, Feb. 27, 1776, *Paps. GW, RWS,* 3:381–82; BA to SD, Camp before Quebec, Mar. 30, 1776, *AA,* 4 ser., 5:549–50, which contains BA's general orders of Feb. 12 as well as his Mar. 30 return of troops. BA's troop strength reports may also be found in the GW Paps., microfilm reel 35, 4 ser., LC.

34. BA to Col. James Clinton, Holland House, Mar. 26, 1776, Autograph Catalogue of A. S. Rosenbach, *History of America* (1949), 74–75, Am. Mss. Colls., AAS. On smallpox inoculation or "variolation," see Duffy, *Epidemics,* 23–42.

35. Desperate for troop strength at this juncture, BA was even willing to accept some Green Mountain Boys. See BA to SD, Camp before Quebec, Mar. 30, 1776, *AA,* 4 ser., 5:549. On the serious problem of short-term enlistments more generally, see GW to Joseph Reed, Cambridge, Feb. 1, 1776, *Paps. GW, RWS,* 3:238; and Martin and Lender, *A Respectable Army,* 69–78.

36. Haskell Diary, Jan. 15, 1776, *MQ,* 487; Ainslie, Jan. 29, 1776, *Canada Preserved,* 45–46; "Journal of the Siege," Jan. 29, 1776, Würtele, ed., *Blockade of Quebec,* 22.

37. Ainslie, Feb. 9–12, 1776, *Canada Preserved,* 48–49; BA to [possibly HA or SD?], Holland House, Mar. 26, 1776, *AA,* 4 ser., 5:512.

38. Ainslie, Jan. 25, 1776, *Canada Preserved,* 45; "Journal of the Principal Occurrences," Jan. 25, 1776, and "Journal of the Siege," Jan. 25, 1776, Würtele, ed., *Blockade of Quebec,* 75, 22.

39. Ainslie, Jan. 25, 1776, *Canada Preserved,* 44; "Journal of the Siege," Jan. 27, 1776, Würtele, ed. *Blockade of Quebec,* 22.

40. "Journal of the Siege," Feb. 18–19, 1776, ibid., 26; Ainslie, Feb. 20, 1776, *Canada Preserved,* 51–52.

41. Ainslie, Jan. 23, 1776, ibid., 44. On Mar. 9, Ainslie (62) accurately reported that Quebec's defenders had one hundred more artillery pieces than did the rebels. BA had only fifteen pieces, a major disadvantage in any proposed assault, as he reported to [possibly HA or SD?], Holland House, Mar. 26, 1776, *AA,* 4 ser., 5:512.

42. BA to Continental Congress, Camp before Quebec, Jan. 24, 1776, *MQ,* 117.

43. BA to SD, Camp before Quebec, Mar. 30, 1776, *AA,* 4 ser., 5:550.

44. BA maintained regular communications with McNeill. See BA to Capt. Hector McNeill, Holland House, Jan. 18, 1776, *MQ,* 116; BA to Mrs. Hector McNeill, Holland House, Jan. 27, 1776, "Mimeo," 957, Am. Mss. Colls., AAS; BA to Capt. [Hector] McNeill, Holland House, Mar.[?] 1776, *The Collector* (n.d.), 76, Am. Mss. Colls., AAS; and BA to Capt. Hector McNeill, Holland House, Mar. 21, and Mar. 29, 1776, Ford Coll., NYPL.

45. Ainslie, Jan. 25, 1776, *Canada Preserved,* 45, noted BA's troops transporting rum from the brigantine back to their camp. See also Ainslie's entries of Apr. 25 and May 3, 1776, ibid., 83–84, 87–88. The latter entry suggests that the brigantine was BA's. That BA had a vessel in the vicinity is confirmed in HA to SD, New Haven, Feb. 1, 1776, *Colls. Ct. Hist. Soc.,* 2 (1870): 358.

46. BA to [possibly HA or SD?], Holland House, Mar. 26, 1776, *AA,* 4 ser., 5:512; BA to SD, Camp before Quebec, Mar. 30, 1776, ibid., 4 ser., 5:549.

47. BA to the Inhabitants of the District of Quebec [original in French], Mar. 4, 1776, AAS. BA had warned Congress about the dangers of running short of hard money in regard to maintaining the *habitants'* allegiance.

48. BA to SD, Camp before Quebec, Mar. 30, 1776, *AA,* 4 ser., 5:549–50.

49. Moses Hazen to PS, Montreal, Apr. 1, 1776, ibid., 4 ser., 5:751. See also PS to GW, Albany, Mar. 9[–10], 1776, *Paps. GW, RWS,* 3:442–43.

50. Haskell Diary, Jan. 30–Feb. 1, 1776, *MQ,* 488–89. Of the 2,505 troops present before Quebec, BA estimated that 1,500 were "at liberty" to go home on Apr. 15. He thought about half that number could be persuaded to stay until after any attempted assault. See BA to SD, Camp before Quebec, Mar. 30, 1776, *AA,* 4 ser., 5:550.

51. Sundry Officers of the Army to Benedict Arnold, under his command, Headquarters before Quebec, Mar. 11, 1776, John R. Williams Paps., RUL; BA to GW, Camp before Quebec, Feb. 27, 1776, *Paps. GW, RWS,* 3:382.

52. BA to JH, Pres. Congress, Camp before Quebec, Feb. 1, 1776, *MQ,* 119–20.

53. BA to JH, Pres. Congress, Camp before Quebec, Feb. 12, 1776, ibid., 121; BA to GW, Camp before Quebec, Feb. 27, 1776, *Paps. GW, RWS,* 3:382.

54. Ainslie, Mar. 5, 1776, *Canada Preserved,* 57–58, considered the flag ridiculous, a symbol of the "imaginary evils" and manipulating devices used by "leaders of the American rebellion" to keep "the lower class of people in ignorance" about the advantages of British rule.

55. BA to [possibly HA or SD?], Holland House, Mar. 28, 1776, *AA,* 4 ser., 5:512; BA to SD, Camp before Quebec, Mar. 30, 1776, ibid., 4 ser., 5:550.

56. The best description of the escape scheme may be found in Henry's Memoir, n.d., *MQ,* 396–410. See also Melvin Journal, Mar. 26–Apr. 1, 1776, ibid., 446–47; Morrison Journal, n.d., ibid., 538–39; Stocking Journal, n.d., ibid., 566–67; and Fobes Narrative, n.d., ibid., 593–97.

57. Ainslie, Mar. 31–Apr. 1, 1776, *Canada Preserved,* 69–71. Just before the end of April the officers also plotted to escape, but that effort also failed at the last moment.

58. BA to [possibly HA or SD?], Holland House, Mar. 26, 1776, *AA*, 4 ser., 5:512; BA to SD, Camp before Quebec, Mar. 30, 1776, ibid., 4 ser., 5:549–50.

59. As late as Feb. 25, DW had spoken well of BA in a letter to GW. He wrote of his plans to travel to Quebec "in a few days" to "join General Arnold who has to his great honor kept up the blockade with such a handful of men, that the story when told hereafter will be scarcely credited." See DW to GW, Montreal, Feb. 25, 1776, *Paps. GW, RWS*, 3:362. No doubt DW later found out that BA had asked for the presence of someone like Charles Lee at Quebec, which would help explain DW's changed attitude regarding BA's martial competence. Then again, DW had treated PS, his commanding officer, with sustained contempt, as he had also done with virtually everyone in Montreal. Thus DW did not single out BA for unusually haughty treatment. For descriptions of DW and BA, see Ainslie, Apr. 2, 1776, *Canada Preserved*, 71–72, who commented on their appearance as they visited advanced rebel positions.

60. BA to PS, Montreal, Apr. 20, 1776, *AA*, 4 ser., 5:1098–99.

NINE: *Reduced to a Great Rabble*

1. BA to GW, Camp before Quebec, Feb. 27, 1776, *Paps. GW, RWS*, 3:381; BA to GW, Montreal, May 8, 1776, ibid., 4:230. Secondary works informing this chapter include French, *First Year of the Revolution*, 693–98; Hatch, *Thrust for Canada*, 175–228; Jones, *Campaign for the Conquest of Canada*, 33–98; Lanctot, *Canada and the Revolution*, 124–48; Leroy, "Sir Guy Carleton as a Military Leader," 1:144–81; George A. Rawlyk, ed., *Revolution Rejected, 1775–1776* (Scarborough, Ontario, 1968), 55–128; Salsig, ed., *Parole: Quebec; Countersign: Ticonderoga*, 93–144; Smith, *Struggle Fourteenth Colony*, 2:294–444; Stanley, *Canada Invaded*, 109–33; Ward, *War of the Revolution*, 1:196–201; Charles P. Whittemore, *A General of the Revolution: John Sullivan of New Hampshire* (New York, 1961), 1–31; and Wrong, *Canada and the Revolution*, 308–16.

2. BA to PS, Montreal, Apr. 20, 1776, *AA*, 4 ser., 5:1098–99. See also MH to PS, Montreal, Apr. 1, 1776, ibid., 4 ser., 5:751.

3. BA to PS, Montreal, Apr. 20, 1776, ibid., 4 ser., 5:1099.

4. Ibid.; BA to Timothy Bedel, Montreal, Apr. 21, 1776, Gratz Coll., HSP; BA to GW, Montreal, May 8, 1776, *Paps. GW, RWS*, 4:230.

5. Col. Joseph Reed reported to GW from Phila. on Mar. 3, 1776 (ibid., 3:406), that "Arnold is to be entrusted with the affairs of Canada—Wooster having either resigned or been superseded I know not which." Then, on Weds., Mar. 6, 1776 (*JCC*, 4:186), after effective lobbying by the Mass. delegates, Congress gave the assignment to John Thomas after promoting him to maj. gen. See also James Duane to Robert R. Livingston, Phila., Mar. 6, 1776, *LDC*, 3:337; JA to John Thomas, Phila., Mar. 7, 1776, ibid., 3:347; and Joseph Reed to GW, Phila., Mar. 7, 1776, *Paps. GW, RWS*, 3:429. For GW's soothing words, see GW to BA, Cambridge, Apr. 3, 1776, ibid., 4:21–23.

6. Ibid. On the British disposition of troops for the 1776 campaign, see Martin and Lender, *A Respectable Army,* 48–54.

7. BA to PS, Montreal, Apr. 20, 1776, *AA,* 4 ser., 5:1099; BA to John Thomas, Montreal, May 1, 1776, Misc. BA Paps., MHS; Commissioners to Canada (BF, CC, and SC) to PS, May 6, 1776, *LDC,* 3:630; BA to GW, Montreal, May 8, 1776, *Paps. GW, RWS,* 4:230.

8. CC to His Father, Charles Carroll of Annapolis, Montreal, Apr. 30, 1776, CC Paps., MdHS. On the commissioners and their journey to Canada, see *The Journal of Charles Carroll of Carrollton,* ed. Allan S. Everest (Fort Ticonderoga, N.Y., 1976), 1–15.

9. BA to PS, Montreal, Apr. 30, 1776, *AA,* 4 ser., 5:1155; CC to Charles Carroll of Annapolis, Montreal, Apr. 30, 1776, CC Paps., MdHS.

10. BA to GW, Montreal, May 8, 1776, *Paps. GW, RWS,* 4:229–30.

11. Commissioners to Canada to JH, Pres. Congress, Montreal, May 1, May 6, and May 8, 1776, *LDC,* 3:611–12, 630, 639–40.

12. BA to PS, Montreal, May 10, 1776, *AA,* 4 ser., 6:452–53; John Thomas to GW, Point Deschambault, May 8, 1776, *Paps. GW, RWS,* 4:231–33; Commissioners to Canada to JH, Pres. Congress, Montreal, May 10, 1776, *LDC,* 3:645–46; Commissioners to Canada (CC and SC) to BF, Montreal, May 11, 1776, ibid., 3:349. The commissioners' initial reaction was to have Thomas pull his whole force back to Sorel, but BA convinced them to consider the possibility of making a stand at Deschambault. See BA to John Thomas, Montreal, May 11, 1776, PML.

13. Commissioners to Canada to JH, Pres. Congress, Montreal, May 10, 1776, *LDC,* 3:646; Commissioners to Canada to BF, Montreal, May 11, 1776, ibid., 3:649; Commissioners to Canada (CC and SC) to PS, Montreal, May 11, 1776, ibid., 3:650–51; Commissioners to Canada (CC and SC) to BA[?], at Col. Livingston's, May 12, 1776, ibid., 3:664–65.

14. BA to PS, Montreal, May 11, 1776, *AA,* 4 ser., 6:480–81.

15. BA to PS, Montreal, May 10, 1776, ibid., 4 ser., 6:452.

16. John Thomas to BA, Point Deschambault, May 8, 1776, ibid., 4 ser., 6:482; John Thomas to Commissioners of Congress, Three Rivers, May 15, 1776, ibid., 6:588–89.

17. BA to PS, Montreal, May 11, 1776, ibid., 4 ser., 6:481.

18. BA to John Thomas, Sorel, May 14, 1776, MHS; BA to Commissioners, Sorel, May 15, 1776, *AA,* 4 ser., 6:579–80. For the experiences of one regt., John Greaton's 24th Continentals, that traveled to Canada under Gen. Thompson, see Henry Winchester Cunningham, ed., "Journal of Lieutenant-Colonel Joseph Vose, April–July 1776," *Publications of The Colonial Society of Massachusetts,* 7 (1905): 3–20. Greaton's regiment reached Sorel on May 9.

19. BA to PS, Montreal, May 11, 1776, *AA,* 4 ser., 6:481; Commissioners to Canada to PS, Montreal, May 11, 1776, *LDC,* 3:650–51; BA to Commissioners, Sorel, May 15, 1776, *AA,* 4 ser., 6:579–80; BA to SC, Sorel, May 15, 1776, ibid., 4 ser.,

6:580–81; BA to Commissioners, Sorel, May 17, 1776, ibid., 4 ser., 6:592–93; William Thompson to Commissioners, Sorel, May 25, 1776, ibid., 4 ser., 6:593–95.

20. BA to Commissioners, Sorel, May 15, 1776, ibid., 4 ser., 6:579–80; BA to SC, Sorel, May 15, 1776, ibid., 4 ser., 6:580–81.

21. Senter Journal, May 6, 1776, *MQ*, 236–39; GC to GG, Quebec, May 14, 1776, *DAR*, 12:137–38; Ainslie, May 3, 1776, *Canada Preserved*, 87–88.

22. Commissioners to Canada (CC and SC) to John Thomas, Montreal, May 15, 1776, *LDC*, 3:680; "Journal of a Physician [Lewis Beebe] on the Expedition against Canada," May 20–June 2, 1776, *PMHB*, 49 (1935): 328–32.

23. BA to SC, Sorel, May 15, 1776, *AA*, 4 ser., 6:580. See also BA to Col. James Clinton, Montreal, May 12, 1776, Emmet Coll., NYPL. In this set of instructions, BA stated that if the Montrealites attempted to "molest" the patriot force as it prepared for retreat, Clinton was to "set fire to the town." Also, he was to warn Bedel when the enemy force from Quebec approached Montreal, so that Bedel's regiment could safely retreat overland from the Cedars to St. Johns.

24. Commissioners to Canada (CC and SC) to JH, Pres. Congress, Montreal, May 17, 1776, *LDC*, 4:22–24; Commissioners to Canada (CC and SC) to JH, Pres. Congress, May 27, 1776, ibid., 4:80–86.

25. JW to NG, Lachine, May 24, 1776, *Paps. NG*, 1:217–18; BA to Commissioners, Lachine, May 25, 1776, *AA*, 4 ser., 6:595. See also JW's self-promoting *Memoirs of My Own Times* (4 vols., Philadelphia, 1816; reprint, New York, 1973), 1:38–44.

26. BA to Commissioners, St. Ann's [Anne], May 27, 1776, *AA*, 4 ser., 6:595–96.

27. Ibid.; JW *Memoirs*, 1:45. JW was only nineteen years old when he participated in these events, which may explain why he could not perceive what BA was doing. In addition, JW grew to despise BA, even before the treason incident, probably because BA recognized JW for what he was: a shallow, self-indulgent person whose only goal was to serve himself. Whatever the case, JW's *Memoirs* contain a strong anti-BA bias.

28. BA to Commissioners, St. Ann's [Anne], May 27, 1776, *AA*, 4 ser., 6:596; JW *Memoirs*, 1:45–46.

29. Ibid., 1:46 (JW's italics removed). Even though I have chosen to follow JW's recollection, researchers must be careful when using his *Memoirs* because of the innumerable inaccuracies contained therein. The content of the "reproachful" comments is not known.

30. BA to Commissioners, St. Ann's [Anne], May 27, 1776, *AA*, 4 ser., 6:596. BA claimed the officers were "unanimous" in favoring an attack. Perhaps BA was covering up an ugly scene or, more likely, did not want to betray badly divided sentiments among the patriot commanders, just in case the enemy captured his letter.

31. Ibid.; CC to Charles Carroll of Annapolis, Montreal, May 28, 1776, CC Paps., MdHS; JW *Memoirs*, 1:46–47, continued his dunning of BA by suggesting that he suffered from "indecision" in his handling of Forster. Before the appearance of Sherburne and Parke, wrote JW, BA "had the enemy completely in his power, . . .

and much moreso afterwards." In reality, among the senior patriot officers present at Fort Anne, BA was almost singular in favoring aggressive action.

32. For the terms of the cartel with various modifications, see *AA*, 4 ser., 6:597.

33. BA to Commissioners, St. Ann's [Anne], May 27, 1776, ibid., 4 ser., 6:596; JW *Memoirs*, 1:47, for a brief, garbled account; BA to Commissioners, Montreal, June 2, 1776, *AA*, 5 ser., 1:165.

34. Commissioners to Canada to JH, Pres. Congress, Montreal, May 27, 1776, *LDC*, 4:81–82. See also CC's diary entries for May 21–29, 1776, *Charles Carroll Journal*, 52–55.

35. Commissioners to Canada to JH, Pres. Cong., Montreal, May 27, 1776, *LDC*, 4:82. Typical of such requisition orders is CC and SC to DW, Montreal, May 25, 1776, CC Paps., MdHS.

36. Commissioners to Canada to JH, Pres. Cong., Montreal, May 27, 1776, *LDC*, 4:81. On May 31, before leaving Canada, SC wrote to PS from Chambly (ibid., 4:105): "It is a million to a shilling that General Thomas will die, General Wooster leaves this place this day. General Arnold is first in command until General Sullivan arrives. I esteem and respect both these gentlemen, but neither of them are competent to the supreme command." It is not entirely clear what SC meant, since both he and CC maintained positive feelings toward BA. In the best sense, he may have thought BA too incapacitated by the effects of his wound; the worst sense would be that he considered BA too mercurial in dealing with immediate subordinates. Most likely, SC was concerned about BA's lack of overall command experience. His words may also have been an exhortation to PS to take direct charge of the northern command in Canada.

37. Council of War Proceedings, Chambly, May 30, 1776, *AA*, 5 ser., 1:164; BA to Commissioners, June 2, 1776, ibid., 5 ser., 1:165. In his *Memoirs*, 1:47, JW claimed to have carried the message from De Haas to BA regarding the results of De Haas's council. JW reported that BA "expressed great indignation," stating that "none but cowards would hesitate to obey a positive order" (JW's italics removed).

38. BA to HG, Chambly, May 31, 1776, *AA*, 4 ser., 6:649; BA to Commissioners, Montreal, June 2, 1776, ibid., 5 ser., 1:165.

39. On Sullivan's career before the Revolutionary War, see Whittemore, *John Sullivan*, 1–19; GW to JH, Pres. Congress, New York, June 17, 1776, *Paps. GW, RWS*, 4:20–21.

40. JS to GW, Sorel, June 8[–12], 1776, ibid., 3:463–64. BA explained why he was detaining De Haas's regt. in BA to JS, Montreal, June 5, 1776, *AA*, 4 ser., 6:924. He had first ordered De Haas's regt. to Sorel, as JS wanted, but then called these troops back because of intelligence reports regarding additional threats against Montreal.

41. GC to GG, Montreal, June 20, 1776, *DAR*, 12:152–53. GG had earlier written GC, dated Whitehall, Feb. 17, 1776 (*DAR*, 12:56–57), that a relief regt. would soon be sailing for Quebec and that a much larger force, to include five thousand foreign troops, would follow at the end of March. All told, the British sent more than ten

thousand soldiers to Quebec for the relief of Canada. At Three Rivers, British casualties were negligible, amounting to twelve or thirteen soldiers.

42. BA to JS, Chambly, June 10, 1776, *AA*, 4 ser., 6:796–97.

43. Ibid.; BA to PS, Montreal, June 10, 1776, ibid., 4 ser., 6:976–77; BA to PS, St. Johns, June 13, 1776, ibid., 4 ser., 6:1038–39. In his *Memoirs*, 1:47–49, 58, JW asserted that BA, whom he described as "a half-breed apothecary," intended all along to steal the "booty" for himself "under the pretext of providing for the officers of the army." At the time, however, JW denied emphatically that BA stole any of the requisitioned goods. For further information, see chapter 10, notes 44–46 below. Major Scott's first name remains unidentified.

44. BA to PS, Chambly, June 13, 1776, *AA*, 4 ser., 6:1039.

45. For GC's seemingly unaggressive behavior as a reflection of supply shortages, see R. Arthur Bowler, *Logistics and the Failure of the British Army in North America, 1775–1783* (Princeton, 1975), 212–25.

46. BA to JS, La Prairie, June 16, 1776, *AA*, 4 ser., 6:930; BA to PS, St. Johns, June 16, 1776, ibid., 4 ser., 6:930. JW claimed in his *Memoirs*, 1:49–51, that he was responsible for warning BA that the British were nearing Montreal; BA acknowledged the same in his letter to JS.

47. BA to GW, Albany, June 25, 1776, *Paps. GW, RWS*, 5:96; JS to PS, Isle aux Noix, June 19, 1776, *AA*, 4 ser., 4:1103–4.

48. JW *Memoirs*, 1:54–55.

49. "Journal of a Physician [Lewis Beebe]," June 17, 1776, *PMHB* (1935):335–36. To this day no marker or plaque recognizes the hundreds of American patriot soldiers who died on Isle aux Noix.

50. BA to GW, Albany, June 25, 1776, *Paps. GW, RWS*, 5:96–97. BA indicated that about one-half of the estimated seven thousand patriot troops on Isle aux Noix were "sick and unfit for duty."

TEN: *Malevolent Spirits in the Summer of 1776*

1. JS to PS, Isle aux Noix, June 19, 1776, *AA*, 4 ser., 6:1103–4. Secondary works informing this chapter include Don R. Gerlach, *Proud Patriot: Philip Schuyler and the War of Independence, 1775–1783* (Syracuse, 1987), 132–72; Hatch, *Thrust for Canada*, 224–36; Jones, *Campaign for the Conquest of Canada*, 90–140; Paul David Nelson, *General Horatio Gates: A Biography* (Baton Rouge, La., 1976), 52–70; Rossie, *Politics of Command*, 96–117; Salsig, ed., *Parole: Quebec*, 140–203; Stanley, *Canada Invaded*, 133–36; and John A. Williams, "Mount Independence in Time of War, 1776–1783," *Vermont History*, 35 (1967): 89–108.

2. JW *Memoirs*, 1:60–61.

3. PS to GW, Albany, June 25, 1776, *Paps. GW, RWS*, 4:104–5. See also GW to JH, Pres. Congress, New York, June 27, 1776, ibid., 5:120–21.

4. PS to JS, Albany, June 25, 1776, *AA*, 4 ser., 6:1107.

5. BA to GW, Albany, June 25, 1776, *Paps. GW, RWS*, 5:96.

6. On Britain's Hudson Highlands strategy, see Martin and Lender, *A Respectable Army,* 48–53. See also GG to GC, Whitehall, March 28, 1776, Cruikshank, ed., *Military and Naval Forces,* 2:150–51; GG to WH, Whitehall, March 28, 1776, *DAR,* 12:95–96; and GG to GC, Whitehall, Aug. 22, 1776, ibid., 12:187–88.

7. BA to GW, Albany, June 25, 1776, *Paps. GW, RWS,* 5:96–97.

8. PS to GW, Albany, June 12, 1776, ibid., 4:509–10.

9. BA to GW, Albany, June 25, 1776, ibid., 5:96–97.

10. On HG's promotion, see Thurs., May 16, 1776, *JCC,* 5:448. On HG's life and career up to June 1776, see Nelson, *Horatio Gates,* 1–57.

11. SC to HG, Phila., June 13, 1776, *LDC,* 4:201–2; JA to HG, Phila., June 18, 1776, ibid., 4:261–62. Rather ironically in the context of PS's concerns, some New England delegates wanted their emerging favorite HG to take command in their region, now that GW had moved the main Continental army to New York City. When HG visited Congress on GW's behalf to share intelligence about the king's rumored hiring of thousands of Hessians, HG stated that the Canadian campaign might well have enjoyed greater success had PS provided frontline generalship. HG then drew up a plan for a separate Canadian command department. The delegates responded by asking him to serve as the campaign's savior. On HG's appointment, see Mon., June 17, 1776, *JCC,* 5:448–50.

12. SC to HG, Phila., June 13, 1776, *LDC,* 4:201–2. The New England delegates were very churlish about any criticism of patriot soldiers from their region. When SC suggested that lack of discipline and commitment among these troops represented one reason for failure in Canada, JA became apoplectic. He wrote to HG and denounced SC. See JA to HG, Phila., Aug. 13, 1776, ibid., 4:670–71.

13. PS was also an Indian commissioner for the Northern Department. He had to concern himself with the Six Nations of Iroquois Indians, hoping to maintain their neutrality. He was already planning a conference to be held at German Flats in the Mohawk Valley in mid-July. Thus to have HG assume direct command of the Northern Department force would make it easier for PS to deal with his other responsibilities in the northern New York region. For the German Flats conference and its significance, see Barbara Graymont, *The Iroquois in the American Revolution* (Syracuse, 1972), 104–13; and *Citizen-Soldier: The Revolutionary War Journal of Joseph Bloomfield,* Collections of the New Jersey Historical Society, vol. 18, ed. Mark E. Lender and James Kirby Martin (Newark, N.J., 1982), 73–100.

14. Mon., July 8, 1776, *JCC,* 5:526. HG to JH, Pres. Congress, Ticonderoga, July 29, 1776, *AA,* 5 ser., 1:649, stated, "I have this day written to General Schuyler to assure him . . . of my unalterable resolution to obey his commands."

15. "Journal of a Physician [Lewis Beebe]," June 1, 7, 10, and 13, 1776, *PMHB* (1935): 331, 333, 334.

16. July 9, 1776, ibid., 341–42. For Beebe's life, see *Biographical Sketches of the Graduates of Yale College, 1701–1815,* comp. Franklin Bowditch Dexter (6 vols., New York, 1885–1912), 3:403–4.

17. Sat.–Mon., June 15, 17, 20, 21, 24, 1776, *JCC,* 5:446, 454–58, 468, 472, 474–75.

18. Weds., July 10, 1776, ibid., 5:533–39. Thomas Jefferson was responsible for writing much of the draft report. See Boyd et al., eds., *Paps. TJ,* 1:400–404, for the first draft (Mon., June 17) of the July 10 statement adopted by Congress. See also Maj. Henry Sherburne's testimony before the committee, also in Jefferson's handwriting (ibid., 1:396–400); and Thomas Jefferson to Francis Eppes, Phila., July 15, 1776, ibid., 1:459–60.

19. William Whipple to John Langdon, Phila., June 10, 1776, *LDC,* 4:186. For other criticisms, see Gen. William Thompson to GW, Sorel, June 2, 1776, *Paps. GW, RWS,* 4:427–29.

20. Thomas Jefferson's committee notes, July 10 [James Price], July 2 [Hector McNeill], Boyd et al., eds., *Paps. TJ,* 1:450, 435.

21. Tues., July 30, 1776, *JCC,* 5:617–20.

22. Fri., Apr. 12, Fri., Apr. 26, 1776, ibid., 4:275, 312–14.

23. JE to JH, Pres. Congress, Phila., May 8, 1776, *AA,* 4 ser., 5:1234–35. Congress had already advised JE to settle his monetary claims with patriot military officials in Quebec Province.

24. Fri., June 28, Weds., July 31, Thurs., Aug. 1, 1776, *JCC,* 5:489, 623, 626.

25. JB's Petition to Congress, n.p., June 26, 1776, *AA,* 5 ser., 1:1219–20; Thurs., June 27, 1776, *JCC,* 5:485.

26. Tues., July 30, Thurs., Aug. 1, 1776, ibid., 5:618–19, 626. The congressional committee on Canada stated that some "licentious persons" had plundered the baggage of the British officers, "in violation of the faith of the capitulation." The delegates agreed and called on PS to determine who the culprits were, so that they could receive "due punishment." Thus the delegates implicitly seemed to accept JB's and JE's alleged innocence, but they still expected PS to hold courts of inquiry regarding their behavior (Tues., July 30, 1776, ibid., 5:618–19). In his dealings with Congress, JB named other culprits, including the thoroughly discredited Timothy Bedel who, like BA, was in no position to defend himself. Who actually plundered the goods remains unresolved.

27. SC to BA, Phila., Aug. 7, 1776, *LDC,* 4:633.

28. PS to GW, Albany, July 12[–13], 1776, *Paps. GW, RWS,* 5:286–88; JS to PS, Crown Point, July 6, 1776, *AA,* 5 ser., 1:234; GW to JH, Pres. Congress, New York, July 17, 1776, *Paps. GW, RWS,* 5:356–57; HG to GW, Ticonderoga, July 12, 1776, *JW Memoirs,* 1:62–63.

29. Council of War Minutes, Crown Point, July 7, 1776, *AA,* 5 ser., 1:233; HG to GW, Ticonderoga, July 29, 1776, *Paps. GW, RWS,* 5:498–500. The fifth person present at the council was Brig. Gen. Frederick William, Baron de Woedtke, who was known for his heavy alcohol consumption and continual drunkenness while on duty in Canada. Woedtke soon came down with a fatal disease and died at the Lake George hospital encampment on July 28, 1776.

30. Remonstrance of Col. [John] Stark and Others to PS, Crown Point, July 8, 1776, *AA,* 5 ser., 1:233–34; PS to Field-Grade Officers, Ticonderoga, July 9, 1776,

ibid., 5 ser., 1:234–35. Twenty-one officers signed the remonstrance. PS also informed GW of the decision, and GW asked his own ranking officers to comment. NG wrote that "to quit Crown Point" was "one of the most mad resolutions I ever heard of." GW did not overrule his northern generals, but he did relate his officers' sentiments to PS and HG. An irritated HG responded that GW's officers lacked the means to evaluate actual conditions at Ticonderoga and Crown Point and had used poor judgment in attempting "to censure the conduct of those, who are in nothing inferior to themselves." Overwhelmed as GW was in preparing to meet a British force four times the size of GC's, he dropped the matter. See NG to Nicholas Cooke, Long Island, July 22, 1776, *Paps. NG,* 1:260; GW to HG, New York, July 19, 1776, *Paps. GW, RWS,* 5:380–81; HG to GW, Ticonderoga, July 29, 1776, ibid., 5:498–500.

31. PS to GW, Albany, July 12[–13], 1776, ibid., 5:286. On the German Flats conference, see note 13 above.

32. BA to HG, Crown Point, July 10, July 12, 1776, *AA,* 5 ser., 1:207, 238–39. See also Thomas Hartley to BA, Crown Point, July 10, 1776, ibid., 5 ser., 1:207–9.

33. BA to GW, Crown Point, July 14, July 15, 1776, ibid., 5 ser., 1:340, 358; HG to JH, Pres. Congress, Ticonderoga, July 29, 1776, ibid., 5 ser., 1:649; HG to GW, Ticonderoga, July 29, 1776, *Paps. GW, RWS,* 5:500.

34. HG to JH, Pres. Congress, Ticonderoga, July 29, 1776, ibid., 5 ser., 1:649.

35. Orders of the Day, Ticonderoga, July 20, 1776, ibid., 5 ser., 1:655. The four colonels whose regts. formed Arnold's brigade had signed the remonstrance against abandoning Crown Point.

36. HG to BA, Ticonderoga, July 13, July 17, 1776, ibid., 5 ser., 1:261, 397; HG to JH, Pres. Congress, Ticonderoga, July 29, 1776, ibid., 5 ser., 1:649; HG to GW, Ticonderoga, July 29, 1776, *Paps. GW, RWS,* 5:498–500.

37. HG to JH, Pres. Congress, Ticonderoga, July 29, 1776, *AA,* 5 ser., 1:649.

38. GW to PS, New York, July 15, 1776, *Paps. GW, RWS,* 5:330; HG to JH, Pres. Congress, Ticonderoga, July 29, 1776, *AA,* 5 ser., 1:649. On July 15, HG informed BA that Hazen was complaining "of several irregularities in the proceedings against him," not the least of which was that BA was attempting to determine who would serve on the hearing board. Given the results of the inquiry and BA's many pressing obligations, this charge seems spurious. See HG to BA, Ticonderoga, July 15, 1776, ibid., 5 ser., 1:357–58.

39. BA Lists of Requisitions, July 20, July 24, Aug. 3, 1776, ibid., 5 ser., 1:745–46; BA to HG, Skenesborough, July 24, 1776, ibid., 5 ser., 1:563–64; BA to HG, Skenesborough, July 25, 1776, *NDAR,* 5:1210–11; and BA to RV, July 26, 1776, CHS.

40. "Diary of Col. Elisha Porter, of Hadley, Massachusetts," July 18, 20, 27, 1776, *MAH,* 30, part 2 (1893): 202–3.

41. "Diary Col. Elisha Porter," July 27, 1776, ibid., 203.

42. "Diary Col. Elisha Porter," July 28–31, 1776, ibid., 203. Self-absorbed as he was with his own problems, as well as with various court-martial proceedings, Col. Porter did not mention the Declaration of Independence celebration.

43. "Diary Col. Elisha Porter," Aug. 1–3, 1776, ibid., 203. MH Court-Martial Documents, Ticonderoga, Aug. 1–2, 1776, *AA,* 5 ser., 1:1272–73.

44. BA to HG, Ticonderoga, Aug. 7, 1776, ibid., 5 ser., 1:1274–75; Benjamin Thomson's Account of Goods Taken at Montreal by B. Arnold, n.p., n.d., PCC, microfilm reel 71, item 58:397, NA. MH could likewise be more than a verbal bully. In its various resolutions relating to the patriot failure in Canada (Tues., July 30, 1776, *JCC,* 5:619), Congress resolved to have PS inquire into MH's alleged abusive conduct in assaulting two prominent French Canadians. One of these gentleman, François Cuillot de la Rose, a militia captain, stated before the Canadian investigating committee that he had "hired and paid for four wagons to remove his effects." At Chambly, MH "stopped, . . . insulted, and beat the deponent, and took the wagons." In addition, one of MH's troops fired his weapon at Cuillot de la Rose. Then MH threw him in a guardhouse, from which he was later freed by JS. For this testimony, given on July 18, 1776, see Boyd et al., eds., *Paps. TJ,* 1:452.

45. JW *Memoirs,* 1:60. JW to RV, Mount Independence, Aug. 5, 1776, *NDAR,* 6:61. JW spent a lifetime manipulating reality to serve himself. He had forgotten about his own exoneration of BA's character when he wrote much later in life about MH's court-martial with this conclusion: "Such was the popularity Arnold had acquired by his abortive enterprise across the wilderness, . . . that in this instance, the principles of justice were subverted, and the best interests of the army sacrificed." See JW *Memoirs,* 1:70–75.

46. JW to RV, Mount Independence, Aug. 5, 1776, *NDAR,* 6:61; HG to PS, [Ticonderoga], Sept. 11, 1776, *AA,* 5 ser., 2:294–95.

47. "Diary Col. Elisha Porter," Aug. 3, 1776, *MAH* (1893): 203; Col. Enoch Poor [on behalf of the hearing board] to HG, [Ticonderoga], Aug. 6, 1776, *AA,* 5 ser., 1:1273–74.

48. "Diary Col. Elisha Porter," Aug. 10, 12, 13, 1776, *MAH* (1893): 204.

49. HG to JH, Pres. Congress, Ticonderoga, Sept. 2, 1776, *AA,* 5 ser., 1:1268, which served as a covering letter for a whole packet of materials relating to the MH court-martial and other pressing matters on Lake Champlain.

50. PS to HG, German Flats, Aug. 3, 1776, ibid., 5 ser., 1:747; GW to HG, New York, Aug. 14, 1776, *Writings GW,* 5:433.

51. GG to GJB, Kew Lane, Aug. 23, 1776, *Stopford-Sackville Mss.,* 2:39. This letter was in response to GJB to GG, Montreal, June 22, 1776, ibid., 2:37, in which GJB mentioned his disappointment in almost overtaking but not bagging a most valuable catch, BA, just north of St. Johns.

52. Field Officers at Ticonderoga to JH, Pres. Congress, Ticonderoga, Aug. 19, 1776, *AA,* 5 ser., 1:1072; BA to HG, Ticonderoga, Aug. 7, 1776, ibid., 5 ser., 1:1275. Of the twelve officers who signed the protest to Congress, seven had put their signatures on the remonstrance against vacating Crown Point.

53. SC to BA, Phila., Aug. 7, 1776, *LDC,* 4:633.

54. BA to HG, Windmill Point, Sept. 7, 1776, *AA,* 5 ser., 2:354.

ELEVEN: *A Most Tenacious Naval Commander*

1. Orders and Instructions, Ticonderoga, Aug. 7, 1776, *AA,* 5 ser., 1:826–27. Secondary works informing this and the subsequent chapter include Gardner W. Allen, *A Naval History of the American Revolution,* 2 vols. (Boston, 1913), 1:161–84; Harrison Bird, *Navies in the Mountains: The Battles on the Waters of Lake Champlain and Lake George, 1609–1814* (New York, 1962), 164–85; Oscar E. Bredenberg, "The American Champlain Fleet, 1775–77," *Bulletin of the Fort Ticonderoga Museum,* 12 (1968): 249–63, and Bredenberg, "The *Royal Savage,*" ibid., 12 (1966): 128–49; William M. Fowler Jr., *Rebels under Sail: The American Navy during the Revolution* (New York, 1976), 153–86; Hatch, *Thrust for Canada,* 229–46; Jones, *Conquest of Canada,* 128–98; Alfred Thayer Mahan, *The Major Operations of the Navies in the War of American Independence* (Boston, 1913), 6–28, and Mahan, "The Naval Campaign of 1776 on Lake Champlain," *Scribner's Magazine,* 23 (1898): 147–60; Martin and Lender, *A Respectable Army,* 53–63; Nathan Miller, *Sea of Glory: The Continental Navy Fights for Independence, 1775–1783* (New York,1974), 164–79; Paul David Nelson, "Guy Carleton versus Benedict Arnold: The Campaign of 1776 in Canada and on Lake Champlain," *New York History,* 57 (1976): 339–66; and Stanley, *Canada Invaded,* 133–44.

2. BA to HG, Skenesborough, Aug. 7, 1776, *AA,* 5 ser., 1:825–26.

3. Ibid.; BA to PS, Skenesborough, Aug. 8, 1776, ibid., 5 ser., 1:1033. Over the years, a debate has occurred over whether BA's fleet at Valcour Island had eight or nine gundalows. In these letters he suggested the construction of only eight; however, other records indicate that nine gundalows were built, including the *Success*—the extra craft in question. Wallace, *Traitorous Hero,* 111, 348, argued in favor of nine gundalows. Fowler, *Rebels under Sail,* 183, 288n, claimed there were only eight. I have concluded that the weight of evidence sustains nine as the correct number.

4. As with all vessels in the Champlain fleet, the actual weaponry on board varied slightly from this standard consignment. One gundalow, the *Philadelphia,* which sank shortly after the Oct. 11 battle, was raised in 1935 and belongs to the collections of the Smithsonian Institution. For its history, see Philip K. Lundeberg, *The Continental Gunboat Philadelphia and the Northern Campaign of 1776* (Smithsonian Publication 4651, Washington, D.C., 1966), *passim.*

5. A List of the Navy of the United States of America on Lake Champlain, Aug. 7, 1776, *NDAR,* 6:96–97, lists four row galleys, including the cutter *Lee,* and states that four more galleys "will be completed by the middle of September." (When retreating from Canada in June 1776, BA had seized the materials of a partially assembled vessel at St. Johns. Completed at Skenesborough, this craft became the cutter *Lee.*) Into early Oct., BA kept hoping to get more galleys than those listed here. The rapid spread of various diseases among the workers at Skenesborough, however, made the delivery of these additional galleys a moot point. See also A List of Continental Vessels on Lake Champlain, Aug. 18, 1776, ibid., 6:224; and A List of

the Armed Vessels in Lake Champlain, prepared by RV, Oct. 12, 1776, *AA*, 5 ser., 2:1039.

6. BA to HG, Skenesborough, Aug. 7, 1776, ibid., 5 ser., 1:825–26; BA to PS, Skenesborough, Aug. 8, 1776, ibid., 5 ser., 1:1033.

7. One of the British vessels, the radeau *Thunderer,* alone carried six 24-pounders. In addition, GC's fleet had twenty gunboats, most of which had a 24-pounder aboard. See List of the Enemy's Fleet on Lake Champlain, contained in BA to PS, Ticonderoga, Oct. 15, 1776, ibid., 5 ser., 2:1080; and Capt. Charles Douglass to Mr. Stephens, Quebec, Oct. 21, 1776, ibid., 5 ser., 2:1178–79.

8. PS to JH, Pres. Congress, German Flats, Aug. 1, 1776, ibid., 5 ser., 1:715; Orderly Book of Brigade Maj. Peter Scull, Ticonderoga, Aug. 10, 1776, *NDAR,* 6:139–40.

9. Orders and Instructions, Ticonderoga, Aug. 7, 1776, *AA,* 5 ser., 1:827.

10. Matthias Ogden to Aaron Burr, Ticonderoga, Aug. 11, 1776, ibid., 5 ser., 1:901; Extract of a Letter from Ticonderoga, Aug. 15, 1776, ibid., 5 ser., 1:969. On Sept. 4, the *Pennsylvania Gazette* published an extract of a letter from an officer on board the *Royal Savage,* dated Aug. 21, 1776, which proclaimed specific intentions to "come to action" at St. Johns (*NDAR,* 6:253). If such was known in Philadelphia, word surely had reached GC and others in Canada.

11. These words appeared in HG's Orders and Instructions, Ticonderoga, Aug. 7, 1776, *AA,* 5 ser., 1:827.

12. BA to HG, Crown Point, Aug. 16, 1776, ibid., 5 ser., 1:988–89.

13. BA to HG, Crown Point, Aug. 17, 1776; Jacobus Wynkoop to HG, Crown Point, Aug. 17, 1776; and relevant copies of Orders, ibid., 5 ser., 1:1002–3.

14. HG to BA, Ticonderoga, Aug. 18, 1776, ibid., 5 ser., 1:1277; HG to BA, Ticonderoga, Aug. 19, 1776, ibid., 5 ser., 1:1073.

15. BA to HG, Crown Point, Aug. 19, 1776, ibid., 5 ser., 1:1277.

16. HG to PS, Ticonderoga, Aug. 20, 1776, ibid., 5 ser., 1:1084; PS to HG, Albany, Aug. 25, 1776, ibid., 5 ser., 1:1277.

17. Petition of Commodore Wynkoop to Congress, Albany, Aug. 27, 1776, ibid., 5 ser., 1:1185–87. See also PS to JH, Pres. Congress, ibid., 5 ser., 1:1217, in which PS stated, "Although I believed Wynkoop to be brave and industrious, and equal to the command of what vessels we had when I recommended him, yet I was so far from being sufficiently acquainted whether he was equal to the command of such a number of vessels as we have now there, that I learned [of] General Arnold's appointment with great satisfaction, and very much approved of it." Wynkoop persisted in his claims to Congress until May 1779 when that body, no doubt worn down by his persistent complaining, awarded him back pay to 1776 at the level of a Continental navy frigate captain. See Tues., May 4, 1779, *JCC,* 14:544.

18. Thomas Jefferson to John Page, Phila., Aug. 20, 1776, *LDC,* 5:33.

19. BA to HG, Crown Point, Aug. 23, 1776, *AA,* 5 ser., 1:1129–30; HG to BA, Ticonderoga, Aug. 23, 1776, ibid., 5 ser., 1:1129. BA's orders, given at Crown Point,

contained in "Journal of Bayze Wells of Farmington, [Ct.,] May, 1775–February, 1777, at the Northward and in Canada," *Colls. Ct. Hist. Soc.,* 7 (1899): 270.

20. "Journal Bayze Wells," Aug. 5, 7, 1776, ibid., 268.

21. HG to PS, Ticonderoga, Sept. 23, 1776, *AA,* 5 ser., 2:481, stated bluntly: "The powder, lead, and flints . . . is not yet even in part arrived. Pray hurry it up. The moments are precious, and not one of them should be lost." See also HG to BA, Ticonderoga, Sept. 26, 1776, ibid., 5 ser., 2:555–56, indicating the same and advising that "economy is the word."

22. BA to HG, Buttonmould Bay, Aug. 31, 1776, ibid., 5 ser., 1:1266–67; "Journal Bayze Wells," Aug. 26–28, 1776, *Colls. Ct. Hist. Soc.,* 7 (1899): 271–72.

23. "Journal Bayze Wells," Aug. 29, 1776, ibid., 272.

24. "Journal Bayze Wells," Sept. 2, 1776, ibid., 273; BA to HG, Windmill Point, Sept. 7, 1776, *AA,* 5 ser., 2:223.

25. BA to HG, Willsborough, Sept. 2, 1776, ibid., 5 ser., 1:1267. Some commentators, such as William Henry Smith, who edited *The St. Clair Papers . . .* (2 vols., Cincinnati, 1882), 1:372n, have claimed that St. Clair's "promotion excited the jealousy of Arnold who, although a brigadier, did not like to see any other officer of ability placed on the same plane with himself." This conclusion does not square with extant historical documents.

26. BA to HG, Willsborough, Sept. 2, 1776, *AA,* 5 ser., 1:1267; "Journal Bayze Wells," Sept. 4–6, 1776, *Colls. Ct. Hist. Soc.,* 7 (1899): 274–76.

27. BA to HG, Windmill Point, Sept. 7, 1776, *AA,* 5 ser., 2:223–24. The offending gundalow was the *Boston* under Captain Sumner.

28. Ibid.; BA to HG, Bay St. Amand, Sept. 21, 1776, ibid., 5 ser., 2:441.

29. Those punished were men serving on the gundalow *Providence,* as recorded in "Journal Bayze Wells," Sept. 20, 22, 1776, *Colls. Ct. Hist. Soc.,* 7 (1899): 279, 280.

30. William Gilliland to BA, n.p., Sept. 1, 1776, *AA,* 5 ser., 2:112–13.

31. BA to HG, Valcour Island, Sept. 28, 1776, ibid., 5 ser., 2:592.

32. HG to BA, Ticonderoga, Sept. 12, 1776, ibid., 5 ser., 2:303; BA to HG, Isle la Motte, Sept. 15, 1776, ibid., 5 ser., 2:531.

33. Weds., Sept. 18, through Tues., Sept. 24, 1776, *JCC,* 5:780–812.

34. BA to HG, Isle la Motte, Sept. 8, 9, 1776, *AA,* 5 ser., 2:354, 265.

35. HG to BA, Ticonderoga, Sept. 5, 1776, ibid., 5 ser., 2:186; BA to HG, Isle la Motte, Sept. 9, 1776, ibid., 5 ser., 2:265.

36. HG to BA, Ticonderoga, Sept. 5, 1776, ibid., 5 ser., 2:186. Accepted casualty figures are 367 for the British and 1,097 for GW's force, including rebel soldiers captured. See Peckham, ed., *Toll of Independence,* 22.

37. BA to HG, Isle la Motte, Sept. 9, 1776, *AA,* 5 ser., 2:265.

38. BA to HG, Isle la Motte, Sept. 15, 1776, ibid., 5 ser., 2:531.

39. BA to HG, Isle la Motte, Sept. 18, 1776, ibid., 5 ser., 2:481.

40. "Journal Bayze Wells," Sept. 19, 1776, *Colls. Ct. Hist. Soc.,* 7 (1899): 279; BA to HG, Bay St. Amand, Sept. 21, 1776, *AA,* 5 ser., 2:440.

41. Ibid.; "Journal Bayze Wells," Sept. 20, 1776, *Colls. Ct. Hist. Soc.,* 7 (1899): 279; BA to HG, Valcour Island, Sept. 28, 1776, *AA,* 5 ser., 2:591.

42. "Journal Bayze Wells," Sept. 11, 1776, *Colls. Ct. Hist. Soc.,* 7 (1899): 277; BA to HG, Bay St. Amand, Sept. 21, 1776, *AA,* 5 ser., 2:440; BA to HG, Valcour Island, Sept. 28, 1776, ibid., 5 ser., 2:592.

43. BA to HG, Isle la Motte, Sept. 18, 1776, ibid., 5 ser., 2:482.

44. BA to HG, Bay St. Amand, Sept. 21, 1776, ibid., 5 ser., 2:440; "Journal Bayze Wells," Sept. 26, 1776, *Colls. Ct. Hist. Soc.,* 7 (1899): 280–81.

45. HG to BA, Ticonderoga, Sept. 26, 1776, *AA,* 5 ser., 2:556.

46. BA to HG, Valcour Island, Oct. 1, 1776, ibid., 5 ser., 2:834.

47. Memorandum of Articles . . . from BA to HG, Valcour Island, Oct. 1, 1776, ibid., 5 ser., 2:835.

48. BA to HG, Valcour Island, Oct. 1, 1776, ibid., 5 ser., 2:834–35.

49. Ibid.; "Journal Bayze Wells," Sept. 26–Oct. 1, 1776, *Colls. Ct. Hist. Soc.,* 7 (1899): 281–82.

50. BA to HG, Valcour Island, Sept. 28, 1776, *AA,* 5 ser., 2:592; HG to BA, Ticonderoga, Oct. 2, 1776, ibid., 5 ser., 2:847; BA to HG, Valcour Island, Oct. 7, Oct. 10, 1776, ibid., 5 ser., 2:933, 982.

51. "Journal Bayze Wells," Oct. 6, 1776, *Colls Ct. Hist. Soc.,* 7 (1899): 283.

52. BA to HG, Valcour Island, Oct. 7, 1776, *AA,* 5 ser., 2:933.

53. HG to BA, Ticonderoga, Oct. 3, 1776, ibid., 5 ser., 2:861.

54. Committee of Secret Correspondence [BF and Robert Morris] to SD, Phila., Oct. 1, 1776, *LDC,* 5:279.

55. JE to JH, Pres. Congress, Albany, Oct. 5, 1776, *AA,* 5 ser., 2:911. See also JB to PS, Albany, Aug. 27, 1776, with various attachments, ibid., 5 ser., 1:1218–19.

56. "Journal Bayze Wells," Oct. 11, 1776, *Colls. Ct. Hist. Soc.,* 7 (1899): 283–84.

57. HA to BA, New Haven, Aug. 17, 1776, AAS.

T W E L V E : *The Valiant Defense of Lake Champlain*

1. "Orders and Instructions," Ticonderoga, Aug. 7, 1776, *AA,* 5 ser., 1:826–27. Besides those sources cited in chapter 11, note 1, secondary works informing this chapter include Bird, *Navies in the Mountains,* 186–219; R. Arthur Bowler, "Sir Guy Carleton and the Campaign of 1776 in Canada," *Canadian Historical Review,* 55 (1974): 131–40; Art Cohn, "An Incident Not Known to History: Squire Ferris and Benedict Arnold at Ferris Bay, October 13, 1776," *Vermont History,* 55 (1987): 97–112; Leroy, "Sir Guy Carleton as a Military Leader," 442–99; J. Robert Maguire, "Dr. Robert Knox's Account of the Battle of Valcour, October 11–13, 1776," *Vermont History,* 46 (1978): 141–50; Charles M. Snyder, "With Benedict Arnold at Valcour Island: The Diary of Pascal De Angelis," ibid., 42 (1974): 195–200; and Ward, *War of the Revolution,* 1:384–97.

2. David Waterbury to JH, Pres. Congress, Stamford, Ct., Oct. 24, 1776, *AA,* 5 ser., 2:1224.

3. No less a naval authority than Alfred Thayer Mahan wrote, "Waterbury's advice evidently found its origin in that fruitful source of military errors of design, which reckons the preservation of a force first of objects, making the results of its action secondary. With sounder judgment, Arnold decided to hold on. A retreat before square-rigged sailing vessels having a fair wind, by a heterogeneous force like his own, of unequal speeds and batteries, could result only in disaster. . . . The correctness of Arnold's decision not to chance a retreat was shown in the retreat of two days later." See *Major Operations of the Navies*, 19–20.

4. BA was following HG's command dispositions. See HG to BA, Sept. 5, 1776, *AA*, 5 ser., 2:186, in which HG hoped to "prevent any confusion or dispute about command in case an unlucky shot or other accident should take off the general [BA]."

5. GG to GC, Whitehall, March 28, 1776, Cruikshank, ed., *Military and Naval Forces*, 2:150–51; GC to GG, Quebec, May 14, 1776, *DAR*, 12:137–38; GG to GC, Whitehall, June 21, 1776, ibid., 12:153–54; GC to GG, Chambly, July 8, 1776, Cruikshank, ed., *Military and Naval Forces*, 2:178–79.

6. GC to GG, Quebec, Aug. 10, 1776, ibid., 2:184. In this letter, GC suggested his approach to waging war against the American rebels. He thought that "valor and good conduct in time of action with humanity and friendly treatment to those who are subdued . . . at our mercy" represented the best means to break rebel resistance and effect a lasting reconciliation. As such, more than supply shortages held GC back (see chapter 9, note 45). GG, by comparison, favored more decisive action; he wanted the rebels crushed, which he believed would prevent future warfare. In this sense, GC thought more like the Howe brothers, who intended to follow "a strategy of careful advances," expecting "to create the impression of British invincibility" and "destroy the colonists' faith in the Continental army," their objective being to "produce a genuine reconciliation." See Ira Gruber, *The Howe Brothers and the American Revolution* (Chapel Hill, 1972), 156. The issue was really over what degree and intensity of force to employ, and GG ultimately found the field performance of both the Howes and GC frustrating. Stephen Conway, "To Subdue America: British Army Officers and the Conduct of the Revolutionary War," *WMQ*, 3 ser., 43 (1986): 381–407, divides the ranking British officers into conciliationists and hard-liners. Clearly GC belonged in the former group.

7. Capt. Charles Douglass to Mr. Stephens, Quebec, Oct. 21, 1776, *AA*, 5 ser., 2:1178.

8. A List of His Majesty's Naval Force on Lake Champlain, prepared by Capt. Charles Douglass, Quebec, Oct. 21, 1776, ibid., 5 ser., 2:1179.

9. Ibid.; *The American Journals of Lt. John Enys*, ed. Elizabeth Cometti (Syracuse, 1976), 16–18; *A Journal Kept in Canada and Upon Burgoyne's Campaign in 1776 and 1777, by Lieut. James M. Hadden, Roy. Art.*, ed. Horatio Rogers (Albany, 1884; reprint, Boston, 1972), 18–21.

10. GC to GG, Chambly, Sept. 28, 1776, *DAR*, 12:232–34. GC laid out his strategy for careful advances in this letter. GG, already concerned that GC would

not move expeditiously, had convinced George III to have GJB or some other ranking officer of GC's choosing to take charge of military operations, thus freeing GC to concentrate on civil affairs in Quebec Province. See GG's delicately worded letter to GC, dated Whitehall, Aug. 22, 1776, ibid., 12:187–88, which effectively removed GC from military command. GC did not receive this letter before sailing south out of Canada, or GJB might well have led the expedition onto Lake Champlain.

11. GC to [Henry] Caldwell, Pointe au Fer, Oct. 6, 1776, Cruikshank, ed., *Military and Naval Forces,* 2:193–94. The tone of this letter, as with that to GG (Sept. 28, 1776) in note 10 above, indicates that GC felt apprehensive about the presence of the rebel fleet, enough so to restrain any desire on his part to pursue anything more than limited objectives during this campaign thrust.

12. Thomas Pringle was from a venerable Scottish family and a son of an eminent West Indian merchant-planter. In 1775 he earned GC's gratitude by carrying dispatches about the rebel invasion back to England. Pringle went on to have a distinguished naval career and gained the rank of vice admiral before his death in Scotland in 1803. For more details, see Hadden, *A Journal,* 17–19n.

13. There is no satisfactory, detailed contemporary battle account. Any reconstruction of the Valcour Bay clash must be drawn from fragments of commentary by the participants, each of whom viewed the engagement from different angles and few of whom agreed on details. For instance, some participants thought BA had fifteen vessels, others sixteen (see chapter 11, note 3). BA, in his after-action account to HG, dated Schuyler's Island, Oct. 12, 1776, *AA,* 5 ser., 2:1038–39, stated that the battle began around 11 A.M. Joshua Pell, a British officer, said the action commenced at noontime. See "Diary of Joshua Pell," Oct. 11, 1776, *MAH,* 2 (1878): 46. Both accounts may be correct, since there was no hourly standardization of time. Other useful descriptions include Capt. Thomas Pringle to Mr. Stephens, *Maria* off Crown Point, Oct. 15, 1776, *AA,* 5 ser., 2:1069–70; Enys, Oct. 11–12, 1776, *American Journals,* 18–22; Hadden, Oct. 5–16, 1776, *A Journal,* 18–30; "Journal of Captain George Pausch," Oct. 11–13, 1776, *NDAR,* 6:1259–60; and "Journal Bayze Wells," Oct. 11–13, 1776, *Colls. Ct. Hist. Soc.,* 7 (1899): 283–84.

14. BA to HG, Schuyler's Island, Oct. 12, 1776, *AA,* 5 ser., 2:1038.

15. James Richard Dacres, born in Cumberland, England, was twenty-seven years old at the time of the battle. He had already served in the British navy for fourteen years. Like Pringle, he went on to have a distinguished naval career, rising to the rank of vice admiral of the white before his death in 1810. See Hadden, *A Journal,* 31–34n.

16. BA to HG, Schuyler's Island, Oct. 12, 1776, *AA,* 5 ser., 2:1038.

17. On the gunboat incident, see "Journal George Pausch," Oct. 11, 1776, *NDAR,* 6:1259–60. BA claimed to have sunk three gunboats that afternoon (BA to PS, Ticonderoga, Oct. 15, 1776, *AA,* 5 ser., 2:1080). Regarding the *Carleton,* Pell claimed that Dacres, "a true British tar," refused to disengage until "the general's [GC's] own boat came on board with positive orders to desist." No one else noted this act, which

seems unlikely. Furthermore, Dacres had been knocked senseless. See "Diary Joshua Pell," Oct. 11, 1776, *MAH* (1878): 46.

18. BA to HG, Schuyler's Island, Oct. 12, 1776, *AA,* 5 ser., 2:1038; Capt. Thomas Pringle to Mr. Stephens, *Maria* off Crown Point, Oct. 15, 1776, ibid., 5 ser., 2:1069; Hadden, *A Journal,* 23; "Journal George Pausch," Oct. 11, 1776, *NDAR,* 6:1259–60.

19. BA never learned that many of his papers were taken by the British boarding party before they burned the *Royal Savage.* Today they are preserved in the archives of Laval University in Quebec and have been published under the title "Documents sur l'Invasion Américaine," *RULQ,* 2 (1947–48): 344–49, 642–48, 742–48, 838–46, and 926–34.

20. Older, more antiquarian studies once espoused the northern escape view, or sailing northward and then around Valcour Island. See Peter S. Palmer, *History of Lake Champlain* (Albany, 1866), 129; and Winslow C. Watson, *The Military and Civil History of the County of Essex, New York* (Albany, 1869), 170. No document supports this remote likelihood.

21. BA to HG, Schuyler's Island, Oct. 12, 1776, *AA,* 5 ser., 2:1038.

22. For a British listing of captured or destroyed patriot craft, see Capt. Charles Douglass to Mr. Stephens, Quebec, Oct. 21, 1776, ibid., 5 ser., 2:1179.

23. "Journal Bayze Wells," Oct. 12, 1776, *Colls. Ct. Hist. Soc.,* 7 (1899): 284. See also BA to PS, Ticonderoga, Oct. 15, 1776, *AA,* 5 ser., 2:1079–80.

24. David Waterbury to JH, Pres. Congress, Stamford, Oct. 24, 1776, ibid., 5 ser., 2:1224.

25. Ibid.; BA to PS, Ticonderoga, Oct. 15, 1776, ibid., 5 ser., 2:1080.

26. Ibid. In this account, BA said the engagement lasted "for about five glasses [two-and-a-half hours]." Pringle sustained BA by estimating the fight at two hours. See Capt. Thomas Pringle to Mr. Stephens, *Maria* off Crown Point, Oct. 15, 1776, ibid., 5 ser., 2:1069.

27. Some commentators have indicated that BA abandoned the vessels in Buttonmould Bay. Cohn, "Incident Not Known to History," *Vermont History* (1987): 111n, 112n, has explained that Ferris Bay, today known as Arnold Bay, was the actual site. During the eighteenth century, Ferris and Buttonmould Bays often bore the latter name together. BA spoke of debarking near a "small creek," which helped to protect his fleeing craft from British fire (BA to PS, Ticonderoga, Oct. 15, 1776, ibid., 5 ser., 2:1080). Such a creek exists in Arnold Bay, close to where remains of the *Congress* have been found.

28. Maguire, "Dr. Robert Knox's Account of the Battle of Valcour," ibid. (1978): 48. Claimed Knox in his account dated Oct. 29, 1776, BA set fire to the five vessels, "burning the wounded and sick with them." Baron Riedesel repeated the same story in his *Memoirs, and Letters and Journals, of Major General Riedesel, during His Residence in America,* trans. William L. Stone (2 vols., Albany, 1868), 1:80. For corrective comments about the rumored slaughter, see the recollections made in 1845 by an aging Squire Ferris, who was present when BA ordered the craft burned (Cohn, "An Incident Not Known to History," *Vermont History* [1987]: 106–10).

29. BA to PS, Ticonderoga, Oct. 15, 1776, *AA,* 5 ser., 2:1080.

30. Ibid. In this letter BA indicated that six craft were "saved," including two row galleys, two schooners, one sloop, and one gundalow. However, this figure included two vessels, the row galley *Gates* and the schooner *Liberty,* not engaged. BA thus lost eleven craft between Oct. 11 and 13: the schooner *Royal Savage* and gundalow *Philadelphia* at Valcour Bay; the gundalows *New Jersey, New York,* and *Providence* at Schuyler's Island; the row galley *Washington* (captured) off Split Rock; and the row galley *Congress* and four unidentified gundalows at Ferris (Arnold) Bay. In addition, on Oct. 15 the British claimed as a prize the cutter *Lee,* whose crew had abandoned this heavily damaged craft on Oct. 13. See A List of the Names, etc. of Rebel Vessels Taken by His Majesty's Fleet on Lake Champlain, Oct. 13, 1776, *NDAR,* 6:1245.

31. BA to PS, Ticonderoga, Oct. 15, 1776, *AA,* 5 ser., 2:1080.

32. On Oct. 10, 1776, BA wrote HG from Valcour Bay (ibid., 5 ser., 2:982), "I am extremely glad you have represented to Congress and General Schuyler the absolute necessity of augmenting our navy on the lake. It appears to me an object of the utmost importance. I hope measures will be immediately taken for that purpose. . . . Perhaps it may be well to have one frigate of thirty-six guns; she may carry eighteen pounders on the lake, and will be superior to any vessel that can be built at and floated from St. Johns." BA was likely reflecting his awareness of the *Inflexible.* Congress, in turn, offered no direction or leadership in calling for the reconstruction of an effective lake fleet for the 1777 campaign.

33. General Orders, Northern Army, Ticonderoga, Oct. 26, 1776, ibid., 5 ser., 3:532.

34. David Waterbury to JH, Pres. Congress, Stamford, Oct. 24, 1776, ibid., 5 ser., 2:1224.

35. GC to GG, On Board the *Maria* off Crown Point, Oct. 14, 1776, *DAR,* 12:237. Like the Howe brothers, GC was attempting to use an appropriate amount of martial force to effect a reconciliation. He had moved forward in careful advances during 1776, seeking to demonstrate the futility of further rebel resistance. GC's decision to release Waterbury and the other captives was part of his strategy; they could spread the message of Britain's clemency. Further, with supplies hardly abundant, GC's force would not have to keep feeding them. Writing from Quebec on Aug. 10, 1776, GC enclosed in a letter to GG (ibid., 12:180–83), an accounting of patriot prisoners taken since the rebel Canadian campaign began. Not including Waterbury's group, the total was 1,283. Most, such as BA's famine-proof veterans, had already been released and were back in the rebellious colonies but not necessarily spreading the word about Britain's humanity. The Aug. 10 list of prisoners may be found in Cruikshank, ed., *Military and Naval Forces,* 2:184–85.

36. HG to PS, Ticonderoga, Oct. 15, 1776, *AA,* 5 ser., 2:1080–81; General Orders, Northern Army, Ticonderoga, Oct. 14, 1776, ibid., 5 ser., 3:529. On munitions supplies, see PS to HG, Saratoga, Oct. 14, 1776, ibid., 5 ser., 2:1039–40; and PS to

GW, Saratoga, Oct. 16, 1776, *Paps. GW, RWS,* 6:579, reporting that "the ammunition arrived at Ticonderoga last night."

37. "Journal Bayze Wells," Oct. 28, 1776, *Colls Ct. Hist. Soc.,* 7 (1899): 286.

38. HG to PS, Ticonderoga, Oct. 24, 1776, *AA,* 5 ser., 3:575; BA to GW, Ticonderoga, Nov. 6, 1776, ibid., 5 ser., 3:550.

39. After GC's pullback from Crown Point to Canada, GJB returned to England for the winter and worked actively to secure for himself the command assignment that GG had wanted him to assume back in Aug. 1776. See note 10 above, and GG to GC, Whitehall, Aug. 22, 1776, *DAR,* 12:187–88.

40. General Orders, Northern Army, Ticonderoga, Oct. 14, 1776, *AA,* 5 ser., 3:527; HG to PS, Ticonderoga, Oct. 15, 1776, ibid., 5 ser., 1080; HG to Gov. Jonathan Trumbull, Ticonderoga, Oct. 22, 1776, ibid., 5 ser., 2:1192.

41. Benjamin Rush to Thomas Morris, Phila., Oct. 22, 1776, *LDC,* 5:365; Richard Henry Lee to Unknown, Phila. Oct. 22, 1776, ibid., 364.

42. Hadden, *A Journal,* 24–25; *The Annual Register, 1777,* in *Rebellion in America: A Contemporary British Viewpoint, 1765–1783,* ed. David H. Murdoch (Santa Barbara, Ca., 1979), 421–23.

43. William Maxwell to Gov. William Livingston, Ticonderoga, Oct. 20, 1776, *AA,* 5 ser., 2:1143. Maxwell was of the Waterbury school of strategy; see note 3 above. This letter, lacking as it did in strategic comprehension, had a serious negative effect on BA's patriot military career. What is clear is that Maxwell, formerly a commissioned regular British officer, resented younger men who stood ahead of him in Continental rank. For Maxwell's sense of pique about Congress promoting Arthur St. Clair, "a younger officer," ahead of him to the general officer corps, see The Memorial of Col. William Maxwell to the Honorable Continental Congress, [Sept. 1776?], PCC, microfilm reel 99, item 78, vol. 15:87, NA.

44. Ibid.; JW *Memoirs,* 1:87, 93. The notion that BA wantonly violated HG's Aug. 7 orders persists. See Paul David Nelson, "Guy Carleton vs. Benedict Arnold," *New York History* (1976): 366. Nelson also criticizes Mahan (see note 3 above) for arguing in favor of BA's vigorous defense of Lake Champlain.

45. HG to BA, Ticonderoga, Oct. 12, 1776, *AA,* 5 ser., 2:1017.

46. JW *Memoirs,* 1:93; Richard Henry Lee to Thomas Jefferson, Phila., Nov. 3, 1776, *LDC,* 5:431.

47. PS to JH, Pres. Congress, Saratoga, Nov. 21, 1776, *AA,* 5 ser., 3:796–97; Council of War Minutes, Saratoga, Nov. 21, 1776, ibid., 5 ser., 3:797.

48. PS to JH, Pres. Congress, Albany, Nov. 27, 1776, ibid., 5 ser., 3:874–75. GC's withdrawal to Canada actually abetted the rebel cause by freeing up patriot soldiers at Ticonderoga to go south and support GW's beleaguered force in eastern Pennsylvania. GC's action thus worked to the detriment of WH's campaign. GC was aware of the need to support WH by keeping the rebel northern force tied down. In GC to WH, Crown Point, Oct. 20, 1776 (*NDAR,* 6:1336), he wrote of his intention to pull back into Canada but hoped "however that our appearance on this side of the

lake will occasion a diversion which may be favorable to your operations." In contrast, GC was ignorant of WH's movements. As GC stated to GG from Quebec on Nov. 17, 1776 (Cruikshank, ed., *Military and Naval Forces*, 2:196–97), "I have heard nothing from General Howe except by a letter containing a request to be supplied with hay and oats and dated the day before an action is said to have happened on Long Island." GC should have made a serious effort to find out about WH's operations, especially since he had orders to work in conjunction with WH. (The same could be said of WH in relation to GC as well.) A real failure of the British generals in America was to communicate effectively among themselves in the orchestration of their campaign efforts. That negligence helped rescue GW from desperate circumstances at the end of 1776.

49. Court of Inquiry on General Arnold, Albany, Dec. 2, 1776, *AA*, 5 ser., 3:1042–43. The hearing panel consisted of General James Brickett, Colonel Edward Wigglesworth, and Colonel Philip Van Cortlandt of New York. Apparently MH had submitted the receipt to the Canadian commissioners for reimbursement before they returned to Philadelphia. They asked BA to comment, and he most likely offered his insulting remark shortly after the Cedars contretemps with MH. General Brickett wrote up the minutes of the inquiry, and his text is none too clear on the matter.

50. "Extracts from the Diaries in the Moravian Archives at Bethlehem, Pennsylvania," *PMHB*, 12 (1888): 394–95; GW to Nicholas Cooke, Camp above Trenton Falls, Dec. 21, 1776, *Writings GW*, 6:412–13.

51. Ibid.; GW to BA, Headquarters Bucks County, Pa., Dec. 14, 1776, ibid., 6:374–75. New Englanders in Congress wanted HG or NG to have the assignment, since they "are greatly beloved in that part of America." See New England Delegates (SA, William Ellery, Elbridge Gerry, and William Whipple) to GW, Phila., Dec. 12, 1776, 5:603. By the time GW received this letter, he had already selected BA and Gen. Joseph Spencer. The decision reflected GW's confidence in BA's demonstrated capacity to hold a critical independent command. Furthermore, GW wanted HG and NG to help him plan and execute what became his masterful attack on Trenton. At the same time, GW was trying to find a suitable assignment for the aging Spencer, a ranking Connecticut militia officer at the outbreak of the war. Receiving a brigadier general's commission from Congress in June 1775, Spencer felt deeply slighted over not obtaining a higher rank. Eventually he agreed to serve, and Congress made him a major general in August 1776, despite lackluster service. Spencer was characteristic of the ranking generals from Connecticut who would block BA's upward movement in the Continental general officer corps. To no one's particular regret, Spencer finally resigned his commission in 1778.

THIRTEEN: *Fundamental Matters of Military Rank and Personal Honor*

1. GW to John Augustine Washington, Camp near the Falls of Trenton, Dec. 18, 1776, *Writings GW*, 6:398–99; Henry Clinton, *The American Rebellion: Sir Henry*

Clinton's Narrative of the Campaigns, 1775–1782 . . ., ed. William B. Willcox (New Haven, 1954), 55. Secondary works informing this chapter include Cress, *Citizens in Arms*, 34–66; James Kirby Martin, "The Continental Army and the American Victory," in *The World Turned Upside Down: The American Victory in the War of Independence*, ed. John Ferling (Westport, 1988), 19–34; Martin and Lender, *A Respectable Army*, 57–78; Charles Patrick Neimeyer, *America Goes to War: A Social History of the Continental Army* (New York, 1996), 8–26; Nelson, *Horatio Gates*, 74–82; Rossie, *Politics of Command*, 135–53; Royster, *Revolutionary People at War*, 86–95; Shy, "American Strategy: Charles Lee and the Radical Alternative," in Shy, *A People Numerous and Armed*, 135–62; John Todd White, "Standing Armies in Time of War: Republican Theory and Military Practice during the American Revolution" (doctoral dissertation, George Washington University, 1978), 181–223; and William B. Willcox, *Portrait of a General: Sir Henry Clinton and the War of Independence* (New York, 1964), 115–29.

2. *The American Crisis*, I, *The Writings of Thomas Paine*, ed. Moncure D. Conway (4 vols., New York, 1894–1896), 1:170.

3. New England Delegates (SA, William Ellery, Elbridge Gerry, and William Whipple) to GW, Phila., Dec. 12, 1776, *LDC*, 5:603. Gerry in particular was upset with GW's seeming obstinacy in not appointing HG or NG. He could not understand why GW "is not complying with our request" and indicated he would call upon Congress to investigate the matter. See Elbridge Gerry to James Warren, Baltimore, Dec. 23, 1776, ibid., 5:641.

4. Charles Lee to HG, Basking Ridge, Dec. 13, 1776, *The Lee Papers*, Colls. of the N-YHS for the Years 1871–1875 (4 vols., New York, 1872–1876), 2:348.

5. On Thurs., Dec. 12, 1776, Congress, just before adjourning to Baltimore, resolved that "General Washington be possessed of full power to order and direct all things relative to the department, and to the operations of war" (*JCC*, 6:1027). The delegates thus gave GW virtual dictatorial powers, leaving for themselves the option to decide whether they approved of his decision making, should he somehow repel the British onslaught.

6. JH, Pres. Congress, to PS, Baltimore, Dec. 30, 1776, *LDC*, 5:702. The argument that health problems caused HG to abandon GW and the Continental army at this crucial juncture is that of Nelson, *Horatio Gates*, 75–77. After all, JH reported to PS from Baltimore on Jan. 30, 1777 (*LDC*, 5:702), that HG was already "much recovered" in health, an impressive recovery rate for a man apparently so desperately ill, especially after so long a journey southward to Baltimore.

7. SA to JA, Baltimore, Jan. 9, 1777, ibid., 6:65; Petition Addressed to the Honorable HG, from JB, Albany, Dec. 1, 1776, *AA*, 5 ser., 3:1158–59.

8. The rhetorical concept of recognizing and rewarding citizens of proven merit, as opposed to deferring to bloodline aristocrats and entrenched elites in matters of leadership, was an inherent part of the republican ideology of the Revolution. Wrote JA in his *Thoughts on Government* in 1776, for example, leadership positions should naturally be accorded to "the most wise and good" in the community, by which he

meant an aristocracy of acknowledged talent. See *The Works of John Adams,* ed. Charles Francis Adams (10 vols., Boston, 1850–1856), 4:194.

9. BA to GW, Ticonderoga, Nov. 6, 1776, *AA,* 5 ser., 3:550. HA had earlier informed BA that Oswald in particular was having a problem getting formally exchanged. See HA to BA, New Haven, Aug. 5, 1776, "Documents sur l'Invasion Américaine," *RULQ* (1948): 644. See also Return J. Meigs to BA, Middletown, July 29, 1776, ibid., 642–43, who likewise asked BA to "exert" himself on behalf of getting the prisoners exchanged.

10. Leake, *Life of John Lamb,* 152–53. On BA's efforts to find a suitable post for Mansfield, who had served on Lake Champlain where he "behaved with great prudence and bravery," see BA to GW, Providence, Jan. 13, 1777, *CAR,* 1:327. BA agreed to underwrite Lamb about a month later after Oswald visited with him.

11. HA to BA, New Haven, Sept. 1, 1776, "Documents sur l'Invasion Américaine," *RULQ* (1948): 746–47.

12. BA Wastebook, Jan. 1777 entries, NHCHS, 92–93; BA to Capt. Hector McNeill, Providence, Jan. 18, 1777, Misc. BA Paps., MHS.

13. NG to Nicholas Cooke, Coryell's Ferry, Pa., Dec. 21, 1776, *Paps. NG,* 1:376.

14. Petition Addressed to the Honorable HG, from JB, Albany, Dec. 1, 1776, *AA,* 5 ser., 3:1158. See also HG to JB, Albany, Dec. 2, 1776, ibid., 5 ser., 3:1160. HG promised JB to "lay your petition before Congress, who will, when they see fit, give such redress as they think necessary thereupon." Brown apparently did not fully trust HG to deliver the petition, so he sent another copy to Congress. See JB to JH, Pres. Congress, Albany, Dec. 10, 1776, ibid., 3:1158.

15. Petition Addressed to the Honorable HG, from JB, Albany, Dec. 1, ibid., 5 ser., 3:1158–59; JB to HG, Albany, Dec. 2, 1776, ibid., 5 ser., 3:1159–60.

16. JB to Theodore Sedgwick, Albany, Dec. 6, 1776, Sedgwick Paps., MHS.

17. GW to Joseph Spencer, Headquarters, Bucks County, Dec. 14, 1776, *Writings GW,* 6:373–74; GW to BA, Headquarters, Bucks County, Dec. 14, 1776, ibid., 6:374–75.

18. Willcox, ed., *Clinton's Narrative,* xvii, 54–58.

19. BA to GW, Providence, Jan. 13, 1777, *CAR,* 1:326–27; Martin and Lender, *A Respectable Army,* 65–78. Because recruiting went so poorly in early 1777, Congress resolved to have the states consider conscription (Mon., Apr. 14, 1777, *JCC,* 7:261–63). See Mark Edward Lender, "The Conscripted Line: The Draft in Revolutionary New Jersey," *New Jersey History,* 103 (1985): 23–45; and, more generally, Neimeyer, *America Goes to War,* 108–29.

20. BA to GW, Providence, Jan. 31, 1777, *CAR,* 1:335.

21. GW to BA, Headquarters, Morristown, Feb. 6, 1777, *Writings GW,* 7:115.

22. BA to GW, Providence, Feb. 7, 1777, GW Paps., microfilm reel 40, 4 ser., LC. The General Return, dated May 21, 1777, for GW's main Continental force showed only 10,003 Continentals on the muster roll, with 7,363 present and fit for duty. See *The Sinews of Independence: Monthly Strength Reports of the Continental*

Army, comp. Charles H. Lesser (Chicago, 1976), 46–47; Martin and Lender, *A Respectable Army,* 75–78.

23. BA to GW, Providence, Feb. 10, 1777, GW Paps., microfilm reel 40, 4 ser., LC.

24. BA to Paul Revere, Boston, Mar. 1, 1777, Misc. BA Paps., MHS.

25. For a family's sense of Elizabeth De Blois, with implications that she never would have been so foolish as to take the future traitor seriously, see Lewis A. De Blois to James T. Flexner, Sharon, Ct., Nov. 19, 1954, Misc. Docs., MHS.

26. BA to Lucy Knox, Watertown, Mar. 4, 1777, *HM,* 2 ser., 2 (1867): 305.

27. BA to PS, Providence, March 8, 1777, PS Paps., NYPL.

28. BA to NG, Providence, Mar. 10, 1777, *Paps. NG,* 2:42.

29. A summary of GW's thinking may be found in GW to JH, Pres. Congress, Heights of Harlem, Sept. 24, 1776, *Writings GW,* 5:106–16.

30. SA to James Warren, Phila., Jan. 7, 1776, Ford, ed., *Warren-Adams Letters,* 1:197–98. See also the essay by "Caractacus," entitled "On Standing Armies," Aug. 21, 1775, *AA,* 4 ser., 3:219–21; Cress, *Citizens in Arms,* 36–50.

31. Fri., Dec. 27, 1776, *JCC,* 6:1045–46.

32. GW to JH, Pres. Congress, Morristown, Jan. 22, 1777, *Writings GW,* 7:49–51. For Congress's authorization of what proved to be a fanciful force of seventy-five thousand troops in eighty-eight regiments, see Mon., Sept. 16, 1776, *JCC,* 5:762–63.

33. Thomas Burke's Notes of Debates, Feb. 12–19, 1777, *LDC,* 6:263–64; Benjamin Rush's Notes of Debates, Feb. 19, 1777, ibid., 6:323–24; Weds., Feb. 19, 1777, *JCC,* 7:133; Francis Lewis to New York Convention, Baltimore, Feb. 18, 1777, *LDC,* 6:314.

34. Roger Sherman to Jonathan Trumbull, Phila., Mar. 4 [i.e. 6], 1777, ibid., 6:404–5. See also Elbridge Gerry to Joseph Trumbull, Phila., March 26, 1777, ibid., 6:494, for the standard public explanation regarding BA's nonpromotion.

35. The date of BA's brig's. commission was Jan. 10, 1776. Lord Stirling, named a brig. gen. on March 1, 1776, had fought valiantly during the Battle of Long Island, where he was captured and exchanged before again performing ably at Trenton. His record after 1777 was solid although undistinguished. Thomas Mifflin became GW's quartermaster gen. in August 1775. Awarded a brig.'s commission on May 16, 1776, Mifflin performed ineffectively in that post during 1777 and is often blamed for the supply shortages at Valley Forge. He resigned from the army in 1779. Arthur St. Clair, whose brig.'s commission bore the date Aug. 9, 1776, served HG ably at Ticonderoga during the fall of 1776. In July 1777 he suffered the embarrassment of losing Ticonderoga to the British, for which he would ultimately be exonerated after a court of inquiry. Adam Stephen was named a brig. gen. on Sept. 4, 1776. He was allegedly drunk while in command of a Continental division at the Battle of Germantown in Oct. 1777. A court-martial board recommended Stephen's dismissal from the service, which both GW and Congress sustained. Lincoln, of whom GW had spoken favorably, would prove himself competent, even though he had to

surrender the main Southern Dept. force under his command at Charleston, S.C., in May 1780. The sum total record of these five officers, both before and after Feb. 19, 1777, indicates that Congress did not exercise its best judgment about those patriots who should be preferred to BA for maj. generalships in the Continental army. See chapter 17 for additional retrospective comments.

36. Thomas Burke's Notes of Debates, Feb. 12–19, 1777, *LDC,* 6:264; Roger Sherman to Jonathan Trumbull, Phila., March 4 [i.e. 6], 1777, ibid., 6:404.

37. Francis Lewis to New York Convention, Baltimore, Feb. 18, 1777, ibid., 6:314; Benjamin Rush's Notes of Debates, Feb. 19, 1777, ibid., 6:323–24.

38. Roger Sherman to Jonathan Trumbull, Phila., March 4 [i.e. 6], 1777, ibid., 6:404–5. Connecticut had named six delegates to Congress, but only two, Sherman and Oliver Wolcott, were present. As further evidence of the hold that a select few gentlemen had on Connecticut's affairs, Sherman seemed most concerned about getting the all-but-censured DW a maj. generalship. See Collier, *Roger Sherman's Connecticut,* 11–14. Sherman's focus on DW, especially in comparison to BA, suggests that he had little comprehension of the qualities making for outstanding generalship.

39. Benjamin Rush's Notes of Debates, Feb. 19, 1777, *LDC,* 6:323.

40. JA to AA, Baltimore, Feb. 21, 1777, ibid., 6:334–35. On this same Fri., Feb. 21 (*JCC,* 7:141), Congress selected ten new brig. generals: Enoch Poor of New Hampshire; John Glover and John Paterson of Massachusetts; James M. Varnum of Rhode Island; John Cadwalader, John Philip De Haas, and Anthony Wayne of Pennsylvania; and John Peter Gabriel Muhlenberg, George Weedon, and William Woodford of Virginia. At least two, Glover and Wayne, represented superb appointments. In contrast, De Haas had already demonstrated his many limitations while serving under BA in Canada. Poor, who had chaired the MH court of inquiry, had not yet done anything to distinguish himself, especially in comparison to Col. John Stark, who was senior to him in the New Hampshire line. For BA, the elevation of De Haas and Poor no doubt represented further proof of Congress's lack of perspicacity in its selection of general officers. De Haas chose either to retire or to become invisible after his promotion, which was probably in everyone's best interest. Poor would emerge as a useful general officer.

41. Thomas Burke's Notes of Debates, Feb. 12–19, 1777, *LDC,* 6:263–64; JA to AA, Baltimore, Feb. 21, 1777, ibid., 6:335.

42. GW to BA, Morristown, Mar. 3, 1777, *Writings GW,* 7:233–34.

43. GW to Richard Henry Lee, Morristown, Mar. 6, 1777, ibid., 7:251. Some officers made discreet inquiries to congressional delegates about BA's case. They were not so much advocating BA's promotion as they were asking themselves: What, indeed, must a person accomplish to become a general officer in the face of such arbitrary standards for promotion? See, for example, Col. Joseph Trumbull to Elbridge Gerry, Hartford, Mar. 10, 1777, Gerry Paps., N-YHS, and Gerry's soothing response to Trumbull, dated Phila., Mar. 26, 1777 (*LDC,* 6:494), in which he described BA "as a brave and deserving officer" who eventually "will meet a timely promotion." Gerry was sanitizing Congressional politics because, among other rea-

sons, he knew that Trumbull would share his response with many other worried officers who were now wondering about the meaning of performing meritorious service.

44. BA to GW, Providence, Mar. 11, 1777, *CAR,* 1:353–56; BA to GW, Providence, Mar. 26, 1777, ibid., 1:360.

45. In Mar. 1777, BA found himself in the same position as the talented Col. John Stark of New Hampshire, who had distinguished himself at Trenton and Princeton. Rather than seeking a redress of grievances, however, Stark resigned his col.'s commission on Mar. 23, 1777. Soon thereafter he accepted a maj. gen.'s militia commission from New Hampshire. He again showed his extraordinary fighting capacity at the Battle of Bennington (Aug. 16, 1777), so much so that an embarrassed Congress responded by commissioning him a brig. gen. Having the self-assurance not to fret about matters of seniority in relation to his personal reputation, Stark accepted the commission but remained very independent in his actions, acting as if the judgments of Congress, especially in its evaluation of meritorious service, were not worthy of an intelligent person's consideration. BA would have better served himself in the long run if he had shown the same confidence in his own reputation.

46. BA to HG, Providence, Mar. 25, 1777, Gates Paps., NY-HS.

47. BA to GW, Providence, Mar. 26, 1777, *CAR,* 1:359–60.

48. GW to BA, Morristown, Apr. 3, 1777, *Writings GW,* 7:352–53.

49. Ibid., 7:352.

50. Lucy Knox to Henry Knox, Boston, Apr. 3, 1777, Knox Paps., MHS. Betsy De Blois tried but failed to elope with stay maker Martin Brimmer in Aug. 1777, soon after her sixteenth birthday. Brimmer was about BA's age. Betsy apparently never married. See Lewis A. De Blois to James T. Flexner, Sharon, Nov. 19, 1954, Misc. Docs., MHS. In Henry Knox to William Knox, Morristown, Mar. 23, 1777, Knox Paps., MHS, GW's artillery chief stated of Congress's decision not to promote BA, "This most infallibly pushes him [BA] out of the service. I hope this affair will be remedied."

51. GW to Richard Henry Lee, Morristown, Apr. 24, 1777, *Memoir of the Life of Richard Henry Lee, and his Correspondence,* comp. James C. Ballagh (2 vols., Philadelphia, 1825), 2:14 (*Writings GW,* 7:462–65, reprints the text of GW's letter but not the postscript in which these comments appear); Richard Henry Lee to GW, Phila., Apr. 29, 1777, *LDC,* 6:677.

52. GW to PS, Morristown, Feb. 19, 1777, *Writings GW,* 7:163.

FOURTEEN: *The Humiliating Part of a Faithful Soldier*

1. BA to Alexander McDougall, West Redding, Ct., Apr. 27, 1777, PCC, microfilm reel 186, item 169, vol. 3:191–92, NA. A compelling account of the Danbury raid remains Leake, *Life of John Lamb,* 154–64. Secondary works informing this chapter include Richard Buel Jr., *Dear Liberty: Connecticut's Mobilization for the Revolutionary War* (Middletown, Ct., 1980), 93–116; Gerlach, *Proud Patriot,* 211–33; Gruber, *Howe*

Brothers, 189–230; H. James Henderson, *Party Politics in the Continental Congress* (New York, 1974), 100–118; Kohn, "American Generals of the Revolution," in Higginbotham, ed., *Reconsiderations Revolutionary War,* 104–23; Max M. Mintz, *The Generals of Saratoga: John Burgoyne and Horatio Gates* (New Haven, 1990), 119–30; Nelson, *Horatio Gates,* 78–88, and Nelson, *William Tryon and the Course of Empire: A Life in British Imperial Service* (Chapel Hill, 1990), 1–17, 148–54; Rossie, *Politics of Command,* 141–53; John S. Pancake, *1777: The Year of the Hangman* (University, Ala., 1977), 87–101; and Ward, *War of the Revolution,* 1:325–33; 2:492–95.

2. A British Officer's Account of the Danbury Raid, Apr. 21–28, 1777, *NDAR,* 8:455; Alexander McDougall to GW, Peekskill, N.Y., Apr. 29, 1777, *CAR,* 1:373–74; Ralph Isaacs to Lucy Knox, Wallingford, Ct., Apr. 30, 1777, Knox Paps., MHS.

3. Jedidiah Huntington to Alexander McDougall, n.p., Apr. 28, 1777, PCC, microfilm reel 167, item 52, vol. 4:143, NA; William Carmichael to Charles W. F. Dumas, Paris, June 20, 1777, *The Deane Papers,* Colls. of the N-YHS for the Years 1886–1890 (5 vols., New York, 1887–1891), 2:74.

4. *The Annual Register, 1777,* Murdoch, ed., *Rebellion in America,* 454–57; A British Officer's Account, n.p., Apr. 21–28, 1777, *NDAR,* 8:456; *Connecticut Journal* [New Haven], Apr. 30, 1777, Moore, comp., *Diary Am. Rev.,* 1:423–25. See also Paul Wentworth to the Earl of Suffolk, [London?], May 18, 1777, Stevens, ed., *Facsimiles,* 2, no. 155, for an intelligence report that bears a strong similarity to the British officer's account.

5. Hugh Hughes to Alexander McDougall, Saugatuck Bridge, Apr. 28, 1777, PCC, microfilm reel 167, item 152, vol. 4:141–42, NA.

6. Hugh Hughes to Horatio Gates, Fishkill, N.Y., May 3, 1777, Gates Paps., N-YHS.

7. BA to Alexander McDougall, Saugatuck, Apr. 28, 1777, PCC, microfilm reel 186, item 169, vol. 3:197–98, NA.

8. Ibid.; Thomas Burke to Richard Caswell, Phila., May 2, 1777, *LDC,* 7:13; GW to JH, Pres. Congress, Morristown, Apr. 28, 1777, *Writings GW,* 7:490. In regard to casualties, each side inflated the losses of their opponent, perhaps as a way of asserting victory. According to A British Officer's Account, n.p., Apr. 21–28, 1977, *NDAR,* 8:456, patriot losses were about three hundred dead and about half that number taken prisoner. By comparison, he stated that the British lost seventy killed but returned to New York with all their wounded. See *NDAR,* 8:456. NG maintained that total British casualties amounted to six hundred. See NG to JA, Morristown, May 2, 1777, *Paps. NG,* 2:65. More accurately, Peckham, ed., *Toll of Independence,* 33, lists patriot casualties at twenty killed and seventy-five wounded. The British fared somewhat worse with 25 killed, 117 wounded, and 29 missing or captured. Had more patriot citizens come out for the fight, the result could have been much worse for the British, as at Lexington and Concord.

9. Fri., May 2, 1777, *JCC,* 7:323; JA to AA, Phila., May 2, 1777, *LDC,* 7:12; JH, Pres. Congress, to GW, Phila., May 3, 1777, ibid., 7:22. Congress also decided that the army needed another brig. gen. and on Mon., May 12, 1777 (*JCC,* 7:347),

elevated Col. Jedidiah Huntington of Connecticut, whom GW considered a very able officer and who had fought with distinction against Tryon's raiders. Like BA, Huntington had been passed over the previous Feb.

10. JA to NG, Phila., May 9, 1777, *LDC,* 7:49. Of the remaining seven medals, HG would receive recognition for the Saratoga victory later in 1777; Anthony Wayne and two others for Stony Point in 1779; "Light Horse" Harry Lee for Paulus Hook in 1779; and Daniel Morgan and one other for the Cowpens victory in 1781.

11. GW, to JH, Pres. Congress, Morristown, May 5, 1777, *Writings GW,* 8:16.

12. GW to BA, Morristown, May 8, 1777, ibid., 8:30.

13. NG to JA, Bound Brook, N. J., May 7, 1777, *Paps. NG,* 2:71.

14. GW to JH, Pres. Congress, Morristown, May 12, 1777, *Writings GW,* 8:47–48.

15. BA to Jeremiah Wadsworth, New Haven, May 6, 1777, PML.

16. Handbill, reprinted in Smith, comp., *History of Pittsfield* 1:73–74. Since JB was one of the few known Revolutionary leaders Pittsfield could claim, portions of this volume serve as a glorification of JB, as well as an assault on the "treasonous" BA. Portions of the material are apocryphal at best.

17. BA to Jeremiah Wadsworth, New Haven, May 6, 1777, PML. Congress accepted JB's resignation on Sat., March 15, 1777, *JCC,* 7:181.

18. On May 16, 1777, GW wrote to Brig. Gen. Alexander McDougall from Morristown (*Writings GW,* 8:67) that BA had journeyed to Philadelphia to settle some issues "previous to his accepting of the rank lately conferred on him."

19. GW to JH, Pres. Congress, Morristown, May 12, 1777, ibid., 8:47–48.

20. CC to Charles Carroll Sr., Phila., May 14 [16], 1777, *LDC,* 7:85; Corner, ed., *Autobiography of Benjamin Rush,* 158. In what were undoubtedly post-treason comments, Rush also said of BA, "His conversation was sometimes uninteresting and sometimes indelicate. His language was ungrammatical and his pronunciation vulgar." If such were the case, surely someone such as the very sophisticated CC would have corroborated Rush's observations.

21. BA to JH, Pres. Congress, Phila., May 20, 1777, PCC, microfilm reel 179, item 162: 86–87, NA.

22. Tues., May 20, 1777, *JCC,* 7:372–73; Richard Henry Lee to Thomas Jefferson, Phila., May 20, 1777, *LDC,* 7:95.

23. JA to AA, Phila., May 22, 1777, ibid., 7:103–4.

24. Board of War, Report to Congress, Fri., May 23, 1777, PCC, microfilm reel 157, item 147, vol. 1:177–79; *JCC,* 8:382.

25. BA to Jeremiah Wadsworth, Phila., May 30, 1777, Wadsworth Paps., CHS.

26. PS presented his credentials to Congress on Apr. 7. On the committee to inquire into PS's conduct, see Fri., Apr. 18, 1777, *JCC,* 7:279–80.

27. Since early in 1777, Congress, with New Englanders in the lead, had employed various devices to get PS to resign his command. A typical action was the removal of his close friend, Dr. Samuel Stringer, from the post of head physician and director of Northern Department hospitals. When PS protested, the delegates said they were under no obligation to explain themselves. Further, they considered PS's

rejoinder "highly derogatory to the honor of Congress." They "expected his letters . . . [to] be written in a style more suitable to the dignity of the representative body of these free and independent states" (Sat., Mar. 15, 1777, ibid., 7:180; JH, Pres. Congress, to PS, Phila., Mar. 18, 1777, *LDC,* 6:460). Wrote PS from Philadelphia to his chief aide, RV, on Apr. 16, 1777 (ibid., 6:597–98), "some people here are greatly disappointed. They were in hopes I would have resigned immediately upon my receiving certain very unaccountable resolutions of the 15th ult."

28. Tues., Mar. 25, 1777, *JCC,* 7:202. JH, Pres. Congress, wrote to HG, dated Phila., Mar. 25, 1777 (*LDC,* 6:486–87): "I have it therefore in charge to direct, that you repair to Saratoga immediately, and *take the command* of the army in that department." This Congressional directive could obviously be read that HG was to supplant PS as head of the Northern Department. On St. Clair's appointment, see Tues., Apr. 1, 1777, *JCC,* 7:217. That Congress ordered St. Clair "to repair to Ticonderoga, and serve under General Gates," was another skillfully designed play on words by the anti-PS delegates. With HG setting up his standard in Albany, St. Clair thus became the de facto frontline commander at Ticonderoga.

29. The charges being leveled at PS became abundantly clear in late July after the loss of Ticonderoga. See Charles Thomson's Notes of Debates, July 26 and 28, 1777, *LDC,* 7:382–83, 388–89.

30. Board of War Report, Thurs., May 15, 1777, *JCC,* 7:364, and Thurs., May 22, 1777, ibid., 7:375; JA to AA, Phila., May 22, 1777, *LDC,* 7:103.

31. JA to AA, Phila., June 8, 1777, ibid., 7:175.

32. On the evolution of WH's thinking with respect to conducting the 1777 campaign, see Gruber, *Howe Brothers,* 174–88, who places less emphasis on WH's desire for a "decisive action" in New Jersey than do Martin and Lender, *A Respectable Army,* 78–83.

33. Whatever caused WH's procrastination, GW's advance to Middlebrook Heights served as an opening challenge. Had GW not moved, WH might well have waited to commence operations until after receiving GG to WH, Whitehall, May 18, 1777 (*DAR,* 14:84–85). In this letter, GG approved WH's invasion of Pennsylvania so long as his objectives were "executed in time for you to cooperate with the army ordered to proceed from Canada." GG's letter seemed to reassure WH that he could accomplish both goals in the same campaign season. See also Gruber, *Howe Brothers,* 224–29.

34. JS to BA, Princeton, May 31, 1777, *Letters and Papers of Major-General John Sullivan,* ed. Otis G. Hammond, *Collections of the New Hampshire Historical Society* (3 vols., Concord, N.H., 1930–1939), 1:350.

35. BA to JS, Phila., June 1, 1777, ibid., 1:355.

36. GW to BA, Middlebrook, June 7, 1777, *Writings GW,* 8:195–96.

37. BA to JS, Phila., June 9, 1777, Hammond, ed., *Sullivan Paps.,* 1:376.

38. BA to JH, Pres. Congress, Phila., June 10, 1777, PCC, microfilm reel 179, item 162: 90–91, NA; Tues., June 10, 1777, *JCC,* 8:432; JH to BA, Phila., June 11, 1777, *LDC,* 7:182–83.

39. BA to JH, Pres. Congress, Phila., June 13, 1777, PCC, microfilm reel 179, item 162: 92–94, NA.

40. BA to Thomas Mifflin, Coryell's Ferry, June 15, 1777, *The Literary Diary of Ezra Stiles, D.D., LL.D,* ed. Franklin B. Dexter (3 vols., New York, 1901), 2:176. For additional information on BA's communications to Philadelphia, see CC to Charles Carroll, Sr., Phila., June 16, 1777, *LDC,* 7:197–98; Committee for Foreign Affairs (Benjamin Harrison, Thomas Heyward, JL, Robert Morris, and John Witherspoon) to Commissioners at Paris (SD, BF, and Arthur Lee), Phila., June 18, 1777, ibid., 8:259–62.

41. JA to AA, Phila., June 18, 1777, ibid., 7:207; GW to PS, Middlebrook, June 16, 1777, *Writings GW,* 8:253–54; GW to BA, Middlebrook, June 17, 1777, ibid., 8:259–62.

42. Ibid. See also BA to GW, Coryell's Ferry, June 16, 1777, *CAR,* 1:384–86, in which he stated: "The enemy must be desperate indeed if they attempt to push for Philadelphia." However, BA has hoping WH would try to do so.

43. Lucy Knox to Henry Knox, Boston, June 3, 4, 8, 1777, Knox Paps., MHS.

44. Henry Knox to JH, Pres. Congress, Middlebrook, July 1, 1777, Knox Paps., MHS. See also NG to JH, Pres. Congress, Middlebrook, July 1, 1777, *Paps. NG,* 2:109.

45. Mon., July 7, 1777, *JCC,* 8:537.

46. JA Diary, Sept. 18, 1777, *Diary and Autobiography of John Adams,* ed. Lyman H. Butterfield et al. (4 vols., Cambridge, 1961), 2:263.

47. Weds., June 18, 1777, *JCC,* 8:476–79, does not mention HG's appearance; Horatio Gates's Notes for a Speech to Congress, [Phila., June 18, 1777], *LDC,* 7:213–15; James Duane to PS, Phila., June 19, 1777, ibid., 7:225; William Duer to PS, Phila., June 19, 1777, ibid., 7:228–30.

48. Tues., July 8, 1777, *JCC,* 8:540.

49. George Morgan to BA and Board of War, Phila., July 6, 1777 [original submitted June 28, 1777], PCC, microfilm reel 157, item 147, vol. 1:255, NA; BA to Richard Peters and Board of War, Phila., July 5, 1777, PCC, microfilm reel 157, item 147, vol. 1:259, NA. BA reviewed the June 28 proposal, which resulted in slight modifications. Congress debated Morgan's plan on Sat., July 19, Thurs., July 24, and Fri., July 25, 1777 (*JCC,* 8:566–67, 578, 579), before postponing further discussion. See also Charles Thomson's Notes of Debates, July 24, July 25, 1777, *LDC,* 7:371–72, 373–75.

50. BA to JH, Pres. Congress, July 11, 1777, PCC, microfilm reel 179, item 162: 106–7, NA.

51. GW to JH, Pres. Congress, Morristown, July 10, 1777, *Writings GW,* 8:377.

FIFTEEN: *An Unsettled Return to the Northern Theater*

1. GW to JH, Pres. Congress, Morristown, July 10, 1777, *Writings GW,* 8:376–77. Secondary works informing this chapter include Bowler, *Logistics and the Failure of*

the British Army, 225–40; Gerlach, *Proud Patriot,* 256–307; Richard J. Hargrove Jr., *General John Burgoyne* (Newark, Del., 1983), 101–62; Henderson, *Party Politics,* 100–129; Mintz, *Generals of Saratoga,* 131–83; Nelson, *Horatio Gates,* 89–112; Rossie, *Politics of Command,* 154–68; Hoffman Nickerson, *The Turning Point of the Revolution, or Burgoyne in America* (2 vols., Boston, 1928; reprint, Port Washington, 1967), 1:129–223; 2:224–97; John S. Pancake, *1777,* 114–45; and Ward, *War of the Revolution,* 1:398–431; 2:477–91, 495–503.

2. Fri., July 11, 1777, *JCC,* 8:545; JH, Pres. Congress, to BA, Phila., July 12, 1777, *LDC,* 7:338; BA to JH, Phila., July 12, 1777, PCC, microfilm reel 179, item 162:108–9, NA. On July 14, Congress received a letter from GW confirming the fall of Ticonderoga. He again asked for the services of BA "without a moment's loss of time," and the delegates even advanced BA $2,700 to cover campaign expenses. See GW to JH, Pres. Congress, Pompton Plains, N.J., July 12, 1777, *Writings GW,* 8:386; Tues., July 15, 1777, *JCC,* 8:553.

3. GW to PS, The Clove, July 18, 1777, *Writings GW,* 8:426–27.

4. GW to Brig. Gens. of Militia of Western Mass. and N.H., The Clove, July 18, 1777, ibid., 8:429–30. GW to JH, Pres. Congress, The Clove, July 18, 1777, ibid., 8:433. See also GW to Robert R. Livingston, The Clove, July 18, 1777, ibid., 8:434.

5. GW to JH, Pres. Congress, The Clove, July 18, 1777, ibid., 8:433.

6. Richard Frothingham, *History of the Siege of Boston, and of the Battles of Lexington, Concord, and Bunker Hill* (Boston, 1849), 114n.

7. *Notes* of General Burgoyne's Speech to the House of Commons, London, May 26, 1778, *Stopford-Sackville Mss.,* 2 (1910): 110–15. See also GJB's "Thoughts for Conducting the War from the Side of Canada," Hertford Street, London, Feb. 28, 1777, *DAR,* 14:41–46, which he used to help solidify his case as the best available general. GJB received the assignment only after HC, who did not want to embarrass GC, declined.

8. GG to GC, Whitehall, Mar. 26, 1777, ibid., 14:53–56. WH convinced himself that GJB would not need much assistance. He wrote, "The friends of government in that part of the country [upper New York] will be found so numerous and so ready to give every aid and assistance in their power that it will prove no difficult task to reduce the rebellious parts of the province" (WH to GG, New York, Apr. 5, 1777, ibid., 14:66). WH was very wrong. For some of the reasons why, see Martin, "Continental Army and American Victory," in Ferling, ed., *World Turned Upside Down,* 25–28.

9. Simon Fraser to [John Robinson], Skenesborough, July 13, 1777, Stevens, ed., *Facsimiles,* 16, no. 1571; *Notes* of General Burgoyne's Speech, May 26, 1778, *Stopford-Sackville Mss.,* 2 (1910): 112.

10. GJB's Proclamation, Camp at Bouquet River, June 22, 1777, *For Want of a Horse, Being a Journal of the Campaigns against the Americans in 1776 and 1777 Conducted from Canada, by an Officer Who Served with Lt. Gen. Burgoyne,* ed. George F. G. Stanley (Sackville, New Brunswick, 1961), 103–4. Various muster rolls for GJB's

force appear in ibid., 170–75. The best analysis of fluctuating troop strength for the contending forces is in Nickerson, *Turning Point,* 2:435–51.

11. Arthur St. Clair to PS, Ticonderoga, June 13, 1777, *St. Clair Paps.,* 1:399–400.

12. Arthur St. Clair to PS, Ticonderoga, June 18, 1777, ibid., 1:401–2; Arthur St. Clair to James Wilson, Ticonderoga, June 18, 1777, ibid., 1:402–4.

13. Camp at Crown Point, June 30, 1777, *For Want of a Horse,* 107; Hadden, July 1, 1777, *A Journal,* 82. Even though nine hundred militiamen had recently arrived at Ticonderoga, Burgoyne's force still had an overwhelming advantage in numbers.

14. Phillips, quoted in Nickerson, *Turning Point,* 144; Simon Fraser to [John Robinson], Skenesborough, July 13, 1777, Stevens, ed., *Facsimiles,* 16, no. 1571; Hadden, July 2–5, 1777, *A Journal,* 83–85. The British soon renamed this promontory Mount Defiance.

15. Council of War Minutes, Ticonderoga, July 5, 1777, *St. Clair Paps.,* 1:420–21; Hadden, July 6–12, 1777, *A Journal,* 85–95; July 6–July 12, 1777, *For Want of a Horse,* 108–18; and the detailed account contained in Simon Fraser to [John Robinson], Skenesborough, July 13, 1777, Stevens, ed., *Facsimiles,* 16, no. 1571. Hubbardton, where the patriot rearguard under Col. Seth Warner fought off the advancing British, represented a relatively short battle with heavy casualties. Peckham, ed., *Toll of Independence,* estimated rebel losses at 30 killed, 96 wounded, and 228 captured. In turn, the British lost about two hundred troops.

16. GJB to GG, Skenesborough, July 11, 1777, *DAR,* 14:133–40; GJB to GG, Skenesborough (Private), July 11, 1777, ibid., 14:140–42; Simon Fraser to [John Robinson], Skenesborough, July 13, 1777, Stevens, ed., *Facsimiles,* 16, no. 1571.

17. *Notes* of General Burgoyne's Speech, May 26, 1778, *Stopford-Sackville Mss.,* 2 (1910): 113.

18. John Welles to James Milligan, Albany, July 21, 1777, Welles Misc. Mss., N-YHS.

19. General Return Compiled by JW, Fort Edward, July 20, 1777, *Memoirs,* 1, Appendix, Item B. The defensive works at Fort Edward, designed to control an easily fordable point on the Hudson River, lay in ruins after years of neglect following the Seven Years' War. Nor did the site provide natural protection, since the works were on the river's flood plain. Enemy artillery fire from the surrounding hills would have rendered the position indefensible.

20. GJB to GG, Near Fort Edward, July 30, 1777, *DAR,* 14:153; *Notes* of General Burgoyne's Speech, May 26, 1778, *Stopford-Sackville Mss.,* 2 (1910): 112–13.

21. Brockholst Livingston to Gov. William Livingston, Fort Edward, July 21, 1777, *CAR,* 2:515.

22. BA to GW, Snook Hill, July 27 [28?], 1777, GW Paps., microfilm reel 43, 4 ser., LC; Riedesel, *Memoirs,* 1:125. See also PS to BA, Moses Creek, July 24, 1777, and PS to BA, Moses Creek, July 28, 1777, PS Paps., NYPL; and PS to John Jay, Moses Creek, July 27, 1777, Morris, ed., *Unpublished Jay Papers,* 1:432–33.

23. BA to GW, Snook Hill, July 27 [28?], 1777, GW Paps., microfilm reel 43, 4 ser., LC. The older woman was Sarah McNeil, a cousin of General Fraser.

24. Among the scholars who have persuasively downplayed the importance of Jenny McCrea's brutal death in rallying New Englanders against GJB's force is Pancake, *1777,* 152–54.

25. BA to GW, Snook Hill, July 27 [28?], 1777, GW Paps., microfilm reel 43, 4 ser., LC.

26. Charles Thomson's Notes of Debates, Phila., July 26, 1777, *LDC,* 7:382–83.

27. These were the words of Elbridge Gerry. See Charles Thomson's Notes of Debates, July 28, 1777, ibid., 7:388–89. See also SA to James Warren, Phila., July 31, 1777, ibid., 7:396–98.

28. Tues., July 29, 1777, and Fri., Aug. 1, 1777, *JCC,* 8:585, 596.

29. NG to Catherine Greene, Ramapo Clove, July 17, 1777, *Paps. NG,* 2:121–22; New England Delegates (JA, SA, Eliphalet Dyer, Nathaniel Folsom, Elbridge Gerry, Henry Marchant, and William Williams) to GW, Phila., Aug. 2, 1777, *LDC,* 7:405; GW to JH, Pres. Congress, Phila., Aug. 3, 1777, *Writings GW,* 9:8–9.

30. Mon., Aug. 4, 1777, *JCC,* 8:603–4; JH, Pres. Congress, to GW, Phila., Aug. 4, 1777, *LDC,* 7:412; GW to HG, Headquarters [Phila.], Aug. 4, 1777, *Writings GW,* 9:11–12.

31. JA to AA, Phila., Aug. 4, 1777, *LDC,* 7:411–12. See also SA to Samuel Freeman, Phila., Aug. 5, 1777, ibid., 7:413–14.

32. PS to GW, Saratoga, Aug. 1 [2?], 1777, PCC, microfilm reel 167, item 152, vol. 4:447–48, NA.

33. BA to HG, Stillwater, N.Y., Aug. 5, 1777, Gates Paps., N-YHS.

34. Fri., Aug. 8, 1777, *JCC,* 8:623–24. PS's close friend, James Duane, did support BA, but William Duer and Philip Livingston, also of the New York delegation, did not.

35. JL to William Whipple, [Phila.], Aug. 8, 1777, *LDC,* 7:443. JL was also miffed that Rhode Island delegate Henry Marchant asked for a roll-call vote. Despite his high-sounding republican principles, he apparently did not like being held accountable for his actions.

36. HL to Robert Howe, Phila., Aug. 9, 1777, ibid., 7:446; HL to John Rutledge, Phila., Aug. 12, 1777, ibid., 7:469.

37. JL to William Whipple, Phila., Aug. 11, 1777, ibid., 7:458–59; see also JL to Oliver Wolcott, Phila., Aug. 21, 1777, ibid., 7:524.

38. GJB to GG, Near Fort Edward, July 30, 1777, *DAR,* 14:153; GJB to GG (Private), Near Fort Edward, July 30, 1777, ibid., 14:154–55.

39. GJB to GG, Fort Edward, Aug. 6, 1777, ibid., 14:156–57.

40. July 27, Aug. 5, 1777, *For Want of a Horse,* 122–23, 126.

41. GC to GG, Quebec, Aug. 11, 1777, *DAR,* 14:157–58.

42. GJB to GG, Nearly Opposite to Saratoga, Aug. 20, 1777, ibid., 14:162.

43. *Baroness von Riedesel and the American Revolution: Journal and Correspondence of a Tour of Duty, 1776–1783,* trans. Marvin L. Brown Jr. (Chapel Hill, 1965), 55–56. The name of the alleged mistress has not been identified. See also GJB to GG, Nearly Opposite to Saratoga, Aug. 20, 1777, *DAR,* 14:163–65.

44. GJB to Lieut. Col. Frederick Baum, [Fort Edward], Aug. 9, 1777, PCC, microfilm reel 167, item 152, vol. 4:553–56, NA.

45. GJB to GG, Nearly Opposite to Saratoga, Aug. 20, 1777, *DAR,* 14:163–65; GJB to GG (Private), Nearly Opposite to Saratoga, Aug. 20, 1777, ibid., 14:165–67. For a contemporary account of the Bennington battle by an eyewitness, see Col. Philip Skene to the Earl of Dartmouth, Camp at Saratoga, Aug. 30, 1777, Stevens, ed., *Facsimiles,* 18, no. 1665.

46. PS to JH, Pres. Congress, Five Miles South of Stillwater, Aug. 15, 1777, PCC, microfilm reel 173, item 153, vol. 3:246–49, NA.

47. PS to BA, Stillwater, Aug. 13, 1777, PS Paps., NYPL. As early as July 24, GW had recommended BA "or some other sensible, spirited officer," to go west in aid of Fort Schuyler (GW to PS, Ramapo, July 24, 1777, *Writings GW,* 8:459–60). BA held back at the council meeting because taking charge of only a regt. of troops plus assorted militiamen and Indians was more in line with the duties of a brig. gen. Also, he was serving as PS's chief assistant while Lincoln was performing detached duty in Vermont trying to organize militia resistance. PS would have preferred to keep BA in camp, but like GW he realized there was no one more capable of executing the assignment.

48. HG to BA, Albany, Aug. 19, 1777, HG Paps., N-YHS. See also HG to BA, Headquarters [Van Schaick's Island], Aug. 22, 1777, HG Paps., N-YHS.

49. BA to HG, German Flats, Aug. 21, 1777, *CAR,* 2:518–19.

50. BA to PS, German Flats, Aug. 21, 1777, HG Paps., N-YHS.

51. Council of War Minutes, German Flats, Aug. 21, 1777, signed by BA, Pres., HG Paps., N-YHS; BA to HG, German Flats, Aug. 21, 1777, HG Paps., N-YHS. This document is a separate, postcouncil summary to HG, which accompanied the minutes (not the same item as listed in note 49 above).

52. Barry St. Leger to GC, Oswego, Aug. 27, 1777, *DAR,* 14:173–74. Hon Yost Schuyler remains a mysterious figure. Most descriptions of him are derived from William L. Stone, *The Campaign of Lieut. Gen. John Burgoyne and the Expedition of Lieut. Col. Barry St. Leger* (Albany, 1877), 209–19. Assigning respective parts in the ruse is difficult, but most credit BA with the concept, since Hon Yost was supposedly a half-wit.

53. Peter Gansevoort to BA, Fort Schuyler, Aug. 22, 1777, HG Paps., N-YHS; BA to HG, Mohawk River, Ten Miles above Fort Dayton, Aug. 23, 1777, *CAR,* 2:519.

54. BA to HG, Fort Schuyler, Aug. 24, 1777, HG Paps., N-YHS; BA to HG, German Flats, Aug. 28, 1777, *CAR,* 2:521.

55. HG to JH, Pres. Congress, Headquarters [Van Schaick's Island], Aug. 28, 1777, HG Paps., N-YHS. See also HG to JH, Pres. Congress, Headquarters [Van Schaick's Island], Aug. 25, 1777 (PCC, microfilm reel 174, item 154, vol. 1:236–37, NA), in which HG specifically acknowledges Gansevoort, Willett, and the soldiers defending Fort Schuyler. "I cannot too warmly recommend them to Congress," HG wrote, without mentioning BA's role.

56. GW to JH, Pres. Congress, Wilmington, Sept. 1, 1777, *Writings GW,* 9:151,

which was in response to JH, Pres. Congress, to GW, Phila., Sept. 1, 1777, *LDC,* 7:584–85; General Orders, Wilmington, Sept. 1, 1777, *Writings GW,* 9:157.

57. HG to BA, [Van Schaick's Island], Aug. 29, 1777, HG Paps., N-YHS; HG to Benjamin Lincoln, Headquarters [Van Schaick's Island], Aug. 31, 1777, Lincoln Paps., MHS; BA to John Lamb, Half Moon, N.Y., Sept. 5, 1777, Leake, *Life of John Lamb,* 171.

SIXTEEN: *The Battles of Saratoga*

1. Sept. 11, 1777, *Revolutionary War Journals of Henry Dearborn, 1775–1783,* ed. Lloyd A. Brown and Howard H. Peckham (Chicago, 1939), 104; Sat., Aug. 16, 1777, *JCC,* 8:649. Secondary works informing this chapter include Gerlach, *Proud Patriot,* 308–29; Hargrove, *John Burgoyne,* 163–205; Higginbotham, *Daniel Morgan,* 55–77; John F. Luzader, "The Arnold-Gates Controversy," *West Virginia History,* 27 (1966): 75–84; David B. Mattern, *Benjamin Lincoln and the American Revolution* (Columbia, S.C., 1995), 41–56; Mintz, *Generals of Saratoga,* 183–213; Paul David Nelson, "Legacy of Controversy: Gates, Schuyler, and Arnold at Saratoga," *Military Affairs,* 37 (1973): 41–47; Nelson, *Horatio Gates,* 112–56; Nickerson, *Turning Point,* 2:298–403; Pancake, *1777,* 146–62, 179–91; and Ward, *War of the Revolution,* 2:504–31. This chapter's interpretation differs markedly from those of Luzader and Nelson above.

2. BA to John Lamb, Half Moon, Sept. 5, 1777, Leake, *Life of John Lamb,* 172; HA to Jeremiah Wadsworth, Middletown, Oct. 4, 1777, Wadsworth Coll., CHS. See also Arnold, *Arnold,* 205–6; JW *Memoirs,* 1:274. BA's sister had sent him a large sorrel stallion and a sorrel mare via the military supply base at Peekskill. Neither animal had yet arrived at Loudon's Ferry, which compelled BA to make arrangements for the services of a muscular gray Spanish mount and a large dark brown mare. Whether BA still was using the horse awarded him by Congress is unclear.

3. BA to HG, Camp Stillwater, Oct. 1, 1777, JW *Memoirs,* 1:259; BA to HG, Camp Stillwater, Sept. 22, 1777, ibid., 1:254–55. The originals of these faithfully reproduced letters may be found in the HG Paps., N-YHS.

4. BA to HG, Camp Stillwater, Sept. 23, 1777, ibid., 1:257.

5. Bemis Heights, which the patriot troops apparently called "the site," remains a misnomer. The property actually belonged to John Neilson, who farmed portions of the heights at the time of the Revolution. Neilson's barn was on the northwest corner of the Bemis Heights entrenchments and became known as Fort Neilson after the rebels constructed a redoubt in front of the barn and placed a number of artillery pieces at this most extended point in their line. Invariably adept at claiming more than his due, JW (*Memoirs,* 1:232) stated that he was the first to recognize the advantages of this site. No authority sustains JW's boast. BA and others had carefully noted the heights as an excellent defensive location during the patriot retreat in August.

6. Strength Report, Saratoga, Sept. 15, 1777, *For Want of a Horse,* 172. On Sept.

7, 1777, GJB received misleading intelligence that HG's force contained fourteen thousand to fifteen thousand troops (Riedesel, *Memoirs*, 1:136).

7. General Orders, Batten Kill, Sept. 12, 1777, *For Want of a Horse*, 142; Sept. 13, 1777, ibid., 143; Brown, ed., *Baroness von Riedesel*, 147; Riedesel, *Memoirs*, 1:140.

8. Thomas Anburey, *With Burgoyne from Quebec: An Account of the Life at Quebec and of the Famous Battle of Saratoga*, ed. Sydney Jackman (Toronto, 1963), 170.

9. GJB to GG, Albany, Oct. 20, 1777, *DAR*, 14:229; JW *Memoirs*, 1:235, stated that BA had only fifteen hundred troops. Despite HG's specific orders about avoiding a general engagement, JW proceeded to fault BA as follows: "After a light skirmish, he [BA] returned without loss or effecting anything more, than picking up a few stragglers." By such logic, BA showed no initiative because he followed orders.

10. Anburey, *With Burgoyne*, 172; Sept. 18, 1777, *For Want of a Horse*, 145–46.

11. Anburey, *With Burgoyne*, 175. See also Sept. 19, 1777, *For Want of a Horse*, 146–47; Riedesel, *Memoirs*, 1:144–45.

12. John Freeman, often described as a loyalist farmer, remains an enigmatic character. At the time of the Saratoga engagements, a Quaker farmer and presumed loyalist by the name of Isaac Leggett apparently owned and was operating the farm. From the point of view of place names, then, the battles actually took place on and around Leggett's farm, with the patriots entrenched to the south on Neilson Heights. To further confuse matters, the battle zone lay within the town of Stillwater and the county of Saratoga. For the sake of clarity, I refer to the engagement of Sept. 19 only as First Freeman's Farm or First Saratoga.

13. RV to PS, Camp [Bemis Heights], Sept. 22, 1777, Arnold, *Arnold*, 179.

14. Unsettled as he was by his possible shortage of troop strength relative to GJB's, HG had received an unnerving blow the previous day (Sept. 18). Gen. Stark had finally led his fifteen hundred militiamen, the victors at Bennington, west across the Hudson River to Bemis Heights. Then Stark abruptly announced that his troops had appeared only out of courtesy and were about to begin marching home, since their enlistments were over that day. Part of the problem lay with Stark, who had repeatedly refused to report to Continental general officers, a reflection of his rebuff for a brig. gen.'s commission by Congress back in Feb. 1777. The Sept. 18 incident also called into question HG's reputation, largely manufactured by congressional delegates from New England, as the one ranking officer who could inspire and rally that region's militia. Most important, the departure of Stark and his troops seemed to have the psychological effect of temporarily immobilizing HG, whose performance on Sept. 19 was that of an exceedingly cautious if not bewildered commander who believed himself hopelessly outnumbered, which he was not. Thus HG held tightly to his lines that day and provided pedestrian, if not ineffective and confusing, leadership at best.

15. Sept. 19, 1777, *For Want of a Horse*, 147; Hadden, Sept. 19, 1777, *A Journal*, 163.

16. JW *Memoirs*, 1:238. That JW was actually in the field at this juncture makes

no sense, given his duties, and likely represents a fabrication about personal bravery that rarely, if ever, denoted his behavior during the Revolutionary War. The story about Daniel Morgan is most likely an apocryphal retelling of the incident, based on hearsay reports in the patriot camp after the battle.

17. Sept. 19, 1777, *For Want of a Horse,* 147.

18. Contemporary British reports almost uniformly describe the principal points of action as occurring an hour later than do American sources. Thus Dearborn, Sept. 19, 1777, *Journals,* 106, had this segment of the engagement commencing at around 2 P.M., whereas GJB (to GG, Oct. 20, 1777, *DAR,* 14:230) cited the time as about 3 P.M. For purposes of consistency, I have adopted the patriot time frame.

19. Letter from Gen. Enoch Poor, [Bemis Heights], Sept. 20, 1777, Moore, comp., *Diary Am. Rev.,* 1:498; "Diary of Captain Wakefield: Unpublished Recollections of 1777," *Visits to the Saratoga Battle-Grounds,* comp. William L. Stone (Albany, 1895; reprint, Port Washington, 1970), 152–53.

20. Colonel Philip Van Cortlandt explained how the positioning of patriot troops worked that day. Poor gave him orders to lead his New York Continentals out from Bemis Heights while "on my parade; and as I was marching also, by General Arnold." BA must have been riding up and down the pathway leading north from the heights to get fresh troops into line for what, despite HG's admonition, had become a general—and potentially decisive—engagement. See "Autobiography of Philip Van Cortlandt, Brigadier-General of the Continental Army," *MH,* 2 (1878): 286.

21. Riedesel (*Memoirs,* 1:150), who knew how derogatory the British could be about the Hessians, wrote of this occasion, "Thus had General Riedesel, with his German troops, once more saved the English from a great misfortune, having unquestionably decided the engagement in their favor." By comparison, GJB (to GG [Private], Albany, Oct. 20, 1777, *DAR,* 14:236), stated that "had the force been *all* British," he could have avoided the disaster of entrapment and surrender.

22. JW *Memoirs,* 1:245–46. Some find it curious that HG apparently placed more confidence in the judgment of staff officers such as Morgan Lewis, who thought that "indecisive progress" equated to "doing well" in the engagement, than in that of his commander in the field. HG thus listened more intently to those who readily said what he wanted to hear. BA was not that kind of person, especially with even a slight prospect for victory at hand.

23. Return of the Killed and Wounded at Freeman's Farm, Sept. 19, 1777, *For Want of a Horse,* 153–55.

24. A Return of the Killed, etc., of the Division under the Command of Major General Arnold, between Stillwater and Saratoga, Sept. 19, 1777, Emmet Coll., NYPL; Dearborn, Sept. 19, 1777, *Journals,* 106–7; Anburey, *With Burgoyne,* 175.

25. GJB to GG, Albany, Oct. 20, 1777, *DAR,* 14:231; *Notes* of General Burgoyne's Speech, May 26, 1778, *Stopford-Sackville Mss.,* 2 (1910): 112.

26. RV to PS, [Bemis Heights], Sept. 22, 1777, Arnold, *Arnold,* 179; "Diary of Wakefield," Stone, comp., *Saratoga Battle-Grounds,* 152.

27. Anburey, *With Burgoyne,* 176; Dearborn, Sept. 19, 1777, *Journals,* 107. For a contemporary account of the battle from the British perspective that also noted the presence of BA, see *The Annual Register, 1777,* Murdoch, ed., *Rebellion in America,* 483–84.

28. RV to PS, Camp [Bemis Heights], Sept. 25, 1777, Arnold, *Arnold,* 184; BA to HG, Camp Stillwater, Sept. 22, 1777, JW *Memoirs,* 1:256. The originals of RV's and HBL's letters to PS, along with the latter's replies, may be found in the PS Paps., NYPL. Like JW, Isaac N. Arnold provided accurate renderings. Both knew that these sources, unless somehow lost, could be checked for accuracy.

29. RV to PS, Camp [Bemis Heights], Sept. 22, 1777, Arnold, *Arnold,* 179; HBL to PS, Camp at Bemis Heights, Sept. 23, 1777, ibid., 180–81.

30. Fri., Aug. 22, 1777, *JCC,* 8:665; JL, a staunch HG advocate in Congress, privately spoke of how he had helped ward off the "foolish rashness about rank" in HBL's case. See JL to Oliver Wolcott, Phila., Aug. 22, 1777, *LDC,* 7:525. On RV's problems with Lieut. Col. Anthony Walton White of New Jersey, see John George Rommel Jr., "Richard Varick: New York Aristocrat" (doctoral dissertation, Columbia University, 1966), 15–17.

31. "Diary of Wakefield," Stone, comp., *Saratoga Battle-Grounds,* 153. HG naturally blamed PS, the source of supplies. In fairness, the Northern Department force had never been better supplied up to that point in the war, thanks to the abundant largesse provided by the French.

32. JW to Arthur St. Clair, Camp Bemis Heights, Sept. 21, 1777, *St. Clair Paps.,* 1:143. JW repeated this fraudulent claim in his *Memoirs,* 1:245. Participants such as Wakefield and scholars of the Sept. 19 engagement have shown JW's assertion to be a fabrication. Typical of the refutations are Nickerson, *Turning Point,* 473–77, and Wallace, *Traitorous Hero,* 326–32. Not even HG specifically denied BA's presence, although he helped distort the record in his Sept. 22 after-action report to Congress.

33. General Order, Sept. 22, 1777, JW *Memoirs,* 1:253–54, which also contains JW's rationale.

34. HG to JH, Pres. Congress, Heights above Bemis, Sept. 22, 1777, HG Paps., N-YHS. Various versions may be found in the HG Paps., including the original draft in what appears to be HG's handwriting. Besides neglecting BA and his division, an additional reason for HG's vagueness was that he had little actual idea of what had happened in the field on Sept. 19. That he included a spurious reference to the wounding of GJB, three days after the battle no less, raises questions about his interest in actually finding out what had actually happened.

35. HG to Benjamin Lincoln, Heights above Bemis, Sept. 19, 1777, *CAR,* 2:525; Benjamin Lincoln to Col. John Laurens, Boston, Feb. 5, 1781, ibid., 2:534–36.

36. BA to HG, Camp Stillwater, Sept. 22, 1777, JW *Memoirs,* 1:256. Puffing up JB was most likely part of a HG/JW strategy designed to drive off BA while restoring the faith of the troops in HG. After the plundering charges leveled against BA in the summer of 1776, JW was especially cognizant of how much BA despised JB. Even in his *Memoirs,* 1:248, JW drew attention to the "handsomely executed" attack under

JB's command. What he did not mention was how HG's orders in calling off the militia had the highly undesirable effect of temporarily clearing a pathway back to Canada for GJB and his force.

37. HBL to PS, Camp at Bemis Heights, Sept. 23, 1777, ibid., 1:253.

38. BA to HG, Camp Stillwater, Sept. 22, 1777, JW *Memoirs*, 1:256. See also ibid., 1:254.

39. RV to PS, Camp [Bemis Heights], Sept. 24, 1777, Arnold, *Arnold*, 179; BA to HG, Camp Stillwater, Sept. 23, 1777, JW *Memoirs*, 1:256.

40. HG to Elizabeth Phillips Gates, Camp on Bemis Heights, Sept. 22, 1777, HG Paps., N-YHS. Given HG's ambitions, this letter may also have been written for consumption by his adoring supporters in Congress. Major Robert Troup, who carried HG's after-action report to Congress, also took this missive with him. Since the controversial report had not yet left camp, HG could likewise have modified his words to assure "justice" in distributing the morsels of glory for First Freeman's Farm.

41. PS to RV, Albany, Sept. 25, 1777, Arnold, *Arnold*, 180; RV to PS, Camp [Bemis Heights], Sept. 25, 1777, ibid., 185.

42. HBL to PS, Camp at Bemis Heights, Sept. 23, 1777, ibid., 181.

43. HG to BA, Sept. 23, 1777, JW *Memoirs*, 1:257; BA to HG, Camp Stillwater, Sept. 23, 1777, ibid., 1:257; HG to BA, Headquarters [Bemis Heights], Sept. 23, 1777, ibid., 1:258.

44. HBL to PS, Camp at Bemis Heights, Sept. 24, 1777, Arnold, *Arnold*, 182.

45. HBL to PS, Camp at Bemis Heights, Sept. 26, 1777, ibid., 183. Chester and BA likely knew each other before the Saratoga campaign. Marital ties existed between the Chesters of Wethersfield and the Huntington clan of Norwich. Also, the dark brown mare that BA rode in the second battle (Oct. 7) probably belonged to Chester, who either loaned or rented the animal to BA.

46. Ibid.; RV to PS, Camp [Bemis Heights], Sept. 24, 1777, PS Paps., NYPL. Arnold, *Arnold*, neglected to reprint this threat, as contained in RV's letter, perhaps to make his forebear look more dispassionate during the controversy. Whatever the case, HG was able to take full advantage of the threat in formally disavowing BA.

47. BA to HG, Camp Stillwater, Oct. 1, 1777, JW *Memoirs*, 1:259–60. The HG camp continued to rankle BA about small matters whenever they could. Sometime before Sept. 27, for example, HG reneged on a bounty payment of $50 earlier promised by BA to a soldier who had killed one of Burgoyne's most ferocious Indians during the patriot retreat from Fort Edward. BA quickly objected, complaining that HG was intentionally making him look "guilty of deceit." HG calmly replied that he was only upholding regulations. See BA to HG, Camp [Bemis Heights], Sept. 27, 1777, ibid., 1:258–59; HG to BA, Camp [Bemis Heights], Sept. 28, 1777, ibid., 1:259.

48. BA to HG, Camp Stillwater, Oct. 1, 1777, ibid., 1:259–60.

49. HC to GJB, [New York], Sept. 11, 1777, quoted in Nickerson, *Turning Point*, 320. In this letter, HC rationalized his lack of assistance in terms of a "poverty" of troop strength. With expected reinforcements, he had about seven thousand troops

to defend Manhattan Island and outposts stretching from Long Island westward into eastern New Jersey. Thus he would proceed up the Hudson River with a diversionary force only when the reinforcements arrived. What HC failed to mention was that no significant rebel force was in the immediate region or threatening his defenses. See also GJB to GG, Albany, Oct. 20, 1777, *DAR,* 14:231; the related communiques between GJB and HC of late September–early October in *DAR,* 14:191–92; and Willcox, ed., *Clinton's Narrative,* 69–80.

50. Anburey, *With Burgoyne,* 181; GJB to GG, Albany, Oct. 20, 1777, *DAR,* 14:231.

51. Correspondence between GJB and HC, Sept. 28–Oct. 5, 1777, n.p., ibid., 14:191–92. HC stressed that he had not "received any instructions from the commander-in-chief [WH] relative to the northern army" and that he was "unacquainted even of his [WH's] intentions concerning the operations of that army excepting his wishes that he [GJB] should get to Albany." He made this statement in response to GJB's request for orders. GJB was also attempting to cover himself, should disaster befall his army, by asking HC for instructions about whether to proceed for Albany or return to Canada. Among the British commanders, no one, it seemed, was to blame except someone else.

52. GJB to GG, Albany, Oct. 20, 1777, ibid., 14:231–32; Riedesel, *Memoirs,* 1:162–63.

53. GJB to GG, Albany, Oct. 20, 1777, ibid., 14:232.

54. JW *Memoirs,* 1:268. A solid contemporary account may be found in *The Annual Register, 1777,* Murdoch, ed., *Rebellion in America,* 485–87.

55. Reminiscence of L. F. S. Foster's Father, n.d., quoted in Arnold, *Arnold,* 204.

56. "Samuel Woodruff's Visit to the Battle Ground in 1827," Stone, comp. *Saratoga Battle-Grounds,* 225–26; GJB to GG, Albany, Oct. 20, 1777, *DAR,* 14:232.

57. "Samuel Woodruff's Visit," Stone, comp., *Saratoga Battle-Grounds,* 226. The story of BA's heavy consumption of rum before entering the battle is that of Dr. Edmund Chadwick of Deerfield, N.H., a surgeon in Col. Alexander Scammell's regt. See ibid., 227–30. That BA, like his father, had a drinking problem emerged as another post-treason tale. On the alleged drunkenness of patriot soldiers, at least in reference to the first battle, see "Diary of Joshua Pell," Sept. 19, 1777, *MAH* (1878): 109.

58. JW *Memoirs,* 1:272. One of JW's more preposterous claims was that he "recommended to General Learned to incline to his right, and attack at that point." Why Learned would need, listen to, or accept the advice of someone so far below him in rank and experience renders this notion absurd, especially in the light of JW's overall combat record, or lack of one, during the Revolutionary War.

59. Henry Dearborn, "A Narrative of the Saratoga Campaign, 1815," *Bulletin of the Fort Ticonderoga Museum,* 1 (1928–1929): 8–9. Most accounts, based on Dearborn's recollections, have BA entering from the northwest; however, the sally port was on the southeast side. BA may well have ridden completely around the back side of the redoubt to get into position, although that would have caused an unneeded

delay in storming the redoubt, especially with darkness coming on. Most likely, he simply rode back over the ground just taken to the American right (British left) of the redoubt.

60. BA was apparently in the southwest corner of the redoubt, and his mount collapsed on its left side. Dearborn, "A Narrative," ibid., 9, described the horse as falling to the right "upon the other leg." If that were the case, then the crippling, deforming wound sustained by BA in his weakened left leg would make no sense.

61. Dearborn, "A Narrative," ibid., 9; Stone, *Campaign of Burgoyne and Expedition of St. Leger*, 66–67.

62. Return of the Killed, Wounded, and Prisoners of the British Troops from Oct. 7 Inclusive to the End of the Campaign, and Return of the Killed, Wounded, and Prisoners of the British Army under the Command of Lieut. Gen. Burgoyne in the Course of the Campaign, 1777, *For Want of a Horse*, 174–75.

63. JW *Memoirs*, 1:269–70.

64. In HG's Oct. 12 after-action report (HG Paps., N-YHS), he also acknowledged the troops of DM and Dearborn, and he singled out Lincoln for special praise. Lincoln had sustained a serious leg wound on Oct. 8 during a skirmishing action with the British. The sense of this report is that HG had little idea of the flow of action during Second Freeman's Farm on Oct. 7. JW *Memoirs*, 1:273, gives BA no credit for anything except getting wounded. Not only did JW repeat the drinking story (note 57 above), but he described BA's behavior as "exceedingly rash and intemperate." Actual participants in the battle saw matters differently, including Dearborn, who prepared his 1815 "Narrative" in response to JW's request for recollections. Wrote Dearborn, "I saw no general officers in either of the actions, except General Arnold and General Poor. I believe that General Gates was not out of our camp on either of the days." JW chose to ignore these comments. See Dearborn, "A Narrative," *Bulletin Fort Ticonderoga Museum* (1928–1929): 10.

SEVENTEEN: *A Violated Right Not Fully Restored*

1. Dearborn, "A Narrative," *Bulletin Fort Ticonderoga Museum* (1928–1929): 9. BA biographers have given little notice to the period of his convalescence at the General Hospital. For BA, this was a critical time of reckoning when he began to deal with his growing disillusionment with the American cause. Arnold, *Arnold*, 205, typified the theme about BA surviving his Saratoga wounds; he wrote, "This was the hour for Benedict Arnold to have died! Had he been so fortunate as to have died of the wound received at the moment of victory, . . . few soldiers in American history would have achieved a prouder fame."

2. Thacher, Oct. 12, 1777, *Military Journal*, 124; Dr. James Brown to Dr. Jonathan Potts, Albany, Dec. 24, 1777, *New England Historical & Genealogical Register*, 18 (1864): 34.

3. Ibid.; L. F. S. Foster to Isaac N. Arnold, n.p., Oct. 29, 1877, Arnold, *Arnold*,

212. The rumor was rife in the American army that BA would have to have his leg amputated if he wanted to survive.

4. RV to PS, Albany, Oct. 30, Nov. 1, 5, 8, 12, 16, Dec. 1, 1777, PS Paps. NYPL.

5. BA to HL, Pres. Congress, Albany, Jan. 11, 1778, PCC, microfilm reel 179, item 162: 110–13, NA.

6. Minutes of a Council of War at Saratoga, Oct. 13, 1777, *DAR,* 14:214. For JW's self-congratulatory account of the negotiations, see JW *Memoirs,* 1:297–302.

7. RV to PS, Albany, Oct. 30, 1777, PS Paps., NYPL.

8. William M. Dabney, *After Saratoga: The Story of the Convention Army* (Albuquerque, N.M., 1954), *passim.* A number of GJB's soldiers, most especially Hessians, were recruited into the Continental army as they traveled southward to Virginia. See Martin and Lender, *A Respectable Army,* 88–93, and, more generally, Neimeyer, *America Goes to War,* 44–64.

9. RV to PS, Albany, Nov. 1, 1777, PS Paps., NYPL. Bernhard Knollenberg, *Washington and the Revolution, a Reappraisal: Gates, Conway, and the Continental Congress* (New York, 1940), 30–36, claimed that HG was quick to send reinforcements to GW.

10. Marquis de Lafayette to HL, Pres. Congress, Albany, Feb. 19, 1778, Idzerda, ed., *Lafayette Letters,* 1:296; HG to JH, Pres. Congress, Camp Saratoga, Oct. 18, 1777, JW *Memoirs,* 1:324.

11. Ibid., 1:323–32.

12. Ibid., 1:333–37; Tues., Nov. 4, 1777, *JCC,* 9:861–62; HL, Pres. Congress, to HG, York, Nov. 5, 1777, *LDC,* 8:235; Arnold, *Arnold,* 213.

13. Fri., Aug. 22, 1777, *JCC,* 8:665; JL to Oliver Wolcott, Phila., Aug. 22, 1777, *LDC,* 7:525; Sat., Oct. 4, 1777, *JCC,* 9:769–70; Thurs., Nov. 6, 1777, ibid., 9:870.

14. See comments summarized in *Letters of Members of the Continental Congress,* ed. Edmund C. Burnett (8 vols., Washington, D.C., 1921–36), 2:545n.

15. NG to Henry Marchant, Camp [Whitemarsh] near Phila., Nov. 17, 1777, *Paps. NG,* 2:199. See also NG to HL, Pres. Congress, Camp at Valley Forge, Jan. 12, 1778, ibid., 2:252–53, in which NG spoke of JW's promotion as a blow to the principle of merit. He likewise mentioned the widespread "discontent" among field- and general-grade officers with "superior claims" to promotion.

16. NG to Jacob Greene, Camp Valley Forge, Jan. 3, 1778, ibid., 2:244. See also Wallace, *Traitorous Hero,* 158, 355.

17. "De Lisle," Fishkill, N.Y., Nov. 20, 1777 [*New Jersey Gazette,* Dec. 31, 1777], *The Papers of William Livingston, 1774–1790,* ed. Carl E. Prince et al. (5 vols., Trenton and New Brunswick, N.J., 1979–1988), 2:150–54. Apparently HBL had not communicated to his father what he had stated in a letter to Robert R. Livingston, Camp Whitemarsh, Nov. 30, 1777, Livingston Paps. N-YHS; HBL complained of HG getting "the credit" that was "due" BA "for our late victories." HBL did give HG credit for "the capitulation alone," but he all but openly mocked JW, who had done nothing "remarkable" at Saratoga and was "ignorant" about his official duties

and showed no "courage" in battle. Among other matters, HBL was upset about JW's promotion.

18. Sat., Nov. 29, 1777, *JCC,* 9:981.

19. Ibid.; At a Board of General Officers, Held Agreeable to the Order of the 14th, by Adjournment from the 15th to the 19th August [1777], Camp Bucks County, GW Paps., microfilm reel 43, 4 ser., LC; Board of General Officers to GW, Camp Bucks County, Pa., Aug. 19, 1777, *Paps. NG,* 2:144; GW to HL, Pres. Congress, Nov. 10, 1777, *Writings GW,* 10:34–35; Weds., Nov. 12, 1777, *JCC,* 9:896–97.

20. JL to John Langdon, York, Oct. 14, 1777, *LDC,* 8:120. For reports suggesting that more than military necessity motivated HG in removing BA from command, see CC to Charles Carroll, Sr., York, Oct. 9, 1777, ibid., 8:86–87, who mentioned that BA "suspects that Gates is envious of him for the share he had in the late action of the 19th." Meanwhile, JL had warned HG about such statements. JL saw the hand of PS in these words. See JL to HG, York, Oct. 5, 1777, ibid., 8:58. See also JW to HG, York, Nov. 4, 1777, *JW Memoirs,* 1:337, who wrote, "Beware of Arnold; he has endeavored to stab you," just as JW was then doing to BA with the delegates.

21. JL's argument was that not all the five maj. gens. had been consulted regarding BA's reelevation over them, a curious position for one who worried incessantly about the military dictating to the civil government. Further, no one in Congress had consulted BA about elevating these same five officers over him. Those supporting BA, according to JL, claimed that they had consulted all five, which was not true in Lincoln's case. See JL to Benjamin Lincoln, York, Feb. 2, 1778, *LDC,* 9:11. JL got Lincoln stirred up about the issue, and he in turn made noises about resigning. See note 28 below.

22. HL, Pres. Congress, to BA, York, Nov. 29, 1777, ibid., 8:343–44.

23. BA to HL, Pres. Congress, Albany, Jan. 11, 1778, PCC, microfilm reel 179, item 162: 110–13, NA.

24. David S. Franks to Lucy Knox, Albany, Dec. 17, 1777, Knox Paps., MHS.

25. Numerous secondary accounts of the "Conway Cabal" exist. The most detailed is Knollenberg, *Washington and the Revolution, passim,* which treats HG as an innocent and comes close to charging GW with needless paranoia. My interpretation varies significantly in emphasis.

26. GW to Thomas Conway, n.p., Nov. 9, 1777, *Writings GW,* 10:29. Neither Conway nor HG ever produced a copy of the former's missive, despite GW's request. On Conway and his motives, see Knollenberg, *Washington and the Revolution,* 37–64. Recent accounts less sympathetic toward HG include Rossie, *Politics of Command,* 174–202; and Martin and Lender, *A Respectable Army,* 103–15. Supporting Knollenberg's pro-HG orientation is Nelson, *Horatio Gates,* 157–85.

27. GW to BA, Valley Forge, Jan. 20, 1778, *Writings GW,* 10:324–25.

28. GW to Benjamin Lincoln, Valley Forge, Jan. 20, 1778, ibid., 10:325–26. Lincoln, no doubt influenced by JL, did not readily accede to GW's advice. See Mattern, *Benjamin Lincoln,* 51–52, and note 21 above.

29. BA to GW, Middletown, Mar. 12, 1778, GW Paps., microfilm reel 47, 4 ser., LC.

30. General Orders, Whitemarsh, Nov. 20, 1777, *Writings GW,* 10:89. Harry M. Ward, *Major General Adam Stephen and the Cause of American Liberty* (Charlottesville, 1989), represents the first modern, even-handed study of Stephen's life.

31. Kenneth R. Rossman, *Thomas Mifflin and the Politics of the American Revolution* (Chapel Hill, 1952), remains the standard account. Rossman focused more on Mifflin's role in the Conway Cabal and passed over his subject's failures as quartermaster general by describing that post as a position Mifflin "intensely disliked" (105).

32. St. Clair has not yet attracted a modern biographer. The standard account may be found in Smith, ed., *St. Clair Paps.,* 1:1–256.

33. Paul David Nelson, *William Alexander, Lord Stirling* (University, 1987), represents the most useful of the modern Stirling biographies.

34. Until the appearance of Mattern, *Benjamin Lincoln,* a very useful study, the standard account was Clifford K. Shipton, "Benjamin Lincoln: Old Reliable," in *George Washington's Generals,* ed. George A. Billias (New York, 1964), 193–211.

35. Bellesiles, *Revolutionary Outlaws,* 245–66, and Jellison, *Ethan Allen,* 314–34, allow for greater merit in their subject than presented herein.

36. On JB, see Dexter, comp., *Biographical Sketches Yale College,* 3:404–7. More detailed but less trustworthy is Smith, comp., *History of Pittsfield,* which also contains scattered references to JE.

37. Everest, *Moses Hazen,* and Higginbotham, *Daniel Morgan,* ably summarize their respective subjects.

38. No modern biographer has yet grappled with JW. Somewhat useful is James Ripley Jacobs, *Tarnished Warrior: Major-General James Wilkinson* (New York, 1938), as well as vol. 1 of JW's less-than-trustworthy *Memoirs.*

39. Conflicting interpretations of HG's role in the Newburgh Conspiracy may be found in Richard H. Kohn, "The Inside History of the Newburgh Conspiracy: America and the Coup d'Etat," *WMQ,* 3 ser., 27 (1970): 187–220; Paul David Nelson, "Horatio Gates at Newburgh, 1783: A Misunderstood Role," ibid., 3 ser., 29 (1972): 143–58, which also contains a reply by Kohn; and C. Edward Skeen, "The Newburgh Conspiracy Reconsidered," ibid., 3 ser., 31 (1974): 273–98, again with a reply by Kohn.

40. Nelson, *Horatio Gates,* presents HG in a much less critical light than does this volume.

41. Gerlach, *Philip Schuyler,* and *Proud Patriot,* carry PS's story through the Revolutionary War. For PS's full life, see Benson J. Lossing, *The Life and Times of Philip Schuyler* (2 vols., New York, 1872–73).

42. GW to BA, Valley Forge, May 7, 1778, *Writings GW,* 11:359–60. See also GW to Pierre Penet, Valley Forge, Apr. 30, 1778, ibid., 11:325–26, thanking him for the gift and explaining his intention to share the extra sets with BA and Lincoln, the

other general officer wounded during the Saratoga campaign. Thacher, *Journal,* 468, stated that GW presented BA with a brace of pistols. Most likely, Thacher confused pistols with the epaulets and sword knots.

43. Dearborn, May 21, 1778, *Journals,* 121.

44. From the Philadelphia parade denouncing BA, Sept. 30, 1780. Description in *Pennsylvania Packet* [Phila.], Oct. 3, 7, 1780, and "Procession in Honor of Arnold," *HM,* 1 ser., 5 (1861): 276–77.

EPILOGUE: *The Current Coinage of Ingratitude*

1. *Military Journal of George Ewing,* May 6, 1778 (Yonkers, N.Y., 1928), quoted in *Writings GW,* 11:356–57n; After Orders, Valley Forge, May 5, 1778, ibid., 11:354–55; GW to BA, Valley Forge, May 7, 1778, ibid., 11:359–60.

2. On diplomatic aspects of the Revolution, see Samuel Flagg Bemis, *The Diplomacy of the American Revolution* (rev. ed., Bloomington, Ind., 1957); and Jonathan R. Dull, *A Diplomatic History of the American Revolution* (New Haven, 1985). Dull places less emphasis on the importance of Saratoga in triggering a formal alliance than do Bemis and other scholars. See also Orville T. Murphy, *Charles Gravier, Comte de Vergennes: French Diplomacy in the Age of Revolution, 1719–1787* (Albany, 1982), 232–60.

3. On the ways in which the intervention of European powers affected the war, see Stephen Conway, *The War of American Independence* (London, 1995), 103–60; R. Ernest Dupuy et al., *The American Revolution: A Global War* (New York, 1957); *passim,* and Mackesy, *War for America, passim.* Eric Robson, *The American Revolution in Its Political and Military Aspects, 1763–1783* (London, 1955; reprint, New York, 1966), 93–174, analyzed whether the British had any chance to win after formal European intervention. See also Martin and Lender, *A Respectable Army,* 118–26, 136–58.

4. John Paterson to William Heath, West Point, Mar. 31, 1780, *The Heath Papers,* Massachusetts Historical Society *Collections,* 7 ser. (5 vols., Boston, 1898–1907), 5:44–45; Ebenezer Huntington to Andrew Huntington, Bush Huts near Passaic Falls, N.J., July 7, 1780, "Letters of Ebenezer Huntington, 1774–1781," *American Historical Review,* 5 (1900): 725–26; BA to NG, Headquarters, Robinson's House, Sept. 12, 1780, *Paps. NG,* 6:282. Mounting ire in the Continental army toward the civilian populace and its leadership reached its most dangerous points in 1779 and 1780, with a flurry of line mutinies and with the Newburgh Conspiracy of 1783. See Kohn, "American Generals of the Revolution," in Higginbotham, ed., *Reconsiderations Revolutionary War,* 104–23; James Kirby Martin, "A 'Most Undisciplined, Profligate Crew': Protest and Defiance in the Continental Ranks, 1776–1783," in *Arms and Independence: The Military Character of the American Revolution,* ed. Ronald Hoffman and Peter J. Albert (Charlottesville, 1984), 119–40; and Neimeyer, *America Goes to War,* 130–58.

5. BA to Mercy Scollay, Phila., July 15, 1778, Arnold, *Arnold,* 216. See also Mercy Scollay to BA, Boston, Aug. 5, 1778, and BA to Dr. David Townshend, Phila., Aug. 6, 1778, Misc. BA Paps., MHS.

6. BA to Mercy Scollay, Peekskill, N.Y., Aug. 3, 1780, Arnold, *Arnold,* 218–19; Sat., July 1, 1780, *JCC,* 17:581.

7. BA to Margaret Shippen, Camp at Raritan, N.J., Feb. 8, 1779, Arnold, *Arnold,* 230–31.

8. BA to GW, Phila., May 5, 1779, *CAR,* 2:290–92.

9. *Proceedings of a General Court Martial for the Trial of Major General Arnold* (New York, 1865), contains documents relating to this subject. For GW's reprimand, see General Orders, Morristown, Apr. 6, 1780, *Writings GW,* 18:222–25.

10. BA to Samuel Holden Parsons, Robinson's House, Sept. 8, 1780, APS.

11. The British paid BA a stipend of £6,315 for lost property, which compensated him for such items as the brigantine *Peggy* (the fireship at Quebec) as well as his residence in New Haven and the mansion, Mount Pleasant, that he had purchased in the Philadelphia area. Ranked as a cavalry colonel in the regular British army, BA's annual salary was £450 plus perquisites. (As a brig. gen. in America, his salary was £650.) His postwar half-pay pension was based on his colonel's salary. In 1782, Peggy began receiving an annual pension of £500, and each of her children would get £100 per year. BA's three sons by Margaret Mansfield obtained commissions in the British army and received annual pensions until their deaths. In 1798, BA also gained title to some 13,400 acres in Canadian lands reserved for loyalists.

12. Generally speaking, HC's immediate subordinates did not like BA. Their reasons varied from the patriot hanging of their fellow officer and friend John André to jealousy over BA's being ranked over many of them. HC, of all people, seemed to worry about BA's fighting determination. Without BA's knowledge, he gave BA's immediate subordinates, Lt. Cols. John Simcoe and Thomas Dundas, blank commissions to supersede BA in Virginia, should BA die or become incapacitated. The latter term held many meanings, including taking over command from BA simply if he did not act forcefully enough against his erstwhile American brethren.

13. Based on BA's official report, Peckham, ed., *Toll of Independence,* 90, lists patriot casualties, most at Fort Griswold, at eighty-five dead, sixty wounded, and seventy captured. All but a handful of the deaths occurred after the Americans had surrendered the fort. BA took nearly two hundred casualties during the raid. Some 143 buildings were burned in New London, along with twelve privateering vessels (another fifteen escaped).

14. Thoughts on the American War—By an American—(Gen. A.) 1782, Arnold, *Arnold,* 419–27. Some have questioned whether BA actually composed this plan.

15. Wallace, *Traitorous Hero,* 295.

16. Peggy Arnold to Edward Shippen Arnold, Gallywood, July 1, 1801, quoted in J. G. Taylor, *Some New Light on the Later Life and Last Resting Place of Benedict Arnold and of His Wife Margaret Shippen* (London, 1931), 59.

17. Quoted in Wallace, *Traitorous Hero,* vii. This story may well be another apocryphal tale, but the governor of Virginia, Thomas Jefferson, did offer a handsome reward of five thousand guineas for BA's capture.

18. "An Acrostic—On Arnold," Oct. 1780, Misc. BA Paps., MHS.

19. The words on the monument to BA's boot conclude with "and for himself the rank of Major General." BA had already obtained that rank; what he regained, but not necessarily because of Saratoga, was his seniority. Bible quotation from Ezekiel 28:18 [New International Version].

Index

Abenaki Indians, 347

Acland, Maj. John Dyke, 394–395

Adams, Abigail, 326, 334

Adams, John, 21, 306–308, 322, 326, 329, 334, 338, 354–355

Adams, Samuel, 41, 43, 57, 184, 295, 304, 408

Ainslie, Thomas, 153–154, 160–161, 163, 168, 190–191, 193, 196

Albany Committee of Correspondence, 81

Alexander, Maj. Gen. William. *See* Stirling, Lord

Algonquin Indians, 347

Allen, Col. Ethan: at Fort Ticonderoga, 64, 66–67, 69–73, 75–83, 85, 87–93, 98, 102, 199, 230, 387, 419; opponent of Arnold, 399, 414. *See also* Green Mountain Boys

Allen, Heman, 64, 66

Allen, Lt. Solomon, 1

Amherst, Sir Jeffrey, 109

Anderson, Capt., 177

André, Maj. John, 1–3, 5–6, 428

Armstrong, Maj. John, 400

Arnold, Absalom King (brother), 24

Arnold, Benedict I (son of William, great-great grandfather), 15, 55, 413

Arnold, Benedict II (great-grandfather), 15–16

Arnold, Benedict III (grandfather), 16, 27

Arnold, Benedict IV (father), 16–19, 21–27, 413; as merchant, 16–18, 21, 26; community leader, 17, 19, 30–31; death of, 31; drinking problem, 25, 30

Arnold, Benedict V (elder brother), 18, 24

Arnold, Benedict: advises Board of War, 339–340; appeals to Congress for Canadian invasion, 92; appearance, 2; apprenticed to Lathrops, 29–30; as military commander of Philadelphia, 426–428; as New Haven merchant, 33–39, 42–44, 47–48, 50, 57–58; as *Veritas*, 96–97; assault on St. Johns, 74–78; at Montreal, 199–217; at Saratoga, 372–402; attacks Quebec, 143–173; becomes

captain of Footguards, 62; becomes colonel in Continental Army, 114; becomes colonel in Massachusetts militia, 65; character attacked by Brown, 298–299; childhood, 13–15, 18–29; commander in Rhode Island, 291–292, 298–303, 312–314; condemns Brown and Easton, 194–195; conflict with Ethan Allen, 80–84; conflict with Hazen, 218–219; courts Elizabeth De Blois, 302–303, 314; death of, 431; death of first wife and father-in-law, 101; defends Ridgefield, 317–321; denied promotion by Congress, 306–314, 356–358; formal education, 22, 26–27; general character, 27–30, 242, 414; Hazen's court martial, 237–238, 242–243; in British army, 430; joins Connecticut militia, 61; leads patriot fleet on Lake Champlain, 246–257, 259–284; leads trek through Maine wilderness, 115–140; life with Peggy Mansfield Arnold, 49–50, 52, 54; marries Peggy Shippen, 427; Masonic ties, 49, 65; meets with Washington at Cambridge, 106–109; meets with Washington at Morristown, 323–325; moves to London, 430–431; opposes British policy, 44–46; orders burning of St. Roch and St. John's, 191–192; promoted to brigadier general, 184–185; promoted to major general, 321–322; religious values, 19, 21–25, 414; renounces American cause, 1–10, 429; resigns Continental army commission, 341, 343; resigns Massachusetts commission, 95; returns home to New Haven, 296–298, 314–315; seeks restoration of seniority in rank from Congress, 323–329, 332–341; seizes Fort Ticonderoga, 70–73; seizes St. Johns, 74–75; wounded at Quebec, 170–172; wounded at Second Freeman's Farm, 400

Arnold, Benedict VI ("Ben") (son), 50–51, 104, 296

Arnold, Caleb (uncle), 16

Arnold, Elizabeth (sister), 24–26